THE WADSWORTH CONTEMPORARY ISSUES IN CRIME AND JUSTICE SERIES
Todd Clear, Series Editor

Convict Criminology

JEFFREY IAN ROSS

University of Baltimore

STEPHEN C. RICHARDS

Northern Kentucky University

THOMSON

™

WADSWORTH

Australia • Canada • Mexico • Singapore • Spain
United Kingdom • United States

Senior Executive Editor: Sabra Horne
Editorial Assistant: Lee McCracken
Marketing Manager: Dory Schaeffer
Marketing Assistant: Neena Chandra
Project Manager, Editorial Production:
  Katy German

Print/Media Buyer: Rebecca Cross
Permissions Editor: Stephanie Keough-Hedges
Copy Editor: Sue Carter
Cover Designer: Sue Hart
Text and Cover Printer: Webcom Limited
Compositor: G&S Typesetters, Inc.

Printed in Canada
1 2 3 4 5 6 7 06 05 04 03 02

For more information about our products, contact
us at:
**Thomson Learning Academic
Resource Center
1-800-423-0563**
For permission to use material from this text,
contact us by:
Phone: 1-800-730-2214
Fax: 1-800-730-2215
Web: http://www.thomsonrights.com

Library of Congress Control Number:
2002104945

ISBN 0-534-57433-5

Wadsworth / Thomson Learning
10 Davis Drive
Belmont, CA 94002-3098
USA

Asia
Thomson Learning
5 Shenton Way #01-01
UIC Building
Singapore 068808

Australia
Nelson Thomson Learning
102 Dodds Street
South Melbourne, Victoria 3205
Australia

Canada
Nelson Thomson Learning
1120 Birchmount Road
Toronto, Ontario M1K 5G4
Canada

Europe / Middle East / Africa
Thomson Learning
High Holborn House
50/51 Bedford Row
London WC1R 4LR
United Kingdom

Latin America
Thomson Learning
Seneca, 53
Colonia Polanco
11560 Mexico D.F.
Mexico

Spain
Paraninfo Thomson Learning
Calle/Magallanes, 25
28015 Madrid, Spain

Contents

I WHAT'S WRONG WITH CORRECTIONS? 15

1 THE USE OF SCIENCE TO JUSTIFY THE IMPRISONMENT BINGE 17

James Austin

2 (MIS) REPRESENTING PRISONS: THE ROLE OF OUR CULTURAL INDUSTRIES 37

Jeffrey Ian Ross

III SPECIAL POPULATIONS 227

11 UNDERSTANDING WOMEN IN PRISON 231
Barbara Owen

12 ASPIRIN AIN'T GONNA HELP THE KIND OF PAIN I'M IN: HEALTH CARE IN THE FEDERAL BUREAU OF PRISONS 247
Daniel S. Murphy

Foreword

A generation ago, there were about 200,000 people locked in America's prisons. Today, after over 30 years of steady and historically unprecedented growth in the U.S. jail and prison population, there are over 2 million incarcerated. This upsizing of the penal system has been one of the signal characteristics of contemporary American culture: we are used to the idea that politically and socially, a prison term is seen as a solution to a social problem.

This growth has had myriad social consequences. Money that might have been spent on higher education has instead been diverted to pay to open new prisons—at the premortgage cost of about $100,000 per cell. People of color have been the social group hardest hit by prison expansions. About 14 percent of African American males aged 20–45 are locked up on any given day; nearly one-third of African American males born today can expect to serve time in prison on a felony. As many as 2 million people of color are prohibited from voting as a result of felony convictions, a number large enough to have changed the outcome of at least two presidential elections and dozens of congressional elections.

Numbers such as these lead some observers to see a reverberation of a modern kind of slavery through the prison system. In some neighborhoods, the concentration of prison experience is so high that nearly every family has a member who has been (or is) behind bars, and geographers have estimated that upward of $3 million is spent locking up residents of a single block in New York City in a single year. In those locations, as much as 13 percent of the parent-aged men go to prison or jail each year.

Most of the growth of the penal apparatus has come by locking up more poor people, more people of color, and especially more men, who were already marginal to the political economy of modern America. As the system grew, gobbling up more and more of these men who start out as socially marginal, not many people noticed—at least not those who shape public opinion and inform public consciousness. To a large degree, the enormous growth in the U.S. prison and jail system has been invisible because it has affected only those who lack a voice and a presence in the dominant culture, anyway. But it is simply not possible to grow the penal system by 600 percent without affecting a lot of people.

Some of these exconvicts have become criminologists. And some of these convict criminologists have started to call attention to the problem of prisons in contemporary society.

As editor of the *Wadsworth Series on Contemporary Issues in Crime and Justice,* I am delighted to introduce *Convict Criminology,* edited by Jeffrey Ian Ross and Stephen C. Richards. The Wadsworth Series publishes books that address important issues in crime and justice in ways that go well beyond the coverage provided by typical classroom textbooks. It is the aim of this series to deepen students' understanding of important questions facing criminology and criminal justice, and the series has, over the years, published some of the most important books on current topics of interest to the field.

This book is about prisons and prisoners, but there are many books on this topic. What makes *Convict Criminology* different is that the authors draw upon a broader base than most scholars about the penal system. Most of these authors have spent time inside the walls serving sentences for crimes, and so they can describe the realities of the prison experience with an expertise not available to those of us who have never been confined. All of these authors adopt a perspective on prisons that is at once critical of the assumptions used to justify incarceration as an institution and also deeply affirming of the humanity of those who are confined.

This last point deserves elaboration. We come, in this culture, to routinely demonize those who go to prison. It is not unusual to hear prisoners refereed to as "animals," or "scum," and this kind of talk can seem to excuse those in charge if they treat prisoners with something less than respect and dignity. Those who have spent time behind walls have many grievances about prison life and prison regimes, but the central difficulty is the way prisons dehumanize. All who enter prison, including those who are paid to go in and work, are affected by the raw power, the total authority, and the human hierarchy that serves as the basis for the existence of the prison.

This book is offered as a statement about prisons, a strong and in some ways controversial statement. It is also a unique, and therefore important, voice in the public conversation about prisons and prison practices. Many who read this book will begin with a different take on the value and social significance of prison—most of us come to accept, rather unquestioningly, that prisons are necessary and that, even if hard for those who stay there, are good for society. After reading this book, even the most ardent advocate of prison time will have to agree that a different, articulate, and informed voice exists on the question of the prison. This is obvious from the title of the opening section: "What's Wrong with Corrections?" It is a point that becomes ever more deeply made, as the book explains the way people who go to prison experience confinement, and how confinement affects different social groups in prison settings.

The editors of this, the very first volume to explain and explore "convict" criminology, close with an invitation and a challenge to those who study criminology and criminal justice. It is a challenge that, if met, will help new generations of students to understand the penal system in an entirely different light. I hope and expect that each reader of this volume will feel stimulated and, yes, challenged, by its message.

Todd R. Clear

Preface

In summer of 1997, I received a call from an exconvict, Chuck Terry, who was completing his doctorate in sociology at the University of California at Irvine. He told me that he had read some of my writing and wanted to meet me—the original felonious sociologist. We met and became instant friends. He also introduced me to Alan Mobley, a second excon, also finishing a Ph.D. at Irvine. Chuck said he had been in contact with several other former prisoners who had completed their advanced degrees in criminology or sociology and were teaching around the country; persons such as Richard S. Jones, Stephen C. Richards, and Edward Tromanhauser. Damn! It seemed to me that convicts were springing up like toadstools in the clean and pure fields of academe; one of the unintended consequences of laws recently casting a larger and larger net and catching, in addition to the usual suspects, a whole bunch of more educated and educable felons.

After we met and talked several times, Chuck brought up the idea of organizing a special "Convict Criminology" session for the upcoming 1997 American Society of Criminology (ASC) annual meetings. He ran the idea past Joan Petersilia, the program chair, and she gave him the green light. I liked the idea of a bunch of us exconvicts getting together, but I didn't fully appreciate the possibilities or the importance of this undertaking. But then, as I began thinking about it, I realized how important it would be for us, "criminals," to start pushing criminologists to do "inside" prison studies again. After all, the major development in criminal justice was the unprecedented expansion of prison populations that started around 1980 and was still accelerating.

I scanned the recent editions of *Criminology* to get an indication of the focus of mainstream criminologists and found articles on crime, crime causation, police work, recidivism, juvenile delinquency, but over a two-year period not one article on prisons or prisoners. There was no examination of the increase in prison population, changes in convict social organization, prison conditions, parole, or the after-prison experiences of the hundreds of thousands of exconvicts returning to society each year. Some other journals, particularly the *Critical Criminologist,* had taken up some of these issues, but not our number one journal, *Criminology.*

Throughout the eighties and nineties, I wondered what the hell was going on in the crowded prisons in which racial hostilities and violence were so intense, where most educational and vocational training programs had virtually disappeared, and prisoners' mobility and privileges had been so drastically reduced. What was happening to the thousands of prisoners held in total isolation in the maxi-maxi penitentiaries? What was going on with released prisoners who, with virtually no preparation and with meager resources, were returning to a society where they were feared and despised? Of course we need a convict criminology! Like African Americans, women, and other minorities, exconvict criminologists are going to have to play a major role in pushing our discipline to critically examine the issues surrounding incarceration in the United States and elsewhere.

But before we can get the attention of our academic colleagues, we have another task. This is dispelling the "Willie Horton" image of the convict as a dangerous, violent predator who, when released from prison, will inevitably rape, rob, and steal. It was the propagation of this image that has allowed criminologists, even those who claim to be "liberal," to ignore what has been happening to prisoners and turn their total attention to the "crime problem." (Of course, scurrying after government funds and favor also diverted them away from their earlier interests.) I knew we were in for it when, in 1991, I presented a paper at the annual meeting of the ASC on the negative consequences of the ongoing prison expansion. After the session, a close associate of mine, a prominent criminologist who had the reputation of being a sound liberal, but as I knew, was an alert follower of trends, came up to me and said, "John, are you still worrying about those convicts?"

So, there is an important task for us in trying to swing the attention of our colleagues back to what we, us exconvicts, know are the most pressing issues in criminal justice. Not only do we have to push, but we have to guide them. They generally do not understand the convict. This is one of the major reasons that the Willie Horton myth has been sustained. Convicts are not animals or monsters, but they are different.

When we first met, Chuck and Alan told me about their dissatisfaction with a great deal of the reading material they were encountering in the prison courses they were taking or teaching. I remembered back to 1960, when I was sitting in Don Cressey's undergraduate criminology course at University of California, Los Angeles, and he was lecturing on the "inmate social organization." (The fact that they were referring to it as the inmate social organization revealed that they were not getting it.) My disagreement with the theory that prevailed at that time inspired our article, "Thieves, Convicts and Inmate Culture" (Irwin and Cressey, 1962).

Prisons in some ways are like exotic, isolated island societies with their own language, worldview, and cultural patterns. Skilled anthropologists have come close to these primitive societies and produced good ethnographies. But it takes time and a special effort. To do it with indigenous people or convicts one has to go native. (Nowadays, few sociologists want to put in the effort and mix with this pack of "disreputables.") But even when they do, they don't get it quite right.

But so what? They come close, don't they? And close is good enough. The trouble with this is that they often misunderstand crucial meanings and motivations of convicts. And this leads to the most important reason for a convict criminology. The general public, most functionaries in the criminal justice system, and many criminologists fail to fully understand and appreciate the viewpoint of the convict and because of this see them as less than human, as inferior or evil deviants. Consequently, they tolerate or participate in the inhumane and counterproductive treatment of them that is occurring today.

We exconvicts know that most prisoners are relatively harmless persons who have done stupid things and perhaps committed a lot of minor, bothersome offenses. Even though these crimes may be petty, most conventional people attribute mistaken meanings and motives to their acts and perceive them as serious criminals. For example, two psychiatrists, Stanton Samenow and Samuel Yochelson (1977), who had been working at St. Elizabeth's Hospital in Washington, D.C., published a study, *The Criminal Personality,* based on research they had conducted on a group of felons whom they had been clinically treating. One of the major points of their book was that these patients had profound "criminal tendencies" that could not be rooted out, even after months of therapy. The doctors' major evidence for this conclusion was the fact that these prisoners, whom they had befriended during the treatment, threw them a party for which the convicts had pilfered most of the food and refreshments from the institution. Samenow and Yochelson were apparently unaware of the fact that many, probably most, ordinary employees regularly steal from their employers and that the majority of persons held in situations of deprivation such as prisons and mental hospitals pilfer whenever they get a chance. Their theft of food is not an indication of flawed character, but a normal response to the control of institutional confinement. This may be seen as deplorable, but the fact that this group of prisoners appropriated institutional food does not prove that they are a special class of deviants. In fact, most convicts were pretty ordinary folks before they went to prison. What distinguished them was their race, class, and demeanor, rather than their criminal behavior. Most of their uniqueness is a result of "prisonization."

A minority of convicts have committed serious crimes. But even in these cases the imagery of the vicious, conscienceless predator isn't very useful. It has been my experience that most of the time, even horrendous acts make some sense if you fully appreciate the perpetrators' viewpoints or the full contexts of their crimes. Recently, I listened to an interview of Timothy McVeigh, the convicted bomber of the Federal Building in Oklahoma City. He argued that the government had committed heinous murder against the Weaver family (Ruby Ridge, Idaho, 1992) and the Branch Davidians (Waco, Texas, 1993) and had conducted terrorist-like activities against other people, such as the Iraqis. So, from his viewpoint, counter-terrorism was appropriate. He said he was unaware of the children being there and argued that it was the government's fault for housing a day-care center in that building. This is twisted and dangerous logic. But so was the logic of Johnson, MacNamara, Kissinger, and many of the other architects of the Vietnam War, particularly in ordering the bombing raids of Hanoi and Cambodia. In either case, invoking simplistic, mistaken interpretations of the motives of individuals who commit dastardly acts frequently results in a lot of unjust and counterproductive policies.

Many of the chapters in this book are written by individuals who served sentences in state or federal prisons, continued their education after release, pursued Ph.D.'s, and have become academics and practicing criminologists. It is important for me to note that, except for one of them, Edward Tromanhauser, they accomplished their transition from prison to academe during the recent, excessively punitive era when most rehabilitative resources were reduced or had disappeared. I, like Tromanhauser, made the transition many years ago when the rehabilitative ideal still dominated penological thinking and there were more educational opportunities inside prisons.

I served five years for armed robbery in the mid-1950s at Soledad Prison in California. Soledad was planned to be the model rehabilitative prison in the California system. We prisoners were forced to participate in educational and vocational training programs. I repeated many high school courses (I had graduated from high school with all D's in my senior year) and earned 24 college units from the University of California Extension Division. Though after release from prison I was discouraged by parole authorities, I immediately entered San Francisco State College, then transferred to UCLA and earned a B.A. in sociology.

I was encouraged to finish a Ph.D. and become a professor by Donald Cressey, with whom I published my first journal article. I received a Woodrow Wilson Fellowship through the recommendation of Lewis Yablonsky, another criminologist who had faith in me. I earned my doctorate at the University of California, Berkeley, where I received significant support from Erving Goffman and David Matza. Then I immediately got a job from Donald Gibbons, another criminologist, who was the chairperson of the Department of Sociology at San Francisco State, where I stayed until I retired in 1993.

The point is, I made my transition from the life of a thief, drug addict, and convict to one of a "respectable" professional during a period when there was growing tolerance toward us condemned wrongdoers. The doors were opening. Then, in the mid-1970s, they slammed shut again. So most of the authors in this book passed through prison and returned to outside society in an excessively punitive era. Many of them fought with administrative policies to continue their educations inside prison. Then, upon their release from incarceration and return to the community, they struggled with arbitrary parole rules

and the hostility of the public to complete their formal education. Their accomplishments are remarkable.

They have a lot to offer criminology. In the first place, they obviously have
extensive direct experience with the stages of the criminal justice system. This
experience, along with their academic training, provides them with the unique
ability to write insightful essays about crime and prisons. Also, they have extensive "participatory" contact with many different "deviant worlds," particularly
that of the prison. They know the walk and talk, and questions to ask. This allows them to interact with prisoners in a relaxed manner, compared with the
condescending or patronizing behavior of most prison researchers.

Second, they have unusual determination and commitment. These were required to get them over the hurdles they had to cross. Also, they have that special strength and perseverance many persons acquire when they have survived
the experience of being abruptly extricated from free society and cast into its
punishment pit—the prison. In recent years many "respectable" people, after
having been thrown into prison and made to serve even short sentences, have
emerged with a burning and sincere desire to "reform" the prison. Many of
them, such as Charles Colson, one of the Watergate defendants who served a
short sentence in a federal minimum-security prison, have kept their promise and continued to work for this honorable purpose. The exconvicts who
write these chapters are not famous, highly placed public figures, but they have
experienced the same indignities and outrage and acquired similar commitment. Many of them served very long sentences in federal or state medium-
and maximum-security prisons.

Each of the authors in this book has supplied a short biography that reveals
his or her background and the source of his or her interest in criminology, and
also announces "where they are coming from"—that is, their "bias." In studying sociology, I discovered that the idea of a value-free social science was an insidious myth. My reading of Max Weber and C. Wright Mills, as well as the
influence of David Matza, taught me that researchers' personal values invariably
intrude into what they study and their collection and analysis of data. More important, what they discover is colored by their or their sponsors' values.

For example, James Q. Wilson and Richard J. Hernstein (1985) reviewed
existing research on crime and offered a theory suggesting that crime in America had nothing to do with the general economic and political arrangements
in our highly stratified society, but was the outcome of criminals' genetic pre-
dispositions or faulty upbringing. Critics of their book, *Crime and Human Nature,* pointed out that they blew little bits of evidence out of proportion and
misused and selectively reported other evidence linking crime to individual and
inherited characteristics (Kamin, 1986). It is apparent that their politically conservative agenda corrupted their research and analysis.

The exconvict authors are straightforward on this issue. They have confronted the full force of the criminal justice system and understand its shortcomings, injustices, and idiocies. They are emphatic: it needs to change. The
other authors in this book—William G. Archambeault, Bruce A. Arrigo, James
Austin, Michael T. Brooks, Preston Elrod, Marianne Fisher-Giorlando, Bar-

bara Owen, Jeffrey Ian Ross, and William S. Tregea—also understand the failings of the prison, not from having been incarcerated, but from having had close personal contact with prisoners, whether through research, teaching, or work in the criminal justice system. Their contact with the prison world has been close up rather than armchair, and thus they keenly appreciate the astonishing gulf between what they see (human beings) and what mainstream criminologists, policymakers, and the public see (animals, scum). It is for this reason that their contributions are included in this book.

John Irwin, Ph.D.
Emeritus Professor, San Francisco State University

Acknowledgments

We want to thank John Irwin and James Austin for their generous participation and support. In addition to our contributors, we are grateful to
Melissa Hickman Barlow, Todd Clear, Susan Dearing, Chris Eskridge, Jeff Ferrell, Bob Gaucher, Gilbert Geis, Warren Gregory, Victor Hassine, Richard G.
Hogan, Michael J. Lynch, Richard McCleary, Richard Quinney, Jim Thomas,
Ron Simons, Jon Marc Taylor, Michael Welch, and the late Richard A. Wright,
all of whom provided either encouragement or sound reflection about our mission and direction.

Many of our students, who tolerated our daily rantings, have provided us
with the opportunity to try out our ideas in the classroom. We also appreciate
the hard work of Dan Alpert, Sabra Horne, and Lee McCracken at Wadsworth,
who adopted and shepherded this project through its many stages. And we are
also thankful to Gretchen Otto and her crew at G&S Typesetters, who took care
of production matters. Stephen wishes to thank his wife, Donna, for her steadfast devotion while he was in prison, and through the years. He also hopes his
son Andre will read this book. Jeff dedicates the book to his wife, Natasha, who
has always been there to "bail him out."

Contributors

William G. Archambeault is a professor and criminologist with the School of Social Work, Louisiana State University (LSU) at Baton Rouge, where he has been on the faculty for over two decades. Archambeault earned his Ph.D. in criminology from Florida State University. He is a former chair of the Department of Criminal Justice at LSU and served for four years as a member of the Louisiana Board of Pardons. His research has focused on comparing public and private prisons, the use of volunteers in courts, correctional management theory and practice, justice administration and computer applications, and Japanese and Asian criminal justice. Over the last six years, his research focus has centered on Native American crime and justice issues, which link him to his Chippewa, Cherokee, Lakota, and French Métis ancestry.

Bruce A. Arrigo is professor and chair of the Department of Criminal Justice at the University of North Carolina—Charlotte, with additional faculty appointments in the Psychology Department, the Public Policy Program, and the Center for Applied and Professional Ethics. Formerly the director of the Institute of Psychology, Law, and Public Policy at the California School of Professional Psychology in Fresno, Dr. Arrigo began his professional career as a community organizer and social activist for the homeless, the mentally ill, the working poor, the frail elderly, the decarcerated, and the chemically addicted.

Dr. Arrigo received his Ph.D. from Pennsylvania State University and holds a master's degree in psychology and in sociology. He is the author of more than 100 journal articles, academic book chapters, and scholarly essays exploring theoretical and applied topics in critical criminology, criminal justice and mental health, and sociolegal studies. He is the author or editor of *Madness, Language, and the Law* (1993), *The Contours of Psychiatric Justice* (1996), *Social Justice/Criminal Justice* (1998), *Introduction to Forensic Psychology* (2000), and *Punishing the Mentally Ill: A Critical Analysis of Law and Psychiatry* (2002), and is coauthor of *The Dictionary of Critical Social Sciences* (with T. R. Young, 1999), *Law, Psychology, and Justice* (with Christopher R. Williams, 2001), *The Power Serial Rapist* (with Dawn J. Graney, 2001), and *Criminal Competency on Trial* (with Mark C. Bardwell, 2002). Dr. Arrigo is the past editor of *Humanity & Society* and founding and acting editor of the peer-reviewed quarterly *Journal of Forensic Psychology Practice*. He was recently named Critical Criminologist of the Year (2000), sponsored by the Critical Criminology Division of the American Society of Criminology. He is also a fellow of the American Psychological Association through its Law-Psychology Division (Div. 41).

James Austin is the director of the Institute on Crime, Justice and Corrections at the George Washington University (GWU) in Washington, D.C. Before he began working at GWU, he was the executive vice president of the National Council on Crime and Delinquency, where he was employed for 20 years. He began his career in corrections in 1970 when he was employed by the Illinois Department of Corrections as a correctional sociologist at the Joliet and Stateville penitentiaries.

Austin has directed studies that entail projections of correctional populations based on current and proposed sentencing reforms in 25 states. He has also conducted evaluations of local jail systems and how various drug control law enforcement programs have impacted the jail system. He has authored many publications, was named by the American Correctional Association as its 1991 recipient of the Peter P. Lejin's Research Award, and received the Western Society of Criminology Paul Tappin award for outstanding contributions in the field of criminology. He has coauthored three books. In 2001 the third edition of *It's about Time: America's Imprisonment Binge* appeared, coauthored with John Irwin and first published in 1994. He was recently appointed as the chair of the American Society of Criminology National Policy Committee.

Michael T. Brooks holds a B.S. in criminal justice. He is now completing his M.S. in criminal justice at the University of North Carolina at Charlotte, where he works as a graduate assistant. He plans to begin work on his doctorate in public policy analysis. His primary academic interests are in the development and evaluation of programs designed to reduce juvenile and adult crime.

Preston Elrod is a professor in the Department of Correctional Services at Eastern Kentucky University, where he teaches courses on adult and juvenile corrections and juvenile justice. Among his published works are studies on juvenile justice policy development and the effectiveness of interventions for juvenile probationers. He is also the coauthor of *Juvenile Justice: A Social, Historical, and Legal Perspective*. His primary research interests focus on the development and evaluation of delinquency reduction efforts. In addition, he worked as a juvenile probation officer for six years. He received his Ph.D. from Western Michigan University.

Marianne Fisher-Giorlando is a professor of criminal justice at Grambling State University. She completed her M.A. and Ph.D. at Ohio State University. Fisher-Giorlando's interest in prisons began when she was a graduate student in 1981. With her colleague Shanhe Jiang, she has conducted research on prisoner disciplinary reports, but her primary project is the history of the women in the Louisiana State Penitentiary. She has published two articles about women serving time before the Civil War in the Baton Rouge Penitentiary. Louisiana Endowment for the Humanities recognized Fisher-Giorlando as an outstanding scholar on Louisiana prisons. She also serves as vice president for the Louisiana State Penitentiary Museum Foundation at Angola.

John Irwin is an exconvict and emeritus professor of sociology at San Francisco State University. Irwin is widely acknowledged by academic scholars as the leading authority on ethnographic research on prisoners and the conditions of confinement. His published work includes classics in the field: "Thieves, Convicts, and the Inmate Culture" (with Donald Cressey), in *Social Problems* (1962), *The Felon* (1970), *Prisons in Turmoil* (1980), *The Jail* (1985), and *It's about Time* (1994/1997/2001) (with James Austin).

Richard S. Jones is an associate professor of sociology at Marquette University. He was incarcerated at the Minnesota Correctional Facility-Stillwater (a maximum-security prison) for possession of marijuana with intent to distribute. Released from prison in 1980 and unable to secure employment, he started the master's program in sociology and corrections at Mankato State University. His began graduate study with a summer internship as a research assistant with the Ramsey County Criminal Justice Planning Department and spent the summer interviewing village and city chiefs of police. After completing his M.A. in sociology at Mankato, still unable to find a "real job," he enrolled in the Ph.D. program in sociology at Iowa State University, earning his degree in 1986. His research on the male and female prison experience has been published in *The Prison Journal, Journal of Contemporary Criminal Justice, Perspectives on Social Problems, Women and Criminal Justice, Symbolic Interaction,* and the *Journal of Contemporary Ethnography.* Jones's most recent work includes *Doing Time: Prison Experience and Identity* (with Thomas J. Schmid, 2000).

Charles S. Lanier is an assistant editor of the *Sourcebook of Criminal Justice Statistics,* Hindelang Criminal Justice Research Center, and a doctoral student at the School of Criminal Justice, State University of New York at Albany. Charlie entered the New York State maximum-security prison in 1979 with some college credits but no degree and exited 12 years later with an M.A. in sociology. Once released from prison, he began work on a Ph.D. in criminal justice. During the last period of his incarceration and the early phase of his doctoral program, his research efforts were directed toward exploring affective states of fathers in prison and developing programs for that previously neglected subgroup of the prison population.

He is coeditor of *America's Experiment with Capital Punishment: Reflections on the Past, Present, and Future of the Ultimate Penal Sanction* (with James R. Acker and Robert M. Bohm, 1998). He also coauthored a series of *Criminal Law Bullet-*

in articles (with James R. Acker), analyzing death-penalty statutes in the United States. This work formed the basis for *Legislating Death: Capital Punishment Statutes in the United States* (with James R. Acker, forthcoming). He has published over 20 journal articles, primarily on incarcerated fathers and capital punishment. His current research interests include capital punishment, corrections, and serial murder.

Alan Mobley pleaded guilty to distributing cocaine in 1984 and served 10 years in medium-security federal prisons. Since his release in 1994, he has worked on rehabilitation issues with current and former prisoners and attended graduate school at the University of California at Irvine. He completed his Ph.D. in 2001.

His major research interests include the sociology of law, criminal justice systems, and ethnography. His published work includes "The Corrections Corporation of America: AKA The Prison Realty Trust" (with Gilbert Geis), in David Shichor and Michael J. Gilbert (eds.), *Privatization in Criminal Justice: Past, Present, and Future* (2000), and "Private Prisons, Criminological Research, and Conflict of Interest: A Case Study" (with Gilbert Geis and David Shichor), in *Crime and Delinquency* (2000).

Daniel S. Murphy has suffered four reconstructive spinal surgeries. The fourth, in 1976, ended a promising collegiate basketball career. In 1984, Dan earned a B.S. in sociology from the University of Wisconsin at Madison. In 1985, while stopped at a red light, a drunk driver plowed into the rear of his vehicle. The progress gained through four reconstructive spinal surgeries was undone in an instant. His life became a nightmare of unending pain. Several months after the accident, a friend stopped by his home. Murphy was in tears due to the relentless agony. His friend suggested that he smoke marijuana to alleviate the pain. At first he refused, but he was so desperate for pain relief that, begrudgingly, he smoked the marijuana and the results were nothing shy of miraculous. The muscle spasticity relaxed and the pain was dramatically reduced. From that moment forth, he smoked marijuana on a regular basis and was able to discontinue the use of prescribed narcotics.

In the summer of 1992, he was arrested and charged with the manufacture of marijuana; he pleaded guilty when threatened by the prosecutor with a sentence of 20 years and a $2 million fine. As a first-time, nonviolent offender, and because of the severity of his medical condition, he was sentenced to a Federal Medical Center. Murphy served approximately three years at FMC Rochester (Minnesota) and one year at FMC Carville (Louisiana). Released from prison in 1997, Dan completed his M.A. in sociology at the University of Wisconsin at Milwaukee (1999). He is expected to complete his Ph.D. at Iowa State University in 2002.

Greg Newbold is an excon and senior lecturer (tenured professor) in sociology at the University of Canterbury in Christchurch, New Zealand. In the late 1970s, he served five-and-a-half years of a seven-and-a-half year sentence for drug dealing, three years of which was served in a maximum-security prison. He completed his M.A. in sociology at Auckland University while incarcerated.

After his release from prison, he received his Ph.D. from Auckland University, writing a dissertation on the history of the New Zealand maximum-security prison.

Newbold has written five books on crime, criminal justice, and rehabilitation, and is currently coauthoring a sixth, on women in gangs, with Glennis Dennehy; his other titles include *The Big Huey* (1982), *Punishment and Politics: The Maximum Security Prison in New Zealand* (1987), *Crime and Deviance* (1992), *Quest for Equity* (1995), and *Crime in New Zealand* (1999). He has also published articles in *Deviant Behavior, Federal Probation, Crime, Law and Social Change,* and the *Journal of Criminal Justice Education.* Newbold has worked voluntarily for 10 years on the board of governors of a halfway house in Christchurch and is frequently consulted by police and correctional authorities on matters relating to crime control and criminal justice.

Barbara Owen is a nationally known expert in the areas of women and crime, substance abuse, and program evaluation, with extensive experience in conducting large-scale studies, ethnographies, and program evaluation. A professor of criminology at California State University in Fresno, she obtained her Ph.D. in sociology from the University of California at Berkeley, in 1984. She received a National Institute of Justice Graduate Research Fellowship in 1982 and was a National Institute on Alcohol Abuse and Alcoholism Post-Doctoral Fellow with the Alcohol Research Group, School of Public Health, University of California at Berkeley, in 1986.

Before returning to academia, Dr. Owen was a senior researcher with the Federal Bureau of Prisons. In the past 10 years, Owen has concentrated her work in the areas of women, prisons, and crime, and gender-responsive programming and policy. She has conducted numerous studies on women and girls in the California prison system. Her ethnography of women in prison, *In the Mix* (1998), describes the struggle and survival of imprisoned women and is the first full-length study of women prisoners in 30 years. Along with Barbara Bloom, she is co−principal investigator of a National Institute of Corrections project, "Gender-Responsive Strategies: Research, Practice, and Guiding Principles for Women Offenders."

Stephen C. Richards is an associate professor of sociology and criminology at Northern Kentucky University. He is a Soros Senior Justice Fellow (2001), served on the American Society of Criminology National Policy Committee (2002−2001), and the American Correctional Association National Research Council.

Arrested in 1982, he was threatened, and then charged, with 10 counts of Conspiracy to Distribute Marijuana, a total of 150 years if convicted (15 years for each count). Upon being convicted of one count, he appealed the case to the U.S. Court of Appeals in 1983 and the U.S. Supreme Court in 1984. Although his federal parole guidelines were 12 months, he was sentenced to nine years and designated to maximum-security penitentiary (USP Atlanta).

Altogether, he stood trial in three federal courtrooms (U.S. District Court, U.S. Court of Appeals, U.S. Supreme Court), served 11 years of correctional custody, including time in two jails (South Carolina), nine prisons in six different states, one work release center, and had six different parole officers. As a federal prisoner he did time in maximum-security behind the wall of penitentiaries (USP Atlanta, USP Terre Haute, USP Marion, USP Leavenworth), in medium-security within the razor-wire perimeters of correctional institutions (FCI Talladega, FCI Oxford), and minimum-security in three different federal camps (FPC Terre Haute, FPC Leavenworth, FPC Oxford).

Richards completed his B.S. in sociology while at FPC Oxford (University of Wisconsin at Madison, 1986). Released from federal prison in 1987, he completed his M.A. in sociology (University of Wisconsin at Milwaukee, 1989) and Ph.D. in sociology (Iowa State University, 1992). He has published work on tattoos, prisons, structural impediments to reentry, community punishments, state crime, and female correctional officers. His most recent book is *Behind Bars: Surviving Prison* (with Jeffrey Ian Ross). He is currently completing *USP Marion: The First Super Max Penitentiary.*

Jeffrey Ian Ross is an assistant professor in the Division of Criminology, Criminal Justice and Social Policy, and a fellow, Center for Comparative and International Law, at the University of Baltimore. He has conducted research, written and lectured on national security, political violence, political crime, violent crime, corrections, and policing. His work has appeared in many academic journals and books, as well as popular magazines. He is the author of *Making News of Police Violence* (2000), *The Dynamics of Political Crime* (2002) and coauthor with Stephen C. Richards of *Behind Bars: Surviving Prison* (2002). Ross is the editor of *Controlling State Crime* (1995/2000), *Violence in Canada: Sociopolitical Perspectives* (1995), *Cutting the Edge: Current Perspectives in Radical/Critical Criminology and Criminal Justice* (1998), and *Varieties of State Crime and Its Control* (2000). He is the coeditor with Larry Gould of *Native Americans and the Criminal Justice System* (forthcoming). Ross worked almost four years in a correctional facility. And for the past decade, he has instructed students, some of whom are incarcerated, through the University of Colorado correspondence division. Ross received his Ph.D. in political science from the University of Colorado.

Charles M. Terry spent over 12 years in correctional custody. His crimes included possession and sale of heroin, burglaries, and shoplifting. Over the course of those years, Terry's ideas, thoughts, and perspectives about life went through a process of dramatic change. Terry's shifting perception was greatly affected by taking advantage of the opportunity to attend two years of college classes inside the Oregon State Penitentiary.

Released on parole in 1990, he took classes at Santa Barbara City College and then completed his B.A. in sociology at the University of California at Santa Barbara. In 1999, Terry completed his Ph.D. at the University of California at Irvine, in criminology, law, and society. He is now an assistant professor of sociology and criminal justice at St. Louis University.

His published work includes "The Function of Humor In Prison," *Journal of Contemporary Criminal Justice* (1997), "One Man's Journey inside the Criminal Justice System and Beyond," in George Cole and Christopher Smith's *Criminal Justice in America* (1999), "Beyond Punishment: Perpetuating Difference from the Prison Experience," *Humanity and Society* (2000), "Exploring the Paradox of the (Un)Reality of Richard Quinney's Criminology" (with Alan Mobley and Harold Pepinski), in *Crime and Delinquency* (2002), and *The Fellas: Rocky Roads toward Addiction, Prisonization, and Reintegration* (forthcoming with Wadsworth).

William S. Tregea is an associate professor of sociology and criminal justice at Adrian College. He holds a B.A., M.A., and Ph.D. in sociology and an M.A. in criminal justice from Michigan State University. Tregea's experience and expertise is in designing and operating prison education programs. He has a long career teaching college classes inside prisons. Since 1981, Tregea has taught courses in some of the toughest penitentiaries in the United States, including both the Southern Michigan complex at Jackson and the Ionia prison complex, and Soledad Penitentiary in California. Tregea's publications include articles in the *Science Journal* and *Perspectives on Social Problems*. Recently, he has been editing a prisoner education advocate publication.

Edward Tromanhauser is a retired (1997) professor and chairperson of the Department of Criminal Justice, Chicago State University. He dropped out of school in the 10th grade, was convicted of attempted robbery at age 19, and served two years; convicted of armed robbery at age 23 and served six years; convicted of robbery at age 30 and served three years; convicted of robbery at age 33 and served two years. Tromanhauser was a "four-time loser" who has served prison time in three states (Michigan, Illinois, and Indiana). While incarcerated he completed his high school education and obtained an associate of arts degree. Serving his final sentence, he began freelance writing and co-authored a book about prison life entitled *An Eye for an Eye* (1969).

Upon release from prison, he obtained employment at a Chicago-area university as a civil service employee. While there he completed a bachelor's degree and his first master's degree. He began teaching criminal justice courses in 1974 and continued to work on a second master's degree. He obtained his Ph.D. in 1989. Tromanhauser was elected president of the Illinois Academy of Criminology in 1974, cochaired the 1975 meeting of American Society of Criminology, and is a former president of the Midwestern Criminal Justice Association. He has been a consultant to the Illinois Department of Corrections; Federal Bureau of Prisons; U.S. Departments of Justice, Education, and Labor; Chicago Public Schools; and the Chicago Police Department. His published work includes 27 journal articles and three coauthored books. His seminal work on school crime, *Chicago Safe Schools Study,* won him the Wexler Award for Criminal Justice Research of the Illinois Academy of Criminology and the Silver Medallion Award of the Central States Education Association. He is the father of five children and grandfather of six and presently lives in Oak Park, Illinois.

INTRODUCTION

What Is the New School of Convict Criminology?

JEFFREY IAN ROSS AND
STEPHEN C. RICHARDS

"That's the reality, and to hell with what the class-room bred, degree toting, grant-hustling 'experts' say from their well-funded, air-conditioned offices far removed from the grubby realities of the prisoners' lives."

RIDEAU AND WIKBERG,

1992: 59

The correctional system in the United States, and most other countries, is unquestionably flawed. Efforts to reform jails, prisons, and other correctional facilities have largely failed and the number of individuals incarcerated is at its highest historic level. There is also something wrong when criminology/criminal justice research is dominated by government funding, conducted by academics or consultants who have had minimal contact with the criminal justice system, or by former employees of the law enforcement establishment (correctional, probation, parole, or former police officers). These individuals appear content to conduct research from the safety and comfort of their offices, often in an effort to simply increase the revenue of their firms, improve their status inside their companies, enhance their chances of tenure and promotion, or improve the working conditions in correctional institutions. Much of this "managerial research" routinely disregards the harm perpetrated by criminal justice processing on individuals arrested, charged, and convicted of crimes (Clear, 1994; Cullen, 1995).

If legislators, practitioners, researchers, and scholars are serious about addressing the corrections crisis (e.g., Clear, 1994; Welch, 1996, 1999; Austin

We wish to thank Bruce A. Arrigo, James Austin, Susan Dearing, Preston Elrod, Marianne-Fisher Giorlando, John Irwin, Richard S. Jones, Greg Newbold, Charles S. Lanier, Daniel S. Murphy, Barbara Owen, Chuck Terry, and William S. Tregea for their contributions to this discussion. An earlier and brief version of this chapter appeared as Stephen C. Richards and Jeffrey Ian Ross (2001), "The New School of Convict Criminology," *Social Justice*, 28, 1: 177–190.

et al., 2001; Austin and Irwin, 2001; J. Ross and Richards, 2002; Richards, 2003), we need to be more honest and creative with respect to the research we conduct and the policies we advocate, implement, and evaluate. In an effort to promote this objective, the present chapter introduces what we are calling "convict criminology" and reviews the theoretical and historical grounding, current initiatives, and dominant themes of this emerging school of social thought and movement.

THEORETICAL AND HISTORICAL GROUNDING

In order to appreciate the context of convict criminology, we need to understand its background. Six interrelated movements, factors, and methodologies led to the birth of convict criminology: theoretical developments in criminology, writings in victimology and constitutive criminology, the failure of prisons, the prisoners' rights movement, the authenticity of insider perspectives, and the centrality of ethnography.

THEORETICAL DEVELOPMENTS IN CRIMINOLOGY

The history of criminological theory consists of a series of reform movements (Vold and Bernard, 1996). As early as the 1920s, biologically based arguments of criminal causation were being replaced by environmental, socioeconomic, and behavioral explanations. Even in the field of radical and critical criminology there have been a series of divisions (J. Ross, 1998b; Lynch, 1996). Since the 1970s, critical criminology has splintered into complementary perspectives including feminism (e.g., Chesney-Lind, 1991; Faith, 1993; Daly, 1994; Owen, 1998), postmodernism (e.g., Arrigo, 1998a, 1998b: 109–127; Ferrell, 1998), left realism (e.g., Young and Matthews, 1992), peacemaking (e.g., Pepinsky and Quinney, 1991; Quinney, 1998), and cultural criminology (e.g., Ferrell and Sanders, 1995a; Ferrell, 1996). This multiplicity of perspectives suggests that radical and critical criminology has broadened its intellectual scope. And, although these diverse discourses and "metanarratives . . . open up some new conceptual and political space" (Ferrell, 1998: 64), they too often remain the intellectual products of the well meaning yet privileged, with only minimal reference and relevance to the victims of the criminal justice machine.

VICTIMOLOGY AND CONSTITUTIVE CRIMINOLOGY

In the 1960s and 1970s, criminologists realized that victims' voices were almost totally ignored as casualties of criminal justice processing. This initiated a subtle paradigm shift resulting in a fledgling social movement and subdiscipline in criminology called "victimology" (Karmen, 2001). In appreciation of victims' voices, a new branch of criminology began to develop. Constitutive criminology advocates "replacement discourses"; researchers need to listen to the messages of the oppressed who are seeking expression (Henry and Milovanovic, 1996: 6; Milovanovic, 1996; Richards and Jones, 1997; Richards, 1998). These are "directed toward the dual process of deconstructing prevailing structures of meaning and displacing them with new conceptions, distinctions, words, and phrases, which convey alternative meanings" (Henry and Milovanovic, 1996: 204). This method helps to give "voice to personal everyday experiences . . . of . . . marginalized groups" (Renzetti, 1997: 133). Perhaps in the new millennium criminologists and other social scientists might also realize that convict[1] voices, in many instances, have been forgotten, marginalized, or simply ignored (Gaucher, 1998: 2–16).

THE FAILURE OF PRISONS

Many prominent criminologists have discussed the failure of prisons to correct criminal behavior. The differential effects of incarceration are well known. According to Sutherland, Cressey, and Luckenbill (1992: 524), "Some prisoners apparently become 'reformed' or 'rehabilitated,' while others become 'confirmed' or 'hardened' criminals. For still others, prison life has no discernible effect on subsequent criminality or noncriminality." Johnson (1996: xi) suggested that "prisoners serve hard time, as they are meant to, but typically learn little of value during their stint behind bars. They adapt to prison in immature and often destructive ways. As a result, they leave prison no better, and sometimes considerably worse, then when they went in." Similarly, Reiman (1995: 2) argued that the correctional system was designed to "maintain and encourage the existence of a stable and visible 'class' of criminals."

Needless to say, we should not assume all prisoners are criminals, or that committing crime has anything to do with going to prison the first time, and even less the second or third. Considering the dramatic growth in prison populations (Austin and Irwin, 2001: 1–16; Richards, 1998: 125–126), the numbers of "innocent" victims will also continue to grow. The first failure of correctional institutions is that they hold hundreds of thousands of prisoners who, although they were convicted of a crime, are not violent felons and pose little if any threat to the community. The second is that they hold people too long; as Austin and Irwin (2001: 143–146) demonstrated, it is about time, not just "hard time" (Johnson, 1996), but "long time" and "repeated time" in prison. The third tragedy of prisons is "they don't do more to rehabilitate those confined in them" (Rideau, 1994: 80). Instead, prison systems function as vast depositories for drug offenders, minorities, and petty offenders (J. G. Miller, 1996: 10–47; Austin and Irwin, 2001: 17–62). One cursory look at the gun towers, walls, and razor wire is evidence that prisons were built to warehouse and punish and not to rehabilitate.

PRISONERS' RIGHTS MOVEMENT

At several points in history, well-meaning individuals and organizations (e.g., American Civil Liberties Union, American Friends Service Committee, Amnesty International, Human Rights Watch, International Conference on Penal Abolition, etc.) have advocated improvements in prison conditions through both conventional and unconventional political participation. As a result of the prisoners' rights movement, "correctional institutions have been forced to rely less on coercive mechanisms to control inmates and to resort to bureaucratic measures instead. Today, prison officials must formally respond to grievances and lawsuits by producing their own reports concerning the alleged violations" (Welch, 1996: 370). "Inmates themselves also are affected by the prisoners' rights movement; they have become acutely aware of their constitutional rights and other legal safeguards. This movement has promoted a higher level of political and legal consciousness among prisoners" (Welch, 1996: 370).[2]

INSIDE PERSPECTIVE

The existing literature that provides an "inside perspective" on crime and convicts can be divided into six groups. First are edited anthologies by prison reform activists (e.g., Rosenblatt, 1996; Burton-Rose, with Pens and Wright, 1998). Embedded in these works are chapters or short pieces written by political activists, lawyers, journalists, and prisoners. The second collection of writings are journalists' accounts of life inside prison (e.g., Mitford, 1973; Wicker, 1975; Earley, 1993; Bergner, 1998; C. Parenti, 1999; Conover, 2000; Hallinan, 2001; Abramsky, 2002). Third, prison journalism (J. Morris, 1998), written by convicts, appears in prison newspapers, like the *Angolite,* or in narrowly focused academic journals (e.g., *The Journal of Prisoners on Prisons*). The fourth group includes edited collections of authentic convict writing (e.g., Martin, with Sussman, 1995; Franklin, 1998; R. Johnson and Toch, 1999; Leder, 1999; Chevigny, 2000). The fifth group includes sole-authored books or edited works by academics that may employ observation and/or interviews of criminal offenders or convicts (e.g., E. Miller, 1986; Fleisher, 1989; Churchill and Vanderwall, 1992; R. Johnson, 1996; Cromwell, 1996; Walens, 1997; May, 2000). The last and most prominent category is composed of monographs written by convicts about life in prison (e.g., Genet, 1949a, 1949b; Chessman, 1954, 1955, 1957; Cleaver, 1968; G. Jackson, 1970, 1972; Abbott, 1981; Rideau and Wikberg, 1992; Abu-Jamal, 1995; Hassine, 1996; Peltier, 1999).

The first four groups of writers, be they convicts, activists, journalists, or academic editors, write "stories" or investigative reports, rarely connecting their discussion to the debates found in the scholarly literature. The fifth collection of authors are academics, who, though they support their research with excerpts from prisoner interviews, and may themselves at one time have been employed inside prisons, are still writing from a privileged perspective as compared to the lived experience of convicts. The final group of authors write authentic and compelling accounts of prison life, but generally do not ground their discussion in academic research (Gaucher, 1999). Missing or underutilized are research accounts by academics who themselves have served prison time.

CENTRALITY OF ETHNOGRAPHY

Convict criminology is also the logical result of criminologists (e.g., Newbold, 1982/1985; Fleisher, 1989; Ferrell, 1993; Richards, 1995a; Ferrell and Hamm, 1998) using ethnographic methods in order to better understand their subject matter. Clearly, the use of ethnographic methods is not new in the field of penology or corrections (e.g., Sutherland, 1937; Sykes 1956, 1958; Sykes and Messinger, 1960; J. Jacobs, 1977; Peak, 1985; Lombardo, 1989; Farkas, 1992). For example, during the 1930s Clemmer (1940/1958), while employed as a sociologist on the prison mental health staff of Menard Penitentiary (Illinois), collected extensive information on the convict social system. More recently, Fleisher (1989) spent a year working as a "mainline" federal correctional officer (a guard assigned to cell blocks and housing units) as a means to compile observation and interview data about both "cons" and "hacks."

Exconvict academics have also carried out a number of significant ethnographic studies. Irwin, who served prison time in California, drew upon his experience as a convict to interview prisoners and analyze jail admissions and subtle processes in prison in a series of articles and monographs (Irwin and Cressey, 1962; Irwin, 1970, 1980, 1985a; Austin and Irwin, 2001). McCleary (1978/1992), who did both state and federal time, wrote his classic "sociology of parole" through participant observation of parole officers at work and on the street. Terry (1997), a former California and Oregon state convict, wrote about how prisoners used humor to mitigate the managerial domination of penitentiary authorities. Newbold (1982/1985, 1989, 2000), having served prison time in New Zealand, used both qualitative and quantitative methods to analyze crime and corrections in his country. Richards and Jones (1997), both former prisoners, used "inside experience" to inform their observation and interviews of Iowa convicts upon their transfer to community work release centers. Finally, Richards, Terry, and Murphy (2002) wrote about the relationship between male prisoners and female correctional officers. Each of these studies have benefited from the inside experience of the investigators.[3]

CURRENT INITIATIVES

Having outlined the factors contributing to the formation of the new school of convict criminology, we can consider the initiatives that our collective effort has taken to date. We begin by describing the new school of convict criminology, and then discuss (1) the collaborative nature of our project, (2) inclusion criteria, (3) who the convict authors are, (4) the preeminence of John Irwin, (5) the little-recognized fact that criminologists also commit crimes, (6) the field's objectives, (7) the school's issue-oriented nature, and, finally (8) the specific questions addressed by the authors in this book.

DEFINING THE NEW SCHOOL
OF CONVICT CRIMINOLOGY

The emerging field of convict criminology consists primarily of essays and empirical research conducted and written by convicts or exconvicts, on their way to completing or already in possession of a Ph.D., or by enlightened academics who critique existing literature, policies, and practices, thus contributing to a new perspective on criminology, criminal justice, corrections, and community corrections. This is a "new criminology" (I. Taylor, Walton, and Young, 1973) led by exconvicts who are now academic faculty. These men and women, who have worn both prison uniforms and academic regalia, served years behind prisons walls, and now, as academics, are the primary architects of the movement. The convict scholars are able to do what most previous writers could not: merge their past with their present and provide a provocative approach to the academic study of criminology, criminal justice, and corrections. These authors, as a collective, are the future of a realistic paradigm that promises to challenge the conventional research findings of the past.

The exconvict professors have endured years of lockup in penitentiaries and correctional institutions, lived in crowded, noisy, violent cell blocks, and emerged to complete graduate degrees and become professors of sociology, criminology, criminal justice, and related disciplines. They have an intimate knowledge of "penal harm" (Clear, 1994), which they carry in their heads and hearts, and in some cases wear as scars and tattoos upon their skin. They are like Steinbeck's character Tom Joad in *The Grapes of Wrath* (portrayed by Henry Fonda in the movie); they are people with something to say, with an anger that will not betray them. They do not write merely for vitae lines, promotions, or tenure. They write so that one day the ghosts will sleep.

Together, exconvict graduate students and professors are now working together to build their expertise in both subject and methodology. The editors of this book assembled the current cohort through an elaborate network of contacts, numerous phone calls, e-mails, and faxes. We now number over a dozen excon professors of sociology, criminology, and criminal justice from Anglo-American democracies. To this we add a growing cohort of exconvict graduate students that are joining us as they complete their dissertations, as well as established criminologists without criminal records who are well known for their critical orientation toward managerial criminology, criminal justice, and corrections.

The dramatic expansion in arrests, convictions, and the rate of incarceration guarantees that the number of professors with profound and traumatic firsthand experience with the criminal justice system will continue to increase. In addition, some of the most important members of our growing group are prominent critical criminologists who, though not excons, have contributed to both the content and context of our new school. This growing pool of talent, with its remarkable insight and resources, is the foundation of our effort.[4]

COLLABORATIVE NATURE

This school is a collaborative effort of enthusiastic participants. Over the last few years, most of these convict criminologists have met, socialized together, and participated in a number of panels and roundtables (e.g., "Convicts Critique Criminology" and "Convict Criminology") at the American Society of Criminology (ASC, 1997, 1998, 1999, 2000) and the Academy of Criminal Justice Sciences (ACJS, 2000, 2001) annual conferences. This provided us with a means to get to know one another, become familiar with our published work and current projects, and discuss future initiatives.

One of our first group decisions was concerned with the proper direction and title of the project that eventually yielded the present book. Two choices emerged: "Convicts Critique Criminology," with all the authors having served time, or the preferred choice, "Convict Criminology," a perspective that emerges not only from prisoners' experience but also from efforts to control state criminality (e.g., Barak, 1991; J. Ross, 1995/2000, 2000b), the radical/critical literature (e.g., Taylor, Walton, and Young, 1973; J. Ross, 1998b), and the input of enlightened academics. Thus, we agreed, a person does not have to be a convict to write convict criminology. Nevertheless, the majority of contributors are exconvicts.

INCLUSION CRITERIA

Those writing in the convict criminology tradition are at various points in their academic careers. Some of them are established scholars, whereas others are just completing their graduate studies. Many of them are accomplished researchers and writers; some are just beginning. Convict experience and a terminal degree were not the only criteria for inclusion. As we know, there are plenty of folks who are part of our club (the Ph.D. one) who are poor researchers and/or do not write well. Conversely, there are lots of individuals who have not gotten past their B.A. who can write circles around the best of us. Additionally, only including persons with Ph.D.'s would be elitist, something that we would not tolerate given our personal and political dispositions.

WHO ARE THE CONVICT AUTHORS?

In terms of academic experience, the convict authors fall into three distinct cohorts. The first are the more senior members, full and associate professors, some with distinguished research records. A second group of assistant professors is just beginning to contribute to the field. The third are the graduate student ex-convicts.

Regardless of academic status, the exconvicts belong to two distinct groups with different personal dispositions toward our collective project, with considerable overlap. The first group supported the "new school" with little if any hesitation. Some of these members are known excon academics (e.g., Robert Gaucher, John Irwin, Richard Jones, Charles Lanier, Greg Newbold, Stephen Richards, Chuck Terry, Edward Tromanhauser). The second group are excon professors and graduate students who share our perspective and provide those of us who are "out" with encouragement, but who for a number of personal and professional reasons have elected to remain anonymous, "in" the closet, where only their trusted friends know of their past. Some of their personal reasons include their reluctance to revisit a painful time in life, and a wish to put the past behind them. Professionally, a number of convict professors expressed concerns that by appearing in this book they might be denied fair access to government research grants. A few of the graduate students were concerned about "coming out" while still in graduate school, before they have tested the job market. All the contributors respect these decisions.

The excons undoubtedly provide convict criminology with unique and original experiential resources, but some of the most important contributors may yet prove to be scholars, who though having never served prison time, may have or will, at some time in the future, be arrested, charged, and or convicted of crimes. This situation may lead them to be reasonably empathetic. Some of the early nonconvict recruits to the new school, as either supporters or contributors, include William Archambeault, Bruce Arrigo, James Austin, Michael Brooks, Preston Elrod, Jeff Ferrell, Marianne Fisher-Giorlando, Barbara Owen, Jeffrey Ian Ross, Randy Shelden, Jim Thomas, Bill Tregea, and Michael Welch. The inclusion of non-excons in the new school's original cohort provides the means to extend the influence of this emerging perspective, while also supporting existing critical criminology perspectives.

It should be noted that although the sample is too small to draw significant conclusions, the majority of excon scholars are educated in sociology and criminology, with a smaller number in criminal justice, and a few more in social work, public administration, and education. This may indicate the relative acceptance and level of support provided excons as students in different disciplines, or how graduate programs may be struggling to recruit new students. Of course, there may be other excon academics whom we have failed to count in disciplines unrelated to criminology or criminal justice, for example chemistry or math, who would have little professional interest in our projects. Finally, three departments should be recognized for producing a handful of exconvict professors over the years and having a few more in the pipeline: the Department of Sociology at the University of California, Berkeley (Irwin); the Department of Criminology, Law and Society at the University of California, Irvine (Mobley, Terry); the Department of Sociology at Iowa State University (Jones, Murphy, Richards); and the School of Criminal Justice of the State University of New York at Albany (Lanier, LeBel, Lockwood).

The outlines of the new school of convict criminology's mission and purpose emerged as writers shared the experiences they have had with prison and academia. This represents an effort to revitalize the criminological literature with research validated by personal experience. Together, these academic authors critique existing theory and present new research from a convict or insider perspective. In short, they "tell it like it is." In doing so, they hope to convey the message that "it's about time" (Austin and Irwin, 2001)—time served, time lost, and time that taught us the lessons we share. In demarcating the field of study for this new approach to criminology, the contributors recognize that they are not the first to criticize the prison and correctional practices. They pay their respects to those who have raised critical questions about prisons and suggested realistic humane reforms. The problem is that, as Clear wrote in the foreword to McCleary's (1978/1992: ix) *Dangerous Men,* "Why does it seem that all good efforts to build reform systems seem inevitably to disadvantage the offender?" The answer is that, despite the best of intentions, reform systems were never intended to help convicts. The real problem is that the reformers rarely even bothered to ask the convicts what reforms they desired. The new school of convict criminology corrects this oversight because its scholars are primarily educated "con-sultants" (Mitford, 1973: 15).

THE PREEMINENCE OF JOHN IRWIN

The most prominent exconvict criminologist is John Irwin. His work and professional conduct over the years have inspired the group. In 1997, in San Diego, we had our first panel (organized by Chuck Terry) at an ASC annual meeting. That evening, over dinner, Irwin, along with James Austin, Stephen Richards, and Chuck Terry, discussed the potential of convict criminology. Irwin (Irwin and Cressey, 1962; Irwin, 1970, 1980, 1985a; Austin and Irwin, 2001) recalled how he had always wanted to assemble a group of excon scholars to write criminology from a convict perspective. However, over the last forty years, there have only been a few exconvicts holding academic positions. Ironically, the drug war, and the concomitant dramatic increase in prison populations in the last two decades, added to our numbers and provided the opportunity to assemble this group.

Irwin has mentored and supported the group from the beginning. We have held informal meetings at ASC and ACJS conferences, with Irwin generously spending time getting to know each member of the group. He would ask each one of us about our criminal past, academic status, and future plans. Irwin's counsel has been for us to honestly declare who we are, to articulate what we experienced and observed, and to do ethnography that tells the truth (Ferrell and Hamm, 1998; J. M. Miller and Tewksbury, 2000).

CRIMINOLOGISTS COMMIT CRIME TOO

In the past five years, some criminologists have reaffirmed the idea that the commission of crime is widespread, and that what separates most individuals from becoming "criminals" is the fact that the latter have been detected and processed by the criminal justice system whereas the former have never been caught (Gabor, 1995). Moreover, Robinson and Zaitzow's (1999) recent study indicates that academic criminologists have engaged in a variety of "criminal, deviant, and unethical behaviors," with varying levels of commitment based on their age and type of behavior. These findings demonstrate that many people in our profession have a more intimate relationship with deviance and crime than they would care to admit, or that they would want the public to know. The fact is there may be a fine line between who is a criminal and who is not. Many criminologists may be more than just curious or fascinated by crime. They may even reflect on, or remember, their occasional, be it past or present, flirtations with criminal violation.

OBJECTIVES OF CONVICT CRIMINOLOGY

Convict criminology challenges managerial criminology, criminal justice, and corrections. Research and publication by this group (e.g., Richards and Jones, 1997; Terry, 1997; Richards, 1998; Richards and Avey, 2000; Newbold, 2000; Austin and Irwin, 2001; Richards, Terry, and Murphy, 2002; Ross and Richards, 2002) should be viewed as a dramatic attempt to critique, update, and improve the critical literature in the field. We have two goals. First, to transform the way research on prisons is conducted. Second, to insist that our professional associations (e.g., ASC, ACJS) begin to articulate policy reforms that will make the criminal justice system humane.

ISSUE-BASED NATURE
OF CONVICT CRIMINOLOGY

Convict criminology is issue based and not necessarily structured by the traditional disciplinary divisions assumed by criminology, criminal justice, or corrections. These subjects describe the etiology of crime, stages of the criminal justice system, and correctional control as separate entities. Unfortunately, this approach has too often resulted in piecemeal research and analysis conducted by armchair technicians and theorists with precious little practical understanding of crime, criminals, and corrections (Austin, this volume).

Most academic criminologists fail to penetrate and comprehend the lived experience of defendants and prisoners, or are simply misinformed. In comparison, convict criminology is research carried out by our "felonious friends," who have both personal and abstract knowledge of the criminal justice machinery. Our work is held together by a number of themes, including, but not limited to, understanding the convict experience, forming convict identity, issues of survival in the convict world, transforming academic criminology/criminal justice, and proposing realistic policy alternatives.

QUESTIONS ASKED
AND ANSWERED BY THIS BOOK

A series of questions are answered by the convict criminology authors in this book. What is wrong with the criminology, criminal justice, and corrections literature? What is missing from the literature and discipline? How do the views of excon academics differ from those without insider status? What is it like for exprisoners to read academic material about crime, criminals, and corrections? What did the writers learn about the criminal justice system from being processed through arrest, court, jail, prison, and release? What unique research methods did the convict authors employ in their research? Why do authors need to be honest and truthful about themselves as they approach their research and writing? Did the prisoners' views on crime and corrections change when they became scholars? What obstacles did these excons experience as university employees? As exconvict professors, how do colleagues perceive them? What suggestions do former prisoners have for the reform of criminology, criminal justice, and prisons? Needless to say, in editing an endeavor like this one, we could not cover every possible subject connected to corrections and incarceration. Our hope is that we have covered the most important issues.

The structure of this book reflects the three core themes of convict criminology: critiquing corrections; forming the convict experience and identity; and understanding special populations in jails, prisons, and other correctional facilities. The chapters analyze existing theory and present new research from a convict or insider perspective. In short, they "tell it like it is." The book is divided into three parts: "What's Wrong with Corrections" (Austin; Ross; Fisher-Giorlando), "Convict Experience and Identity" (Tromanhauser; Terry; Richards; Newbold; Lanier; Jones; Mobley), and "Special Populations" (Owen; Murphy; Arrigo; Archambeault; Tregea; Elrod and Brooks).

Part I opens with Austin's chapter, which outlines how government-funded research studies were used to justify the dramatic increase in prison admissions. Ross explores how important cultural industries have misrepresented prison and prisoners as a means to increase corporate profits. Finally, Fisher-Giorlando underscores the importance of personal contact with the prison world. "In this day and age of a 'get tough' mentality and the public fear of criminals," she writes, "it is important to expose criminal justice students and the lay public to the prisoner as a person, not the horrible monster that the press paints."

Opening Part II, Tromanhauser talks about the problems of defining crime and understanding recidivism, and also tells the story of his 40 years of experience with the criminal justice system as armed robber, convict, and professor. Terry, perhaps more than any other writer in this volume, relates the personal dimension in his journey from West Coast surfer and occasional drug user to habitual offender, convict, university student, and now professor. He highlights his own self-discovery and the way he found new reference groups as a cushion against social alienation. Then, Richards shares his incarceration experiences and takes the reader on a journey through the federal prison system. His chapter introduces a new convict typology and emphasizes the active resistance of prisoners to long-term incarceration. Newbold discusses his time served in a New Zealand penitentiary, and how it contrasts with what we know about U.S. prisons. Lanier addresses the very painful subject of convict fathers. Jones looks at the problems of managing the disclosure of having a prison record, especially in light of his own experience as a graduate student and professor. Last, Mobley describes his personal dilemma of being an exconvict while entering a private prison to conduct research. In short, the convict criminologist contributors emphasize how their life experience transformed their self-concept and identity.

In Part III, Owen starts off the examination of special populations with her discussion of how women do time. Her study illustrates the need for ethnographic studies of females in prison. Murphy reviews how he and other prisoners with serious health concerns, despite inadequate medical services, managed to survive and maintain their dignity in federal medical prisons. Arrigo shares stories about how he, as a mental health caseworker, visited homeless people, many of whom had prison records, as they struggled to survive after being shifted from one institutional environment to another (transcarceration). He also documents how he tried to help his clients cope with the personal damage they had sustained and interpret that experience. Archambeault educates us about human diversity and the experience of Native Americans in prison. Tregea relates his experience teaching in a variety of correctional settings, outlining how he and a number of other college instructors, although starting their jobs out of economic necessity, were transformed by the experience and became advocates for higher education programs in prisons. Elrod and Brooks discuss how they learned by observing and interviewing in jail that children were being socialized to become future adult prisoners. They recommend that children and adolescents be immediately removed from adult jails.

The tone of the discussion may be somewhat more dramatic than what is expected in an academic text. All the contributors in this book are profoundly disappointed with much of what passes for respectable scholarship in this field. Unfortunately, the discipline is rarely grounded in reality and continues to be dominated by researchers that serve political masters rather than the needs of prisoners. The contributions in this book, we hope, will serve as a wake-up call to criminologists, policymakers, and the public.

CONCLUSION: DEVELOPMENT
AND SUPPORT OF CRITICAL
CRIMINOLOGICAL PERSPECTIVES

As the field of criminology matures, it will continue to incorporate new voices, challenge established hypotheses and theories, and develop new ones. Critical criminology, in particular, continues to contribute innovative theoretical developments. It is our hope that the new school of convict criminology will encourage critical criminologists to "ground" their theory in ethnographic accounts. This, we hope, will inform specific policy recommendations.

As the prison population continues to grow, so too will the number of individuals released back to the community. Many of these persons, as they reenter conventional society, will attend universities and study criminology, criminal justice, and corrections.

Stanley Cohen (1988/1992: 299) suggested this scenario in "The Last Seminar":

> Then Bridges, who I thought had been deliberately avoiding me, walked up to the desk at the end of the class in which he had participated with his usual intense stare. "You don't know anything about it, do you? It's all a game to you." I asked him what he meant. "Prison," he said, "You think because you've spoken to a few cons you understand it all. Well, you don't, you just don't." He was slowly shaking his head. The tone was polite but condescending. I'd heard that tone before. "How do you know?" I asked. "Because I've been inside, that's why. I don't want to talk about it now." He was already moving out of the room. He turned around at the door. "Didn't you know there were two of us in your class?"

As this process continues, some of these former prisoners will complete their graduate educations and become the future cohorts of the new school. We predict that over time, this new school of convict criminology will provide the public with a more realistic understanding of crime, criminal justice, and corrections that is based on experience and cutting-edge research.

NOTES

1. Throughout the text we have tried to be consistent in our use of the terms "convict" and "exconvict." Convict refers to a person in prison, whereas exconvict identifies an individual as once having served prison time and now residing in the free community. However, the public often assumes "once a convict always a convict" and discriminates against persons with prison records. Additionally, we have attempted to avoid the use of the terms "inmate" and "offender." Inmate generally refers to persons confined to an institution, such as a prison, hospital, or asylum. Thus, the term implies that prisoners are persons who are somehow physically or mentally impaired or suffering from some sort of sickness. Too often the term "inmate" is used by correctional workers to demean and dehumanize persons. From the convict's perspective, "inmate" is a managerial term that is used to insult prisoners. And, when convicts call another person an inmate, it is understood to be disrespectful. Inmates are understood to be prisoners that conform to institutional policy, follow the rules, obey orders, and betray the trust of other prisoners. They may be too familiar with or dependent on staff, or operate as snitches. We also avoid the term "offender," because a person may be convicted of a criminal offense but may not be an offender. The term also suggests that the person so identified is in some way offensive (as in "offensive odor"). We prefer the use of the term "prisoner" or "convict." Thus contributors consciously try to refer to men and women in prison as prisoners, convicts, or individuals. Alternatively, though somewhat unwieldy, would be to refer to "men or women convicted of a particular offense."

2. See also J. Jacobs (1980), J. Fox (1983), Cummins (1994), and Welch (1999: 187–215).

3. For a detailed discussion of the use of ethnographic methods to do prison research, see for example Peak (1985) and Farkas (1992).

4. It is instructive that with the exception of Irwin, Tromanhauser, and Lanier, all the exconvict contributors in this volume were convicted of drug-related offenses. This may lead critics to charge us with a subtle bias. Although this may be true, many of our academic colleagues—who we know have been convicted of misdemeanors or felonies—were not prepared to make public their convictions.

PART I

What's Wrong with Corrections?

INTRODUCTION

From the early days of the muckraking of Jessica Mitford (1973), to the contemporary analysis by scholars (Clear, 1994; Johnson, 1996; Austin and Irwin, 2001), corrections has been studied for all its shortcomings and inhumanity. Part I of *Convict Criminology* extends this work in three chapters.

Jim Austin, in "The Use of Science to Justify the Imprisonment Binge" (Chapter 1), argues that criminology has played a significant role in providing the scientific basis for justifying the historic increases in prison and jail populations. Beginning in the 1970s, a small number of studies by a conservative group of criminologists and organizations, funded by different federal agencies, were done to determine the impact of incapacitating offenders who fit the profile of a career criminal. This chapter reviews the methodological weaknesses and mistaken analyses in these studies. This research has been used to justify legislation and policy designed to widen the use of incarceration through truth in sentencing, abolition of parole, and mandatory minimums. A more appropriate interpretation of the career criminal research, if taken at face value, is that most prisoners are not career criminals, pose little threat to public safety, and should not be sentenced to prison or should serve much shorter prison terms.

Jeffrey Ian Ross, in "(Mis)Representing Corrections: The Role of Our Cultural Industries" (Chapter 2), discusses the many myths about jails, prisons, and prisoners. These misrepresentations, misconceptions, and stereotypes are conveyed through a series of symbols and images that influence how the public perceives and misunderstands corrections. At the same time, the number of individuals being incarcerated is at its highest historic level. In order to be part of the solution to this prison crisis, rather than contribute to the problem, we must be able to distinguish the myths from the reality. This chapter reviews the most dominant myths produced by various cultural industries, examines the role of popular culture and style in creating these images, and then deconstructs these powerful messages.

In "Why I Study Prisons: My Twenty-Year Personal and Professional Odyssey and an Understanding of Southern Prisons" (Chapter 3), **Marianne Fisher-Giorlando** discusses how her first teaching position in a prison college education program nearly two decades ago resulted in a career studying conditions of confinement. She credits her professional and personal commitment to prisoners as the basis for many of her academic accomplishments. This chapter includes a description of Fisher-Giorlando's early teaching experiences in both men's and women's prisons in Ohio; the teaching, research, and community service agenda that emerged; and her years of experience inside "infamous" Angola and other state correctional institutions in Louisiana. A brief history of the plantation prison model, with an emphasis on Louisiana, is included, illustrating the unique development of prisons in the South, a subject rarely included in corrections histories (Carleton, 1971; Rideau and Wikberg, 1992; Mancini and Lomax, 1996; Oshinsky, 1996). Fisher-Giorlando discusses the many tasks and issues involved in conducting research in prisons, teaching about them, introducing students to prisons through trips and research projects, and encouraging friends, students, and colleagues to visit prisons and participate in prison programs (Fisher-Giorlando and Jiang, 2000).

1

The Use of Science to Justify the Imprisonment Binge

JAMES AUSTIN

I got involved in the study of prisons by accident. Raised in a white middle-class culture (Wheaton, Illinois; the home of John Belushi, Billy Graham, and Bob Woodward), I was graduating from Wheaton College in 1970, with less than a stellar academic record, in search of work and a career. One of my sociology professors was a consultant for the Illinois Department of Corrections at the Joliet and Stateville maximum-security penitentiaries. He knew I was looking for a job and mentioned that the Illinois prison system was hiring college graduates to work as counselors; I applied, and was immediately hired, along with several other naive college graduates and a few middle-aged men with college degrees and checkered pasts in search of a new mission. Many of these individuals were religious types who had committed some moral transgression and could no longer be affiliated with organized religion. I marveled at how the inmates often appeared to be more "normal" than their counselors. Put differently, we had no experience in prisons, criminology, or skills in treating hardened criminals. Maybe, as the late Robert Martinson lamented before he committed suicide, "nothing works" in prison?

I spent the next four years bouncing between the Joliet and Stateville prisons (later relabeled as "correctional centers") helping to provide the illusion of rehabilitation and treatment. These were "real" prisons with a rich history of American penology. Most of the prisoners were young, uneducated, street-wise blacks being managed by middle-aged, uneducated white males from the rural farms of Illinois. It was truly a culture clash.

During those four years, I saw it all, including a couple of major prison riots. I also worked on death row, one of the country's first high-security control units, designed by the legendary Karl Menninger and Norval Morris. I spent time with James Jacobs as he wrote *Stateville,* and watched inmates "volunteer" for experimental drugs for TB, malaria, and who knows what else (they earned about $25 a month). I interviewed hundreds of convicts as they paraded before the parole board petitioning for their freedom. I also had the opportunity to get to know some of Chicago's most notorious gang members, who, sent to prison in record numbers by an aggressive Chicago prosecutor, were wreaking havoc on the way these prisons were managed. I even saw the famous convict turned university professor, John Irwin, make a cameo appearance at Stateville peddling his book *The Felon.* But, like so many "experts" before him, he came and went, and nothing really changed at Stateville and Joliet.

All of this was interesting for someone raised in the protected suburbs of Chicago. What struck me the most about prisons was how normal the convicts were in terms of their behavior and values. I rarely encountered prisoners who were as criminal as most people perceive them to be, or as portrayed on HBO's *Oz* series. Rather, they seemed to express conventional values and aspirations such as settling down, getting married, having children, owning a home, having a regular job, and going straight. What made "them" different from the "rest of us" was the color of their skin and their lack of education, social skills, and employment skills—a combination that would seriously limit their attempts to reach those shared middle-class goals. And, it became increasingly clear to me that their incarceration would do little to help them make it in the outside world.

After four years of the same routine (working in a prison can be like doing time), I grew bored and escaped to San Francisco out of the fear that I would end up working 30 years at Stateville, owing the prison credit union a ton of money and slowly losing my mind. Soon, I was hired by the National Council on Crime and Delinquency, a well-known liberal think tank. There, I mastered the craft of writing successful research proposals, which allowed me to live off of "soft research money" for the next 25 years.

At the same time, I navigated my way through a Ph.D. in the sociology program at the University of California at Davis, where I had the opportunity to study with Travis Hirschi and Ed Lemert (two extremes in criminological theory). In 1980, I completed my doctorate, with Lemert as dissertation chair. My "claim to fame" was that I had actually worked in a prison—a rare experience for almost all criminologists. Today, I work at George Washington University, where I have joined with a talented group of devoted colleagues and graduate students who are engaged in a number of major studies on juvenile and adult corrections at the Institute on Crime, Justice, and Corrections.

Throughout my career, I have been amazed at how many of our most distinguished criminologists—those who dominate the discourse on criminal justice policy—have so little firsthand knowledge or experience with prisons and prisoners. In my view, criminologists have become increasingly distant from what they are supposed to have expertise in: criminal behavior and the criminal justice system. They are spending less time observing their subject matter firsthand. Instead, they rely upon official records, despite the rich scholarly literature documenting the bias inherent in relying exclusively on agency-constructed data.

This trend toward "armchair" quantitative criminology has resulted in a flawed and incomplete understanding of criminal behavior and the advocacy of the so-called benefits of imprisonment. Unfortunately, this situation has contributed mightily to the imprisonment binge—the dramatic increase in the number of people sentenced to prison—that is the topic of this chapter.

THE ROLE OF SCIENCE IN ADVOCATING CRIMINAL JUSTICE POLICY

The American public is increasingly exposed to a barrage of information and facts all designed to influence their minds, money, and votes. Each day we hear about the results of new studies showing that something is amiss in our water, atmosphere, food, drugs, laws, and social institutions. Commensurate with the "major findings" is a recommended reform of some legal or bureaucratic policy or social institution that promises to correct our problems.

Increasingly, in order to advocate a particular reform, one must have some scientific evidence that "supports" the proposed policy. It matters little how this evidence is generated. The important requirement is that it be gathered and analyzed by respectable scientists and institutions that are qualified to issue such opinions on social policy. These designated opinion makers can be seen on the major television talk shows, read in the editorial pages of important newspapers, or heard at the plenary sessions of professional organizations.[1]

Too often, this information is what Cythnia Crossen (1994) has coined as "tainted truth." In the rush to justify one's ideology, studies and "significant findings" are manufactured to gain the upper hand in the battle for ideas with Congress, local and state policymakers, courts, and the media. As Crossen noted, scientific studies and their carefully orchestrated dissemination to the public have already influenced government decisions; for example, to allow the corporations that manufacture tobacco and silicone breast implants to distribute their goods while withholding factual information on the possible deadly effects on our health. Similarly, Pentagon estimates of enemy body counts during the Vietnam and the Gulf Wars illustrate the fabrication of truth that may serve to mold mass opinion rather than honestly inform the public. As noted by Jack Douglas (1992: 72), the situation has gotten far out of hand:

> Fraudulent activities pervade all forms of official information we have studied . . . Sonar reports, body counts, efficiency reports, preparedness reports, population (census) studies, crimes reported to police, university personnel records, and all others involve many fraudulent practices . . .

prefiguring, file building, unrepresentative glossing, unrepresentative windowing, outright lying, and many other forms of deceit.

The crime issue has been subject to a similar battle of "truth." In the past two decades, the United States has witnessed a truly remarkable, but horrific, escalation in the use of imprisonment to control crime. In 1980, for example, there were 330,000 persons in prison, a figure that has since increased to over 1.3 million—a rise of 300 percent. This historic change in the use of imprisonment did not happen by accident.

Even though numerous studies have repeatedly shown that most prisoners are neither career criminals nor dangerous, the vast majority of scientific attention has focused on what a few, but highly influential, criminologists have referred to as "persisters," "super predators," or the "truly dangerous." This bias has influenced policymakers to uncritically accept the notion that incarceration works and that reducing the prison population by even the smallest margins is both expensive and dangerous to public safety.

Unfortunately, few of us have the time, interest, or knowledge to examine the science that has been used to justify the imprisonment binge. This is understandable given the hectic work and family schedules of most people today as well as the daily deluge of facts and studies. Consequently, we only have time for truncated summaries of studies with little critique of the research. It has been taken for granted that the science is sound and need not be questioned.

RESEARCH-BASED "THINK TANKS"

In order to have political influence, one must have considerable resources and access to the media. This has resulted in the development of sophisticated, research-based "think tanks" and institutes that conduct research and provide policy recommendations that favor one particular ideological perspective over another. Most of these organizations are privately funded and unabashedly serve the interests of the funders. The most well-known institutions that fall into this category are the Heritage Foundation (conservative), the Manhattan Institute (conservative), the Cato Institute (libertarian), the Brookings Institute (centrist), and the Lindesmith Center (liberal). These organizations (with the exception of the Brookings Institute) rarely accept government funding, preferring private patron donations in order to preserve their ideological bent.

On the other hand, there are a larger number of nonprofit research centers and university-based institutes that are primarily staffed by well-known scientists and are funded by federal and state governments. By virtue of this public subsidy, they are expected to serve the interests of government. Unfortunately, their research is often used to advance policy initiatives favored by the majority political party. Beginning in the 1990s, for example, when the Republican party took control of the House of Representatives, they tried on several occasions to strip various liberal research centers of their nonprofit status so as to restrict their access to and support by federal funds.

FEDERAL CONTROL
OF RESEARCH DOLLARS

Federal money now dominates the criminal justice research agenda. Government-sponsored research is also inherently tied to the political interests of those politicians and bureaucrats who control the use and distribution of research funds. For example, the Office of Justice Programs (OJP), within the U.S. Department of Justice, is the primary source of funds for academicians conducting criminal justice research. The attorney general, who oversees the OJP, is nominated by the president to the Congress, which also must endorse the appointment. Finally, virtually all of the directors of the various agencies within the OJP are presidential appointees and must be approved by Congress.

In the long history of the National Institute of Justice (NIJ), which is the primary source of research funds for most academic research in criminal justice, the director has never been a trained criminologist. This is not to say that all research results emanating from these funding sources are tainted. Nevertheless, one should recognize a persistent bias in the research topics selected, the funding awarded, and the organizations and persons invited to produce scientific studies (see Ross, 2000a).

In the area of criminal justice reforms, this is certainly the case. Both liberal and conservative advocates have taken advantage of the politicized nature of funding to further their own political agendas. Under the Clinton administration, the Democrats also developed conservative policies. The major criminal justice initiatives were 100,000 more cops for community policing, three strikes you're out, truth in sentencing, the establishment of drug courts, programs to prevent violence against women, and prison construction. There was no Democratic initiative designed to reduce the prison population or reverse the dramatic rise in the incarceration of blacks and women.

Many criminologists have either supported or remained silent about the incarceration binge (Austin and Irwin, 2001).[2] A highly influential group of criminologists and organizations with considerable funding from the Reagan, Bush, and Clinton administrations has provided an ill-founded scientific basis to justify mandatory minimums, truth in sentencing, elimination of indeterminate sentencing (replaced by either sentencing guidelines and/or determinate sentencing), and the abolition of parole. The justification for increasing the use of prison sentences (disposition) and the length of incarceration (duration) can be summarized as follows:

1. There is a small but identifiable group of career criminals who are responsible for most of the crime being committed in each year.

2. These habitual criminals cannot be deterred, they do not respond to any forms of treatment, and their criminality does not decline with age.

3. The costs of their crimes far exceed the costs of incarceration.

These assumptions, I will argue in the following, are based on a combination of flawed research methodology and distorted interpretation of research results.

CRITERIA FOR ASSESSING RESEARCH

In their formal training, criminologists are taught to adhere to certain standards to ensure their research findings are valid and worthy of guiding policy. These standards are designed to ensure that theories of crime causation and responses to crime are rigorously tested by independent researchers at multiple sites before they can be brought to market. Some of the major tenets are as follows:

1. The application of rigorous experimental designs with random assignment to control for alternative hypotheses and factors that may confound the internal or external validity of the research.

2. Within the studies themselves, adequate and representative sample sizes with minimal sampling attrition to reflect the population in question so that the findings can be generalized to other physical settings or groups of people.

3. Multiple measures of the independent and dependent variables in question using both qualitative and quantitative data (triangulation).

4. Reanalysis of the reported findings by independent researchers to verify their statistical procedures and conclusions.

5. Additional studies conducted by other researchers at other sites to determine if the original findings can be replicated.

These requirements, however, are rarely applied to research used to formulate criminal justice policy. The more frequent procedure is to bring the untested "product" to market. Only later is it evaluated—by a sympathetic researcher using a weaker quasi-experimental design at a single site. This faulty research and development process has fostered such popular innovations as boot camps, drug courts, residential drug treatment programs, electronic monitoring, mandatory drug testing, and many other forms of what Stephen Richards (1998) has referred to as "community punishments."

A recent example will illustrate the problem. The Minneapolis police department adopted the policy of mandatory arrest and detention for persons charged with domestic violence. Using a rigorous experimental design to evaluate this policy, Larry Sherman and Richard Berk (1984) concluded that mandatory arrest reduced subsequent domestic violence incidents. On the basis of this single study, many police departments adopted the policy. Further experimental studies conducted by independent researchers in other cities, however, did not replicate the original positive findings. The mandatory arrest policy nonetheless remains in effect in many jurisdictions.

Several major studies have been used to support policies designed to incapacitate career criminals. A closer look at this research reveals some startling facts. Rather than being supportive of incarceration, this work shows that the number of habitual or career offenders is quite small, the future criminal behavior of these persons cannot be predicted, and most are already in prison. More important, this research reveals that most prisoners are not dangerous or habitual offenders; they have committed few crimes, most of which are petty and pale in comparison to the costs of incarceration.

THE MAJOR STUDIES

The Early Search for Career Criminals
and Their Incapacitation

In the 1950s, Marvin Wolfgang and his colleagues (Wolfgang, Figlio, and Sellin, 1972) at the University of Pennsylvania discovered that if you track a cohort of approximately 10,000 Philadelphia boys born in 1945, you will find that about 35 percent will be arrested at least once and most of them will have at least one arrest, but that a small percentage will account for most of the arrests associated with the cohort. Of the 3,475 who were arrested at least once, 1,613 had only one police contact as a youth. Put differently, about 80 percent of the cohort had very limited contact with the police. It is the remaining 1,862 that caught career criminologists' attention. It turns out that these youth were being arrested quite often. Specifically, the researchers found that 6 percent of the cohort (or 18 percent of all arrestees) was responsible for 52 percent of the cohort's entire number of arrests.

This pioneering study launched a modern effort to identify what John Irwin (1985b) referred to as the never-ending search for the "bogeyman." Led by a small group of criminologists who have published numerous reports (mostly reanalysis of a limited number of longitudinal cohort studies), a medical model perspective evolved that assumed criminals are different (abnormal) from the rest of us, cannot be treated, and need to be isolated from society for a very long time. These criminologists assumed that if they could establish a scientific basis for identifying the high-rate offender, the crime problem would be largely contained. Farrington, Ohlin, and Wilson (1986: vi) asserted that

> the idea no doubt sounds elusive and grossly affected to any reader unacquainted with research in this field, but in the main it is a simple theme: Let us follow the careers of groups of children, youths, and young adults over time, particularly the careers of those who are likely to be involved in crime, in order to try to distinguish those who are likely to be involved from those who are not, to discover which of them persist and which desist, and to learn which treatments seem to work and with whom. This is a well-known strategy in medical research; it is time for its importance to be appreciated and pursued with new vigor in criminological research.

This particular research methodology, which employed arrest records and involved little face-to-face interaction with offenders, despite its merits, had serious shortcomings (see, e.g., Weis, 1986).

Most "convicts," in fact, have episodic careers that begin at about age 15 and terminate by age 30. More important, it is not possible to separate the "good" from the "bad" using quantitative methods that rely only on official or self-reported measures of criminal behavior. Moreover, narrowly focusing on the quest for the career criminal ignores a more fruitful course of inquiry regarding the structural criminogenic attributes of American society (rather than convicts) to explain criminal behavior.

The 1970s Studies

There were five major publications in the 1970s that provided conflicting views on the merits of incapacitation (i.e., confinement to jail or prison). One of the first modern studies was conducted by two engineers (father and son) who were concerned about high crime rates in New York City and wanted to see how incarceration could reduce these rates. Shlomo and Reuel Shinnar (1975) developed a simplistic model that assumed that (1) offenders had distinct careers that began and ended (or in the language of social scientists, "initiation and termination"), and (2) during their careers they had constant rates of offending that were reflected in police reports. The Shinnars suggested that increasing the time of imprisonment for these convicts early on in their careers would have a direct impact on suppressing crime rates. Put differently, if a career criminal is incarcerated for 50 percent of his/her active career, the amount of crime reduced will also be 50 percent. They went even further, predicting that if all persons convicted of a violent crime were imprisoned for five years, the violent crime rate in New York would drop by as much as 80 percent.

Shortly thereafter, Joan Petersilia and Peter Greenwood from the Rand Corporation initiated their careers as career criminal researchers with a 1978 report claiming that a mandatory five-year prison term for convicts convicted of violent crimes in Denver, Colorado, would have reduced crime in the Mile High city by 30 percent.

In 1974, Stephen Clark published the first study to temper these promises of dramatic crime reduction through incapacitation with his analysis of the incapacitation effects on a cohort of nearly 10,000 Philadelphia boys. He concluded that current incarceration policies were averting only 5–15 percent of all juvenile Uniform Crime Report (UCR) crimes, and only 1–4 percent of all UCR crimes (adult and juvenile).

This publication was followed by a study of people convicted of violent crimes in Franklin County (Columbus), Ohio, by criminologists Steve Van Dine, Simon Dinitz, and John Conrad. Their publication, released in 1992, concluded that if all of these people had received a mandatory five-year sentence, the crime rate in Columbus for these crimes would have dropped by no more than 4 percent.[3]

That same year, the respected physicist turned criminologist David Greenberg published national estimates of incapacitation effects that would be derived by either increasing or decreasing the nation's prison population by 50 percent. He concluded that such a policy would only increase or decrease the crime rate by less than 4 percent (Greenberg, 1975).

These conflicting studies encouraged a small cohort of influential criminologists to develop their own models of career criminality and incapacitation effects using either self-report or arrest data.[4] Their view would push major funding of studies in pursuit of the career criminal instead of understanding why so many convicts were *not* career criminals. This career criminal research so dominated federal funding that two prestigious but noncareer criminal criminologists, Michael Gottfredson and Travis Hirschi (1986: 213), openly complained about the lack of opportunity for other criminologists:

> On March 26, 1982, 14 leading members of the criminology community in the United States met in Washington, D.C. to discuss the future of criminal justice research in this country. The priority area for future research listed by this panel was "criminal careers" . . . Four years later, the criminal career notion so dominates discussion of criminal justice policy and so controls expenditure of federal research funds that it may now be said that criminal justice research in this country is centrally planned.

The intellectual climax of this movement occurred in 1986 with the publication and widespread dissemination of two volumes of research by the National Academy of Sciences (NAS). This occurred at the height of the Reagan administration, whose Department of Justice was under the direction of Edwin Meese, who funded the studies through the National Institute of Justice (see Blumstein, Cohen, Roth, and Visher, 1987). It is ironic that this body of science, which later fueled the imprisonment binge, was initially defined by the panel's chair, Alfred Blumstein, as a possible means for reducing the prison population as well as crime rates. From the onset, these criminologists recognized what others had been saying for some time—that most convicts sentenced to prison were not career criminals and contributed to the crime rate. In the introduction to their volume, Blumstein, Cohen, Roth, and Visher (1986: vii) wrote:

> In 1983, when the Panel on Research on Criminal Careers was convened, the U.S. prison population had experienced a rapid growth—more than doubling from 196,000 in 1972, to 437,000 in 1983—and the crime rate had just passed its 1980 peak of 13 million reported index crime, or almost 6,000 crimes per 100,000 population. There was strong policy interest in finding alternatives to rapidly escalating imprisonment costs and what was perceived as a relatively ineffective crime control. One approach that was widely considered was to direct attention at "career criminals," high rate or long duration offenders, who contribute to higher crime rates.

Somehow, the original goal of using career criminal research to develop new sentencing policies that would reduce the prison population never materialized. It is even more than ironic that since the 1986 report was released, crime rates have continued to rise and the prison population has tripled in its size. The NAS monograph presented new findings on the nature of career criminals and the likely effects of their incapacitation. The report focused on a new type of criminal career (the "persister"), and the Rand Corporation's research, also funded by NIJ, focused on the utility of "selective incapacitation."[5]

The Persisters

The search for career criminals and their incapacitation was sanctioned as a promising research endeavor by the 1978 NAS Panel on Deterrence and Incapacitation Effects. The NAS was staffed by some of the leading proponents of career criminal research, who had reached the conclusion that most "offenders" have a relatively brief and modest criminal career, but a small group of "persisters" were actively involved in serious crime for long periods of time (well beyond age 40). This research contradicted the other major studies by claiming that age (or the maturation effect) did not diminish these offenders' pattern of criminal behavior; it followed that these persisters were prime candidates for long-term incapacitation.

The studies relied upon by the NAS were simply the same ones that the panel members themselves had published earlier. In general, the research consisted of cross-sectional samples of adults arrested in a given year in two cities (Washington, D.C., and Detroit). "Persisters" were identified from this data. Because of the criteria for being selected as a possible persister (one must have had at least two arrests, with one in the year for which the sample was drawn and a second at age 18, 19, or 20), a very small sample was constructed. For example, in 1973, of the 5,338 persons arrested in Washington, D.C., less than 200 met the selection criteria. For 1974–1977, of the 18,635 people arrested in Detroit, less than 150 were analyzed. Even within these extremely small samples, the average number of arrests for serious crimes was about one for every five to seven years of street time.

The policy implications of this finding alone seem to have received short shrift by the career criminal researchers. These results showed that the vast majority of people arrested each year do not persist and are, at best, episodic criminals. It also sets up a situation where, due to an extremely low "base rate," it would be virtually impossible to develop a risk instrument or scale that could predict or separate the "persisters" from the "desisters" (see Table 1.1).

Such methodological issues should have prevented the researchers from reaching firm conclusions. Or, they might have made the more obvious inference: The so-called persister is a very rare and fortunate breed of criminal— "fortunate" in the sense that it would be truly remarkable that anyone who is repeatedly arrested for serious crimes over a 20-year period would somehow escape long periods of incarceration. Even with a relatively low police clearance rate (crimes cleared by arrest) of approximately 20 percent, it would be virtually impossible to comprehend a benevolent prosecutor that would allow any adult offender to be arrested on a regular basis for two decades and not be "put away" for a substantial period of imprisonment.

These "persisters" probably reflect pathetic persons whom the police use to pad their arrest records. Or they could be "snitches" rather than "persisters," whom the police rely upon to inform on others, and are then rewarded for their snitching by having the charges dropped. The failure to recognize these possibilities reflects an incredible level of naiveté on the part of these scientists. And these practices have been going on for many decades.

Table 1.1 A Closer Look at the "Persisters"

CAREER CRIMINAL STUDIES		
Key Attributes	**Washington, D.C.**	**Detroit**
Year	1973	1974–1977
Attributes of arrestees	Adults, 92% non-white, 90% male, 75% under age 35	Adults, 43% non-white, 96% male, 83% under age 35
No. persons arrested	5,338	18,635
Crimes adults have been arrested for	Homicide, rape, robbery, aggravated assault, burglary, auto theft	All crimes
Average arrest rate per year	1.09	0.55
Sample sizes of possible persisters	Under 200	Under 200
Percentage of original cases	3.7	1.1
Estimated annual crime rates	25.9 per year	14.6 per year

SOURCE: J. Cohen (1986: vii).

In a recent study of prisoners released from a boot camp program in Chicago, I first tracked the number of times a released person had been returned to the jail as a measure of "failure." One high-ranking law enforcement official was bemused by my effort at quantitative social science:

> Don't you know what's going on here? These poor mopes are the ones standing on the corner and getting roused by the vice squad [drugs, prostitution, gambling] to pad their monthly numbers. If you look at the dispositions of these repeat offenders, you'll see they're getting dropped either by the DA or the judge.

Sure enough, when I restricted my measure of recidivism to court dispositions, I found that about half had been dropped by the prosecutor (no probable cause). It was enough to show that instead of a 40 percent failure rate, the actual 12-month rate was about 20 percent. An arrest or return to jail does not prove criminal behavior. People are arrested but not indicted for a crime, or the charges are dropped for lack of evidence, misidentification, or false complaint.

This raises the obvious question of why the NAS researchers failed to further investigate or reveal the court's handling of the persistent arrestees. After being arrested, were the defendants released, jailed, acquitted, or found guilty by a court of a crime? A major reason for the lack of court disposition data is that they don't exist. Many of those arrested had no official court disposition recorded, which made it impossible to distinguish "criminals" who were incarcerated from those who were not. Many of those arrested were released without appearing in court or being convicted of a crime.

Those familiar with police practices understand that police can easily manufacture an arrest pattern that fits the profile of a "persister." Namely, the police routinely round up the "usual suspects" for any crime reported in a particular neighborhood. These individuals are typically poor, young, and/or members of minority groups that cannot afford legal counsel, who are easy victims for police frustrated by high inner-city crime rates. Minorities were especially at risk in Detroit and Washington, D.C., which at the time had dismal reputations for shoddy police practices and corruption.

The NAS researchers then amplified the amount of crime that could be attributable to the "persisters." For each arrest, an estimate of the "actual amount of crime" committed by each arrestee was based on the ratio of aggregate reported crimes to the aggregate arrests for the two cities. For example, if the ratio of reported index crimes to arrests was 13 to 1, it was assumed that a person who had been arrested for any index crime in D.C. in 1973 had committed 13 index crimes.

In the research literature, this is commonly known as an "ecological fallacy," where the attributes of a group are ascribed to individuals. Because the ratio of reported crimes is much higher than arrest rates, anyone arrested must be committing more crimes at exactly the same ratio of his/her community, city, state, or country. This may be true or false, but we really don't know unless we get closer and better observations of the person's behavior and lifestyle. But that would require the researchers to interview and observe the identified "persister."

Despite these limitations, the NAS recommended that these "persisters" were prime candidates for lengthy periods of incarceration—apparently, something they believed was not occurring in the 1980s. Blumstein, Cohen, Roth, and Visher (1986: 92–93) concluded that this

> pattern has important implications for incapacitation policies applied to older more established offenders. The sharp decline in aggregate arrest rates by age 30 has conventionally been interpreted to mean that incarceration would be wasted on 30-year-old offenders because they are about to terminate their careers . . . . The few persistent offenders who begin their adult careers at age 18 and remain criminally active into their 30s appear to represent prime candidates for incarceration.

Given the dubious quality of the data used to reach such a conclusion, it would be prudent to further investigate why these "persisters" were not being incarcerated even though they were frequent visitors to the squad car and local jail.

Collective and Selective Incapacitation

The NAS work fit nicely with the well-financed Rand career criminal research program and its support for incapacitation as public policy. The Rand studies began in the 1970s as the public was becoming increasingly concerned with the rising crime rates. Over a 10-year period a number of influential reports were funded by what is now known as the National Institute of Justice and published by the Rand Corporation. These studies received widespread attention among politicians looking for a scientific basis for the building of more prisons. The titles of these reports reflect the tenor of the times: *Criminal Careers of Habitual Felons* (Petersilia, Greenwood, and Lavin, 1978), *The Prison Experience of Career Criminals* (Petersilia and Honig, 1980), *Who Commits Crimes: A Survey of Prison Inmates* (Peterson and Braiker, 1981), *Varieties of Criminal Behavior* (Chaiken and Chaiken, 1982), and *Does Crime Pay?* (Wilson and Abrahamse, 1992).[6]

The Rand researchers, like the NAS, believed they too had discovered the scientific means for identifying habitual or career criminals. Still, they went further to argue that incapacitation, and in particular, "selective incapacitation" (locking up people before they commit crime) would be an effective policy to reduce crime. The idea of using incapacitation was not new. This school of thought had already produced scientific findings that imprisonment would reduce crime.

For example, NAS researcher Jacqueline Cohen (1978) calculated that by imposing a mandatory two-year period of imprisonment on all adult convicts convicted of robbery in the District of Columbia (the jurisdiction where some of the highest incarceration and crime rates in the country) would reduce the number of robberies by 8 percent and increase the prison population by only 7 percent. Zimring and Hawkins (1995) noted that the uncritical acceptance of incapacitation as public policy was troubling given that it was based on so little research. The Rand studies sought to fill that gap.

The Rand researchers conducted a number of studies in search of the career criminals who would be candidates for lengthy prison terms. The first study involved interviews with 49 prisoners serving time for robbery convictions at a single California prison. Enthused by the results of this study, a larger study, funded by the U.S. Department of Justice, consisted of 624 California inmates housed at five prisons. A third and final study, also funded by the U.S. Department of Justice, consisted of conducting these surveys in California again and two other states (Texas and Michigan), with even a larger sample (2,190 convicts).

The methodology employed in these studies can be summarized as follows (see Table 1.2): The researchers who administered the surveys to the prisoners drew random samples of the daily population. Elaborate statistical manipulations of the sample were conducted by Rand's statisticians, who "simulated" an admissions sample. These inmates were asked how many crimes they had committed during the past two to three years. This is known as a "retrospective study," meaning the inmates were simply recounting how many crimes they had committed before coming to prison.

For the second study, two exconvicts were hired to develop a rapport with some of the more suspicious prisoners, who were told their responses would be treated anonymously. They received $5 each for completing the 25-page questionnaire. In retrospect, one wonders if the respondents were aware that their responses would lead to recommendations to keep them incarcerated more often and for longer periods of time (i.e., informed consent).

Generally, the Rand studies produced methodologically suspect findings that were then interpreted in a questionable manner to support selected incapacitation. The results of all three surveys yielded two major findings. First, the vast

Table 1.2 A Closer Look at Rand's Incapacitation Studies

Year	1975	1976	1978–79
Correctional facility location	One California prison	Five California prisons	Prisons in three states (California, Michigan, Texas)
Type of inmates	Inmate population convicted for armed robbery with at least one previous prison term	Entire inmate population	Prison and jail population that was "weighted to simulate admissions cohort"
Original sample size	60	1,323	2,190
Final sample	49	624	1,270[a]
Attrition rate (%)	18	53	42
Type of data	Retrospect and self-reported crimes for time periods ranging from 3 to 11 years	Retrospect and self-reported crimes for the 3 years before current incarceration	Retrospect and self-reported crimes for 13–24 months before current incarceration
Results	Most inmates report an "intermittent" pattern of crime with long periods of crime-free activity	Most inmates report no or very few previous crimes and very few report high rates	Most inmates report no or very few previous crimes and very few report high rates

[a]It is difficult to determine the sample size in the study; in a note Cohen reported that 42 percent of cases were excluded because of "bad data."

SOURCE: J. Cohen (1986).

majority of inmates were low-rate criminals. They rarely committed crimes (none to two or three per year), most of their crimes were nonviolent, and most were of little economic value. As reported by Pierre Tremblay and Carlo Morselli (2000), the median annual income derived from these crimes for the surveyed inmates (in 1976) was only $546 (at 1997 values). Nevertheless, like the NAS panel, Rand paid very little attention to this finding, even though Rand's samples were of prisoners serving lengthy prison terms.

In another Rand study, Petersilia and Honig (1980) sought to discover if "career criminals" behaved differently than "noncareer criminal" convicts in prison with respect to serious disciplinary incidents. On the basis of prevailing theory, Petersilia and Honig expected that these convicts, who were assumed to be violent predators, would be the most difficult persons to manage in prison. However, the researchers found that these "career criminals" behaved just like the "normal" convicts. It should be noted that Rand classified nearly half the prison population in the three studies as "career criminals" on the basis of one prior prison sentence. This questionable definition of a career criminal no doubt contributed to their finding of no difference in convict behavior.

Regardless of the findings in the follow-up studies, public attention was riveted on the second finding: a very small portion of the sample reported committing a very large number of crimes per year (well over 100 crimes per year). By narrowly focusing on these "outliers," the Rand researchers argued the bene-fits of selective incapacitation. Greenwood and Abrahamse (1982) predicted that crime rates could be reduced by 20 percent, without increasing the prison population, by extending the period of incarceration by the magical five years. They developed a simple, seven-item additive scale they claimed accurately sep-arated the "good" from the "bad" and urged its adoption by courts for sentenc-ing purposes. Despite severe methodological problems, the Rand studies were also hailed by fellow criminologists (and prosecutors) as a major advance in our knowledge of criminal behavior.

The collection and analysis of these data were seriously compromised. To be classified as a career criminal, each sampled convict (selected on the basis of willingness to participate) was asked to respond to a list of 15 questions, which the Rand researchers assumed reflected criminal behavior. Regardless of the number of years they had been in prison, the prisoners were asked to remem-ber how many times in the last three years, before they were incarcerated, they had committed the following acts:

1. Threatened someone with a weapon in order to get money or some-thing else.
2. Totally lost your temper.
3. Beat or physically hurt someone badly.
4. Hustled or conned someone.
5. Cut someone with a knife or shot someone with a gun.
6. Broke into a home or business in order to take something.
7. Got into a fist fight.
8. Forced someone to have sex with you.
9. Got drunk and hurt someone.
10. Threatened to hurt someone with a gun, knife, or other weapon.
11. Tried to kill someone.
12. Forged a check or other paper.
13. Stole a car.
14. Sold hard drugs.

Because many of the surveyed prisoners had served more than two years be-hind bars, they had to recall events that had occurred five years or more in the past. Calendar cards were used to help the prisoners determine when the crimes occurred. But Visher (1986: 175, 180), in her reanalysis of the Rand data, re-ported that despite these efforts to get complete responses, "incomplete or am-biguous responses in this set of questions were fairly common," and that "many inmates had trouble filling out their calendars."

Each prisoner was asked to estimate how many crimes he had committed in the past three years prior to incarceration using preset categories of either 10 or under or 11 or more. If it was 10 or under, the prisoners had to say exactly how many crimes they had committed. However, 17 percent of the inmates failed to provide any number. Rand decided to assign an average of 5.5 even though the typical convict reported 2–3 crimes, thus producing an exaggerated average. For the prisoners who reported 11 or more, Rand used estimation methods that the NAS had used to inflate the number of crimes reported by the inmates (Visher, 1986: 205).

Later, Visher, with Spelman (1986: 206), reanalyzed the Rand data and the Greenwood/Abrahamse selective incapacitation scale using more conservative estimates of the retrospective rates of offending as self-reported in the surveys. Visher and Spelman concluded that the estimated crime reduction benefits were excessive and that the concept of selective incapacitation was not warranted as a suitable and practical sentencing public policy. Two additional studies also failed to validate the Rand survey results. One study, funded by NIJ, was conducted by Peter Greenwood, the primary advocate of selective incapacitation, and another Rand associate, Susan Turner. It is instructive that NIJ did not issue any requests for proposals to other researchers not associated with the original selective incapacitation studies to attempt replication studies of the scale and to validate the scale on released inmates.

Greenwood and Turner (1987) followed California inmates from the third Rand survey, some of whom had been classified as high-rate convicts and had been released from custody. The title of their report says it all—"Selected Incapacitation Revisited: Why the High-Rate Offenders Are Hard to Predict." Basically, Greenwood and Turner discovered what others had noted before; it is virtually impossible to predict future offending among those few ex-prisoners classified as high-risk convicts. Thus, many of the inmates Greenwood had originally wanted to lock up for five more years in his previous studies turned out to be low-rate offenders, persons that matured out of crime. So, Greenwood changed his mind, but the damage had already been done, as his previous research was used to support stiffer sentencing laws.

The second validation study, by Auerhahn (1999), was conducted on a 1991 sample of 2,188 California inmates. Her study was instructive because she was using official data available from the courts and prison system to score the prisoners, as opposed to using self-report survey information. In this sense, her application of the selective incapacitation scale was a more practical and independent test of the instrument's utility. She found that most prisoners would score as low- (41 percent) or medium- (31 percent) rate offenders. Her analysis suggested that the Rand study did quite poorly in terms of actually predicting the future behavior of prisoners with extensive prior criminal records. Auerhahn (1999: 703) concluded that, especially for the high-rate convicts, "the selective incapacitation scheme advocated by Greenwood and Abrahamse performs extremely poorly in terms of both reliability and validity, thus precluding the implementation of such schemes." Auerhahn (1999: 727) marveled that some criminologists still clung to the idea that incapacitation of high-rate convicts (who could not be identified on a retrospective basis) was a worthy idea: "Their statement that their support of selective incapacitation as a strategy that 'works' is based not on the available empirical research, but rather on the theory and philosophy that underlies selective incapacitation proposals."

The Costs of Crime

The second part of the pro incapacitation argument is that it's "cheaper to keep 'em." During the Reagan administration, Zedlewski (1987), a NIJ staffer with a Ph.D. in economics, published a report, widely disseminated by NIJ, stating that incarcerating high-rate convicts as defined by the Rand studies would result in significantly reduced crime, and society would reap enormous economic benefits. Specifically, each year of additional incarceration for each prisoner would cost $25,000, but society could avert $430,000 in social costs. Zedlewski assumed that each incarcerated offender would have committed 187 crimes per year, costing about $2,300 per crime (the combined costs of the victims of crime and the criminal system).

A related study that attempted to quantify the "true" costs of crime was conducted by Mark Cohen and his colleagues. An initial report was published in 1988, with another version released in 1996 by NIJ. Cohen and colleagues (2000) took the cost of crime one major step higher by adding the costs of "pain and suffering" to the cost/benefit equation. Remarkably, this piece of research claimed that the true cost of national street crime was actually $450 billion per year, with $345 billion being linked to so-called quality of life issues. These cost figures are well above the government's own estimates of $17.6 billion suffered by victims.

These two studies allowed many politicians to argue that increased incarceration would significantly reduce crime and yet save money; in fact, hundreds of billions of dollars. DiIulio, using the NAS and Rand career criminal research findings, claimed that "prisons were a bargain." "Truth in sentencing," "three strikes and you're out," and other efforts to lengthen prison terms were advocated by many politicians who now had the scientific basis to support their "get tough on crime" ideology. For example, California's then Governor Pete Wilson's chief economist promised that passing the "three strikes and you're out" legislation would reduce the crime rate in California by 20 percent and the state would save $55 billion (Romero, 1994). Conversely, policies that might serve to reduce prison sentences, for example, diversion to community supervision, were criticized as "ineffective."

THE NUMBERS DO NOT ADD UP

These career criminal and incapacitation studies have been roundly criticized because the numbers do not add up to what is well known regarding the number of crimes and their costs. With respect to the number of crimes associated with incarcerated felons, Zimring and Hawkins (1988) have noted that assuming the 187 crimes per convict was true, given the large increase in the prison population, crime would have been eliminated in the United States many years ago. Clearly, the numbers do not make sense.

And, as I have pointed elsewhere with respect to Mark Cohen's cost/benefit claim, using rarely issued jury awards for "pain and suffering" for all crimes, regardless of their relative pettiness, is absurd:

These estimates are applied to all crimes despite the fact that virtually none result in jury awards. Even if one assumes that the $345 billion estimate of "quality of life" is accurate, what does it mean in real dollars? The answer is very little. The number is only a monetary symbol, it has nothing to do with real dollars, and has no economic significance. (Austin, 1996: 10)

Similarly, Zimring and Hawkins (1995: 138) wrote:

The specific cost estimates are opportunistic, arbitrary, inconsistent, and too high. The schema lacks an articulated theory of either public or private cost. Moreover, Cohen's analysis reveals no relationship between the cost estimates and his conclusions about the cost-effectiveness of the investment in further crime control resources.

CONCLUSION: WHO'S AFRAID OF THE BOGEYMAN?

It is time to terminate the search for the bogeyman. Children who are afraid of the dark sleep with a night light on. Science demands that we examine the facts in the light of day. There is no criminal hiding under the bed or in the closet. The convict is not the bogeyman. Maybe what is truly frightening for many people is to realize, as I discussed earlier in this chapter, that prisoners are normal, not unlike you or me. The fact is, we still have no empirical evidence that career criminals represent a significant number of individuals in our prison population. Despite years of scientific studies, we still have no reliable means to predict the behavior of men or women after release from prison. For better or worse, past behavior does not necessarily determine the future.

To summarize, the NAS and Rand studies on career criminals had the following methodological issues, which compromise their utility as a rational basis for public policy:

1. Few if any of the researchers have conducted studies that are based on direct field observations of convicts relative to their pre-prison, imprisonment, or postincarceration behavior.

2. The major published studies are retrospective and use prior arrests and self-reported crimes, all of which have the following methodological problems:
   a. Severe sampling attrition rates.
   b. Few independent replication studies funded by nongovernment sources in other jurisdictions by researchers who do not share the well-published ideological perspective of the pro-incarceration scientists.
   c. Severe errors in the prediction of the impact of increasing incarceration policies on future crime rates and on the criminal justice system.
   d. Where independent reanalysis and replication studies have been conducted, the research does not support selective incapacitation as a means to lower crime rates.

Along with these methodological shortcomings, what is most striking is that conservative social scientists have selectively focused on career criminals and the possible benefits of incarcerating them. Their own data clearly show that most people arrested and incarcerated are not career criminals, persisters, or high-rate convicts. My complaint is that this finding has been ignored and silenced, and the silence has been deafening. As politely noted by David Greenberg (1991), the public and policymakers have been given the impression that many career criminals remain at large and are causing most of the crime problem. Greenberg (1991: 39) warned:

> This potential for bias becomes even stronger because of the tendency of naive lay persons to oversimplify, misunderstand, or lose distinctions and qualifications that criminologists make about their work and consider important. This point was brought home to me when a scientist-colleague who is not a criminologist told me that he heard Al Blumstein speak about criminal career research. He "learned" that we now have the capacity to identify "career criminals" with high precision while they are still very young, and he added that it was much to be regretted that public senti-mentality about young children stood in the way of solving the crime problem through very long periods of preventive imprisonment for such precareer criminals.

What is most startling is the recklessness of these researchers in their pro-motion of these dubious findings and recommendations as worthy for imple-mentation as public policy. Rather than trying to incarcerate the elusive (and in fact already imprisoned) career offender, our science should be directed toward a massive decarceration effort by reducing prison terms rather than extend-ing them. Because we are still afraid of the bogeyman, there are hundreds of thousands of men and women wasting away in prison who could be productive citizens. This is what our science is telling us. But thus far, that science is losing badly.

NOTES

1. It goes without saying that these "high priests" of science do not reflect our soci-ety but are heavily skewed toward white males who come from privileged families and academic institutions supportive of the status quo.

2. Where questions have been raised, they have been raised in a very timid manner.

3. Apparently, this figure was computed by discarding many cases with missing information. If one assumes the missing cases had the same attributes as the known cases, the amount of violent crime reduced by incapacitation increases to 26 per-

cent (personal communication with Steve Van Dine).

4. The leading career criminal research-ers in this cohort of criminologists were Alfred Blumstein, Delbert Elliott, David Farrington, Albert Reiss, and Marvin Wolfgang, plus those associated with the Rand Corporation, which include Allen Abrahamse, Jan Chaiken, Marcia Chaiken, Peter Greenwood, Joan Peter-silia, and Mark Peterson.

5. In reviewing this chapter, Steve Van Dine (personal communication) expressed the view that I have misrepresented the intentions of the Rand researchers and

Professor Blumstein, all of whom I know quite well. He thought that they were actually bent on using the "selective incapacitation" as a means for reducing the unnecessary incarceration of many convicts. This suggested that whereas the Shinnars and Wilson advocated a more wholesale approach, the other researchers believed that "selective incapacitation" could be used to maximize crime control with little or no prison growth. Perhaps this is true, but it is noteworthy that these same researchers have never published this perspective or provided testimony at congressional or legislative hearings stating that in the 1980s there was no need to expand the prison population.

6. For a detailed listing of the LEAA-funded studies for Rand, see Petersilia and Honig (1980).

2

(Mis)Representing
Corrections

The Role of Our
Cultural Industries

JEFFREY IAN ROSS

The correctional system in the United States and elsewhere suffers from numerous problems (Welch, 1996; Austin and Irwin, 2001). One of the most important issues is that it is hard to obtain accurate information about corrections, incarceration, and prisoners.[1] Consequently, many falsehoods, myths, misconceptions, misrepresentations, and stereotypes about this field have been developed by individuals, organizations, and institutions.[2]

To address this problem, I identify the common myths of corrections, review the most important cultural industries that are responsible for developing the misconceptions, and provide appropriate examples from the respective industries that demonstrate how the myths are used.[3] To do this, it is necessary to situate this endeavor in an appropriate epistemology. I use the radical/critical perspective, which I believe best informs this topic (e.g., I. Taylor, Walton, and Young, 1973; Lynch and Groves, 1986/1989; J. Ross, 1998b).

In general, the critical perspective, as applied to corrections, involves

> questioning, challenging and examining all sides of various problems and
> issues. Instead of uncritically accepting punishment and corrections as
> natural extensions of society, the critical approach delves under the sur-
> face of punishment to explore corrections at greater depths . . . it dispels

Special thanks to Natasha J. Cabrera, Richard S. Jones, Charles Lanier, Greg Newbold, Stephen C. Richards, Charles S. Terry, and the anonymous reviewers of this book for helpful comments. This chapter was presented at the annual meetings of the American Sociological Association, Anaheim, California, August 2001.

many myths and misconceptions surrounding corrections . . . it demysti-
fies the objectives, processes and outcomes of correctional intervention
and offers alternative interpretations and solutions (Welch, 1996: 7).

This kind of ideology and methodology looks for the hidden meanings behind
myths and explores their utility, purpose, and function, and thus better informs
this subject matter. I do not suggest that one *needs* to adopt a radical or critical
perspective to examine issues at a deeper level, but this is a central feature of
such an approach. More specifically, in this chapter I explore the importance of
mythmaking about crime, criminal justice, and corrections; look at why myths
are successful; examine the important role of cultural industries, such as fashion,
advertising, documentaries, fictional treatments, motion pictures, and the mass
media/news media; and offer some concluding thoughts about remedying this
problem.

THE IMPORTANCE OF MYTHMAKING
ABOUT CRIME, CRIMINAL JUSTICE,
AND CORRECTIONS

Most people have never been in a holding cell, jail, or prison as an arrestee, convict, correctional officer, support staff, administrator, teacher, or visitor. Thus,
the general public depends on secondary sources of information and their own
(often inadequate) inferences about correctional facilities and the individuals
who live and work there (R. Freeman, 2000: 3).[4] Too often this material is conveyed in the form of folklore or myths (Pepinsky and Jesilow, 1985; Kappeler
et al., 1996), thus increasing its transmission and consumption.

   Myths are not necessarily arbitrary, false, or the result of poor research or
differences of opinion. Rather a myth is "a traditional story of unknown authorship, with a historical basis, [that] explain[s] some event." Myths "exaggerate . . .
'ordinary' events in life. [They are] nonscientific, spoken or written fiction used
as if it were a true account of some event" (Kappeler et al., 1996: 2). These authors add, "These crime fictions often take on new meanings as they are told
and retold—and at some point [are accepted as] truth for many people" (2).
Myths are powerful windows into the beliefs of a society. They are not always
false, but they may exaggerate or simplify particular aspects of reality.

   The notion that the criminal justice system (e.g., Pepinsky and Jesilow,
1985; Kappeler et al., 1996; "America's Prisons," 1997; Reiman, 1995), corrections in general (e.g., R. Freeman, 2000), and various dimensions of corrections
(e.g., Kolfas and Toch, 1982; Schicher, 1992; McAuley, 1994; Saum, 1995; Peterson and Palumbo, 1997) have their fair share of myths is not new. Needless
to say, much of what we know about the criminal justice system has some basis
in fact or reality. Indeed, "Many of our contemporary issues of crime and justice are the product of some real event or social concern. Whether or not these
events are based on 'truth' is largely irrelevant" because they gain a "larger-

than-life" reality (Kappeler et al., 1996: 2). "As crime-related issues are debated and redebated, shaped and reshaped in public forums, they become distorted. Once transformed and repeatedly played out in public arenas, the mythical social problems are incorporated into the public consciousness" (Kappeler et al., 1996: 3). Perhaps nowhere is mythmaking more prominent than in the field of corrections. According to Roberts (1994: 1), "Prisons, as debated in political campaigns, dissected in university classrooms, and portrayed in newspapers and motion pictures, are often a caricature. The truth about prisons is at once less dramatic, less fixed, less utopian, less dystopian, and less frightening than stereotypes would suggest." To expand upon this discussion, I examine the interrelated topics of what the myths are, how they are created, the effects of crime and corrections myths, and who perpetrates the myths.

What Are the Myths?

There are at least 12 interrelated myths about prisons and convicts (ordered from least to most damaging):

the amount of punishment that convicts receive;

the quality of the facilities that house prisoners;

the cost of certain amenities;

the frequency of sex in prison;

the physical appearance of convicts;

the violent nature of prisoners;

the uncaring disposition of correctional officers;

the deterrent nature of incarceration;

the relationship between incarceration and crime rates;

the viability of mandatory minimums;

the utility of punishment as a deterrent; and

the effectiveness of community corrections.[5]

In short, these issues deal with facilities, processes, prisoners, and sentences.[6] Although the myths themselves deserve special attention, the focus of this chapter is on myth creation and the vehicles by which this is accomplished.

How Are the Myths Created?

Myths have deep roots in folklore and culture. They are often timeless. Stories get passed on from generation to generation and often are accepted without much regard to (or knowledge about) the evidence that often challenges them.

Several components need to be present for myths, particularly those about crime and criminals, to be developed. These criteria include proper presentation and dissemination; following certain well-known themes; targeting unpopular groups in society; making victims appear helpless and innocent; and most important, using a variety of dissemination vehicles. According to Kappeler and his colleagues (1996), myths about crime and criminals "must be properly packaged and marketed," and they need to be "depict[ed] . . . as pervasive" (15). "Only by exaggerating the magnitude of the problem," they write, "can public attention be sustained for prolonged periods, fear be instilled, calls for institutional control be made, and public support be mustered to institute formal sanctions—all the ingredients required for a myth to reach its full potential" (Kappeler et al., 1996: 15).

To achieve these goals, they add, "Myths must be accompanied by certain characterizations" (18). Crime myths are successful if they prey on people's fears and are perceived to affect a large segment of a population. "Modern crime myths must follow certain themes for success. There must be 'virtuous heroes,' 'innocent' victims, and 'evil' villains who pose a clear and certain threat to the audience" (Kappeler et al., 1996: 18).

Moreover, "Crime myths are often built around unpopular groups in society [including] those that are easily distinguishable from the dominant social group." This includes identifying features such as race, ethnicity, religion, national origin, political or ideological views, immigration status, and sexual preference. "This characterization in the construction of crime myth has been used by hate groups, proslavery advocates, supporters of prohibition, and advocates of the death penalty" (Kappeler et al., 1996: 19).

It is important for the mythmaker to portray victims of crime as "'helpless,' 'innocent,' and very similar to the average American" (Kappeler et al., 1996: 20). Some of the victims that have been showcased include "women, children, law enforcement officers killed in the line of duty, prison officials who contract AIDS from criminals, or unwitting business people who become the victims of 'organized' crime" (Kappeler et al., 1996: 20).

The portrayal of victims as innocent legitimates "the implementation of stiff criminal sanctions against the deviants—accompanied by feelings of moral superiority and satisfaction over retribution" (Kappeler et al., 1996: 20). According to Kappeler and colleagues (1996: 26),

> A criminal event or series of events cannot become a myth unless a sufficient number of people contribute to its transformation. . . . Crime myths are unique in that they are a product of the social, political and economic atmosphere of a time . . . the audience must be ready or made ready to accept a crime myth. A criminal event that has the potential for becoming a crime myth at one given moment may not be a viable myth at another point in time. Myths are constructed within a given context and that context includes existing myths of crime and justice.

Finally, "Mythmakers . . . structure reality by selecting and characterizing events —thereby cultivating images of crime" (Kappeler et al., 1996: 22). They do this through various conduits.

In sum, ideas and beliefs are socially created (Berger and Luckmann, 1966). The social construction of reality literature informs us that orientations do not exist in a vacuum, but are shaped by a variety of individuals and organizations.

The end result is similar to what happens in the game of "broken telephone," where the original communication often bears little resemblance to the final message. And, in regard to corrections, it is understandable that our opinions are generally based upon mediated truths because we lack firsthand knowledge.

Effects of Crime Myths Concerning Corrections

Crime myths "have numerous effects on our perceptions; we may not even be conscious that they are at work." Crime myths have six main purposes. First, they "organize our views of crime, criminals, and the proper operation of the criminal justice system" (Kappeler et al., 1996: 3).

Second, they "support and maintain prevailing views of crime, criminals, and the criminal justice system, strengthening the tendency to rely on established conceptions of crime and justice" (Kappeler et al., 1996: 3).

Third, these misrepresentations "reinforce the current designation of conduct as criminal, support existing practices of crime control, and provide the background assumptions for future designation of conduct as criminal" (Kappeler et al., 1996: 3–4).

Fourth, the myths are "convenient[ly] used to fill gaps in knowledge and to provide answers to questions social science either cannot answer or has failed to address" (Kappeler et al., 1996: 5).

Fifth, the stereotypes "provide for an outlet for emotionalism and channel emotion into action" (Kappeler et al., 1996: 5). In general, they "seem to follow a series of recurrent patterns. These patterns allow a disproportionate amount of . . . attention to be focused on a few isolated criminal events or issues" (Kappeler et al., 1996: 5).

Finally, with respect to corrections, myths about prisons prevent rational discussion from emerging and getting a fair hearing in public. The acceptance of such myths also means that the same types of mistakes will continue to be made in this policy arena.

Who Perpetuates the Myths?

Although criminals, convicts, and excons have a role, powerful groups with vested interests are mainly responsible for developing, crafting, shaping, disseminating, and perpetuating the majority of myths about corrections. Many of the misrepresentations originate in or are reinforced by the mass media, government (through its various bureaucracies; see Austin, this volume), correctional institutions and their staff, interest groups, universities, consulting companies, and public relations. These interests can have competing or complementary agendas.

A number of constituencies disseminate myths about jails, prisons, and convicts in order to promote policies and practices that are favorable to their own objectives and constituencies. They often try to minimize external involvement in their programs and operation of facilities and to sell products or services to increase their firm's revenues. This gives them a greater degree of autonomy than they otherwise would have.

WHY ARE MYTHS ABOUT CORRECTIONS SUCCESSFUL?

There are roughly four interrelated reasons why myths about crime and corrections are so effective. They include the power of those doing the mythmaking, the costs involved in getting accurate information about prisons, the apathy of the public, and the convincing nature of the myths.

Those promoting myths about corrections possess a considerable amount of resources (i.e., money, personnel, expertise, and access). The American Correctional Association (ACA), for example, is a large dues-paying organization with many influential members. The stated goal of the ACA is to "improve the image of those who work in corrections [through] improving the conditions of corrections professionals and those who are incarcerated through the development of standards" (R. Freeman, 2000: v). However, the ACA also shapes dialogue on prisons. Government and many media outlets are also well funded through tax revenues and sales of their products and services.

One way to gather accurate information about corrections is through ethnographic research and other qualitative studies. This work inside prisons is extremely difficult. One of the biggest problems is access. Complex and protracted negotiations with prison officials needs to be completed before researchers can interview prisoners. Even if access is granted, gaining the trust and cooperation from prisoners is a challenge.

Because correctional facilities are usually located in rural areas, policymakers and the media are rarely motivated or have the opportunity to conduct independent research and find out firsthand about prison conditions. The public is also overburdened with the problems of making a living, taking care of children, and so on; thus attention to many social problems becomes a luxury, especially when it involves taking the time to find accurate information (J. Ross, 2000c: 119–120).

Finally, myths appear convincing. Mythmakers are very skilled at getting the message across, tapping into issues the public feels are realistic, and using many effective channels of communication (Beckett and Sasson, 2000).

The Role of Style and Self-Presentation in Perpetrating Myths

Dissemination of information about corrections is often part of an interaction between deviant/criminal subcultural groups and authorities. Building on the subcultural theories of crime literature (e.g., A. Cohen, 1955) and recent interpretations concerning the role of style in crime causation (e.g., Ferrell, 1993,

1996; Ferrell and Sanders, 1995a, 1995b), in its simplest formulation, "deviant" or "criminal" subcultural groups (e.g., gangs, prisoners, etc.) interact with criminal justice authorities (e.g., police, correctional officers, support staff, and administrators) who identify and/or recognize membership and participation in deviant/criminal groups by their outward appearance (or style). In turn, members of subcultural groups often amplify their defining characteristics, which are often superficial but identifying styles (i.e., speech, language, signals—written, spoken, and body), appearance (body customization—tattoos, piercing, increasing muscle mass, haircuts), and fashion (through the altering of clothing).

Ferrell (1995: 169–170) argues that style is the

> most delicate but resilient of connecting tissues between cultural and criminal practices . . . style is considered here not as a vague abstraction denoting form or fashion, but as a concrete element of personal and group identity, grounded in the everyday practices of social life. Style is in this sense embedded in haircuts, posture, clothing, automobiles, music, and the many other avenues through which people present themselves publicly.

According to Ferrell (1995: 174), "Style defines the social categories within which people live, and the communities of which they are apart . . . style serves as a ready and visible medium for negotiating status, for constructing both security and threat, and for engaging in criminality." He adds,

> When members of a community each choose particular haircuts, clothes, or postures, they . . . engage in collective behavior. . . . Collective style serves . . . as the social glue that holds subcultures and communities together; . . . stylistic codes and conventions constitute a significant portion of the 'techniques' and 'motives' learned within a criminal community.

This is not to suggest that style is a monolithic concept. In fact, it is easy to be confused over prisoner style, gang style, and styles adopted by African Americans and Latinos, who make up the bulk of our jail and prison populations. A rich literature focusing on inmate subculture exists (Bowker, 1977). Three dominant explanations of this phenomenon are prisonization (Clemmer, 1940/1958), deprivation (Sykes and Messinger, 1960), and importation (Irwin and Cressey, 1962).

Ferrell and Sanders argue that "many social groups and events traditionally conceptualized as criminal are in fact defined in their everyday operations by subcultural meaning and style" (1995b: 3). Thus, whether we are talking about property offenders, bikers, prostitutes, or white-collar criminals, they can have defining features that incorporate special styles of clothing, hair, and speech.

Our knowledge of corrections is formed through a complex interaction of mythmakers (i.e., initiators, sources, propagandists, gatekeepers), mediums, and recipients. This information is predicated on shared or misinterpreted meanings among convicts, reporters, researchers, prison information officers, and the public. These messages or communications are transmitted through a vast array of cultural industries.

THE CONTRIBUTION
OF CULTURAL INDUSTRIES

Many businesses exploit the styles of deviant subcultures to generate corporate profits (Lopiano-Misdom and De Luca, 1997; Klein, 2000: chapter 3). This process is often referred to as the commodification of culture. Some cultural industries use images and symbols about jails, prisons, correctional officers, and incarceration to convey a particular lifestyle, to sell their products, and consciously or unconsciously to perpetrate and perpetuate myths about corrections.

Cultural industries do not simply exist in a vacuum; they function within a social context and have ideological implications, too. Schiller (1989: 30), identified a number of cultural industries that "provide symbolic goods and services," dividing them into two tiers. The first one he categorizes as "publishing, the press, film, radio, television, photography, recording, advertising, sports, and . . . the information industry" (30).[7] The second category includes "services . . . displayed in relatively permanent installations" like "museums, art galleries, amusement parks . . . shopping malls, and corporate 'public spaces'" (30–31). Schiller notes that "all economic activity produces symbolic as well as material goods. In fact, the two are generally inseparable" (31).[8]

Cultural industries reflect and shape public opinion. This has a number of effects. For example, they influence policymakers and legislators, thus affecting the laws that are debated, introduced, and ultimately passed. In some cases cultural industries glamorize or romanticize prison life, making it seem better than it really is. Often, however, the settings, individuals, and plots are dramatized for entertainment value. For instance, the camaraderie with or conflict between officials (e.g., correctional officers) and prisoners is often glorified or exaggerated, giving the public a false impression of the subtleties of relationships inside correctional facilities.[9]

Cultural industries are important in constructing the popular culture of corrections, a culture that is the "product of a complicated, ongoing evolutionary process organized around the creation and consistent reinforcement of a core set of negative stereotypes and their associated imagery. This core of negative stereotyped imagery defines the constructed image template of corrections" (R. Freeman, 2000: 10).

In the main, there are eight interwoven cultural industries that perpetuate myths about incarceration.[10] From least to most important, they are advertising, fashion, documentaries, music, fiction, television, motion pictures, and the mass/news media.[11] Understanding that the styles of deviant or criminal subcultures are often glorified may strip away the appeal of prison to those who have never served time.

Advertising

Prisoners or prisons are often used in advertising campaigns for shock and/or entertainment value. By grabbing the public's attention, commercials enable corporations and political organizations to gain attention, sell products, and promote and gather support for certain points of view. Convict and correctional themes are traditionally used in magazines and forums that sell products to the "correctional industrial complex" (see, e.g., Christie, 1993). Four relatively recent efforts include display and TV commercials released to the general public by Pot Noodle, Benetton, Camel Cigarettes, and the Republican National Party.

In 1999, Pot Noodle, a Bestfoods snack that is popular in the United Kingdom, started an advertising campaign that "features a prisoner who has built a cardboard puppet theatre in his prison cell" (Newland, 1999). Additional ads used segments from well-known Hollywood films taking place in prisons ("Pot Noodle," 1998).

Also in 1999, United Colors of Benetton, an international clothing company, started a $20 million global advertising campaign, "We, on Death Row," which "sympathetically portray[s] American murderers awaiting execution, conveying what's on their doomed minds" (Stuever, 2000: C1). In an effort to garner attention, photographs of 26 different prisoners "appear[ed] on billboards, posters and print ads across the country . . . some not so far from the communities where they killed, or where they're imprisoned—along with their quotable sentiments in large type" (C7). One of the most influential places where this appeared was a 96-page insert in the now defunct *Talk Magazine*. Needless to say, friends and families of victims murdered by these convicts were shocked to open magazines to see these individuals being glorified by Benetton. Many families filed suit against the clothing manufacturer, while others started a boycott of the company's products (Della Famina, 2000).

During the late 1990s, following their controversial Joe Camel advertising campaign, Camel Cigarettes (or more simply Camels), popularly known for running ads containing sexual innuendo that would appeal to teenage smokers, launched a series of print commercials depicting cardboard cutouts of a prisoner standing in his cell, while a frustrated guard looks on discovering that he has been duped by an escape. The cutouts had been fashioned out of used Camels cartons. The message contains several strands of meaning: if you are a prisoner (perhaps metaphorically), Camels will help you in your escape; if you smoke Camels, you are likely to be resourceful and clever; and smoking Camels is antiauthoritarian.

In the political advertising arena, U.S. advertising agencies and media outlets have been handmaidens to promoting misrepresentations of corrections. Nowhere was this most prominent than in the 1993 presidential race, when the Republican campaign depicted Democratic hopeful George Dukakis, former governor of Massachusetts, as being lenient on crime by linking him with the Willie Horton case.[12] The Horton myth was promoted by the Republicans to cast doubt on Dukakis's ability to handle criminal justice matters and to convince the American public that because Dukakis was "soft on crime," the country would suffer if he were elected (D. Anderson, 1995).

The potential to use prisons and corrections for advertising campaigns and branding is limitless. This process largely depends on the creativity and ability of commercial artists and copywriters to link the symbols and images of this environment with the products and services they need to sell.

Fashion

It has long been recognized that our clothing, jewelry, and accessories consciously or unconsciously project or reflect our values, mood, or image, and/or provide us with a sense of belonging or identity. Clothing can also be used to separate people and categorize them into groups, thereby providing a type of psychological and later physical distance between real, imagined, or potential antagonists. It should be noted that clothing, fashions, and style are not simply embedded in dress, but can extend to speech, hair, and body customization (Goffman, 1959; J. Miller, 1995). Scholars have long recognized that members of particular subcultures wear characteristic styles of clothing (e.g., Tunnell, 2000: 48–51). Three issues are relevant to this particular discussion: what prisoners wear, the origins of popular ideas of prisoner clothing, and how prisoner styles have been co-opted by mainstream clothing manufacturers.[13]

Whereas most subcultural groups can exercise choice in what they wear, prisoners have little say in this matter. Nowadays, some minimum security institutions allow convicts the freedom to wear their own clothing. Up until around 1900, they had to wear striped clothing. This helped authorities to identify prisoners if they tried to escape. The types of stripes (vertical or horizontal) and the combinations (e.g., vertical on pants and horizontal on shirts) also denoted the privileges and seniority of convicts.

Later, prison "blues" and jumpsuits were introduced. Prison blues are usually cheap work clothes made of cotton denim. Jumpsuits (or overalls) come in a variety of different colors (white, orange, red) and usually denote the pod or unit in the facility where an inmate is housed. This alternative to bar coding is useful for correctional officers in determining if a convict is not where he/she is supposed to be in the facility, and/or if he/she has to be transferred back to his/her appropriate cell house. Federal convicts are "dressed" out in worn military fatigues, some of which is army surplus gathered after World War II or the Korean or Vietnam wars.

Not only do prisoners incorporate certain styles into their dress, but agents of social control react to them and perhaps amplify the effect as well. For instance, a newspaper article quoted the warden of a juvenile detention facility saying that they give prisoners "identical yellow jumpsuits" to "break down gang ties based on colors and clothing styles" (quoted in Ferrell, 1995: 173). Nonetheless, prisoners still modify their state-issued uniforms to differentiate themselves from one another.

Style often goes beyond clothing and haircuts. The most visible style that outsiders notice about many convicts and excons is their tattoos (Howell et al., 1971; Sanders, 1989; Richards, 1995b) and distinctive forms of speech (Clemmer, 1940/1958). Tattoos done in prison are often rudimentary and made with india ink or ashes from Bible paper. In most jails and prisons, tattooing is against the rules and the violator can be sanctioned. Tattoo artists receive the respect of their fellow convicts for the sophistication of their work and the risks they take. Although many prisoners (especially bikers) come into the institutions with tattoos, a greater number come out with fresh artwork. Speech is used to show group solidarity, and separateness from authorities, in this case correctional workers. It is also a way of preventing those in authority from understanding what prisoners are talking about or planning to do (e.g., Clemmer, 1940/1958; Cordozo-Freeman Diez, 1984).

Commercial fashion has always co-opted images and styles from popular culture (F. Davis, 1992; Rubenstein, 1995). Clothing companies wanting a bigger market share have looked to street fashions, gangs, criminals, and those incarcerated in jails and prisons as sources of ideas for new clothing and accessories (e.g., Trebay, 2000: A23). As Trebay (2000: A23) notes,

> Incarceration chic is everywhere lately, in the orange jumpsuits worn by the staff at the hip Chelsea nightclub Centro Fly (nearly identical to models wholesaled to [jails or] penitentiaries) and the jailhouse denims worn by the rapper master P on the cover of the June 2000 issue of *The Source,* a hip-hop magazine. It is also in the county-lockup look of kids at Brooklyn's Fulton Mall, who sport generic blue or green uniform trousers, white sleeveless T-shirts and gang bandannas.

The original source of such styles is difficult to determine. Echoing Irwin and Cressey's (1962) early work about the importation and exportation thesis, Alphonse McCulough, a senior editor at *The Source,* recently said, "Let's face it, there's a lot of incarcerated people in the United States, and a lot of those are young people." They "come out of jail, and they take a part of that culture with them. Folks I've known who were locked up get released with their prison gear on, so they keep it. Folks in L.A. have been wearing county blues for a long, long time" (Trebay, 2000: A23).

Adding to this mystique is the manufacture and sale of items that are made by convicts (see Terry, this volume). Prison Blues, a clothing label owned and operated by the Oregon Corrections Department, reports that a considerable amount of their jeans were sold each year to the public.[14] During the 1970s, but less so today, people wear shirts with slogans that proclaim "escaped from Alcatraz," the now-defunct federal maximum security prison in San Francisco Bay. Alternatively, "PNB nation, an urban-wear subsidiary of Perry Ellis, with annual revenues of $20 million, has produced a runway show full of jailhouse looks, including denims that resemble prison yard suits and T-shirts with fake docket number on the front" (Trebay, 2000: A23).

In the end, commercial fashion integrates the styles and images of inner-city youth and jail and prison culture. Because the articles of clothing are interpreted as hip, they are adopted by mainstream culture, often through a process of middle-class voyeurism. In turn, this can make prison seem acceptable and those who wear the articles somewhat radical or rebellious.

Documentaries

A growing number of documentaries and docudramas that attempt to present the reality of prisons have been produced. Some of these have been made for television news magazines such as *48 Hours, Primetime,* or stations such as cable-based Court TV. To accomplish their goals, these productions often trace the history of different institutions; cite statistics (including the number of cells, cost to house prisoners, etc.); use archival photographs, newsreel footage, reenactments, and interviews with prisoners or former prisoners, correctional officers, chaplains, and so forth; present copious footage of the prison, including its graveyard, cell blocks, and so on; use dramatic language to describe individuals and incidents; and play haunting music as a backdrop. Some are narrated by news personalities like Ted Koppel, Bill Kurtis, Hedrick Smith, Mike Wallace, and Tom Wicker, or actors like Andre Braugher, Tim Robbins, or Paul Sorvino. Others mainly consist of a series of "talking heads," including convicts, guards, prison wardens, reformers, and judges.

In the past two decades, two organizations have been responsible for producing the lion's share of this work: the Arts and Entertainment Network and the American Correctional Association (ACA). Not only have many of these documentaries aired on television, but because they are available as videos for sale to the public, many criminology and criminal justice instructors use these products as an aid in teaching corrections classes. Typically, faculty are inundated with flyers from companies like "Films for the Humanities & Sciences," Insight Media, or NIMCO, Inc., to purchase these videos.

Kurtis, a producer and broadcaster with Cable Company Arts and Entertainment (A & E), has spent a considerable amount of effort making documentaries on prisons. As part of his series "American Justice," he has produced at least 20 documentaries dealing with prisons, corrections, or community-based corrections.

A large number of expensively priced documentaries are also produced by the American Correctional Association (ACA). Often shorter in duration, the ACA videos tend to be used as training aids. These are very conservative in tone.

Regardless of who produces and distributes these documentaries, they routinely feature stereotypical images of prisoners who are tattoo laden, pumped up from lifting weights, and sporting brutal demeanors. Although students may enjoy these videos more than the class lecturer, often these films serve to reinforce the myth of convicts as violent predators.

Music

The connection between music and prisons is hardly new (see Fisher-Giorlando, this volume). Famous musicians have done time, and several individuals who have been incarcerated have been released only to go on to successful music careers. Moreover, a handful of musicians have been granted access to correctional facilities to play concerts and a number of well-known musicians have written popular protest songs focusing on the plight of those incarcerated. Hence, some of these musicians write and record songs based on their experiences inside.

In fact, a number of the more successful rap artists (e.g., Tupac Shakur) have used prison themes in their music videos. Naturally, this begs the question of why these individuals become successful musicians and what the role of prison was in their career. In short, did it help or hinder their abilities? They turned it into something positive, but this does not necessarily imply their prison experience led to their success.

This post-prison phenomenon has occurred across a number of different music genres including country and western, rock and roll, blues, and bluegrass (Tunnell, 1992, 1995). In 2000, Boston-based band "Godsmack" released their CD and song called "Awake." The video, which accompanied the music, depicts the members of the band playing their instruments while incarcerated in a prison. Other prisoners are shown sitting in the mess hall and acting disorderly. Alternatively, in 1999 Tommy Lee, formerly of the rock band Motley Crue, after spending six months in the Los Angeles County Jail, released an album entitled "Methods of Mayhem." Two of the songs were highly critical of the criminal justice and correctional system, including the Los Angeles police and courts.

As Meatto (2000: 81) notes, "From Folsom to Soledad, concerts for convicts have spawned legendary performances, and there's a strange ring to each one." Many songs, and sometimes entire concerts, have been recorded in prison, including artists such as country singer Johnny Cash; blues artists The Prison-aires, B. B. King, Little Milton, and John Lee Hooker; and punk rockers the Sex Pistols.

Today, a large number of rap artists are writing and singing about controversial aspects of the American criminal justice system (Hamm and Ferrell, 1994). Some of these individuals have spent time in correctional facilities. Many rap artists, particularly through their videos, tend to glorify prisons and convicts. The average viewer, after seeing these depictions, might get the erroneous impression that correctional facilities are great places to be for African Americans and Hispanics. Everyone appears to be singing, dancing, and generally having a good time. Who would not want to be inside?

Not only have prisoners and excons written songs about their previous experiences while incarcerated, but popular singers have written "protest songs" about jails, prisons, and prison disturbances. John Lennon, for example, wrote "Attica State" (1972), which criticized then-governor Nelson Rockefeller's approach to ending the 1971 convict rebellion at the infamous New York State prison with a police assault that murdered dozens of prisoners and correctional officers. Graham Nash (of the group Crosby, Stills, Nash, and Young) wrote "The Prison Song," a haunting tune about people sentenced to prison for selling marijuana. Bob Dylan, an icon of the 1960s, penned "The Ballad of George Jackson" about the famous inmate in California's Soledad prison who wrote a best-selling autobiography and was later killed in a failed prison escape. Dylan also wrote the music that documented the plight of middle-weight professional boxer Rubin "Hurricane" Carter, who Dylan contended was falsely accused of murder and spent the better part of his life locked up in a New Jersey prison.

Fictional Treatments

Each year, fictional treatments of life in prison are written and published (Franklin, 1982, 1998; Massey, 1989). This includes poems, short stories, and novels. Perhaps the most important type of fiction is books because of the possibility that they can be transformed into movies, videos, or television series. In general, "the prison novel balances attention on the bureaucratic or institutional setting or atmosphere with a focus on the character caught up in it" (Massey, 1989: 3). "Some, like *Cool Hand Luke* by Donn Pearce or Edward Bunker's *No Beast So Fierce,* received recognition when movies based on the novels became popular. The vast majority of these novels appear briefly, often only in paperback, and then . . . [go] out of print" (Massey, 1989: 2).[15] Fictional books on prison can be divided into two camps: those novels written by "professional writers who have not served extensive time behind bars" and those works produced by convicts or exconvicts (Massey, 1989: 2). The first category includes Stanley Elkin's *A Bad Man;* John Cheever's *Falconer;* Stephen King's series *Two Dead Girls, Mouse on the Mile, Night Journey, Coffey's Hams, Bad Death of Eduard Delacroix,* and *Coffey on the Mile;* and Tim Willocks's *Green River Rising.* Some books written by nonconvicts are done by crime reporters (e.g., Katzenback's *Just Cause).*[16]

Just because the authors have not spent time in a correctional facility does not mean that they are unable to write with a degree of realism concerning what has taken place. To research their novels, these writers typically read studies on prisons and interview convicts about their experiences. Alternatively, they may work as teachers or correctional officers inside these institutions.[17]

There is also a growing number of books written by American convicts or excons, including Jack London, Malcolm Braly, and Edward Bunker. Massey (1989: 5–6) reviewed fictional books written by convicts or excons. He identified "a progression of experiences found in virtually all prison novels": entry, the world of prisons, and crisis. Additional themes are repeated in each novel: "the alien world of the cell block, the animosity between the convict and his keepers, the macho inmate in a violent social environment, and the criticism of a country that treats humans this way" (Massey, 1989: 6).

Although some of this work is printed by major publishers, "the bulk of the literature by Black convicts . . . is put out by small presses and Black publishers." One of the more prominent publishers in this context is "Holloway House, a Black publisher specializing in 'Black experience' books and largely supported by the works of Black convict authors" (Massey, 1989: xv).

Most of this writing is done by men. "The literature of female prisoners . . . is not voluminous" largely because they represent a smaller percentage (5– 10 percent) of the state and federal prison population. The work of female excons or "connets" (Dearing, 2000) is more typically "found in anthologies gathered from the local and county jails, where women are more often incarcerated" (Franklin, 1982: xviii).

The prison, in such accounts, "is often pictured as a refuge from the trivial or prosaic" (Duncan, 1996: 13). As a refuge its importance lies in the "prison as the quintessential academy and prison as a catalyst of intense friendship" (Duncan, 1996: 13). Given that the reading public is much smaller than the mass media, it is difficult to say how influential prison fiction is in terms of shaping public perceptions.

Television

For the average viewer, television is cheap to access and relatively pervasive (e.g., bars, airports, etc.). Anyone who has access to it receives its message. Many people watch hours of television each day. Viewers do not have to be literate or even speak English to understand the content of a program. It is also a power-ful disseminator of style, which is often visual.

Two basic types of programs that are relevant to corrections have been pro-duced for television broadcast: so-called infomercials, and series. First, during the 1980s a number of criminal justice "reality TV" shows started to be made (e.g., *Cops, Top Cops, Stories of the Highway Patrol*). "Following the format of information commercials [infomercials] . . . television crime programs began to blend entertainment and government-sponsored messages" (Kappeler et al., 1996: 11). These series depended on the access and statements of "government officials, well-known relatives of crime victims, and law enforcement officers to inform the public about crime" (Kappeler et al., 1996: 11). Most of these "reality-based" television programs, regularly shown on Court TV and A & E, allowed broadcast journalists to accompany police officers as they performed their duties. Often these episodes would include reenactments of crimes and ar-rests. Most have been about police work, with only a few about prisons. It is un-clear whether there was minimal or no public demand for correctional themes to be depicted in this manner, or it was too difficult filming inside prisons.

By the same token, "Television has produced few 'prison' series that last be-yond one season. Indeed, even since the advent of cable television, dedicated movie channels, and made-for-TV movies, most presentations of prison life on television have been via the movie format rather than the series format" (Cheat-wood, 1998: 210). In 1997, Home Box Office (HBO) cable station introduced a prison series called *Oz,* which is in its fifth season. Created by Tom Fontana and produced by both Fontana and Barry Levinson (well known for his series *Homicide*), the program looks at the lives of convicts and prison guards in an urban correctional facility. This series too often portrays prisoners as predatory homosexuals or psychopathic killers suffering from severe psychological prob-lems engaged in an ongoing soap opera. Only six to eight shows have been aired each season. Many criminal justice practitioners and prisoners believe that *Oz* is a gross distortion of prison reality. They do not accept this program as an hon-est representation of prison life. In fact, in the spring of 2000, *Saturday Night Live,* a popular television comedy show, parodied the show.

Motion Pictures

Our attitudes and beliefs about prisons are also shaped by films produced by the motion picture industry (Crowther, 1989; Parish, 1991; Rafter, 2000: Chap-ter 5). "The prison film, a claustrophobic offshoot of the gangster film, was by 1933 a thriving sub-genre in its own right" (Shadoian, 1979: 169). "Public at-titudes toward criminals in general, the types of people who are or should be incarcerated, and prison conditions that should be tolerated become evident through the treatment of criminal characters in film" (Munro-Bjorklund, 1991: 56–57).

Motion pictures are powerful purveyors of images of prisons and prisoners. Prison movies, according to Rafter (2000: 123), enable viewers "to identify with the perfect man; . . . to participate in perfect friendships; . . . to fantasize about sex and rebellion; and . . . to acquire insider information about the ap-parent realities of prison life." According to Rafter, "Traditional prison films invite us to identify with heroes, even superheroes" (123). Prison films contain an abundant supply of "ideal companions, buddies more loyal and true than any on the outside" (124). She adds that "prison films with male inmates often have a homosexual subtext in which the buddy gets both a perfect friend and a lover" (125). Finally, prison films "offer the inside scoop, a window onto the inaccessible but riveting world of the prison" (127).

Rafter (2000: 117–123) suggests that stock characters, plots, and themes are prevalent in all prison films. With respect to characters, there are typically "convict buddies, a paternalistic warden, a cruel guard, a craven snitch, a bloodthirsty convict and the young hero" (118). In terms of repeated plots, we see riots, escapes, or the planning that goes into these events (120). Other common themes include "rebellion against injustice. Innocents . . . are being punished by diabolical officers and nasty fellow convicts . . . To restore justice, the prisoners sometimes take matters into their own hands . . . At others, someone comes to their rescue" (121–122).[18]

Many of the images we have about prisons come from movies (R. Jones and Schmid, 2000). Whether the films are screened in movie houses, transferred to videotape and sold to television networks, or sold on the video market,[19] Hollywood movies present us with some of our definitive images of prison life.

Since the 1930s, there have been over 100 films on male adult prisons alone (Cheatwood, 1998). Like television, movies are accessible to most people. One need not have special skills like being able to read in order to understand the message. And, of course, the most important motivation behind the message is economic. Cheatwood (1998: 210) notes that "the goal of motion pictures is to make money—not to educate, to deliver messages, or to present realistic portraits of prison life. If these things are done, they are by-products of the primary demand for financial return."

That the process of making prison films would entail misrepresentation is understood. "As products for a mass audience, these films present society's baseline attitudes about corrections at specific times and places, undisguised by academic jargon or political rhetoric. As such, they are almost pure 'morality plays' that allow us to see the optimism or pessimism society holds toward the 'system' and toward 'individuals' at that time" (Cheatwood, 1998: 210).

Few people have systematically investigated films about prisons. Munro-Bjorklund (1991: 56–61) examined the motion pictures that were made in the aftermath of the Attica riot, but it was not until Cheatwood that we had a relatively comprehensive treatment of all Hollywood movies on incarceration. As Cheatwood (1998: 210) notes, "much of the research that does exist is highly impressionistic or treats only one film, one national event, or one limited time period." According to Travisino, "Hollywood and the television writers continue to portray the vilest aspects of prison life, and the public is led to believe that nothing can be accomplished because that's 'the way it is' with the system" (Travisino, 1980: 1, quoted by Cheatwood, 1998: 210).

In an analysis of movies about adult, male civilian prisons that were produced between 1929 and 1995, Cheatwood classified the films by era: Depression, 1929–1942; Rehabilitation, 1943–1962; Confinement, 1963 to 1980; and

Administration, 1981–1995. He claims that "prison era films . . . revolve around the themes of confinement, justice, authority and release. These components . . . enable us to see how our theories and public positions are translated and presented to the public" (Cheatwood, 1998: 210).

Cheatwood (1998:211) believes that Hollywood films on prison have a "subtle" rather than an "immediate" impact on the viewing public. He states, "People see pictures that support their established and currently held views of the world, and films can only gradually reshape or crystallize amorphous visions, perceptions, or ideas that the viewing public holds" (211).

Films about prisons "have varied from military prison escape films to musicals about maximum security institutions" (211), but Cheatwood limited his sample to "films whose predominant subject was incarceration in a male, adult, civilian correctional facility. There are several pragmatic reasons for this limitation. In the public, the 'prison problem' tends to be identified with adult, male, civilian facilities. So few 'probation and parole' films exist that they do not constitute a genre at all. Although there are quite a few films about women's prisons, many are sexploitation films" (211).

Cheatwood (1998) argues that

> within each of these eras, the treatment of distinct elements and the manner of their combination has been relatively consistent through the films produced. Further, the nature of these films displays a relationship both to the academic theories of corrections predominant in the era and to changes and events in the pragmatic operations of corrections in the nation. (215)

Despite the interesting points that Cheatwood marshals, there are a number of problems with his work. To begin with he assumes that there is no overlapping in the times. One of the most serious misrepresentations embedded in motion pictures is of female prisoners (Morey, 1995; Faith, 1997), which Cheatwood almost categorically dismisses by his focus on male prison movies. Few Hollywood films give accurate accounts of incarcerated women. Those that are available are generally pornographic in nature and considered as B movies. They typically have busty blondes and butch guards, and emphasize themes of domination, lesbianism, lust, and voyeurism. In general, all prison movies misrepresent reality as they fail to convey the boredom and drudgery of life behind bars (J. Ross and Richards, 2002).

Mass Media/News Media

Americans receive their news from a variety of sources: television, radio, magazines, newspapers, and increasingly, the World Wide Web. In fact, according to Cheatwood, "Most people in the general public have formed their images of what prison life is 'actually' like from the mass media" (1998: 210). This section will look at the importance of the news media, the empirical research on the media's coverage of corrections, and the problems of the mass media.

In the twentieth century, because of advances in communications technology, the mass media gained enormous influence over what messages are communicated, heard, and seen, as well as in interpreting important events. In fact, the mass media are probably the most important vehicle for conveying and shaping the cultural construction of crime and criminals. The news media, in particular, are in a perfect position to communicate these misrepresentations.

By the same token, the news media serve a variety of functions including (in order of increasing importance) providing information, educating the public about what is taking place (M. Parenti, 1995: 165), sharing opinions, stimulating debate, reinforcing dominant stereotypes (Lichter et al., 1986; Barak, 1995; Brownstein, 1995), and, most of all, making a profit for their owners (Brownstein, 1995).

The way crime/corrections stories are covered by the mass/news media is shaped by a number of factors. In any given newspaper there are a variety of reporters. The variability is largely a function of the resources the organization has, which in turn is fueled by revenues and perceptions of market share (J. Ross, 1998c, 2000c: Chapter 2). In larger newspapers there is typically a crime or police reporter. Some, like the *New York Times,* may have upward of 10 police or crime reporters.

Unfortunately, few crime reporters are assigned to cover the prisons or jails on a full-time or even part-time basis. According to Chermack, "News media do not have a corrections beat that fulfils the same function as a police or court beat" (1998: 97).

One must also recognize that in most news organizations, crime reporting is often an entry-level position. As part of a natural career path, most reporters may begin with this beat, and then graduate to covering city hall, state politics, and eventually, if they are lucky or so inclined, to covering federal politics. According to Kappeler and his colleagues (1996: 6),

> Prompted by the nature of the media industry, television and newspaper reporters focus on "hot topics" of entertainment value. In the early stages of myth development, a media frenzy develops which allows for expanded coverage of isolated and unique events. Typically, the appearance of an uncritical newspaper or magazine article exploring a unique social problem starts the chain of events.

The journalist has "uncovered a 'new' social evil. Other journalists, not wanting to be left out, jump on the band wagon" (Kappeler et al., 1996: 6).

It is difficult to assess corrections coverage, however, because few actual content analyses of newspaper coverage of corrections have been performed. First, J. Jacobs and Brooks (1983) examined newspaper, periodical, and television news broadcasts about prison that appeared in 1976. R. Freeman (1996/1998) examined "the content of 1,546 newspaper articles concerning corrections that appeared through the United States between September 8, 1994 and November 24, 1995" (203). Finally, J. Ross (1999), in an attempt to understand the issues that corrections reporting focuses on, the prominence of the stories, the reporters covering this topic, and the sources of the stories, performed a content analysis of a year's worth (i.e., 1999) of criminal justice reporting appearing in the *Baltimore Sun.* Unfortunately, these studies are mere snapshots in the overall picture of corrections reporting. Moreover, the latter two studies might depict regional patterns of corrections reporting better than they do national content. Further content analyses of crime reporting are needed.

Even in the absence of such studies, however, many observers have noted serious problems with mass/news media coverage of crime and corrections. In fact, the media have been accused of a whole host of sins, including sensationalism, bias (selectivity), censorship, lack of interest in serious and complicated questions, and superficiality. Needless to say, the media face a number of obstacles in trying to research articles or stories on correctional facilities.

According to C. Davis (1998), "Much has been written about the emergence of the correctional 'boom' in America, yet for all the media attention, prisons remain a largely unchecked arm of American governance. In many states, corrections is among the largest budget items, yet coverage of correctional facilities and the convicts incarcerated in them is scarce."

The amount of access reporters have to jails and prisons varies according to the type of facility, and jurisdiction (Talbot, 1988, 1989; "Corrections," 1989; Hincle, 1996; Kindel, 1998; "Access Prisons," 1998; "Freedom," 1998b). Each correctional institution has its own policies and procedures and some are stricter than others. Most prisons rarely or never allow prisoners to be interviewed by reporters. And, much of what is reported often comes from limited or biased sources, such as prison public information officers.

In most cases, the media are not allowed access to correctional facilities and convicts housed in them. For example, there are almost no press releases regarding prisoners murdered or sexually assaulted. The Supreme Court has derived "three major principles concerning prison access": (1) The First Amendment "does not guarantee the public or the press a right to obtain information from prisons"; (2) "journalists have no greater rights of access than the general public"; and (3) "the public's need for access to information will be balanced against other societal needs, such as law enforcement interests and personal privacy" (*Saxbe v. Washington Post,* 1974; *Pell v. Procunier,* 1974).

Despite the United States having the highest incarceration rate, and a so-called prison crisis, in the main, corrections is not a hot topic of news media interest. Why is corrections avoided by the news media? Although nobody knows for sure, there could be a self-fulfilling prophecy operating. In other words, the news media does not report on corrections, thus the public is not interested, and because a wider audience does not care, the media is not interested, either.

CONCLUSION

How can we change things? There are about seven possible solutions, listed here from least to most important, that would minimize or counterbalance the production and dissemination of myths produced by the cultural industries. We must also appreciate the limitations of these approaches.

First, prisons need to be more open to inspection, investigation, and interviews of prisoners by the media, and academic researchers. These reports, we hope, will document how brutality, corruption, and illegal activities of prison personnel are commonplace.

Second, correctional facilities need to submit to periodic open houses so that the public can see what actually happens in jails and prisons. Admittedly, not all parts of prison should be open to the public. But encouraging outsiders to see as much as possible about what happens behind the razor wire will help them get a better picture of the concerns of convicts and corrections officers.

Third, the mass media and Hollywood need to make more of an effort to produce films with more accurate and less sensational portrayals of convicts and the criminal justice system. Likewise, criminology and criminal justice instructors should endeavor to use realistic accounts of life in prisons (e.g., documentaries, autobiographies, etc.).

Fourth, we should help reporters gain access to prisons. They also need to be better educated about the conditions of prisoners, as well as the powers of guards and administrators. Schools of journalism could be helpful in this respect.

Fifth, guest lecturers who have done time or who have worked in correctional facilities should be used more often and effectively to talk about the reality of prisons. We should caution them against the overuse of sensationalism and avoiding a succession of "war stories." Excons, correctional employees, and administrators should be invited to speak to news organizations and groups of students. They can bring much more realism to the classroom than many of the academic texts we currently use.

Sixth, we can also depend more heavily on autobiographical books written by convicts and excons (e.g., G. Jackson, 1970; Abbott, 1981; Abu-Jamal, 1996; Ross and Richards, this volume).

Seventh, perhaps a public relations campaign against the powerful cultural institutions could be conducted. Building on the success of the ad-busters campaign (documented in books like *No Logo;* Klein, 2000), it should hold these powerful institutions' feet to the fire.

We live in a time when more is demanded of the public because the issues are so numerous, complex, and interrelated. Some people "tune out," but a modern representative democracy demands a public that is alert and well informed. Ability to critically analyze controversial evidence is needed. Finally, the misrepresentation of corrections, the misinformation, and the outright lies propagated by the government and media need to be challenged. This book, and the accumulated publications of the authors in this effort, represents a serious attempt to deconstruct public misperceptions of corrections.

NOTES

1. I use the term "corrections" to refer to "prisons, jails, probation, parole, and a [variety] of other forms of intervention [including the] institutions, policies, procedures and other nuts and bolts of the system" (Welch, 1996: 3). Also, to the extent possible, this chapter focuses on the practice of incarceration in the United States and draws the majority of its examples from this single country. In sum, bad information leads to bad policy and legislation.

2. This chapter uses the following words interchangeably: myths, misconceptions, misrepresentations, and stereotypes.

3. This chapter's interpretation is mainly confined to the United States; however, I believe that the findings can easily be generalized to many of the advanced industrialized democracies.

4. Surrette (1998: xvii) suggests that there are actually three "dominant social construction of reality engines," but a discussion of this issue is beyond the scope of this chapter. Additionally, secondary sources may or may not be accurate.

5. Perhaps the best statement on the myths of prison and incarceration is Kappeler et al. (1996). Unfortunately, even they can be accused of perpetrating some myths. They state, "The basic survival needs are met: inmates do not go hungry or die from exposure to the elements. In addition, inmates generally receive adequate health care and are provided with an opportunity to exercise. However, prisoners are confined to the bare minimum, with enormously restricted opportunity to seek higher levels of satisfaction" (266). What Kappeler et al. fail to mention is that the bare minimum may cause a person to get sick and/or die.

6. It is difficult to identify something as a myth. In other words, there are no acceptable criteria for an issue to be labeled as a misconception, misrepresentation, or stereotype. For example, the Prison Discipline Study (PDS) (1996) titled its research "Exposing the Myth of Humane Imprisonment in the United States." I doubt that most Americans believe that prisons are humane institutions.

7. Noticeably absent is visual art. According to Ferrell and Sanders (1995c: 319–320), "From the shared symbolism of prison tattoos to the slippery linguistic codes designed to evade the grasp of prison authorities, from the 'envelope art' of Latino/Latina prisoners in the U.S. to the republican art that has emerged in the prisons of Northern Ireland, the culture of imprisonment embodies the lived politics of the prison."

8. He adds, "A community's economic life cannot be separated from its symbolic content. Together they represent the totality of culture. Still, it is observable in the development of capitalism from its feudal origins that specific categories of symbolic goods and services have been withdrawn from their place in community and individual existence. They have been organized much like other branches of individual activity, subject to the same rules of production and exchange" (Schiller, 1989: 31).

9. It must be acknowledged, however, that opinions do not necessarily predict human behavior. A considerable literature, much of which is situated in the field of social psychology, demonstrates this point. In short, the cultural industries do not portray prison in a realistic fashion.

10. Cultural industries are often analyzed through the prism of cultural studies or research on popular culture. The areas of radio and sports are not covered in this chapter.

11. For example, it is difficult to separate the origins of the messages conveyed in a movie set in a prison and the book upon which the film was based (e.g., *Dead Man Walking*).

12. Convicted killer Horton, while released on a furlough, traveled out of state, where he raped and then killed his victim.

13. A handful of scholars have identified what might be referred to as a gang style (e.g., J. Miller, 1995). Not only do gang members identify with this type of clothing or its nuances (i.e., particular types of haircuts), but, as Miller indicates, probation officers use gang style as indicators of gang membership and sanction individuals under their supervision who sport those kinds of looks (225). She adds, "Gang style is seen as a reflection of an outlaw lifestyle adopted by gangs and their members. The reading of the youths' symbolism in these ways allows for the construction and maintenance of 'the gang' as trouble, danger, and violent threat. Viewing gangs only via this narrow construct justifies formal intervention that is punitive, mean-spirited and surprisingly individualistic in its solution (e.g., GANGS = PRISON)" (Miller, 1995: 230).

By Miller's account, "Hairstyles provide another example of the adoption of gang members of a defiant stance, drawn from the look found in penal institutions." One probation officer interviewed by Miller said that "a lot of hispanic gang members will wear their hair . . . shaved really close, some almost bald. . . . They keep it like that to give them the look like as if they're in state prison" (1995: 222). They also wear shaved heads to look tough and avoid having their hair pulled in a fight.

14. Needless to say, advertisements for these jeans portray inmates, thus buttressing the use of convicts for shock value.

15. Others include *Brubaker* and *Shawshank Redemption*.

16. Some outsiders have criticized these professional writers "as writing primarily for profit. . . . Needless to say, those profits, even for the most famous novelists . . . have been meagre" (Massey, 1989: 2).

17. Their books, unlike those of the convicts or excons, "usually contain substantial sections of flashback or revery covering the former life, distinctly non-criminal or at least non-inmate, of the central charac-

ter," and "several . . . of these novels by non-convicts answer the most commonly question asked by visitors to inmates in prison: what did you do to get here?" (Massey, 1989). This type of flashback is not as common "in the novels written by convicts or ex-cons. The past is there, of course, although rarely associated with the kind of total remorse which the Quakers hoped for" (Massey, 1989).

18. Not only have academics commented on the stereotypical images presented by Hollywood films but so has the correctional industry (e.g., Zaner, 1989).

19. The video market, an offshoot of the Hollywood movie industry, is particularly crucial in shaping the minds of teenagers. They are impressionable, and may lack, but desire, many of the entertainment venues available to adults. Bored silly by family TV shows, they may look for excitement at the video store. Video stores rent numerous bad movies, often X or R rated, about prisons, some of which have been aired on television.

3

Why I Study Prisons

My Twenty-Year Personal and Professional Odyssey and an Understanding of Southern Prisons

MARIANNE FISHER-GIORLANDO

INTRODUCTION: A WHITE FEMALE YANKEE PH.D. IN PRISON

As I was driving home from the annual Human Relations Club function at Wade Correctional Center, one of Louisiana's satellite prisons, with two colleagues from the university, one of them asked me, "Why do we get excited about going to the prison?" "Why do I keep going to the prison?" and "Am I doing enough for the men and women incarcerated there?" These are questions I have been asking myself in one way or another almost every time I leave a prison, since summer 1981.

Before I get to the answers, I think it is important to understand how I have developed the habit of visiting prisoners, and why I look forward to spending an evening or an afternoon at a local prison. I want to tell the short story of how I, a white woman with a Ph.D. in sociology, started going to prisons in

I want to thank the editors of this book for giving me the opportunity to share my experiences over these last 20 years. I know that some of my colleagues, especially Billy L. Williams and Daniel L. Dotter, are tired of listening to the stories. I especially want to thank Dr. Susan Roach, who gave me my first copy of Carleton's *Politics and Punishment* and encouraged me to stay in Louisiana to do research. Thanks also to the Emmanuel family for their food and friendship. Most important, I want to thank all the men and women who live and work in the prisons I have visited and researched. They continuously support my professional successes, even though they may not know it.

the first place, and how I now find myself visiting and doing research in and about prisons in the Deep South, including the Louisiana State Penitentiary at Angola, one of the most infamous prisons of them all. Because the history of Southern prisons, particularly Angola, differs from traditional corrections history, I will also include a brief history of Southern prisons with an emphasis on Angola.

EARLY BIOGRAPHICAL HISTORY

I was born in Newark, New Jersey, and raised in East Orange, New Jersey, often looked upon as a suburb of New York City. Reared Irish-Catholic, I attended Catholic schools, both grammar and high school. My Father worked in New York City and commuted there every working day of his life.

As a Catholic-educated teenager of the 1950s, I dreamed about getting married and having children. I married in December 1959 and left New Jersey with my husband, a second lieutenant in the U.S. Air Force. That was the beginning of my travels, literally all around the world and back.

I do not remember how many states we lived in those first few years, but the moves outnumbered the years. By April 1962, we had two girls, born 17 months apart. Eventually, we got the coveted European assignment and spent almost three years in Wiesbaden, Germany, where our son was born. At that point, my husband decided to resign his commission with the military, and I suggested he look for a job in Europe someplace, since we were all enjoying the experience so much. He obtained a civilian contract job with Raytheon Corporation and we packed up and went to Aviano, Italy, for the next two years to live in an Italian village with the Italian survivors of a dam disaster. We came back to the states to live in Concord, Massachusetts, for one year, Willingborough, New Jersey, for two years, and finally settled in Dayton, Ohio. By the mid-1970s, when the youngest was starting school, I became bored with my home-making role. Although it is difficult to believe in the telling now, I was one of those women who had gone from my father's house to my husband's house and had never completely supported myself. I had attended college, but for two years only, when I dropped out to save money to get married.

COLLEGE, GRADUATE SCHOOL,
AND DIVORCE BETWEEN 40 AND 42

In the fall of 1977, I started taking college classes at Wright State University, in Dayton, Ohio, in order to complete the college program I had quit almost 20 years before. I was getting a degree so I could get a job to earn enough money for the family to go on vacations.

After receiving my B.S. in sociology in the spring of 1979, I began graduate studies at Ohio State University. I fell in love with sociology. As I finished my master's degree, I also received a divorce after 21 years of marriage.

TEACHING IN PRISON, THE END OR THE BEGINNING?

In the summer of 1981, I had a brand new master's in sociology in one hand and a dissolution decree in the other (another term for no-fault divorce in Ohio). I did not receive the teaching assistantship, which I had expected. I needed a job. My undergraduate social theory professor suggested I go down to the prison, Lebanon Correctional Institution, in southern Ohio, two hours south of Columbus. The director of the college program there was a graduate of the sociology program at Ohio State. I was told he always needed teachers and he would especially like to have a female one. Even the feminists weren't interested in teaching in the men's prison.[1]

Not surprisingly, I got the job. I loved teaching at the prison. To this day, I compare every new class with the students in that first class—social theory— I taught in the men's prison at Lebanon. The convict students were outstanding. They participated. They asked questions. They had answers. They had read more Karl Marx and other social theorists than I had. I immediately became intrigued with prisons and how these young men managed their lives in such institutions.

I drove down to the prison that summer with a man who had previously taught there. During the four-hour round trip, we talked about the prison, the men, and my novice experiences in the prison classroom. He asked me to do a guest lecture on sex roles in his introductory sociology class.

Influenced by my new awareness of feminism, I told the men about traditional sex roles and how restrictive they are for both sexes. As one example, I used my own personal experience with divorce and how I did not ask for any alimony or any part of my ex-husband's retirement benefits. I thought we were equal, and we divided all the material possessions equally. They listened politely and asked a few tentative questions about why I would do such a thing. My friend told me that in their next class meeting, they voiced their honest opinions about my beliefs. They thought I was crazy! I slowly discovered that men in prison hold the most conservative of beliefs, at least in the area of sex role behaviors.[2]

During the long rides, my friend and I also talked about my divorce, and in the midst of many tears, I even considered not pursuing my doctorate. However, I had already lost the marriage; I would not give up my education. I decided to switch my concentration from social theory to criminology, specifically, corrections, for the Ph.D. course work. I had to support myself for the first time in my life and believed I should be doing something more practical than social theory, which I had emphasized in my master's program.

PRISONERS TEACH THE TEACHER

Now that I look back, I think the men taught me more than I taught them. Men who had been locked up for years helped restore my self-esteem, which had crashed because of the divorce. I felt that they literally put me on a pedestal— as a teacher and as a woman. I had the sense that they treated me almost too well. Their extreme, exaggerated politeness made me uncomfortable. As I told my colleagues in a graduate class, I had never been treated by any man like this. Of course the joking response was: "How have men treated you, Marianne?" Now, of course, I realize the prisoners' treatment of me came from the formality and super politeness that the structure of the prison system almost demands. Prisoners live in a simple world of few material possessions. They focus their attention on people and conversation, and therefore their conversations with free-world people are particularly intense.

In fall 1981, I began the Ph.D. course work in my new area of concentration, criminology and corrections. While all my friends were attending happy hour, I was heading to the prison to spend Friday evening teaching the men at Lebanon Correctional Institution. This time I traveled alone, and as I left the prison every night, I thought about how those men dealt with their incarceration. As I was driving home from the class I taught before Thanksgiving break, I cried for the men who would be without their families on this holiday.[3] I thought about how the men who would be released would adapt to the free world. How would they make decisions about waking up in the morning, what they would eat, where they would go? What would the experience of driving a car be like for them again? (I am still asking the same questions.)

While learning as much as I could academically about prisons, especially the inmate subculture, I also taught a college course in the Women's Reformatory at Marysville, Ohio.[4] My most vivid memory from that class is the day the parole board met. One of the women sat there with a Kleenex box and cried and cried. I initially tried to teach whatever the subject was, but finally stopped and asked her what was wrong. That day, the women prisoners gave me a very simple, but complicated, explanation. When the parole board makes decisions, some people go home and some do not. This young woman had been denied, and would have to serve three more months to complete her sentence. She was devastated. I couldn't understand—three more months was such a short time. But three months is not a short time in prison. The women also explained to me that some of their friends were going home, so although they might be happy about getting their parole, at the same time they were unhappy about leaving their friends behind.

Teaching that class, I also came to appreciate that well-known expression "There but for the grace of God go I." Another woman in that class had a very similar life history to mine. She had been married to a navy officer and divorced after at least 15 years of marriage. In the immediate throes after the divorce, she became involved with the wrong type of man and got caught up with the "drug scene." I could have been that woman.

I also taught a short history of corrections to a group of potential employees for a prerelease center that was under construction at the time. Some of those students were married to long-time prison employees. They shared some of the class information with their spouses and told me how their spouses wished they had known prison history before they started to work in prisons. Now they understood the institution in which they worked in a different way.

A GIFT FROM PRISONERS:
MY DISSERTATION

As my classes were coming to an end, it was time to choose a dissertation topic. I was intrigued with the fact that Ohio was developing its prison industry programs and opening stores for their products in selected Ohio cities. I couldn't understand how this was possible. How could Ohio legislators pass laws to allow prisoner-made products to be sold on the open market in the middle of a recession? Weren't there federal laws that restricted sales of prison products—the Hawes-Cooper Act (1929) and the Ashurst-Sumners Act (1935)? My advisor thought this was a good idea, so I read the literature on prison industry. By the end of that quarter, I knew that this subject could not be my dissertation topic. I was so bored with the topic that I was falling asleep reading. Panic almost set in. I had wasted almost 10 weeks and still didn't know what my Ph.D. thesis would be. A student friend of mine had seen me do a class presentation on prison music collected by folklorists in the early part of the 1900s (Gellert, 1936, 1939; Lomax and Lomax, 1936, 1966; and Oster, 1969). She encouraged me to change my dissertation topic to prison music.

I went to my advisor and told him that I wanted to do a content analysis of songs written by prisoners. This time, I had to persuade him. I listened to a lot of country, blues, work songs, and many different kinds of music that I had never heard before. I studied the folk music that had been collected in prisons in the 1920s and 1930s, on up to Bruce Jackson's (1972) 1960s study of prison work songs in the Texas prison system. The historical part was not enough, and I was directed to go into contemporary prisons to collect music written by the prisoners in the 1980s.

Did prison music exist in Ohio prisons of the 1980s? I wrote a proposal and submitted it to the Department of Corrections and the university's research review committees. They approved my proposal and off I went to all the prisons I could gain entry to in Ohio.

What a wonderful experience it was! However, after the first couple of visits, talking to convicts, hearing their stories about the music they wrote, I realized that these incarcerated men and women would be giving me my "green card" to the academy through the data they provided for my dissertation (Fisher-Giorlando, 1987). If they didn't talk to me, I would not be able to obtain a degree. I was overwhelmed with this gift. What could I give back? I asked my friend who taught at Lebanon Correctional Institution with me that first summer. He tried to convince me that I was giving back to them by paying attention to something good the men and women were doing with their lives. I was giving them time. I was listening to them.

Upon completion of my Ph.D. course work I left Ohio State, All But Dissertation (ABD), and went off to a temporary full-time appointment at the University of Northern Iowa in Cedar Falls. I was to be responsible for teaching social theory and corrections courses. Corrections students at that university annually toured the famous prison at Stateville, Illinois. As the junior faculty member, I was the sponsor for that trip. I still remember standing on the ground floor of the one surviving panopticon cell block and looking up at the cells in that wall with a low iron fence as the only separation from a possible deadly fall for the prisoners. I also remember the shock of seeing an armed guard in the central control post on the ground floor level.

Although renewed for another year, this academic appointment was rapidly coming to an end, and I needed another job. I put out my applications and was called by the chair of the Criminal Justice Department from Grambling State University in Louisiana, one of the historically black colleges and universities in the Deep South. As a born and bred Yankee, I was not sure that I wanted to move to Louisiana. The job was to begin January 1986. As it is unusual to leave an academic appointment midyear, I spoke to Northern Iowa's dean, who gave me his blessings. I left Cedar Falls, Iowa, on a January day when the temperature read 26 degrees below. As I got out of bed that morning, I remember thinking I would never have to face such temperatures again, not realizing I would have to face extreme heat and humidity, which would be equally brutal.

Still anxious about living in the Deep South, I figured that things had to have changed since I had spent a year in Montgomery, Alabama, in the early 1960s. A small town such as Grambling would be a good place to finish the dissertation. I would only stay a little while and go back to the Midwest or out East. I am still in Louisiana 16 years later. My children will probably bury me here. But I digress; back to the prisons.

At Grambling, I would be teaching an undergraduate corrections course and one graduate-level course in penology: Correctional Administration and the Law. For the latter course, I knew I needed help. The natural thing to do was to invite the warden from the state prison, Wade Correctional Center, located approximately 50 miles away, to speak to the class. I was invited to speak to the Human Relations Club at that same prison by a student in my class who was a correctional officer and sponsor of the club.[5] I was flattered to be asked. I started taking students on field trips to Wade and to the Louisiana Correctional Institution for Women at St. Gabriel in southern Louisiana. Finally, I went to the Louisiana State Penitentiary at Angola, for the annual Arts and Crafts Festival.[6]

Now a trip to Angola is at least an annual if not biannual trip, which students are asking me about the first day of classes in the fall. Some 10 years later, I still travel to Wade, on an average of at least once a month, sometimes more.

However, now, rather than doing presentations myself, I constantly try to find other volunteers for the different organizations that exist at this facility. Somehow, I was also asked to assist the Vets' Incarcerated II group at Wade. (Vets' Incarcerated I is at Angola). So I attend their two functions, one on Veteran's Day and the other on Memorial Day. I also try to help the veterans' volunteer literacy tutoring project by asking my university colleagues to recycle paper for the men to use, as they have no funding and are constantly in need of paper and pencils.

Grambling State University's Army Reserve Officer Training Corp (ROTC) color guard routinely performs for the two veterans' functions and two years ago, the Air Force (ROTC) taught the prisoners how to perform the Missing in Action (MIA) Ceremony for Veterans' Day. Watching the young AFROTC student cadets teach the older prisoners the proper routine, with such patience, brought tears to my eyes. It is an image I will carry with me for a long time.

A couple of years ago, I brought some students to speak to one of the prisoner groups at Wade. As is usual, the room was set up in a very formal way with a table for the four presenters at the front. When we walked in the room and the students saw this, they were just a little intimidated and nervous about being given such status. However, on the way home, they were so elated, I thought they would fly. The respect the prisoners gave them by the arrangement of the room and the attention they gave during the presentation was immeasurable. One of the women, particularly, talked about how important it made her feel. As with my own first experience in prison, the prisoners had helped raise the students' self-esteem.

To this day I am conscious of how much prisoners give me. Prisoners gave me my dissertation, and continue to give me legitimacy in the classroom, in addition to the status and prestige I have earned in the profession as a recognized prison scholar. I still believe that this is too one-sided.

RESEARCH IN PRISON

As noted, I interviewed prisoners for my dissertation, but after that, I resisted the idea of prison research because so much of it can be used to exert greater social control over prisoners. Yet somehow, another faculty member and I organized a research project on inmate disciplinary reports at the local prison (Fisher-Giorlando and Jiang, 2000). Approximately 10 graduate students participated in collecting the data and gained invaluable experience in doing research. The warden at Wade Correctional Center provided the records we needed to do the project. We were also given the correctional officers' roll-call room to do the work; lunch was provided gratis. When researchers talk about the difficulties of obtaining entrance to prisons to do research, I marvel at the open-door policy of this institution.

WOMEN IN THE LOUISIANA STATE PENITENTIARY: THE ROAD TO THE *ANGOLITE* OFFICE

One-and-a-half years after I arrived at Grambling, the dissertation was finished. Here I was, a 49-year-old Northern white woman in a black university in the Deep South with a brand new Ph.D. I was in Louisiana, the home of one of the most infamous prisons in the South—Angola. A folklorist colleague of mine gave me Mark T. Carleton's (1971) book, *Politics and Punishment: The History of the Louisiana State Penal System,* as a gift for my graduation, with the following inscription: "In hopes that you'll be doing more research in Louisiana." A couple of years later, I traveled with this friend to Baton Rouge, and while she attended a professional meeting, I spent the day perusing Louisiana's early penitentiary records in the state library. What a shock! What I saw in the 1859 Board of Control Annual Report on the Louisiana State Penitentiary has led me to the major research project I have been involved with for the last 10 years, and surprisingly the opportunity to spend time in the *Angolite* office, the famous prison news magazine at Angola.

Contrary to historians' belief that there were no slaves or women in Southern prisons before the Civil War, there they were on Louisiana's 1859 annual report (Board of Control, 1859; Ayers, 1984; Rafter, 1990; Fisher-Giorlando, 1995). I saw all these people listed by first name only, followed by a comma and the term "slave." And there were the women, 18 of them. Furthermore, 16 of the women were black (slaves and free women of color); 2 white women were listed. Moreover, a third of the 330 prisoners, or 109 men and women, were slaves. I couldn't believe it and 10 years later, I still am amazed that Louisiana differs so from other Southern states.

How could I find out more about this unique history of Louisiana's penal system? Which group would I study—slaves or women? I chose women, but the work evolved into a study of slavery also, as the majority of women prisoners were slaves. Even Carleton (1971) hadn't mentioned this phenomenon in Louisiana. He concurred with other historians that slaves did not enter the official criminal justice system and certainly not the penitentiary before the Civil War, as their owners regulated their punishment.

In order to find out more about the history of women in the penitentiary, one of our graduate students suggested that I contact Burk Foster, one of his former teachers at the University of Louisiana at Lafayette. Foster referred me to prisoner Ron Wikberg, then coeditor of the *Angolite*. Wikberg told me about an unpublished manuscript written by the former deputy warden, Roger Thomas, which chronicled the history of Angola using prison documents, registers, and all sorts of archival data. The *Angolite* office had a copy. Wikberg suggested that I get permission to visit the *Angolite* office so that I could examine Thomas's work. I wrote to Warden John P. Whitley in the spring of 1992, and he granted my request. By the time I was able to get to Angola (four hours door-to-door from my house), it was summer and Wikberg had been released.

Before I describe my experiences at the *Angolite* office, it is important to give a short overview of the history of Southern imprisonment. It is particularly important to understand how and why prisons in the Deep South, like Ramsey, Ellis, and Wynne in Texas, Cummins and Tucker in Arkansas, Parchman in Mississippi, and Angola in Louisiana, still look like slave plantations to this day.

BRIEF HISTORY OF SOUTHERN PRISONS

Historically, the South did not follow the pattern of penitentiary, reformatory, correctional institution, community corrections, and warehousing, which is the traditional development of imprisonment found in most introductory corrections textbooks. The practice and philosophy of Southern imprisonment has differed greatly from the standard history of corrections. First of all, the penitentiary tradition, the "black flower of civilized society," as Nathaniel Hawthorne called it, did not blossom in the South as it did up North (Ayers, 1984: 34).

Ayers (1984) and Carleton (1971) noted that there were a variety of reasons for the South's reluctance to accept the idea of the penitentiary. Three are primary. First, the development of the penitentiary up North was a reform movement closely tied to the abolition of slavery. Understandably, Southerners were suspicious of anything that was connected to eliminating slavery. Second, and equally important, was the fact that slavery was an institution that controlled the lower classes of the South. The South did not need a walled fortress to control its lower classes; the South had slavery. Third, the South was primarily an agriculturally based culture and economy that didn't support a factory-based urban system. Accordingly, Southern state legislatures debated long and hard about building penitentiaries in their states.

Although most of the Southern states eventually relented and built some kind of penitentiary before the Civil War, it was often done only to save the state the expenses of paying local facilities for housing convicts. When asking the legislature to increase appropriations for building the original penitentiary at Baton Rouge, Louisiana's Governor Roman clearly noted that even if the penitentiary system did not change the prisoners, it would not only save the taxpayers money, "it will be a great source of economy in the public expenses"(Senate Journal, 1833: 6). The governor had already told the legislature, in his initial request to build a penitentiary, that Wethersfield, Connecticut, had a surplus of $8,713.13 over the cost of prison expenses (Senate Journal, 1832: 7). Louisiana had spent $179,631.88 in expenses for state convicts since 1819, when the penitentiary was first suggested. Roman concluded, "We can see no good reason why that which is accomplished elsewhere cannot be as well done in Louisiana" (Senate Journal, 1832: 7).

Prewar penitentiaries were generally reserved for white men, although some slaves and free people of color could be found in some Southern prisons. As noted, Louisiana was an exception; both slaves and women were found in the penitentiary in significant proportions. In fact, slaves represented one-third of the total prison population. Women also constituted 5 percent of the total prison population for the decade of the 1850s, a figure comparable to that of the 1980s, when female imprisonment was supposed to be at an all-time high (Fisher-Giorlando, 1995).

When penitentiaries failed to make a profit, "authorities shifted the burden of maintaining prisons to the first person who offered to assume it (McKelvey, 1977: 45). Kentucky was the forerunner by turning its state penitentiary over to a lessee in 1832, and Missouri, Louisiana, Alabama, and many of the other Southern states soon followed suit (Sellin, 1976: 141). Louisiana has the record for granting the longest running lease—21 years.

As a result of the Union Army's occupation during the Civil War, most of the Southern penitentiaries were greatly damaged, if not totally destroyed. The former Confederate states then turned to unfettered leasing to save the expenses of incarceration and to deal with the newly freed slaves, who were rapidly filling up the prisons. Almost overnight, Southern prisons became populated predominantly by black convicts. Without any penitentiary building in some cases, the prisoners generally labored outside the walls, wherever the lessees could use them. Unlike the North, where prison authorities contracted prison labor but maintained control inside the walls, Southern states turned over the prisoner population to lessees who were then responsible for supplying food, clothing, housing, and security for the prisoners.

Leased prisoners were used to rebuild the roads and railroads and to repair other damage resulting from the Civil War. They worked in coalmines and lumber and turpentine camps, in addition to doing agricultural work on former plantations (Mancini and Lomax, 1996; Oshinsky, 1996). Women also were found in Alabama's coalmines and on former plantations. Louisiana's lessee, Samuel L. James, who moved most prisoners to Angola in the late 1870s, even subleased state prisoners back to the state so they could be used to work on the state levee system.

Eventually, leasing came to an end. Several factors led to its demise. The railroad boom, which used convict labor, spent itself. The states also became aware of how much money the lessees were making with labor that the states had provided, and they wanted that profit. Additionally, abuses of some inmates did rile both official and public temperament. However, it was often abuses suffered by white inmates that were of concern to most Southerners (Murton and Hyams, 1969; Carleton, 1971: 131, 151–153; Fierce, 1994; Mancini and Lomax, 1996; Oshinsky, 1996: 55–84).

Even when the states took control, the prisoners probably could not tell the difference. In Texas, Louisiana, Arkansas, and Mississippi, the lessees had placed most of the prisoners on plantations, and when the states resumed control of them, they often bought the plantations, and prisoners continued doing the same agricultural tasks that they had performed under the former lessee. In Louisiana, the state even hired some of the former lessee's employees (Carleton, 1971: 81). Under state control, the prison operation was still based upon the plantation model; as Carleton (1971: 7) points out, "The survival of agricultural operations within the penal system into the 1960s suggests the terms 'convict,' 'slave,' 'Negro,' and 'farm worker' have remained unconsciously interchangeable in the mind of institutional Louisiana." In fact, Burk Foster (1995: 4) observes that if Major Samuel L. James, the former lessee, walked around Angola in 1969, a hundred years after he had purchased the lease, he would have observed few differences.

Southern state prisons eventually changed with the federal court orders of the late 1960s and early 1970s. When the federal courts intervened in the Southern states, they pronounced their prisons deplorable and sufficient to "shock the conscience of reasonably civilized people" (Bartollas and Conrad, 1992: 453). The horrible conditions that were found by the federal courts no longer exist. Although Texas, Arkansas, Louisiana, and Mississippi still maintain their prison farms and have the appearance of a slave plantation, they are just one type of facility in a network of correctional institutions throughout their respective states. Ironically, Louisiana was the "only jurisdiction in the country that was accorded the American Correctional Association's (ACA) distinction of being a fully accredited state correctional system at the community and institutional levels in 1995," and Angola, formerly the "worst prison" in the United States, was the first and oldest maximum security prison to be accredited by ACA (C. Douglas, 1996: 70).

ANGOLA AND TWO DAYS
IN THE *ANGOLITE* OFFICE

I finally set up the appointment to go out to Angola. Angola is "nestled" in a bend of the Mississippi River and surrounded by the river on three sides. On the fourth side it is bordered by the rugged Tunica Hills. Composed of 18,000 acres, the farmland is some of the most fertile in the state. The first job for incoming prisoners to Angola is to do some kind of agricultural work for 90 days, and many of them do so for decades. Driving out to the main prison, you see row after row of men working in the fields, watched over by armed guards on horseback. When prisoners come in at night, you see a "long line" of primarily black men with farming implements on their shoulders, mostly hoes. The sight of the "line" is almost "spine chilling"; it looks like slavery to me.[7]

I couldn't believe that of all places, I was really going to the *Angolite* office. As a graduate student, I had heard about the *Angolite,* one of the most famous prison publications. I was checked through the front gate and went to announce myself at Warden Whitley's office. Eventually, I was escorted to the main prison by one of the assistant wardens and went down the Walk to the prisoners' organizations offices, where the *Angolite* office was located. I was introduced to Wilbert Rideau and the other members of the *Angolite* staff. The warden stayed awhile, talking to Rideau and the other men. They seemed to have an easy relationship and respect for one another. They were people who had known each other and had worked together for a long time. Finally, the warden left. Rideau, the paper's award-winning editor, had cleared a space for me at Wikberg's former desk.[8]

Rideau said: "Here you are Doc"—pointing to the desk. Former Assistant Warden Thomas's manuscript was neatly placed in the center. Rideau thought I hadn't seen the papers and pointed to the desk again. I came out of my stupor and sat down. I spent the next couple of days systematically going through Thomas's research and talking with the *Angolite* staff (all prisoners) and the occasional officer who came in to chat. There wasn't a lot of information about women prisoners in the manuscript. I asked Wilbert and the *Angolite* staff a lot of questions. I remember at one point that an officer, a young woman, stuck her head in the door and asked if everything was all right and Rideau said yes. Within seconds after she left, I realized that she was the prison employee who was responsible for my physical safety in the main prison. I asked Rideau if this was true; he said yes and we all laughed. She was smaller in size than I am—less than 5 feet, 4 inches, and probably no more than 110 lbs.

I ate a noon meal, just like the one that the prisoners received. It was bland looking and tasteless, a muddy gray color. The vegetables were raised on Angola, but cooked to death. There were no women's bathrooms along the *Angolite* corridor. The hallway contained mostly security and classification offices. I had to go up front and ask the guard to let me into their office to use the bathroom. The bathroom looked outside on a space where prisoners worked. A window allowed people on the outside to see the upper part of the body of anyone who was in there. I had been warned about this by Anne Butler, who had spent time in the *Angolite* office when she and C. Murray Henderson were interviewing prisoners for their books (Butler and Henderson, 1990, 1992). Even though other women, employees, Butler, and other visitors had been to the *Angolite* office, Rideau claimed I was the first female university professor to spend a full two days in the office with the men, without an escort physically present in the room.

Wikberg and Rideau became my colleagues and friends. Wikberg, who had been paroled even before I got to the *Angolite* office, invited me to his wedding in August. Rideau and I talked on the phone monthly, sometimes more often. Both men continued to answer my unending questions about the women in Louisiana's prisons, and when I exhausted their knowledge they gave me names and phone numbers of people to contact. Wikberg asked me to be a critic for one of the first "Author Meets the Critics" panels at the American Society of Criminology annual meeting, November 1992, in New Orleans. The authors would be Wikberg and Rideau and we would be discussing *Life Sentences*. I told Wikberg that I was supposed to be helping him. He wasn't supposed to be doing so much for me. My participation in this panel led to a publication for me: a book review of *Life Sentences* in the *Criminologist* (May/June, 1992: 24–25).

In the course of a phone conversation with Rideau, he detailed the places to see when I brought students and colleagues to Angola. Accordingly, Grambling State University gets special tours of the Louisiana State Penitentiary at

Angola.[9] Rideau is assigned as our prisoner tour guide along with the required classification officer, and we have permission to stay as long as we like—at least until the afternoon count.

Foster, Rideau, and Douglas Dennis (an *Angolite* staff writer) encouraged me to write my first article about the history of the women in the Louisiana State Penitentiary for the book they coedited, *The Wall Is Strong* (Foster, Rideau, and Dennis, 1995: 16–25). Clearly, I have benefited, both personally and professionally, from my relationships with Rideau, Wikberg, and Dennis in addition to other men like them. I hope they also have gained from their relationship with me.[10]

INVITATION TO CORRECTIONS PROFESSIONALS

If you have not already understood the many reasons why I continue to visit and research prisons, let me say it again in a different way. In April 2000, the Bureau of Justice Statistics reported that at midyear 1999, the United States surpassed Russia's incarceration rate (Beck, 2000). The state I live in, Louisiana, still has the highest incarceration rate in the United States, which means that I live in the state that has the dubious distinction of imprisoning a greater proportion of citizens than any country in the Western world.

I simply do not understand how I could not give back something to those women and men of the prison world, upon whom my success rests. These are my individual justifications for doing volunteer work in the prison. I believe there are other important reasons for why we as a society must continue to visit prisons, even beyond individual personal and professional explanations.

I am convinced that it is absolutely necessary for me to do this work, to keep myself conscious of prisons, their operations, and the faces in prison, both the keeper and kept, and to be there just to observe. The stories I collect about what I see and experience in prisons continue to give me the credibility with my students and to keep me conscious of the fact that real live men and women live in and work in the correctional institutions of this country. In this day and age of a "get tough" mentality and the public fear of criminals, it is important to expose criminal justice students and the lay public to the prisoner as a person, not the horrible monster that the press paints. And, at a historically black university such as Grambling, it is especially important to remind the students that these men are their brothers, fathers, cousins, and uncles. They are, literally and figuratively, all our families. A former president of Grambling has a nephew at Angola. I met a former student who had completed his college degree at the Lifers' meeting at Wade. Every time we go to Angola, our group members are always meeting someone from the neighborhood. Even on the trip sponsored by the university police, a couple of the police officers talked to folks they knew from back home.

When we visit Angola, our young African American women exclaim that the men they see are "so young." And I think, yes, a great number of young, marriageable-age African American men are locked up—these women are so right. According to the Bureau of Justice Statistics: "On June 30, 1999, 12.3% of black non-Hispanic males age 20 to 25 were in prison or jail" (Beck, 2000: 10). Visits to prisons make those statistics come alive in such a real way for Grambling's young women and men.

OPPORTUNITIES IN PRISON: VISITATION AND SUPPORT

As already noted, my entree into prisons was through teaching in various higher education programs offered at prisons in my immediate locality. By 2000, however, many states have eliminated their higher education programs or significantly cut back on them because the federal Pell Grant was eliminated for prisoners. Accordingly, access through teaching in prison higher education programs is now limited. However, there are various other ways to make contacts with administrators and employees in order to gain entree to the prison as a volunteer/expert and to bring prison employees/experts into your classrooms. I have used a variety of methods and continue to do so.

GUEST LECTURERS

Criminal justice instructors can invite local experts to guest lecture in their university classes. Even small communities have local detention centers with employees and administrators who are often flattered when asked to speak at the university. Moreover, some of these facilities have teams of prisoner trustees, who come into the community often to speak primarily to juveniles in trouble, but are also available to speak to college classes.

Asking someone in corrections to guest lecture is often the first step to gaining entrance to a local prison. In fact, my most successful introductory course included a number of guest speakers in the different areas of criminal justice. My initial contact, however, with the state prison closest to our university, came from an invitation by a student/correctional officer who was a sponsor for one of the inmate clubs. My next step was to ask the warden of that same facility to talk to my graduate-level correctional administration and law class. The next logical step is to bring the class to the prison in order to see the environment in which the person is working. This often gives students a good idea about how consistent the prison official is in matching what they say with what they actually do.

Faculty who teach corrections courses are not the only ones who benefit from a working relationship with the prison. I always arrange to take the guest lecturers to lunch or dinner if their time permits. I also invite my colleagues from other departments such as sociology, psychology, and social work, who may be interested to attend. These informal sessions create a network of professionals upon which a variety of research projects can be built. They also link the prison administrators to the university in a variety of ways. Better public relations may be what the warden wants, but as you become trusted by the administration you may eventually get to do the research you really want to do.

COMMUNITY SERVICE

Even if you are not interested in conducting research about prisons, or are not a criminal justice or a criminology professor, faculty are required to perform community service at some universities. Thus volunteer work at a prison fulfills this obligation. I have taken colleagues up to Wade Correctional Center to speak to prisoners' organizations on any manner of subjects. A biology teacher gave a presentation about fossils. I watched the prisoners who were genuinely fascinated with her exhibits and the *National Geographic* magazines she brought along to demonstrate the subject matter she was discussing. A friend of mine told me about an anthropology professor at a predominantly white university. This woman goes to Africa every year and has an extensive collection of artifacts from different countries. The white students on her campus do not connect with her stories and lectures about Africa the way black students would. So she has developed a voluntary anthropology course about Africa that she teaches at the prison to a predominantly African American population. There she gets feedback unlike anything she is able to receive at the university where she is employed.

TRADITIONAL PRISON
VOLUNTEER GROUPS

Presumably the very first volunteers in American penitentiaries were ministers and members of religious organizations. Under the Pennsylvania model of imprisonment, the only visitors allowed to talk to those isolated silent prisoners were members of the Prison Society, who came to check on and encourage their penitential progress (Welch, 1996: 68). Different religious denominations probably represent the largest number of volunteer groups in any prison. The range of spiritual groups varies depending upon the area of the country, the religious denominations in the free community, and the spiritual orientations of the prison population.

Although prisoners' rights to practice their faith has been firmly established, only Catholic, Protestant, and sometimes Jewish and Muslim clerics are actually part of the employed staff at most prisons. Yet prison chaplains have little status in the prison and have an even smaller budget. Overwhelmingly they depend on legions of volunteers (Pace, 1993: 114; H. Allen and Simonsen, 1995/1998: 560/495–496). Not only do volunteers conduct worship services, religious studies, Sunday schools, and various study classes, workshops and retreats, some, who are qualified, provide counseling (Pace, 1993: 114).

Volunteers also augment the prison chaplain staff. In fact, a completely volunteer staff runs a faith-based Prison Fellowship program in one wing of "the Jester II facility, a minimum-security prison outside Houston." Only state guards are hired to provide security. Although this program is starting small with only a few volunteers offering round-the-clock Christian education and training to two dozen prisoners, it is projected that eventually 300 volunteers will work with 200 prisoners—well over the present prisoner population at this unit (Loconte, 1997: 12–13).

If you're averse to proselytizing, religious organizations often do a variety of practical things for prisoners and their families. Some of the many services they provide include transportation on visiting days, adopting a prisoner to visit, purchasing gifts for prisoners to give to their children at Christmas, and running a children's corner in the visiting room. If you want to visit and do some community work, it is easiest to gain access to prisons through religious organizations.

However, many secular programs such as Jaycees, Veterans' associations, Toastmasters Clubs, Dale Carnegie Clubs and various types of substance abuse groups such as Alcoholics Anonymous and Narcotics Anonymous also constitute a major part of prisons' organizational activities. For examples of these many organizations, see any issue of any prison newspaper or magazine, especially the *Angolite,* and the *Corrections Today* special issue on volunteers, August 1993. If you happen to be a member of any one of these organizations in your community, you have a simple entry to the prison through the same or comparable groups that exist in the prison. You also can encourage the members of your free-world group to coordinate activities with the prisoners inside.

Volunteer work can serve multiple functions. You are fulfilling community service requirements of your academic appointment, you are observing a small part of the prison world, and at a minimum you are supplying yourself with stories to tell about this world in your classroom lectures.

CONCLUSION: AN INVITATION

Before you accept my invitation to enter the prison, I want to warn you that this experience will be unlike anything you have ever done before. As I have reiterated several times in this chapter, there are multiple benefits. This is important work. Realize however, that this endeavor is time-consuming, it is physically and emotionally draining, but it is the most rewarding work you may ever do.

The advantages for me have been the innumerable insights that I have gained into the prison world. This knowledge made me a better teacher, researcher, and human being. In addition to my ethical obligation to give back to those who have given me so much I keep going to the prison, because I am constantly amazed at how some people, both the keeper and the kept, manage to become the best of who they can be, even in the middle of such a potentially violent and cruel world. The prison is a constant paradox for me as I see the best and worst of humanity.

Prisoners have taught me and given me more than I can ever give back. They have educated me about patience and humility, and about the inextinguishable hope in human beings.

NOTES

1. See G. Wojda, Wojda, Smith, and Jones (1991) for more recent images of Lebanon Correctional Institution. They bring back some bittersweet memories for me.

2. As I retell this story, I realize that the men were correct. I was, at the least, naive. How could I be economically equal with someone who had a twenty-two-year work history, when I was not even finished with my educational preparation at the age of 42? On the other hand, I have always wondered if I would have been so driven to become financially solvent if I had received alimony.

3. I was probably crying for myself also, as this was the first Thanksgiving I would spend without my family.

4. See R. Wojda and Rowse (1996) for more recent images of the Women's Reformatory at Marysville. These images are not as familiar for me as the ones from Lebanon.

5. The Human Relations Club is one of the many prisoner organizations in Wade Correctional Institution. This club has traditionally been composed of primarily black convicts. Clubs play a major role in prisoners' social lives (Rideau, 1995: 107–110).

6. The Arts and Crafts Festival at Angola occurs annually in the spring. A variety of inmate-made products are sold, including jewelry, leather items, paintings, sketches, and wooden furniture, to name just a few. Most of the funds are deposited into the respective inmates' accounts and the men use the money to buy more raw materials

and to buy personal items at the prison canteen. During the year, the men often spend all their free time in the hobby shop making these items to sell at the next fair.

7. Images of the famous "line" at Angola are depicted in the Arts and Entertainment movie *The Farm: Angola USA* (Stack, Garbus, and Rideau, 1998). I have not included any reference or discussion of *God and the Rodeo* (Bergner, 1998) for a couple of reasons. First of all, I do not support Angola's prison rodeo. I concur with Burl Cain, who didn't want to see the prisoners hurt (Bergner, 1998: 19). Rodeos are not entertainment for me because of the possible injuries. I think they are inhumane. Second, except for my frequent daylong tours through the years and my time at the *Angolite* office, I have never had the opportunity to "hang out" at Angola, as Bergner did. Furthermore, I am not interested in the crimes that prisoners have committed per se. I am more interested in how both women and men work and live in prisons and still maintain their humanity.

8. Rideau's "Sexual Jungle" won journalism's distinguished George Polk Award in 1980 (Rideau and Wikberg, 1992: 107).

9. Phone calls were routinely connected to the *Angolite* office when I first met Rideau. In recent years, phone calls have been connected only occasionally. Professor Burk Foster at the University of Louisiana at Lafayette actually was the first to receive extensive tours at Angola with Rideau as the convict tour guide. Foster also has been extremely supportive of me by initially including me in the small

circle of Louisiana scholars and continuing to encourage my research efforts. He too gave me hints on what to ask for in a tour (though he is neither convict nor exconvict).

10. Sadly, Wikberg died of bladder cancer in the fall of 1994, a little more than two years after his release. My first reaction was that it was the result of poor medical care in prison. Wikberg told me no. He had no symptoms until after he was released. See Cline's (1995: xv–xvi) moving eulogy, originally published in the *New York Times*, October 9, 1994: A45.

PART II

□

Convict Experience
and Identity

A number of accounts of life inside prisons (Clemmer, 1940/1958; J. Jacobs, 1977b; Fleisher, 1989; Hamm, 1995; Walens, 1997; Owen, 1998) have been conducted by outside researchers or prison employees, who while they may have had empathy for prisoners, went home every day to the safety and comfort of the free world. Although these studies constitute a valuable insight into prison, our research extends this previous work, both in depth and breadth.

Closely connected to the discussion of convict experience is convict identity (Irwin, 1970: 82–85; R. Jones and Schmid, 1993, 2000). Classic and contemporary prison research (Clemmer, 1940/1958; Sykes, 1956, 1958; Sykes and Messinger, 1960; Giallombardo, 1962; Irwin and Cressey, 1962; Ward and Kassebaum, 1965; Irwin, 1970, 1985a; J. Jacobs, 1977a) has investigated this topic. Prisoners develop a specific set of orientations (i.e., values, beliefs, language) that provides the means of retaining a sense of dignity and self-respect amidst degrading and dehumanizing conditions (Hassine, 1996). Those who internalize and live by this perspective are convicts. Those who do not are "square Johns" (Irwin, 1970: 32–33). Attention is given to the distinction made between "us" and "them" and how this is perpetuated by prison staff, prisoners, and the prison experience itself. These illustrations demonstrate how convicts see themselves and their world, both inside and outside prison walls. To the extent that one "becomes a convict," he/she will do easy prison time. Conversely, the more one sees the world from a convict perspective, the more difficult it will be to "make it" in the outside world (Irwin, 1970: 174–204). Convict experience and identity are explored in seven chapters.

Edward Tromanhauser discusses his career in "Comments and Reflections on Forty Years in the American Criminal Justice System" (Chapter 4). He tells his story of how, as a young man, he did four stretches in prison for armed robbery and emerged to pursue an academic career (professor and later chair of a department of criminal justice). Tromanhauser reflects on his experience with the criminal justice system as criminal, convict, and criminal justice professor. He shares his insight on the existential moment of rehabilitation, shifting allegiances and sympathies, and on his 25 years as a change agent and teacher.

Charles M. Terry, in "From C-Block to Academia: You Can't Get There from Here" (Chapter 5), reviews the transformation in his life from being a drug addict, then a convict serving prison time in California and Oregon, to becoming a university professor. He emphasizes how his convict identity helped him survive his prison experiences, yet acted as a formidable limiting factor in adjusting to life beyond the walls. He illustrates how the conceptions he had of himself and the world were radically altered after attending college classes in prison, and how his understanding of these processes of change helped him adapt to life in academia and the outside world. He notes how criminologists, and the field of criminology in general, are far removed from the reality of the social worlds that serve as their subject of expertise.

In "My Journey through the Federal Bureau of Prisons," **Stephen C. Richards** (Chapter 6) discusses growing up as an orphan, describes his education, and then reflects upon 11 years of federal custody, taking the reader on a guided tour of federal justice and incarceration. He takes the reader through some of America's most infamous prisons, including federal penitentiaries, correctional institutions, medical centers, transfer centers, metropolitan correction centers, and prison camps.

In less than 20 years the Federal Bureau of Prisons (FBOP) prisoner population has grown by more than 400 percent, to become the toughest prison system in the United States, with the most dangerous prisoners and the highest security prisons. What would federal prisoners want the public to know about federal courts and the FBOP? The chapter concludes with a few stories about prisoner resistance and a call for an end to the war on drugs.

Greg Newbold's "Rehabilitating Criminals: It Ain't That Easy" (Chapter 7) explores why so little works in corrections, even when optimal conditions apply. Drawing on his personal experience with incarceration and research in New Zealand, he argues that in spite of that country's long history of liberalism and reform in corrections, recidivism rates are still high. More than half of New Zealand's prison inmates are in minimum security and only 5 percent are in maximum. There is a wide range of rehabilitative and treatment programs in prisons, and living conditions are generally humane. Sentences are relatively short, parole allows many inmates to work in the community or live in halfway houses upon release back to the community, and there is a variety of intermediate sanctions, such as community service and weekend detention, available to sentencing judges.

In spite of this, recidivist levels are high, with more than 70 percent of inmates reoffending criminally within five years of release. These figures are not significantly different from those in the United States, where prison conditions are much harsher. This high rate of recidivism, Newbold asserts, occurs because the life chances of many prisoners have been irredeemably destroyed long before they enter prison, through inadequate and abusive parenting. He also points out that rehabilitative programs in the community often fail because they don't deal effectively with the real-world pressures that exconvicts must face (coping with the ready availability of alcohol/drugs, reentering the workforce, dealing with sexual and other relationships).

In "Who's Doing the Time Here, Me or My Children? Addressing the Issues Implicated by Mounting Numbers of Fathers in Prison" (Chapter 8), **Charles S. Lanier** asserts that as the American prison population swells larger each year, it envelops increasing numbers of parents. National statistics document the considerable rise in state and federal prisoners during the 1990s. Not surprisingly, then, increases in the number of people imprisoned have resulted in larger numbers of fathers in prison. This chapter focuses on this subgroup of the prison population, on which the scholarly literature has been sparse.

In "Excon: Managing a Spoiled Identity," **Richard S. Jones** (Chapter 9) describes the difficulties convicts encounter upon the completion of their sentence as they reenter the "free world." Some of the problems identified in the literature include loss of intimacy with family and friends (Holt and Miller, 1972), loss of parental rights (Burton et al., 1987), unemployment, and other structural impediments to successful reentry (Richards, 1995a, 1998; Richards and Jones, 1997; J. Ross and Richards, 2002: 155–179). An equally compelling problem confronting all exconvicts is the meaning that the term "exconvict" holds for society in general, and how those occupying this role manage this spoiled identity. Exconvicts expect to be treated differently than "noncriminals." Dilemmas confronting the excon include whether to reveal or not reveal their status, to let on or not to let on, to lie or not lie, and under what circumstances a particular strategy might be employed.

Finally, **Alan Mobley,** in "Convict Criminology: The Two-Legged Data Dilemma" (Chapter 10), examines the paradox of being an exconvict and a criminologist. He explores his own identity crisis as he compares his experience serving 10 years in federal prison with his new career as an academic. His past and present identities collide in a postmodern duel that leaves him with a new person he does not recognize. His anomie only intensifies as he tours a private prison, unsure of the role he should play as he attempts to assess the comparative merits of public and private corrections.

4

Comments and Reflections on Forty Years in the American Criminal Justice System

EDWARD TROMANHAUSER

In January 1998, after 28 years in criminal justice education, I retired. Add to that about 12 years as a part-time criminal, with a large percent of that period spent on probation or parole, or in a county jail or state prison, and it adds up to 40 years of fairly intimate contact with the criminal justice system.

There are those who would say, and I would agree, that having observed the system from both sides of the fence, I was able to bring something a little different to my university classroom, writing, and research; a perspective that was at variance with the dominant thinking in criminal justice.

In spite of having been a part-time criminal before becoming a criminologist, I do not have the answers to the major questions asked by individuals in the discipline. I cannot, for example, offer a definitive explanation of what causes crime or why one becomes a serious lawbreaker. Nor can I tell policymakers the "right" way to prevent crime or to go about changing lawbreakers into law abiders.

What I will do, however, is offer some observations based upon my years of experience in the field. What I am not going to do is offer a heavily footnoted discussion that cites the written work of others. I leave that to the other authors in this book. Nor will I comment upon all of the works of the pantheon of architects who have slowly constructed criminological theory. To do so would take volumes, not a chapter. These are my personal reflections.

An earlier version of this paper was presented at the American Society of Criminology meeting, Toronto, Canada, November 1999.

THE CRIMINAL ACT IN PERSPECTIVE

Deviance is a characteristic of any social group. If you live alone on an island far from what is called civilization, there can be no deviance, using this expression as a reference to the norm. What you do is the norm. But let a few survivors of a shipwreck reach the island and things change. The seed of deviance has been planted.

The larger the social group, the more deviance. The more heterogeneous the group, the more deviance. Some deviance within a social group is tolerated whereas other forms will be punished. The sanction may be mild, for example, chastisement or avoidance of the deviant. But other kinds of deviance are so threatening to the group that the severity of punishments will be escalated. Group rule violations, which are considered to be serious deviations from the established norms, are usually called "crimes" and are the most harshly punished (Becker, 1963; Durkheim, 1964; Lemert, 1967).

If all social groups contain deviants, and crimes are one form of deviation, then all social groups have individuals who commit crimes. The larger the group, the larger the extent of crime within the group. Crime is here to stay. Any attempt to eradicate crime must be interpreted with caution. Wars on crime are, by definition, unwinnable, if the object of a war is to *win* it. Declaring war on crime is like declaring war on human nature.

Moreover, each individual in a society is, or has been, deviant at some time in his or her life. From a farmer in a rural area, to the urban dweller in a large city, each and every one of us deviates from expected group norms in some area of life. In a country such as the United States, with singular exceptions, we have all violated criminal laws and therefore are technically lawbreakers. Granted, the lawbreaking may not be viewed as serious by the majority. If known, they may be overlooked.

Every cop on the street knows you cannot officially intervene every time a law is broken. Ranging from jaywalking, spitting on the sidewalk, playing loud music on a bus or subway, driving without a license, consuming alcohol while under age, skipping school, smoking marijuana, or an 18-year-old having sexual relations with a 16-year-old, on the one hand, to shoplifting, driving while intoxicated, vandalism, destruction of property, or failure to declare all earned income on your tax return, on the other, most people are, or have been, lawbreakers. There is no big difference between the person labeled criminal and the average citizen (Becker, 1963; Lemert, 1967).

The gulf exists, however, when it comes to certain felony crimes. Few people commit auto theft, burglary, serious assault on others, or robbery. Even fewer commit homicide or rape. Only by understanding this can rational social policy really begin to address the problems created by crime and criminals.

AMERICAN CRIMINOLOGISTS

At a time when society needs to broaden its intellectual perspective on crime, the level of public debate on this issue has deteriorated. American criminologists have basically remained silent or murmured polite disapproval as politicians, the media, and vested interest groups in law enforcement and corrections have established the ground rules for the debate, gained the high ground and the public's attention, and shaped public policy with respect to the problem of crime and its punishment. As a result, the misinformed public is led down the garden path (see Ross, this volume).

No politician ever lost an election by being "tough on crime" or wants to have an opponent accuse him or her of being "soft on crime." And, as a result, lawmakers and policymakers unhesitatingly, sometimes with little thought, support and pass futile laws, establish poor public policy, and continually ratchet up punishments. It is common knowledge among criminologists that the United States has more criminal statutes per 100,000 population than any other country in the world. We also have the highest incarceration rate and the most draconian sentences. Many criminologists in other parts of the world are dumbfounded by the length of our prison sentences. The United States also has the highest crime rate among countries that keep official crime statistics.

Criminology is to a large extent an academic endeavor. Most people who call themselves criminologists are teachers and researchers. As such they strive for objectivity and a process of critical analysis. Nevertheless, most of the knowledge they gain is not made widely available to the public. Moreover, those in our profession may be reluctant to take a public stand on the very issues they study and claim to know.

Most criminologists disagree with a large part of criminal justice policy in the United States. They find fault with the "war on drugs," harsh sentencing laws, operation of the correctional system, and much else. We talk about this among ourselves at professional meetings and write about such things in our professional journals. But we are, for the most part, content to let politicians, media, and vested interest groups dictate American criminal justice policy.

THEORIES ABOUT THE ORIGINS
OR ETIOLOGY OF CRIMINAL BEHAVIOR

There are individuals all over the world who can call themselves "criminologists," in that they study various aspects of crime. Nevertheless, it has been American criminologists who have provided the world with the richest and most varied explanations of criminal behavior. Thus, we have a variety of theories competing for our attention, including biological, psychological, strain, social control, Marxist, conflict, economic, ecological, and anomie, to list but a few.

If the key characteristic of a scientific theory is that it makes statements that can be disproven, then none of the theories mentioned above, standing alone, explain a great deal about criminal behavior, since all have been shown to have only limited utility. That is to say, none of the theories demonstrate why some people commit crime and others do not. Further, none of the theories, standing alone, account for the majority of crimes committed on a daily basis. Finally, none of the theories have been sufficiently tested, either in a laboratory setting or a field or natural setting, for most criminologists to feel comfortable accepting one or several of them as satisfactory.

Many criminologists would, I think, agree that criminal behavior is learned behavior. I do not know any colleagues who would argue that people are "born with criminal tendencies." What you do and how you think are shaped, quite literally, by the millions of sensations and observations taken into the brain from birth to maturity. One could argue, as some have, that level of intelligence, endocrinal output, and other factors within the individual may make some contribution to etiology. The question is, how much? And under what circumstances? In many ways, we are only at the threshold of our understanding of the origins of crime.

When teaching criminology, I have often posed this question to my students: What do you think causes crime? The replies come fast and furious. "Poverty causes crime," say some. My reply: Why aren't most poor people in jail or prison? My second reply: Why do we convict wealthy people of crimes? "Ah," says another student, "greed causes crime." My reply: Then why do so many people not commit crimes, even though it is obvious that there is a great deal of greed in the world? What causes one greedy person to obtain more of something in a socially approved fashion while another rapacious person is willing to take unlawful paths to the same end?

What about crimes that generally do not lead to economic gain? What causes one person to assault, rape, or murder, while another, in similar circumstances, does not? By the end of the class I have a blackboard filled with responses to my question, including hate, love, greed, envy, lust, poverty, economic inequality, pride, ego, failure to internalize normative values, faulty parenting, and bad role models. The list seems endless. The point is that defining the causes of criminal behavior is extremely complicated. I want my students to recognize this essential fact and learn to view with skepticism any simplistic explanation of such behavior, whether it comes from a politician, a police chief, or a criminologist.

WHY DID I BECOME A CRIMINAL?

With respect to my own criminal career, why did I, as a young man, become a criminal? Poverty, social class inequality, and economic deprivation could be used as explanations, but what about my peers in school and the neighborhood, from the same working-class background, who did not get in trouble with the law? Broken homes and alcoholic parents can be thrown in. Still, most people raised in families with an alcoholic parent do not wind up in prison. Faulty role models abounded in my neighborhood, but why did I adopt them as role models when others did not? Did my failure to bond to socially acceptable groups such as school, church, and family explain the criminal behavior? Perhaps, but why did most of my peers form these bonds and commitments, even though they were poor and came from what could be described today as dysfunctional families? Does failure to internalize socially acceptable norms and values cause crime? Perhaps, but why did a few of my friends and I get convicted of crimes, whereas the majority of my peers did not?

Why did some of my friends commit crimes with me but were never caught? One explanation that comes to my mind is that these friends stopped committing crimes on their own without the intervention of the criminal justice system. It is the law of averages; the more often you repeat criminal violations, the more likely it is that you will eventually be apprehended.

The causes of crime are complicated and difficult to analyze. Explanations fall easily from the lips, especially when you are familiar with all of the theories. But in spite of years of introspection and reflection, I cannot provide myself, or you, with an explanation that rings true, an interpretation that I know intuitively is the real answer. Still, you may find it hard to believe that a lot of people, including myself, who have committed crimes cannot provide a definitive explanation for why they did what they did.

CRIME AND THE LAW

In my criminology class, after a long discussion about the "causes" of crime, I made a statement: "I know what causes crime: the law. If we did not have the law, we would not have crimes." That statement may seem facetious, and it is always guaranteed to start a stimulating class discussion. But, to try to explain crime, it is not enough to talk about theories of criminal behavior. We must also examine the theories that attempt to explain how and why criminal laws are made. So, a discussion ensued about the minimum rules that a society requires if it is to remain a coherent unit, for example, laws concerning personal safety and private property.

Granted, no society can exist where murder, rape, and pillage go unpunished. But can there be wrongful laws? Can there be laws that are immoral? Historically, there were criminal statutes that forced citizens to adopt a state religion or kill their own children, or that made criminals out of moral and ordinary citizens. In Nazi Germany, it was a serious crime not to report your Jewish friends and neighbors to the police! In many Southern states in the United States before the Civil War, it was illegal to teach a black person how to read! In Kansas at one time it was public policy to sterilize females who had been convicted of petty economic crimes, such as shoplifting!

Yes, the students agreed, there could be, and are, laws that are wrongful and immoral. Are citizens convicted under these laws criminals? Of course they are. If the state convicts you of a crime, you acquire the label of criminal.

Are there criminal laws that are nonsensical? Most students agreed that there are. I said, "Give me an example." Some laws are brought up having to do with illegal drug use and sexual behavior among consenting adults. Is a person suffering from glaucoma (eye disease that can cause blindness) a criminal because he or she smokes marijuana to relieve the pressure on his or her eyes when no other medication will do? "Yes," says the federal government. Is a married couple that engages in oral sex in the privacy of their bedroom criminal? Yes, says the state of Georgia.

American criminologists have for too long accepted the criminal law as given, and then attempted to find a theory that will explain the criminal violation. It is much easier and professionally safer to focus on theories of the behavior of those labeled criminal.

A major challenge for criminologists is to explain the process by which legislators write laws that criminalize common social behavior. This is a form of macrolevel research that is politically difficult and that has been neglected in our endless pursuit of minutia about criminals. Today, we know so much about the phenomenon of crime that we are unable to make sense out of what we already know.

CORRECTIONS IN AMERICA

Following the Revolutionary War, with the birth of the new country, Americans were, if nothing else, optimists. They sought to shake off the European approach to punishment for crimes that relied so heavily on corporal and capital punishments. By 1800, attempts had been made to abolish or greatly reduce the use of torture and death as criminal penalties.

In its place, confinement for long periods—at least, lengthy in the understanding of the times—was substituted. Thus, two years in the Walnut Street jail (Philadelphia) was considered a rather hefty sentence. Eventually what emerged from the various early U.S. systems (i.e., Pennsylvania solitary confinement system or Auburn congregate system) were penitentiaries and prisons as a way to punish serious offenders.

As originally conceived, these institutions were to be humane and rational places where prisoners were expected to reflect upon their past deeds and learn new ways of behaving. I am not going to provide even a brief history of the American prison system, for others have done so (Teeters, 1955; Sykes, 1958; Rothman, 1971; Sellin, 1971; Killinger and Cromwell, 1973). It should be noted, though, that some of these authors have referred to this new experiment in punishment as a noble endeavor gone wrong.

By the early 1800s, the New York Prison Association and the Boston Prison Discipline Committee, two of the most prominent prison oversight groups of the era, were proclaiming that prisons were largely a failure in that they (1) did not make prisoners penitent, (2) failed to reform the inmates, (3) were havens of political patronage, and (4) were truly horrible places to be in for both the keepers and the kept (Fogel, 1975).

The history of the American prison is not a pleasant one. Observers have called them "human zoos," human warehouses," "pits of shame and degradation," and "the finest example of man's inhumanity to man." Moreover, they have always been schools for crime. They often take in rather naive first-time offenders and generally release individuals much more sophisticated in criminal attitudes and behaviors.

It does not make much sense to put the young man who burglarized a neighborhood store into a penitentiary where he interacts 24 hours a day with sophisticated criminals. If he desires, that naive teenager can come out in a few years with a wealth of knowledge about illegal entry, burglar alarms, safes, burglary tools, and where to fence his stolen goods. Possessing this information, he is a much greater threat to the community than when he first entered prison.

Since the 1800s, there have been numerous attempts to reform prisons, including the reformatory movement that began in the 1860s, innovations such as the industrial prison of the 1920s, and the introduction of counselors and caseworkers in the 1950s. Still, the prisons of the 1990s are remarkably similar to those of the 1890s, which were not much different from those of the 1790s. The basic goals are, of course, the same: to hold offenders in a secure environment, while they serve their sentences, and thereby protect society during their incarceration, coupled with efforts to reduce the likelihood of recidivism upon release. Nevertheless, correctional institutions are also places that degrade, brutalize, and make insensitive the very individuals they purport to assist, and are in some part at least, as Menninger (1968) said several decades ago, "monster breeding factories."

I served sentences in the prisons of the 1950s and 1960s. Later, as a professor of criminal justice, I visited prisons in 24 states, from Florida and Texas in the South, to California and Oregon on the West Coast, to New York and Massachusetts on the East Coast. I spent a week, as an observer, in United States Penitentiary Marion (Illinois), the federal prison hailed as the "new Alcatraz" before that institution went on 23-hour-a-day close security lockdown. When I compare what I have seen and heard to what I have read about prisons of 100 or 150 ago, I find that the more things change, the more they stay the same.

Americans, by and large, have placed their faith in fortress-like "big house" penitentiaries, "super-max" prisons, and lengthier sentences in response to crime. The climate of public opinion and politics lends itself readily to this approach. So, today we have over 2 million people in our prisons, most serving longer sentences than in the past, and we lead the world in the percentage of our population that we put in these places.

DOES SENDING MORE PEOPLE TO PRISON REDUCE CRIME?

Researchers have never established a direct relationship between incarceration rates and crime rates. It is a confusing picture. Some countries with small numbers of people incarcerated, relative to population, have low crime rates (most advanced industrialized nations; e.g., France, England, Japan). United States and Russia have both large numbers of people in prison and high crime rates. In some countries, an economic downturn is coterminous with less crime, whereas in others it may be related to more crime.

Most criminologists do not believe there is a clear relationship. Locking up more people for longer periods may not reduce crime. Social and economic class inequalities may have a more direct association with crime rates than do rates of incarceration or length of sentences. Crime rates tend to go up when the population of young adults is denied opportunities for employment.

American criminologists have been fundamentally remiss in failing to hammer relentlessly at the real truths about the relationship between our correctional system and crime. Too many criminologists in this country serve as apologists or handmaidens for our flawed sentencing and correctional policies, even though they know the system does not work effectively in the prevention of crime (see Austin, this volume).

I have been told by some criminologists that politicians set the policy agenda, and they are not consulted; thus, it is not their fault. Others say that the funding is not available for research that may contradict the prevailing policies. Finally, some of my colleagues tell me that it is not the job of academic criminologists to attempt to formulate criminal justice policy, only to contribute their knowledge when asked.

CRIMINOLOGISTS AND PUBLIC POLICY

Nevertheless, criminologists can and do contribute information and knowledge that may advance fundamental changes in public policy. In the 1960s, Lloyd Ohlin and a group of prominent criminologists contributed to President Johnson's Report on Crime and Justice in America (President's Commission on Law Enforcement and the Administration of Justice, 1967). This government-sponsored study influenced crime policy for the next decade.

There are a number of other examples of criminologists having their arguments seized and exploited by conservative policymakers. In the 1970s, David Fogel's development of the "justice model for corrections" again shaped American crime policy for a decade (Fogel, 1975). Unfortunately, his model was embraced, then warped, by conservatives, resulting in longer prison sentences and a reduction of rehabilitation programs. Fogel and I were on the same lecture circuit. He would speak before a legislative body presenting his justice model. I would follow and point out the dangers. I warned Fogel that law-and-order hardliners would seize upon his model and distort it, using it as an excuse for both longer sentences and reduction of rehabilitation programs. I did not want to be proven right. But I was.

Also in 1970s, the Quakers' seminal work, *Struggle for Justice* (American Friends Service Committee, 1971), argued against the arbitrary and capricious operation of the indeterminate sentence and used this as justification for a return to determinant or "flat time" sentences. But, to the dismay of the authors, what was originally intended by the Quakers and academics (including John Irwin, this volume) to be a humanitarian reform was distorted by conservative policy makers: the elimination of indeterminate sentences was coupled with longer imprisonment periods and the abolition of parole. In a similar fashion, Robert Martinson's (1974) work examining the effectiveness of rehabilitation programs was used to reduce or eliminate many correctional initiatives (e.g., education, drug and alcohol, group therapy), sweeping out the effective with the ineffective.

Key buzzwords in the early years of prisons were "reform" and "penitence." They were later replaced by "work ethic" and "education." These, in turn, were changed to "rehabilitation," "resocialization," and "correction." In each case something was to be done to, or for, the prisoner by the prison. Each effort largely failed. The shortcomings can be traced, I believe, to many factors, but especially to the place that was chosen to perform these tasks: the prison. I cannot think of a less therapeutic and more artificial environment than the typical prison. Correctional facilities regiment, control, punish, deprive, and often brutalize prisoners. It is not an easy place to conduct adequate programs to rehabilitate, resocialize, or correct. I survived the prison. That is about the best that one can hope for given the environment.

PRISON AS A BLACK BOX

Consider the prison as a "black box." Society desires that lawbreakers enter the institution and law abiders exit. The basic question, then, is what takes place within the prison that can result in the desired output? This has been the central debate ever since the prison was created. Few would expect that for 100 criminals who enter prison, 100 rehabilitated citizens will exit. No institution could possibly be that successful. Our schools have large dropout rates. Some students may even graduate without learning to read. People leave mental institutions only to return. We are not looking for utopia with respect to the desired outputs from these institutions. Nevertheless, taxpayers are looking for something a whole lot better than they are getting. So, they continue to buy the empty promises of politicians, who tell them that more prisons, longer sentences, and a more austere existence within the prisons will do the job.

From two perspectives, one can argue that the prison is doing its job. First, those criminals who are confined are not, during the period of their confinement, preying upon society. But of course, 95 percent (5 percent serve life sentences without parole) of them will be returning to the community. This raises a fundamental question. Do they come out a greater or lesser threat to the public than when they went in? Second, and here we return to the idea of the black box, for every 100 lawbreakers who enter the box, probably only 50 will come back. One can argue that if 50 out of 100 do not return, the prison has "rehabilitated" the 50. Problem is, criminologists have rarely examined the 50 who did not return to determine why they stayed out. The focus of research has always been the 50 who returned to prison.

A few of those who never returned were so traumatized by the existential moment of being arrested that they would not commit further crimes, regardless of the outcome of their court case. A few more were so shaken by the county jail experience while awaiting disposition that they never wanted to risk returning to such a place. Some, following conviction and its impact on their lives, would not have returned to criminal activity even if they had only been given a suspended sentence, or simply ordered to pay a fine or to make restitution. Still others would not have returned to criminal activities because of the impact of arrest and conviction on their friends, family, and neighbors. Of course, we do not know what percentage of the 50 these individuals represent.

How many of these 50 who did not return to prison decided to abandon lawbreaking because of the prison experience itself? Again, we do not know. Most people believe that if the prison experience is made especially harsh and degrading, it will scare or deter the individual from returning to criminal activity. I am certain that this works in a small percentage of cases. Some state departments of corrections have a reputation as being exceptionally severe and brutal. Other systems have a reputation as being much less so. Some make prisoners serve 10 years for crime X and others make them serve only three years for the same offense. Nevertheless, generally speaking, the "posted" or announced rates of recidivism are pretty much the same in the hard-time states and the easy-time ones. So, longer and harsher sentences in cruel environments do not seem to make a difference. This is another area of research generally neglected by American criminologists.

In fact, the whole topic of recidivism can be confusing, even for criminologists. And for good reason. No one can agree on a definition for recidivism. Definitions range from a parole violation for failing an alcohol or drug test, to getting convicted of any crime, misdemeanor or felony, anytime subsequent to a prior conviction, to getting arrested within five years of discharge from a previous incarceration. There are a lot of definitions in between. In many states, the word "recidivism" refers to any prisoner released from that prison system who returns with a new conviction to that same system. If the released offender commits a crime in another state and is subsequently convicted, it may not count. Finally, some states only count parole violators as recidivists. If a prisoner is discharged from prison without parole or successfully completes his or her parole period, and then returns to the same prison system later on a new conviction, he or she may not be counted as a recidivist.

One last return to the example of the black box. Because no one knows the national recidivism rate and each of the 50 states makes up its own definition, I will use the following definition (and I know there are problems with it): anyone who is convicted of a new felony (sentenced to more than one year) and receives a sentence of jail, prison, probation, or other community sentence, and who is subsequently convicted for a new felony is, by definition, a recidivist. This definition does not include persons returned to prison for technical parole violations (violating parole rules) or convicted of misdemeanors (sentence less than one year).

Returning to our previous example, for the sake of argument, let us consider a hypothetical situation where 50 out of 100 released prisoners do not return to prison, but 50 do when convicted of a new felony. The rate of recidivism is 50 percent. Further, let us presume that the 50 that do return to some form of correctional jurisdiction are all released again after serving their second stretch in prison. Fifty percent of the group, or 25, will not return a third time. Two sentences are enough. This leaves 25 who will be convicted a third time. Finally, assuming that they are all eventually released, once again about half will stay out and half will return as "four-time losers." So you see, there is attrition. Based on the attrition rates one can argue that the prisons are serving their purpose. Still, there must be a better, more effective, economical, and humane way.

WHY DO PEOPLE RETURN TO PRISON?

There are many reasons why people return to prison. Many no longer fear serving time. It is no longer an unknown experience. They have served a prison sentence and survived. Of course they do not want to do more time, and will do everything they can to avoid going back to prison, except, perhaps, become law-abiding citizens.

Some people are committed to criminal activity. It is a mind-set, a collection of attitudes and beliefs. They may believe only suckers work straight jobs. Chumps carry a lunch bucket. For these individuals crime is work and they have a career. Going back to prison is a risk that is factored into the "life." They expect that from time to time they will take a fall. For these convicts what is done to them, or for them, in prison may not alter their behavior.

Nevertheless, the vast majority of prisoners in our prisons are not committed to crime. They are generally situational offenders who are not dedicated to criminal occupations. Circumstances, situations, environments, peers, and sometimes just survival dictate that they commit criminal acts. For these people, returning to prison is not something they desire. Most leave prison with the belief that they will not return because they will not commit crimes that will get them sent back. Almost all leave the prison optimists in this regard.

A TYPICAL PAROLE STORY

A member of the Illinois Board of Pardon and Parole once told me this story. Appearing in front of them was a first-time offender burglar with no prior convictions. He was in his early 20s and had dropped out of school in the ninth grade. He had been unable to hold jobs because of his drinking. Apparently, he could not get out of bed in the morning after a night on the town. About a year before his arrest and conviction he got married. Sentenced to a 2- to 15-year term, he was now before the parole board after serving 18 months in prison.

Based on actuarial tables indicating level of risk for parole release, he had the following positives: first-time offender, married, had been attending AA meetings regularly in the prison; had learned a job skill (auto body and fender repair); had been offered a job upon release by a friend in a neighborhood gas station; and his wife would provide him with a place to stay. The negatives included the following: his pre-parole report indicated that he was still somewhat immature and had difficulty handling crisis situations.

The parole board weighed the positive and negative indicators and decided to release the young man back to the community. The day he was released from prison he was picked up by his brother and told that he no longer had a place to stay. His wife had begun an affair with someone else and he could no longer live with her. She had not informed him of this change in their marital relationship, and had not informed the parole officer who had stopped by to talk with her. She did not want to jeopardize her husband's chance for release.

His brother told him that with a one-bedroom apartment, a wife, and two children, he could not offer a bed, only a few nights on the living room floor. Then, he would have to find lodging elsewhere.

His brother drove him to the neighborhood gas station where his friend was going to give him a job. The employer informed him that because his parole release had been delayed for several weeks, he had been forced to give the job to someone else. He was very sorry.

In his appearance before the parole board, this prisoner's likelihood of success was determined to be above average. He had a job, a place to stay, a wife who had stuck with him during his period of incarceration, and he appeared to be dealing with his drinking problem.

As things turned out, he had no place to stay, no job, and because of his resentment of authority he was not inclined to turn to his parole officer for assistance. He went into a bar and started drinking. A month later he was back in the county jail, charged with another burglary and on his way back to prison.

REENTRY PROBLEMS:
THREE BASIC NEEDS

After several years in a prison, reentry problems are extremely difficult for many ex-prisoners (Richards, 1995a, 1998; Richards and Jones, 1997; J. Ross and Richards, 2002: 155–171). Released offenders need temporary support from the society that has placed them in prisons. I strongly believe that in the majority of cases, it is not what is done to, or for, an offender in an institution that determines whether or not he or she returns. It is what happens to him or her in the first weeks or months following release from prison.

A person getting out of prison has three basic needs. First, a place to stay is obviously of critical importance. The community corrections movement has attempted to meet the needs for shelter or a place to stay, at least temporarily. Nevertheless, halfway houses have a multitude of problems. They have their own set of rules and requirements, many of which create difficulties for recently released prisoners.

A better way would be to subsidize the housing of recently released offenders for a limited period of time, such as 90 days. Prisoners could be provided sufficient funds to pay rent for three months. This would cost much less than returning them to prison. These "welfare funds" could be administered by parole officers or community counselors. Again, the alternative is high rates of recidivism and much greater costs to the society.

Second, the former prisoner needs employment, a job that will pay for daily living expenses. Many persons just released from prison experience great difficulty with employment applications, interviews, and discrimination. Employee computer background checks now make it nearly impossible for some exconvicts to secure employment. Community corrections agencies need additional support for job counselors to assist ex-prisoners with their search for employment.

The third need that those released have is for someone who believes in him or her and will provide support, emotionally, psychologically, and, if necessary, limited financial support or shelter. By far, the greatest need is emotional and psychological support. Parolees need a "significant other," a believer, or counselor—someone to turn to when things seem hopeless.

Finally, the released offender needs a stake in the future. He or she has to have something to lose. If he or she has a job, a little money in his or her pocket, friends in the neighborhood and at work, he or she begins to have a stake. The climb back is difficult, but if the ex-prisoner receives some help, and the time to get "back on his or feet," he or she might just "make it" (see Jones, Mobley, Murphy, Newbold, Richards, Terry, this volume). He or she will succeed, and not return to prison.

CONCLUSION: WHAT I HAVE LEARNED

Over the years, I have, like many criminologists, been frustrated by federal and state crime policies and practices, which I know are largely ineffective. These include draconian sentences, brutal prisons, virtually nonexistent postrelease assistance, and a constant focus on suppressive measures as opposed to true crime prevention, which would entail a serious examination of the structure and form of our society, which generates so much crime.

Criminologists have a vast store of information and knowledge that could be applied to our crime problem. Only some of this gets the attention of policymakers. More often the "hired guns" of criminology rush to respond to "requests for proposals" for ever more suppressive crime measures, which offer, at best, only limited short-term protection for the public, while investigation of major etiological issues and structural inequalities is basically ignored.

The timidity of American criminologists in confronting the truly serious issues is equaled only by their willingness to sell out for a federal or state research
dollar, regardless of the problem to be investigated. Still, some progress has been
made. At least we, as criminologists, are no longer doing much research on psy-
chedelic drugs for incarcerated offenders, or the best way to use military tanks
and armored personnel carriers to suppress crime.

During the decades I have called myself a criminologist, I have met many
individuals who really wanted to make a difference. And, I have also met good
people who disagreed with my positions. As a matter of fact, some of my views
have changed over the years. I no longer believe, as I did as a young man, that
the cops and correctional officers are the enemy. Both groups have a difficult
job to do, and in the main, I think they do it well.

It is easy to single out particular groups and proclaim that they are the problem, whether that group may be legislators, law enforcement, corrections, or
courts. The real problem is a societal one. As long as we have an indifferent and
uneducated public with respect to crime issues, the deplorable state of American criminal justice policies and practices will continue. Sometimes I think that
the public has contributed as much to our crime problem as the offenders themselves. We need to become much more vocal advocates of rational and just policies based upon the knowledge that we possess.

5

From C-Block
to Academia: You Can't
Get There from Here

CHARLES M. TERRY

A sense of inclusiveness surrounded me at our convict criminology panel at the American Society of Criminology (ASC) meeting in Toronto (1999). Instead of feeling out of place and alienated, as I often do in "professional" settings, I felt comfortable, like I belonged there. Of the hundreds of criminological "experts" at the conference, here were a few colleagues who shared my own perspective and sense of purpose, and realized that beyond the ivory towers of academia, something insidious is happening in this country. They recognized and discussed many of the horrors found within the American system of criminal injustice and within the discipline of criminology itself. They had enough heart to publicly acknowledge that the majority of research on crime is driven by politics, economics, government funding, and special interests. That some of it is at best meaningless and at worst detrimental for many vulnerable people. A common denominator of the panel members was a sense of integrity and first-hand experience within the social worlds of confinement. Like myself, most were exconvicts. The others had been involved in either research or some form of volunteer work in prison. Implicit within each of their presentations was the idea that all of us, including those defined as criminal, are human beings and deserve to be treated as such.

An earlier version of this paper was presented at the Academy of Criminal Justice Sciences meeting, New Orleans, Louisiana, March 2000.

Associating with other academics who have survived the noise, monotony, and madness of America's prisons is inspirational. Their presence reminds me that I am not alone. Watching them during the panel was enjoyable.

Stephen Richards, a central force behind our effort, looking serious, professional, and humble. Greg Newbold discussed prison problems in his New Zealand accent; the only person in the hotel clad in a tight-fitting white T-shirt. Edward Tromanhauser, reserved and dignified, an academic for many years, shared his wisdom. Warren Gregory, a recent Ph.D., openly acknowledging his own limitations by saying he was "still trying to find himself." Rick Jones, as always, communicated profound ideas using easy-to-understand language. Those who were not exconvicts were also moving. Bruce Arrigo, young, brilliant, and passionate about the plight of the mentally ill. Jim Austin, impressive and motivational as he called for battle against the "big boys" of criminology. And, Marianne Fisher-Giorlando quietly shared with us her love for the oppressed.

John Irwin, our "gang leader," was really "on" that day. Placing the American imprisonment binge within a historical context, he gave a brief overview of some of the major changes that have taken place in the past 30 years—the main one being the dramatic increase in the numbers of incarcerated bodies (Austin and Irwin, 2001: 1–5). He held up the ASC conference program, entitled "Explaining and Preventing Crime: The Globalization of Knowledge." As Irwin turned the pages, he commented that 20 or 30 years from now a historian like Douglas Hay or Robert Hughes[1] will come along and, looking back at us during this period, say, *"What the fuck were they doing?"* He pointed out how the majority of research being done by criminologists today does not even address the fact that there are now 2 million people behind bars in the United States; let alone the ravaging effect this is having on communities, families, and individuals, most of whom are poor, minority, uneducated, and unemployed and/or underemployed. With passion, he pleaded for help in getting people to recognize the tragic damage being done to hundreds of thousands of individuals, as we build more prisons and lock up more people.

As he has in the past, Irwin (1980: 240) conceded that there are times when prison sentences are necessary. Nevertheless, trips behind bars should be short, safe, and humane. Moreover, resources should be available for prisoners who wish to make an effort to better themselves. Finally, he suggested that perhaps the most disastrous effects of the prison experience are related to what happens after people are released from confinement.

The issue of making the transition from prison to the outside world is in dire need of attention by criminologists. Based on my own experiences, and those of others, I view "making it" (Maruna, 2001; Jones, this volume) after being released as an almost insurmountable obstacle.[2] The general effects of spending time (especially long sentences) in prison can be overwhelming. This is especially true for those of us who developed and internalized a convict identity.[3]

My "criminal career," which stemmed from an inability to successfully support a heroin habit without getting arrested, spanned a period of two decades (1970–1990). During that time, I survived four prison sentences and spent roughly 12 years behind bars, in prisons and county jails in California and Oregon. By doing so, I participated in and witnessed[4] a world known best by those who have been there. This chapter is a synopsis of my experiences, perceptions, and behavior. Building on Irwin's *The Felon* (1970), this chapter is a quasi-autoethnographical (Hayano, 1979) illustration of what took place before, during, and after my years in prison. Emphasis is given to the processes that affected my changing self-concept, the rewards and difficulties I encountered along the way, and my thoughts about academia and convict criminology.

PRISON SOCIAL WORLDS, MEANINGS, AND REFERENCE GROUPS

Having at least some idea about the meanings common to the social worlds from which people come is crucial to understanding their behavior. Each is characterized by special languages, norms, values, prestige ladders, and common outlooks. The way we define situations and the actions we take are a reflection of the perspectives we have learned in these worlds through a process of ongoing social interaction and communication. Perhaps the greatest sense of identification and solidarity can be found in deviant communal structures such as a motorcycle gang or prison. The bottom line here is that in order to know why people do what they do, we need to understand their perspectives, which are a reflection of the social worlds from which they come (Shibutani, 1955).

The conceptual foundation of *The Felon* utilizes the notion of perspectives (subcultural beliefs, values, meanings, and worldview carried by some group of actors), identities (one's self-conception relative to a particular perspective), and systems (or patterns) of behavior peculiar to different groups of prisoners within the convict social world. The meanings and behaviors common to these groups are identified as ideal types (e.g., thief, dope fiend, head, state-raised youth, square john). Irwin (1970: 7) suggested that although the various patterns of behavior fluctuate and often overlap due to cultural diffusion, an understanding of their importance is necessary "because they do exist as relatively distinct entities in the minds of some of the participants, and they operate, therefore, distinctly and differentially on an overall and long-term basis."

The concept of a reference group is used throughout Irwin's book as a descriptive tool.[5] A reference group "is that group whose outlook is used . . . as a frame of reference in the organization of [a] perceptual field" (Shibutani, 1955: 565). To the extent that one identifies with people from a particular social world, the meanings and values of that world become the basis for making judgments and decisions in everyday life.

Those at the top of the social hierarchy in prison see and refer to themselves as convicts or "regulars." Idealistically, they adhere to what is often referred to as the "convict code" (Irwin, 1970: 83) or the norms of the culture. These include projecting an image of fearlessness in the way they walk, talk, and socially interact, not cooperating with authorities, minding their own business, and never backing down from violent confrontations. It is my belief that the more time one does in prison, the more likely one will identify himself/herself as a convict. This will make his/her time inside easier, and a successful transition to the outside world harder, because his/her primary reference group becomes the convict social world. In other words, even though he/she gets released, he/she may still continue to define situations from a standpoint shared with those he/she left in prison.

MY LIFE BEFORE PRISON

My teenage years were spent hanging around other white, working-class youngsters with similar interests in my southern California hometown by the beach. During high school, which most of us completed, we became involved in activities that were popular in the later 1960s. We grew our hair long, surfed, listened to rock music, went to concerts, had girlfriends, got high on the popular drugs of the time (e.g., marijuana, LSD), and tried to keep our actions hidden from figures of authority. Though not always successful in this regard, few of us got into serious trouble with the law or had to spend any time behind bars.[6]

By the time I was 19 years old, I was shooting heroin daily. Explaining why is impossible. What I will say, however, is that it *made me feel good!* Suddenly I found myself doing nice things for little kids and saying hi to old ladies on the street. Heroin made me feel alive, like I was connected to the universe. I remember telling the person I was with, shortly after the first time I tried it, "I can't believe I have been wasting my life doing anything besides shooting this stuff." My love for heroin propelled me into social worlds and a lifestyle I never knew existed.

Going from a surfer/hippie kind of guy to a heroin addict did not take long. My associations and actions quickly changed. I avoided old friends and family and quit surfing completely. Before I knew it, I was interacting with street-level addicts, many of whom were desperate and struggling to survive. Images remain of aged hookers with scarred, sore-covered bodies; poor, ethnic neighborhoods; people "nodding," overdosing, being arrested, getting out of prison, and dying. As my social world changed, so too did my self-concept, which eventually led me to being arrested and locked up for burglary.

At first, jail was a frightening place to be. Strange things happen in those environments. The sight of pain and suffering is common. I remember winos going through DTs, guard and prisoner violence, screaming at all hours of the day and night, addicts suffering from withdrawals, people having epileptic seizures, and homosexual activity that was sometimes consensual, sometimes not. Over time, the daily routine became familiar: chow lines, court lines, shower lines, holding tanks, strip searches, thoughts about the outside, and a lot of time to play cards or dominoes, write letters to girlfriends, and tell war stories about the streets.

In the Los Angeles County jail, we washed our clothes in toilets because they contained the best source of running water. We made wine (pruno) out of water, fruit, sugar, and yeast. We drank hot chocolate brewed by mixing melted Hershey bars and water. Using matchlit, tightly rolled toilet paper as fuel, we cooked grilled cheese sandwiches on the steel slabs we slept on. We also gambled, bought and sold cigarettes and candy bars for profit, and did everything we could to obtain drugs whenever possible. As I became more comfortable in "jail,"[7] my fear and anxiety about living among the "rabble" of society (Irwin, 1985a) became almost nonexistent. Over time, what once seemed like the caverns of hell became more like home.

MY EARLY YEARS IN PRISON

County jail experiences and associations helped prepare me for my eventual journey into the California prison world of the 1970s. Still, the differences were dramatic. Jails are community facilities, close to family, where inmates serve short sentences. In comparison, prisons are places where people spend many years. The men, both prisoners and guards, are bigger and tougher, many with tattoos (Sanders, 1988; Richards, 1995b). Penitentiaries, maximum-security "big house" institutions, are huge complexes, filled with thousands of men, and known for high levels of violence, blatant racism, and hatred. I remember the pain I felt deep down in my guts when I observed the de facto segregation that existed in the chow halls and in the yard; blacks with blacks, whites with whites, browns with browns. I recall the fear I felt when we thought a race riot was about to start. In those days we would hear that a lot. Sometimes, it actually happened.

The way I saw the world and myself continued to change during my early prison years. I became a lot like those I saw around me who seemed to be doing the easiest time. These were the guys who were respected; the ones with tattoos all over their bodies, lifting weights, drinking coffee with cream and sugar, smoking tailor-made cigarettes, getting high, and laughing all the time. My developing convict identity was learned from those men I associated with, the meanings we shared, the things we did, our use of language and prison humor (Irwin, 1980: 6–8; Terry, 1997), and how we were seen and treated by others.

Topics of conversation were often about groups and individuals who did not live up to our standards and expectations. We depicted them as weak, untrustworthy, subhuman, snitches, child molesters, "dings" (mental cases), and scared. We told stories about the outside world that reinforced and validated our convict self-concepts. We never talked, at least in public, about being lonely or afraid ourselves. To do so would be unacceptable. The more I saw myself as a convict, the more alienated I became, not only from nonconvicts inside the prison, but from people I would meet in the outside world.

EARLY YEARS ON PAROLE

The things I did after being released from prison had a great deal to do with the meanings I developed while still inside. There were times when my plans to "make it" centered around staying away from heroin. If I just don't use, I thought, I will be able to stay out of prison. On other occasions I had no such plans at all. The only thing I wanted to do was get loaded and have sex as soon as possible. Whatever my plans, the beliefs and values I learned in prison continued to affect my judgments, decisions, and actions.[8]

My relationships with parole officers varied. Some were more understanding than others. Urinalysis tests were the center attraction of all our encounters, whether they took place at the parole office, home, or work. Immediately after I was paroled, I tested positive for heroin eight weeks in a row. Because I was working at the time, and my parole officer (PO) did not believe I was doing felonies to support my habit, she encouraged me to get on a methadone maintenance program. Once on methadone, I managed to quit using heroin every day, continued working, and completed the parole supervision.[9]

A few years later, upon finishing another stretch in prison, on my first day out, I was assigned a PO who told me he did not think I was fit to live in the free world. He wanted me to immediately enter a long-term, live-in drug program. I told him the idea of doing more time right then was not appealing; that I was clean, planned on doing good, and had no intentions of going into any program. He responded by saying, "Terry, you belong in San Quentin [maximum-security penitentiary], and I will do everything within my power to send you there." The guy hounded me to urinate in bottles three and four times a week to see if I was using heroin. Each time I reported to his office, he examined my arms with a magnifying glass in the hopes of finding needle marks.

That time, I stayed clean for about a month. Once I started using dope again, I did what many parolees do when they know they will be sent back: I quit reporting to the parole office. Like Irwin (1970: 113) said, "Many parolees careen and ricochet through their first weeks and finally, in desperation, jump parole, commit acts which will return them to prison, or retreat into their former deviant world." Within 90 days I was jailed again for another crime and on my way back to prison.

The more time I did inside prison, the more alienated I felt around nonconvicts. It got to where I couldn't even relate to most of the heroin addicts I met in the outside world.[10] Only a minority had been to prison. It became increasingly difficult to relate to conventional people in any context. Even when I was doing everything I could to "do good" (e.g., stay clean, work, not commit crimes), I felt out of place and uncomfortable. The reason, of course, is that

my reference group had become the convicts. The movement from one meaning world to another, from prison to the outside, was simply overwhelming.

MOVE TO OREGON

In 1981, I left a California prison and moved to Oregon. It was my hope that
a change in scenery would help me "stay out." My plan failed. As it happened,
I made it nearly three years before receiving another prison sentence.

Using heroin was not a problem because I became involved with a woman
who had access to enough money to support both our habits. Consequently, I
lived a relatively normal life for about two years. I worked regularly, ate good,
slept OK, did not lose weight (as many of us do when we get addicted), and,
except for purchasing and using the narcotic, did not break any laws. In the eyes
of the people I interacted with who did not use heroin, I was likely seen as a
normal, law-abiding citizen.

Eventually, the money supply dried up, and the script for another return
to prison was written. I began shoplifting. Before long I was doing burglaries
again. Out of control and not wanting to return to prison, I tried to "clean up"
on my own. I made calls to numerous "substance abuse centers." I told the drug
counselors I was addicted, had already been to prison three times for heroin-
related crimes, was doing felonies every day, and could not stop! The response
was always the same, a Catch-22 situation: "Do you have insurance?" "No,"
I answered. "Well," they would say, "If you don't have insurance the charge is
$500.00 a day." Right! If I had that much money I wouldn't have to stop doing
heroin! Addicts with money get "treated" by medical personnel and spiritual
advisors. The rest of us get locked up.

THE OREGON STATE PENITENTIARY:
MY LAST PRISON SENTENCE

Out of money, addicted to heroin, unable to get drug treatment, and doing
crime to support my habit, I was busted again. Now, it was time for a trip inside the Oregon state prison system, most of it spent behind the walls of one of
those old, nineteenth-century, maximum-security pens. I served time in Oregon from 1984 to 1990. It was during those years that my perceptions about
the world and myself began to change dramatically.

The Oregon State Penitentiary (OSP) was different from any California
prison I had ever seen. When I first stepped onto the yard I thought they might
have sent me to the wrong place. The men looked more like mental patients
than convicts (many were). Roughly 75 percent of the population was made up
of sex offenders.[11] The racial mix was approximately 15 percent black, 6 per-

cent brown, and the rest white (personal observation). Prisoner power was restricted. For example, in California we bought our jobs from convict clerks in exchange for cigarettes. Here, all job placements were made by a guard. The first few years I was there, thanks to the guards who brought it in, there was an abundant supply of marijuana. Plus, they fed us well. To my surprise, I found myself in an institution where violence was almost nonexistent. Compared to California prisons, the Oregon State Penitentiary of the 1980s was a relatively safe place to be.

As soon as I arrived, I was greeted by convicts I had known in the California system. My social network and place in OSP was quickly established. As "California boys," the prison staff labeled us as threats to "institutional security." I remember being interviewed by an old sergeant. Looking at both me and my central prison file with obvious contempt, he said, "So, you are from California. I see you were sentenced to 20 years with a recommendation that you do 10 before being eligible for parole. I hope you do every day of it." Prisoners, on the other hand, treated us with respect.

After a couple of years of doing what I had always done in prison (work, hustle, exercise, and get high whenever possible), I found myself becoming bored. Little changes in those places. We ate, slept, showered, worked, and exercised at the same times every day. The food, though good compared to California, got old as well. Only so much can be done with that "mystery meat" they called "hamburger steak," "Swedish meatballs," or "meatloaf," depending on which day it was being served. The constant laughter we engaged in, along with the marijuana or other drugs we managed to use, was always a welcome source of relief. Eventually, though, I was motivated to seek something different to break up the monotony. It was at that time I decided to sign up for college classes in the education department.

PERSONAL TRANSFORMATION
THROUGH COLLEGE EDUCATION

In the 1980s, due to the availability of Pell grants, it was possible for Oregon convicts to pursue college educations. Instructors came from the local community. We were able to earn valid, transferable, academic credits for our course work. During my stay it was possible to obtain up to a bachelor's degree. This source of funding has since been discontinued for prisoners (Stolberg, 1995; Tregea, this volume).[12]

Having the opportunity to be formally educated was amazing. School provided us with the chance to take classes in algebra, anatomy, anthropology, computers, biology, ethics, health, psychology, religion, and sociology. Our teachers were, for the most part, dedicated, competent, and caring people. Besides teaching, they treated us like human beings, as equals. Once we left the education floor we were again subjected to the rules and realities of prison life.

Nevertheless, in class, at least temporarily, we got a reprieve from the prison oppression.

For nearly two years I attended classes as a full-time student. During this period my self-concept and ideas about life began taking a radical shift. Perhaps the greatest impact came from taking cultural anthropology classes, which helped me recognize how the diversity of the human experience reflected the varieties of cultures found throughout the world. Each culture makes sense and works according to its own meanings, values, and customs. Here was evidence that life involved much more than freeways, cars, fast food, drugs, prisons, and being a "stand-up guy." I began to get a sense of history; that the way things are has everything to do with what came before. Ultimately, I began to question my own way of thinking.

During those school years I experienced many new ideas. Never before had I thought of myself within a broad sociohistorical context. Seeing prison as a distinct culture, as one that was basically synonymous with the world of the street (Irwin and Cressey, 1962; E. Anderson, 1999: 66–106) was something I recognized almost immediately. The "reruns in the yard" stories I had been hearing since my earliest prison days were now boring, shallow, and meaningless. My perception of others became noticeably different. Just as my initial use of heroin propelled me into an alien social world, the new ideas and thoughts I was exposed to in school were, in effect, altering my reality and preparing me for a future I never imagined.

In retrospect, it seems clear that the major effect of my prison college experience was an ability to critically examine my self-conceptions and views of the world.[13] What I began to see was troublesome. At that point I saw myself as a white, mid-30s aged convict, a heroin addict from California. My friends were other white convicts. We spent the majority of our time talking bad about others and reinforcing our convict self-images with the use of humor and stories about the streets. I began to realize that my status and place in prison was made possible because of the identity and meaning system I had learned to embrace. Trusting others outside my social circle had become nearly impossible. For the most part, we either hated or distrusted anyone we saw as different. This, combined with having a sense of being part of an elite group to whom I felt great loyalty, characterized my perspective. These thoughts led me to realize that I was basically cut off from almost everyone on the planet. My newfound ideas provided motivation to continue seeking a way out of my dilemma.

After my prison classes ended, I continued the introspection process by reading books about spirituality and self-awareness.[14] Over time, I learned that my thoughts, feelings, and emotions were a reflection of my self-concept, perceptions, and desires. Anger, hostility, rage, impatience, envy, and jealousy came about because I wanted things to be different than they were. I learned that how I see others is a reflection of how I see myself. Moreover, what I see in them I *increase* in myself. My consciousness was permanently altered when I realized that the negative, hateful thoughts I projected onto others usually had little effect on them. Instead, I learned, I was the one who felt the effects of my thinking. When I projected anger, I felt anger. When I extended kindness and love, I was answered with kindness and love.

The process of realizing these ideas took time, effort, and motivation. The eventual outcome was an increased ability to notice when I am generating hatred, anger, or any type of alienating feeling. This awareness allowed the pain I experienced, when I am involved in these projections, to dissipate. Another effect was an increased sense of empathy for others. Where before I would condemn and criticize the pariahs that lived within the prison (e.g., snitches, child molesters), now I felt empathy for them. Like never before, I saw their pain, suffering, and miserable existence as tragic realities of the human condition. As a result of my efforts and new understandings, my hatred was gradually replaced with compassion.

Ripples from the "War on Drugs" taking place in the wider society became increasingly noticeable during my last few years at OSP. Access to drugs dried up considerably. The warden who had greeted us when I first arrived was no longer around. The guards who previously brought in marijuana had been caught and fired. Instead, those who smuggled drugs into the institution brought in methamphetamine and heroin, because they were easier to conceal and had more value. Drug testing became part of institutional policy. This led to many of us spending months in disciplinary segregation units (the hole) for having drug-contaminated urine. Though I still got high occasionally, I spent most of my time clean, exercising, hanging out in the yard, reading, and getting to know myself.

My motivation to learn through formal education, growing older, and changing perceptions, among other things, led to an unanticipated experience that today I would call a major turning point (Ebaugh, 1988: 123–148). About 90 days before I was scheduled for release on parole, I injected a good dose of heroin (I had gone for several months without using any). The first thing I thought of after perceiving the effects of the drug was, "I can't believe I wasted so much of my life for this feeling." The next thing I realized, and this thought seemed unquestionably clear, was "this stuff isn't giving me anything. Instead, it's taking away from what I have." For the first time, I realized I liked being straight more than the way I felt using heroin. My world turned upside down. Today, looking back at that significant event, I think I had developed a new self-concept that was negatively affected while I was high. One thing was certain: the meaning of being under the influence of heroin had changed.

My parole plans were vague. Unlike times in the past, I did not feel anxious about getting out.[15] My contacts and orientation with the world beyond the prison walls, other than those I had maintained with my family and convict associations, were tenuous. Somehow, I sensed that I would never have to spend more time behind bars. Yet, how this would be possible was unclear. I realized I was institutionalized, that I had never lived as "normal" person, and that making the transition from where I sat in C-block to the outside world would be difficult. One day a thought crossed my mind: "I know I am institutionalized. School is an institution. I like school. Maybe I will get out of prison and go to college. I will just switch institutions."

MY LAST PAROLE

Withstanding the Initial Impact of Reentry

Leaving prison after all those years was like entering a strange new world. Inside I was a respected convict. I knew where I stood with others, how to act, and what to expect. Once outside in the "free world," everything changed. Moreover, my self-concept and orientation got flipped on its head. Irwin (1970: 113–114) described the process:

> The exconvict moves from a state of incarceration where the pace is slow and routinized, the events are monotonous but familiar, into a chaotic and foreign outside world. The cars, buses, people, buildings, roads, stores, lights, noises, and animals are things he hasn't experienced at first hand for quite some time. The most ordinary transactions of the civilian have dropped from his repertoire of automatic maneuvers. Getting on a street-car, ordering something at a hot dog stand, entering a theater are strange. Talking to people whose accent, style of speech, gestures, and vocabulary are slightly different is difficult. The entire stimulus world—the sights, sounds, and smells—are strange.

Walking into a supermarket was like entering Disneyland. All those things —lights, products, lines of people—anything you wanted, right there at your fingertips. And, I'm supposed to pay? Compared to the caged-in prison canteen, this place was wide open. Eating in restaurants was awkward. So many choices. I quickly learned that, unlike in the prison chow hall, making efforts to trade for food was taboo. "Excuse me, would you like to trade those green beans for these mashed potatoes?" After being looked at like I was from Mars and politely being told no, I realized that it's not OK to ask strangers in line at the college admissions office if they want a drink of my soda. The difficulty of my initial entry was mitigated by my family, the 12-step program of Narcotics Anonymous, and associations with people I met at Santa Barbara City College.[16]

Family and Home

My step-mom and a family friend met me at the prison gate to bring me "home." The differences of meanings in our respective social worlds became immediately obvious. It was strange to be riding with them in a car that seemed to be traveling fast, talking to them, and listening to their conversations. My dad greeted me with a smile and a handshake after we arrived at the house, yet seemed unsettled about my presence. Who could blame him? Here was his 38-year-old heroin addict son coming home after completing his fourth prison sentence. We talked a bit and did our best to communicate. As difficult as that may have been, my folks made it clear that they would do anything they could to support me. The familiarity of the surroundings and their warm welcome was comforting.

Never before had the differences in living conditions between prison and the outside world been so apparent. Of course, this time I had been locked up a long time, having served six-and-a-half years. In prison we had only steel chairs or wooden stools, concrete or tile floors, and thin mattresses on a steel rack. At home everything was soft, with cushioned sofas, carpets, and thick comfortable beds. The walls, instead of penitentiary green, yellow, or brown, were painted in pastel colors and decorated with paintings and family photographs. And, at home there was silence and privacy! No more cell block sounds: the constant noise, screaming, yelling, steel doors slamming shut, and guards aiming flashlights at my head at all hours of the night. Suddenly, I could eat on plates instead of steel trays, shower, sleep, turn off the lights, use the phone, come and go whenever I wanted! Compared to C-block, this was paradise.

Despite the lavish comfort I found in my immediate physical environment, I was still a stranger in a strange land. In order to "make it," I would have to overcome a number of serious obstacles and barriers. This process was facilitated not only by my family but by the 12-step program of Narcotics Anonymous (NA).

NARCOTICS ANONYMOUS

An Intermediary to the Outside World

My Uncle Joe came to see me my first day home. He had been a member of Alcoholics Anonymous (AA) for several years, and suggested I go with him to a meeting. I agreed. As I entered the meeting place I felt awkward. The group was made up of predominately white, working- and middle-class people who appeared to be members of mainstream society. However, once they started telling stories about themselves and their drinking days, I began to notice the similarities instead of the differences between us. Of particular interest was their focus on spirituality and learning how to become serene instead of insane and selfless rather than self-centered. I was excited to learn that they were talking about the same ideas I had been studying in prison. This realization, and the warm welcome I felt by the time I left, inspired me to "keep coming back."

My first trip to the parole office was routine. "Lock 'em up Tom," as my new PO was called, let me know that he saw me as trouble and would be keeping an eye on me. He said, "One of the conditions of your parole is to attend at least three AA or NA meetings a week." I said, "I don't think that is really necessary because I no longer have a drug problem." Chuckling, he said, "Well, that may be true. But you also don't know how to live out here either. Remember the first time you went to jail?" After I said yes, he continued. "When you first went in there [prison] you didn't know what was going on. You had to learn how to survive. You had to learn what you could do and couldn't do. After awhile you knew what was happening and got along quite well." I agreed. "Well," he went on, "this is like that in reverse. Now you have to learn to live in the outside world. The people in those meetings will help you do that if you let them." I had already been introduced to AA by my uncle and liked what I had seen. Tom's directive provided me with additional motivation to participate.

Eventually, Uncle Joe took me to an NA meeting, where people identified as drug addicts instead of alcoholics. I could not really relate to many of them at first; most had not been to prison, were not heroin addicts, or streetwise, and had done things like work all their lives. Yet I immediately felt more comfortable there than I did at AA meetings. The use of language was familiar and likely increased my sense of connection with the group (Lindesmith and Strauss, 1972; Maurer, 1981). Before long, I discovered there were people in NA who had backgrounds like myself.

After being out 28 days, I went to an NA convention at the St. Bonaventure Hotel in downtown Los Angeles. Roughly 4,000 recovering addicts from all over southern California were in attendance. What I experienced there had a powerful effect on the conception I had about NA. This group had little in common with the one I had been exposed to in Santa Barbara. Instead, I saw Chicanos from East L.A., blacks from South Central, and a whole lot of exconvicts.

As in prison, people hung out together depending on where they were from. Over here were some from Pomona. Over there was the crowd from Long Beach. It was almost like being in a prison yard (except there were women). The look of the street, the cell blocks, and the tiers was everywhere. The difference, though, was that here people were hugging each other, regardless of their race, talking about doing things to stay clean, helping other addicts, and getting their lives together.

On Saturday night I sat in a room with about 1,500 people and listened to an old Chicano heroin addict (with 15 years clean) who had spent years in prison share his experience, strength, and hope with the audience. As might be expected, I could relate to almost everything he said. He honestly talked about the joys and pains he had experienced since being clean. His story, like the presentations by my convict criminologist colleagues at the ASC, gave me hope, a sense of purpose, and a feeling of being a part of the people in the room.

By the time I returned to Santa Barbara, my evolving self-concept as a recovering addict and member of NA had taken on new meaning. The people I met at NA meetings served as intermediaries between prison and the outside world. They linked my past to the present and gave me direction for the future.[17]

EMPLOYMENT?

BEFORE SCHOOL ORDEALS

When I got out of prison, my plan was to attend school at Santa Barbara City College as soon as possible. As it happened, I was paroled in early October, and the new semester did not begin until the following January. During that two- to three-month period, I helped my folks around the house and attended 12-step meetings daily. I was also able to acquire a few odd jobs that helped me pay a little rent money and have some change in my pocket.

Finding a real job was difficult. My record of employment was not exactly favorable, and filling out applications seemed less than promising. What can you say when asked about where you worked during the past 10 years, skills, how much you were paid, and why you left your last job? I figured that not much credibility was given for knowing how to stand in lines, lift weights, play dominoes, or tell war stories in the prison yard. I decided that honesty was the best way to go, so on several occasions, I admitted working for the state department of corrections as a "furniture factory finishing man," "firefighter," "tier sweeper," and "file clerk," for wages that never exceeded $3.00 a day. After several rejections, I finally landed a driving job for a new car dealership. The only thing they were interested in was the status of my driver's license. I assured them I had a perfect record, not a single ticket in seven years! The job was mine, but within two weeks the business folded.

My next stop was a temporary service agency. Once again I was honest while completing the application. Before long, I was sitting in front of an attractive woman who said, "I have helped exconvicts get jobs before and I've been burned. I had a guy in here one time who threatened my life and scared the holy hell outta me. If you ever threaten me in any way, I guarantee, I'll get you arrested. And know this, the district attorney is one of my best friends. I can get you a job beginning in the morning, but you must never tell the people where I send you anything about your past or where you came from. Remember, you are working for me, not them." Nice lady. The next day I began earning the minimum wage for a business that provided mail services. For eight hours a day we stuffed papers into envelopes as fast as possible. Most everyone who worked there drank alcohol during breaks. Several had been to prison.

STARTING COMMUNITY COLLEGE

Before the beginning of the semester, I made several trips to Santa Barbara City College (a two-year community college) to take assessment tests, meet with counselors, fill out stacks of forms, choose which classes to take, and apply for financial aid. These journeys to campus were stressful because there were so many people, strange conversations, new places to go, and much to do. I remember walking through campus, with hundreds of people rushing to their next class, and becoming so overwhelmed that I had to pull off to the side, stop, breathe awhile, and get hold of myself. Fortunately, several people I met during these expeditions lessened the strain.

Part of my student aid came in the form of work-study. I was eligible to work 19 hours a week on campus for a paid wage. This required finding out what was available and applying for an open position. Eventually, I walked into the campus transfer center, an office that exists to help students move on to four-year colleges, and met a woman who became a very close friend. I told her I was an exconvict trying to do good and would not let her down if she gave me the job. Later, she told me how intimidated she felt by my presence during that first meeting. She claimed that my level of intensity, language, and brutal honesty was discomforting. Luckily, she recognized that her feelings were due to her own insecurities and expectations and decided to give me a chance.

Once the semester began, I settled into a routine, something convicts do well. There was a time to be at work, in class, attend NA meetings, or go to sleep. Feelings of alienation were lessening with time. Positive social support surrounded me almost everywhere I went. Because of the efforts I was making, the opportunities I had, and the help of those around me, I was actually "doing good" on the outside. For the first time in my adult life, I was developing a straight routine.

A CONVICT GOES TO UNIVERSITY

My new routine left me with a sense of living in two different worlds. I learned that others from NA, including a few exconvicts, were also students at City College. We would see each other on campus, drink coffee together, and compare what we were doing to our past lives in the streets or in the prison yard. Seeing them was always a boost and reminded me that I was not alone. They were welcome links with my past, helping me move ahead.

That following summer I met Debbie, my wife, and Annie, her nine-year-old daughter. Before long we were all living together. Annie, always trustworthy and bright, has been like a guiding light ever since I met her. Debbie has been good for me because, among other things, she knows how to live out here. She has helped me learn everything from how to pay bills to what kind of clothes I should wear. Lovingly, she has pointed out that striped pants and checkered shirts do not match, and that it is not OK to remove a fake tooth from my mouth and set it on a restaurant table while I eat. For three years she told me I should put a shirt on when I enter a supermarket. "Why?" I wondered. It was hot. I never wore a shirt in the prison yard when it was hot. One day she finally got through. She said, "Look at it like this. How many other guys do you see in the store without their shirts on? Especially ones with tattoos all over their bodies?" Ding. Ding. Lights going off in my head. I got it that time. Today, I wear shirts almost everywhere in public. One of the most important elements of our relationship is our ability to laugh together.

In 1992, I transferred to the University of California, Santa Barbara (UCSB), as a sociology major. While I was there, the person who had the greatest impact on me was Denise Bielby, a professor who knew little about crime, drugs, or convicts. She was my instructor in a yearlong senior seminar—another guide out of nowhere. Her hands-on teaching style was extremely beneficial. For me it was also inspirational. One day, as I was sitting in her office while she read something I had written, she looked up and said, "Chuck, you write well. I think you should seriously consider getting into a Ph.D. program after you graduate." Her words of validation surprised me and made me feel uncomfortable. What she was saying was not consistent with my outside world negative self-evaluation. Convicts are no good. Convicts don't get Ph.D.'s. According to mainstream standards, convicts don't do *anything* well. Previously, I had received good grades and words of praise from others, but it never had much meaning. Somehow, I imagined that the only reason they were telling me I was doing good was so I would not start shooting heroin again. Nevertheless, when Professor Bielby told me that, I believed her. Her words encouraged me to think about graduate school.

During the year I worked with Denise Bielby, I became familiar with the prison literature, especially the work of John Irwin; completed a research project about prison humor; and applied to graduate school. As fate would have it, I got accepted at the University of California at Irvine (UCI). For the next five years, I commuted between Santa Barbara and Orange County, California, in pursuit of a Ph.D.

GRADUATE SCHOOL: "MAKING IT" WITH A LITTLE HELP FROM MY FRIENDS

My time at UCI was spent learning what the "experts" think and say about the general subjects of criminology, law, and society. Although the beliefs and ideas of my instructors varied, they all supported my efforts and treated me with respect. I learned about "operationalizing" variables, program evaluations, criminological theory, how to look at crime from a policy perspective, and some of the critical perspectives used to study "law and society." Regardless of which course I took or with whom I interacted, I never kept my views or where I came from a secret. Then, as now, I complained about what I see to be the major missing "factor" in most criminological research. That is, most statistical and theoretical research presented and quoted in journals, books, and classes has little to do with the real-life situations of human beings.

Part of my routine at UCI included working as a teaching assistant (TA), which I saw as a great opportunity. It meant getting paid for working with undergraduates and learning about what I'd be doing after graduate school. Several times I was given the opportunity to do guest lectures. On these occasions I talked about my life, heroin addiction, prison, and always attempted to humanize the people who inhabit these deviant social worlds.

Convicts, like war veterans, or cops, often develop close relationships with each other. Alan Mobley, who did time in the federal prison system, began his graduate education at UCI during my second year. Though our stories are dramatically different, we immediately became friends. In subsequent years, we spent time together talking about what was going on in school, things we had done and seen in prison, and about the ongoing dramas of our lives. Alan was, and is, not only a good friend, but also a solid link to the past. His presence during graduate school was a major means of support. Again, there was a convict in my life doing what I was doing; I was not alone (see Mobley, this volume).

Irvine's faculty had a positive influence on my education, and especially on my changing self-concept and future. In about my third year, Henry Pontell humorously said they had me about 75 percent socialized, but that I still had a ways to go. Paul Jesilow, who acted as my dissertation advisor, had the most lasting impact. Like Denise Bielby had done at UCSB, he provided me with hands-on experience as a researcher and writer. I often complained to him about the so-called empirical content of the discipline, which failed to include real-life representations of people who got caught up in crime and the criminal justice system. He encouraged me to follow my heart. Today, as I write, I hear his voice telling me "too many words" or "what's the point?"

As time passed, my relationships and familiarity with academics beyond the Irvine Ph.D. program broadened. Often, this had to do with finding literature not included in the curriculum. Symbolic interactionism, for example, was not included in any theory or methods classes I took. Unfortunately, despite the fact the UCI professors taught critical analysis, they were, for the most part, comfortably distant from their subject.

ATTENDING CRIMINOLOGY AND CRIMINAL JUSTICE CONFERENCES

My eyes were really opened at my first American Society of Criminology meeting. I learned that criminology is not only an academic discipline, it is also a profession, and for some people, a business. After living in the "belly of the beast" (Abbott, 1981), exposure to these alien-like, privileged social worlds is highly disturbing. My perceptions at this particular event, which reflected my convict background and graduate student status, left me feeling uneasy and out of place. This is common for many graduate students, especially attending a conference for the first time.

Criminology and criminal justice conferences always take place in what appears to me to be lavish, luxurious hotels, replete with extravagant furniture, floor covering, lighting, and restaurants that charge exorbitant prices. "Experts" come from all over the country and world. Social networks are built. Authors of books wander, meeting with old friends and colleagues they may only get to see on these occasions. Their travel and conference expenses, at least in part, are usually paid for by the organizations they represent; for example, universities, research institutes, or government agencies.

Now comes the hard part. Reflecting on John Irwin's earlier statement, *"What the fuck were they doing?"* The value of some of their research is highly debatable. Much of their work, which may have been undertaken as a result of the lure of grant money, does little more than elevate their status. Presentation of "data" is dominated by factor analysis and multivariate correlations. Problems associated with prisons and the lives of people who get released, if mentioned at all, are said to be management related. The widespread damage of crime-related politics and policies is seldom discussed. Issues related to humanity, morality, and virtue are oddly missing.

Early conference encounters were difficult. Panel after panel left me feeling empty inside. Over and over I would think, "Nobody is talking about the people who suffer. Nobody is talking about the truth." What I saw was a group of people benefiting at the expense of human misery beyond their comprehension. The reality of the human condition as it related to those defined as criminal, their definers, and the worlds in which they live was seldom heard. Strolling through the book display I noticed few of the books were about prisons. One thing was sure, this was a long way from C-block. And the guys in the yard are still there. The addicts, homeless, poor, and mentally ill on the streets are still suffering. Where is the "data" about their lives?

At my first few conferences, I was assigned to panels based on the type of abstract I submitted. Typically, most of what was said by session participants supported the views of those with interests in maintaining the social order. Looking at overheads filled with tables and charts was always painful. It reminded me of being in school when I was a kid. I couldn't wait to leave.

Once, at an Academy of Criminal Justice Sciences (ACJS) annual meeting, I was placed on a panel that drew less than 10 people. Sitting at a table before it began, I saw a man enter the room wearing a nametag indicating he was a prison warden. Seating himself across from me, he immediately made a comment about the tattoos on my arms. "Well, I see where you've been. You must be doing good now." Then, in an obviously condescending tone, he said, "Are you going to get those things removed now?" With great pleasure I told him, "Hell no. Rewards for doing good?" The sweet taste of vengeance? No wonder I don't wear long sleeves more often.

At another ACJS session, I talked about the relationship between crime and desperation. Before my presentation we heard from two academics and a man who worked for the National Institute of Justice (NIJ). His sterile, mindless words and unmistakable arrogance turned my stomach. He was clearly far removed from the real lives of people who live on the streets or in prison. Like many other middle-class professionals at the conferences and in the halls of academia, he left me with the impression that he had led a sheltered, antiseptic existence his entire life (J. Ross, 2000a).

When I had my chance to speak, I suggested that instead of viewing "criminals" as rational calculating machines (Cornish and Clarke, 1999), we might try to see them as human beings doing the best they can with what they have to work with. HIV-infected, drug-addicted parents don't choose to leave their kids home without food while they hustle money for dope. Armed robbers, usually addicts, are not necessarily "seduced into crime" (Katz, 1988). In reality, there are many ways to unravel the causes of criminal behavior, yet any explanations that fail to include politics (crime is politically defined), economics, ideology, and historical context are basically meaningless. Finally, I said, recognizing the desperation involved in many criminal activities might put a different dimension on how we conceptualize criminal behavior. It would, perhaps, allow us to see our own culpability rather than blame it all on "them." During my short talk I noticed the man from the NIJ avoiding my eyes and squirming in his chair as if it was on fire. As soon as I finished, before any questions could be asked, he hurriedly left the room.

I was having a hard time making sense of these conferences. Why am I here? What do I have to offer? Joan Petersilia supported me from the beginning of my graduate school days. Early on she knew my feelings about the failure of criminologists to recognize the dehumanizing conditions of the criminal justice system and the lives of those defined as criminal. She always listened as I told her about my frustrating conference experiences. One day, she suggested I contact some other exconvicts turned academics and attempt to put a panel together for an upcoming ASC meeting. I contacted John Irwin, Stephen Richards, Rick Jones, and Ed Tromanhauser. Convict criminology was born, and now I enjoy conferences.

ASSISTANT PROFESSOR

What's It Like Now?

In the fall of 1999, I began working as an assistant professor at the University of Michigan at Flint. My wife and I left Annie, then 17 years old, behind in Santa Barbara to live with her father while she finished high school. The move to Michigan has been both stimulating and painful. We are enjoying the novelty of the Midwest and the excitement of new beginnings. On the other hand, uprooting ourselves from relationships that took years to develop has been difficult. Serious change is never easy.

After arriving in Flint, I immediately became involved in the local NA meetings. Doing so helped me to enter a new social network of recovering addicts, who act as a major means of support. As they did in California, they also give me a grounded, nonacademic glimpse into social worlds that revolve around the negative effects of illegal drug use, the law, and imprisonment.

What I do today is a far cry from the controlled environment of the prison. As time passes, I find myself getting increasingly involved in problems that other academics struggle with: interdepartmental conflicts, deadlines, health insurance, retirement funds, car problems, issues about money, and so on. Still, some of the most simple aspects of life, like not having to worry about cell house violence, are not forgotten. Strength is gained by recollecting the past, which is never further than a thought away.

Compared to being a convict, life as an academic is incredible. I live in a nice home with Debbie. The food we eat—though we have to buy it, prepare it, and clean up the dishes afterward (much easier to just get in line)—is of a much higher quality than the mystery meat served behind prison walls. I love my job, and especially enjoy teaching. As I write this I can look out my window at squirrels scurrying around the snow-covered ground. There are no bars on the windows, or guards walking by counting me like I am part of a cattle herd.

The opportunity I have today allows me to tell what I know about the ways many of us, inside prison and out, are living as a result of warped ideologies, politics, economics, racism, sexism, homophobia, social class inequality, and a market economy that generates an extreme form of self-centeredness, rampant competitiveness, and lack of compassion for others.

In prison, I saw men shot by authorities for no reason whatsoever. I have seen convicts stab each other because they felt they must. Failure to do so would have meant being seen as weak, and therefore, no good, in the eyes of other convicts. I have seen men in penitentiary psychiatric units drugged out of their minds because they were deemed "dangerous" by prison doctors. I remember them walking around in circles for hours after being let out of their cells holding hands, sticking their tongues in each other's ears, stumbling forward to take step after step, and they had been there for years. I have seen the hopelessness, degradation, monotony, and real conditions of prisons in this country, and the courage, fortitude, and humor that have helped a few of us survive and maintain some degree of sanity. We need to tell about what we know. Isn't that our job?

ALL IN A DAY'S WORK: FROM THE BELLY OF THE IVORY TOWER TO THE HEART OF THE INNER CITY

It is not always easy for this convict criminologist to be an assistant professor. Before the semester started, I happened to run into a university dean as I was dropping some paperwork off at her office. As the cheerful secretary introduced us, I noticed her checking out the ink work on my arms. Feeling strange and not knowing how to respond, I asked, "How do you like my tattoos?" She responded, "Well, I guess they kind of go with the design on your shirt." I regretted not wearing long sleeves on that occasion. Awkward moments come and go.

One particular day, I was obliged to attend a new faculty meeting. Feeling extremely out of place, I sat and listened as those of us who had just gotten hired were introduced. From there I was invited to a welcoming luncheon at the home of the chancellor. The festivities took place on a spacious lawn area at a mansion-like house. My feelings of alienation deepened as I made my approach. Members of the faculty, or royalty as they appeared to me, were sitting, talking, and eating at colorfully decorated tables. Adjacent to the lawn was a porch area with several more long tables covered with different kinds of foods and drinks. Servers, dressed in white clothes and hats, waited on the tables and helped with the food. Not knowing a single person there, and feeling like I was what they used to call "out of bounds" in prison, I awkwardly scooped up some food, found a table, indulged in some very brief small talk, finished eating, and left within 10 minutes. Driving away, I wondered what I was getting myself into. Again, this was a long way from C-block.

That night I went to an NA meeting near downtown Flint. It was held in a church basement in a predominantly black neighborhood, within four miles of the chancellor's house, in an area full of vacated, boarded-up houses. Bars covering the windows and doors of people's homes give them the appearance of miniature jail cells. As happens in many AA and NA meetings where people tell it like it is, stories of pain and hope were shared. Lots of tears and hugs.

Never in California had I heard a woman in an NA meeting talk about one of her children being murdered. That night I heard two people, both black, grieving over the shooting deaths of their adolescent sons. Along with the tears came humorous presentations of life experiences that conveyed a sense of belonging. Tears and laughter are cathartic, a means of healing for people in pain. Nowhere else, except maybe at a funeral, do I hear such truthfulness, people exposing their vulnerability. While in the presence of such honesty, I am not a convict, addict, or academic. During these special moments, at least temporarily, I am just another living, breathing person, nobody special or different. Realizing this helps me see more clearly that underneath our facades, we are all really the same.

INSIDIOUS CONSEQUENCES OF THE PRISON EXPERIENCE: COHORTS AS EVIDENCE

John Irwin recently suggested to me that the ruined lives of the majority of the people we met in our respective prison cohorts is evidence of the damaging effects of imprisonment. I agree. Criminologists have told me that what I saw and talk about is merely anecdotal and, therefore, can have no effect on social policy, which should be the true aim of our work. I disagree. The truth needs to be told. The truth of deviant social worlds—obscured by government-funded statistics, the corporate-owned media, and arrogant middle-class academics— is screaming to be heard.

Stories of people making successful transitions to the streets after spending years behind bars are unusual. The effects of incarceration turn many of us into violent, relatively fearless individuals who hardly care whether we live or die once we get out of prison. While inside, we became psychologically and socially impaired. Once released, those who "do good" generally fall into some conventional social world, usually with the help of family, friends, prisoner assistance programs, and a great deal of individual effort. Many become dependent on families and social welfare. Others cross back and forth, within and outside the law. They may work menial jobs, then drift back into drug habits, spending time in detox wards and county jails. Unknown numbers of us who fail to find some conventional niche gravitate toward dereliction (Austin and Irwin, 2001: 152–157), characterized by homelessness, cheap wine alcoholism, poor health, and despair. We sleep where we can—in bushes, under bridges, on sidewalks, inside cardboard boxes, and in a variety of other locations, beyond the sight of the public. As when we are locked up, we are characterized by many as lazy, morally deficient, and burdensome.

Success stories of my own convict cohort are few and far between. Many died from overdoses. A few were stabbed to death while inside. It was not unusual to hear about a guy who upon getting out of prison was shot to death.

Meanwhile, more and more of us are dying from health problems related to cancer, AIDS, and hepatitis C. Too many, like a friend who was given 32 years to life for possession of a spoon containing traces of heroin residue and less than a quarter gram of cocaine, are doing what is commonly called "all day" by convicts; meaning he will never be released from prison again.

The fear of getting out and the difficulty of "making it" need acknowledgment. From what I have seen, the following words from a friend who wrote me just before being released by a parole board are not unusual for seasoned prisoners:

> I have a lot more shit to trip on than the [parole] board. Like getting out. I was laying on my rack this morning thinking about the streets, stomach in knots, palms all sweaty. I hate it here. But I'm also scared to get out. Don't know why bro, just makes me scared. Remember how you felt on the van riding to Chino [trip from jail to prison] or wherever? Well, that's how I feel when I'm about to get out. My guts all in a knot. Remember the last time I got out? You met me at Carrow's [restaurant]? Well, right before that at the Greyhound station I felt like crying when I got off that bus. Not cause I was happy either!

Within two months after being released, he was murdered in a Phoenix area "homeless camp."

Particularly painful for me was the story of a guy I met in NA. Except for a brief amount of time spent behind bars for heroin possession, he was gainfully employed his entire adult life. When I met him he had just been released from prison and was attending meetings to satisfy his parole officer. The eventual resurgence of his heroin habit led to another drug conviction, which meant he would spend more time living amidst the madness of California prisons. I saw him a few times after he bailed out of jail, waiting for trial, anticipating being returned to prison. His usual, joyful personality was gone. It was as if the life had gotten sucked out of his body. To resolve his dilemma, he killed himself by jumping off a freeway overpass bridge, bouncing off a car traveling between 65 and 70 miles per hour. Rather than being afraid of getting out, he didn't want to go back. Sometimes deterrence really does work. From what I have seen, tragic stories never seem to end.

One day while driving from Santa Barbara to Irvine, I stopped in Hawthorne for gas. As I was waiting for a left turn light to get back on the freeway, I saw a filthy, obviously homeless man standing next to me holding a sign that said, "To hell with lying, I need a drink." Though he looked older than he likely was, I figured we were about the same age. Rolling down my window, I began talking to him as I handed him a couple bucks. "How's it going man? You staying warm at night?" Looking at some bushes perched on the side of the freeway off-ramp, his home on the other side of the street, he said, "Yeah, well, it's going all right. I got some blankets and shit. It's fucked up when it starts raining though. Other than that it's OK. Know what I mean?" I responded, "Yeah, I know."

This guy looked like he hadn't bathed in months. His white skin and clothes were crusty dirty. Yet somehow we seemed instantly connected. After glancing at the bushes again, he asked, "Hey, you want to come over and have a drink?" I replied, "I'd actually kind of like to, but I gotta keep going." "What are you doing, anyway?" he wondered. "Well, I'm going to school right now. I spent a lotta time in 'those places' and I'm staying clean these days so I don't have to go back," I told him. He immediately knew what I meant. "I've been in those places too," he said. "And, I ain't never going back." The light turned green, I said goodbye, and continued on my journey. Back on the freeway I felt saddened. The man I just left reminded me of others I had to leave behind, in prisons, detox wards, rescue missions, and funeral parlors. Somehow, what I was leaving seemed to be part of what I am.

CONCLUSION

I have a few ideas about what might be done to improve the lives of people who spend time in prison and their chances of "doing good" after release. Real solutions would be geared toward improving the social circumstances of those most likely to get incarcerated: the poor, the undereducated, the unemployed —mostly minorities from America's inner cities. Improved employment and educational opportunities, better housing, health care, and a dismantlement of Draconian drug laws would be a good place to start.

As convict criminologists, we can do our part without selling out. Rather than seek government funding to study things like the varying rates of marijuana use, or how to better identify, isolate, and track members of "gangs," we can align ourselves with others who provide critical representations of the many issues related to our field.

As the rate of imprisonment continues to climb, more prisoners are getting out of prison. In 1995, about 463,000 people were released from prison. Estimates indicate those numbers will reach 660,000 by the end of 2000 and hit the 1.2 million mark by 2010 (Abramsky, 1999: 32–33). Instead of figuring out how to better "manage" this population, be it inside or outside prison walls, perhaps part of what we can do is study and write about their experiences and lives. Such efforts might help them be seen as human beings instead of animals, as they are continually depicted in the popular culture. By doing so, maybe we can help generate the beginnings of a compassionate criminology, a criminology that does more than help maintain the social order. As Richard Quinney said one time at an ASC panel, "It is not enough to be critical. We must also be proactive."

Addressing the structural impediments (e.g., loss of civil rights, blocked employment opportunities) that hinder the chances of "doing good" after release are important (Richards, 1995a, 1998; Richards and Jones, 1997) and should continue. Yet how we see ourselves and how we think others evaluate us after we get out greatly affects our actions. Some typical comments I heard from exconvicts about their release experience illustrate this dilemma. One man, for example, told me, "Everyone looked at me like they were scared to death." He figured they thought, "Jesus Christ. Charles Manson just got out." Another said, "Soon as I got out, I noticed everyone looking at me. It was like everyone knew I'd been to prison. It was like being from another planet." Efforts to reduce such feelings are drastically needed and might be achieved if prisons were more humane.

Encouraging the humanization of the worlds behind bars should be a major concern for all of us. Even prison administrators should be concerned with the unnecessary, counterproductive, punitive practices commonly found in penal institutions across the country. In this regard, prison policies should be geared toward reducing cruel and unusual punishment and increasing the level of prisoner safety. Moreover, they should provide adequate health care and rehabilitation programs for those who are motivated to help themselves (Murphy, this volume).

In my view, humanizing *all* contemporary deviant populations should be a fundamental goal of convict criminology. After all, prisoners represent only a fraction of the "dangerous classes," which are increasingly subject to formal social control (Mandell, 1975; Gordon, 1994; Shelden, 2001). We should also remind others that people do change with experience, age, and education. This transformation is facilitated by forgiveness, understanding, and compassion.

Instead of focusing so much on the deviant as the cause of all our social problems, we might benefit by looking at the part each one of us plays in either reducing or increasing human suffering. If harm reduction were our true concern, then "the realization of peace in our own everyday lives [would be] the best social policy" (Quinney, 1995: 148). Our "wars" on drugs and crime are really wars on ourselves. An excerpt from the spiritual text *A Course in Miracles* suggests the value of peace:

> Peace, looking on itself, extends itself. War is the condition in which fear is born, and grows and seeks to dominate. Peace is the state where love abides, and seeks to share itself. Conflict and peace are opposites. Where one abides the other cannot be; where either goes the other disappears (*A Course*, 1992: 489).

We all affect each other. Striving to look upon others without condemnation, especially those we fear, is perhaps the greatest harm-reducing effort each of us can make.

NOTES

1. See Douglas Hay (1975) for a scathing critique of England's escalation of punishment, especially the death penalty, during the eighteenth century. As is the case today in the United States, those being punished most often came from what was viewed as the "dangerous classes." Also, Hughes (1988) portrays the history of the European colonization of Australia as being rooted in the suffering and brutality of England's convict system of transportation.

2. For more on "making it," which simply means staying out of prison, see Irwin (1970: 88–89) and Jones (this volume). See Richards (1995a, 1998), Richards and Jones (1997), and J. Ross and Richards (2002: Chapter 12) for an in-depth look at some of the obstacles faced by prisoners after they are released.

3. See Irwin (1970: 82–85) for a discussion about convict identity.

4. For an excellent discussion regarding the idea that criminologists can be witnesses to atrocities, see Quinney (1998).

5. Shortly after the ASC meeting, I called John Irwin on the phone. During our talk, I asked him why academics today seldom use concepts like social worlds and reference groups anymore. He answered, "You don't need to when you're doing survey research and using computers for data analysis."

6. The people I knew who did get into trouble with the law began using heroin regularly while still in high school and were not my close friends during that period.

7. See Irwin (1970: 74–76) for a descriptive analysis of jailing.

8. See Irwin (1970: 86–106) for a discussion about looking at the streets from the inside.

9. I "did good" that time for almost two years. Unfortunately, when I attempted to get off methadone I began using heroin again. Shortly thereafter, I returned to prison.

10. Both the heroin and the types of people who used it began changing by the beginning of the 1980s. A newer, stronger form known as "tar" heroin became prevalent at that time. In the 1970s, the heroin addicts I knew were mostly street- or criminal-oriented. In the 1980s, I began seeing individuals with more conventional perspectives using the drug.

11. This statistic was corroborated by an article I read in the local paper at that time.

12. One night in 1995, I turned on a television news show that helped justify the removal of Pell Grants from prisons. The show questioned why certain kids (images of pitiful looking, young white faces covered the screen) are denied government funds for education while criminals (images of black prisoners sitting behind computer terminals) receive support.

13. Classes that critiqued politics, economics, history, or the law and society were not offered. The effects of the curriculum, a good proportion of which was made up of psychology classes, took my attention inward rather than outward.

14. Examples include Watts (1957), Keyes Jr. (1975), Levine (1979), and Lozoff (1985).

15. See Irwin (1970: 104–105) for a discussion about "getting short."

16. For a discussion about social organizations that help buffer the problems related to reentry, see Irwin (1970: 126–130).

17. Cressey (1955) outlined the processes that can affect the changing behaviors of criminals. Applying differential association theory (Sutherland), he suggested that the alteration of criminal behavior can be enhanced when people identify themselves and become involved with non–criminal-oriented groups.

6

My Journey through
the Federal Bureau
of Prisons

STEPHEN C. RICHARDS

"In all of his life he could never have been as frightened as at this moment,
but he had a dignity and presence that spared him from humiliation
and a genuine elegance that was defeated only by tarnished hands
and nails that had been shattered by rough work."

MARQUEZ
1970: 265

"Races condemned to a hundred years of solitude did not have
a second opportunity on earth."

MARQUEZ
1970: 383

Like it or not, some things are decided before birth. I never knew my father,
and my mother had been seriously disabled years before I was born. She
spent her brief adult life in and out of hospitals, suffering from a terminal condition. Each time she was admitted to another medical facility, my sister and I
were alone, waiting for her return. She fought bravely to keep each job she lost,
support her children, and fight off the inevitable. I remember her as gentle and
soft spoken.

As small children we learned to stand at the mailbox waiting for welfare and
child support checks, come home to a cold and dark apartment when the util-
ities were turned off, stall the landlord when we did not have the rent, and to
pack our meager belongings each time we were evicted. After years of living in

I would like to thank Daniel S. Murphy, Donna H. Richards, and Jeffrey Ian Ross for their
comments and suggestions on this chapter. An earlier version of this paper was presented
at the American Society of Criminology meeting, Toronto, Canada, November 1999.

public housing projects, hotel rooms, and rented apartments, our family broke up when my mother was hospitalized again. My sister was sent to live with "her" father, and at age seven, I became a "ward of the state."

I was placed in a children's home, an orphanage for displaced children. As a "state-raised youth" (Irwin, 1970: 26–29; Abbott, 1981: 3–22), I have a couple dozen orphan brother and sisters. We grew up together, sometimes sleeping as many as five children to a room. Eating meals at long noisy tables, the rule after dinner was, we would first clear the dishes, then sit back down to study, the older children helping the younger. We were not allowed to leave the dinner tables, to watch television or play outdoors, until everyone's homework was completed. Some evenings we sat at those tables until bedtime.

As orphans, we wore nametags in our clothes, had no parental protection or family privilege, and were raised to be self-sufficient. Professional childcare workers, many of them college students, served as surrogate parents and were devoted to our needs. I had the advantage of being able to selectively model myself after a collection of diverse adults, from different social, economic, racial, and religious backgrounds. Some of my favorite "staff" were African American. As an orphan, I am the child of many "parents."

Every year, as I grew up, I watched the older children leave the institution. On the day of release, there was a party, the child was allowed to select the menu, and the director of the children's home would give going-away presents; it was always the same, a five-dollar bill and a cardboard suitcase. At the conclusion of the party, the child would walk to the bus stop and leave, never to return. I remember one director, with tears in his eyes, whose final words to the assembled children were, "At 18 your funding is finished, you leave here with the clothes on your back, and all the education you were able to complete."

In 1969, at age 17, I graduated from high school early and left the orphanage to attend the University of Wisconsin (UW-Madison). During this time, UW-Madison was one of the lead campuses in the Civil Rights and antiwar movements. As a sociology student, I remember our professors leading us from the lecture halls to join peace marches in the streets. I participated in Students for a Democratic Society (SDS), marching for welfare mothers' rights, the Black Student Union strike, the Teaching Assistants' Union strike, and numerous mass demonstrations, with tens of thousands of students, against the Vietnam War.

The police and National Guard occupied our campus every year and gassed us from helicopters and military vehicles. An important part of our education was learning how to differentiate between tear, blister, and pepper gas. The UW-Madison students fought the police with sticks and stones, and filled the county jail and hospitals after each "spring offensive." I served a couple of short sentences in jail for participating in these activities, then left school to join the "revolution."

Orphans are tough, they have to be. As sad as it sounds, the children's home and my experiences with radical politics at UW-Madison prepared me for life, instilled a deep appreciation of learning, and gave me perseverance, the ability to struggle against the odds, and the social-collective skills to weather adversity. Later in my adult life, this preparation would serve me well to survive and even prosper in both the penitentiary and academia.

PRISON EDUCATION

I am a convicted felon and former federal prisoner. I was arrested in 1982, when I refused to cooperate with the Drug Enforcement Agency, was threatened with, and then indicted on, 10 counts of Conspiracy to Distribute Marijuana. Facing 150 years, if convicted on all charges (15 years for each count), I stood jury trial in the Federal District Courthouse in Charleston, South Carolina. In 1983, upon being convicted of one count, and while on bail, I appealed the case to the U.S. Court of Appeals, and in 1984, the U.S. Supreme Court. Although my federal parole guidelines were only 12 months, I was sentenced to nine years and designated to maximum security at the United States Penitentiary Atlanta (USP Atlanta).

Altogether, I stood trial in three federal courtrooms (U.S. District Court, U.S. Court of Appeals, U.S. Supreme Court), and completed two years on close bail supervision, three years incarcerated, and six years on parole, for a total of 11 years in correctional custody. During my personal journey I served time in two jails (South Carolina), eight Federal Bureau of Prisons (FBOP or BOP) institutions in six different states, one work-release center, and had six different parole officers. As a federal prisoner I did time behind the walls of United States penitentiaries (USP Atlanta, USP Terre Haute, USP Marion, USP Leavenworth), within the fence of medium-security federal correctional institutions (FCI Talladega, FCI Oxford), and minimum security in three different federal prison camps (FPC Terre Haute, FPC Leavenworth, FPC Oxford). There is no substitute for experience.

UNIVERSITY EDUCATION

In 1984, while I was still on bail, the U.S. Supreme Court responded to my Writ of Certiorari by inviting my attorneys to give written and oral arguments. The U.S. Supreme Court reviews cases that raise serious questions about due process, trial procedures, and judicial misconduct. Meanwhile, I resumed undergraduate studies at UW-Madison. During final exams in my last semester, my bail was revoked and I was jailed. I do not think the federal district judge in Charleston, South Carolina, wanted me to graduate from college.

In 1986, while in prison, I managed to complete a B.S. in sociology by taking correspondence credit through the University of Wisconsin-Extension, which I paid for by working as a clerk at UNICOR (federal prison industries). As the FBOP does not offer college courses or support prisoners who pursue higher education (Lanier, Philliber, and Philliber, 1994; Tregea, this volume), it was a struggle completing college credit by correspondence. Every "joint" (prison) I was in had a small group of men who were taking classes by mail. We were subject to a number of security restrictions that complicated our student activities, including no more than five books in our cells, limited use of typewriters or photocopy machines, and restricted mail procedures. For example, all mail, coming and going is opened, read, and copied by guards. Books mailed to prisoners have the covers ripped off by prison employees to prevent the entry of contraband (drugs or weapons) into the institution.

In addition, because we were taking college classes, we were subject to frequent cell shakedowns (searches), and disciplinary transfers to "administrative detention" (solitary confinement) or other institutions. Prison wardens usually considered educated convicts to be a threat to their authority because they have the ability to write letters to the media reporting inhumane conditions and corruption. As students, we were considered dangerous because we were using the mail and phones to communicate with "outside" university personnel—people that might have influence with the press or political system. Upon receiving my college diploma in the mail, knowing full well the answer to the question, I went to a prison case manager and asked for permission to attend the graduation ceremony at UW-Madison. I was told no, and that if I asked again, I would go straight to the "hole" (solitary confinement).

In 1987, while on a six-day furlough from Federal Prison Camp Oxford (FPC Oxford), I visited the Department of Sociology at the University of Wisconsin-Milwaukee (UW-Milwaukee) and asked to see the department chairperson, Professor Gregory Squires. Upon introducing myself, and informing him I was interested in applying to the master's program, I gave him two file folders; one contained my undergraduate university transcripts, the other my prison furlough papers. Squires asked, "Can you teach criminology?" He then called the dean of arts and sciences for permission to admit me to the program with an appointment as a graduate teaching assistant (GTA). His next step was to have his secretary type my application to their graduate program in his office, waive the application fee, and introduce me to some of the faculty (Don Green, Nason Hall, Ellie Miller, and Joan Moore). When I returned to FPC Oxford, I used the UW-Milwaukee admission and GTA appointment to secure a six-month halfway house. The UW-Milwaukee sociology faculty broke me out of prison early.

Released from federal prison in 1987, I entered the master's program at UW-Milwaukee, where Ellie Miller introduced me to Rick Jones (a contributor to this volume), who was an exconvict and an assistant professor of sociology at Marquette University. In 1989, upon completing the M.A., with the help of Jones, I entered the Ph.D. program in sociology at Iowa State University, graduating in 1992. Today, I am an associate professor of sociology and criminology at Northern Kentucky University.

INTRODUCTION: JOURNEY THROUGH THE FEDERAL GULAG

My experience with incarceration and academic studies has taught me that convicts are the real experts on prison conditions. In comparison, many prison employees, despite their work experience, do not have a clue or a care about what corrections is or could be. They simply are not interested in considering the potential prisoners may have for personal growth and transformation. Instead they operate penal facilities that focus almost exclusively on inmate management and control.

The reality is that correctional officers behave like parking lot attendants, doing little more than controlling the movement of inmates throughout the institution, for example, directing prisoners to enter or exit cells, stand in line, or walk through metal detectors. It is rare for guards to have any meaningful interaction, even conversation, with individual prisoners. The guards operate as zoo custodians, not as correctional workers. They are members of a blue-collar occupation that despite its claim to expertise and professional pretensions has failed to develop the standards and skills required to do corrections.

Unfortunately, academics probably know even less about prisons because they have little firsthand knowledge and simply parrot the outdated correctional descriptions, theories, and so-called empirical evidence they learned from other sheltered scholars. Most of these "experts" have spent precious little time inside of penitentiaries or conversing with convicts.

If you want to know how the criminal justice and penal machinery functions, then ask a convict. What is it like to be prosecuted and imprisoned by the U.S. government? Reflecting on my own experience as a convict, visits to and tours of numerous BOP facilities, and conversations with hundreds of federal prisoners over the last 15 years, I will focus on the way a typical federal convict might remember court, jail, and prison. This is what I believe a person might experience as a prisoner of the U.S. government.

Many federal prisoners have a story to tell about their journey through the federal system of courts and prisons. Each one travels the "stations of the cross," as they are processed through arrest, jails, courts, prisons, and release to parole or community supervision. New federal prisoners learn of "another America" where there are no states, only six BOP administrative districts (North East, Mid-Atlantic, South East, North Central, South Central, West). The men and women are sentenced into a prison system that has officially repudiated rehabilitation, has the longest sentences in the world, and no parole (for persons convicted since 1987) (Richards, 1990).

Forget the nonsense you have read in correctional textbooks about the "criminal justice system,"[1] correctional facilities, and programs of rehabilitation. Instead, come with me on an unauthorized tour of the federal gulag (Richards, 1990), a world of prisons that stretch across America, of "cons" patrolled by "hacks" (prison guards), and security perimeters defended by high walls, razor and concertina wire (rolls of barbed wire five feet tall that encircle prisons), and gun towers. The journey traces my steps through some of America's most infamous prisons, institutions identified by their acronyms, including administrative detention maximums (ADXs), United States penitentiaries (USPs), federal correctional institutions (FCIs), federal prison camps (FPCs), federal medical centers (FMCs), federal detention centers (FDCs), metropolitan correctional centers (MCCs), and federal transfer centers (FTCs). The chapter discusses the federal war on drugs and federal prosecution and describes doing jail time, transport of prisoners, BOP prisons, classification of prisoners, a typology of federal prisoners, and prisoner resistance.

THE FEDERAL WAR ON DRUGS

The U.S. government is fighting a war on drugs (Richards, 1990, 1998: 122–144; Johns and Borrero, 1991: 67–100; Currie, 1993: 9–35; J. G. Miller, 1996; Welch, 1999: 51–67; C. Parenti, 1999: 45–66; Beckett and Sasson, 2000: 64–68; Richards and Avey, 2000; Hallinan, 2001; Abramsky, 2002; J. Ross and Richards, 2002: 173–179). The government does not report that this war has human casualties (Gaucher, 1998); millions of people are arrested and hundreds of thousands of people sentenced to long prison sentences every year. The federal crusade against illegal drugs is a holy war, a "jihad" that is the engine driving the dramatic increase in federal expenditures on police, courts, and prisons. This is a war the "drug czars" have fought in earnest since the beginning of the Reagan administration (C. Parenti, 2000: 58–62).

The war effort allows the government to declare a national emergency and extend police powers with military tactics. The "rules of engagement" include the following: (1) The federal government has invented new laws that allow it to conduct search and seizure of homes, cars, boats, businesses, and financial instruments, including funds designated for legal defense; (2) severe sentencing of convicted drug offenders provides the government with the means to compel cooperation of defendants and witnesses against their own friends and family; and (3) the government will not allow itself to lose criminal cases, despite the fact that it is not a war federal authorities can win, as the supply and popularity of illegal drugs continues unabated.

Reiman (1995: 4–5) defined a "Pyrrhic victory" as a "military conquest purchased at such a cost in troops and treasure that it amounts to a defeat." He also argued, however, that the failure of the criminal justice system yields such benefits to those in power that it amounts to success. It matters little if the drug war is ineffective at suppressing the supply and distribution of controlled substances, as long as federal law enforcement budgets grow fat on confiscated property and increased appropriations. The drug war is an entitlement program, the administrative dole for the growing "thug bureaucracy" (Richards and Avey, 2000).

TAKE DOWN:

CATCHING A FEDERAL CASE

It began with a phone call from an old friend who told me he had a business proposition I could not refuse. He suggested we have lunch and discuss his "great idea." Later, I would learn that he had been busted in a drug deal I knew nothing about. My "friend" decided to work for the government and "roll over" to lighten his own sentence.

I went to meet my "friend." On that fateful day my head was in the clouds. My wife had just given birth to our son. I failed to pay attention to my surroundings—strange noises on the phone and unfamiliar cars parked down the street. I never expected to be set up by a friend and assaulted by federal agents. Without warning, no knock, my "friend" hid under a table, shaking in fear, as the door flew off the hinges and a dozen federal agents (Ferrell, 1994: 161; Richards and Avey, 2000), armed with automatic weapons and shotguns, stormed the premises. In all the confusion, I was lucky not to be shot.

The room filled with large men representing a federal strike force wearing military dress, including flak vests and helmets. Their uniforms identified them as belonging to numerous federal agencies: Drug Enforcement Agency (DEA); Federal Bureau of Investigation (FBI); Immigration and Naturalization Service (INS); Bureau of Alcohol, Tobacco, and Firearms (BATF); and Customs. I learned later that they had dozens of officers hiding in trees, on roofs, and crawling around in the bushes. The officers had no search or arrest warrants, and found no weapons or drugs.

As a federal prisoner, I was told many stories by fellow convicts about "take down procedures," federal search and destroy schemes, and early morning raids on homes and offices. The feds employ overwhelming force as a means to both protect their own and eliminate resistance. Unfortunately, drug raids do go awry. Incorrect addresses are entered, innocent people are arrested, personal property is destroyed searching for evidence, and occasionally, people get injured or killed. Thus, it should not come as a surprise to learn that the U.S. Department of Justice does not publish statistics on the number of illegal entries and searches, homes damaged, or people injured or murdered in drug raids, some of them innocent bystanders.

The federal government, with all of its statistical reporting on crime (e.g., Bureau of Justice Statistics; National Institute of Justice, etc.) goes to great lengths to conceal the violence of its military-style arrest operations. For example, the 1993 mass murder at Waco, Texas, of the Branch Davidians illustrates the carnage, cover-up, and federal double-talk that may result from military-style police raids (Hamm, 1997). As a federal prisoner, I have met many men, some of them with amputated limbs who will spend the rest of their lives in wheelchairs, who were wounded by police gunfire in drug raids.

CONSPIRACY CONVICTIONS

The drug war is being fought at the federal level with conspiracy convictions. "The federal courts use conspiracy laws coupled with secret grand juries to indict defendants for indiscriminate associations, thoughts, and alleged attempts to violate federal law" (Richards, 1990: 22). A common complaint of prisoners is the way they were prosecuted under these statutes. Conspiracy is defined as the discussing, overhearing, or having knowledge of a plan to violate federal law; a person is indicted for having "knowledge thereof." It is not necessary for the prosecution to prove direct involvement or that a crime actually happened. In other words, the mere intention to commit a crime is a crime. Because the federal criminal code does not require the possession or sale of drugs for conspiracy indictments, prosecutors can construct cases out of circumstance, association, and hearsay, and then invent their own sentencing guidelines (Tonry, 1993: 131–149) based on imaginary quantities of controlled substances.

STING OPERATIONS

Despite the lack of physical evidence in conspiracy cases, the arresting officers and court functionaries, working together, rarely lose a case. The wheels of justice turn on breaking the will of the defendants, "rolling them over," and "turning them" into government witnesses. One of the more insidious inventions of federal agents is the strategy of coupling the "weak burden of proof" required by conspiracy laws with the bag of tricks and deceit used to work "sting operations." Federal judges, prosecutors, and police design and employ stings and reverse stings to cast a wide net. The more defendants indicted, the easier it is to get a conviction by coercing one or more codefendants to testify against the others. "Sting" refers to undercover agents attempting to purchase drugs, weapons, stolen goods, or political influence. "Reverse stings" are when police agents pose as smugglers, distributors, or dealers offering to sell drugs; this is a tactic often used by federal authorities. These operations are particularly nebulous when pursued as conspiracy cases, which do not require the completion of a drug transaction.

Federal agents "design a crime," a criminal scenario, and then entice and trap persons to participate. The agents are most successful when the activity is vague, ill defined, and limited to casual conversation, as opposed to specific business arrangements, transactions, exchanges of product for cash, or deliveries of controlled substances. Criminal indictments are based on a person's agreeing to participate in something—whether that something actually happened or not. For example, a federal agent can solicit a person to buy drugs in a crowded bar with loud music, and the victim, not understanding the offer, can simply nod his or her head, and be arrested. No display or exchange of drugs for money is required.

EXORBITANT BAIL IS USED
TO FORCE COOPERATION

After being arrested and jailed, persons go before a federal court, where the bail is intentionally set in excess of what the defendant can reasonably be expected to afford, depending upon the lack of "cooperation." Many defendants indicted in criminal charges give oral or written statements, what are called confessions, or what the feds call "debriefing," as a means to get out of jail, because they cannot raise bail. Some plea "nolo contendere" (no contest); others, so-called friendly defendants, who have already established their role as informants (or those that will) walk out on personal recognizance. In comparison, uncooperative defendants spend many months, even years in jail, awaiting trial, if they are unable to raise bail.

INFORMERS

"Cooperating" individuals will name and "denounce" acquaintances and associates as participants in the alleged conspiracy. Manning (1997: 235) reported that informants or "snitches" are recruited by the police and paid in money or reduction of charges in exchange for their cooperation. The feds simply employ the "arithmetic of terror" to bully defendants into pleading guilty and or becoming informers. U.S. attorneys threaten the accused with multiple counts, indictment of family members, and possible life sentences.

Under federal law, prisoners have no possibility of parole, and must do at least 85 percent of their legal commitment or mandatory release at the expiration of sentence (100 percent); state prisoners, by contrast, may be paroled after serving, for example, a fourth or a third of court-ordered time. Many indicted suspects are so intimidated by the possibility of being sentenced to decades in prison that they plead guilty and make up stories about friends or even people they have never met as a means of reducing their own sentence. It is common to see coconspirators read prepared or recite rehearsed statements on the witness stand, and if they hesitate or deviate from the script, they are threatened again with the withdrawal of their plea bargain. Despite the objections by defense counsel that government witnesses have extensive criminal convictions or that testimony has been coerced and paid for with a reduced sentence or money, the judge nearly always rules in favor of the prosecution.

The pressuring of federal defendants to identify and testify against codefendants is reminiscent of tactics employed by the Soviet KGB, German Gestapo, or congressional committees during the McCarthy period. Konrad (1982: 177) wrote about Soviet methods used to compel testimony in postwar Hungary, "Even the names of casual acquaintances who might have been drawn into the conspiracy were squeezed out of the hapless schemers. Soon these people were also moaning on the basement floor; even though they knew nothing about the conspiracy. And they named names, too; if you beat someone he'll talk sooner or later." The feds do not need to physically torture defendants, which is messy, primitive, and would eventually provoke the moral indignation of the public. The U.S. government is more sophisticated; its agents need only threaten arrest of family, termination of parental rights, confiscation of assets, and audit by the Internal Revenue Service (IRS) to compel confessions, collaborating testimony, and plea bargains. "After all, one can only be crucified in the name of one's own faith" (Koestler, 1941: 174). No wonder federal prisoners refer to the DEA as the KGB and the FBI as the Gestapo.

The federal government also has special facilities where they train professional informers and prepare them for future court appearances. At FCI Sandstone, Minnesota, a large medium-security prison, the BOP has a specially constructed "snitch compound" consisting of dormitories with private rooms, wall-to-wall carpet, and color televisions for the internment of their informers. Federal prisoners have told me these "professional witnesses" are flown in and out of their privileged confinement by helicopter, on their way back and forth to federal courts around the country. As they enter or exit their prison dormitory they wear black hoods to conceal their identities from the general population prisoners in the main prison (Richards, 1990: 19).

STANDING UP TO
FEDERAL PROSECUTION

A "stand up" defendant is a person that, upon being arrested, keeps his or her mouth shut, does not confess or give statements against others, pleads not guilty, demands a trial, and refuses to cooperate with prosecutors. Remember, a defense attorney can only represent a client in a trial if the defendant retains his or her right to "remain silent" (*Miranda v. Arizona*).

The federal courts' day-to-day participation in the drug war effort has compromised its claim to judicial impartiality. The feds punish defendants who exercise their Constitutional rights to due process (Fourteenth Amendment): right to remain silent, bail, an attorney, jury of your peers, and appeal. These "noncooperative conspirators" may be subject to aggressive federal prosecution, which includes confiscation of assets, trial by press, intimidation of legal representation and family, and threat of multiple indictments. They may spend months or years in county jail, as the federal court delays proceedings through numerous pretrial hearings.

A few defendants will actually raise the hundreds of thousands of dollars required for bail by piecing together a surety bond based on a collection of mortgage equities, usually belonging to relatives. Then, because they had the audacity and resources to "make bail," they will be determined by the federal judge to be "flight risks" (i.e., they may fail to appear in court), and are thereby denied bail, or upon be bailed out of jail, assigned to "supererogatory" or "close bail supervision." This means they will be required to report daily to a federal parole office and restricted in travel, usually to the federal court district. The federal judge will order the parole office to conduct a presentence investigation (PSI), which in the federal system is just another variation of police interrogation. When the defendant refuses to cooperate with the PSI, the parole officer may resort to intimidation and threats of bail revocation. As the months pass, and the defendant proceeds through the federal district trial and appeals, his or her phones may be tapped, mail monitored, house kept under surveillance, and relatives, friends, and neighbors questioned.

In 1982, upon being arrested, I was charged with 10 counts of "Conspiracy to Distribute Marijuana," and bail was set at $1 million. I refused to cooperate. After a number of weeks in the Charleston, South Carolina, county jail, I was able to arrange a surety bond, which provided for my release to bail supervision in Madison, Wisconsin. I spent two years on "supererogatory bail supervision," which required me to report daily to the federal parole office, as the judge declared I was a flight risk, despite the fact I had no adult criminal record (other than the Madison arrests for antiwar demonstrations), was employed, and was married with a child.

As an out-of-state defendant, I needed more than one lawyer—a trial attorney I trusted and a local legal counsel to represent me in pretrial hearings. Later, I would hire additional legal talent for appeals and tax court. Lawyers' fees and travel expenses added up quickly. I paid for airline tickets, rented cars and hotel rooms for my legal staff as we traveled to and from court in South Carolina, Virginia, and Washington, D.C. Each of the many court appearances (arraignment, preliminary, numerous pretrial, bail revocation hearings, and three trials) cost thousands of dollars. I knew part of the prosecution's strategy was to deplete my legal defense fund. The IRS would later assess a 100 percent tax levy on their approximation of these legal expenditures, deciding arbitrarily that I financed my defense with undeclared income.

In 1983, I stood trial in the Federal Court House in Charleston. I remember how surprised and upset the judge was that I demanded a jury trial, and then, upon being convicted of one count, appealed the lower court's decision. In my defense, it should be noted that federal courts do not grant appellate bail unless there is reason to believe the case may be overturned when reviewed in a higher court.

The two years I experienced on bail were existentially painful. It was like being a living ghost, a deceased person still walking and talking. Like attending my own funeral, it was surreal listening to in-laws and friends make future plans without me, dividing up the spoils, as if I was already dead and buried. My wife, on the verge of a nervous breakdown, abandoned our marriage and disappeared with my son, leaving no phone number or address. In 1984, after I lost in Federal District, Appellate, and Supreme Court, my bail was revoked and I was jailed again.

DOING FEDERAL JAIL TIME

All trips to prison begin with some jail time (Irwin, 1985a; J. A. Thompson and Mays, 1991; Welch, 1994). This is usually, if computed properly, later deducted from prison "time to be served." "Going down" means descending into a "nether world" where you no longer have any control or influence on what happens above in the "free world." Everything you left on the street is up for grabs. The longer you stay incarcerated, the more you lose, including spouse, children, friends, home, job, and personal possessions. Stay in prison long enough and even your own family will forget you ever existed.

Most prisoners consider city and county jails to be worse than prison, especially facilities in large cities and the Deep South. Generally, jails have only holding cells, cell blocks with day rooms, and solitary confinement. Cells are crowded with bunk beds stacked two or three high, with a dozen or more men in each cage. These facilities have very little, if any, medical, recreational, or educational services.

Upon being arrested in 1982, I spent a few weeks in the Charleston jail (I returned to this jail two years later). This was a local facility staffed by "turn-key" guards[2] who were paid minimum wages (they actually showed the prisoners their paycheck stubs), and appeared nearly as economically desperate as the prisoners. The place was jammed with men sleeping in the day rooms and on mattresses along the hallway floors. The cells were filthy, with several species of cockroaches covering the ceilings, rats foraging in the dark, and the worst jail food I have ever had the pleasure of refusing. Each day, at every meal, the food was cornbread, grits, and coffee. In the evening they would serve fish heads (eyeballs and teeth) that were said to be donated by the nearby naval base. You could smell the stench coming down the hall on the dinner carts. Even the guards were embarrassed to serve the food. Feeling sorry for the prisoners, because they knew we were starving, and probably so they could make some money on the side, they would make their rounds late at night with a grocery cart selling potato chips and candy bars.

I had been in jail before, years ago for participating in civil rights marches, antiwar demonstrations, and labor strikes. But this was different. South Carolina is one of the poorest states in the country. The jail population was disproportionately black and young, many of the prisoners only children. The cells were filled with poor, illiterate juveniles who had been arrested for petty offenses but were facing years in prison. Their public defender lawyers were white and appeared to be going through the motions without much concern for what happened to their clients. I did what I could interpreting their legal papers, preparing them for court, and comforting them after they had pled guilty and been returned to the cell blocks with long sentences and tears running down their faces. Very few of these prisoners had the nerve and financial resources to fight their cases. They pled guilty to get out of jail, to be released to the street for "time served," or to be moved to the state prison system.

My first cellmates were a crew of two dozen Colombian sailors who said they had been arrested when their 200-foot freighter was boarded by the U.S. Navy on the high seas. They were attempting to deliver a ship full of marijuana to Europe. The captain of the "mother ship" (a large boat or ship that would off-load to smaller speed boats), a fine fellow who spoke a number of languages and who had been educated in America, told me that his vessel had been stopped and boarded illegally by the U.S. Navy in international waters. He'd been bound for Gibraltar, where he would begin his first run delivering pot outside Marseilles (France) and later the Dalmatian coast, a region of Croatia along the Adriatic Sea (what was then Yugoslavia). His intention was to open a trade route for smuggling marijuana into southern Europe and the Soviet Union. The crew, who stood at attention, wore uniforms, and saluted their officers, were brown, black, and white. They were given long federal sentences; later I would meet a few of them traveling the FBOP.

As a federal prisoner, and a Yankee, I was less than popular with the guards. They had read about my case in the newspaper, and would visit my cell to verbally threaten me, warning me not to get any ideas about escaping. It seems the last federal prisoner in this county jail had bribed the guards to open his cell and give him the keys to a squad car; he made good his escape but was recaptured in another state. That story was later confirmed when I met both the guards and the escaped prisoner in a BOP prison.

With my bail revoked, I returned to the same jail in 1984 to begin my federal sentence. This was a racially segregated facility, with different sections reserved for white and black prisoners. This time I was placed in the cells with the black prisoners, which was considered to be unusual—a form of punishment reserved for whites that were foolish enough to converse with blacks. I was more comfortable with the black prisoners anyway; they expected no favors from their keepers, as the local whites did.

The 30 boys and men in my cell block were a rowdy bunch. For fun and games they liked to save paper cups and fill them with grits and urine, which they lined up and stored on the top bunks. When they had collected enough ammunition, they would summon the guard they hated the most, and then pummel him with this disgusting brew. The "screw" would blow his whistle, and the rest of the "good old boys" would "come a running" armed with clubs. The prisoners, who had tied the cell block door with wet towels, would continue to barrage the officers, who were desperately attempting to open the door so they could subdue the rebellion. When the door opened, it was "off to the rodeo," with the prisoners, led by the youngest, surging forward to battle the guards with fists and food trays. When it was over, the guards would handcuff the worst offenders and tie them to the bars to be beaten some more with truncheons.

A month later I was transferred to another county jail in Columbia, South Carolina. This jail had better food and more modern architecture, but was just as loud and dirty as Charleston. The first two days there I spent in a holding cell with 50 men. At night we would sleep on the floor, using each other's hips as a pillow, to keep our heads off the soiled concrete. In the next cell, somewhere down the hall, a black man with a beautiful voice sang us to sleep with a nightly lullaby of sweet and soulful blues.

A few months later, I was picked up by federal marshals for transport by car to USP Atlanta. I was glad to get out of South Carolina and those wretched county jails. In full restraints (handcuffs, belly chain, and leg irons), I was loaded into the back seat of a Ford sedan with two other federal prisoners. The marshals appeared to be decent fellows. They said they knew how bad the food was in most jails, and it might be a long time before we were fed at Atlanta. The marshals stopped at a fast-food drive-through to feed us before we arrived at the federal penitentiary.

When I arrived at USP Atlanta there was a riot going on, the first Cuban rebellion; the prison was on fire and smoke was pouring out of the main building (Hamm, 1991). Although I was "designated" to Atlanta, I never entered general population and was again transported, this time to FCI Talladega, Alabama.

TRANSPORT TO AND WITHIN
THE FEDERAL GULAG

Most federal prisoners are transported from county jails, or state or military prisons into the federal gulag by U.S. marshals in cars, buses, or planes (Richards, 1990: 23; Murphy, this volume). A few are allowed to "self-surrender" at camps. Prisoners refer to prison transports as "con-air," "dog buses," "diesel therapy" (Richards, 1998: 123), or "bus therapy" (Levinson, 1994: 104). Prisoners are subject to numerous transports, most of them unwelcome, as they are transferred from one institution to another across the breadth of the country. The BOP transports 40 prisoners on Greyhound-type buses that have blacked-out windows secured with iron bars. These vehicles cruise the nation's interstate highway system, stopping along their routes at lockups to pick up or drop off prisoners. They only travel during the day and may be escorted by security or chase cars (Earley, 1993: 64). On board, the prisoners wear khaki uniforms, paper slippers instead of shoes, leg irons, and handcuffs attached to belly chains. High-security prisoners wear double handcuffs and "black boxes," a device worn over the handcuffs to prevent the picking of the locks.

Prison transports are always tense. These BOP buses are staffed with three guards, a driver, and two more officers that occupy gun cages at the front and back of the vehicle. The officers are usually armed with pistol grip, short-barrel pump shotguns. They are responsible for the loading, transport, and delivery of prisoners. They do not tolerate interference with their duties during the long trips. There are no stops for food or restrooms. Prisoners are expected to use the bus toilet while still in restraints. It is not unusual to see men wet their pants. The bus trips are especially dangerous for elderly or medically frail prisoners. Not surprisingly, the BOP does not publish the number of men and women who have died on these transports.

In addition to buses, the BOP has its own fleet of airliners, reported to be planes confiscated from commercial airlines for smuggling drugs. These large jets have been converted, much as the buses, to the requirements of prisoner transport. The BOP operates its own mini-airports all over the country where prisoners are transferred from buses to be airlifted to the next destination. These planes are used to transport as many as 90 prisoners at a time from one side of the country to another. Generally, prisoners prefer airlift to buses because the trip is shorter. Finally, the BOP has invented a new prison type called federal transfer centers. For example, FTC Oklahoma City is a medium-security prison where BOP planes land and taxi through the razor-wire fence to unload their prisoners inside a giant hangar that is part of the prison.

According to the BOP, prisoners may request transfers to be "closer to home," to receive medical attention at a federal medical center (e.g., MCFP Springfield, FMC Rochester, FMC Fort Worth, FMC Lexington), or for participation in institutional programs (e.g., education, UNICOR). The BOP also uses frequent transfers to discipline (Hamm et al., 1994) prisoners, redistribute population to new or less crowded facilities, racially balance institutions, and protect snitches. Another common reason is to disable or obstruct convict legal talent. Prisoners who file "administrative remedy" (Fleisher, 1989: 88–90) paperwork (called BPs) as a means to address their complaints or concerns or as a prerequisite for filing lawsuits or motions to court are routinely treated to a trip on the "writ bus."

As a federal prisoner, and a jailhouse lawyer, I was transferred many times. In fact, prisoners who filed legal briefs knew that they should always be prepared for a midnight transfer. We knew that once our motion or appeal, which may have been filed for another prisoner or group of prisoners, was received at court, especially if it had legal merit, we would be transferred to another prison. The prison administrators would move the writ-writing prisoner out of the federal or appellate district as a means to suppress his or her legal motion. When the prisoner arrived back in general population at another federal institution he or she would then have to resubmit the motion to a new court. If the convict litigant was particularly dangerous—that is, if he or she was trained in the law, had a record of success with legal procedures, or a specific issue that might overturn existing federal code—the BOP could dump him off at a particularly bad jail or keep him perpetually riding the buses, in some cases for years at a time (Richards, 1990: 22).

The BOP transports thousands of prisoners every week. Every night these men and women are housed in different prisons that are officially called "holdover" prisons. Various federal prisons provide different accommodations for these "guests." In the penitentiaries and correctional institutions they are usually confined in "holdover units," "bus stops" (dormitories for new prisoners), R&D (receiving and departure) holding cells, or administrative detention (the hole), if there is room available (the hole is usually filled with prisoners). In camps, the visiting prisoners may sleep in crowded dorms, hallways, or recreational areas (Richards, 1990: 23).

Generally, federal prisoners are allowed fewer material possessions than state convicts. Individuals serving time in state prisons may have their own televisions, collections of books, music, clothes, and posters or pictures hung on their cell walls. Federal prison cells are more austere. The prisoners are restricted to only basic items, for example, five books, toiletries, a few changes of institutional clothes, and no television; all of it must fit in one small locker.

Upon being assigned to transport, federal prisoners are required to pack all of their personal property (i.e., everything in their foot locker) into a "federal box" made of cardboard. They discard or give away items to cellmates that will not fit in the box. This container, which has their name and official prison number on it, has a property list that inventories the contents; for example, two pen-cils, five stamps, and one photo of your children. Any item found in the box that is not listed, and thereby not authorized by prison authorities, is cause for disciplinary action ("shot"), and the convict gets a trip to the hole; for example, a single unauthorized penny or a dollar bill results in an automatic lockdown in solitary confinement. Included in this one box, and critically important to many prisoners, is a smaller container or file folder labeled as legal papers.

Transport and holdover prisoners travel with the clothes they wear and their one "federal box," which is loaded in the cargo bay of the bus or plane. While in transit, which may last for weeks or months, prisoners do not normally re-ceive mail, have access to phones, or have opportunities for outside visits. They do not work, participate in prison programs, receive institutional pay, or have commissary privileges. The prisoners are denied regular communication with the outside world (family, friends, press, and legal representatives). They are re-duced to depending on the generosity of general population prisoners for nec-essary items.

It is a tradition among federal prisoners to share personal property with holdover prisoners. Many times, I have seen, in violation of institutional rules, cell blocks and dormitories full of prisoners provide entire busloads of "hold-over" prisoners with personal hygiene items, clothes, blankets, sheets, commis-sary food, stamps, and smokes. Each of these convicts risked being "written up" for a disciplinary infraction. Having spent the better part of a year in tran-sit on those damn buses, and as a holdover in six different prisons, I remember well the kind and supportive hospitality of the many men who opened their lockers to divvy up their meager possessions with those of us who needed clean clothes, a pair of shoes, soap, shampoo, writing supplies, or a can of tuna.

FEDERAL BUREAU OF PRISONS

Historically, the FBOP was created to incarcerate gangsters, racketeers, kidnap-pers, bank robbers, drug smugglers, white-collar criminals, tax protesters, and political prisoners. Congress created the first federal prisons with the Three Prisons Act in 1891, which authorized the U.S. Department of Justice to estab-lish three autonomous "big house" penitentiaries. For the next 30 years, most federal prisoners were held at Leavenworth, Kansas; Atlanta, Georgia; or Mc-Neil Island, Washington (Roberts, 1994: 7). In 1930, thanks to the Harrison Act of 1914 (narcotics), the Volstead Act of 1919 (prohibition), the Deyer Act of 1919 (interstate automobile theft), the beginning of the Great Depression, and the growth in organized crime, Congress passed legislation to create the FBOP (Hershberger, 1979: 13–23; Keve, 1991: 98; Roberts, 1994: 9; Carlson et al., 1999: 81).

Prohibition provided Congress with the primary rationale for the first ex-pansion of the federal prison system. The Bureau moved quickly by building another penitentiary at Lewisburg, Pennsylvania; hospital prisons at Springfield in Missouri, Lexington, Kentucky, and Ft. Worth, Texas; a youth reformatory at Chillicothe, Ohio; and a number of minimum-security camps for all those thirsty consumers and purveyors of illegal distilled spirits.

When I entered the BOP in 1984, at the beginning of the drug war, the entire system had only 32,000 prisoners. Today, the BOP operates 96 prisons, with a total population exceeding 143,000. Approximately 20,000 of these men and women are "on the bus," in local jails, or confined in privately operated facilities. The BOP (BOP Home Page, www. bop.gov/: July 2000) reports the following:

> The 1980s brought a significant increase in the number of Federal in-
> mates—the result of more Federal investigations, prosecutions, judicial
> activity, and new legislation that dramatically altered sentencing in the
> Federal criminal justice system. Most of the Bureau's growth since the
> mid-1980s has been the result of the Sentencing Reform Act of 1984
> (which established determinate sentencing, abolished parole, and reduced
> good time) and mandatory minimum sentences enacted in 1986, 1988,
> and 1990. From 1980 to 1989, the inmate population more than doubled,
> from over 24,000 to almost 58,000. During the 1990s, the population
> more than doubled again, reaching 140,000.

The BOP prisoner count is scheduled to grow to 200,000 over the next few years (BOP Home Page, www. bop.gov/: July 2000).

BRIEF DESCRIPTION OF FEDERAL
PRISON INSTITUTIONS

The pride and joy of the BOP is the Federal Correctional Complex at Flor-ence, Colorado, which includes four new prisons: a minimum-level camp, a medium-security correctional institution, a maximum-security penitentiary, and an administrative maximum-security detention facility. The ADX Florence is a supermax prison (Ward, 1994: 81–93), what the prisoners call the "Hell-hole of the Rockies" (Annin, 1998: 35). This is the highest security prison in the system and a replacement for the control unit at USP Marion, which has been in lockdown since 1983 (Ward, 1994).

ADX Florence, like the USP Marion control unit and the administrative segregation units in the "mainline" penitentiaries (e.g., USP Leavenworth, USP Atlanta, USP Lewisburg), enforces a strict discipline, with few privileges, that does not allow for the normal "controlled movement" of prisoners from cells to the dining hall, work assignments, and recreation. These convicts are kept locked in their cells all day and night.

ADX Florence, which I toured in 1998, years after completing my own prison sentence and becoming a criminology professor, has 550 permanently locked down one-man cells, but only half the cells are occupied (Levasseur, 1998a: 201). The empty cells are reserved for intake prisoners that may be trans-ferred in from rebellious or rioting institutions. You enter the facility by de-scending a 50-foot staircase. Each day, the prisoners are locked in their cells for

23 hours and may be allowed one hour of exercise in a private room. They eat all their meals in their concrete "boxcar" cells. Levasseur (1998b: 206–211), a prisoner in ADX Florence, wrote about four-point spread-eagle restraints, forced feedings, cell extractions, mind control medications, and chemical weapons used to incapacitate prisoners.

This prison was built not only to eliminate escapes, but also to defend from outside attack. The "outrider" (a guard that patrols outside the fence or wall) at medium- and maximum-security facilities is a correctional officer in a pickup truck armed with a shotgun who drives around the prison perimeter. The ADX Florence outrider is a white armored personnel carrier (a tank without a cannon). Upon completing the tour of the facility, as we exited the institution, we were challenged in the parking lot by three guards carrying automatic weapons who demanded we show identification.

The old "big house" United States penitentiaries (USPs) are maximum-security prisons that hold as many as 3,000 prisoners (USP Atlanta) and that are guarded by high walls and gun towers. The newer maximum-security prisons have double or triple fences and sophisticated detection devices instead of walls (Fleisher, 1989: 33). These "mainline" penitentiaries (Fleisher, 1989: 33) are colleges of higher learning in crime (Earley, 1993: 30).

USP Leavenworth (Abbott, 1981; Richards, 1990: 18–19; Earley, 1993), the oldest and most famous USP and the "geographical center of the BOP" (Richards, 1990: 19), is known for its advanced training in criminal occupations, available from old cons: bank robbery, securities fraud, counterfeiting currency. This penitentiary can hold as many as 2,000 prisoners in four cell houses (ABCD), each of which consists of five tiers stacked to a 150-foot-high ceiling. The prison walls are 35 feet high and extend 35 feet into the ground to prevent tunneling, 12 feet wide, and protected by six gun towers. Leavenworth has no air-conditioning in the cell blocks and has been described as the "Hot House" (Earley, 1993) because of the extreme temperatures endured by prisoners during the long Kansas summer. As I remember, the cell houses were also freezing cold in winter, with ice on the floor and walls.

The night I arrived at USP Leavenworth, with 200 men on five buses, we carried three old men over the snow-covered ground and up the stairs to the entrance into the prison. The federal "pens" are reserved for older prisoners (at least 26 years old) doing long sentences. A large number of the convicts in Leavenworth are older men, many of them having spent most of their lives incarcerated. After months in holdover status traveling through Atlanta (USP), Talladega (FCI), Terre Haute (USP), and Marion (USP), I was sick with fever and my ankles were badly infected from the cuts I received wearing leg irons. My left leg was frozen, and I stumbled as we were being processed through R&D. I remember being placed in a holding cell, and an old man asked a hack if he could attend to my bleeding legs. That old convict cleaned and dressed my wounds with soap and a T-shirt and demanded I get medical attention.

Federal correctional institutions (FCIs) are called "gladiator schools" (Abbott, 1981: 74; Earley, 1993: 30) because they are populated by younger adult prisoners. These medium-security prisons have no walls and are guarded by heavy razor-wire fences and gun towers. Many of the newer institutions have modern pod architecture—separate buildings holding 200 prisoners in what the Bureau refers to as "unit management" (Lansing, Bogan, Karacki, 1977: 43–49; Levinson, 1994: 101–103).

Federal prison camps (FPCs) are minimum-security facilities that are composed of dormitories, some with fences, some without, that may be satellites to a neighboring FCI or USP or may stand alone. These camps, with populations ranging from a few hundred to several thousand, are the cheapest to build and operate and least secure institutions. Many of these men or women are serving their first prison sentence (Jones and Schmid, 1993, 2000) and could easily be moved to probation or community facilities without any danger to the public.

Federal medical centers (FMCs) (Fleisher and Rison, 1997; Murphy, this volume) are camps (FMC Rochester), correctional institutions (FMC Lexington), or penitentiaries (MCFP Springfield) that are classified as administrative facilities and staffed by U.S. public health medical staff. These facilities are used for elderly, ill, and dying prisoners. Each of these medical prisons houses hundreds of men in wheelchairs, dying from cancer, AIDS (Blumberg, 1991; Welch, 1999: 217–251), or other serious illnesses. There are cell blocks and housing units filled with elderly (Kratcoski and Pownall, 1989; Flynn, 1992; Flanagan, 1995; Vaughn and Smith, 1999) and mentally ill (Toch, 1982; Arrigo, this volume) persons. When prisoners die from old age or medical neglect, they are quickly transported to a nearby private hospital, where they are declared dead on arrival. This administrative trick allows the FBOP to seriously underreport the number of prisoners that "expire" in their custody.

Metropolitan correctional centers (MCCs) are high-rise prisons that resemble corporate office buildings, many of which are located in large cities (e.g., MCC New York, MCC Chicago). The roofs are used for helicopter pads and exercise areas for prisoners. These facilities serve as both prison and courthouse. Many federal prisoners are housed at MCCs during trials, either when they are to serve as witnesses or when they are being charged with new indictments.

In addition, the Bureau also operates federal detention centers (FDCs) and metropolitan detention centers (MDCs), which are prisons for foreign citizens who have completed their BOP sentences and are being deported to their home countries. In 1986, FDC Oakdale, Lousiana, just months after it was opened, was burned to the ground by Cuban prisoners (Hamm, 1991, 1995).

Probably the most unusual prison in the FBOP is the federal transport center (FTC) at Oklahoma City. This facility processes thousands of prisoners each year that arrive and depart on federal marshal prison planes and buses.

PRISONER CLASSIFICATION
AND DEMOGRAPHICS

The BOP uses an "inmate classification system" (Levinson and Williams, 1979: 37–43; Janus et al., 1986: 35–41; Fleisher, 1989: 32–33; Levinson, 1994: 95–109) as a means to segregate, punish, and reward prisoners. This is a "classification ladder" with maximum security at the top and minimum security at the bottom. Ideally, if the FBOP operated to facilitate rehabilitation, prisoners would work their way down the ladder with good conduct and program participation. As they completed their sentences and got "short" (which means a year to release), they would be moved to minimum-security camps or community custody. Unfortunately, most men and women move up the ladder from minimum to medium, or medium to maximum, rather than down. Few medium- and maximum-security prisoners ever make it to the camps.

The classification designations have changed over the years to accommodate the growth in BOP prisons and population. The old system had six security levels, with 6–5 being maximum, 4–2 being medium, and 1 being minimum. USP Marion (the first supermax penitentiary) was the only level 6 institution. United States penitentiaries were level 5 (e.g., USP Atlanta, USP Leavenworth, USP Lewisburg, USP Lom Poc); the federal correctional institutions ranged from 4 to 2 (e.g., FCI Talladega, FCI Sandstone, FCI Oxford, etc.), and the federal prison camps were 1. Security levels 6–2 are "in" custody, which means inside the fence or wall. Level 1 is "out" custody, which means federal camps that do not have fences. Level 1 community custody refers to prisoners in camps who were eligible for community programs—work assignments or furloughs.

In the 1990s, the BOP collapsed these six security designations into five: high, medium high, medium low, minimum, and administrative. The BOP prisoner population is approximately 10 percent high (USP), 25 percent high medium (FCI), 35 percent low medium (FCI), and 25 percent minimum (FPC), with the rest not assigned a security level; many of these men and women are in administrative facilities (medical or detention), transit, or held in local jails or private prisons. "Administrative" refers to Administrative Detention Max (ADX) Florence in Colorado (the highest security prison in the country), FTC Oklahoma City (a medium-security transport prison), and the federal medical centers (which may be maximum, medium, or minimum security).

The federal prisoner population can further be described as 92 percent male and 50 percent white, the rest being black, Hispanic, Asian, Native American, or "other." The BOP reports that 70 percent of prisoners are American citizens, with 20 percent being Mexican, Colombian, or Cuban, and 10 percent unknown or from other countries. Seventy-five percent of these men and women are serving sentences over five years, with nearly 50 percent doing 10 years or more. Fifty-eight percent are doing time for drug convictions. The average age of a federal prisoner is 37 years (BOP Home Page, www. bop.gov/: July 2000).

BOP CENTRAL INMATE
MONITORING SYSTEM

All federal prisoners have a "jacket"—their official prison file, which includes their presentence investigation (PSI report), commitment papers, and institutional records. Each prison keeps large loose-leaf notebooks containing mug shot photos of each prisoner. When the "hacks" mess up the "count" (the entire population is counted several times each day and night), they march through each "unit" (cell block or dormitory), stopping before each prisoner to compare the notebook photos with individual faces. This method is used to determine who is missing, escaped, or dead.

The Central Inmate Monitoring System (CIMS) is a computer system that tracks nine special categories of prisoners (Fleisher, 1989: 59–72):

1. "Witness Security" prisoners are government informers that have testified, are testifying, or will testify in court cases.

2. "Special Security" prisoners are prison snitches cooperating in internal investigations.

3. "Sophisticated Criminal Activity" prisoners are those inmates identified as being involved in large-scale criminal conspiracies, for example, organized crime, drugs, or white collar. They may be men or women who were targets of the federal Racketeer Influence and Corrupt Organization (RICO) or Continuing Criminal Enterprise (CCE) prosecution, which carry life sentences (Richards, 1998: 133). Many of these convicts are suspected of being connected to major drug-smuggling organizations, or they may have refused to plead guilty, cooperate, and inform on other persons. (My jacket said "Sophisticated Criminal Activity.")

4. "Threats to Government Officials" prisoners have been convicted of writing letters, making phone calls, or issuing verbal remarks that convey the intent to do bodily harm to public officials.

5. "Broad Publicity" prisoners are those inmates involved in high-profile cases. For example, I remember a former U.S. attorney convicted of selling heroin, and the attorney general of a Midwestern state serving time for bribery.

6. "State Prisoners" are inmates serving state sentences who were transferred into the fed system because they were "difficult." At FCI Talladega, I met juvenile prisoners from state prisons, covered in tattoos, who because of their institutional history of violence had been reassigned to the FBOP.

7. "Separation" prisoners are those who have been moved to another institution because they are government witnesses, institutional snitches, gang leaders, or persons in danger of being killed or killing someone else.

8. "Special Supervision" prisoners[3] are cops, judges, and politicians who are provided protective privilege (Barak, 1991: 3–16; Kappeler et al., 1994; J. Ross, 1995/2000, 1998, 2000b; Richards and Avey, 2000). These men and women are usually designated to camps (they would not survive long in a penitentiary).

9. "Disruptive Groups" prisoners may include members of organizations, such as street or prison gangs and political groups (e.g., Black Panthers, Communists).

FEDERAL PRISONER TYPOLOGY

The official BOP classification of prisoners is designed to separate prisoners into security levels. I suggest that a more useful means of thinking about different groups of prisoners might be the following typology: amateur, professional, reservation, and political.

"Amateurs" are persons with only a part-time or occasional involvement with criminal activities. These are men and women, many of them married with families, who held legitimate employment and lived conventional lives before imprisonment. Most federal prisoners convicted of petty property crimes or minor drug offenses are amateurs. Some of them are serving short sentences for minor offenses, such as failure to pay student loans or income tax, Social Security fraud, or violation of immigration laws. This is the largest group of prisoners. The longer they stay in prison, the more likely they are to learn and assume the ways and means of professional crime.

"Professionals" are prisoners who when they lived in the "free world" had occupational positions that required special training and experience, be it legal or illegal. For example, doctors, lawyers, politicians, corporate personnel, as well as successful drug smugglers, bank robbers, members of organized crime, and counterfeiters are professionals (see, e.g., Sutherland, 1937; H. King and Chambliss, 1984; Friedrichs, 1996).

When I was a prisoner at FPC Oxford, the convict population included a number of judges and dozens of attorneys, as well as ministers, priests, medical doctors, dentists, bankers, stockbrokers, elected officials, even three university professors. One measure of professionalism, be it legal or illegal, is the income or fortune derived from employment. BOP prisons contain numerous individuals that were considered "pros" because of the resources and assets they retained from either legal or illegal enterprises.

"Reservation" refers to land reserved for federal uses. Native American, military, and District of Columbia prisoners convicted of crimes on federal property are considered reservation inmates. All crimes committed on Indian reservations or military property or within the District of Columbia come under federal jurisdiction. Therefore, the FBOP is home to many Native Americans, military personnel, and D.C. residents who found themselves incarcerated in distant federal prisons for relatively minor offenses, such as misdemeanors. The growing number of reservation inmates, because of their relatively short sentences, compared to the typical federal convict, tends to artificially lower the officially reported average sentence of BOP prisoners.

I remember federal prisoners who were Native Americans sentenced for drunk driving or petty theft. They usually spent less than a year and were released back to the reservation. The BOP is also receiving an increasing number of military prisoners, many of them transferred in from the Leavenworth detention barracks, army stockades, or navy brigs. These prisoners complained that BOP law libraries did not have the military case law references needed for them to fight their criminal cases or pursue appellate remedies.

The D.C. prisoners are an ongoing headache for the BOP. These prisoners are shipped in from the District of Columbia, Maryland, and Virginia jails and prisons. They are held under unique legal provisions that provide for parole, assuming they do not catch additional time or lose "good time" while imprisoned in the FBOP. Many of these "DCers" collect disciplinary infractions and are transferred into higher security institutions.

"Political" prisoners include persons from Native American, antinuclear, left- and right-wing political, labor, and environmental groups that are considered dangerous by the BOP because they write press releases, have free-world constituencies, and public credibility. In my travels through BOP prisons, I met numerous clergy, some sentenced to life sentences, for peaceful protests against government military policies.

Historically, the BOP has incarcerated many famous political figures, including Eugene Debs (labor leader and presidential candidate), Wilhelm Reich (author and Sigmund Freud's clinical colleague), Alexander Berkman and Emma Goldman (prominent anarchist authors and speakers), Leonard Peltier (American Indian Movement leader), and thousands of "Wobblies" (Industrial Workers of the World), war protesters, draft resisters, and labor leaders (Richards, 1990: 21–23; Keve, 1991: 133–154).

In my opinion, all convicts serving time for drug offenses, as the result of the failure of the federal drug war policy, are political prisoners. Many of these persons, with the exception of their use, abuse, or trafficking in illegal substances, were, before being imprisoned, law-abiding citizens with no previous criminal record.

HEROES OR CRIMINALS?

Prison is a fascinating place to study "deviant worlds" that overlap with, but may remain hidden, from conventional society. Chambliss (H. King and Chambliss, 1984: 142–143) discussed how "every society has many living worlds that exist side by side in silence." The visible world is that of "normal" people who assume that everybody else, more or less, lives like them, sharing their same norms and values. The invisible world is less accessible than the visible, as it is populated by fewer persons and is located in the silent semi-darkness on the edge of society. Serving time in federal prison, I met interesting desperados who represented the deviant worlds of the international drug smuggler, Mafia, Latino-drug soldier, and motorcycle gangs.

In 1984, the drug war was just getting into full swing. The Reagan-Bush administration was using the U.S. Air Force, Navy, and Coast Guard to interdict many ships and planes that engaged in marijuana commerce. As the jails and federal prisons in Florida filled beyond capacity, busloads of men were transported north to USP Atlanta in Georgia and FCI Talladega in Alabama.

When I arrived at FCI Talladega, a level 4 (medium high security) modern prison, many of the men I was housed with were not common criminals convicted of theft, assault, or local street crimes (these are not federal offenses).

"Generally speaking, federal statutes aim to deal with crimes that stretch beyond the borders of a single state or that involve large-scale conspiracies, which are difficult for states to investigate and bring to justice" (Roberts, 1994: viii). Instead, they were prisoners of the drug war, for example, smugglers, pilots, and boat crew members.

Some of these North American and European men were well educated, multilingual, and rich. Their lives have been popularized in Jimmy Buffett songs ("Changes in Latitude, Changes in Attitude") and movies. For example, one of my cellmates was a Royal Air Force pilot (United Kingdom) who had been caught flying a large commercial plane full of Jamaican "ganja" (pot). Another was an American military officer who had an unfortunate landing while parachuting into Florida with a backpack full of kilos of cocaine.

Yes, they were convicted of crimes, but they did not consider themselves criminals, or have criminal identities (Terry; Jones; Tromanhauser, this volume). Rather, they had the swagger of a swashbuckler pirate who sailed the "Spanish Main" (Yul Brynner in *The Buccaneers*) or the dare-devil personality of a galactic smuggler like Hans Solo (Harrison Ford in *Star Wars*), the determination of an Indiana Jones (Harrison Ford) or business savvy of a cocaine importer (Mel Gibson in *Tequila Sunrise*). They were "true-life action heroes," men who enjoyed foreign travel and adventure and who were drawn to risky ventures. Some of them were Vietnam veterans, others mercenaries or soldiers of fortune. They told great stories about crashing planes, boats that sank in hurricanes, and making and losing millions of dollars. In another time, they may have, or could have, been "real heroes," like war heroes, who kill and are awarded medals.

A second group of men, related to the first, were the Hispanic-Latino drug soldiers. The North American–European smugglers worked closely with their Caribbean, Mexican, Central American, and South American partners. My favorite were the Colombian cartel employees, many of whom were middle or upper class, educated in America or Europe, and considered themselves to be "trade representatives." The Colombians considered it their patriotic duty to market their national agricultural products and return to their country with investment capital (reminds me of Marx's "primitive accumulation of capital") so they could sponsor economic development. The Colombians tended to be more serious, successful, and business-like then their Cuban, Jamaican, and Mexican counterparts, who may have also been their colleagues or competitors in smuggling operations.

A third deviant world, which for decades has been an important element of federal prison populations, was that of members of the "outfit" or Mafia. These men, many of them handsome Italians (or at least Italian looking), were the administrators, soldiers, or "wannabes" of the American syndicate. They were the big and little gangsters that ran the rackets in urban America, specializing in a host of illegal activities. Many of them appeared to be acting out film roles, as if they had seen too many *Godfather* movies.

Last, but not least, were the bikers, representatives of the Bandidos, Hell's Angels, Mongols, Outlaws, Pagans, and other assorted motorcycle clubs. These were the "usual suspects," hard-core working-class white boys who dressed in black leather and occupied the attention of police authorities. The U.S. Department of Justice specializes in prosecuting bikers (according to the bikers), and the FBOP confines thousands of these men and women in its penal institutions. They were and continue to be the most significant gang population in many federal prisons.

Another group was the white supremacists. "The Aryan Brotherhood (AB) or Nation is viewed as the most dangerous convict organization in federal prisons" (Fleisher, 1989: 73). They are known for being tattooed[4] with swastikas, SS lightning bolts, and the numbers 666. First formed in 1968 from the ranks of Hell's Angels and "Blue Bird" gang members in San Quentin (Earley, 1993; C. Parenti, 1999: 194, 200–203), they continue to dominate maximum-security prisons. According to prison legend, there is only one way in or out of this gang: blood in, blood out. Convicts become AB members by committing murder and only leave the organization upon their own death. Today, many members of the AB are locked up in supermax federal prisons (e.g., ADX Florence or the control units in USP Marion).

Over the years, I circulated between these groups, listening to stories, getting to know people. I learned a little Spanish playing handball with the Colombians, and the Mafia soldiers taught me how to play bocci. Federal prisons are known for handball (all you need is a wall and a small rubber ball) and bocci courts (Italian-style bowling played in a sand pit with large clay balls). Occasionally, I weight-lifted with the Hell's Angels. Spending time with each group provided me with an opportunity to learn about their worlds and how their different affiliations provided a support system in prison.

DOING TIME AS A PRISONER
OF THE U.S. GOVERNMENT

The FBOP is considered by convicts to operate a better system than most states. The prisons are cleaner, with more desirable food, and the prison staff are better educated, trained, and paid (Fleisher, 1989; Keve, 1991; Roberts, 1994). It is fair to say that most prisoners would prefer to do federal time, day for day, than state time.

The big difference between state and federal prisons is that federal prisoners do more time. The federal sentencing guidelines defy all logic, punishing nonviolent offenders more than those convicted of violent offenses. Under federal law, a person may be sentenced to more prison time for growing or distributing marijuana or selling cocaine than bank robbery or murder. BOP cell blocks are filled with prisoners doing life sentences for drug convictions, with no possibility of parole. It is not uncommon to hear federal prison staff comment on the insanity of drug war sentences.

The first lesson I learned in prison is that you cannot judge a person by the uniform he or she wears. You have to get to know people one at a time. Some convicts are honorable and decent persons, while others are not. The same can be said of the "hacks." I do remember "good officers" who came to work every day and treated prisoners with courtesy and respect.

Correctional officers are known as "hacks" or "cops" by the prisoners. A "hack" is an officer who collects his or her paycheck, does as little as possible, and goes home. A "cop" is a hack that is always on patrol trying to bust prisoners for petty infractions of the rules. Most guards are hacks, some are cops, and a few brave souls actually try to relate to and help prisoners. A cop would send me to the hole and another officer, a man that deserves my thank-you and respect, would get me out. The best officers were men and women who kept their cool and behaved humanely.

A few correctional officers risk their careers and the wrath of BOP administrators to defend the best interests of prisoners. In 1985, upon arrival at USP Terre Haute, I was placed in solitary confinement. The previous six months in county jails, USP Atlanta, FCI Talladega, and repeated bus trips had taken their toll. I was still in holdover, with no assignment to general population and ineligible for regular commissary, phone, visitation, or work privileges. I was withdrawn and pissed off, sick from the poor diet and food poisoning. The door of my cell opened and in walked an officer with a file in his hands. He said, "Your name Richards?" I said, "Yeah, what's it to you?" The officer responded, "Richards, what are you doing here?" I said, "What do you mean?" He said, "You have a first offense marijuana conviction, a central file labeled 'Sophisticated Criminal Activity,' and you are designated level 5 [maximum security]. How come?" I told him that I had gone to the U.S. Supreme Court. Upon confirming what I said by checking the contents of my file, he said, "No wonder. Pack up. I'm taking you out of here [the hole]."

The officer escorted me through the front security gate of USP Terre Haute and over to FPC Terre Haute (the satellite camp). On the way I asked him why he bothered to help. He said that he checked the files of all transit prisoners arriving at the penitentiary looking for new prisoners that did not belong in maximum security. He explained that some of these men were prisoners being punished by federal judges for exercising their right to due process and refusing to cooperate with federal investigations. I spent 30 days at FPC Terre Haute, enjoying the relative freedom of the camp. Then, as things happen, I was transported back into maximum security at USP Marion.

FEDERAL CONVICT PERSPECTIVE

Ironically, some convicts have a perverse pride in being prisoners of the U.S. government. Federal prisoners are considered the elite of the prison world. These are the men and women who local authorities were unable to corner, arrest, and convict. Some of them actually "beat" state charges with expensive attorneys and were then reindicted under federal law (this is called "federal oversight"), whereas others were simply too quick and sophisticated for city, county, or state police agencies. Many of the members of organized criminal groups were insulated, or even enjoyed relative immunity, because of payoffs or political influence, for their activities in certain cities.

Federal prisoners, because of the frequent transit to different institutions all over the country, tend to share information about how the system is growing, the conditions at prisons they have been to (food, clothing, architecture, and population counts), and news about old friends. Upon arriving at a different institution, the convict establishes his reputation with the new population by relating stories about the previous facilities he has been in and the people he knows. For example, a prisoner from one of the supermax or high-security penitentiaries is given respect by other men when transferred to one of the correctional institutions or camps.

Ideally, the system is supposed to move individuals from high- to medium- to minimum-security facilities as they complete their sentences. Unfortunately, the opposite is usually the case, with men being transferred for disciplinary reasons from camps to FCI, or FCI to USP. Each serious institutional violation, written up as an "incident report" by the staff and called a "shot" by the convicts, is paid for with a trip to the "hole" or reassignment to a higher security prison.

I have seen many men in medium-security joints, with relatively short sentences (10 years or less), defend themselves in a fight, with another con or a hack, and find themselves with more time to serve as the result of new charges, and a midnight transport to Leavenworth or Marion. Many of the men serving life sentences in ADX Florence or USP Marion are there because of the pressure prison conditions created to settle scores or defend themselves. There is a saying in the BOP, "The only man who wins a fight is the one who walks away." The BOP does not recognize self-defense. No matter who starts the brawl, all participants are severely punished.

The BOP prides itself on operating orderly institutions. Unfortunately, the Bureau propaganda does not match the reality. In my experience, many of the older federal prisons were plagued by rampant staff corruption and theft. In one penitentiary, I saw hacks steal food, building supplies, and tools. The prison was dominated by cliques of guards, many of them blood relatives or related by marriage. Despite the best efforts of internal affairs officers, hacks continued their illegal activities. It was not unusual to see the dinner menu change, or the mess hall run out of food, because of the theft.

Moreover, the BOP cannot even win the drug war in its own institutions. Every joint I was in was flooded with drugs and alcohol. It was common to see convicts smoking pot, snorting cocaine, shooting heroin, or drinking either homemade or commercial liquor. The introduction of illegal drugs or alcohol into prisons is usually attributed to visitors or staff.

Unfortunately, convicts, who can be quite innovative, have developed additional schemes to defeat the most sophisticated security. At FCI Talladega low-flying planes did airdrops at night. Every morning prisoners would check the "yard" looking for rubber balls or waterproof packages filled with dope. A less high tech approach, used at many prisons, was to simply throw or use slingshots to deliver tennis balls with drugs inside over the wall or fence. Another problem endemic to BOP facilities was the common practice of gambling, espe-

cially sports betting, which was probably responsible for more institutional violence than drugs or gang affiliation.

The most common complaint voiced by federal convicts is that their sentences are too long (Richards and Jones, 1997). Determinate sentencing, with
no parole, has resulted in tens of thousands of men and women, convicted of
nonviolent offenses, being forced to serve decades in federal penitentiaries and
correctional institutions. These men and women are growing impatient and
the tension is building inside the fence and behind the wall.

A FEW STORIES
OF PRISONER RESISTANCE

The long federal prison sentences, with no parole and little opportunity for
earning "good time" (reduction in sentence), breed revolt. Somewhere, at this
very moment, a "disturbance" is going on in a federal correctional facility.
Needless to say, the BOP enforces a "black out" of news coverage because they
fear bad publicity will create contagion, the spreading of rebellion to additional
institutions. The only time the media reports on a prison riot is when prisoners
take hostages or set an institution on fire. Most "cell block uprisings" and "minor disturbances" go unnoticed by "free world" reporters.

In 1984, after the first Cuban rebellion at USP Atlanta, when I was shipped
out to FCI Talladega, I remember being placed in the hole, along with 100 or
more men. As I was standing in front of the cell door, while the correctional
officer removed my leg shackles and belly chain, another prisoner, one of the
orderlies distributing food trays to the cells, came up behind me and stuck a
pack of Camels under my arm and a copy of *One Hundred Years of Solitude* (Marquez, 1970) inside the waistband of the back of my pants. Upon entering the
cell, I turned back to face the door and stuck my arms through the "wicket"
(small slot in the cell door) so the hack could remove my handcuffs. My new
friend returned to tell me he would stop by my "house" once a day with more
books and smokes.

After 30 days in solitary, we were released and lined up to move to the chow
hall in another building. Having been in the hole, with limited rations and no
commissary, we were hungry and in a foul mood. As holdover prisoners, still
wearing the "carrot suits" (orange-colored jumpsuits reserved for disciplinary
segregation prisoners), we marched with our fists clenched and arms in the air,
swearing at the guards. The hacks were leery. They stood 50 feet off our line
and motioned us forward. Arriving at the mess hall, we were met with grins
from the prisoners serving dinner. As we went through the serving line, the
kitchen staff, with guards attempting to stop them by holding back their arms,
gave us double portions of food. Sitting down at the tables, we pulled back the
chairs and found cartons of gift cigarettes on every seat. The Talladega prisoners were rewarding us for the burning of Atlanta.

The dramatic growth in the number of BOP institutions has only complicated the problem. In October 1995, during one week, WBET radio in Wash-

ington, D.C., reported that 38 federal prisons had "disturbances." The Prison Activist Center in Berkeley, California, listed at least 15 rioting federal prisons.[5] The national media covered the story of the FBOP riots for one day, and then the feds issued their media prohibition. Shortly after the rebellion subsided, one BOP correctional officer told me he was reassigned to emergency duty at FCI Memphis, where the riot damage was so extensive that the government had to bulldoze the entire prison. This hack told me the prison population was being temporarily housed on school buses while they arranged for transportation to other prisons. A few months later, I interviewed a federal prisoner who said, "As fast as the BOP builds new prisons, we will burn them down."

CONCLUSION: ENEMIES OF THE STATE

I have used my own journey to give you a brief tour of the FBOP, offering a convict perspective on the war on drugs, federal prosecution, doing jail time, transport to the federal gulag, prisons, prisoners, doing federal time, and prisoner resistance.

The drug war continues to define citizens as "enemies of the state," persons to be indicted, convicted, and sentenced to spend years in government confinement. Meanwhile, the men and women doing federal time wait for the American public to demand justice, including the release of nonviolent prisoners. The only just reason for locking a human being in a cage is that that person presents a physical danger to other persons. All wars must come to an end, eventually.

NOTES

1. The phrase "criminal justice system" is an abstract concept used in the academic literature, and refers to the intended coordination of police, courts, jails, and prisons. In fact, there is no criminal justice system; no address, phone number, or central organization. Instead, there remains a hodge-podge of numerous city, county, state, and federal agencies, jurisdictions, and facilities, operating under different authority and law.

2. "Turnkey" refers to a device (which looked like a round tape measure) the jail guards wore on their belts that contained a roll of paper that was marked in time increments. Each cell block corridor had a key that hung on the wall. As the officer made his rounds, he would take each key and insert it in the device to record the time. This procedure was used to

ensure that the guards actually visited each cell block in a timely fashion, as required.

3. At FMC Oxford, where I finished my sentence in 1987, there were a half-dozen judges (Gray Lord case), numerous attorneys, congressmen, cops, and DEA (Drug Enforcement Agency) agents.

4. Motorcycle gangs, for example, Bandidos (Texas), Hell's Angels (West Coast), Mongols (California), Outlaws (Midwest), Pagans (East Coast), are all characterized by club tattoos. These specific tattoos are openly displayed on forearms as signs of membership. They may include initial enrollment dates or remembrances of deceased members.

   Motorcycle club tattoos are common on prison inmates. I recall one graphic example of an inmate at Leavenworth Federal Penitentiary (Richards, 1985), a member of the Hell's Angels, who wore a large tattoo on his right bicep. The tattoo was of a police officer down on all fours, doggie style, in blue uniform. Standing upright behind the cop was a "biker" with long hair, dressed in black leather. When the Hell's Angel clenched his fist and pumped his bicep, the tattoo would move like a cartoon. Below the tattoo was the inscription "Fuck Pigs." The prisoner would stand in the dinner line at Leavenworth, hold his arm high in the air, and work the cartoon tattoo for the pleasure of the other convicts and the considerable displeasure of the prison guards. The

"biker" cartoon figure was tattooed like his human host, with the Hell's Angels insignia (Richards, 1995b: 19).

5. Including FCI Talladega (Alabama), FCI Terminal Island (California), FCI McKean (Pennsylvania), USP Lewisburg (Pennsylvania), FCI Allenwood (Pennsylvania), FCI Memphis (Tennessee), FCI El Reno (Oklahoma), FCI Greenville (Illinois), MCFP Springfield (Missouri), USP Leavenworth (Kansas), FCI Marianna (Florida), USP Atlanta (Georgia), FCI Raybrook (New York), FCI Fairton (New Jersey), and FCI Dublin (California) (Pens, 1998: 244–249).

7

Rehabilitating Criminals: It Ain't That Easy

GREG NEWBOLD

For more than 200 years, prison reformers have been trying to rehabilitate criminals and reduce recidivism. In 1764, Cesare Beccaria wrote *On Crimes and Punishments,* ushering in a new era in corrections. Criminal justice, Beccaria reasoned, should not just punish, it must also be committed to producing a better society. Beccaria's proposal was founded on simple notions of deterrence and social sanitation, but it became immediately famous because, for the first time, a systematic rationalist-utilitarian approach to the problem of crime control had been crafted.

After Beccaria, the idea that the judicious use of punishment could reform criminals and improve society grew rapidly. In the late eighteenth century English liberals John Howard (1777–1929) and Jeremy Bentham (1789–1961) worked vigorously for a prison system that was humane and effective. A consequence was a series of laws between 1779 and 1791 that improved prison conditions and attempted to establish reformist principles. Finally, in 1791, Bentham conceived the famous panopticon, a model prison that, in seeking to simulate the conditions of a perfect society, was designed to reform criminals by bringing out their natural "goodness."

In America, the development of corrections was affected by the same themes. In 1787, the first prison reform society was formed in the Quaker state of Pennsylvania and three years later, Philadelphia's Walnut Street Jail, Amer-

An earlier version of this paper was presented at the American Society of Criminology meeting, Toronto, Canada, November 2000.

ica's first penitentiary, was opened. Walnut Street, subscribing to the Quaker postulate that goodness lies at the heart of every person, was dedicated to rehabilitating criminals through a regime of complete solitude and Bible study. Then, in 1819, a similar but competing system was developed at Auburn prison in New York State. Here convicts, although allowed to congregate and work, were prohibited from speaking to one another. Eventually all American jurisdictions adopted the penitentiary system, generally preferring the Auburn model.

It was these American developments that the Europeans followed and finally emulated. By the mid-nineteenth century most countries in Europe had taken on the penitentiary idea. In 1842, Britain, a relatively late starter, opened its first penitentiary, Pentonville. It was followed by many others. In fact, the British were so confident in the penitentiary that in the next six years, 54 new prisons containing 11,000 separate cells were established (Du Cane, 1885: 6).

Initially, the new system received high praise from observers, but it was not long before flaws appeared. Allegations of inhumanity, overcrowding, and psychosis caused by prolonged misery and solitude threw the effectiveness of the penitentiary into doubt and spawned a search for alternatives. In the 1840s, for example, Captain Alexander Maconochie, warden of the Norfolk Island Penal Colony (just off the coast of Australia), developed a system whereby prisoners earned or lost marks in progressing toward their freedom. Welcomed by reformers, the principle was applied to prisons in the form of indeterminate sentencing, with release contingent on conduct. Later, in Ireland in the 1860s, Sir Walter Crofton conceived a four-stage liberty system, where freedom and privileges were awarded according to behavior. The final of Crofton's stages, "ticket of leave," introduced revocable parole, which today is a familiar component of correctional systems around the world.

In 1876, the first reformatory, a product of Maconochie and Crofton's insight, was established at Elmira, New York, for offenders aged 16–30. In 1905, the British created the Borstal system for juveniles in Borstal, Kent. Here, indeterminate sentences, systematic education, and trade training were intended to equip offenders to survive in the free world. Unfortunately, the ideals of both schemes became corrupted and they proved unable to overcome problems of internal violence and high recidivist rates.

Since the nineteenth century, in spite of the failure of early searches for an effective formula, the quest to find something that really does "work" has continued. In the twentieth century, there were numerous initiatives in Western industrialized countries to try to control recidivism and stem the tide of crime. Among them have been shock probation, boot camps, "three strikes," chain gangs, halfway houses, weekend detention, release-to-work, "scared straight" programs, and determinate sentencing provisions. Each of these has been designed, in one way or another, to reduce reoffending by reforming miscreants and/or by deterring them from crime. But, as Robert Martinson (1974) found, few, if any, of these ideas have proven capable of consistently achieving these goals.

"NOTHING WORKS"

Martinson was an early skeptic of rehabilitation programs, but he was not the first. Between 1937 and 1945, a group of 650 boys in Boston were divided into two matched cohorts to study the effects of treatment. For a period of two to eight years, one group was subjected to a regime of intensive counseling, while the other received no treatment at all. The results were less than encouraging: no significant difference was found in subsequent delinquency between the two groups (Powers and Witmer, 1970). This research, known as the Cambridge-Somerville study, became world famous and generated cynicism about the prospects for rehabilitating criminals.

By the early 1960s, some British sociologists were talking regularly about the "interchangeability" of penal measures (N. Morris and Hawkins, 1970: 118). But the biggest bomb was Martinson's when, having participated in an assessment of 234 programs reported worldwide, he concluded, "With few and isolated exceptions, the rehabilitative efforts that have been reported so far have had no appreciable effect on recidivism" (Martinson, 1974: 25). In other words, nothing works.

Martinson's disclosure excited such spirited rebuttal that he later modified his opinion to acknowledge that some things can work, sometimes (Martinson and Wilks, 1977; Martinson, 1979). This idea that nothing, or nothing much, works is an unpalatable one. A number of criminologists (e.g., Gendreau and Ross, 1986; T. Palmer, 1986; J. Q. Wilson, 1986) have argued that some things can work, as long they are done right. But it is clear that there is no universal, generally applicable, recidivism-reducing formula.

Such strategies that have worked usually involve intensive and often expensive intervention strategies that are applied to offenders with specific, identifiable behavioral problems. For the majority of prisoners, no such remedy exists. Recidivism levels remain high. Thus in America, for example, Bureau of Justice Statistics (BJS) figures demonstrate that within six years of release, more than 70 percent of ex-inmates are rearrested and nearly half are reincarcerated (cited in Schmalleger, 1991: 426). After all, America's system is quite severe; sentences are long, and prison conditions are harsh. High recidivism might be expected. Surely a system that was more committed to prisoner reform would do better?

NEW ZEALAND:
A CASE STUDY IN LIBERALISM

An example of a nation with a tolerant tradition in the treatment of offenders is New Zealand. For years my country has taken pride in its ability to minimize what Sykes (1958) termed "the pains of imprisonment" by adopting imaginative correctional initiatives. This makes it a worthy candidate for a case study in the relationship between liberal methods and reoffending.

New Zealand's tradition of correctional humanism began in 1909. By the 1920s, although 30 percent of all convicts were held in the maximum-security prison (Census and Statistics Office, 1925: 247), 70 percent were employed in outside work schemes (Newbold, 1989: 4). The issuing of firearms to officers ceased in 1918, and by 1925 schoolteachers had been appointed, libraries had been enlarged, and hours of unlock increased. In an attempt to make the New Zealand prison system "as efficient as any existing anywhere in the world" (cited in Missen, 1971: 10), a sincere effort was made to replace the original regime of punitive confinement with one of humane custody and reformation.

The ethic of indulgence in prisons continued in the ensuing decades. In 1941, capital punishment for murder was abolished experimentally, then, in 1961, done away with for good. Educational, social, and psychological services continued to develop. And as early as 1953, maximum-security convicts were first allowed outside prison walls to participate in debating competitions. By 1969, when Paremoremo Prison, a new maximum-security facility based on the supermax United States Penitentiary at Marion, Illinois, was opened, fewer than 10 percent of the total prison population was held in maximum security. Within a few years, Paremoremo Prison had become a showpiece of humanitarianism and progressiveness in the treatment of prisoners.

DOING TIME AT PAREMOREMO

As it happens, in the late 1970s, I served time at Paremoremo Prison during its period of greatest liberalism. As such, I was in a unique position to experience the operation of a maximum-security prison at its best, and also to observe some of its effects on fellow convicts. My story starts in the winter of 1975, when I was a 23-year-old drug dealer in Auckland, New Zealand's biggest city. One sunny afternoon the tranquility of the day was shattered when the doors and windows of the house I was at exploded inward, and the place filled up with cops and dogs. Arrested for offering to sell an ounce-and-a-half of almost pure heroin, I was taken into custody, denied bail, and tried five months later. In November 1975, I was sentenced to seven-and-a-half years' imprisonment. This was considered a long sentence at the time. The following day I was unlocked from my cell at Mount Eden Prison and put on the escort to Paremoremo.

In 1975, Paremoremo prison had an awesome reputation. It held the hardest and most violent criminals in the country, and for its first few years it had been wracked by continuous strikes, fires, riots, and hostage taking. A lot of blood was spilt and thousands of dollars worth of damage done. However, by the time I arrived a new superintendent, Jack Hobson, had been in place for three years and the troubles of the early years had largely been resolved. An experienced and competent manager, Hobson had a reputation for a firm-but-fair approach to prison government. He listened to convicts as well as staff, was decisive, bold, and consistent, and within weeks of his arrival the seething atmosphere of the prison had begun to settle. As this occurred, Hobson eased his grip and extended inmate privileges.

By the end of 1975, conditions were as relaxed as they ever have been. Physical security was tight and prisoners were never permitted outside without a special escort, but within the institution levels of freedom were relatively high. Prisoners, contained in five blocks of 48 cells each, all had their own cells and the majority, comprising the general population, were unlocked between the hours of 7:00 A.M. and 8:30 P.M. Men were employed in the well-equipped workshops, prison laundry, kitchen, or bakehouse. Those who showed a serious interest in education could get relief from work duties and be assigned to full-time studies. Meals were of a high standard and prisoners had access to the exercise yards and a good gymnasium at least once a day and all day on weekends. The library was available each night of the week. Prisoners could write and receive as much mail as they wanted, and contact visits, normally lasting two hours, were permitted once a week. In the evening and on weekends, convicts had hobby rooms where the principal activities included woodcarving, basket weaving, and oil painting.

The prison was well patronized by outside groups. During most weeks there would be visits from basketball or badminton teams, a Maori (native) culture group would attend, and competition debates with teams from the Auckland region were held regularly. A number of years the prison won the city's A-Grade and/or the B-Grade debating trophy. In addition, there was a weekly inmate-organized football (i.e., soccer) contest held between the cell blocks in the gymnasium. The football contests and the debates were particular highlights of inmate life.

During this time, relations between staff and prisoners were relatively open. Although conflicts occurred from time to time, for the most part, prisoners and staff were on a first-name basis and lived in harmony. Inmate-inmate relations, too, were easygoing. The small size of the cell block communities meant that everybody knew each other. Prisoners became intimately acquainted and friends assisted one another through hard times. An ethic of egalitarianism pervaded the prison and there was no active convict or gang hierarchy.

The men had a high level of commitment to a code of social behavior similar to that described by Sykes and Messinger (1960), and in confrontations with the authorities, group solidarity was strong. Importantly, and in apparent contrast with reports from American prisons (e.g., Wooden and Parker, 1983; Hassine, 1996), predation upon weaker prisoners by the physically powerful was infrequent and was actively discouraged by other prisoners (see Newbold, 1982/1985). Homosexuality was rare and homosexual rape was almost unheard of. Sometimes men fought and many had knives, but actual use of weapons was infrequent. In fact, there have been only two homicides (in 1979 and 1993) in the maximum-security prison's 30-year history. Both deaths were caused by stabbings.

When I arrived in the prison, as a relative novice, I was already known because of the high profile of my trial. The case had involved heroin from a major ring known as the "Mr. Asia Gang," and I was one of the few who had refused to talk and testify against codefendants. This got me the heaviest sentence, but it also made me immediately acceptable to the inmate community.

As soon as I entered the cell block, I was taken under the wing of a robber-cum-drug-dealer named Pete, a career criminal who is still one of my closest friends. He introduced me to others in the block, explained the rules and routine, and generally assisted me through the difficult period of adjustment to prison life. When I started studying a few months later, the guys turned their radios down and brought me cups of tea at "smoke" time. Within a year I was fully integrated within the cell block, and had become an active member of the debating and football teams. By the time I was transferred to lower security in 1978, I was captain of the debating club, had led the A team to victory in the Auckland debating competition, was organizer of the Christmas sports activities, had participated in a couple of strikes, and had acted as block spokesman. I had a B.A. degree when I entered prison; by the time I left, I had completed an M.A. degree in anthropology. The day I left was a sad one; prisoners visited me in my "slot" (cell or room) with going-away gifts, including tokens of friendship, a Maori (native) neck pendant, a piece of carved greenstone, a favorite cassette tape, and a couple of joints (marijuana cigarettes). I treasure these things to this day, except the joints, of course, which I smoked with my mates in the back of the escort van, on the way home to Auckland.

THE MODERN CORRECTIONAL SYSTEM

Partially for political reasons, things have now changed at Paremoremo, and the prison today is run much more tightly than it was when I was there. But, until very recent times, Paremoremo reflected the general humanity that is still the hallmark of New Zealand's correctional philosophy. Its population seldom exceeds 240 and many inhabitants, not classified as maximum but as high-medium security, are awaiting places in less secure facilities. In the last New Zealand prison census, in 1997, of 4,700 prisoners in the entire system, only 5 percent (235) resided in maximum security and only 1.2 percent (56) were so classified. Thirty-six percent had a medium-security classification and more than 60 percent were minimum (Lash, 1998: 30). In contrast, the figures for American prisons are approximately 33 percent maximum, 48 percent medium, and 19 percent minimum (H. Allen and Simonsen, 1998: 230).

In New Zealand, the bulk of prisoners live in small, 60-bed units for both minimum and medium custody. Most prisoners have their own cells, and the squalid dormitory warehousing that is so much a feature of medium and minimum institutions in the United States does not exist in New Zealand. My country does not have a penitentiary that compares with the massive high-security prisons with thousands of prisoners, known for high levels of violence and brutality, that are operated by federal and state authorities in the United States.

By and large, the social conditions I have described in Paremoremo are still replicated elsewhere in the New Zealand correctional system. The exception is the old institutions, which hold about 1,000 prisoners, many of them temporary residents awaiting trial, transfer, or release. But relatively new accommodations, built within the last 20 years, contain the majority of prisoners. These institutions have organized work and welfare programs, are run on a full-fledged unit and case management basis, and contain facilities for education, hobbies, and other activities. Most institutions have rugby football, soccer, softball, and cricket playing fields, and many have sports teams consisting of minimum-security prisoners who play in local and regional competitions. Sometimes prison staff play alongside prisoners in these teams or against them in opposing teams. As noted, many minimum-security prisoners are also permitted a 72-hour furlough with their families every two months.

COMPARING NEW ZEALAND
WITH THE UNITED STATES

Compared with the United States, sentences in New Zealand are short. A lifer doing time for murder is normally paroleable after 10 years, and the average time served is about 13 years. Since 1993, the courts have been empowered to impose non-parole minimums greater than 10 years, but the longest non-parole period ever given for murder is 17 years, awarded to two gang members in 1997 for shooting a Crown (prosecution) witness, and to another man in 1999 for murdering two teenagers. In 1997, 6.2 percent (305) of New Zealand prisoners were serving life sentences; 1.9 percent (92), nondeterminate sentences of preventive detention (10 years to life) for sex offending; and only 4.8 percent (238), finite terms of more than 10 years. About 87 percent were serving 10 years or less. Two-thirds were serving five years or less and most of these could expect to be released after serving a third to a half of their total terms (Lash, 1998: 27).

New Zealand does not have a major addictive narcotics problem (see Newbold, 2000), and unlike America, New Zealand has light sentencing for drugs (Mays and Winfree, 1998: 189–190; Schlosser, 1998). Only 7 percent of all New Zealand prisoners are serving time for drugs as their most serious offense compared with 22 percent in the United States (U.S. Bureau of Justice Statistics, 1995; Lash, 1998: 28). And, although just over half of those convicted of dealing in drugs other than cannabis (marijuana) go to prison, the average prison sentence is less than three years. The average cannabis-dealing prison sentence is about one year, but only 16 percent of those convicted go to prison (Spier, 1998: 54). Prisoners serving time for nonviolent offenses are eligible for parole after doing one-third of their sentences and they normally serve about a half.

The longest sentences in New Zealand are for serious violence. The average armed robber receives about 3.5 years, attempted murder draws an average of almost 7 years, and the average rapist receives about 7.5 years (Spier, 1998: 45). Violent offenders sentenced to finite terms of more than two years are not eligible for parole and must do two-thirds of their sentences before release on remission (good time). Fifty-six percent of prisoners are serving sentences for violence as their major offense (Lash, 1998: 28).

The prison population of New Zealand is growing quickly. Since 1989, the total prison "muster" (count), including "remands" awaiting trial, has increased by 62 percent, from 3,500 to 5,600. And, although New Zealand has one of the highest incarceration rates in the Western world (Criminal Justice Policy Group, 1998), with a total population of 3.6 million (156 per 100,000), its rate is still far below that of the United States. In comparison, America's inmate population has roughly doubled since 1989 and in 1999 stood at 1.8 million (720 per 100,000). New Zealand has an overall crime victimization rate that, apart from murder and armed robbery, is slightly higher than that of the United States. Serious assaults, for example, are reported considerably more frequently in New Zealand (Harland, 1995).

Part of the reason the New Zealand incarceration rate is comparatively low is the extensive use of intermediate sanctions, which are specifically designed to divert petty offenders from prison. The Criminal Justice Act of 1985 says that minor cannabis offenders and property offenders punishable by imprisonment of seven years or less shall not be incarcerated except in unusual circumstances. The act also provides that when any nonviolent offender commits a felony, he/she shall not be imprisoned unless a community sentence is deemed undesirable because it would endanger public safety. Prison sentences, the law says, shall be as short as is consistent with the interests of public safety. The result is that a large number of men and women in New Zealand, convicted of imprisonable offenses, are doing periodic detention or other intermediate sanctions such as community service and residential community programs. For every person sent to prison in New Zealand, six get sentenced to one of these alternatives (*Appendices to the Journals of the House of Representatives* E.61 FR 1998: 19).

THE EFFECTIVENESS OF NEW ZEALAND'S CORRECTIONAL MEASURES

The objective of this brief summary of New Zealand's correctional program, which is described in more detail in Newbold and Eskridge (1996), has been to establish that for the greater part of its history, my country has recognized the need to avoid incarceration wherever possible and to emphasize rehabilitation. Imprisonment is used sparingly, sentences are brief, and conditions are good. With such a focus on the welfare and training of criminal offenders, one might think, recidivist rates would be low. However, this is not the case.

Until recently, no comprehensive survey of recidivism in New Zealand had been completed, but today there are enough data to give a reasonable picture of reoffending and the circumstances surrounding it. Currently, the New Zealand Ministry of Justice is collecting information about recidivism. Unpublished figures released to me show that 82 percent of all offenders sentenced to prison in 1991 were reconvicted of an offense within two years of release. These include serious traffic offenses, such as dangerous or drunken driving, which by law require a court hearing rather than an instant fine. Interestingly, "boot camps," to which young offenders are sent for two to three months, have a recidivist rate of 95 percent.

But the most comprehensive information on New Zealand comes from Bakker and Riley (1999), who considered recidivism in two large groups: 31,985 individuals convicted of an imprisonable criminal offense in 1990, and 4,785 offenders released from prison in 1990. These groups were followed until May 1996, and all who had recorded a criminal reconviction before May 1996 were designated as recidivists. In this survey, traffic and minor offenses were excluded. Bakker and Riley found a 72 percent recidivist rate among those convicted in 1990 and an 84 percent rate for the prisoners discharged in that year. Fifty-three percent of those released from custody in 1990 had returned to prison by May 1996.

Offense and sentence type were relatively poor predictors of reoffending. Even noncustodial and therapeutic-type sentences, which are generally given to less serious offenders, had recidivist rates ranging between 64 and 84 percent. Apart from sex offenders, whose crimes tend to be specific and whose reoffending rates averaged between 35 and 50 percent, other types of offenders tended to be generalists and recidivated more than 70 percent of the time.

The most accurate predictor of reoffending was age, with young offenders being far more likely to reoffend than older ones. In this study, 95 percent of those released from prison under 20 years old recidivated, compared with just 53 percent of those aged 40 or over. Another important correlate of reoffending was previous convictions. Only 20 percent of first offenders sentenced in 1990 recidivated. Likelihood of reoffending increased sharply with each subsequent conviction, but began to flatten out after five previous convictions and leveled at about 70 percent.

An even stronger relationship was found with previous incarcerations. Those with more than two previous incarcerations had high probabilities of reconviction. Another predictor of reoffending was ethnicity, with Maori convicted in 1990 reoffending 80 percent of the time, Pakeha (Caucasian) 70 percent, Pacific Island people 64 percent, and other groups (principally Asian) 30 percent. Less important was gender, with men only slightly more likely to reoffend than women.

Interestingly, in this study, the length of incarceration had little effect on chances of reconviction. Prisoners who spent just a few months in prison were less likely to reoffend than those who served longer. However, once an individual had spent more than a few months in prison, the likelihood of reconviction flattened out. Past this point, persons behaved similarly, irrespective of whether they served one year or five years. Presumably, however, those who served more than 10 years would be less likely to reoffend, because they would be significantly older when released.

Different studies of course produce different results, so making sense of comparative material can be difficult. Nevertheless, the New Zealand data all have one thing in common: recidivist rates are high, irrespective of the correctional method used. Earlier I cited BJS figures indicating that over 70 percent of American prisoners are rearrested within six years of release and nearly half are reincarcerated. These figures are almost identical to New Zealand's, and suggest that the quite different approaches to corrections in the two countries have little apparent effect on recidivism. It seems, therefore, that a person's chances of reoffending have small or no relation to the correctional treatment that he or she received. Of greater significance are factors like age, offending history, ethnicity, and to a lesser extent, gender.

WHY DO CORRECTIONS FAIL?

The reasons that correctional attempts often fail are manifold. A major part of the explanation is simply procedural: if prisoners are released on restrictive parole provisions and authorities are quick to revoke even for minor violations, then recidivist rates will inevitably be high. In California, for example, due largely to compulsory urine testing and rigid policing of parolee behavior, 62 percent of all offenders admitted to the state's prisons in 1992 were parole violators (H. Allen and Simonsen, 1998: 244).

Human Rationality

Still, the reason for high recidivism rates is more complex than this. Part of the explanation lies at the heart of the human condition. Eighteenth-century rationalists believed that human beings are logical and driven to seek pleasure and avoid pain. Therefore, a reasonable person should be deterred from committing crime because the pains of imprisonment would exceed any gains that might be derived from offending. In other words, a rational person will realize that "crime does not pay."

There are two major and related flaws with this assumption. First, not all offenders get caught. In many cases, in fact, the chances of being captured are slim. Illegal drug taking, for example, is seldom detected, and only a small proportion of the large number of users are ever prosecuted. Even drug dealing is a relatively low-risk occupation, though the profits can be high. Indeed, the higher a person is on the dealing scale, the greater the profits, and because the big-time dealer normally distances himself personally from the crime itself and can often pay off corrupt officials, his chances of being caught are especially low.

Other offenses are similar. Burglary has a low clearance rate. In New Zealand only about 16 percent of reported burglaries are cleared, and the better a person is at it, the more money he makes and the more likely he is to avoid arrest. Such also is the case with fraud. Sophisticated fraudsters make millions, they are difficult to catch, and they get relatively small penalties even if convicted (see Newbold and Ivory, 1993).

Indeed, if a person is unqualified and unable to get a decent job, the rewards of crime—financial, social, and psychological—might seem rather attractive. The "pains" threatened by possible imprisonment may be little worse than the loathsome drudgery of a boring, low-paying, and low-prestige job. Crime might "pay" after all, and be a truly reasonable choice.

Moreover, people are not always logical, and this is the second flaw to the rationality thesis. Social analysts like Michels (1911–1962), Pareto (1916–1935), and Hoffer (1951–1980) observed that people behave nonrationally a good deal of the time. For much of their lives, people are driven by whim or emotion. Often they make critical life decisions when they are intoxicated by drugs, alcohol, excitement, love, or lust. Rational considerations may play little or no part in these decisions.

If people were by nature rational, surely they would all believe in the same God, or none at all. They would not smoke cigarettes, which they know are expensive, addictive, and life threatening. They would not risk life and limb volunteering to fight for abstract ideals like duty, justice, or patriotism. And they would almost certainly never get married and have kids. Far from being a deterrent to behavior, high risk and the thrill associated with it are what attract many people to certain activities. If sports like boxing, mountain climbing, bungie jumping, white-water kayaking, and big-wave surfing did not have adrenaline-pumping, life-threatening risks attached to them, those sports would have little participation.

So it is with crime. As Katz (1988) so eloquently demonstrated in his book, *Seductions of Crime,* many career criminals are drawn to their offending as much by the attendant danger and the thrill of getting away with it as by the available profits. For many, crime has an emotional appeal in itself, which transcends conventional morality and logic. Like rock climbers who constantly seek steeper and tougher routes up the same face of a mountain, burglars, robbers, and thieves are often increasingly audacious in the crimes they commit. They seek bigger, riskier, more exciting jobs. They are driven by the will to dare to plan and execute high-risk offenses because they love the exhilaration of the act and the escape, and they enjoy the kudos they get from the criminal community. Professional criminals are no more deterred by the fear of imprisonment than the boxer is by the fear of concussion and brain damage, the surfer or the kayaker by the fear of drowning, or the climber by the fear of falling, frostbite, and avalanche (see Richards, this volume).

Criminal Subculture

Social control theorists like Hirschi (1969) argue that one reason criminals offend is that they have weak social bonds, often due to undersocialization. Because of this, they are said to lack the internalized inhibitions against offending that a socially bonded person possesses. Similarly, John Braithwaite (1989) suggested that a principal explanation for predatory offending is that criminals are inadequately integrated within society, and thus do not feel "ashamed" of the crimes they commit. These theorists say the solution is to instill strong community values in criminals, whereby the sense of shame they feel upon committing an offense would be a deterrent in itself. The problem with such theories, which are similar to those of Bentham, who designed the Panopticon, is that they are inclined to be tautological: offending is taken as evidence that undersocialization has occurred.

In fact, criminals may not be undersocialized at all; rather, they may be differentially socialized. As Sutherland and Cressey (1960) observed, social values are not homogeneous. Modern society consists of numerous subcultures, and what may be morally condemned in one subculture may be approved of in another. If a person is raised in a criminal subculture, his values are likely to be different from those of the mainstream. An ability to steal cleverly, con plausibly, and fight readily may add to, rather than detract from, his social value. And in the cultural world of the prison, where criminals are sent for "correction," ideals such as these are not weakened but reinforced.

Certainly, one of the goals of prison rehabilitation programs is to change those values and teach cognitive, coping, and job skills that might assist a convict to survive crime-free after release. Prisoners might work hard in these programs, attempting to transform their lives, but achieving long-term effectiveness is difficult. Overcoming subcultural identities and affiliations, including those learned in prison, remains a major obstacle.

A number of authors have identified factors that impede postrelease chances. Clemmer (1940/1965: 300) discussed "prisonization," which depending upon length of sentence and conditions of confinement, may "make a man characteristic of the penal community and so direct his personality that a happy adjustment in any community becomes next to impossible." Richards (1998: 140) coined the term "joint mentality" to describe how a person assumes the walk and talk of a convict, living day to day in prison, unable to plan a future. Austin and Irwin (2001: 100–112), for example, described how profound alienation and bitterness result from the perception of injustice, and noted the psychological and social impairment precipitated by long-term confinement. Richards and Jones (1997) discussed the problems excons face when they are released; they have almost no money and face serious difficulties finding a job. Rideau (1994) remarked that because many prisons offer so little in the way of programs, prisoners are released unskilled and unprepared to succeed on the outside, just as when they went in. Finally, Duncan (1988) commented that life in prison offers a number of affirmative conditions, such as security, certainty, refuge, freedom from responsibility, comradeship, and social status, conditions that for many prisoners are absent on the outside. Consciously or unconsciously, therefore, some released prisoners who may struggle with the harsh anonymity of life at liberty are drawn back to the prison's protective womb.

Family Circumstances

Apart from the fact that many convicts have been raised with criminal thinking patterns from an early age, the majority also have had childhoods that were far from ideal. There is an old Jesuit adage that holds that once a child is seven years old, his or her personality, intellect, values, and temperament are firmly set. In the first years of a child's life, factors like parental contact or lack of it, peer group affiliation, mass media input, and trauma set the path of the emerging adult. Character becomes more rigid and difficult to change the older a person gets. By the time someone first goes to prison, he or she may have experienced a lifetime of unemployment and alcoholic and violent adult role models, accompanied by deviant values, parental neglect, and possibly physical abuse. If we look at the family background of those in prison, we find that a large proportion of prisoners come from these types of circumstances.

In New Zealand, the makeup of the prison population was profiled in 1986 by a census that asked questions relating to prisoners' backgrounds. All 120 females who were in prison at the time, as well as a random sample of 879 males (a third of the total sentenced male population) completed the questionnaire. The survey found that 11 percent of prisoners either did not know their parents or did not know their parents' marital status. Thirty-eight percent had parents whom they knew were married. The remainder was single-parented as a result of death, divorce, separation, or their parents never having lived together.

In over 56 percent of cases there was a record of family tension. Major problems identified were marital discord, alcohol abuse, and violence toward children. In almost a quarter of all cases, family discord had been sufficient to require intervention from state welfare agencies and/or the police. About a third of the prisoners had been placed under the guardianship of the Department of Social Welfare before they reached 15. By age 19 over 70 percent had come to the notice of police or welfare officials. Almost a quarter had been taken into pre-prison custodial care (Braybrook and O'Neill, 1988: 119–169). Although no precise comparisons with the general population are possible, these figures seem extremely high.

The family backgrounds of prisoners are reflected in their personal histories, and here some valid comparisons can be made. Eighty-eight percent of prisoners had left school without any qualifications (degrees), and only 11 percent had taken any training after leaving school. Very few, about 3 percent, had any professional or trade qualifications. In comparison, in the general population of New Zealand, only 37 percent had left school without qualifications, and 36 percent had postschool qualifications (Statistics New Zealand, 1997: 55–56). So, the inmate sample was considerably less educated than the population at large.

Approximately 44 percent of prisoners had required psychological assessment at some time in their lives, in many cases as a result of drug or alcohol abuse, and about half had experienced difficulties with personal alcohol abuse in the past. About 44 percent had had problems with drug abuse. By way of comparison, a 1998 survey of drug use among New Zealanders aged 15–45 found fewer than 10 percent used alcohol to the point where it had threatened their health. Only 15 percent were regular cannabis users, and use of other illegal drugs was relatively uncommon (Field and Casswell, 1999: 14, 21, 40). The incidence of drug and alcohol problems among prisoners was thus very high relative to that of the general population.

Sixty-five percent of convicts had been unemployed at the time they were sentenced and almost half had been unemployed for over a year (Braybrook and O'Neill, 1988: 119–169). Nationwide, the unemployment rate at the time was much lower, about 7 percent. So, the 1986 prison census gives a useful snapshot of prisoners, showing that they come largely from disadvantaged family backgrounds, and through lack of education, substance abuse, and unemployment, are unable to overcome the handicaps they face.

Not all people with bad family backgrounds become criminal and not all criminals have bad family backgrounds, but a history of parental neglect or abuse is highly predictive of maladjustment later in life (Fergusson and Horwood, 1997; Fergusson, 1998). In their late teens or early twenties, by the time they get a prison term substantial enough for "rehabilitative" efforts to be effective, the years of emotional and psychological conditioning make the chances of success remote. Some prisoners, haunted by family dysfunctions and trauma, may be unable to overcome past history without considerable professional services.

The Reality of Life Outside

An added burden to changing people inside is the harsh reality of life on the outside. It may be all very well, through the use of programs such as Narcanon, Alcoholics Anonymous, Anger Management, and so on, to get a commitment from people in prison to give up drugs, to drink sensibly, or to stem their aggression (see Terry, this volume). In the sterile and controlled atmosphere of maximum security, such resolutions may be made with absolute sincerity and commitment. But, on the outside things are different. Here the therapist or social worker is not the primary influence. There is the added problem of peer group pressure, and the temptations of alcohol, drugs, sex, and consumer advertising. And of course, food has to be bought and bills have to be paid. When a person who has "reformed" in prison is cast back into the same impoverished, gang-dominated world where drugs and drink are easy temptations, resolutions made in another world at another time can easily dissolve.

When I was in prison in the 1970s there were many young, middle-class kids like me, locked up for relatively long periods for dealing drugs (depending on whether the conviction was for hard or soft drugs). This was a new phenomenon in the 1970s, but in prison we were not much different from other prisoners. Prison, the great leveler, reduced us all and apart from a general absence of tattoos and the fact that most of us were white, it would have been difficult to tell much about our backgrounds. The long-termers all mixed together, irrespective of class and often of race. We talked the same way, we thought the same way, and we identified with one another. The middle-class prisoners tended to get more regular visits and to study or do hobbies in some of their spare time. In contrast, the lower-class or underclass prisoners gambled or sat around talking all day and listening to music. Certainly we got drunk, stoned, and socialized. But not all the time.

Nevertheless, the class differences showed after we got out. Almost without exception, the middle-class prisoners moved into the workforce after release. Today, the majority I know are successful, ordinary people with jobs, wives, and families. The men from underclass backgrounds, who already had adolescent histories of violence, drunkenness, and criminality, are doing what they always did: living unpredictable, hedonistic lives, surviving from day to day on the money they hustle through drugs, theft, gambling, or "pulling rorts" (scams).

Some of them, many of them intelligent men who I am good friends with still, or whose names I see in the court sections of newspapers from time to time, make more money than I do as a university professor, but their material assets are largely restricted to a flashy car, a few fancy clothes, and odds and ends of gaudy jewelry (see Tunnell, 2000).

The Allure of the Prison

For career criminals, prison is a hazard that many accept, although with less tolerance as they get older. Apart from their freedom, they may have relatively little to lose by going to prison. For example, they may have had no career, reputation, mortgage, marriage, or children. Recidivists do not like prison. Ask them and they will tell you they hate it. But, they are used to it and adjust quickly. In prison they know many people, among the staff as well as the prisoners. Initially a sort of reunion takes place, as the man returned to prison renews old acquaintances and trades in the latest gossip. If the recidivist is older, he will have a degree of ready-made prestige, not have to establish his bona fides to people he does not know, and will move straight into one of the respectable cliques. He is likely to have immediate access to the perks of the prison, including pressed clothes, a better cell, a good job, drugs, and the odd drop of alcohol to keep him warm on a cold night. For the old "boobhead" (con), the pains of imprisonment will not be as sharp as they are for the hapless first timer.

So, for the recidivist, as Duncan (1988) has outlined, prison offers a number of attractions. It provides friendship and status within a tight primary group. It gives predictability, physical comfort, and freedom from many of the stresses of life. Meals appear ready-cooked, three times a day. There are no dirty dishes to worry about. Laundry is all done free of charge, every week. When clothing gets shabby, it is replaced. The power is always on, the showers are hot, the rooms are warm. There are no bills to pay, landlords to appease, long hours of work, or nagging wife and screaming kids. The inmate is free to socialize, read, watch TV, do crossword puzzles, or engage in gambling or hobbies, for much of his week. The principal enemy is chronic boredom, but limited psychological stimulation can be taken from entering the eternal intrigue of prison politics or by improving one's material status through the underground economy.

I know of no one who would exchange liberty in preference for life in the slammer. But, for men and women with long histories of incarceration, who find the pressures of existing outside difficult, who often go without food or a roof over their heads, the quality of life in the free world may not be so much greater than that inside the prison walls.

SO WHY HAVE PRISON PROGRAMS?

If the foregoing is true, and if in spite of their vastly different correctional philosophies, New Zealand and the United States both have depressingly high recidivist rates, then a case could be made that prison programs are little more than an expensive waste of time. It could easily be argued that programs should be dispensed with altogether. In my judgment, this would be a mistake. There are a number of reasons why correctional and welfare programs are an essential component of any modern prison system. Perhaps surprisingly, the first has to do with recidivism.

The problem with measuring recidivism in terms of reconviction rates is that it gives only a crude indication of reoffending (see Austin, Tromanhauser, this volume). Some measures discriminate in various ways between serious offending and minor offending; others do not. But, the difference between what is serious and what is not is subjective. As noted, drug offending is considered much more seriously in America than in New Zealand, where violence draws the heaviest penalties. Another factor that recidivist figures often ignore is intensity of offending. A person reconvicted for 20 offenses within a two-year follow-up usually appears just once in the recidivist figures, alongside others who have reoffended once or twice.

Moreover, some types of crime have far higher detection rates than others. For example, a bank robber who becomes a drug dealer after release is much less likely to appear as a recidivist than a drug dealer who becomes a bank robber. Likewise, a person who studies the criminal law and the law of evidence while inside is arguably less likely to be reconvicted than someone who does a course of, say, anger management, because although both may reoffend, the former is less likely to leave culpatory clues. Getting smart has a lot to do with not getting caught, and this is one reason career criminals appear less often in recidivist statistics than naive ones. As they get older, criminals may get smarter.

So, the effectiveness of prison rehabilitation programs might be confused rather than revealed by recidivist statistics. Maybe, for example, the exconvict will reoffend but he will do so less often. In this case, a program may have been effective, but that may not show in the data. Or maybe the exconvict will offend less seriously. Maybe he/she will reoffend just as often and just as seriously, but will not get caught. We cannot know. If a man or woman gets out of jail and smokes a joint, he/she commits a criminal offense. Technically, they have reoffended, and I would imagine that at least 90 percent of New Zealand prisoners and probably Americans, too, fall into this category.

Maybe, however, although a woman reoffends, she now looks after her kids properly. Maybe a man no longer beats his wife up. Perhaps he now takes his kids to football every weekend instead of spending it boozing up with his mates. Maybe, although he is reoffending, he appears to be just a nice guy who is polite to his neighbors, helps old ladies cross the street, and gives money to the homeless. Breaking the law is not everything, and perhaps this active criminal is just a better person because of the humane treatment he received in prison.

The second good reason for programs in prison is that they humanize people, or at least reduce the deleterious effects of long terms of imprisonment. As we know, one thing that many chronic offenders have in common is terrible childhoods. Many have experienced years of suffering from abusive, uncaring parents. Having never known compassion as children they are likely to have little conception of what empathy means. As adults, abused children often become merciless, violent, and predatory.

The classic New Zealand example is Joseph Thompson, who although softly spoken and intelligent, had in his childhood been frequently beaten by his father and regularly raped by a neighbor. When he grew up, Thompson applied the lessons of his youth, bashing and sexually exploiting the weak and vulnerable. Over a 12-year period, he raped and terrorized dozens of women in the working-class suburbs of Auckland. In 1995, he received the longest term ever given by a New Zealand court: preventive detention with a non–parole period of 25 years.

Prison is one chance the state has to try to repair some of the damage done to a prisoner before he was incarcerated. Perhaps, for the first time in his life he will experience fair treatment, be given respect and humanity, and be shown the compassion he never knew in his youth. To continue with the familiar pattern of brutality and dehumanization in prison is to perpetuate the circumstances by which dangerous criminals are made. Some day, most of these men will be released, and if their violent inclinations are not curbed, innocent people will suffer.

Jack Henry Abbott (1981) is an example. Released in 1981 after serving a total of 24 years in U.S. state and federal prisons, within six weeks he had wantonly stabbed a waiter to death outside a New York City restaurant. The death of the victim, 22-year-old Richard Adan, may or may not have been preventable (see Abbott and Zack, 1987). But, for me, it seems that an obvious duty of the state is to protect its citizens by making every effort possible to humanize the men and women it takes into custody on serious criminal charges. If any such effort was made with Abbott, it plainly and tragically failed.

A third reason for having programs in prison is that, irrespective of whether or not rehabilitative effects are statistically discernible, some convicts will make use of them, to their own advantage and to the overall advantage of society. There is a time in most prisoners' lives when they get sick of crime and are ready to make a change. Often that point is reached in prison. It is essential, in my view, that prisons be prepared for such occasions and be equipped with facilities to assist sincere prisoners on their way to self-improvement.

I can use my own case to illustrate. In 1975, I was 23 years old when I was sentenced to seven-and-a-half years for heroin trafficking. I knew that by the time I got out my 20s would be finished. So, I began thinking immediately about how I could salvage what was left of my life. If the facilities had not been there for me to study while I was inside, this could not have happened. I would not have been released with an M.A., completed a Ph.D., become a university professor, and written a chapter for this book. There is a strong likelihood that I would have returned to a life of crime and would be either dead or locked up at this very moment. The fact that I am not, and am able now to contribute in a unique way to the understanding of criminality and corrections, is a tribute to the policies of senior management at Paremoremo's maximum-security prison and to the prisoners who assisted and supported me along the way.

The final reason for including programs in the routine of a prison is simply that it is sound management practice. For not only is fair and humane treatment likely to create compassionate ex-prisoners, but the presence of such facilities also makes prisons easier to control. Convicts who recognize that prison staff have a real and active concern for their overall welfare are likely to be far more sympathetic to the overall objectives of management than those who do not.

Studies of prison riots indicate that in a large number of cases, the underlying cause of these disturbances is bored, resentful, dissatisfied, overcrowded prisoners, produced by inconsistent, careless, incompetent, and arbitrary management (MacCormick, 1954; V. Fox, 1956; Schrag, 1960; Colvin, 1982; Useem and Kimball, 1991). Well-organized prisons have fewer escapes, strikes, fights, and suicides than those that are not (DiIulio, 1987; Newbold, 1989; McLellan, Newbold, and Saville-Smith, 1996). Unfortunately, few American prisons are well managed, and the result has been unrelenting violence and a history of prison disturbances and riots that continues to this day (see Richards, this volume).

Again, I use an example from New Zealand. In 1990, the country introduced a new philosophy into its prisons called *He Ara Hou* (A New Way) that consisted of improving institutional programs and reducing authoritarian barriers between prisoners and staff. After the introduction of *He Ara Hou* and, presumably as a result, assaults dropped, suicides became less frequent, and escapes declined (Newbold and Eskridge, 1996: 470 – 472). Prisoners still did not like being locked up, but they responded positively to management initiatives. One of the reasons, I believe, that homosexual rape in New Zealand prisons is rare is that prisoners, treated with a measure of respect from staff, treat one another with respect as well. The social environment within New Zealand prisons simply will not tolerate the abomination of homosexual rape. For this reason, men who are predatory and recalcitrant in other contexts must behave completely differently when they get to prison.

EXAMPLE OF HUMANE TREATMENT

My point is well illustrated by a man I met in prison called Wayne. He was a former boxer who for years had made a living through theft, burglary, and robbery. When he was in his twenties, Wayne went to Australia, where he eventually did time in the states of Queensland, New South Wales, and Victoria. In prison he was a "hock," an aggressive homosexual, and he developed a reputation for violence that earned him long stretches in administrative segregation (the hole). In his last sentence before being deported to New Zealand, Wayne spent the greater part of a six-year sentence locked in seclusion in the Victorian prison of Pentridge.

When he was deported to New Zealand, Wayne had a five-year sentence to serve for a bank robbery committed some years before. He was sent straight to segregation in D-block at Paremoremo maximum-security prison. The superintendent of Pentridge, wishing to warn Jack Hobson, superintendent of Paremoremo, about Wayne's intractable character, sent Hobson a memo. In it he described Wayne as one of the most vicious and dangerous criminals he had met in his time in the prison service. He described Wayne as totally unpredictable and completely untrustworthy. He said he was likely to attack without warning at the slightest provocation. He advised Hobson to give Wayne no quarter and keep him in solid lockup for the duration of his sentence.

Two days after he arrived in Paremoremo, Hobson visited Wayne in his segregation cell. He gave Wayne a copy of the memo and asked him if the description was fair. Wayne said it was. Hobson then said, "Well, I take every man as I find him. I'm moving you over to the standard blocks today and if you behave yourself, you can stay there."

That afternoon, Wayne arrived in A-block, occupying a cell a few doors down from mine. A little tense at first, he soon settled into the routine of the block. It was easy to see the latent aggression below Wayne's surface, but he respected Hobson for the trust he had placed in him. He was not a model inmate —none of us were—but for the duration of his sentence Wayne committed no assaults and received no misconduct reports. Removed from the oppressive environment of the Australian prisons and treated with decency and respect, Wayne became a pretty ordinary inmate. I remained friends with him until he died of a heart attack in 1998.

Wayne's is not an isolated case; it is typical. When Hobson arrived at Paremoremo in 1972, by adopting a firm-but-fair approach to the handling of prisoners, in a matter of months he turned a violent, riot-ridden, tension-filled institution into one of the best in the country. Prisoners were happier and so were staff. Good staff do not like working in an environment where they know they are hated by the men they have to deal with and who may attack them at any time. Staff become brutalized by such experiences as well, and it is their families who often feel the brunt of their frustration, hatred, and fear when they come home at the end of the day. Prisons with programs professionalize staff and make their jobs easier. So, staff become nicer people too. In a well-run prison morale is high on both sides of the line, people get along, and trauma is reduced to a minimum. Rehabilitation and welfare programs are thus an essential component of the successful prison formula.

CONCLUSION

When the prison was first conceived of as a principal sanction for offenders, it was because of a belief that something could be done to correct the behavior of criminals. Early prisons were designed to relieve society of its crime problem by subjecting offenders to reformative influences, thus deflecting them from their predatory lives. So, the campaign has continued.

Nearly 200 years of correctional experimentation has yet to reveal a prison program that is effective in reducing recidivism in a significant and generally applicable way. Irrespective of what treatment convicts receive, it seems that recidivist rates remain high. Even New Zealand, with its 80-year history of correctional liberalism, has recidivist figures that, on the face of it, are little different from those of the United States.

Part of this is due to the inaccuracy of recidivist data. Most studies using these data are not sensitive enough to pick up many of the subtle changes that occur while a person is in prison. But this notwithstanding, it is nonetheless true that the majority of released prisoners do reoffend after they are discharged —more even than official figures indicate. The reasons why rehabilitation programs are apparently so ineffective are various, but they reflect the complex nature of the human organism itself. We have seen that personality characteristics are usually well established by the time a person first enters prison and that the characters of criminals have often been inured by years of neglect and abuse. This makes achieving radical change very difficult. When a prisoner is returned to the realities of free society, situational factors often impel him or her to discard lessons that have been learned or commitments that have been made in the artificial environment of a cell block.

Nevertheless, this does not deny the necessity for prison programs. Prisons are agencies of the state, funded by the taxpayer, and as such they are bound to serve the interests of all citizens, including prisoners, prison staff, and the general public. The interests of convicts are served by prison programs because they soften the impact of incarceration and the hardening effect that years in prison may produce. Moreover, they provide the opportunities for prisoners who are committed to change to take the steps necessary to make themselves into productive citizens. Likewise, the interests of prison officers are served because programs make prisoners easier to manage and they improve the quality of the working environment. Hostility and the threat of physical danger are reduced in a good prison, and the caustic effects of daily subjection to hatred and threat are removed.

Finally, and perhaps most important, humane treatment and prison programs are of a direct benefit to the community. Discontented prisoners riot, and this type of violence is expensive. Property is destroyed and people are often injured. So, well-run prisons, which are not subject to strikes, riots, and sabotage, ease the burden on the taxpayer. In addition, well-run, humanely organized prisons reduce the threat to the public of violent criminal victimization. Nearly all prisoners will some day be returned to the mainstream of society. If an inmate has been brutally or callously treated during his years in prison, there is every possibility that he or she will be a desperate or dangerous individual when released. This person will be somebody's next-door neighbor. This situation should be avoided if possible and it is the duty of the state to protect its citizens as cheaply and effectively as it can from the threat of such crime. If this is the case, then one of the primary tasks of corrections must be to devote at least a portion of its resources to programs that are designed to mellow, moderate, and rehabilitate the people who the state takes into its care.

8

"Who's Doing the Time Here, Me or My Children?"

Addressing the Issues Implicated by Mounting Numbers of Fathers in Prison

CHARLES S. LANIER

Two weeks before my 29th birthday, I stood stoically (but listened intently) as the county court judge slammed me with 12½ to 25 years in state prison for committing an armed robbery. I "blew trial"[1] several weeks before, and was expecting a respectable hit by "Maximum John"—the local magistrate who bragged he would hand out "a million years" while dispensing justice from the bench in New York. He gave me the maximum, sure enough, while noting he was "unimpressed" by anything good that anyone had to say in the presentence reports. He knew "bad" when "bad" crossed his path. Sure enough!

First stop on my magical mystery tour was the Clinton Correctional Facility[2] in Dannemora (formerly known as the Dannemora State Hospital, which opened on November 15, 1900). Back in 1979, the maximum-security Clinton was considered "reception" for convicts going directly to prison from any upstate New York region. It also was considered "Siberia" because it was located in the far north, a few miles from the Canadian border. My codefen-

The title of this chapter comes from a comment by a young Scottish offender (Tripney, 2000). I would like to thank Adriana Fernandez-Lanier, Creasie Finney Hairston, Stephen C. Richards, Jeffrey Ian Ross, and Hans Toch for their comments and suggestions on earlier drafts of this chapter.

dant and I were met at the gates of the prison by the resident "goon squad" and treated to a devastatingly simple lecture ("Your release date says 2004 and as far as we're concerned, that's how long you'll be here") and a shaved head. Half an hour later I was dressed in prison greens, sitting on a dirty mattress, on an empty bunk, in a small barren cell, musing, "What the fuck am I doing here?"

After "enjoying" the upstate surroundings at Clinton for almost a year, I returned to court for another trial on a separate "weapons" charge. Soon after that case was dismissed, I was shipped to the "box"—a.k.a. the Special Housing Unit (SHU)—in the Green Haven Correctional Facility in Stormville, New York. I was "in transit," on my way to Attica, the historical "max," which in 1971 was made infamous by the state-sponsored slaughter of 43 guards and prisoners.[3] It was an arduous, grueling, all-day trip to reach this notorious institution, a trek prolonged by stopping on the way at Auburn prison (home of the "Auburn system"[4]) to pick up a few more convicts. Once we reached the prison, the whole "boat" of 60 or so prisoners was met with a sizable force of hacks, whereupon we were stripped naked en masse and told that Attica was a "tough camp" where "wolf tickets"[5] would be "cashed in"[6] by the guards.

Soon after my arrival, I learned that my grandfather had died. I asked to see my "counselor" in order to request a funeral trip home, so I could be with my family as they mourned. It was a simple decision for my counselor: "You should've thought of that before you came to prison." Shortly afterward, I requested a transfer to the Green Haven Correctional Facility, still maximum security, but about six hours closer to home. I finally made it to The Haven, at is was called, in 1981, and started to receive regular visits from my family and friends, my wife at the time, and our one-and-a-half-year-old daughter. At Green Haven I attended college classes and eventually graduated with a bachelor's degree in political science.

In 1985, I shipped out again, this time to the maximum-security Eastern Correctional Facility (which in 1921 became the world's first institution for "defective" delinquents), so I could participate in a novel master's degree program at that prison. Eastern was about the same distance from home, so I still saw family and friends on a fairly regular basis. I did a "good bid"[7] at Eastern, and only left there when I finally received approval for "education release." I had been accepted to the doctoral program at the School of Criminal Justice, University at Albany, and was slated to begin classes in January 1991.

In January, I was taken for another taxing journey around the state, and finally ended up at the Hudson Correctional Facility. "Work" or "education" release prisoners were housed in the basement of an old church on the grounds surrounding the facility, which was about 30 minutes from Albany. From here, each day, I would travel on a bus back and forth to school. After 11½ years "behind the wall," Hudson was my first stay in a medium-security prison. One moment I was behind 30-foot walls, where guards with M16's in menacing turrets watched my every move, and in the next moment I was walking freely across the grounds without any concrete or razor wire to obstruct my path.

A year of attending classes on education release passed before I was scheduled for my first parole board hearing. After 12 years and 4 months under the custody and control of the Department of Correctional Services, I returned to prison for the day to sit in front of the parole board, where I would be judged once again. Their words were not harsh, but surprisingly rather apologetic. They'd lost my paperwork ("We're sorry, but you'll have to come back"), so I had to return again, the next month, to finally learn my fate. I did as they directed and finally was paroled on February 14, 1992.

GENESIS

"Look, I'm taking Jessica, changing our names back to my maiden name. You can just forget about us, and when you get out you can start your own family." Those words launched an early-morning surprise visit, from what was then my wife of four years. She had traveled to Green Haven early that beautiful, bright summer morning, to tell me "Adios" from her and our daughter. Little did either of us know that those words would later inspire me to navigate a line of scholarly inquiry about prisoners that had mostly been neglected by academics, researchers, and policymakers.

There are no secrets in prison! Thus it was that everyone, guards and prisoners alike, knew my wife had left me, and that my young daughter no longer came to visit her "Daddy." Friends who greeted us—and with whom we visited in the prison visiting room and on family picnics—knew, when regular visits halted and I no longer discussed my wife and daughter, that the prison walls had claimed another family. My silence and my avoidance of others were viewed, most likely, as a period of mourning, and I was given a wide berth. My grief was my own; everyone else in population had their own problems to confront.

As I soon learned, though, many others shared the same loss as I, and in fact wanted to talk about "our common condition." When the mother of my daughter stopped her from visiting not only me, but my parents as well, I challenged the action in the New York State family court system. My impertinence lasted three long years, until my ex-wife's objections to visitation were trumped only by her desire to remarry and get on with her life. At that point, we settled the case, and I established joint legal custody in addition to regular contact with my daughter. Concerns about regular visitation and family reunion visits[8] evaporated, and my daughter and I were allowed to resume our relationship.

What also occurred during those years of court action was that I became a source for other prisoners who were desperately trying to maintain ties with their children and/or cope with the loss of their family. As such, I was privy to many stories of family breakups, as well as the overwhelming sense of loss and despair that ravaged the fathers who walked the prison yard with me. Before I left the prison at Green Haven, I had conferred with dozens of these convict fathers who had lost all contact with their offspring, about both their concerns for their children and their own day-to-day well-being. There were times I felt

like a Pied Piper, attracting men searching for a wisp of the positive, some assurance that they would be able to confront and survive their immense and
ubiquitous loss.[9]

FROM QUESTIONS TO QUESTIONNAIRES

As alluded to above, I enrolled in college classes once imprisoned. I began college classes while in Attica in 1980 and completed the requirements for a bachelor's degree in 1984, after I had been moved to Green Haven. Bored after my
college program ended, and enticed by the thought of continuing formal study,
I applied to an advanced degree program at another prison. I applied to, and was
accepted to, the master's degree in the sociology program at the Eastern Correctional Facility in Napanoch, New York. Fortunately, my transfer to nearby
Eastern to attend classes in this unique master's degree program behind bars
(Lanier et al., 1994) occurred just before higher education programs in New
York State were abolished at the hands of politicians.

The master's program at the prison was sponsored by the College at New
Paltz, State University of New York. The curriculum of the prison program was
identical to the one at the main campus in New Paltz. That is, everyone had
core classes, some additional elective classes taught by adjunct professors, and required courses in various techniques (i.e., research methods and statistics). Professors would travel to the prison at night and offer classes in research methodology (both qualitative and quantitative design), statistics, sociology of the
family, foundations of sociological theory, and other subjects. In addition, graduate students at the prison were expected to write a thesis in order to fulfill the
requirements for the degree.

Some sought out extant data sets for their thesis research (e.g., comparative
attitudes of native- and foreign-born blacks, the deemphasis of formal hierarchy
in the regulation of the airline industry, the changing conceptions of ethnicity),
but many chose to write about issues related to the prison setting. Because none
of the prisoners were allowed to travel to the other side of the wall to collect
their data, even though we all asked for such permission, developing research
questions for a prison survey became the norm for those who chose to focus on
the prison in their thesis. Given the opportunity to conduct research on a question of growing importance to me, I began to explore the previously ignored
domain of fathers in prison.

I was nudged along, gently, in this adventure by Creasie Finney Hairston,
now the dean of the Jane Addams College of Social Work in Chicago, who
shared with me an interest in this field. What I first thought was a "hokey" idea,
one that no one had ever even bothered to examine before, was, she told me,
"on the cutting edge." Invested with her sage counsel, as well as the support of
the professors at New Paltz, I set out to survey maximum-security prisoners at
Eastern about the status of their relationship with their children. It was mostly
virgin territory, but I had plenty of ideas about the scope and relevance of the
issues and problems in this area. After all, I was an incarcerated parent myself,

and had discussed similar concerns with countless other prisoners who sought me out for advice and understanding about a terribly debilitating problem that we jointly shared.

IMPORTANCE AND SCOPE

Although I felt this was a worthy arena of study on a personal level, I wondered about whether it was really that important to others. How would focusing on the concerns of incarcerated fathers contribute to the overall body of knowledge about prisons and prisoners? What were the policy implications for such a study, if any, and how could they best be addressed? Who reposed within the ambit of this research—was it fathers in prison, alone, or did their children, their families, and the prison community inhabit this domain as well? In short, why was examining the plight of fathers in prison important?

As noted elsewhere (Lanier and Fisher, 1989, 1990; Lanier, 1991, 1993; Hairston, 1995), research about incarcerated fathers has important ramifications for institutional safety and stability, the adjustment of convicts to institutional life, and to prisoners' postrelease success. Not only does prior research suggest that these considerations are valid, common sense does as well. It is logical to assume that men who are tethered tightly to their families, and who are aware of their special responsibilities as parents, will act in a more pro-social manner both behind prison walls and in the free world. A better understanding of the incarcerated father also might help his children cope with their loss and overcome the absence of the parent from the home.

There is a legal foundation for ensuring a father's access to his children when the paternal parent is incarcerated (Barry, 1985; Fleischer, 1998; Zealand, 1998; Patton, 1999). This right can be located in Supreme Court decisional law: "The Supreme Court has unanimously held that 'the interest of parents in their relationship with their children is sufficiently fundamental to come within the finite class of liberty interests protected by the Fourteenth Amendment,' and, accordingly, has provided *de minimis* procedural safeguards for parents" (Zealand, 1998: 266).[10] The Court also noted that due process protections are in order for those confronted with the destruction of their family at the hands of the state.[11] Several authors have explored legal and other issues involved in termination proceedings ("On Prisoners and Parenting," 1978; Genty, 1991/1992; J. Brooks and Bahna, 1994; Fleischer, 1998; J. Johnson and Flowers, 1998).[12]

Beyond the legal considerations noted above, focusing on this subgroup of the prison population just might be, simply, "the right thing to do." One author (Bauhofer, 1985) suggests that it is morally correct to encourage and help imprisoned parents interact with their families. Perhaps to bring together and assist prisoners and their families, rather than condemn and destroy, is a better direction for "correctional" policy. Of course, it may be that some family bonds are not salvageable, and others may be better off "left alone" (i.e., without resuscitating), yet such decisions should be made individually, on a case-by-case basis, not on the basis of either incarceration or gender.

Moreover, the overall importance of this question cannot be adduced without examining the scope—that is, the number of lives impacted—of this issue. As the American prison population swells each year, increasing numbers of parents are swept along in its wake. National statistics document the considerable rise in state and federal prisoners during the 1990s. Government numbers reflect that the combined state and federal prison population, for males and females together, expanded from 739,980 in 1990 to 1,305,393 in 1999 (Maguire and Pastore, 2000) [13]—approximately a 76 percent increase.

Among those prisoners, according to a recent bulletin put out by the U.S. Department of Justice, Bureau of Justice Statistics (BJS) (2000), are people who have left their children behind in the free world. BJS reports an increase of over 250,000 parents serving prison sentences during the period 1991–99. Of course, male prisoners compose the majority of all citizens serving time behind prison walls. For example, there were 1.2 million men as opposed to 82,594 women incarcerated in state and federal prisons as of December 31, 1999 (Maguire and Pastore, 2000). Not surprisingly, then, increases in the number of people imprisoned overall have resulted in larger numbers of fathers in prison.

BJS estimates that by year-end 1999 there were about 721,500 parents in state and federal correctional institutions (compared to 452,500 in 1991) (U.S. Department of Justice, BJS, 2000: 2). The majority of these imprisoned parents —667,900, or about 93 percent—were fathers (2).[14] The same document notes that these 667,900 incarcerated fathers left behind approximately 1.4 million children under age 18 (2). What this means is that an enormous number of fathers and their young children are touched by the criminal justice system, in general, and prison programs and policies, in particular. These large numbers suggest a significant population with important needs.

"WHAT" DO WE KNOW AND "WHEN" DID WE KNOW IT

Beyond establishing the magnitude and importance of this problem, prudence dictates inquiring whether this topic previously has been the focus of any formal inquiry. In short, what have academics and researchers discovered about men in prison, and their role as parents?

The extant research on incarcerated fathers can be categorized as (1) that which deals with actual survey findings and semistructured interviews (i.e., more analytical and descriptive in nature) and (b) that which focuses on policies and programs (i.e., more impressionistic and prescriptive in nature).

Survey Research

Survey research on fathers in prison appears to be scarce. In an early article, one author explored "whether women were uniquely affected by the disruption of the family or whether incarcerated men and their children suffered equally" [15] (Koban, 1983: 173). A nonrandom sample of minimum- and medium-security female prisoners in Kentucky, as well as an equal number of men matched on selected characteristics, participated in the study (95 and 111, respectively).

Respondents were queried on things like "preincarceration" and current placement of their children, perceptions of children's happiness, frequency and length of visits, and reunification plans with children after release. The author concluded that (1) "female offenders had closer relationships with their children prior to their incarceration" (181), and (2) "women's relationships with their children and the family structure are more stressed by incarceration than are men's families" (182). The researcher appears to champion better programs for imprisoned mothers because of women's "greater commitment to and responsibility for their families prior to incarceration" (182).

The first survey in which I explored this topic occurred in 1987 at Eastern Correctional Facility. This initial research formed the basis for my master's thesis, and was both descriptive and analytical in nature (Lanier, 1987).[16] In this study, a random sample of male prisoners was surveyed about their relationships with their children. A total of 302 men completed the protocol, for a response rate of 80 percent. The information was gathered by myself and other prisoners trained in data collection. In addition to descriptive information about these fathers and their offspring, we also queried respondents about their psychological state.

I hypothesized that men whose relationship with their children was poor would be more likely to experience negative psychological consequences. In short, I theorized that the status of the father-child relationship (FCR)[17] should be associated with the father's overall affective state. My measures for affective states included depression, the father's concerns,[18] anxiety, and somatic complaints. I found statistically significant relationships for both depression and concerns about the father-child relationship. Descriptive data also illustrated that about two-thirds of the prisoners reported having children.

Additional research based on this prison population focused on dimensions of father-child interaction (Lanier, 1991), and both affective states (Lanier, 1993) and self-concepts (Parker and Lanier, 1997) of incarcerated fathers. The thesis sample of 302 male prisoners formed the basis for my 1991 and 1993 articles. A second prison survey at Eastern, which also yielded approximately 300 male prisoners for a response rate of 80 percent, formed the basis for the 1997 article (Parker and Lanier, 1997).

Among the dimensions of interaction explored in 1991 were the following: exchanging cards and letters, visits (including family day picnics and family reunion overnight visits), and telephone calls home. Preimprisonment relationships (i.e., did the father live with his children), as well as the father's current perception of his post-imprisonment residential status with his children (i.e., whether the father will live with his children after his release), were examined as well (Lanier, 1991). Not surprisingly, fathers who lived with their children before prison had higher levels of interaction while incarcerated (33–34); they also had greater expectations of living with their children after their release from prison (35). A subsequent article revisited the findings on the affective states of fathers in prison, albeit in a much abbreviated fashion (Lanier, 1993). It concluded that among fathers in prison "the potential for negative psychological consequences . . . are greater among men with poor father-child relationships" (60–61).

Several policy initiatives were proposed as a way to ameliorate the problems faced by incarcerated fathers, particularly those arising from divorce/separation and lack of visitation. First, I suggested that a legal services program for incarcerated fathers could be established to help prisoners assert their legal rights to maintain ties with their children. I also recommended establishing a cadre of trained mediators to assist those fathers behind bars who were prevented from seeing their children as a path by which to avoid full-blown legal action between estranged parents or other caregivers. Another solution I urged involved implementing counseling programs that would help fathers in prison with their unique problems.

Data for the 1997 report (Parker and Lanier) came from another prison survey at Eastern, which was conducted in 1992. In this research, the association between the father-child relationship (i.e., as measured in the earlier studies) and self-concepts (i.e., both self-esteem and self-efficacy) was explored. We hypothesized that the self-concepts of imprisoned fathers would be directly related not only to the status of their parent-child relationships, but to the status of actually being a parent as well. Findings suggested partial support for the hypotheses: (1) being a father appears to be directly related to self-esteem, and (2) the status of the FCR is directly related to self-efficacy. Both relationships were statistically significant. As with the earlier study at Eastern, a random sample of the prison population was surveyed, resulting in similar findings regarding the overall numbers of men reporting they were fathers.

Another, more exploratory, study employed a qualitative design, using semi-structured interviews, among a small population of prisoners and their children (Ransom, 1993). Fathers and their children were queried mostly around the nature and extent of their interaction. Among the findings, the author discovered that the children were more likely to misstate the level of communication from the father, and the fathers were more likely to misrepresent the status of their relationship with their children. In short, the children were more likely to falsely claim that their fathers wrote to them, and the fathers were more likely to falsely claim a "close" relationship with their children.

In an attempt to gather information for program purposes, as well as to add to the base of knowledge on incarcerated fathers, one researcher collected survey data from a nonrandom sample of 115 men housed in a southeastern United States maximum-security facility (Hairston, 1989). The sample included all prisoners who volunteered to participate, regardless of marital or parental status. Open-ended questions explored parenting and family relationships (e.g., frequency of visitation), as well as respondents' desire to improve parenting skills. The author noted that the respondents "[saw] themselves as not just convicts, but as current and future fathers" (28). As such, the men were interested in participating in parenting programs while incarcerated.

A subsequent research endeavor by this same scholar likewise set out to "define the nature of prisoners' family ties, to determine their family and parenting issues, and concerns, and to assess their interest in organized family programs" (Hairston, 1995: 32). Data were collected from a nonrandom sample of 126 men, at both a minimum- and maximum-security facility, using a self-administered questionnaire. The researcher found that contact between incarcerated fathers and their children was limited, in part because no one was available to bring their offspring to visit. As with the earlier study mentioned above (Hairston, 1989), these men also were concerned about their children, wanted to be better parents, and were interested in programs that might facilitate that end.

Program and Policy-Oriented Articles

The literature has seen a much greater focus on policy-oriented articles, which are prescriptive and palliative in nature, and deal with policy issues, particular programs, and general reviews. For example, one author confronts "visiting policy guidelines," specifically (Hairston, 1996b), and in another paper more generally discusses the maintenance of parent-child relationships and responsible parenting among incarcerated fathers (Hairston, 1998). Among the strategies for change proffered in the latter article are the following: national standards to govern policy toward incarcerated parents and their children that would be part of the accreditation process; state- and federal-level leadership among child welfare agencies to help develop policy toward children involved in the child welfare system whose parents are in prison; a national research and dissemination agenda about incarcerated parents and their children, supported by family advocates as well as child welfare and criminal justice professionals; and leadership from social service organizations and practitioners in developing policy and programs to assist parents in prison maintain ties with their children (632–636).

A number of articles have explored parenting programs for incarcerated men. For instance, one early examination focused on an intervention in the minimum-security unit of the Idaho State Correctional Institution (Marsh, 1983). The goal of the pilot program was simply to improve the parenting skills of parents in cases where the father was incarcerated. Three sets of parents and their 10 children were involved in the eight-week program and assessment. Volunteer instructors worked with the children in the child development classroom, while parents jointly received their instruction in a parent training class; both parts of the intervention occurred in rooms set up in the minimum-security unit. The results suggested that both communication (in all parents) and child management (in two of three families) skills improved. Interestingly, though, the author noted that for the parents, "the crucial problem in their lives was the strain of incarceration on the marital relationship" (Marsh, 1983: 162).

Hairston and Lockett (1985) described the program rationale and components for another parenting intervention—this one in the Tennessee State Prison for Men—called "Parents in Prison." The focus of this initiative was to reduce the potential for child abuse and neglect among men who left prison. The authors revisited the program in a subsequent article, but were unable to determine whether the effort actually reduced or eliminated an ex-offender's propensity to neglect and/or abuse his children after his release (Hairston and Lockett, 1987).

Additional studies discussed both programs that actually have been implemented (Lanier and Fisher, 1989) as well as theoretical proposals for a more comprehensive parenting project (Lanier and Fisher, 1990). One parenting intervention, developed by prisoners, was called the Eastern Fathers' Group (EFG). Its implementation came only after a long period of striving and arm twisting by interested prisoners; its demise was signaled when prison bureaucrats hijacked the enterprise for their own ends (see below). The EFG consisted of "mutual support meetings, monthly educational seminars, and a certified parenting education course" (Lanier and Fisher, 1989: 159). Although future plans called for establishing a parenting reference library and conducting an evaluation of the program, those projects never materialized.

Still, a much more ambitious and comprehensive model emerged from the EFG parenting initiative. What was called the Prisoners' Parenting Center (PPC) advocated joining educational instruction with various therapeutic techniques to create a multifaceted resource center—that capitalized on the parental role—within the prison (Lanier and Fisher, 1990). The PPC approach was "designed to assist in the voluntary socialization and moral development of incarcerated fathers, as well as to improve the quality of life of children whose fathers are in prison" (Lanier, 1995: 35). Although this intervention offers a logical and sound program model, it has never actually been implemented.

Several additional studies have examined existing parenting programs for prisoners. For example, one article described a book-sharing program for fathers and their children in a medium-security United States correctional institution (Genisio, 1996). The purpose of the Breaking Barriers with Books initiative was to improve relationships between incarcerated fathers and their children by addressing two needs arising from their separation: "the child's need to experience memorable, positive experiences with her/his father and the father's need to maintain an active relationship with his child" (92). The three-part program attempted to accomplish this goal through weekly instructional classes, visits between the fathers and their children, and a weekly parent support group. Using anecdotal reports, the author concluded that the book-reading effort was a success.

Another study explored the effects of a six-week parenting education program at the minimum-security Jackie Brannon Correctional Center in McAlester, Oklahoma (Harrison, 1997). Using a volunteer sample of 30 men and their children, Harrison sought to determine whether parental training leads to (1) improved child-rearing attitudes among fathers, (2) increased self-esteem in fathers, and/or (3) more positive self-perceptions in children (589). Prisoners who volunteered for the study were randomly assigned to either an experimental (those receiving parenting education and behavior management training) or control (those receiving no parenting education or behavior management training) group. Support for only one hypothesis (i.e., parent training led to improved child-rearing attitudes) was found.

A more recent study explored a "filial therapy" parent-training program among male prisoners housed in a medium-security federal prison (Landreth and Lobaugh, 1998). Developed originally by Bernard and Louise Guerney in the early 1960s, this remedial technique was inspired by a lack of mental health services for families and children. Landreth and Lobaugh note that "the objective of this approach is to help the parent become the therapeutic agent in the child's life by using the naturally existing bond between parent and child, thus the term "filial therapy" (1998: 158).

The researchers selected 16 fathers and 16 children[19] each for both the experimental and the control group. Results indicated that the perceived acceptance of their children among fathers in the experimental group increased significantly. Fathers in the experimental group also reported both fewer problems with their children's behavior and less stress over their role as parents. The self-concepts of the children in the experimental group also were significantly higher than those of the children whose fathers were in the control group. The authors concluded that filial therapy is an effective intervention for incarcerated parents.

Another recent study examined a parenting program for males who were housed in a minimum-security federal prison (Wilczak and Markstrom, 1999). This study employed an experimental research design, with 21 prisoners each in the experimental (pretest, eight-session parenting intervention, posttest) and control (pretest and posttest only) groups. The study attempted to investigate the relationship between parenting education,[20] and locus of control and parenting satisfaction. The findings were mixed: experimental group members scored significantly higher on knowledge tests and on some subsets of the satisfaction and locus of control measures. The authors found enough support to conclude that "parent education for inmates is a small effort with potential beneficial outcomes for all family members and institutions of society" (Wilczak and Markstrom, 1999: 101).

The National Center on Fathers and Families (NCOFF) also recently reviewed some of the available data on fathers in prison. Among the information presented in the NCOFF report were specific initiatives for incarcerated fathers in eight states (Brenner, 1998). These programs were designed to "enhance the parenting skills of incarcerated men on a statewide basis" (2). The NCOFF report also addressed the "link" between incarcerated fathers and current welfare reform and child support enforcement policy. The author suggested that employment and parenting skills programs *both* can lead to a reduction in recidivism as well as positive outcomes for children (i.e., a reduction in child welfare roles and an increase in child support payments).

Several observations concerning the studies mentioned above are in order. First, prior research primarily has utilized small samples, where respondents have been selected on a volunteer or some other nonrandomized basis. As such, the findings are limited in nature and have little generalizability to other populations. Second, the "treatment" period for the program assessments may be too brief to accurately reflect any true effects of the intervention. Third, many of the studies appear to have occurred in a vacuum, that is, without benefit of previous research in the field. In short, promising and relevant studies have not been replicated or continued over time to explore longitudinal effects. There also has been little integration of the literature, either in theory or in actual application. Fourth, and perhaps most significantly, prior research in this area has not been adequately funded.

Nevertheless, the growing body of research on fathers in prison provides a sound "point of departure" for future inquiry. Numerous authors have scouted this terrain, in spite of the lack of a solid base of extant literature and adequate funding for their research. As such, they have laid the groundwork, and culti-vated seminal issues—both of which are essential for additional scholarly study in this area. Furthermore, practitioners now also have an idea of what programs and what content "work," and as such can approach program implementation from an informed perspective. Thus, although the literature on incarcerated fa-thers remains slim at present, there are signs that work in this area is expanding.

NEW DIRECTIONS, NEW INSPIRATION

Research on incarcerated fathers, and the programs and policies that rule their lives behind bars, has expanded over the last 15 years. Importantly, it is poised to feature significantly on the research agenda in the near future. For example, BJS has for the first time taken an interest in fathers as well as mothers when it comes to discussing parents in prison. As noted above, government authors discuss this previously unappreciated population in a recently released Bulletin (U.S. Department of Justice, BJS, 2000). Their report provides descriptive sta-tistics on fathers in state and federal prisons (e.g., race, age, education, marital status); in addition, it offers offense and sentence data for these men (e.g., cur-rent offense, sentence length, time left to release). The document also presents information on substance abuse (e.g., preimprisonment drug and alcohol use), as well as type and frequency of current contacts (e.g., letters, telephone calls, visits) between imprisoned parents and their children.

In another exciting development, the Vera Institute of Justice in New York City has implemented the Incarcerated Fathers Initiative (http://www.vera .org/index.html), which is supported by both the Bureau of Justice Assistance and the Charles Stewart Mott Foundation. This study will review programs for fathers—both those who are still serving time as well as those who have been released. Among the queries explored by the Vera survey will be the effective-ness of different programmatic approaches; the rationale for parenting programs for male prisoners; institutional obstacles, if any, to parenting programs for men; and results of such programming on men who have been released. A report will offer recommendations for some pilot programs for fathers.

Karen Looney, a doctoral student at Trinity College in Dublin, Ireland, also is investigating fathers in prison as part of the requirements for her doctorate in clinical psychology. The dissertation research will focus on the father's perspec-tive on how the prison environment influences both fatherhood (i.e., identity) and fathering practices (i.e., roles). Using identity theory as a model, the study will examine aspects of the prison context—like "no touching" rules during visitation, geographical proximity, telephone restrictions, associated stigma—and then explore their impact on two associated constructs: (1) the fathers' iden-tities (i.e., their views of themselves as parents), and (2) their roles as parents (e.g., disciplinarian, caregiver, role model). Data collection will involve the use of largely qualitative interviews with about 30 prisoners, as well as with a se-lection of prison staff. Information was gathered during September and Octo-ber 2000 at the Wheatfield and Mountjoy prisons in Dublin.[21]

There also is movement among some organizations to explore the issues triggered by fathers serving time in prison. For example, the Task Force on Families with Parents in Prison is planned within the scholarly community. This interdisciplinary task force is being organized by Diane J. Willis, Ph.D., under the auspices of Division 29 of the American Psychological Association. It will focus on both mothers and fathers behind prison walls and their children. Additionally, the Family and Corrections Network (FCN)[22] plans to create a national advisory board, which will focus on issues affecting incarcerated fathers and their children. Part of the agenda of this board will be to produce easily accessible articles (perhaps via an online library) designed and written to help imprisoned parents and their offspring navigate life both behind bars and in the free world.

The FCN recently also helped organize a fatherhood conference attended by over 200 practitioners, ex-offenders, and researchers. This watershed event was held September 13–15, 2000, in Durham, North Carolina. The first ever North American Conference on Fathers behind Bars and on the Street was co-organized and cosponsored by the Family and Corrections Network and the National Practitioners Network for Fathers and Families (NPNFF). The meeting presented "an in-depth exploration of the practice, research and policy issues that impact fathers who live in the community and fathers who are incarcerated in local, state, and federal corrections institutions" (http://www.fcnetwork.org/). According to organizers, the gathering was intended to advance the larger goal of "bring[ing] together individuals and organizations dedicated to serving the needs of fathers and their families, and to addressing the major social, cultural, and economic factors that contribute to the increasing number of children growing up in single-parent homes and in fragile families" (http://www.fcnetwork.org/).

The meeting offered a wide variety of presentations and workshops. For example, one plenary session was entitled "Issues in Funding and Assessing Outcomes of Fatherhood Programs." Another panel consisted of a video project that offered a screening of "Voices of Incarcerated Fathers." Issues confronted in workshops and seminars focused, primarily, on specific program models (e.g., "The Georgia Fatherhood Program," "Fatherhood Training for Prisoners: North Carolina's Pilot Project"), policy issues (e.g., "Fatherlessness: Its Effects on Families, Communities, and Society"), and child support matters (e.g., "Child Support Policy and Practice during Incarceration"). Generally, the conference was devoted to an overview of the issues implicated by the intersection of parents with prisons, with discussions of programs and policy high on the agenda. What was less focused on was the future direction for scholarly inquiry in this area. Still, based on previous research, as well as the discussion at Durham, some suggestions for future study are in order.

FUTURE STUDY

Setting a research agenda can help to pull extant research together and at the same time clarify and sharpen thinking about the direction of future work in a particular area. Some of the following suggestions have been made but not pursued:[23] Such research probably should (1) cut across a variety of jurisdictions, (2) ideally encompass all members of the family unit, and (3) involve both prison and free-world settings. Both quantitative and qualitative research methodologies profitably could be used to explore this area more thoroughly.

Future investigation might begin with surveys that are designed to identify the precise numbers of incarcerated parents and their children in this country. Such a review would target state and federal prison systems, as well as local jails and other lockups where unsentenced and short-term prisoners are housed. A comprehensive discussion of visiting practices and parenting programs for both male and female prisoners in each jurisdiction also might be included in this effort. The number and types of resources and programs in the community that are supportive of children with parents in prison also could be ascertained. Making racial, ethnic, gender, and other comparisons is essential to the analysis.

The scope of inquiry also might extend to the international arena as well. For example, what are the practices in other countries when parents are sent to prison? Are there special programs for helping these people and their offspring? Is there any formal support—either from community or government organizations—for family members left behind when a parent enters the prison system? What are the visitation practices in other countries, including frequency, duration, and type of visit? Are there any statistics, reports, or even anecdotal reports about the failures or successes of extant parenting programs or other family-oriented policies for prisoners in these countries?[24]

The effects of parental incarceration is another important area. How are the various members of the family impacted when a father is sent to prison? For instance, in what ways are children influenced when a father leaves the home and is imprisoned? Are children affected differentially, based on age, pre-incarceration residential status of the father, and/or type of community, for example? Can any developmental differences among these children be identified, and are they attributable to parental imprisonment, specifically, or father absence, more generally? Is there a link between paternal incarceration and a child's subsequent negative involvement with the criminal justice system? What are the economic ramifications on the family when a father is sent to prison? What role do extended families play in tempering the loss of a father to the prison system?

In terms of incarcerated fathers, more research needs to focus on the psychological and emotional impact of their loss. Are fathers in prison at greater risk of suffering adverse psychological ailments and, if so, what are the potential consequences for the prison environment? How might these negative affective states impact their current family and other social relationships, as well as their eventual release into the community? Complementary issues to be explored should focus on the nature of the father-child relationship, both before and during incarceration. Moreover, what, if any, are the effects of long-term incarceration on this relationship?

Research also must be directed toward the impact of fathers on the prison system. For instance, is there a link between the status of the father-child relationship and institutional adjustment? Can the prisoner's status as a parent be used to help ensure stability in the institution, both among prisoners as well as among prisoners and staff? Furthermore, how does growing scholarly interest on the imprisoned paternal parent mesh with what is known about convicts in general? What does knowledge about incarcerated fathers do to help inform— if at all—the abundant body of previous research on prisons and prisoners?

In terms of "prison programs," might parenthood be a useful and genuine avenue by which to engage prisoners on a constellation of issues, like substance abuse, worthwhile employment, education, and pro-social behavior, in general? Moreover, what makes certain parenting programs work and others fail? Is there a way by which institutional officials and prisoners can collaborate in the development, implementation, and operation of such programs? Can common ground be located between convicts and institutional administrators so that programs remain meaningful for each group (substantive programs and public relations/career advancement purposes, respectively)?[25] Information on these critical aspects of prison parenting programs remains absent from the literature.

Another area of relevant inquiry concerns the postrelease relationships of incarcerated fathers and their children. Do prisoners return to their families after release? If so, what are the family dynamics like? Did the father resume his presence as well as his status in the life of his children? Do fathers who leave the mothers of their children remain in contact with their children postrelease? What are these relationships like, and are they associated with postrelease success? Are there instances where families actually are more stable and better off when a father leaves the home, and, if so, how can the noncustodial parent be helped to acknowledge and deal constructively with this situation, both during imprisonment and after release?

Beyond that, the breakup of a family and its associated traumas haunt parents and their children, generally—not just prisoners and their offspring. Do the problems, pains, and shattered dreams affect in similar fashion parents in the free world as well as those in prison? Is the suffering and loss experienced by children of prisoners similar to that experienced when a father dies in an accident or leaves home after separation or divorce? Moreover, there is an ever-expanding body of literature on families, in general, that discusses the importance of fathers in their children's lives. Future study should remain keenly aware of the overlap that may exist between that growing body of literature and prison research, and strive to integrate the two fields.

THE EASTERN FATHERS' GROUP: MUGGED BY THE SYSTEM

While still imprisoned at Eastern, with about five years left to serve before my parole board hearing, I attempted to implement a program that evolved out of my fledgling research on incarcerated fathers. The prison administration offered a chilly reception to my policy ideas, and I spent 18 months applying pressure and cajoling officials into allowing the Eastern Fathers' Group to be born (Lanier and Fisher, 1989). At the end of that period, a recently promoted secretary who later became the assistant to the director of the Family Reunion Program was persuaded to work with me on this project. I supplied the model, energy, and participants for the parenting program because—after all—I was a stakeholder in its outcome, and I had lived the need for such a program for years. She supplied the office (i.e., the institutional legitimacy), and thus had the authority to call men together at a specific place in the prison.

The Eastern Fathers' Group became wildly successful, in part, because prisoners developed and ran the initiative themselves.[26] Moreover, local FRP and prison administrators who shunned the idea at first now embraced it wholeheartedly. Important officials from the Department of Correctional Services Central Office in Albany, New York, who knew a good thing when they saw it, traveled to Eastern to congratulate their staff and applaud their efforts in "designing and implementing" a parenting program for men. They even hired a professional film team to capture the support group in action, as part of their vainglorious promotion for this parenting program.

In short, prison staff and higher echelon officials commandeered this parenting initiative, not out of any desire to ameliorate pain and suffering among the men who lived there, but rather, simply, to advance their own interests within the bureaucracy. From this point on, the EFG became a travesty, a sham whose priority shifted from helping men in prison who were crushed over the loss of their families to recording the number of people who attended meetings on a given day. Prisoners were relegated to statistics, rather than stakeholders, when the fire underpinning the program was extinguished by an insincere and unmotivated staff (i.e., the dynamism that energized and sustained the EFG flagged after basically unmotivated, overwhelmed, and disinterested administrative personnel took over its operation).

Not surprisingly, the "legitimacy" of the parenting initiative among prisoners was lost after prison officials expropriated the program, and subsequently advanced it as their own creation. Rather than allowing the program to remain a legitimate source of pride and accomplishment for incarcerated fathers, a commissioner from Central Office told me: "You might not like it but that's the way it has to be." In short, a powerful modality for helping prisoners, and perhaps even their children, was lost because bureaucrats chose to advance their interests over those of the people they were mandated to care for and to help.

The preceding experience provides an important lesson to keep in mind during the development and establishment of prison parenting programs: Prisoners must be among the developers and implementers of such programs. They also must be kept in charge of these programs, in an effort to maintain the dynamism and vitality essential for successful interventions. In fact, one author alludes to this integral role for prisoners in program development by noting: "It is important that a broad-based constituency—social service providers, criminal justice practitioners, academicians, community leaders, prisoners, and families —be involved in defining research needs and approaches and in assessing and interpreting research findings and their implications for policy and practice" (Hairston, 1995: 635).

Beyond this prescription for maximizing prisoner involvement, meaningful parenting initiatives might encourage the participation of guards and other staff members. Capitalizing on the parental role might be a viable strategy to locate the common ground that exists among both "the keepers" and "the kept" behind bars. Importantly, such efforts must focus on the parental role, rather than on an offender's potential to harm or neglect his children once he is released from prison. Programs also should be designed to meet the needs of all types of prisoners over the "life course" of their sentence. For example, strategies to help "short timers" must differ from those designed to assist men who have many more years to serve before their release. In addition to sentence length and differences in age, programs must reflect the diverse racial, ethnic, and cultural variations in the prison population.

Parenting interventions also should be available for all prisoners. Some may argue that parenting programs for convicts should be directed exclusively toward those who are parents, and who eventually will return to their families on release. As noted above, it may be that some families are better off without the father living in the household. If that is the case, and it is legitimately determined to be true, then programs might help those excluded fathers live—and succeed—outside the home on release. Such progressive and sensible initiatives also might prepare them, as well as other prisoners who may start families after release, to be caring and responsible parents in the future.

THE EASY PART

A cogent—yet at the same time dynamic—research agenda devoted to discovering and exploring the issues enveloping incarcerated fathers and their families is overdue. A systematized and focused inquiry should advance the body of knowledge about families, in general, and how they cope with trauma, deprivation, loss, and stigma. It also would contribute to an overall understanding of prisoners—their motives and behaviors, perception of the future, mental and emotional state, and whether they resist institutionalization or surrender to prisonization. Such a body of knowledge also would assist practitioners as they develop programs and search for interventions that might help stem the flow of children into the criminal justice system. A greater, more accurate understanding of fathers in prison would advance our overall body of knowledge on diverse fronts.

It is relatively easy to articulate what needs to be done. Finding the money and the political will to advance such study and program development is what poses such a formidable challenge. Available funds are targeted on razor wire and walls, not parenting education initiatives; on guards and restraints, not family counselors. Moreover, the perception of being "soft on crime" for elected and appointed policymakers is tantamount to casting their lot with the devil. In short, only "tough" prison policies that avoid the "mollycoddling" so popular in the past can insure job security for policymakers and legislators.

The waters turn darker and are further muddied when one considers both societal attitudes and the sentiments of the officials who run the prisons. One of the intractable problems facing incarcerated parents is that fathers on the outside, generally, are also often treated solely, and unfairly, as "economic providers." Until that perception changes, it is highly unlikely that fathers who spend their time behind bars will be allotted any special respect for their status as fathers. In short, they will not get the serious attention they deserve, much as is the case among free-world fathers. After all, if the father's role is viewed as "provider" rather than "nurturer," then once he is unable to fulfill that role his usefulness to his children has expired.[27]

Thus, perhaps most of all, change is required at the societal level. Regardless of all the men's movements and progressive-sounding statements from women's groups, the norm is that mothers equate with "parenting" whereas fathers equate with "earning." This view also can be seen in family court practices and procedures, which probably were designed to attract female voters rather than with any sound family policy in mind. The question thus looms large: In general, how can societal attitudes toward the role of men and women, when it comes to their status and importance as parents, be changed?

Of course, another problem in terms of addressing the needs of fathers in prison is the ruling paradigm under which such institutions generally operate in contemporary society. Punitiveness is up; rehabilitation is down. Public opinion and fear of crime allow prisons to be harsh, and sentences long. Not surprisingly, the mandate for prisons today focuses primarily on custody and security. Visiting and other family-related programs may appease various actors in the system, like prisoners, their supporters, and some social service providers, but their overriding goal is to maintain order in the system. Any benefits that might accrue to prisoners are secondary. Thus, as long as the pendulum remains "hung up" on punitiveness side of the scale, credible "corrective" or "rehabilitative" strategies will remain relegated to some distant future.

Beyond the debates over men's and women's roles, liberal or conservative attitudes, or punishment versus rehabilitation, is another critical arena where differences exist. We see prisoners as an undifferentiated, incorrigible mass, not as individuals, human beings with dreams and aspirations for the future, and people worthy of rejoining society. Curiously, we prefer to maintain this image, and to view them in this desperate, godforsaken congregation, when the opposite tack is the smarter path to follow.

Zeroing in on individuals and actually determining and addressing a family's specific needs is a more beneficial and wiser strategy. Custody and security, while admittedly important, should not be the sole determinant of prison policies. Perhaps a new paradigm might focus on ways diverse needs can be unified, rather than pitted against one another. Further, concentrating on the parental role of male prisoners might be a step along the path to "humanize our prisons" (Austin and Irwin, 2001: 247–249). Allowing for the importance of parents, in general, and encouraging and nurturing the paternal parent's role, specifically, also might just help to humanize the free-world society that exists beyond prison walls.

NOTES

1. That is, I was found guilty by a jury.

2. The use of euphemisms is strictly avoided in this chapter. Nonetheless, some euphemisms, like "correctional facility" and "inmate," have crept into the text when they are used as part of quoted material or are part of an official title.

3. "On the morning of 13 September, in a poorly planned and uncoordinated nine-minute assault, heavily armed state police and corrections officers retook the prison. In the resulting carnage 10 hostages and 29 inmates were killed by the assaulting forces. . . . Adding the one CO and three inmates killed in the initial stages of the riot meant that a total of 43 had died, the largest number ever killed in a United States prison riot" (Winfree, 1996: 44).

4. The "Auburn system" involved a prohibition against communication between prisoners, forced labor, and harsh discipline. It was developed during the years 1821–1824.

5. "Wolf tickets" or "woof tickets" are basically words or comments that offer a challenge either to authority (e.g., "I'm not locking in") or to another person (e.g., "Let's throw down").

6. In essence, any challenge or remonstration would be met with physical force.

7. For example, the services and food were good, visiting conditions were somewhat pleasant, the guards were more laid back than in other maxes, and the prison was located fairly close to home. Moreover, in part because the prison at Eastern placed a lot of emphasis on programs (e.g., academic), the facility was mostly a "static-free" joint (i.e., no major problems, less violence, infrequent lockdowns, etc.).

8. The Family Reunion Program (FRP) in New York State facilitated extended visits (usually two days) in mobile homes, on prison grounds, for convicts and their families. Family members would arrive at the prison, bringing with them food and clothing for several days. Prisoners that had been approved for the program would then join their families in the mobile trailer compound where they could visit uninter-rupted, cook their own meals, and interact as a family.

9. In a similar manner, Arthur Hamilton Jr., a long-term prisoner in Michigan, was sought out for his knowledge on parenting issues after he fought to gain custody of his two children. Elise Zealand writes that "Arthur researched his parental rights in the prison library, and enlisted the help of social workers and relatives. He arranged for the children to be in the temporary custody of two of his sisters. As a result of his work on his children's behalf, Arthur gained a reputation around the prison as something of a family law expert, and began helping other fathers with family issues" (1998: 248). Hamilton also describes some of these experiences in his own autobiographical tome (Hamilton and Banks, 1993). For a similar tale of firsthand accounts of fathers in prison see L. Wolfgang (1999).

10. See *M.L.B. v. S.L.J.,* 519 U.S. 102, 119 (1996), quoting *Santosky v. Kramer,* 455 U.S. 745, 774 (1982), (Rehnquist, J., dissenting). But see also *Caban v. Mohammed,* 441 U.S. 380, 391 (1979) ("best interests" of the child may be served by awarding custody to nonbiological parent over biological parent's objections), and *Stanley v. Illinois,* 405 U.S. 645 (1982) (noting that biology is not determinative because "neglectful parents may be separated from their children" [652]).

11. "The fundamental liberty interest of natural parents in the care, custody, and management of their child does not evaporate simply because they have not been model parents or have lost temporary custody of their child to the State. Even when blood relationships are strained, parents retain a vital interest in preventing the irretrievable destruction of their family life. If anything, persons faced with forced dissolution of their parental rights have a more critical need for procedural protections than do those resisting state intervention into ongoing family affairs. When the State moves to destroy weakened familial bonds, it must provide the parents with fundamentally fair procedures" (*San-*

tosky v. Kramer, 455 U.S. 745, 753–754 [1982]).

12. Not surprisingly, Genty observes: "Despite language in many of the cases that incarceration cannot by itself be a reason for terminating parental rights, a close examination of state court decisions reveals that they often treat incarceration as a sufficient reason for the permanent termination of parental rights even when an incarcerated parent could continue to play a meaningful role in her child's life. Moreover, some state courts have shown a disturbing tendency to streamline termination proceedings in cases involving incarcerated parents, thereby sacrificing important procedural safeguards" (footnote omitted; page numbers unavailable).

13. The focus in this chapter, and thus in the numbers discussed below, is on citizens sentenced to a term of incarceration of more than one year, i.e., those serving sentences in state and federal prisons. Although the discussion and statistics presented here exclude those parents who are in jails or other short-term lockups, the concerns and problems experienced by this group of prisoners is worthy of attention as well.

14. The BJS bulletin notes that "55% of State prisoners and 63% of Federal prisoners reported having a minor child. Among State prisoners, women (65%) were more likely than men (55%) to have minor children. In Federal prisons, similar percentages of men (63%) and women (59%) had a minor child" (U.S. Department of Justice, BJS, 2000: 2).

15. The author prefaced these remarks with the following commentary: "This study of female offenders and their families conducted in Kentucky started with the assumptions that being stripped of the role of mother was one of the most traumatic factors in a woman's adjustment to institutionalization and that a female inmate's failure to maintain contact with her children would negatively affect her chances for rehabilitation and reunification with her family" (Koban, 1983: 173;).

16. A leaner version of this research was presented at the First National Conference on the Family and Corrections and later was published by the Family and Corrections Network (Lanier, 1989).

17. The status of the FCR was established by measuring the amount of contact, communication, and involvement had with their children, both before and during incarceration.

18. The "father's concerns" variable was designed specifically for this study to measure the presence of a subclinical, dysphoric state in respondents. It "was added in an attempt to measure the psychological state that lies within the gray area between normal sadness and clinical depression" (Lanier, 1987: 26).

19. If the participating father had more than one child, he was asked to choose just one of his children for the 10-week training period.

20. This program was adapted from the STEP parenting program (Dinkmeyer and McKay, 1982) to meet the particular circumstances facing incarcerated parents. For instance, the section on parent–child communication dealt with building relationships at a distance through writing letters, telephone calls, and visitation; another section was devoted to helping prisoners provide honest answers about their imprisonment to their children.

21. "Mountjoy Prison is a 'closed' committal prison for male and female prisoners aged 17 and older in Dublin. The prison population is a fairly general one in terms of crimes, though as far as I know there are no sex offenders there. There are a lot of prisoners there on drugs charges and a lot of heroin is used there. . . . 'Committal' refers to prisoners who have been sentenced, i.e., they are not on remand, and 'closed' refers to the level of security. There are three levels of security in prisons here, closed, semi-open and open. Closed . . . is not quite the equivalent of your maximum-security prisons, but pretty close. Wheatfield is another closed committal prison in the Dublin area that caters for male adults and juveniles aged 15 and over. Again the population is general, though not so drug related" (personal communication with Karen Looney, August 11, 2000).

22. "Since 1983 Family and Corrections Network has provided ways for those concerned with families of offenders to share information and experiences in an atmosphere of mutual respect. We have done this through publishing, sponsoring conferences, liaison with other agencies, presentations, and consultation. We have published information on children of prisoners, parenting programs for prisoners, prison visiting, incarcerated fathers, hospitality programs and a variety of other topics" (http://www.fcnetwork.org/).

23. Because many areas previously suggested as part of a "research agenda" for incarcerated fathers (Lanier, 1995, 1996) remain unaddressed, they will be included here (see also Hairston, 1996a).

24. For example, while discussing the development of the "Polmont Positive Parenting scheme," a program officer at Polmont Young Offenders Institution (YOI) in Scotland noted that "we also took into account the recommendations of the recent Social Inclusion Report, which suggested that all YOIs should be presenting 'Parenting Courses' before April 2002" (Tripney, 2000: 5).

25. My thanks to Creasie Finney Hairston and Hans Toch for raising these issues during their review of an earlier draft.

26. In short order, other prisoners were involved in running the EFG, specifically, by taking responsibility for attracting speakers and taking charge in support group meetings, and, generally, in just maintaining its vitality.

27. As one author notes: "Legal notions of fatherhood reflect, to a remarkable degree, fathering divorced from nurturing. The model of fatherhood embedded in law is dominantly biological and economic" (Dowd, 1996: 526).

9

Excon: Managing
a Spoiled Identity

RICHARD S. JONES

Imprisonment carries both direct and indirect consequences for convicts (Rich-ards and Jones, 1997). Direct effects refer to what prisoners may lose when they are incarcerated, including nearly everything that is dear to them in the outside world—spouses, children, employment, homes, and personal possessions (Holt and Miller, 1972; Parker and Lanier, 1997; Richards, this volume). They are confined in institutions that are often characterized by violence (Sawyer et al., 1977; Flanagan, 1983; Fleisher, 1989; Silberman, 1995), sexual victimization (Lockwood, 1980; Nacci and Kane, 1983; Jones and Schmid, 1989), and severe overcrowding (Paulus, 1988).

The indirect outcomes of incarceration may not be evident to prisoners un-til they are released from prison (Richards and Jones, 1997). Among these col-lateral consequences are the physical and psychological effects of imprisonment, including institutional dependency (Walker, 1983; Wormith, 1984; Zamble and Porporino, 1988; Goodstein and Wright, 1989); extended difficulties in relationships with family (Holt and Miller, 1972; Burstein, 1977; Cobean and Power, 1978; Schafer, 1978; Homer, 1979; Conrad, 1981); various disabilities, disqualifications, and legal restrictions (Burton et al., 1987; Gordon, 1990; Rich-

I want to thank Stephen C. Richards, Jeffrey Ian Ross, and Thomas J. Schmid for their generous encouragement and able assistance with previous drafts of this chapter. An earlier version of this paper was presented at the Annual Meeting of the American Society of Criminology, Toronto, Ontario, November 1999.

191

ards, 1990, 1995a; Richards and Jones, 1997); inadequate financial resources at the time of release (Lenihan, 1975; Richards, 1995a); post-prison unemployment (Pownell, 1969; Dale, 1976; Tropin, 1977; Smith, 1984; Dickey, 1989; Grogger, 1989; English and Mande, 1991); and underemployment. Drawing upon these and other analyses, criminologists and other social scientists have declared the prison system to be a failed policy of crime control (Bottoms and Preston, 1980; F. Allen, 1981; Reiman, 1995; Dyer, 1999; Austin and Irwin, 2001).

One measure of this failure is the detrimental effect of stigmatized identity (Warren, 1980; E. Jones et al., 1984). According to Irwin (1970: 135–138), stigma is a complex problem that operates on two levels. First, there is a difference between how an exconvict might perceive his/her stigma (the subjective level) and how it is actually perceived by others. Second, because the person is discreditable rather than discredited (Goffman, 1963), he/she must make decisions about how to manage this stigma in both formal and informal social settings.

EXCONVICT

I am an exconvict. My experience with prison began when I was sentenced on a marijuana conviction to serve a year and a day in the Minnesota Correctional Facility-Stillwater, a maximum-security penitentiary. Ordinarily, one of the most difficult steps in research on prisons is gaining unrestricted access to inmates' day-to-day lives within the convict world. This brief time incarcerated provided me a unique opportunity to study prison conditions and my fellow inmates.

In a conversation with a professor prior to my entering prison, it was suggested that I begin keeping a journal. He said that I might at least try to make something positive come from this experience. One week before I entered prison, I began a record that chronicled my daily life for the next year. My early entries were predominantly personal thoughts, impressions, and a chronology of daily events. I used the "diary-interview" method (e.g., Zimmerman and Wieder, 1977) entries to provide a framework to derive new observational strategies and identify potential themes.

From my first day at Stillwater, I recorded extensive notes describing the everyday interactions with other members of the prison community (both long- and short-term inmates), as well as observations of the entire realm of prison life to which I was exposed. When I completed my prison sentence, I entered graduate school and returned to the same prison to conduct extensive interviews with 20 first-time inmates serving time of two years or less. These individuals were asked a series of questions to focus their discussions of prison life, but were allowed to portray their experiences without the constraints of a formal interview schedule. Over 1,000 pages of data were collected from these two sources and were analyzed based on the principles of "grounded theory" (Glazer and Strauss, 1967).

THE MAKING OF AN INMATE

Doing time in a maximum-security prison is not simply a matter of "being in prison." It is, rather, a creative process through which inmates must invent or learn a repertoire of adaptation tactics that address the varying problems they confront during particular phases of their prison careers. There is an extensive literature on the informal organization of prison life and the socialization processes through which prisoners come to participate in this informal organization (e.g., Cordilia, 1983).

Clemmer (1940/1958) argued that men who are sent to prison experience a socialization process through which their established values, beliefs, and attitudes are stripped away and replaced by the cultural values of the prison, a process he referred to as the "prisonization ordeal." In other words, as inmates come to adopt behavior patterns that are consistent with prison culture, they also become increasingly further removed from conventional behavioral patterns. Within this conceptualization, Clemmer hypothesized that the longer a convict is incarcerated, the more prisonized he would become and therefore the more difficult it would be to alter his behavior in a socially acceptable direction.

The deprivation model, an alternative explanation, is most closely associated with the work of Sykes (1958) and Messinger (Sykes and Messinger, 1960), who argued that the inmate social structure is a functional response to inherent deprivations of imprisonment: the loss of liberty, goods and services, heterosexual contact, autonomy, and security. Although prisoners react to these deprivations individually, Sykes and Messinger observed that they also do so collectively, through the cultural theme of inmate solidarity and the normative prescriptions of the convict code. The various social roles that constitute the inmate social system are essentially a classification system of how individual prisoners respond to prison deprivations, including the extent to which they conform to or violate the inmate code (Irwin, 1970: 82–85; J. Ross and Richards, 2002: 72–74; Richards, this volume).

Other prison researchers have contended that the deprivation model gives insufficient consideration to what convicts bring to the prison environment. This "importation response" emphasized how the experiences and values of prisoners prior to their incarceration affect their adaptations in prison, and ultimately inmate social structure and culture. In an early statement of this model, Irwin and Cressey (1962) identified three ideal-type subcultures within the inmate social structure: the thief, convict, and legitimate subcultures.

Members of the thief subculture identify with a larger criminal subculture that extends well beyond the boundaries of the prison world (King and Chambliss, 1984; Shover, 1996). These men value, at least in principle, the ideas that criminals should not cooperate with police or prison authorities and that they should be reliable and "solid" in the eyes of other thieves. Their interests lie in resolving group conflicts and promoting behavioral norms that contribute to making life easier for them on the street and while serving time. Thieves expect to enter and exit prisons many times over the course of their adult lives, as they are usually sentenced to relatively short sentences (less than 10 years), serve their time, and then return to the streets. The life they live assumes that they must maintain a respectable status in the thieves' world. In effect, they live with one foot in the street and another in prison.

In contrast, members of the convict culture are serving longer sentences (10 years to life), many for violent offenses. They are oriented primarily to the prison itself and seek to acquire status with convict cliques within the prison. These are men who have served extensive prison time behind bars and do not expect to "make parole" or have their sentences reduced by "good time." They may be fearless and have little respect for official prison policy and procedures. Many of them spend months or years in detention cell blocks (the hole). They have no choice but to make a "home" in prison. Some of these are "state-raised" convicts (Irwin, 1970: 26–29; Abbott, 1981: 3–22; J. Ross and Richards, 2002: 70/-72; Richards, this volume), convicts who as children spent time in orphanages and juvenile detention institutions.

A large percentage of the prison population, according to Irwin and Cressey (1962), reject the values of both the thief and convict subcultures, attempt to isolate themselves from these groups, generally follow prison rules, and seek to do their time with as little trouble as possible; these are the men classified as members of the "legitimate subculture." Irwin (1980) has since observed that prisons are no longer comprised of the three dominant subcultures that he and Cressey identified originally. Rather, as a generalized extension of the importation model, inmate social systems are increasingly constituted by specific groups or gangs of prisoners, each with its own identity and purpose (Davidson, 1974; Richards, this volume).

My research on prisoners' experiential orientations does not speak directly to the deprivation versus importation debate, but it is informed by, and contributes to, the same research tradition. Like all of the studies cited, my project examined inmate adaptations to the conditions and deprivations of prison life. Lending broad support to the importation model, this analysis documented the importance of what new prisoners bring with them to the prison; in the case of the individuals studied, an outsider's stereotypic imagery of prison life, and a tentative plan of action grounded in this imagery. More generally, the men studied could be classified as members of what Irwin and Cressey called the "conventional" or "legitimate" subculture in prison, although their inexperience with penal confinement would relegate them to the margins of even this segment of the prison world. However, in contrast to the usual importation model analysis of how outside norms or values are translated into prison adaptations, I examined how new prisoners, as outsiders, defined the problems of imprisonment and then acted on these definitions.

This research adds two sociological themes to the research on prison culture and inmate adaptations. The first is that prisoners' changing orientations to prison life are better characterized as active efforts to interpret the prison rather than as the passive response to prison culture, as was suggested by Clemmer's concept of prisonization and subsequent research on prison socialization. The second is that individuals' orientations, at least for new prisoners, reflect the interplay and continuous influence of both the outside world and the prison world throughout their sentences. This simultaneous influence is inadequately recognized not only by the prisonization pattern of a linear, progressive socialization into prison culture, but also by the U-shaped adaptive pattern (through which prisoners are seen to be prisonized and then deprisonized) suggested by Wheeler's (1961) and Garabedian's (1963) research. It is also insufficiently addressed by the "deprivation versus importation" framework for examining prison culture.

My own research suggests that both of these themes are important in the prison experiences of new prisoners during their pre-prison orientations, in which they attempt to envision and prepare for prison life, and again in their post-prison orientations, when they compare the prison with the free world and endeavor to assess the impact that this experience may have on their future lives. There is, to be sure, a period in the middle of their sentences when their response to the prison routine suggests a more passive form of prison adaptation such as that represented by the term "prisonization." Nevertheless, this takes place only after the inmates have already altered their emotional response to the prison as a result of their own experiences and interpretations. In addition, it is countered by their ambivalent but continuing identification with the outside world.

Prisoners' behavior is not determined solely by rules and values; they recall real events and then interpret these abstractly. Thus, their evolving experiential realities and the changing problems and concerns of everyday prison life provide the basis for the inmates' changing adaptations to the different phases of the prison experience. This involves something more than a passive alternation between conventional and criminal values. Instead, they work to resolve their difficulties with life both inside prison and outside, after they return to the free world. Finding out how prisoners face these challenges can tell us a lot about what might be done to help them.

FROM THE INSIDE LOOKING OUT

Inmates' preparations for their future on the outside begin while they are still in prison. Throughout their incarceration, convicts fantasize about what they will do when they finally get out of prison. Toward the ends of their sentences, they begin to speculate more frequently and to discuss their outside plans with others.

In order to plan for his future, an inmate has to construct an image of the outside world. Irwin (1970) noted that this takes place on two different levels. First, there is that which operates within the general prison community, where their dreams about their future tend toward generalized possibilities, often grandiose and impractical. As their return to the free world becomes more imminent, however, their plans tend to become more specific and realistic. This is more likely to take place on a personal level, in discussion with their close associates or friends.

Beyond their immediate need for a job and a place to stay, inmates are also concerned with other dimensions of their lives outside. Most of the expectations that these prisoners have for the outside world center around escaping the deprivations associated with incarceration. The following interview with a prisoner anticipating release identifies some of these issues. Denial of heterosexual relationships is discussed in the following excerpt:

> The talk of sexual escapades can always be overheard, second only to talk about past criminal behavior. There is much talk of what they [fellow prisoners] are going to do sexually when they get out.

Loss of autonomy is expressed by the following inmate:

> I've wondered what my day would be like once I gained my freedom. . . . What will it be like to not be constantly surrounded by hundreds of males, to not have to listen to the bells ring at 6:00 every morning?
>
> I think there is some danger in the idea that we all expect so much from our new lives. In looking back, my life wasn't filled with total joy and excitement. Yet we seem to think that is what awaits us once we obtain our freedom. I am afraid that many of us may be in for quite a letdown. We have set our expectations much too high. Hell, anything will be better than what we have now, but anything will wear off quickly. It won't take much to put a real damper on things, such as a failure to get a job, or find that woman or women you have dreamed about during incarceration.

Irwin (1970: 88–93) stated that inmates learn three concepts that serve as guides for their planning about the future. The first is "making it," which entails becoming financially viable and coping with the parole system. Making it, in spite of a lack of education, vocational skills, and the stigma of being an ex-con, is thought to require a considerable amount of effort and a little luck. The second is "keeping out of the old bag," which refers to the former life, with its high probability of arrest and conviction. The third is "doing all right," which goes beyond merely staying out of prison and includes the fulfillment of specific desires and goals.

As prisoners think about returning to the "free world," they attempt to make plans. Throughout their prison careers, convicts dream about "doing all right"; for example, having sex with women, buying a car, and finding a good job. But, as they near the completion of their sentences, certain fears and doubts begin to enter their thoughts. The following interview focuses on an inmate's uncertain future:

> I think often about what it will be like when I get out, but can't really imagine it. I know it will be another beginning for me. This starting all over again is just like getting out of high school or the military or whatever. It is kind of scary. Starting out with nothing, not knowing if you're making the right decisions. The parole board asks what your plans are when you get out. I don't know how anyone can know for sure. I think I know what I would like to do but I don't know if I will be able to do it.

Surrounded by many examples of parole failures, this man has good reason to worry about his ability to make it on the outside.

Another prisoner offers an extreme example of a fellow convict's difficulties in reentering the free world:

> One of the inmates out here is a guy well into his 70s, by the name of Pete. From what I've been told, he shouldn't be here [back in prison]. After he was paroled, one day they found him sitting on the front steps crying. Evidently he just couldn't make it on the outside. All of his family and friends were dead and things had changed too much. He was just lost out there. So, they are allowing him to do his parole here in minimum security. It's a rather sad case, though, that once a person's time is up he can no longer function out there in society.

This quotation emphasizes the changes that take place in the outside world while an inmate is incarcerated, and the difficulty he may have after serving many years in prison returning to the community, where he no longer has family or friends.

Another prisoner expresses his concern with the dependency that is induced by the prison system and wonders whether he will be able to make important decisions on his own:

> I just seem to go through the motions every day. It doesn't take much thought to wake up, go to chow, go to work, and go to your cell when the bell rings again. I wonder what effect this has on us when we get out, when we no longer have these bells to tell us what and when to do? It is a shame to let a person who has been totally dependent on an institution for a period of time just go out on his own, ill prepared to make any decisions for himself.

This prisoner expresses a more generalized concern about what impact the prison experience will have on his ability to make it on the outside:

> I'm in a kind of strange mood. I think I'm just a little scared. I've been doing a lot of thinking about my future on the outside and I guess I have some doubts about my ability to make something of my future. I really wonder what impact this prison stay will have.

Another inmate is more concerned about how others might perceive him after his release from prison:

> I had an interesting visit with my friend Joan the other night. She told me that she and two friends were talking about me and the joint. During the conversation with Joan it came out that her friends didn't think much of criminals, but that somehow that didn't apply to me because I was their friend, and I wasn't really a criminal. But it really made me realize that when I get out of here I am going to have to fight the stigma of being an excon. It could be tough to find work and such, and people always seem to act a little weird around excons. I never really thought about this before.

The end of a prison sentence includes a prisoner's efforts to reconstruct a picture of his reintegration in the world outside the prison walls. This look into the future is emotional and includes increasing apprehension about returning to the "free world."

PROBLEMS OF REENTRY

Incarceration creates a number of obstacles that must be overcome when a prisoner is attempting to adapt to life again in the free world (Austin and Irwin, 2001: 139–159). Individuals released from prison must cope with strained personal relationships, poor education, and few job skills, plus the stigma of a felony conviction, which may bar them from many occupations and make it difficult to obtain employment of any kind. In addition to this, they must find housing as well as deal with a myriad of other reentry problems, for example, moving from a highly routinized, controlled environment into the complex, fast-moving world of the streets. Given all of these issues, it should not come as a surprise that many individuals who are released from prison are not successful and are reincarcerated, many for technical violations (Austin and Irwin, 2001: 143–146).

The focus of the remainder of this chapter will be on how excons view the reentry process and develop strategies for coping with stigma. Before doing this, I need to reveal some of my own experiences when I left Stillwater penitentiary.

MY EXPERIENCE WITH REENTRY

I am not the typical excon, whatever that means. In comparison to the other exprisoner academic authors in this book, I have done the least amount of time in prison. Some might argue that I most closely fit Irwin's description of the "square john" in my orientation toward the prison experience. I believe that what is important for readers to understand is that there is no typical exconvict. Although we have something in common in that we have all been rejected by society and sent away to prison, we have not experienced incarceration in the same way. As a result, we shouldn't expect all exconvicts to experience reentry in a similar fashion. I remember my last day in prison:

> I have been waiting so long for this day to come around. I didn't do anything at all today but sit around and watch television. A fitting way to end my prison experience. I have really been watching the clock. Just 10 more hours to go.
>
> I just crossed off the last day on my prison calendar. I just want to scream, I'm so damn happy. I had hoped that I would be more settled on the outside––with a job that is. But at the present time I really don't care. At least I have a place to live [with my family]. I know that I am going

to make it. I have no real plans for today, except that I would like to party with my friends.

Reflected in this final entry in my prison journal are some telling and conflicting images. For many prisoners, including myself, the prison experience is viewed as time wasted, and getting out, then, is an opportunity to make up for lost time. So, one of the first things that I wanted to do was to reconnect and celebrate with old friends and family. On the other hand, getting out of prison is filled with uncertainty and risk: no job, no real plans.

Many individuals leave prison on parole and are required to write a release plan that includes specifying a place to live, family arrangements, and employment. In contrast, because I had served my entire sentence (with deductions for jail time and "good time"), I was released immediately to the street without the encumbrance of parole supervision and any other obligations to the community corrections legal machinery. As a result, I was not required to formulate a release plan, and no one would be checking on me to see that I had a job or a place to live. So, although I had a place to sleep and hang my hat, I had no way of making a living and the prospects for doing so did not seem so bright. But, I was resolved to "make it."

I was lucky for a number of reasons. First, I was busted in Minnesota, a liberal state with relatively lenient penalties for marijuana convictions. If I had been sentenced by a federal court, or in a different state, for example, in the South, I might have been required to do more time. Second, I was able to do my sentence without serious physical injury or catching a new case. Third, I had the support of family and friends.

I served less than one year in prison and was able to maintain fairly close contact with my family and friends, and will be forever grateful for their support. For example, I received a steady flow of mail and visits, even from people that I never expected to hear from. I doubt this would have been possible if I had served a longer sentence, or if I was doing federal time and shuttled constantly from prison to prison across the United States (Mobley, Murphy, Richards, this volume). Research (Richards, 1995a; Richards and Jones, 1997; Austin and Irwin, 2001: 151–153; J. Ross and Richards, 2002: 155–171; Terry, this volume) suggests that the two most important factors in successful reentry into the free world are the strong social support system of family and friends and meaningful employment. Upon my release, I went home to live with my family.

EMPLOYMENT?

The employment situation was a completely different story. Before I went to prison, I had completed a bachelor's degree in sociology from Mankato State University (MSU), but I was reasonably certain that no one in the fields of criminal justice or human services would be inclined to hire a recently released prisoner. So, I limited my employment search to the usual exconvict kinds of jobs, and applied for entry-level positions at foundries, restaurants, and with moving companies. Many exconvicts are forced to hide their criminal status when applying for work; ironically, I found that my college degree was preventing me from being hired for manual labor positions.

For two months I responded to newspaper ads and leads provided by the local unemployment office, as well as those given to me by family and friends. Nothing happened. I kept getting more and more frustrated, having never experienced this kind of rejection before. I had always had a job, whether delivering newspapers as a kid, holding down a variety of part-time positions as a teenager, working my way through college, or serving in the military. This was the first time that I could not secure employment.

Ready to give up, I received a phone call from a former professor who told me about a university-sponsored paid summer internship in a criminal justice planning department that was headed by a friend of his. They were willing to hire me as a research assistant if I would enroll in graduate school, thereby making me eligible for federal subsidies. I had never really given much thought to graduate school until this opportunity forced me to consider this option. I applied to the master's program in sociology at MSU as a part-time student, but with no real intention of attending the university.

At the end of the summer, I was again faced with the prospect of being unemployed. Again, my former professor came to my aid. He offered me a two-year graduate assistantship appointment at MSU. With no other job prospects, I decided to enter graduate school as a full-time student. I was relieved that my next two years were essentially covered. Although I was still not committed to attending graduate school, the prospect did provide a certain amount of certainty in my very uncertain life.

It is important to note that none of these opportunities were created through my own efforts. On my own, I was unable to acquire a job. I always felt that my excon status prevented me from getting on with my life. These gifts were provided by my professor at MSU. They could have been given to other people rather than me. My "spoiled identity" did not prevent me from receiving these positions. Once my foot was in the door, I was able to demonstrate that I could do the work that was required.

GRADUATE SCHOOL

My first year of graduate school was a surreal experience. I breezed through the course work, completed the comprehensive exams, and collected the data for my thesis within the first year. My status as an excon was known by the entire faculty (I had been an undergraduate in this same department before my incarceration) and other graduate students.

I was also asked to speak in a variety of criminology and sociology courses, so it appeared as if everyone at MSU knew who I was and about my history. It also seemed as if my past was viewed in positive terms; my prison experience was presented as a life experience that all could learn and benefit from. My "bad boy" reputation even helped me get dates with women. This was the kind of year that an excon could only dream of with all of these opportunities falling into place and my criminal status actually working for me.

Toward the end of the first year, I felt that I had accomplished all that I could at MSU, and that it was time to move on. I was encouraged to apply for Ph.D. programs. I figured that I was still unemployable, and that going to graduate school would further distance me from my time spent in prison. Fortunately, I was admitted to Iowa State University (ISU) and awarded a teaching assistantship. I moved to Ames to continue my graduate education. Five years later I received my Ph.D. in sociology and was back on the job market.

Graduate school was a wonderful experience. It is so unrelated to the real world. The intellectual atmosphere is accepting and supportive of a wide range of people, beliefs, and values. I had a great cohort of graduate students, many of whom I continue to stay in close contact with. In addition, the faculty at Iowa State was supportive and continued to reassure me that I was on track and that my criminal conviction would not be an issue in the future. After all, for someone who studies deviance and social control, my prison experience would likely be treated as a positive factor. Both my professors and I were soon to learn differently.

After my fourth year of Ph.D. studies, and upon being officially designated as "All but Dissertation" (ABD), I decided to test the academic job market. Although the sociology employment market had been fairly tight, there were quite a few advertised positions for assistant professors with concentrations in criminology and deviance. I applied for 25 positions, many of which appeared as if they had been written for me. Unfortunately, I did not make the short list for any of these openings.

I couldn't understand what was going on. My grade-point average was nearly a 4.0. I had prepped and taught four different courses on my own, as well as having served as a teaching assistant in four other classes. I also had presented a number of conference papers and had a book-length manuscript under review with the University of Chicago Press. My professors consoled me by saying that my ABD status was not helping my job prospects.

I still had another year of funding left at ISU, so I remained and continued to work on my dissertation. I finished collecting my data and began the writing process slowly but surely. October through February was the time when most of the open faculty positions for the following year are advertised. I began to apply for every position that I might fit, as well as some that I didn't. I applied to 45 schools for assistant professor positions. Finally, things were starting to look up. When I attended the Midwest Sociological Society annual meeting in March, a number of criminologists from different universities told me their departments had been discussing me as a possible hire and had me on their short list (three to five persons to interview). They were sure that I was going to be offered campus visits and I would be in a position to choose between job offers.

I was surprised when nothing happened. Then, I was shocked when two other students in my Ph.D. cohort were offered positions and I couldn't even get one campus interview. It was generally thought that I had the stronger vita —more teaching experience, conference papers, and articles under review. I wondered what was going on here. We started doing some comparisons among the three of us. We all had experience in the criminal justice system. One of the persons in my cohort was African American, so it is possible that affirmative action was playing a role, but this individual also had a refereed publication that I did not have at the time. One person was a former prison guard, another had previously been a police officer and probation officer, and I was an exconvict. None of us had degrees in hand, but we were all scheduled to defend our dissertations. This was the first time that I actually began to wonder about my excon status and whether it was affecting my ability to get a job in my chosen profession. I also discovered that two of my references had mentioned my excon status in their letters on my behalf. They believed that this was a positive attribute and played it up. It appears that was not the best strategy.

ASSISTANT PROFESSOR

I had learned something important about the academic hiring process. Being an excon is perceived negatively by many people, even in a relatively liberal discipline such as sociology. I decided that I needed to manage this status differently. I was no longer the crown prince looking for a job. Rather, I was more like a pariah, someone to be shunned.

I was finally offered a tenure-track position at Pittsburg State University (PSU) in southeastern Kansas. Needless to say, I was not their first choice. In fact, PSU called ISU trying to hire one of my graduate student cohort who had already accepted a job. Once they found out that he had been hired by another university, they asked the department chairperson if there was anyone else available. I was recommended, so PSU invited me down to Kansas for a campus inteview. Let's face it, they were desperate. After a brief interview I was offered the job. I put off accepting it for as long as I could, hoping that a better-known university would finally call. They never did and I moved to Kansas.

Upon arriving at PSU, I immediately went back on the job market, but with a different strategy. The faculty at PSU were very supportive of me during my one year there. I just couldn't conceive of myself spending my life in Pittsburg, Kansas, teaching eight courses a year. Meanwhile, one of my PSU colleagues confided in me that he had a friend who was on the faculty of a larger university that had previously shown some interest in hiring me as an assistant professor. It turns out that I had been their number one candidate until it was learned that I was an exconvict. Once that happened, my stock dropped drastically. So, I decided to ask my academic references to rewrite their letters of support, and delete the information that identified me as an excon. I had learned the risk of raising this issue in their letters of recommendation. If they were asked about it in person or on the phone, then they could talk about my exconvict status in a positive way.

This new strategy worked. I had a Ph.D. degree in hand, was sitting on a tenure line at PSU, and was getting offers to interview from a variety of universities. Something interesting took place during one of those interviews. Faculty in the know had a hard time raising the question about my status. And of course, I never knew who was in the know. So, faculty who were unaware of my ex-con status would raise a question about how I got interested in doing prison research, and I did not know if that was a "trick" to see if I would divulge my excon status. Therefore, I was always confused and unsure as to what to say. Ultimately, I ended up telling them the truth about my criminal background, and generally surprised some of the faculty. I also learned later on that my status was an issue that was discussed before I was offered the positions, and that in all cases, the departments felt obligated to inform the administration.

I was offered tenure-track employment at Marquette University. This was a joint appointment in their sociology and criminology programs. What I was not aware of was the faculty warfare that was going on between these two disciplines, that eventually I would be caught in the middle, and that my excon-vict status would become an issue. Having decided to guard my excon status, I only revealed my personal history as necessary for research endeavors and within the academy, but I would not share it in the classroom or with the general public. I wanted to be in control of who knew. What I discovered, though, is that I had been publicly "outed" before my arrival on campus.

When I arrived at Marquette University that summer, and I met returning students as well as alumni, I was often greeted with a phrase that went something like this: "Oh, you're the one. I think that it is great that we have someone like you in the program." I was stunned by this and had no idea of how to respond, other than to say "thank you."

ASSOCIATE PROFESSOR

Later, as my career at Marquette developed and I was preparing to go up for tenure, I was informed that some senior faculty members, who were very critical of me, were spreading the word that I was inappropriately using my excon status to curry favor among the students and glorify my prison experience. This, of course, was not true. Since graduate school, I had always been reluctant to discuss my personal history. Unfortunately, some of my colleagues were not nearly as concerned about protecting my privacy. So, these less than positive faculty observations were included in my tenure file, and I will never know what role they may have played in my tenure denial (which was later overturned after I hired an attorney).

CONVICT CRIMINOLOGY AUTHORS
IN THIS VOLUME

Part of relearning how to act on the outside involves learning how to cope with a spoiled identity. The stigmatized individual must determine what information about himself he will convey. According to Goffman (1963), information control is particularly significant for persons who are able to "pass." This need to control information about personal history will affect the types of relationships he develops, as well as his concept of self in these relationships (Adler and Adler, 1989).

Goffman implied that stigma is the primary factor in determining the nature of all social relationships. He suggested that the motivating force for all behavior is to reduce tensions and/or to withdraw attention from the stigma, thus establishing the most favorable identity possible. This can be accomplished by employing one of the following three coping strategies. First, the exconvict can hide or mask the stigma by applying for and receiving a pardon. This would certainly minimize the degree to which the stigma would intrude upon and disrupt interaction. Second, he/she could develop mastery in areas that might ordinarily be considered closed to someone with this character blemish, such as going to graduate school and earning a Ph.D. And third, one could call attention to his tainted past and use the stigma for secondary gains. The remaining section of this chapter will focus on these latter two coping strategies for managing a spoiled identity, which have been used by many of the exconvict authors contributing to this book.

Convicted felons leave prison knowing that life ahead of them will not be easy. According to one of the exconvict professors appearing in this volume:

> I am a man with limits caused by my identity and there is no way that I can overcome them. I will attempt to get a job in academia. I will use the "cover" of academia to make a living, knowing full well that if my name comes up surrounding a controversial issue—I will be the issue. Only through time and good work do I stand a chance to become active in policy matters.

Another author explained:

> Humiliation and degradation have no limits in the criminal justice system, and when I thought about and planned for the day of release, I did not perceive it as a day of gaining liberty in the free world. Freedom is a tenuous thing, especially for those labeled as felons, no matter how much time passes. Credibility is permanently lost in the eyes of those who are in positions of judgment. I saw the upcoming day of release from prison as the beginning of a struggle to live in the outside, and I know better than anyone that I had no idea how to live in the ordinary world.

So, planning for the future goes beyond finding a job and a place to live; it also involves the expectation that there will be people who will judge you on what you have done in the past, not on who you are or what you are doing in the present.

Awareness of a spoiled identity is common to all exconvicts. How one chooses to manage this identity varies from person to person, and from situation to situation. One question to face is under what conditions one should reveal one's deviant status. One convict criminology associate, not appearing in this collection, wrote about the discrimination she suffered in a sociology master's program:

> I am faced with the decision of whether to reveal the status when applying for Ph.D. programs. Disclosing information here has elicited a reaction I would classify as close to shunning. Disclosure reveals more about the recipients of the information than it does about me. . . . My presence here has been tolerated, just as the presence of blacks here is barely tolerated. The question that I have struggled with . . . is when and to whom to reveal my prior status. Even a good friend or employer can hurt me in their well-meaning desire to help me.
>
> I am applying to Ph.D. programs between semesters. I don't plan to openly divulge my status. There is no need or purpose. Some individuals will know and some will not. I'll be damned if it isn't hard to figure out who should and who shouldn't. But when there is a chance of someone else being affected negatively by it, I tell.

Captured in these quotations are sentiments of uncertainty over when and what to reveal about oneself. On the one hand, exconvicts are aware of the potentially negative reactions if they reveal the deviant status, but they are also cognizant of the moral element involved in not revealing under certain circumstances, like when a friend goes out on a limb to support them. At the heart of managing a spoiled identity is trust, something that inmates have not had a great deal of experience with while incarcerated.

This convict criminology author demonstrates that appearances can be deceiving:

> I have learned that it is not so much what people say to your face as what they whisper behind your back. The problem was the "goody-two-shoe" few who had lived sheltered lives and found my convict background difficult to accept.

For still another member of our group, the decision of when or what to reveal was made for him, as is shown in the following excerpt:

> I refuse to accept that I am stigmatized by the official misdeeds of a government. I am the wronged party and I want everyone to know what the criminal justice system does and why. Of course, my federal probation officer said that I had to inform any employer of my status and prior conviction so secrecy was never an issue.

In this case, having the government decide for you under what conditions you must reveal your deviant status removes one burden in the decision-making process.

Nevertheless, how one goes about revealing is still left up to the exconvict. Another author in this book adds:

> I have used no strategies. When I enrolled at the University [as a Ph.D. student], I informed every instructor that I had, that I am an excon. I am now teaching four classes at the University and my students, when

informed of my background, are amazed that I am an excon. I firmly believe that all but the most right wing professor believe in my innocence. In other words, the criminal justice system is paying every day for this mistake and I will not go away.

Regardless of the strategy chosen, most former prisoners realize that they are going to need some help in making it on the outside. Generally, the assistance is unsolicited and comes from unexpected places. This author reveals how he was helped by academics:

> I do not suffer from the illusion that I have pulled myself up by my own bootstraps. I am one of a very privileged few who happened to encounter the most humane and generous people in a [academic] community. Jobs were offered so that I might make a living, and people were generous with themselves and their time.

One of the interesting aspects of convict criminology is the informal support provided by group members. This individual was an adjunct instructor before going to prison, and while in prison he received visits from one of the exconvict professors who had mentored him:

> In prison, I spent most of my time thinking about how I was going to make a living on the outside. I had it set in my mind that I could no longer write with any authority and certainly not be able to teach again. The only reason I am finishing my doctorate now is because of the support I received from one of the convict criminologists. He convinced me that I could both write and teach again.

Professors in this book have mentored numerous prisoners, literally from prison into graduate school and through graduation. A number of the recent Ph.D. authors in this book are the "academic children" of the more established professors. Convict criminology continues to grow as exconvict graduate students join the group.

The following letter to Steve Richards shows another aspect of mentoring or assistance that has been offered to help former prisoners with problems that they are having in the free world:

> I am writing to you in the hopes that you may be able to help me with a problem. I am aware from attending ASC [American Society of Criminology] conferences that you are a convicted felon and might be able to offer some valuable advice. I am currently completing my dissertation and have applied for a few faculty positions. I have recently been hired very briefly for two positions. That is until I advised the deans that I served time in various federal institutions. One of the deans stated that he admired my candor, but could no longer offer me the faculty position. The other lost his ability to converse intelligibly and sent a letter stating that I was originally offered the position in error. . . . Perhaps it would be better if I did not disclose my [prison] record?

The answer is that although exconvicts are not obligated to reveal their felony record when applying for academic positions, they should do so before signing an employment contract. Failure to do so will only create future problems with colleagues. The difficulty is that no matter who is informed (dean, department chair, search committee), exconvicts cannot control the flow of information, including who may remain uninformed or misinformed. Despite the best intentions for full disclosure, the information may not be shared with everyone in the workplace.

Once the exconvict is established in the profession, he takes on a new identity as professor. This metamorphosis requires many years of hard work. This convict criminology colleague shares his insight:

> Now, 14 years out of prison and a recently tenured professor, I find it more tedious to have to explain my excon status to people who keep their own history hidden. I was a convict, then a graduate student, and now a professor. I dare say that the Dr. title cuts the stigma.

The convict, like every other Ph.D., has devoted many years to completing graduate degrees, overcoming many disadvantages. This may contribute to the exconvict becoming an exceptional university colleague. At the very least, they know well the value of higher education as a medium for personal transformation.

Exconvict professors may be especially talented at teaching across several related disciplines. They have firsthand knowledge of inequality, disadvantaged groups, deviant worlds, and how the criminal justice system operates. This experience with police, courts, jails, and prisons provides them with the ability to teach many different courses. One convict professor writes:

> I continue to employ my excon status in the classroom and my academic research. Over the years, I have taught courses in sociology, criminology, criminal justice, corrections, community corrections, and law enforcement. I dare say, my students learn more than what is read in the standard textbooks or journals.

A number of the convict professors whose writing appears in this book are popular instructors who teach lively courses. Their real-life adventures provide colorful insight and spirited commentary, which challenge students to question their own deep assumptions and stereotypes about criminals and convicts.

For example, few students know that felons are subject to a long list of employment restrictions (Richards, 1995a: 62–72, 1998: 127–130; Richards and Jones, 1997). Many occupations and professions are closed to exconvicts, and felons are routinely barred from both corporate and government positions. Universities remain one of the few places that remain open to hiring exconvicts. A convict professor employed at a state university writes:

> I still enjoy the surprise of students when they learn that their professor is an excon. I tell my students, as a felon, I cannot vote, teach school, or get an occupational license. I cannot even be bonded to work a cash register

at McDonald's. But a felon doesn't need a license to be a professor, just a Ph.D.

Fortunately, universities remain committed to inclusion, equal opportunity, and lifelong learning.

The criminal justice system arrests, convicts, and imprisons millions of people. Despite all of the sophisticated compilation of criminal justice statistics, we have no adequate estimate of the number of Americans that are now felons. Over the years, especially the last 20, as the drug war intensified, millions of people have been "felonized." Today, any crime that carries a possible sentence of "year and a day," or more, is a felony. We now have a growing number of student felons that require our attention and support. A contributor to this volume shared his experience:

> I have a number of students who are excons, some still on parole, who feel a measure of support in my presence. I have come to see us as an "invisible minority," a growing army of former prisoners who will no longer hide silently in the shadows. Damn it, there are millions of us. The "proof is in the pudding" (Marx) and not in Goffman's analysis of strategies to "manage a spoiled identity." The drug war incarceration of millions of Americans has felonized so many people that spoiled identity is an archaic concept.

This final excerpt is a call to arms. In many respects, it is meant to inspire successful exconvicts to come forward and challenge existing policies that hold ex-prisoners down and prevent their successful reentry into the free world.

CONCLUSION:
THE MORAL OF THIS STORY

In our desire to manage the personal image presented to others we attempt to control how our exconvict status is represented. Still, we are not always able to maintain control over what others learn about us. So, each exconvict must decide when, and with whom, to share his or her personal history. And, if he does not, someone else might do it for him. In addition, laws may force us to reveal our status whether we want to or not. And obviously, there are consequences that follow whatever decision is made.

In many ways, this is the hardest essay that I have ever been asked to write. It could be said that I am one of the more reluctant members in the convict criminology group. I am still extremely wary of outing myself, of pronouncing to the world that I am an excon and I am not ashamed of it. For example, my children and neighbors still do not know this little secret that my wife and I keep. Nevertheless, I know that my experience as a penitentiary prisoner has educated me in criminology and provided insights that inform my research in ways that a textbook education could not. Still, I am also aware of the risks that all the exconvict professors in this book are taking by "coming out" and honestly discussing their personal background.

10

Convict Criminology:
The Two-Legged
Data Dilemma

ALAN MOBLEY

As a convict, I had nothing but contempt for prison officials and legal experts. I hated the whole continuum of spit'n'polish, buttoned-down, public-trough-feeding parasites; from hard-nosed and heavily armed corrections officers, through monkey-suited, no-nonsense administrators, and on to supposedly detached and objective academic desk jockeys immersed to their drawers in criminal justice research. To my seasoned and cynical eye, they were a sordid assemblage of minions and thugs, each groveling for that government paycheck. Such folks were in charge of my life, either through direct commands, institutional rules, or their ability to shape public policy, and I despised them for it.[1] Several years have passed since then, mercifully, and there have been some changes. I am out of prison, and now I am one of *them:* a Ph.D., and a member of the criminal justice academic fraternity.

I am still involved with some of the same dirty issues as when I was a convict, but now I keep my hands clean. I probably do not need to tell you that my new role feels kind of strange, even when I manage to convince myself that I have not sold out to the enemy. It seems that my education and interests have separated me from the people with whom I feel the closest connection, those utterly resilient and somewhat civilized convicts I like to call peers. For better and for worse, I often feel like a new man.

My thanks to Gilbert Geis and Richard Perry for assistance throughout the preparation of this chapter, and to Stephen C. Richards and Jeffrey Ian Ross for often enlightening comments. An earlier version of this paper was presented at the Academy of Criminal Justice Sciences meeting, New Orleans, March 2000.

The point of this introduction is to make clear that I am both an exconvict and a criminologist, and the combination of identities has got me disturbed. Although my career as a professional criminologist is just beginning, already I find it difficult to be simultaneously the one who studies and that which is studied. I do not deny that I belong to both categories, criminal and criminologist; the problem lies in getting the two identities to coexist peacefully. Thus far, my dueling incarnations aim to cancel each other out, like opposite-signed but equivalent numbers in an algebraic equation. Not even mathematical precision can hide the fact that this exercise in dissonance reduces me to nothing. Such an imagining might not be so bad, except I can't take being a nothing anymore. I had my share of that in prison. Now a scholar, I am supposed to be somebody. The way things are going, though, I am concerned that while trying to become a somebody I might turn into someone I do not recognize. My identity demons would be trouble enough if they were purely hypothetical, but they are not. They are material, real, and basic to the writing of this chapter.

The last time an identity question came up I was doing research a long way from home, in northeastern Ohio (Youngstown). I hoped to be perceived as just another visiting scholar, touring a prison, and interviewing prisoners and staff. At the prison in question they didn't know about my criminal record, and I was worried about what might happen if they did. I guess I had been in some kind of denial, because it was just after breakfast and raining hard when the nature of my predicament hit me. I paced the already deeply worn carpet in my roadside motel and contemplated the possible scenarios. If they asked at the gate about my background I could lie, but that might be construed as a felony offense. I appreciate irony, but the idea of getting busted and being sent back to prison for trying too hard to get into one was rather much. The legal technicalities were something of a mystery, an unknown quantity to me, because the Youngstown, Ohio, prison was not typical; it was a private prison owned and operated by a for-profit corporation.

The research was for my doctoral dissertation. Up to that point, my formal studies in criminology had been largely restricted to learning the literature. Becoming familiar with this body of work had proved a maddening experience for me, because sometimes the data in black and white conflicted with my lived experience. Still, my time in graduate school was invaluable. It kept me out of real trouble and I survived five years on parole.

NORTHEAST OHIO CORRECTIONS CENTER, YOUNGSTOWN, OHIO

I selected the Northeast Ohio Corrections Center (CCA Youngstown), for my research because the situation there intrigued me. The institution, although only two years old, had already gone through major turmoil. In the first 14 months two inmates were murdered, six escaped, and dozens more suffered from armed assaults. The company operating the facility, the Corrections Corporation of America (CCA), had a record of serious mishaps at its prisons across the country (Mobley and Geis, 2000; Austin and Irwin, 2001: 85). They claimed to be doing something new at Youngstown. I had spoken to staff members and learned that the company was apparently turning things around by shipping out the most risky prisoners and bringing in some excons as counselors to work with those who were left.

Personally, I was encouraged by the presence of excons at Youngstown, although I knew that any legitimacy conferred on them was not likely to be meaningful for my position. The number of ex-offenders working at the prison was modest, and they had to endure background checks, comprehensive training, and periods of probation. I spoke with one of them on the phone when I requested a guided tour. I was tempted to reveal my background then, but something told me that if I came clean I would have no chance of getting inside.

I still had an hour to kill before my appointment at the prison, and that left plenty of time for me to reminisce about my prison years. I remembered that at first I was especially bitter, and that I hated having "tourists" come around and stare. It made me feel like a pornographic exhibit trapped behind mirrored, one-way glass. When they looked at me I knew what they saw and I felt unclean. I was reminded of who I was and where I was. Sometimes I would get angry and I would stare back at them until they turned away. I finally structured my day so that the tourists completely passed me by. Even the women. Especially the women. I didn't want to see them or let them see me.

It had been demeaning to fall under the gaze of "free people." Now, the shoe was on the other foot, but the fit was no better. Now, I would be doing the looking, the probing, asking the questions. How could I do what I had come to do without giving offense?

The rain had slowed some by the time I arrived at the prison. The skies were gray, the landscape monotonous. The Mahoning Valley had been home to some of the largest steel mills in the world and the damage left behind from their operation was apparent (Lynd, 1983; Bruno, 1999). The earth was either torn up in the haste and waste of boomtown construction or pounded down by the weight of massive trucks and heavy machinery. The trees and plants showed the ill health that comes from ingesting industrial pollutants. Now the steel plants were closed, shut down, but the environmental devastation remained.

I was greeted warily at the control center, but no new questions were asked. My escort was notified of my arrival. I was issued a visitor's badge, had my belongings searched, and I passed through a metal detector. I met an assistant warden and the captain of security and eyeballed a few secretaries. My host was the manager of the new experimental housing units, and he was an excon. He said he spent most of his adult years as an inmate in state prisons in the South. He was in his late 40s, African American, wore a white shirt and a conservative tie, and appeared to be a very busy man. I asked him how it felt getting a paycheck from the same people who kept him chained all those years. He answered with an ambivalence I could respect. He said that his goal was to change the lives of inmates. If he had to "lay down with lions to do it, so be it."

As we passed through the stainless steel grills that form security choke points, I felt off balance in the way that pressurized airliners sometimes make me feel. This place had the formidable quality that moves some visitors to wonder if once inside they will be allowed to leave. I understand that fear of being enveloped. In terms of sheer mass, a well-built institution is as weighty as a parking structure and as animated as a deserted morgue. Everything just settles. I felt the strangeness, but then I just let it go. If you can relax and surrender to the rhythm of prison, the place itself will take care of you. The walls are straight and tall, the floors usually clean, and all the tiles point in the same direction. Guards or cameras and squawk boxes are positioned at convenient distances from one another, offering passersby the security and peace of mind of a roadside call box system. It's hard to get lost.

It was something else that confused me. I strode alongside my excon escort, but I could not decide whether to act the convict or the criminologist. He obviously was quite removed from the convict mentality, having already spent a number of years in corrections administration. And academic criminology meant little to him, because he saw himself as a "man of action," a no-nonsense practitioner "with little time for talkers." His heavy drug use had led him into a life of crime, but he "was fortunate" to have done time in a drug treatment program. After his release he worked as a substance abuse counselor in a community halfway house before landing a job with the state department of corrections. He was recruited to the Corrections Corporation of America by another excon, the founder of CCA's drug program.

We rounded a corner and I caught my first glimpse of guys in funky yellow jumpsuits. I thought I was ready for the sight of prisoners, but it was like encountering quail or jackrabbits in the wild; they were like a different species, and so self-conscious. They seemed to want to melt away from the sight of me. They stiffly acknowledged the unit manager and briefly glanced my way. There was a curiosity and a challenge to their look, but what I mostly saw in their eyes was a jumble of anger, excitement, fear, and desire. I recognized something there that made me recall when I first got out of prison. I wanted to take in the whole world with my eyes. Everything different had value for me after all those years of the same. My attentiveness gave me a certain presence. Some women in particular liked the intensity, but most people found it odd and intimidating. Now I knew why.

But these guys were not like me; they were still inside, locked up, and not at liberty to stare. Hard looks might elicit rebukes from supervisors, though when you are inside you try to stop yourself from doing a lot of things, staring included. You try, but you can't help it; something within you strains to peer beneath the surface of everything, because surfaces are all you have and they are not enough. Hard, shiny surfaces sharp with edges, points, and meanings. The effort to see is an exertion, a physical act that requires energy. You notice its buildup and release. When you realize that *desperation* is what that fuels your involuntary looks, and you consider the source of that desperation, that is when it all comes flooding in on you; where you are, what you are, who you are. You feel shame, anger, defiance, self-pity, and impotent rage. All come zigging in toward your heart then zagging out at whomever or whatever instigated the whole messy chain reaction.

Entering the prison as a visitor put me in the position of a reluctant sadist. I felt like the nurse who pulls adhesive tape from a hairy patch of skin. There is no easy way to do it; no avoiding the fact that for the patient, the prisoner, it's going to hurt. Being merciful means being businesslike and getting it over with, fast. Up until then I'd really downplayed the hurtful part of my trip. I was caught up in the drama of my return to prison and, to a lesser extent, in my research. I now knew what I was sparking in those guys just by being there. There's always a price to pay for everything, but for my research, it was the prisoners who would be covering the costs.

I remembered that prison is about pain, and in a way that makes it the opposite of sensation's end, of death. The pains of imprisonment come from all you've lost and all that you can't have. It's a compacted, intensified life. Perhaps that's why prison is so often aligned and juxtaposed with death. Not because it's a debased way of life hardly worth living, but because it's a painfully intense life whose only relief, or respite, lies in death. The other kind of release, the legal one, seems totally out of your hands. Just thinking about it brings on another dose of the blues.

CCA THERAPEUTIC COMMUNITY

The convicts I was to see were participating in a drug program called "Lifeline." It's the CCA version of a therapeutic community (TC). Therapeutic communities are not uncommon in correctional settings, and in the topsy-turvy, double-speak world of prison their purpose is arguably therapeutic. In some facilities, however, there is reason to believe that "drug treatment" may be little more than a euphemism for "inmate management." That is because prisoners enrolled in the TC are kept apart and do not ordinarily mix with the "regular" population. Their days are dominated by group counseling sessions and a wide-ranging schedule of anti–drug abuse education. In this way the time of TC participants is carefully controlled and managed. The Lifeline TC is especially noteworthy within the CCA Youngstown context for its fiscal frugality. Low-wage earning excons contribute to cost savings while serving in positions of trust and authority.

Like many privates prisons, CCA Youngstown is dogged by high employee turnover rates and staff shortages. Low payrolls help keep the facility under budget, but are problematic in maintaining adequate inmate supervision. Employing more, lower paid, supervisors gives administrators a bigger bang for their human resources buck. Excon graduates of TC programs are remarkably well suited for CCA staff positions. Their generally low level of employability outside prisons, and their high level of commitment to the TC program model, eases recruitment problems, minimizes training needs, and permits prison administrators to stay within budget targets.

The Lifeline unit is structured as a collective, with inmates encouraged to look upon one another as "family." Prisoners are held individually accountable for their actions, but TC rules stress each person's duty to the others. Individual responsibilities entail *watching* each other in addition to *watching out* for one another. Prisoners who witness rule infractions are required to report them to authorities. Applying writer John Edgar Wideman's (1984) memorable phrase, TC members serve as both "brothers and keepers."

If "innovations" such as the TC permit private companies to build and run prisons that turn a profit, the corrections world will take notice. The costs of incarceration may come down as public facilities move to emulate the successful privates. Programs such as Lifeline could signal the start of a trend. If so, I wanted to be there and see what it was all about.

Entrepreneurs in Action

CCA Youngstown is a medium-security prison, and I took some comfort in that. All of the places I served time in were medium-security federal prisons. Youngstown is an example of a new type of prison constructed to fit the realities of today's corrections industry. The facility's similarity to many federal prisons was news to me but should have come as no surprise. The place is stocked with prisoners from the District of Columbia. Congress ordered D.C.'s own prisons closed by late 2001 and appointed a federal trustee to oversee the shutdown. The trustee, a former Federal Bureau of Prisons warden, monitors the transfer of prisoners from District to federal control, and he supervised the moves to Youngstown (J. Clark, 1998).

My research would entail an analysis of what went wrong at Youngstown following the arrival of D.C. prisoners. I also wanted to examine what might now be going right. I hoped to poke some holes in the conventional wisdom about criminals doing time, and along the way maybe even put to rest a few personal demons.

My Convict Credentials

One of my goals in this chapter is to provide a personal context. I think that your insights will be deepened if I allow you fuller access to mine. Toward that end, I offer a brief history of my criminal career time in prison, but I am unsure how to proceed. I can "stick to the facts," but I doubt that will be enough. Facts provide a reliable chronology of events, but facts alone do not convey much insight.

Not long ago, I received a telephone call that brought back some of my old life. I will let it set the stage for details of my criminal existence. I am at home on the phone listening to my friend Ron:

> "I'm so proud of you, man. You finished your Ph.D. and settled down and now you have a kid. They couldn't hold you down." He inhales deeply, then boils with anger: "They made you do 10 years and you shouldn't have done a day. You're a goddamn hero."

Although we live just a few miles apart, Ron and I have spoken only once or twice in the past five years. We used to be friends of a sort. Our relationship was based on the business we were in, the cocaine business, and I imagine the friendship persists in large part because we were arrested by federal agents on the same case.

Ron doesn't get around much now. In fact, he has hardly moved at all in 15 years. The arrests went down all over town, and when the feds got him they shot him in the back with a 12-gauge shotgun. It was your standard predawn raid and they caught Ron asleep. They rousted him from bed, dragged him onto the floor and cuffed his hands behind his back, using a plastic sure-lock strap. He was on his knees with his face pressed into the carpet when they shot him. The police shooter was cleared of all wrongdoing and Ron was sentenced, while tied to a gurney, to 15 years probation. The courts refused to grant him any monetary compensation for his injuries.

Although I was glad that Ron called, it scared me to talk to him. I think that shotgun blast affected more than just his body. All he talks about is 1984. It's always 1984. That is the year one lifetime ended for us and another began. Ron is stuck in time and in place, and that is why it was such a coincidence that he should call. I'd been thinking about our federal case and was having a hard time organizing my thoughts.

The "facts" are that I sold cocaine for five years, got busted when I was 24, and was sentenced to 45 years in federal prison. I did 10 years behind bars, five years on parole, and I owe the Internal Revenue Service $7 million. Various civil penalties remain in effect for life.

You might be wondering what living the life of a drug lord (albeit a lesser lord), getting convicted, and doing time have to do with my evaluating prisons. I think I understand such skepticism because academic pursuits usually separate life events from one another so that they appear isolated and self-contained. They say the disciplines do this to assure a more rigorous analysis. The irony is that everything in existence is always linked and fluid, so that holding things separate is a gross distortion of reality, not a simple magnification of it. I credit my life experience for giving me a broadened perspective.

Prisons: Inside/Out

Much of the prison literature refers to prisons as "total institutions" (Goffman, 1961), places sealed off and utterly divorced from the reality of the "real" world. This view has it that the memories and experiences, the cultures and very lives of prisoners never make it inside the walls with them, but fade like dreams at the prison gates. John Irwin, one of the first convict criminologists, put to rest that piece of mythology many years ago (Irwin, 1970). His research revealed how prisoners bring their pre-prison selves into prison with them. People immersed in the subculture of the professional thief, for example, carry their skills, ethics, and loyalties onto the prison yard. Preincarceration identities serve as markers to help prisoners recognize one another and organize themselves into protective groups.

Likewise, when a prisoner's time is up and he or she leaves the institution, the break is not total. Values, attitudes, and prejudices learned in prison remain. High rates of recidivism complicate things by making it difficult to distinguish prison-learned characteristics from either pre-prison or postrelease personas. For some groups in society, the revolving door between prison and the outside seldom stops spinning. For them, separating "prison" culture from "street" culture makes no sense. Prison is an integral part of their lives. Irwin's work notwithstanding, the myth about the hermetic prison experience lingers, both in the literature and in scholarly discourse. I tend to agree with the old saying, "Wherever you go, there you are." I think it applies to researchers, too.

I had all sorts of ideas about prison before I was put into one. I saw prison as an ending, as a sort of suspended animation or ceremonial death. My ideas changed once I got there. For one thing, I didn't die. As much as my heart, mind, and soul suffered, life went on. Sometimes I would awake early in the morning certain that I would die of a broken heart that day. But no, the organism doesn't work that way. The heart beats, breathing continues, you get up and start your day.

I'd been a professional, a cocaine kingpin, and getting over myself was hard. Right from the start I got "respect." Ours was a high-profile case with much media attention, so when I got to the prison yard most everyone knew who I was. I was the guy who ran one of the (so-called) largest drug operations on the West Coast.

Prison is about stripping you down and making you feel worthless, and over time it works. Maybe you break down and start to believe what they want you to believe (that you need them for everything), or maybe you persevere, and put up an inspired resistance (like Rubin "Hurricane" Carter). Either way, or any way in between, the system doesn't care. Once you are caught inside the machine you go along with the program or get chopped to bits. Either way, you are changed forever.

I fought the system for a while. I lied to staff every chance I got, so that I would be an accomplished liar, should I ever need to be. I stole whatever and performed my work assignments to the absolute minimum level of my ability. I watched staff to assess their habits and vulnerabilities, and I planned escape. But, the whole thing fell apart for me about four years in. We had just lost our last criminal appeal when word came that the trial court had restructured my sentence to allow for the possibility of early parole. The unstacking of my sentences didn't guarantee anything, but my sense of optimism seized on the news, and I found myself planning for release. It might not come this year or next, I reasoned, but it seemed inevitable. At least, I knew I would not have to do 45 years.

I'd been fighting, but then they offered me a carrot and I bit. It's typical, and why the system almost always wins. They have the weight of incarceration on their side. It is perpetually there, pressing against you, and it controls you by provoking a response. I could have rejected their advances, stayed strong, maybe even escaped. The system would have sent out its agents, of course, and they would have searched in their steady, methodical way, eventually tracking me down and recapturing me. It's possible that I might have lain low enough and moved slow enough to evade them. But then what would have been the point of escape?

Either way, no matter what I did they had me, and knowing it did me in. Around this same time there was an incident that brought home even more the reality of my situation. Some low-life got into my locker and stole my safety razor and blades. I was livid. Maybe the scumbag didn't know who I was, but I would show him. I wanted to hurt him or have him hurt, but both avenues to revenge had their risks. I decided against involving anyone else and waited for my chance. One day I was out on the track running miles when I saw him. He was walking up ahead of me, oblivious to my presence. How easy it would be to swing by the weight pile and snag a 5- or 10-pound plate. I could crash it upside his head as I ran past, and that would be that.

I didn't do anything. I am not sure if it was the guard towers or the prospect of getting turned in by a snitch, but I just ran on past. My pride was hurt, but it made me think. I started to get over the idea that I was superior and impregnable, and I avoided more time and a transfer to a maximum-security penitentiary. What had kept me out of maximum in the first place was my age. The feds had a rule that says you can't be designated to a maximum-security United States penitentiary unless you are at least 26 years old, are considered violent, or are deemed an especially high escape risk. All I had against me was the length of my sentence. I knew that as long as I stayed clean in the joint I could avoid the madness of the higher security institutions.

COLLEGE EDUCATED
IN FEDERAL PRISON

So, I swallowed my pride, steered clear of trouble, and was nothing special in prison. I fell in line, became a model inmate, and chose schooling as my primary "programming." My first prison was the Federal Correctional Institution (FCI) in Texarkana (TX). There was a college program for an associate's degree run by the local community college. I took classes in the evenings and tried to stay out of the heat and humidity that gripped the place during the day. Two years later I was transferred to a relic of a prison called FCI La Tuna, located near El Paso (TX). Not only was there no college, there was not a blade of grass on the yard. Nothing but sun, sand, and rock.

I took a correspondence course in geography from Utah State University, and studied Spanish on my own. Friends within the overwhelmingly Latino inmate population helped me with pronunciation and vocabulary. I learned enough to eventually earn 12 units of college credit.

My big break came when I was transferred to Colorado. FCI Englewood is located in the Denver-Boulder area, so going there was a sort of return to civilization. A college program that offered a full load each semester was just getting started. I enrolled in classes and asked the adjunct faculty to proctor my correspondence courses and equivalency exams. Within five years, I completed a bachelor's degree in economics and a master's in sociology. For my master's fieldwork I went no further than my own backyard, conducting a participant observation study of a men's medium-security federal prison. It was my first fieldwork experience and it was incredibly powerful. Looking closely at where

I was and at the people around me helped me to see past the labels and explore the depths of whole human beings.

The education paid off in more ways than one. The federal judge who sentenced me heard about my degrees and reduced my sentence to time served. That meant an immediate release, and it came right at the 10-year mark. I am writing this now because of that man and his apparently high regard for education. Do not let anyone tell you that schooling doesn't pay.

Most of my college bills were paid with federal Pell Grant money, money that doesn't exist for prisoners anymore (J. Taylor, 1992; J. Taylor and Tewksbury, 1998; see Tregea, this volume). Congress took away the funding because legislators dread appearing soft on crime. At the same time, they do not mind saving money at prisoners' expense. Today, I doubt there are many places like FCI Texarkana or FCI Englewood, where the prison staff extend themselves and their resources to help educate the prisoners.

BACK TO CCA YOUNGSTOWN

I learned a lot in prison, but it seemed that for the toughest problems, the available wisdom was never enough. Lucky for me there were some correctional workers dedicated to helping me help myself. When I spoke with the guys doing time in CCA Youngstown, I wondered just who was going to help *them*. Their unit manager was sincere enough in his desire to assist them in kicking dope and finding satisfaction within. But, I'd just come from D.C. and had seen the neighborhoods where most of the unit's "crew" had lived. They would be going back to the same ghetto streets. How would their newly acquired skill in positive thinking stand up under the pressures of the "hood?"

Convicts like those at Youngstown know that the deck is stacked against them, and are aware of an American history of steady oppression. After all, a full 98 percent of D.C. prisoners are African American. I had no such knowledge of the underbelly of America when I went to prison. I am white and middle class, and was raised to believe that criminals go to jail, achievement is based on merit, and that I can be whatever I want to be. My prison experiences have shown me the gaps in the American Dream. I have seen up close some of what we as a people have done, and what we have to overcome. If criminology is going to do any real good, we will need to reinvent it. To do so requires that we come to terms with its beginnings.

CRIMINOLOGY
AND "THE WHITE MAN'S BURDEN"

Criminology, like sociology (the discipline with which it is most commonly associated), has its origins in anthropology. American criminology, in fact, was first known as "criminal anthropology" (Rafter, 1992). Anthropological knowledge has long been a valued tool of government. Ethnographic descriptions were integral to the colonial expansion projects of European nations from the eighteenth to the twentieth centuries. Anthropologists were commissioned to venture into "native" lands and collect data on the ways and practices of inhabitants. Scholars then used this information to compile a body of knowledge on a variety of human cultural practices (see Foucault, 1970). This so-called neutral knowledge was also used by state agencies as "intelligence" to manage and control subjugated peoples.

This conflicted legacy of serving two masters—state power and the ivory tower—still haunts both anthropology and criminology. Some criminologists continue the quest to build an objective body of knowledge regarding illegal behavior, while others have turned to more practical objectives in what Donald Cressey called "an attempt *to do something* about crime" (Sutherland and Cressey, 1978).

THE POWER TO NAME

Naming and grouping individuals into value-free aggregates is at the heart of our political economy. In nominally democratic countries, people are called upon to make choices, the results of which may be reflected in social policies that influence the distribution of resources. The way we choose often corresponds to our identification with certain groups. From the voting booth to the supermarket checkout stand, we typically make choices according to who we think we are. From "Banana Republic" to "Republican," from "Coca-Cola" to "Greenpeace," building and retaining brand loyalty is everything in the struggle to control the marketplace, whether of political power and ideas or of consumer products.

What we now call the social sciences began in earnest on the European continent during the Enlightenment period. Classic books, from Steven Jay Gould's *The Mismeasure of Man* (1981), to Michel Foucault's *The Order of Things* (1970), inform us that a principal aspect of the European Enlightenment was to impose order on the chaos of the natural world. An important part of this ordering entailed the naming and categorizing of all manner of things. Plants, animals, insects, and even homo sapiens were divided into categories based on common characteristics. Over the next few centuries taxonomies were refined with scientific precision. Deviant human constructs included "the savage," "the criminal," and "the hysteric."

Many human categories, such as "race," are now understood to be spurious. Human qualities formerly seen as permanent and essential have been unmasked as fully constructed cultural products. The concept of "savages," for example, was created to stand in opposition to "civilized man," the figure Europeans thought that they embodied. So too the "hysteric," almost always a female, was placed opposite the superior "rational gentleman." The "criminal" was made to personify "the citizen" gone wrong. In short, those with the power to name could declare who they were by showing who they were not.

Recent changes in "anthropological knowing" have been instigated by people who were once themselves objects of scientific scrutiny. Stereotypes have been shattered as minorities, women, and colonized peoples have won the right to represent themselves in the arts, sciences, and government the world over (Ashcroft et al., 1989).

This volume may be "another first step" in the debunking of faulty theory about prisons and crime. At the same historical moment that exconvicts are earning the chance to "write back" at those who categorize them, however, social scientific fields of inquiry are moving away from experience-based knowledge. For some time, in fact, "real," substantive knowledge and insights on social phenomena have been devalued in favor of aggregate conceptualizations. When I began my research at CCA Youngstown I had to accept that my findings, whatever they were, would largely be seen as second-rate science. My choice to use qualitative methods, to go and talk to people about contemporary social control, runs against the grain of today's criminology. Unfortunately, today it is not an exaggeration to say that criminology is all about the numbers.

SHIFTING PARADIGMS: ABSTRACT EMPIRICISM

Research detached from actual "people" has meant the elevation of abstraction as the guiding concern of social research. Our terminology reflects this reality. Talk of "research subjects" has replaced references to "social actors," and "populations" have superseded "subjects." Individuals are regarded as collections of risk factors, traits, and even nascent attributes. It is thought that if computer models can calculate the combinations of traits and environmental factors productive of crime, the process of criminality might be reversed. Not only has what Mills (1959) termed "abstracted empiricism" permitted researchers a more orderly, professional existence away from the "geeks, freaks and perverts," but the relative comfort of the lab has permitted a larger number of people to engage in criminal justice research. Announcements for academic positions in the social sciences often carry the line: "proven ability to attract external funding a plus." This caveat advances the chances of quantitative analysts whose work traces the government funding agenda.

SOUND BITE SCHOLARSHIP AND THE COURT OF PUBLIC OPINION

In graduate school I learned that the father of American criminology, Edwin H. Sutherland (1924), once admonished the discipline to look at "the criminal" as "a human being rather than as a concept." This dictum has not taken root in today's research world, where much of the basis for expert authority has shifted from experiential knowledge to technical proficiency. In the 1960s and 1970s concerned thinkers such as Mills (1959) and Gouldner (1968) bemoaned the rise of statistical analysis and its tendency to create cold abstractions from the flesh and bone of human lives. Today's "techno wizards" are not only the "number crunchers" who dominate professional journals, but also agile word smiths skilled at generating fodder for a ravenous media machine. In criminology, where so few real solutions to persistent problems are forthcoming, the multifaceted complexity of the issues is daunting. Professional competition and a desire for coherence can lead to simplistic sound bite scholarship.

Recent years have seen some leading researchers gain much attention by warning of a coming generation of "superpredators."[2] These respected academics advised police officials to combat future crime by targeting young men of minority ethnicity and urban origin. New laws were passed, civil rights restrictions were put into place, and prison building intensified.

The academics' predictions have proven wrong, yet the criminal justice infrastructure they helped to create continues to operate at a staggering level of bureaucratic efficiency (see Austin, this volume). It is today's prison–industrial complex. Young men like those at CCA Youngstown are the raw materials of this industry.

DOING SOMETHING ABOUT CRIME

In the field of prison studies, "doing something" usually means evaluating correctional facilities with an eye to making them work better. What makes for a good prison? Safety and security for all concerned, surely, but one of my convict interviewees put it this way: "A good joint is one with plenty of dope and a lax visiting room. You know, where you can get laid."[3] Clearly, ideas about improving prisons vary depending on whom you ask. My authentic, albeit facetious quote is meant to illustrate how one "expert's" improvement is another's nightmare. The complexity and contentiousness involved in prison reform has opened the way for the rise of a new emphasis in corrections: money.

Today, the good prison is a cheaper prison, and financial matters have come to dominate discussions on imprisonment. My first reaction to reports of cost cutting, consolidation, creating economies of scale, contracting–out, and outsourcing was to cringe in horror. Prisons have always been big business, but now they are being absorbed by Big Business. Initial shock has given way to a more thoughtful approach, however, and prison privatization is now my leading research interest. To my surprise, I am finding that cost-centered penology may encourage us to see that making better prisons may mean completely unmaking prisons as we know them. The form to come, however, is far from certain at this point.

PRIVATIZATION AND THE PARADOX
OF ENTREPRENEURIAL PRISONS

The return of prison privatization is often cast as a solution to the corrupt and inept public administration of prisons. Governing bodies are said to be "too mired in red tape" to make meaningful changes. A major shareholder in a vate prison company put it this way: "If we in the United States are to meet the challenges of an increasingly dangerous and sophisticated criminal client, we had better do it right. In this land, founded as it is on free enterprise, our best bet is the private sector."[4] Private corrections companies aim to do the same job as their public counterparts, only at less cost.

The tendency to expand corrections posed by the privatization movement has attracted the attention of stalwart prison foes, who oppose any attempt to expand the prison-industrial complex. These determined and often eclectic folks typically support moratoriums on prison construction and see any prison as a bad prison. Such organizations include the long-established Citizens United for the Rehabilitation of Errants (CURE), American Friends Service Committee, and the more recently formed Prison Moratorium Project and Critical Resistance groups.

Privatization campaigns have led to the formation of political action coalitions comprised of startlingly strange bedfellows. Of these, none is so strange as the sometime alliance between conservative, free-market privatization hawks and liberal abolitionist doves. What points of commonality could there be between people advocating the improvement of correctional institutions through privatization and those seeking to abolish prisons altogether?

The thinking behind this troubled convergence is downright Machiavellian, driven in no small part by the high financial, ethical, and emotional stakes held by all involved. One depiction of what is happening includes a pragmatic means-to-ends argument. It goes like this. Private prison owners and their sponsors embrace support from any quarter because they see it as consensus building and legitimating. The better entrenched in the public mind they become, the easier it will be to expand portfolios, increase revenues, and generate profits. Entrepreneurs therefore have extended a cautious welcome to traditional reformers by suggesting that privatization itself is the latest phase of progressive prison reform.

Abolitionists usually stand on the other side of the correctional spectrum. They abhor prisons, yet under the proper circumstances, they might be willing to endorse private corrections in order to break the stranglehold public prison bureaucracies have on power and resources. After all, the last 15 years have seen the largest prison expansion in U.S. history. The first order is to weaken the traditional prison operators. After that is accomplished abolitionist groups can turn against the newer kids of the block, the privates. The recent financial mayhem engulfing some private prison corporations provides a strong argument that deficiencies inherent in the private systems will cause many of these companies to self-destruct, bringing antiprison activists that much closer to their goal.

Another rationale for the curious alliance between social policy hawks and doves stems from the pragmatic character of today's entrepreneurial brand of corrections. Wardens who must act as businesspeople, as well as bureaucrats, might be motivated to put "customer service" first and provide better amenities to prisoners. A corrections strategy of appeasement makes sense, considering that a warden's primary concerns are local. Being a good neighbor within often isolated, rural, communities means running a prison that provides jobs, buys services, and perhaps most important, stays out of the news.

Improving the conditions of imprisonment is just one goal pursued by reformers with wide-ranging networks and national agendas. Remember that abolitionists believe that prisons should be changed in a fundamental way or even eliminated because they are dehumanizing and do not meaningfully contribute to the rehabilitation and social reintegration of offenders (CURE, 2000). The die-hard prison foes realize, however, that corporate prisons may have more incentive to treat prisoners humanely than does the state. This incentive does not arise so much from a desire for "repeat customers" as from the experience that peaceful, contented prisoners are less expensive to manage.

State prison systems have shown themselves to be expansionist, arrogant, and often neglectful of prisoners' rights. In the face of such conditions, the logic continues, money-minded prison managers might as well be given a chance. If prisons must exist, it's better that they be run by people motivated toward peace, whatever the underlying basis for the motivation.

It is paradoxical that both capitalists and prison reform activists have found common ground around the realization that it behooves prison operators to treat prisoners with dignity. Similarly, both sides now agree on the importance of rehabilitating the image of prisoners from sound bite degradation (see Ross, this volume). Stories and press releases coming out of private prisons tend to emphasize efforts to rehabilitate prisoners. Recent examples include the widely announced inauguration of large prison therapeutic communities by two major prison corporations (PR Newswire, 2000). Portraying prisons and prisoners in a gentler light also serves the privates' immediate interests, because much opposition to locating private prisons has centered on local residents' complaints against the importation of violent out-of-state inmates.[5]

The warm welcome given to CCA by the city of Youngstown was quickly withdrawn following the disturbing troubles of 1997–1998. Local labor leaders complained about their inability to organize the CCA workers. Law enforcement officials decried the corporation's lack of accountability and poor or nonexistent efforts at communication. Citizen groups protested the placement of rapists and murderers near schools and residential neighborhoods. That the D.C. prisoners were being used as currency, as dollars and cents, was easy to see, but the wave of protests against the prison showed that the commodification had gone much further. Various groups within the community were now using them to pursue moral, political, and ideological agendas as well. I was soon to be next in line, using them to build a career.

CONCLUSION

Criminology is a curious business, and it is not clear where, or if, the convict criminologist fits in. There are several difficulties. The norms of academic discourse discourage the personal. Some professors forbid their students use of the first person altogether, and permit themselves only the plural form. This "we," often referred to as "the royal we," is indicative of the traditional scholarly stance. Scholars are positioned as detached, yet never alone. They stand upon the shoulders of those who went before, writing not as individuals, but as representatives of certain disciplines and master conveyors of a particular body of knowledge. Individual scholars do make contributions to this textual body, but, ideally, personal advancement in any guise is beside the point. The purpose of scholarly work is not self-fulfillment or expression, and certainly not self-knowledge.

To the extent that most scholarly discourse is reflexive at all, it is as a means to an end, a question of methodology. A discussion of methods is central to a discipline like criminology, yet our concern is primarily, once again, as a means to an end. The end under pursuit is expected to be a clearer understanding of the phenomena under study, a portfolio usually said to include crime, criminals, and societal reactions to both. Throughout the decades and the various theoretical epochs, our subject matter has invariably remained something "out there."

The situation of a convict criminologist is much different, as he or she is both speaking subject and object of study. As subject, the authority of the convict criminologist is almost certainly called into question, as he or she clearly lacks credible objective detachment, having "gone native"[6] as a convict long before succumbing to the lure of the academic fraternity. The convict criminologist's claim to the profession thus faces a perhaps insurmountable a priori challenge. Further frustrations await us. Objects of scientific scrutiny are usually frozen in or across time. Through our scientific ingenuity a myriad of life factors is held constant so that we may assess the separate effects of each upon the predicament of interest. The convict criminologist, however, knows from experience that everything happens at once. The effort to unearth the complexity of decisions and circumstances resulting in crime, and from crime, is fragile, and appears undermined by standard methodologies, pushing answers ever further away.

As a speaking subject, the convict criminologist is atypical of criminological objects of study. With rare exception, criminals' voices are muted not only by scholars but by every aspect of the criminal justice encounter. Our American adversarial system of justice all but requires that defendants allow their representatives to speak for them. Following conviction, criminals are legally held incommunicado in a number of jurisdictions. Even when convictions are overturned after many years, such as in the justly celebrated case of "Hurricane" Carter, human subjects other than the accused are credited with principal agency.

The ability to speak and be heard is not the only problem with the convict criminologist construction. The former convict is no longer a convict, but an exconvict. This point may seem of little consequence, as the main aim of convict criminology is to include in the conversation the voices of those experienced in the "customer end" of the criminal justice system. Yet, I consider the distinction an important one. Those of us who emerge from prison after many years know the unsettling sensation of finding ourselves separated from our friends and concerns. People with whom I shared nearly everything lost their immediacy to me almost the moment I stepped outside prison walls. I was shocked by the sensation, but it was there, real, undeniable. Even as I knew in my innards that I was no free man, I was no convict, either. Not anymore.

Any pretensions I had to authentic convict status disappeared when I reentered prison as a researcher. I found that the prisoners operated on a wholly different frequency than either myself or staff, and I recognized the feeling. I was one of them once, but no longer.

The legitimacy of the convict criminologist's claims to special knowledge is thus challenged on both ends. Inclusion within the profession is made only tentatively, at the margins. As for being a prisoner and possessing all of the insights of the imprisoned, well, the convict criminologist does not. The position is separate, neither here nor there, though perhaps through the little understood mechanics of remembrance some of the insights of our former selves may remain. Still, it is doubtful that both subject positions can be fully assumed at once.

Exconvicts can be excused from a desire to hold onto "benefits" accruing from their master status as convicted felons. In this society it is for the most part "once a felon always a felon," and the disadvantages of that are real enough. Criminology itself has helped to build the boxes that constrain ex-felons, but a bitter reading is not at all what *convict* criminology is about. Readers might note the ambiguity in the italicized term, as "convict" can be read as a noun, adjective, or verb. Sometimes I have trouble deciding which usage I prefer, but here the emphasis belongs squarely on the first syllable.

I remain hopeful regarding the field of criminology. As more "two-legged data" (individual researchers) enter the profession, their experienced voices will be heard. Perhaps then the discipline will grow more sensitive to the plight of the men and women caught in the web of the criminal justice machine and professional ethics will preclude the use of dehumanizing methods and language (Richards, 1998: 142–143).

Academics may employ pernicious tactics to garner attention and promote the profession, but they come at the expense of those that have already paid a high price for their transgressions. The law may define "outlaw" social groups in order to demonize and vilify them, but it is shameful for a profession to gain influence by relying upon and perpetuating such harms.

NOTES

1. Among the academic fraternity of criminal justice professionals I am happy to report some exceptions. The work of John Irwin, Todd Clear, and Richard Quinney were particularly encouraging.

2. Three prominent criminologists who have received widespread media attention are responsible for making false predictions about juvenile crime waves. These conservative prophets of doom are James Q. Wilson, John DiIulio, and James Alan Fox. Their predictions have not come true.

3. Interview (1999), Youngstown, Ohio.

4. Interview (1999), Washington, D.C.

5. I am indebted to anonymous activists on both sides of the privatization debate in Youngstown, Ohio, for their help in constructing this analysis.

6. "Going native" is an ethnographer's term signifying a loss of scientific objectivity from becoming overly intimate with the subjects of one's research. The term originated during the time of colonial domination and was pejoratively applied to colonizers who mixed with the colonized in an undignified fashion.

PART III

Special Populations

As most of the contributors imply, prisons are populated by people like you and me. This population mirrors free society, including persons with unique needs, for example, women, medical patients, mentally impaired, students, and children. Special populations are discussed in six chapters.

In "Understanding Women in Prison" (Chapter 11), **Barbara Owen** outlines critical issues that address the consequences of the enormous increase in the female prison population. The experience of women prisoners has long been ignored by researchers and policymakers. Why are so many more women being incarcerated? To answer this, demographic characteristics, pathways to imprisonment, as well as public policy and its specific impact on women must be examined. The elements of these women's lives that may have led them to prison include abuse and battering, economic disadvantage, substance abuse, and unsupported parenting responsibilities. Because many of these women are poor, are from minority communities, and behave in ways outside middle-class sensibilities, prison has become the uniform response to problems created by inequality and gender discrimination. The upward spiral in the number of women convicts represents a serious failure of conventional society and public policy.

Women prisoners have been damaged by the oppression of patriarchy, economic deprivation, and the far-reaching effects of such shortsighted and detrimental policies, for example, the war on drugs and the overreliance on incarceration. Women confined in U.S. prisons are enmeshed in a criminal justice system that is ill equipped and confused about handling their problems—the issues that brought them to prison and the dilemmas they confront while incarcerated.

Although men too have suffered under these policies, the social sciences have not addressed the gendered nature of imprisonment and the consequences of public policy in any concrete fashion. Feminist criminology aims to bring these gendered issues to the fore of public and academic debate in describing the critical concerns of women prisoners, who are victims of the new "get tough" incarceration policy.

Daniel S. Murphy's "Aspirin Ain't Gonna Help the Kind of Pain I'm in: Health Care in the Federal Bureau of Prisons" (Chapter 12) argues that the Federal Bureau of Prisons (FBOP) operates a symbolic medical care system. The FBOP provides minimal health care services in federal camps, correctional institutions, and penitentiaries. Prisoners complain of medical neglect, malpractice, and indifference, resulting in improper treatment of both chronic and critical illness, and unnecessary death.

As the federal prison system grows, overcrowding and graying of the prisoner population create new problems. The result is a growing number of medical prisoners. What are the alternatives? What do federal prisoners suggest needs to be done to improve medical services? How might home incarceration increase the quality of health care provided prisoners, and at the same time reduce the financial impact upon the FBOP? What is the role of compassionate release? These questions are answered in this chapter.

Bruce A. Arrigo's "Convict Criminology and the Mentally Ill Offender: Prisoners of Confinement" (Chapter 13) explores how mentally ill convicts experience transcarceration as they are routinely transferred between prisons and mental health facilities. This method of processing individuals has profound effects on how disordered persons are identified with and assume the role of prisoner. These mentally ill people become part of the systems they are repeatedly channeled through, and in the process, they unknowingly reify the legitimacy of their involuntary participation in transcarceration. As a result, not only do they live roles as both "bad and mad," they are also powerless to free themselves. Mentally ill offenders become prisoners of confinement; that is, they figuratively and literally become hostage to a process that restricts their role performances, leaving little room for them to renegotiate their identities.

This chapter investigates how the activity of transcarceration renders the mentally ill person a prisoner of the confinement process. Particular attention is directed toward the field experiences of the researcher, coupled with the life stories of selected psychiatrically disordered prisoners. Both theoretical and practical dimensions of this phenomenon are considered. The author concludes by speculating on the future research and policy implications of convict criminology for the mentally ill prisoner.

William G. Archambeault, in "Soar Like an Eagle, Dive Like a Loon: Human Diversity and Social Justice in the Native American Prison Experience" (Chapter 14), examines the complex issue of human diversity among America's native peoples and its implications for understanding the difficult adjustment of these people to prison. He also presents a typology of Native American prison roles that illustrates the multidimensional issues involved, which may serve as a basis for future research.

This chapter focuses on the continuing struggle of Native American prisoners to practice their historical, cultural, and religious traditions and to follow their own moral consciences. There is no typical Native American. Neither is there a quintessential prison experience for Native American prisoners. Current government law and correctional policies fail to recognize the differences that exist among native peoples. Consequently, centuries-old patterns of ethnic and religious discrimination continue to be visited upon them, especially those in prison, where such patterns are exacerbated by a void of substantive research about the incarceration of Native Americans.

In "Twenty Years Teaching College in Prison" (Chapter 15), **William S. Tregea** reviews the current research on and trends in U.S. prison education programs. Many prisoners have literacy problems and have not graduated from high school. Today, most labor markets require advanced skills training and postsecondary education. Yet, the majority of prisons offer only adult basic education (ABE) and general equivalency degree (GED) study, and they have eliminated higher education programs.

Do prison college programs work? Numerous studies suggest that prisoners that complete college courses have a lower rate of recidivism. What qualities in program design work best, when, for whom, and why? Tregea concludes his chapter with a discussion of recent political coalitions working to secure postsecondary education programs for prisoners.

In "Kids in Jail: 'I Mean You Ain't Really Learning Nothin [Productive]'" (Chapter 16), **Preston Elrod** and **Michael T. Brooks** discuss the history of jails as the most commonly used correctional institution in the United States. Indeed, the jail is usually the first, and in many cases, the only experience that many people have with incarceration. Not only are jails being used to house

adults suspected of or convicted of a variety of crimes; they are also being employed to hold increasingly large numbers of children, adolescents, and juveniles. This trend is the product of several factors, including, in some states,
legislation that has lowered the age of criminal court jurisdiction, the transfer
of increasing numbers of juveniles to adult courts for trial, and the continued
placement of juveniles in adult jails.

Despite the increasing use of jails for both adults and adolescents, relatively little
is known about jail prisoners in general or adolescent prisoners in particular.
Who are jail prisoners? What are they like? Where do they come from? How
do they experience jail? What services do jails offer? What unique problems do
children encounter in adult jails? This chapter examines the jail from the perspective of those persons who live or work inside. The authors explore the social policy implications of our increased reliance on jails as a crime control and
correctional strategy.

Stephen C. Richards and **Jeffrey Ian Ross** conclude the book in "An Invitation to the Criminology/Criminal Justice Community" by summarizing
the main themes discussed by the contributors and tying the diverse strands together. They invite scholars, researchers, and concerned citizens to join them
in developing not only a new school but a heightened consciousness or social
movement called convict criminology. The task is to write criminology that in-
corporates the experience and perspectives of persons who have been processed
through the criminal justice machinery. Embedded in this objective is to go beyond ideal types and theoretical constructions and to challenge the overuse of
imprisonment.

These chapters build upon existing research but have the added benefit of ethnographic research primarily conducted by insiders, convicts, or exconvicts.
This gives voice to those who may be excluded, minimized, or marginalized in
academic discourse. At the same time, it provides an opportunity, as well as an
invitation, to our colleagues to expand their existing thinking about research
and policy options. It is not a time to retreat or withdraw. It is a time to speak
out, to make a difference.

11

Understanding Women in Prison

BARBARA OWEN

Troy Duster, one of my professors in graduate school, once said, "Scratch an ideology and find a biography." As the chapters in this book attest, many of us came to study the prison community through a personal, rather than an objective, pathway. I became involved with the study of women's prison through a circuitous route, without much early planning and preparation. In the first part of this chapter, I describe this winding road. The second section outlines my understanding of female incarceration and provides some ideas about how women come to prison in ways dramatically different from those of men. I also describe how women do their time in ways distinct from those found in a male prison. As I have argued in *In the Mix* (Owen, 1998), imprisonment is a gendered experience. As the next paragraphs detail, my career as a student of the prison also has been gendered, shaped by my role as a middle-class (and middle-aged) white woman, and a vested interest in the status of women in society.

As an undergraduate, I had plans to become an art historian and had no concept of prison beyond what was manufactured through popular culture (see Ross, this volume). In my second year of college at the then Fresno State College, I was volunteering in a youth center and became briefly involved with a man who (unbeknownst to me) was on the fast track to prison. Although this first liaison was short, his appearance in my life ultimately shaped my future

Appreciation is due to my friends and colleagues who assisted in the development of this chapter: my road dog and research partner, Barbara Bloom; my husband, Vince DiCiccio; Valerie Johnson; Brian Powers; and Bo Saylor. The editors of this volume also deserve mention for their attention to detail.

work. By the end of my sophomore year, I had changed my major to sociology and transferred to the University of California at Davis. When I arrived there, my friend had begun his long career with the prison system, beginning with a stint at the California Rehabilitation Center. By my senior year, my convict friend was doing his second term at Vacaville prison, waiting to be processed and sent on through the California correctional system. He wrote and asked me to visit. I was unsure about this, but felt that since Vacaville was not far from Davis, it would be rude not to go.

This first visit was a critical experience for me. Entering a prison for the first time was overwhelming. It is hard now to reconstruct all the reactions, but I do remember being struck by the size of the facility and how people were divided on either side of the bars into a free world and a captive one. The visit was unsettling—both seeing my friend behind the visiting room glass and confronting the reality of human beings confined in prisons.[1]

This exposure to the institution changed the direction of my studies and put me on the winding path to studying women in prison. In the master's degree program in sociology at San Francisco State, I first met John Irwin and the next critical juncture in my development as a student of the prison. Irwin taught me that research on the prison had two dimensions: epistemological and political. First, I learned that the study of prison itself was indeed a legitimate enterprise. In many academic arenas—then and now—the study of prisons is not held in high esteem. Although high-level theory once addressed the problems of incarceration, most mainstream sociology does not consider the prison as a legitimate area of concern. Most prison research takes place in criminology or criminal justice departments where, even there, the study of prison subculture is largely out of fashion.

Irwin's teachings legitimized both a substantive area and a methodology. First, quantitative research and its magical statistical power have long been held as the true standard for social knowledge, but Irwin is a qualitative methodologist who believes in asking questions of individuals on their terms. As part of a small but vocal minority of scholars, Irwin demonstrated to me that there was indeed power in documenting the worldview and the meaning-systems of social actors. Qualitative description and inductive reasoning continue to be, in my view, a more honest and direct way of studying the social world. Both Irwin and his wife, Marsha Rosenbaum, taught me that ethnography is the better way to understand deviant worlds.

Second, Irwin taught me that the study of the prison could combine advocacy with scholarship. I saw how he mixed his personal experience as a convict with political activism and the use of empirical data to work for social change. When first exposed to his work with the American Friends Committee, I began to understand how empirical research could be paired with the political desire to change an oppressive system.[2] Though I was slow to grasp this lesson, and did not openly address advocacy issues until more recently, it is a lesson that shapes the way I now frame research and its implications.

At the end of my time at San Francisco State, I got a part-time job at a community college teaching a course on social problems to prisoners in Vacaville.

My second exposure to the prison world was as a very inexperienced instructor. I do remember joking that I was assigned to teach a course about social problems to social problems. My memory of that class is not clear: it was small, with about five or six men who were fairly well prepared to take an introductory course in sociology. I don't recall that any one person was highly politicized, but I do remember that it was a lively group.

After completing my M.A., I entered a Ph.D. program in sociology at UC Berkeley. Here too Irwin influenced my work as I passed through the stages leading to the dissertation. I was also very lucky to study with several people in the Berkeley sociology department who shaped my perspective: David Matza, whose brilliance shaped my understanding of subjective experience; Troy Duster, with a sophisticated take on politics and organizations; Arlie Hochschild and her teachings on the self and social psychology; and Michael Burawoy, with his perspective on political economy and ethnography. I am not sure these scholars would claim me as a student, but I am grateful for their contributions to my education. My work was also influenced by friends in graduate school— Brian Powers, who taught me more about qualitative methods and the importance of social structure in producing individual perspectives, and Terry Arendell, who continues to shape my views on gender issues, feminist methodology, and qualitative research.

While at Berkeley, I knew I wanted to study prisons, but I didn't have a clear sense of focus. As I was looking for a dissertation topic, my convict friend arrived at San Quentin. Again, geography dictated my behavior. I went to see him at this facility and, in reconnecting with him, I also saw a selfish opportunity to become involved—in a very small way—with the prison world through the visiting room. I can remember how puzzling it was to think about doing prison research. I recall the frustration of not knowing how to access this world and how to gain entry to a place I wanted to study. For me, taking the role of a visitor seemed to be a first step. My personal life and my academic interests melded together as I visited for two years. My first ethnographic attempt described the prison visiting room and began to focus on the correctional officer world through the brief contacts I had with the staff assigned there. Once again, my relationship with my convict friend placed me within the prison world and here I was to stay.[3]

My dissertation (and first book) rose out of this third exposure to corrections. I somehow decided on extending the work on prison subcultures to the occupational world of the correctional officer. After a long delay, I was able to get permission from the California Department of Corrections. With the support of a National Institute of Justice graduate fellowship and the ongoing influence of Irwin's sociological imagination, I wrote about how correctional officers developed a worldview that was grounded in prison culture (Owen, 1988).

Following my Ph.D., I spent a year at the Alcohol Research Group in Berkeley (conducting a study of parole violators) and taught for a short time in Washington State. I then received a call from a manager at the Federal Bureau of Prisons (BOP) who was interested in my work with prison staff and invited me to apply for a research position. After a lot of red tape, I was hired as a research analyst and assigned to work at one of the federal men's prisons in southern California, FCI-Terminal Island.[4]

Along with my introduction to the personal aspects of imprisonment and my academic education, my time at the BOP was instrumental for understanding prisons. I spent over a year as the researcher at Terminal Island, and learned more about the day-to-day life of an institution than would have been possible in any other role. I was amazed that I got to go to work every day and experience an environment that is typically closed to public scrutiny. I think I have always been comfortable around male prisoners and became even more so in my time there. I was given extraordinary latitude in the development of my projects. Some assignments were set up by the BOP regional and central offices, but I was allowed to develop my own lines of inquiry. As a staff member, I participated in the institutional disciplinary committee meetings, met with prisoners confined to disciplinary segregation, stood "mainline" in the dining hall (and ate there as well), served as "Officer of the Day," and participated in other activities that gave me a real sense of the institution. Of course, I realize that I was only experiencing this prison as a staff member and not a prisoner. But this job gave me a perspective that few academics can experience and one that I feel has made me a better prison researcher.

In the fall of 1987, I was transferred to the BOP central office in Washington, D.C. Initially I was unhappy about the move but it was ultimately beneficial both in experience and perspective. Working with the BOP office of research was an education in itself. At the central office, I learned how research on a national level operates and was again given a fair amount of freedom to pursue my interests. Under Bo Saylor's tolerant supervision, the qualitative perspective was given equal weight even as he encouraged me (with little success) to develop more statistical competence.

During this time, I had some abstract interest in women prisoners, but, like other prison scholars, I focused on the male prison world. I had written one or two articles about women staff from my San Quentin work (Owen, 1985, 1986), but I hadn't thought about the situation of women prisoners. Even though I considered myself a feminist, women's prison issues were not within my research plans. I now feel embarrassed that I ignored this critical prison population and wonder now how it could have taken me so long to recognize the importance of studying women prisoners. There were lots of reasons—none of them good. Perhaps it was the tyranny of the numbers: the sheer volume of male prisoners has forced policy and research attention to male issues. Maybe it was the location: female prisons are few and far between. Or maybe it was the sociological tradition: with some wonderful exceptions, most scholarship has addressed the male prison.

In most studies, from Clemmer (1940/1958) to the essays in this volume, the male experience has captured the attention of prison researchers. And in some ways this makes sense: historically, men have had a much higher rate of imprisonment, with women prisoners a decided minority. Most sociologists were drawn to the dynamics of the male prison, and most of the research was done by men about men. The inattention of academics to women in prison is mirrored by the lack of concern most contemporary prison systems exhibit toward women as well. In the 1980s, many feminist researchers argued that women in prison had become "correctional afterthoughts." Whatever the reason, little attention was given to the issue of women's imprisonment.

By the time I left the BOP in 1990 and returned to Fresno, now as a professor at California State University, a new phenomenon was taking many criminologists and prison managers by surprise. Although still a small proportion of the total prison population, women were coming to prison in unprecedented numbers. Geography once again shaped my research agenda as a new female prison was built in the Central Valley of California, near my new academic home. The Central California Women's Facility (CCWF) was activated in the early 1990s. It was designed to hold just under 2,000 women. It typically holds almost twice that many. With a colleague, I approached the warden, Teena Farmon, asking for access to her population. I explained my background—as an academic and former BOP researcher—and my emerging interest in women's prison. I further explained that there was little research on women prison populations and I had a particular interest in writing an ethnography that described the ways women do time (Owen, 1998). Some results of this study are summarized in the section below.

I continue to be grateful to Ms. Farmon for allowing me into her prison and opening yet another door to my exploration of the prison. As I was conducting this ethnography, other related projects developed. My research partner, Barbara Bloom, and I expanded the prison work to include surveys of adult women in the California system (Owen and Bloom, 1995a, 1995b), girls and young women confined to the California Youth Authority (Owen et al., 1998), and an analysis of gender-specific issues in the juvenile justice system (Owen and Bloom, 1999).

FEMINIST CRIMINOLOGY

In addition to coming later to the substantive study of women's prisons, I have embraced feminist criminology in mid-career. Although I had read the work of the founding mothers of the perspective,[5] I don't know that I had a fully conscious appreciation of what feminist criminology might mean separate and apart from the default masculine perspective that shapes the social sciences. Fonow and Cook (1990) argued that much of what masquerades as sociological knowledge about human behavior is in fact knowledge about male behavior. In defining the subject matter (male prisons, male-based theories), mainstream criminology also dictates the method through which these issues are studied. The positivistic emphasis on "objectivity" and "value free" knowledge has often been translated into quantitative survey methodologies, hypotheses testing, and statistical analysis. In so many ways, these dominant research methods are masculine: in their emphasis on statistical power, "objectivity," and distance from the subject. In contrast, I began to discover feminist methodology, in which subjectivity and context are critical to a real understanding of the world.

Feminist criminology emphasizes the context of women's lives and examines this with an awareness of patriarchy and its impact on the oppression of women in prison. Just as the lives of women in prison are gendered, so is the study of these worlds. Neilson (1990) argued that women know the world differently from men due to gender segregation under patriarchy and that survival under a male-based system attunes women to the perspective of the dominant class. For me, feminist ethnography strives to document the lives and activities of women, understand this experience from their point of view, and conceptualize women's behavior as an expression of social contexts. By investigating the marginalized and stigmatized context of women's criminalized behavior, a feminist analysis of women's prisons describes the lived experience of women, the consequences of this experience on their sense of self, their relationships with other actors, and the meanings they attach to this behavior. I am also convinced that feminist criminology calls for using research as advocacy and as an instrument of social change in applying research data to improving lives.

This does not mean that only women can study women prisoners; instead, I take this to mean that working as a feminist criminologist requires a conscious investigation of gender and its consequences, regardless of the substantive issue at hand. Men can employ gender as an analytic concept and apply it to the study of men's lives. Feminist criminology also means that research is sensitive to gender on all dimensions. Although for the most part this perspective builds on the philosophy of qualitative methodology, feminist methodology has taught me to be mindful of the larger questions about gender and its impact on the research as well as on the social worlds under investigation.

WOMEN AND IMPRISONMENT
IN THE 1990S

An understanding of women's imprisonment begins with a startling fact. Women —and particularly women of color—have been swept into prison at astounding rates (U.S. Department of Justice, Bureau of Justice Statistics [BJS], 1999). In 1970, just under 6,000 women were incarcerated in state and federal prisons. In 1980, this number had doubled to about 12,000 women. By 1996, nearly 75,000 women were incarcerated in state and federal prisons, with another 52,000 in local jails. By 1998, 84,000 women were imprisoned in state and federal prisons, with another 64,000 in jails. In California alone, the female prison population rose dramatically from 1,316 in 1980 to almost 12,000 in 2000.

The reasons for this dramatic climb in women's prison population continue to fascinate me. Women, like men, have been channeled into prison due to the "so-called 'war on drugs' and related changes in legislation, law enforcement practices and judicial decision-making" that has fueled this remarkable increase in the punishment and incarceration of women (Human Rights Watch, 1996). As a result of the misguided drug war and its punitive consequences, women have become increasingly punished as the United States continues to increase criminal penalties through mandatory sentencing and longer sentence lengths.

Crime rates don't account for the huge upswing in the population of women's prisons. According to the Bureau of Justice Statistics, the crime rate for women has risen only about 32 percent in the last two decades, whereas the imprisonment rate has increased 159 percent (BJS, 1999). Steffensmeier and Allan (1998: 10) looked at crime rates and found that most of this rise is "due to the sharp increase in the numbers of women arrested for minor property crimes, like larceny, fraud and forgery." In addition, they see that "rising levels of illicit drug use by females appear to have a major impact on female crime rates" (Steffensmeier and Allan, 1998: 12). The root of female crime, they argued, is found in the "female inequality and economic vulnerability that shape most female offending patterns" (Steffensmeier and Allan, 1998: 11).

In 1994, Barbara Bloom, Meda Chesney-Lind, and I looked at the burgeoning female prison population in California. We argued then that incarceration rates were driven by more than just crime rates. We suggested:

> The increasing incarceration rate for women in the State of California, then, is a direct result of short-sighted legislative responses to the problems of drugs and crime—responses shaped by the assumption that the criminals they were sending to prison were brutal males. Instead of a policy of last resort, imprisonment has become the first order response for a wide range of women offenders that have been disproportionately swept up in this trend. This politically motivated legislative response often ignores the fiscal or social costs of imprisonment. Thus, the legislature has missed opportunities to prevent women's crime by cutting vitally needed social service and educational programs to fund ever-increasing correctional budgets. (2)

Seven years later, little has changed as the impact of these policies continues to drive female prison populations. There is no doubt that men have suffered as the United States has continued its imprisonment binge (Austin and Irwin, 2001), but it is important to note that there has been a measurable gender-based difference in the rates of this increase. This difference is most apparent among women of color. Mauer, Potler, and Wolf (1999) examined the substantial impact of policy on the involvement of women in the criminal justice system, arguing that drug policy affects women differentially because women are more likely to commit drug offenses. In examining the overall rise in prison population between 1986 and 1995, they found that drug offenses account for about one-third of the rise in male prison population but fully half of the increase in the female prison population. During this period, the number of women incarcerated for drug offenses rose an amazing 888 percent; those imprisoned for other crimes rose 129 percent. This difference is particularly marked in states with serious penalties for drug offenses. In New York, Mauer, Potter, and Wolf argue, the notorious Rockefeller drug laws account for 91 percent of the women's prison population increase; in California, drug offenses account for 55 percent; and in Minnesota, a state committed to limiting incarceration to very serious offenses, drug offenses account for only 26 percent. Compared to white women, women of color are also more likely to be arrested, convicted, and incarcerated at rates higher than their representation in the free-world population (Mauer et al., 1999).

Stephanie Bush-Baskette (1998) made a similar point in arguing that poor women of color have been disproportionately penalized by the war on drugs:

> Although the war on drugs has significantly affected the imprisonment of women in general, Black women have suffered from the greatest increase in the percentage of inmates incarcerated for drug offenses. At the state level there was an 828 percent increase in the number of Black women who were incarcerated for drug offenses between 1986 and 1991. For Black men the change was 429 percent, for White women it was 241 percent, and for Hispanic women it was 328 percent. Both their race and their gender exacerbate their plight. (222)

THE CONTEXT OF WOMEN'S LIVES

Understanding women's imprisonment begins with an investigation of the context of their lives prior to imprisonment. As I have argued previously, three central issues shape the lives of women prior to imprisonment: multiplicity of abuse in their pre-prison lives; disrupted family and personal relationships, particularly those relating to male partners and children; and drug use. Given this background, spiraling marginality and subsequent criminality is a common result (Owen, 1998). Combined with a public policy that criminalizes drug-using behavior, the outcome is ever-increasing rates of imprisonment for women.

Even as more women are incarcerated, the overall profile of women prisoners has remained consistent. The majority of these convicts come from poor minority communities. They have few educational or vocational skills and are mostly young mothers with personal histories of substance abuse, unemployment, physical and mental illness, and physical and sexual abuse (Owen and Bloom, 1995a, 1995b).

In the 1990s, substance abuse played a key role in the imprisonment of women and contributed dramatically to their increasing numbers. Women are more likely to use drugs more often, use more serious drugs, and be under the influence of drugs at the time of their crime than males (BJS, 1994, 1999). In the latest national survey (BJS, 1999), almost half of all female prisoners reported being under the influence of drugs or alcohol at the time of their offense compared to just about one-third in 1991 (BJS, 1994). In the 1997 data, around 50 percent reported daily drug use in the month before their offense, again up from 40 percent in 1991 (BJS, 1994). Almost one-quarter of the 1991 sample reported committing a crime to get money to buy drugs (BJS, 1994), with one-third reporting this in 1997. Clearly, drug use and its impact on life chances contribute significantly to these rising imprisonment rates.

In addition to the damage done by substance abuse, the impact of the physical, sexual, and emotional abuse must be recognized. Scholarship on women in prison establishes this fact: women prisoners have been victimized both as children and adults. Studies consistently report a high incidence of physical, sexual, and emotional victimization in the personal histories of women prisoners, with figures ranging from 30 percent to 80 percent of women having an abusive background (ACA, 1990; Pollock-Byrne, 1990; Owen and Bloom, 1995a; Browne et al., 1999). Violent offenders are more likely to have previously experienced this abuse (BJS, 1999). Owen and Bloom (1995a, 1995b) found that physical, sexual, and emotional abuse is a defining experience for the majority of women in California prisons. In this sample, which included the category of emotional abuse, 80 percent of the women interviewed reported experiencing some kind of abuse. With the exception of sexual assault, most women indicated that they were harmed by family members and other intimates.

In a detailed examination of women incarcerated in New York prisons, Browne, Miller, and Maquin (1999) found that a substantial majority of their sample reported sexual molestation or severe violence in childhood and adolescence. Out of 150 women interviewed, 70 percent reported experiencing severe physical violence from a caretaker. Fifty-nine percent reported some form of sexual abuse during childhood. As adults, their lives were also marked by violence: 75 percent of all women reported a history of physical violence as adults by intimate partners, with 35 percent experiencing marital rape or other forced sexual activity. These women also indicated severe victimization by nonintimates as well. Over three-fourths (77 percent) of all respondents reported that they had been a target of violence by others. Most telling is the finding that, when all forms of violence are taken together, only 6 percent of all 150 respondents did not mention at least one physical or sexual attack during their lifetime (Browne, Miller, and Maquin, 1999: 313–315). Browne and colleagues concluded, "These findings suggest that violence across the lifespan for women incarcerated in the general population of a maximum security prison is pervasive and severe" (1999: 316).

THE CONTEMPORARY WOMEN'S PRISON: PROBLEMS AND UNMET NEEDS

Women in contemporary prisons face a multitude of problems; some result from their lives prior to imprisonment, others from imprisonment itself. Without attention to these issues, they are often released from prison unprepared to manage these preexisting problems, not to mention those created by their imprisonment. Several critical problems are faced by female prisoners, and most are aggravated by incarceration. Three critical problems are discussed here: physical and mental health, substance abuse, and staff sexual misconduct.

Most prison systems are unprepared to deal with the complicated physical needs of women prisoners. Acoca (1998) argued that the enormity of health care issues may in fact eclipse other correctional concerns as the female inmate population continues to grow. She found that the majority of imprisoned women have significant health care problems and most are unmet in the nation's prisons. In addition to having conventional health care needs, imprisoned women are often exposed to infectious diseases, including tuberculosis, sexually transmitted diseases (STDs), and hepatitis B and C infections, as well as HIV. Acoca (1998) found that both risky behavior prior to arrest and inadequate prison health care contribute to this problem. Pregnancy and reproductive health needs are another neglected area of health care. Estimates of the percentage of pregnant women in prisons and jails range from 4 to 9 percent. Acoca (1998) argued that pregnancy during incarceration must be understood as a high-risk situation, both medically and psychologically, for inmate mothers and their children. She noted that deficiencies in the correctional response to the needs of pregnant inmates include lack of prenatal and postnatal care, including nutrition, inadequate education regarding childbirth and parenting, and inadequate preparation for the mother's separation from the infant after delivery.

Mental health disorders are equally ignored. Few studies accurately assess the prevalence and incidence of these needs, but estimates suggest that between 25 and 60 percent of the female prison population require mental health services (Acoca, 1998). Many women are often dually diagnosed, experiencing both substance abuse and mental health problems (National Center on Addiction and Substance Abuse [CASA], 1998).

The vast majority of imprisoned women have a need for substance abuse services, but few prisons provide intensive treatment. And, although most research argues that drug use acts as a multiplier in interaction with criminality (Wellisch et al., 1994; CASA, 1998), prison-based services are rarely available. A national survey of drug programs for female prisoners found that a relatively small percentage of women prisoners in prisons and jails receive any treatment while incarcerated (Wellisch et al., 1994). These findings are supported by a study by the National Center on Addiction and Substance Abuse (1998), which found that women substance abusers are more prone to intense emotional distress, psychosomatic symptoms, depression, and lower self-esteem than males.

Although most women prisoners are, ironically, physically safer in prison than on the streets, sexual abuse and staff sexual misconduct can undermine this feeling of safety (Owen, 1998). Human Rights Watch (1996) found that women in prison also suffer from the inability to escape their abusers. They also argued that ineffectual or nonexistent investigative and grievance procedures and the lack of employee accountability (either criminally or administratively) contribute to this problem. Combined with the lack of any public concern, the authors strongly state that "being a women in US state prisons can be a terrifying experience" (Human Rights Watch, 1996: 1). As Bloom and Chesney-Lind (2000) noted, the sexual victimization of women prisoners is difficult to uncover due to inadequate protection of women who file complaints and an occupational subculture that discourages complete investigation of these allegations.

As I have argued previously, society expects the women's prison to address these problems that result from the devaluation and marginalization of women under patriarchy. Prison is the wrong place to address the issues of drug use and personal violence that shape women's pathways to prison. But in pursuing a policy of increasing imprisonment, American society incarcerates women that would be better served in community settings. The current trends toward criminalizing the survival behavior of marginal women can only result in continued numbers of incarcerated women. As these numbers swell beyond rational belief, the study of women's prison culture becomes increasingly important.

STUDYING WOMEN'S PRISON CULTURE

Once women are sent to prison, they must learn to live in an institution that developed as a response to male prison behavior. Because women's experience prior to prison is different, it makes sense that their reaction to prison will be different as well. The study of prison subcultures involves investigating the way prisoners adjust to prison, the way they learn to "do their time," and the resulting prison social structure. By the 1960s and 1970s, scholars were beginning to study the subculture of the women's prison and found that it was much different from life in male prisons. Three important studies provide an initial understanding of the world of the women's prison. Ward and Kassebaum (1965), Giallombardo (1966), and Heffernan (1972) conducted in-depth investigations of three prisons during the 1960s. These studies found striking similarities: (1) the world of women's prisons was quite different from that of the male culture, (2) prison culture among women was tied to gender role expectations of sexuality and family, and (3) prison identities, to some degree, were based on outside identities.

Personal relationships with other prisoners, connections to family and loved ones in the free community, and commitments to pre-prison identities continue to shape the core of female prison culture. In the many months I spent as an active observer in this world, I too found that women organize their time and create a social world that is markedly different from the world of the contemporary male prisoner. Just as offense patterns are tied to differences between men and women, so is prison social organization. The facts of their lives as women and girls, the pervasive influence of patriarchy, and the limitations created by economic and social marginalization combine with the stigmatization of criminality to create the social context of women's offense patterns and imprisonment.

When I entered CCWF in the early 1990s, I realized that everything I knew about "prison" was based on a male model. At CCWF, I found that very little of what I knew about prisons applied here and I needed to employ different analytic categories in order to make sense of this world. Here, I discuss four elements of this negotiation: (1) becoming prisonized, (2) the prison code, (3) the importance of personal relationships, and (4) "the mix," elements of prison life that shape struggle and survival in the modern prison for women (Owen, 1998).

Becoming Prisonized

In 1994, over half of the women in California prisons were first-timers. These individuals have had little experience with imprisonment and must learn the rules and roles of the prison culture to survive their incarceration. For first-time prisoners, incarceration can be frightening and filled with apprehension. Vanessa, a white-collar, first-time offender, describes coming to CCWF from a county two hours away:

> And it's just when I saw those gates, I said, oh my God I'm going to prison. And it finally set in that I was actually going to be here. And we drove through them and I looked around and I said there's no way out of here, they are going to keep me here as long as they want to. (Owen, 1998: 76)

Once a prisoner gets off the bus, she is "processed" into the prison population. This woman describes her experience as she was introduced to the routine and the impersonal handling that characterizes the modern facility:

> Being processed was like an assembly line. Each person had a job to do, you go in there, you weren't a person anymore, you weren't human anymore, they could care less. About 42 of us came in together. They threw us all in the same room, and we four of us, shower together, it was awful. We were in orange jump suits, with no underwear. For some girls it was that time of the month and one girl had to keep a pad on with a jump suit with no panties on. That's just the way it was. And they don't care. The phrase is always, "Welcome to the real world." (Owen, 1998: 77)

Once processed, women discover that prison is filled with uncertainty. To manage this period, they begin to negotiate routines and strategies that allow them to make a life in this new world. Clemmer (1940/1958) called this process of learning how to do time "prisonization," a process of becoming socialized into the behaviors, values, and worldview of prison life. Learning to live in the prison comes primarily through interaction with other prisoners, and relationships are a critical aspect of this new socialization process. As one woman explained, "Some women are way out of their territory here, they need help from someone who knows what is happening." Newcomers are likely to stumble through their first weeks or months in the prison, as they begin to learn "how to do their own time."

One critical aspect of the prisonization process is establishing a new prison identity. As in male prisons, being respected and having a good reputation with other prisoners is important to the women of CCWF. For old-timers, their past behaviors and being known as an "Original Gangster," or "O.G.," are sufficient to establish a place in the prison social system. Newcomers, on the other hand, may have to prove themselves in the subtle stratification system.

The Prison Code

Women adjust to prison in many ways. These accommodations may change over time, evolving throughout the prison term. One woman may become highly prisonized during her sentence, taking on prison-defined ways of acting and feeling, whereas another may maintain her pre-prison identity and not become attached to the values and culture of the facility. The diversity of the population and the complexity of the many backgrounds brought together contribute to a diverse and complex prison culture. One way of learning how to adjust to the struggle of imprisonment is through an allegiance to the prison code. The code is a set of values that outline the conduct of a prisoner who has few attachments to outside values and is fully immersed in her prison community. Among male prisoners, common values include "Don't be a snitch or informer," "Be loyal to convicts," and "Do your own time." Most "old-timers or "Original Gangsters" still adhere to these rules. Although the male prison code seems to be more rigid and based on super-masculine values, there is some overlap between the prison code of male prisoners and that of female prisoners. As Toni, a 48-year-old woman who has served almost 20 years, commented:

> I still go by the code. I won't have a position where I have to work next to an officer. Now people tell [inform to staff]: they don't have common sense; they think they have street knowledge and don't realize that it is different than prison knowledge. (Owen, 1998: 177)

One aspect of the prison code involves teaching newcomers, or "youngsters," the rules of prison life. Toni tells us how things have changed:

> Well, when I first came, I didn't even know how to act. So many youngsters come to prison and [they think] they are going "to kick it on the yard." Youngsters want to be noticed, to put their stuff out . . . they can be loud and obnoxious . . . I used to tell them [the rules, the code], like not to tell on nobody, but I have given up doing that. Years ago, you just didn't tell; I was taught the old way. It's not like the old days. I learned from the old school, in the 60s. The convicts stuck together, if you went down, you just took it—you didn't bring nobody down with you. "Do your own time"—that was the rule. (Owen, 1998: 176)

Personal Relationships: Families Inside and Out

As women adjust to their imprisonment, they develop friendships and other forms of relationships with other prisoners. One common type is the "prison family" or the "play-family." These are a significant part of the social organization in women's prisons. A woman often learns how to do her time through interaction with these social units, becoming prisonized into the ways of behaving, feeling, and thinking. All previous studies of women's prison have found that women in prison organize in these family-like arrangements, replicating common gender roles on the street (Ward and Kassebaum, 1965; Giallombardo, 1966; Heffernan, 1972). At CCWF, these families developed out of complicated emotional relationships, sometimes based on practical or sexual ties. Families have social and material responsibilities, such as providing friendship and support; celebrating birthdays and holidays; providing food, cigarettes, and clothing; and taking care of a member's possessions when she is transferred out of the unit. Divine talks about the types of families she has observed over her three prison terms:

> There are about five people here who called me "Moms" on the street. I would say this is my play-family. Almost everybody is involved in them in

one way or another. It could just be two people or a bunch. It is just like the family on the streets—you start depending on them. Then there is the loose-knit family. That is just what you call each other, but you don't really care that much about each other. All families do not have women who play the male role—some are based on couples, some on friendship. (Owen, 1998: 136)

Another way women in prison are different from incarcerated men is in the degree of attachment to family and friends outside. About 80 percent of women in prison are mothers, with three-quarters having children under 18 years of age. Lord (1995: 266), a prison warden in New York, has stated that whereas men in prison "do their own time," women "remain interwoven in the lives of significant others, primarily their children and their own mothers." They are tied to the lives of their children during their imprisonment, some through contact with phone calls, letters, and visits, others through emotional attachments unrealized in actual contact. For most incarcerated mothers, being separated from their children is the most painful part of their prison term. Many women do not see their children because of the distance, expense, and other hardships traveling to the prison may cause. Maria, a first-timer serving a short drug-related sentence, described how missing her children affected her:

> Missing them is the hardest thing [about doing time]. I have not seen them since I have been locked up because I do not trust anyone to bring my children here. I have letters and pictures to keep me going. The first 15 months were hard, but the next 10 will be easy because I know I will get out to the gate and see them. (Owen, 1998: 127)

Connections to the free world can make it much harder to "do time," particularly for those who have long sentences to serve. As Divine said:

> You cannot do your time in here and out on the streets at the same time. That makes you do hard time. You just have to block that out of your mind. You can't think about what is going on out there and try to do your 5, 10 [years] or whatever in here. You will just drive yourself crazy. (Owen, 1998: 129)

The Mix

A key element in surviving prison life is negotiating an aspect of prison culture known as "the mix." In its shortest definition, this term refers to one aspect of prison culture that can bring trouble and conflict, both with staff and with other prisoners. The mix is the "fast life" or "la vida loca," or the crazy life, lived while "running the yard" in prison. Becoming involved with the mix can lead to violating the prison rules, developing destructive relationships with other prisoners that lead to fights, and generally getting into trouble. A variety of behaviors can put one in the mix: same-sex relationships, known as "homosecting," involvement in drugs, fights, and "being messy," which means making trouble for yourself and others. As Mindy tells us, "The mix is continuing the behavior that got you here in the first place." For the vast majority of the women at CCWF, "the mix" is generally something to be avoided. Most women want to stay out of trouble and do their time in their own way. The majority of prisoners at CCWF serve their sentences, survive the mix, and return to society, resuming their lives in the free community. For many women, their prison life becomes a time for reflection on the trajectory of their lives. One woman said, "Coming to prison was the best thing that ever happened to me. I know I would be dead if I hadn't been sent here. It has made me stop and think about what I was doing to myself and my kids." As Blue, ending a long sentence for kidnapping, tells us:

> I probably would have been dead if I had not come to prison. I was living too fast and I was too young to be living that fast. I should have been already getting my degree from college, and I should have been getting my life together where I had my own apartment and my own job. Instead, I came to prison. (Owen, 1998: 189)

These feelings notwithstanding, it is important to emphasize the damage of imprisonment, as conveyed in these comments by Morgan, a long-termer serving time for violence in and out of prison:

> Prison makes you very bitter . . . and you become dehumanized. I've been in prison since I was 17. I have been abandoned by my family members, and anyone else who knew me out there. Being in prison forces you to use everything that you have just to survive. From day to day, whatever, you know it's very difficult. It's difficult to show compassion, or to have it when you haven't been extended it. (Owen, 1998: 190)

CONCLUSION

Trying to understand women in prison has led many of us to ask why women are incarcerated in the first place. To answer this, one must examine demographic characteristics, pathways to imprisonment, public policy, and its specific impact on women. The problems that lead women to prison—abuse and battering, economic disadvantage, substance abuse, unsupported parenting responsibilities—have become more criminalized as contemporary society ignores the context of these women's lives. Because many of these individuals are poor, are from minority communities, and behave in ways outside middle-class sensibilities, prison has become the uniform response to problems created by inequality and gender discrimination. These issues are best addressed outside the punitive custodial environment, and the upward spiral in the number of women in prison represents a serious failure of conventional society and public policy. Women in prison have been damaged by the oppression of patriarchy, economic marginalization, and the far-reaching effects of such shortsighted and detrimental policies as the war on drugs and the overreliance on incarceration (Owen, 1998). Under current policy, these complex problems are laid at the feet of the prison by a society unwilling or unable to confront the problems of women on the margin. Women confined in U.S. prisons are enmeshed in a criminal justice system that is ill equipped and confused about handling their problems— the issues that brought them to prison and the problems they confront during their incarceration. The prison, with its emphasis on security and population management and its deemphasis on treatment and programs, is unable to respond to the real needs of women victimized by criminal justice policy.

This is not to say that men are faring well under this system. But, as I say to the dismay of many of my colleagues, I can't worry about the problems of men. Social policy and the social sciences have not addressed the gendered nature of imprisonment and the consequences of public policy in any concrete fashion. I'm quite conscious of the fact that, though I work toward documenting the experiences of imprisoned women, my observations and analysis are dependent on my privileged social position as a white, middle-class woman in a society that marginalizes women without these protective credentials. These gendered issues are brought to the fore of public and academic debate as feminist criminologists continue to describe the issues surrounding women's imprisonment to anyone who will listen. We continue to work toward articulating the intersection of women's issues, public policy regarding incarceration, the need for advocacy, and the need to describe the struggle of women who live behind prison fences.

NOTES

1. I probably need to say here that my friend was not an innocent. He came to crime through an all-too-common avenue—early unsettled years touched by family violence, dropping out of high school, starting early and fast in serious drug use and a developing pattern of sometimes violent crime, addiction, and repeated imprisonment. At last count, he has been imprisoned for at least four different commitments and countless parole violations. He now has emphysema and lung cancer—ironically, smoking will kill him before heroin addiction does.

2. He and Jim Austin have continued this approach in their current work (Austin and Irwin, 2001).

3. I am grateful to him for first bringing me into contact with the convict world and teaching me to look for the humanity in all people—even those whose behavior is unacceptable by my standards. Because of my friendship with him, I like to think that I have an empathetic view of the convict world and can see that those behind bars are people worthy of attention and concern.

4. At FCI-TI, Richard Rison was the warden. The world is filled with irony; later Mr. Rison and John Irwin would be opponents in the free speech litigation involving Danny Martin. I continue to count both as my friends.

5. I have been influenced in this regard by Meda Chesney-Lind, Dorie Klein, Nikki Rafter, Kathy Daly, Joy Pollock, and Jo-Anne Belknap, as well as Esther Heffernan and Rose Giallombardo.

12

Aspirin Ain't Gonna Help the Kind of Pain I'm in

Health Care in the Federal Bureau of Prisons

DANIEL S. MURPHY

Are prisoners' rights to medical care, such as those afforded under the Eighth Amendment, which bans cruel and unusual punishment, being met? Are rights provided by the due process clauses of the Fifth and Fourteenth Amendments being upheld? Are standards of health care established by congressional mandate, Supreme Court rulings, and policy directives contained in the U.S. Department of Justice (DOJ) Health Services Manual being met by the Federal Bureau of Prisons (FBOP) health care delivery system? If we care about the U.S. Constitution, what goes on inside federal prisons should worry us.

Having spent five years imprisoned in two federal medical centers (FMCs), I have substantive experience with the health care delivery system of the FBOP. In these settings, I lived the rationing of health care practiced by FBOP medical personnel, saw the organized denial of medical care provided prisoners of the FBOP, and became intimately familiar with the symbolic quality of health care provided prisoners within the FBOP, which operates with minimal expectation of improving prisoners' health. Discretionary medicine is top-down FBOP policy and what prisoners get instead is symbolic health care.[1]

Issues discussed in this chapter are based upon my experiences while imprisoned in the FMCs, conversations I had with prisoners during my incarceration,

This chapter was originally presented as a paper at the Annual Meeting of the American Society of Criminology, San Francisco, November 2000. I would like to thank Mike Bell, Chava Frankfort-Nachmias, Donald Green, Andrew Hochstetler, Daniel Hoyt, Janet Huggard, Stephen C. Richards, Jeffrey Ian Ross, and Ronald Simons for comments.

and interviews conducted with prisoners since my release. Primary data provides an ethnographic description of the health care delivery system within the FBOP. Qualitative description, the spine of this chapter, brings to life the facade of humanistic health care "provided" sick and dying prisoners. This chapter is intended to replace the myth that those incarcerated are nothing but a bunch of tough guys with tattoos who are lifting weights. They are people, thousands of them, sick and dying in indignation. Although the chapter is meant to describe and interpret the health care services inside the FBOP, its larger goal is to suggest practical alternatives in hope of abating the federal prison health care crisis.

METHODOLOGY

As a convict criminologist[2] I had the opportunity to analyze prison culture from the perspectives of participant and observer. Caged within the razor wire of federal prison, I witnessed and chronicled significant deprivations of "normal" life inherent in the warehousing of human beings: an inadequate health care delivery system, the economic system of the imprisoned, the process of spoiled identity, and the prison as the university of crime. I identify variables of interest, bring the topic to life through qualitative (ethnographic) methodology, and compare observations and interview notes with discussion and descriptions contained in the work of other authors (Cressey, 1961; Irwin, 1970, 1980, 1985a; Richards, 1995, 1998; Richards and Jones, 1997; J. Ross and Richards, 2002). Excerpts from interviews conducted with prisoners housed in four FBOP FMCs (FMC Rochester, FMC Carville, FMC Lexington, and FMC Fort Worth) follow.

Secondary data sources are also included: FBOP policy statements, U.S. DOJ policy statements, U.S. DOJ statistics, U.S. General Accounting Office reports, and information provided by the American Correctional Association.

THE RIGHT TO TIMELY
AND ADEQUATE MEDICAL CARE

The FBOP is a big and powerful organization. As Fleisher and Rison (1997: 327) point out, "Today the Bureau is the largest agency in the U.S. DOJ. It has an annual budget in excess of $2 billion and employs nearly 28,000 staff members" (see also Mobley, Richards, this volume). Does a prisoner confined in the FBOP have the right to timely and adequate medical care?[3] Although it is true that prisoners lose many of the rights they enjoyed prior to incarceration, "the one right that they do retain, under the Eighth Amendment, is the right to be protected against cruel and unusual punishment" (*Bell v. Wolfish,* 1979). According to one of the most famous cases, "There is no iron curtain drawn between the Constitution and the prisons of this country" (*Wolf v. McDonnell,* 1974).

In 1972, a U.S. district court ruled that the Alabama correctional system violated inmates' rights under the Eighth and Fourteenth Amendments by not providing "adequate" and "sufficient" medical care for prisoners (*Neuman v. Alabama*, 1974). In *Estelle v. Gamble* (1976), the U.S. Supreme Court ruled that "an inmate must rely on prison authorities to treat his medical needs; if the authorities fail to do so, those needs will not be met. In the worst cases, such a failure may actually produce physical torture of a lingering death." In *Gregg v. Georgia* (1976), the U.S. Supreme Court ruled that the "infliction of such unnecessary suffering [is] inconsistent with contemporary standards of decency."

Estelle v. Gamble sets forth the "deliberate indifference standard to serious medical need" as the measure to determine whether or not a state [or the FBOP] has breached its constitutional duty to provide medical care. "It was established in *Gamble,* deliberate indifference to serious medical needs of prisoners constitutes unnecessary and wanton infliction of pain" (J. McLaren, 1997: 369–371). The court held that "deliberate indifference by prison personnel to a prisoner's serious illness or injury constitutes cruel and unusual punishment contravening the Eighth Amendment" (*Gamble*).

Courts have defined serious medical need as "a condition diagnosed as requiring medical treatment or one for which the need for medical treatment would be obvious even to a layperson" (*Hampton v. Holmesburg Prison Officials,* 1977, 1976); "highly contagious or dangerous conditions for which treatment is mandated by statute" (*French v. Owens,* 1982); "conditions diagnosed as serious and that threaten substantial harm if not treated or that may result in serious injury when requests for treatment are denied" (*Freeman v. Lockhart,* 1974); "injuries that are severe and obvious" (*Smith v. Sullivan,* 1977); and "chronic disabilities and afflictions" (*Barksdale v. King,* 1983).

The Supreme Court, in *De Shaney v. Winnebago County Social Services* (1989), recognized the total dependence of prisoners upon the prison agency for health care and safe conditions of confinement. Justice William Rehnquist clearly enunciated the obligations of prison custodians, stating:

> When the State [FBOP] takes a person into its custody and holds him there against his will, the Constitution imposes upon it a corresponding duty to assume some responsibility for his safety and general well being . . . The rationale for this principle is simple enough: when the State [FBOP] by the affirmative exercise of its power so restrains an individual's liberty that it renders him unable to care for himself, and at the same time fails to provide for his basic human needs—e.g., food, clothing, shelter, medical care, and reasonable safety—it transgresses the substantive limits on State [federal] action set by the Eighth Amendment.

The prisoner is unable to get a second opinion. Life or death of those imprisoned is dependent upon the medical care provided by the FBOP.

Whereas legal precedent applies equally to men and women prisoners, *Women Prisoners of the District of Columbia Department of Corrections v. District of Columbia* (1994) addressed conditions specific to female prisoners. In this case the court found Eighth Amendment violations due to lack of medical care, sexual harassment, and inferior living conditions:

> After an extensive trial, the court concluded that civil rights violations
> were established conclusively by the plaintiffs and that prison officials had
> deviated from the standard of acceptable mental health care for women
> prisoners, had tolerated deficient gynecological examinations and test-
> ing, and had maintained inadequate testing for sexually transmitted dis-
> eases. The court, applying the "deliberate indifference" standard (*Estelle
> v. Gamble* [1976]), further found liability for inadequate health education,
> prenatal care, ineffective prenatal education, and overall inadequate pre-
> natal protocol. In a scathing portion of the opinion, the judge found that
> shackling of female prisoners in the third trimester of pregnancy and im-
> mediately after childbirth violated contemporary standards of decency.
> The belief that adequate medical care exists in women's prisons may be
> on the brink of serious reexamination in light of the revelations of facts
> in this case. (J. McLaren, 1997: 369–371)

The medical needs of women in prison must be provided for at acceptable
community standards (see U.S. Department of Justice [DOJ], 1997; Pollock-
Byrne, 1990; J. Palmer, 1994). The hard reality is that they are not being met.

U.S. DOJ POLICY STATEMENTS: MEDICAL CARE IN THE FBOP

In theory,[4] directives contained in FBOP prisoner health care policy statements
as delineated in the DOJ Health Services Manual (U.S. DOJ, 1997) appear to
rise to the level of humane treatment. Federal directives mandate provision of
necessary medical care at levels comparable to accepted community standards.
DOJ rules mandate that health care requirements take precedent over security
concerns whenever possible. FBOP health care directive (P.S. 6000.05) assures
humane treatment of prisoners, yet true health care in the FBOP is symbolic in
nature.[5] This interpretation is a common theme among prisoners interviewed.
According to one of them,

> These people don't give a rat's ass about you. They don't care if you're sick
> or dying. This so called medical care ain't nothin but a big show. These
> doctors, hell most of em ain't even doctors, fill out their little forms so
> they can say they're doin somethin for ya. They ain't. They don't care if
> you live or die. It's all just a show for the public.

Health care services provided by the FBOP are symbolic because they are predicated upon a system of economic justification, rather than motivated by the
need to provide adequate medical care. "It is all just a show for the public," a
bureaucratic paper trail to justify fiscal expenses. It is the sick and dying prisoners who pay the price, very often the ultimate price: death.

FBOP health care policy portends to provide medical care "consistent with
acceptable community standards." Section 1 of the FBOP Health Services Manual mission statement issues the following mandate:

> The health care mission of the Federal Bureau of Prisons is to provide
> necessary medical, dental, and mental health services to inmates by profes-
> sional staff, consistent with acceptable community standards. (U.S. DOJ,
> 1997: 1)

The stated aim of FBOP health care policy is to provide humane medical treatment for prisoners. When compared to the actual quality of medical services
provided prisoners, health care in the FBOP is symbolic by design. In reality,
health care does not meet the standards delineated in DOJ policy statements.
The vast divide between health care policy stipulated by the DOJ and the reality of health care provided by the FBOP contravenes both Supreme Court
rulings and congressional mandate.

The FBOP medical care mission statement states that health care requirements take primacy over security concerns ("whenever possible"). This is pat-
ently false rhetoric. Maury Greenberg (1988: 167–170) discussed the contradiction between the stated goals of FBOP health care requirements and security
concerns, reporting: "The stated health care policy of the FBOP gives prece-
dence to medical care over security requirements whenever possible. In reality,
the converse is true" (see also Anno, 1991). The normative expectation of adequate health care in the prison setting is diametrically opposed to the security
function of the FBOP. Citing the possibility of "an incompatibility between
medical and correctional guidelines [that] should be resolved, as far as practical,
in favor of medicine," the FBOP presents a front that health care requirements
take precedent over security concerns. The phrase "as far as practical" is an
open-ended, ambiguous definition allowing the FBOP wide latitude in placing security concerns over prisoners' health care needs.

An inherent problem in the DOJ Health Services Manual (U.S. DOJ, 1997),[6]
which delineates the policy directive contained in the FBOP Health Services
Manual mission statement, is the definition of "acceptable community standards." "For example, precisely what do the terms 'adequate,' 'reasonable,' 'appropriate,' and 'acceptable,' mean for prison officials who must design and
deliver inmate medical care?" (Fleisher and Rison, 1997: 329). Definitional ambiguity allows the FBOP free reign to contravene legal obligations contained
in the Constitution of the United States of America, congressional mandate,
Supreme Court rulings, and the U.S. DOJ policy statements. The FBOP puts
forth, for public consumption, an image of compassionate health care for those
prisoners under its charge. Yet within the context of definitional confusion, the
FBOP minimizes and skirts Constitutional, Supreme Court, and congressional
mandate, without legal consequences for such subversion.

SYMBOLIC MEDICAL CARE

Today, the FBOP operates a symbolic medical care system. It is out of legal com-
pulsion, not the welfare of prisoners, that medical care is rationed. This argument extends to the quality of the medical staff. According to one inmate that
I interviewed, "In the health care unit much of the care is provided by ICPs

[inmate care providers]. These are inmates who have received very little training. They are given a fancy diploma that don't mean nothing."

In 1994, the U.S. General Accounting Office (GAO, 1994), generally
known for its pull-no-punches approach, produced a report entitled "Bureau
of Prisons Health Care: Inmates' Access to Health Care Is Limited by Lack of
Clinical Staff." The document provided an assessment of the quality of medical
care provided by FBOP physician assistants. They "lack generally required education and certification and are not receiving adequate supervision from physicians. At the three centers we visited, 11 of 27 physician assistants had neither
graduated from a program approved by the American Medical Association nor
obtained certification from the National Commission on Certification of Physician Assistants" (11).

Moreover, the GAO report describes the inadequate health care available to
federal prisoners at federal medical centers (prisons):

> Inmates with special needs, including women, psychiatric patients, and
> patients with chronic illnesses, were not receiving all of the health care
> they needed at the three medical referral centers we visited [Butner, North
> Carolina; Lexington, Kentucky; Springfield, Missouri]. This situation was
> occurring because there were insufficient numbers of physicians and nurs-
> ing staff to perform required clinical and other related tasks. For example,
> physicians did not always have enough time to supervise physician assis-
> tants who provided the bulk of the primary care given to inmates, and
> nurses did not have sufficient time to provide individual and group coun-
> seling to psychiatric patients. As a result, some patients' conditions were
> not improving and others were at risk of serious deterioration. (2)

Insufficient medical care staff is a function of dual realities: an exploding prison
population in conjunction with proportionately decreasing funds available for
health care services.

For the fortunate few, some sick and dying prisoners are sent to "contract
medical facilities"—public hospitals the FBOP sends prisoners to receive medical care beyond the scope of services the FBOP is able to provide (Fleisher and
Rison, 1997: 327–334). The lucky prisoner may receive an operation or treatment for serious medical conditions at one of these facilities, only to be returned to the "total institution of prison" (Goffman, 1961) and be simply neglected. I knew prisoners who received adequate medical attention at a contract
medical facility only to come back to prison and die under lock and key because appropriate care was not maintained. Postoperative care in the prison setting is at best substandard, and ongoing medical care for serious medical conditions falls well below the level of acceptable community standards.

Perhaps we rationalize the lack of proper medical care provided those imprisoned because, after all, the prisoner can be viewed as somewhat less of a human being. It is society that attaches the label "prisoner," while sublimating the
human being. Berkman (1995) reported:

> The buildup in the prison population has been accompanied by a sys-
> tematic campaign to dehumanize those in prison. Politicians and policy-

makers increasingly use terminology such as "animals" and "sub-humans" to describe street criminals. The intended result is to demonize those in prison, implicitly relieving society of any obligation to supply decent living conditions or medical care. (1616–1618)

The dehumanization process allows the FBOP symbolic presentation of health care to go unquestioned. Dehumanizing justifies substandard treatment. Substandard treatment is cost effective. Reducing expenditures on medical care frees more resources for human warehousing. And the cycle of inhumanity disgracefully rages on.

REALITY OF MEDICAL CARE AT FEDERAL MEDICAL CENTERS: VOICES FROM WITHIN

Many prisoners entering the federal prison system suffer from malnutrition and disease stemming from poverty, drug, and alcohol abuse, and life on the streets. Some may have contracted diseases such as AIDS, TB, hepatitis, and cirrhosis of the liver. The compromised health of many of those going to prison poses a serious challenge to the health care delivery system of the FBOP. What is the response by the FBOP to the medical needs of those entering prison, and what is the long-range plan for medical care of prisoners incarcerated with sentences that span decades? How do FBOP health care workers determine who needs and/or receives medical attention? A comparison of FBOP policy statements, which in theory govern medical care practices, to testimonies of those imprisoned reveals many contradictions.

A prisoner I interviewed described being poor and using drugs beginning at an early age. He is a black man from the ghettos of Washington, D.C. He spent four years, between the ages of two and six, in and out of hospitals receiving skin grafts for burns that resulted when a babysitter placed him in a bath of scalding water. At the time of this interview the individual was 38 and had been locked up since he was 21: "The first time I got loaded-up (high on drugs), God damn, I was 12 or 13 and living in a foster home. I done some crazy shit and now my body's paying the price. Now I just want to be a peaceful old man."

Another convict I interviewed, who was suffering from alcohol abuse was remanded to a FMC for alleged mental health counseling and alcohol/drug abuse treatment. He describes his condition at the time of incarceration: "When I first got to prison I had the DTs—shaking, paranoid, frantic. I could not stand to have nobody touch me or talk to me. The first year was really rough because of the alcohol. Before coming to prison I was doing at least a six-pack of beer every night after work, and two cases on the weekends."

While in the county jail awaiting transport to a FMC, I saw a fellow prisoner who was a 25-year heroin addict. They confined this person, who had become addicted while serving his country in the Vietnam War, in a cell to dry out "cold turkey," as it is called. I watched the horror of someone suffering withdrawal without medical assistance. I will never forget watching this man pace in circles sweating profusely and shivering at the same time, as he described the sensation of a snake trying to crawl out of his belly and up his throat.

POLITICALLY RATIONED
HEALTH CARE IN THE FBOP

Is the delivery of medical care within the FBOP politically rationed? Is someone who complains, desperately attempting to receive treatment, subject to retaliatory denial of medical care? A prisoner who was having difficulty urinating described the politics of health care within the FBOP:

> Navy doctors are politically inclined to go along with the system. [In referencing "navy doctors" the respondent is referring to the government branch of Public Health Services (PHS). These medical technicians support the FBOP medical staff. They wear uniforms similar to those of Naval officers]. A lot of politics involved in getting medical procedures. They look at the background, your PSI [presentence investigation report] and your team reports [evaluations prepared by a prisoner's counselor and unit representative]. This decides what medical procedures you get. Two men died this week. If you don't know somebody on the outside who can step on their feet, the BOP doctors' feet, then they just give you a pill and forget you.

Another convict supports this position, stating, "If you get injured, hurt, or sick, they give you Motrin. It takes months before you get medical attention."

I experienced this kind of rationing of medical care by the FBOP. Becoming very ill while imprisoned; my weight dropped from 214 to 157 pounds. I pleaded with FBOP doctors for medical care and was told I was suffering the shock of adjusting to prison (which they conveniently called "post–traumatic stress disorder"). I was passing blood during 10–14 bowel movements per day. In desperation, I contacted my family, who convinced a U.S. senator to contact the FMC on my behalf. In short order, I was taken to a contract hospital and diagnosed with Crohn's disease (ulcerations of the intestine). This condition is chronic, and if untreated, it is potentially terminal. I was one of the lucky few, for in prison, resources needed to mobilize political pressure are rare.

A prisoner described the quality of the medical care to which he was subjected:

> In this system, medical attention is deliberate indifference. This Federal Medical Center is not a real medical facility. There are over 150 men in wheelchairs. There are maybe 50 men in wheelchairs on the third floor of my unit, and there's only one elevator. If there is a fire, we're all toast. This place has no handicapped bathrooms or showers. Men are always falling out of their wheelchairs on the steep ramps.

Another prisoner echoes description of the inhumane medical care provided by the FBOP: "If you come here in a bad medical state, you go out in a black bag with a tag on your toe. Critical care cases are supposed to go to a different FMC. Yet there are people here with AIDS, cancer, liver disease, TB, and so on. I'd say 70 percent of the prisoners here are on respite [medically unassigned]. They don't have the facilities to care for these men." Medical care provided by the FBOP does not rise to the level of accepted community standards, as required by law. For many imprisoned in the FBOP, their original sentence has been convoluted into a death sentence due to substandard health care.

It is easier for the average citizen to believe that convicts are treated with compassion rather than understand the true nature of medical care provided by the FBOP. To a misinformed public, Congress perpetuates the "get tough on crime" model at the expense of those human beings imprisoned behind the razor wire and gun towers of the FBOP. The following excerpt provides insight into the quality of medical care provided those incarcerated. The prisoner interviewed was in a wheelchair. He was wearing a pair of shorts that did not fit, and a T-shirt. He was not wearing shoes and his feet were bleeding. Yet, an uncomfortable wardrobe was the least of his problems:

> I'd been here a year and because of my large size, I have yet to get clothes, or even underwear. I been sick here 20 times. I came here from a hospital on the streets where I was suffering heart failure. Since I have come here I have had to buy antibiotics and painkillers from other inmates because the prison doctor won't give me any. Recently I woke up about 1:00 A.M. with [congestive] heart failure. The emergency button in the medical wards don't work. I couldn't breathe, my temperature was up, and I was foaming at the mouth. My roommate in the medical-acute dorm, which has 25 men suffering with MS [multiple sclerosis], MD [muscular dystrophy], and so on, and everybody is in a wheelchair, he called the cop. The CO [prison guard] called the nurse. The nurse refused to come check my condition. The CO said she can't do anything for me.

Conflicting with the medical needs of convicts are the security requirements of the FBOP. "Security is a primary concern in corrections, even during the delivery of medical care to inmates" (Fleisher and Rison, 1997: 330; see also Greenberg, 1988; Anno, 1977, 1991). This was underscored in an interview with another prisoner. He was taken to a contract hospital for a five-way heart bypass:

> I'm in the operating room, already prep'ed for surgery. The "hack" [prisoner argot for prison guard] had me handcuffed to the operating table. I couldn't believe it, but this hack was going to stay in the operating room for the whole operation. The doctor comes in and tells the hack to take the cuffs off. The hack refused and said something about security requirements. The doctor explained to this lard head that in addition to being under anesthesia, he was going to cut apart my ribcage and remove my heart from my body. He explained that it was pretty much clear that I

wasn't going nowhere. The fucking hack still refused to take off the cuffs. Now the doctor got pissed. He told the hack that if my heart stopped and they had to hit me with the paddles, the cuffs would conduct electricity and I'd get severely burned. The hack told the doctor that if that were the case, I'd just have to get burned. The doctor went ballistic. He called the warden right from the operating room. I told the doctor that I refuse the operation, and that I was going to sue these bastards. After a shouting match with the warden, the doctor handed the phone to the hack. Next I knew the cuffs were off and the operation was on.

The lengths to which the FBOP goes to ensure security in the face of medical need is amazing. I interviewed a prisoner who is a quadriplegic. He is paralyzed from the neck down and confined to a wheelchair. This individual had made great progress by the time I interviewed him, training his diaphragm to drive the breathing process, whereas previously he had been bound to a mechanical respirator. I witnessed the events described by the convict:

These assholes are totally unbelievable. I have been paralyzed for over a decade and these fuckers still chain me to my chair [wheelchair] when I go out on medical [a trip to a medical contract facility]. I got shot and my fucking spinal cord was busted up. What do these assholes figure, I'm going to escape, I'm going to run the 440, or do these stupid assholes figure I'm goin' to fly away? And they put me through this shit every time. The good news is that the doctors at the hospital make these fucking assholes take the chains off as soon as we show up.

The functional conflict between the medical needs of a prisoner and the security emphasis of the FBOP is further underscored by an excon who is a medical doctor:

Beneath the talk of health care systems and public health planning, there is the stark reality of individuals grappling with illness and possible death in an inhumane environment. During my second bout with cancer, I was almost totally paralyzed from the neck down, able only to breathe and minimally use my hands. Yet, I was kept shackled to the bed, the guard coming by regularly to check the restraints. Prisoners struggle to live, or die, surrounded by people whose primary responsibility is to confine them, not care for them. There is no comforting touch, no human solidarity in the face of suffering or death. (Berkman, 1995: 1616–1618)

Section 1 of the U.S. DOJ Health Services Manual mission statement decrees that the level of health care provided prisoners must be "consistent with acceptable community standards" (U.S. DOJ, 1997: 2). Is a system of health care in which people are struggling to live or die, surrounded by people whose primary responsibility is to confine them, not care for them, consistent with acceptable community standards? Is the FBOP meeting the standards of care ordered by Supreme Court law? Has Congress's mentality of "throw away the key" usurped the Eighth Amendment's guarantee against cruel and unusual punishment? Are convicts human beings, subhuman, or just a number?

GUERILLA HEALTH CARE TECHNIQUES:
SELF-SURVIVAL

While imprisoned, I observed various methods prisoners adapt to survive, despite limited, rationed, symbolic health care service. These methods of self-preservation are routinized behavior patterns convicts implement to maintain and improve their health. Given the lack of adequate medical care provided by the FBOP health care delivery system, four forms of self-maintenance implemented by various prisoners were identified. These include the walker, the health nut, the weight lifter, and the maintenance man. A fifth approach, the sessile state, is the all too frequent destruction of health that results from the soul-crushing despair of incarceration.

The Walker

Many of the elderly convicts are walkers. Their mantra is "move it or lose it." They walk the track several times per day in endless circles going nowhere. Their self-reliance often yields improvements in health. Many of those implementing the walking approach to self-maintenance shed weight. Diabetics interviewed reported their reliance on insulin was reduced. Several indicated their blood pressure was lowered as a result of their walking. An additional benefit to the "walker" is the social and emotional support provided through the interaction with those with whom they walk. Numerous prisoners interviewed explained that they had no choice but to walk. In the face of inadequate medical care, many believed if they did not do something for themselves, they were destined to die in prison.

The Health Nut

The health nut relies on nutrition and vitamins for health maintenance. These convicts practically exist on fruits and vegetables purchased on the prison black market. Prison culture has its own economic system. Cigarettes and stamps, available for purchase at the prison commissary, are the usual forms of currency. These staples are used to purchase commodities ranging from legal services provided by a "jailhouse attorney," to food stolen from the kitchen. The health nut shunned the slop passed off as food in the prison chow hall. In response, the health nut prepared his cuisine in microwave ovens located in some cell units. I was amazed at the gourmet-quality meals many were able to miraculously create with the limited supplies available.

The Weight Lifter

The weight lifter implements a combination of exercise and self-discipline to maintain health. The myth that prisoners are muscle-bound weight lifters was not borne out in my experience. In fact, the vast majority of those I observed lifting weights were not huge, burly men. Instead, they were average guys who found disciplined commitment to a structured activity as their mechanism of survival. For many this was a revelation, a life-changing awakening. In their life on the street, many of the convicts interviewed did not have a firm grasp of what discipline or commitment meant. In the prison setting, these individuals not only used the activity of weight lifting as a method of health maintenance but found meaning through the commitment of daily weight training.

Despite the positive gains associated with weight lifting—commitment, discipline, and improved health—the FBOP has eliminated weight lifting as a tool for self-improvement. In 1996, Congress passed the Zimmer Amendment, which prohibited weight training by federal prisoners. Subsequently, recreation departments of the FBOP were barred from purchasing or replacing weight-lifting equipment (The Zimmer Amendment, 1997).

The amendment was a stopgap measure that expired at the end of the 1997 fiscal year. It was replaced by H.R. 816, *The Federal No Frills Prison Act* of 1997 (105 Congress, February 25, 1997). H.R. 816 states in part:

> No Federal funds may be used to provide any of the following amenities or personal comforts in the Federal prison system: . . . Instruction (whether live or through broadcasts), or training equipment, for boxing, wrestling, judo, karate, or any other martial art, or any bodybuilding or weight lifting equipment, of any sort.

Subsequently, the FBOP has adopted practices that reflect the Zimmer Amendment. The October 1, 1997, to September 30, 1998, budget bill H.R. 2267 contains a provision similar to the Zimmer Amendment that prohibits the purchase or replacement of weight-lifting equipment.

Through legislative action, Congress and the FBOP have taken from the convict far more than just weights. Many of those incarcerated had discovered a sense of commitment and discipline through weight lifting. More than physical development, many grew in strength of character. Additionally, weight training was for many a means of improving and maintaining health. It may be argued that a large sum of money was saved on health care expenditure as a result of improved health associated with weight training. Does it not make sense to provide those incarcerated with the opportunity to improve their health and grow in character through the disciplined commitment to lifting weights?

The Maintenance Man

The maintenance man implements a rounded approach to personal health care. Irwin (1970: 158) describes this approach to surviving in prison as the "gleaner." He stated that "one very important dimension of this style of adaptation [is] the tendency to pick through the prison world (which is mostly chaff) in search of the means of self-improvement" (see also Cressey, 1962; Lemert, 1967).

Rather than committing to one of the categories previously discussed, the maintenance man borrows a bit from each. He frequently walks, is concerned with nutrition, lifts weights, and often engages in aerobic exercise. In addition, the maintenance man spends time in the library, reads, may participate in religious activities, or enrolls in the limited programs provided by the FBOP. He is a Renaissance man, improving not only his body but his mind and soul.

The Sessile State

The fifth approach, relied on by the majority of prisoners, is antithetical to a positive state of health. In the sessile state, the convict seems to grow roots to the seat of a folding metal chair. Stationed in front of a TV, the physiologically beleaguered and often psychologically broken prisoner wastes away in stagnation. They do not receive adequate medical care, and as result, their health spirals downward. It is often a slow, agonizing death, which I observed over and over again.

THE (UN)COMPASSIONATE
RELEASE PROCESS

The indignation of dying in prison is little understood by the public. Isolated from family and friends, the dying convict suffers alone. I witnessed many men pass away in this ultimate denial of human dignity. The following is a prisoner's description of health care and dying within the FBOP:

> Last month, 11 men died from cancer, heart attacks, and leukemia. Most of the navy doctors [Public Health Service] try hard as hell to do what they can do for the men. Most BOP doctors put forth little effort. They'll give an aspirin to a man with a broken leg. When a person gets to a certain stage medically, they are put on a certain floor in the medical wing. And when they get so far along, they put them on a certain wing to die.

Imagine if you, or a loved one, was denied the right of dignity in death. Is being forced to die within the isolation of prison a breach of the Eighth Amendment cruel and unusual punishment clause?

FBOP program statement PS 5050.46 *Compassionate Release, Procedures for Implementation* 18 USC 3582(c)(1)(A), as contained in 28 CFR part 571, subpart G, establishes the criteria for compassionate release for those convicts near death:

> A motion for a modification of a sentence will be made to the sentencing court only in particularly extraordinary or compelling circumstances which could not reasonably have been foreseen by the court at the time of sentencing.

Imminent death meets the criteria of extraordinary or compelling circumstances. Nevertheless, the process of compassionate release is symbolic in nature, for the FBOP is not in business to release prisoners.

Before a recommendation for compassionate release can be made to the sentencing court, a petition for release under 18 USC 3582 must be initiated by the convict, or medical staff, and directed to the warden. The prisoner must comply with each phase of the protracted resolution process. Only after completing this gamut, which can span a year or more and which may be derailed at any one of the bureaucratic levels, can the dying convict request be brought to the sentencing court for consideration of sentence modification. In many cases the petitioner is dead before this process can be completed. Thus, the prisoner is denied the opportunity to die in dignity with his family. How is it possible that the compassionate release process drags on in light of today's technological advances, such as fax machines and computer e-mail?

What does the future hold for the provision of medical care in the FBOP? Six changes, producing a comorbidity, will continue to negatively impact the delivery of services: the increasing prison population, increased poverty, fixed budgets, the continuing war on drugs, the graying prison population, and the increased frequency of sexually transmitted disease and TB (see, e.g., Crawford and Moses, 1995: 120–121).

PRISON POPULATION EXPLOSION: STRAINS ON THE FBOP HEALTH CARE DELIVERY SYSTEM

The prison population is growing exponentially. Between 1990 and 1996, the overall U.S. prison incarceration rate rose 45 percent (Camp and Camp, 1996). In 1997, there were more than 445 adults in prison for every 100,000 residents of the United States (Gillard and Beck, 1998). Due to rapid growth of the prison population, health care for those incarcerated in the FBOP is compromised.

Increasing Number of People Going to Prison

The FBOP operates the "the nation's largest health care system" (Fleisher and Rison, 1997: 327). This federal bureaucracy is forced to provide medical care, operating within a fixed budget, while concomitantly experiencing an exploding population base (Blumstein et al., 1978; Flynn, 1992; Hagan, 1994b; Austin et al., 2001; J. Ross and Richards, 2002).

The FBOP espouses practical health care solutions for meeting convicts' medical needs. Medical care provided by the FBOP is, in part, an economic function of a fixed operating budget, compromised by an increasing prison population. As the federal prison population continues to skyrocket, limited funds available for health care must be used to treat greater numbers of prisoners. Also, medical support staff in the FBOP must care for increasing numbers of patients. As caseloads placed upon medical support staff continue to grow, and money available for health care continues to dwindle, the quality of medical care for prisoners proportionately decreases. The "practical" solution for the FBOP health care delivery system is to reduce health care services.

Correctional health care delivery systems have been viewed as the original managed care setting in the sense that there is a fixed budget for the provision of medical care regardless of prison population size. "Managed care is a health care delivery system in which costs, accessibility, quality and outcomes of care across a continuum of health services are tightly regulated using various rules, guidelines, and oversight methods" (T. Douglas and Mundey, 1995: 98–100). If the segment of the prison population in need of medical care exceeds projection, the FBOP has no alternative than to reduce the quantity and quality of medical services available. Such cutbacks reflect the "practical" application of "symbolic" medical care within the FBOP. For a given fiscal year, Congress allocates the FBOP a fixed budget. Funds available are predetermined whether there are 100,000 prisoners in the system or whether the population expands to 200,000 over the fiscal year.

In 1993, the amount allocated per prisoner for annual health care costs was $2,997 (Maguire and Pastore, 1993; Fleisher and Rison, 1997). A survey conducted by *Corrections Compendium* (1996: 3) reports health care costs averaged $3,431 per convict for fiscal year 1995. The implication is that as the prison population increases, and the cost of medical services increase, the BOP is forced to budget more funds or restrict access to health care.

For fiscal year October 1, 1997–September 30, 1998, the FBOP spent almost $390 million on medical services (*Corrections Compendium,* 1998: 13). Correctional health providers have always had to make decisions and prioritize medical services based on budget. In today's policy of human warehousing, fiscal resources are simply not available to meet health care needs.

The Contribution of Poverty

Before they are imprisoned, many federal convicts do not have access to medical care (Goldsmith, 1975; D. Jones, 1976; Anno, 1977, 1979; L. King and Desai, 1979). "In 1992, a Bureau health services administrator estimated that in his region about 75 percent of the inmates hadn't had medical or dental treatment prior to their commitment in the federal prison system" (Fleisher and Rison, 1997: 328).

And, as J. Jacobs (1977a: 89–107) notes, "Prisoners are not randomly drawn from the larger population, instead a large percentage come from the lower socioeconomic strata of our society." Marquart et al. (1996) observe that there is an inverse relationship between health and income that "suggests that health conditions within the lower socioeconomic segments of the noninstitutionalized population shape and influence population morbidity and mortality within prison settings. In short, to account for the health condition of the institutionalized population, one must examine health conditions within the wider population, especially among those segments of the population that contribute a disproportionate number of individuals to the prison" (331–360).

Because the prison population is disproportionately composed of people with lower socioeconomic status, disease rates in prison are higher than in the general population. Discussing infectious disease rates in U.S. prisons and jails, Krane et al. (1998) state:

> Infectious disease rates are higher among inmates than in the general population. The Bureau of Justice Statistics discloses in its report *HIV in Prisons and Jails,* 1995, that the AIDS case rate in prisons is six times higher than the overall U.S. AIDS case rate. Syphilis rates among female inmates

in some facilities range from 5.4 percent to 35 percent. Gonorrhea rates in juvenile facilities are 152 times higher among girls and 42 times higher among boys than among girls and boys in the general population. In some facilities, 14 to 25 percent of the inmates are infected with TB. And while just 0.9 percent of the general population is infected with hepatitis B, experts suggest that the infection rate is as high as 8.0 percent in the prison population. (124)

These figures underscore a problem inherent in the FBOP health care delivery system. Given the exploding prison population and the fiscal restraints imposed by Congress, how can the FBOP adequately provide medical care to convicts who are disproportionately from low socioeconomic backgrounds, and who come to prison infected with disease?

The ("Civil") War on Drugs

The drug war has resulted in the imprisonment of many people for simple possession. They may have used legal or illegal substances in an effort to self-medicate, attempting to deal with their latent physical and mental health issues. For the manifest symptom of drug abuse, many are condemned to the horror of prison due to the latent symptomatology of physical and mental health challenges.

The war on drugs has had the net effect of incarcerating many people who suffer with physical, mental, and drug abuse problems. Many are being imprisoned for the manifest symptom of drug use due to the latent causes of physiologic and mental disorders.

There are currently more critically, chronically, and mentally ill convicts in the FBOP than in any other period in U.S. history (Federal Bureau of Prisons Fact Card-1995). *Corrections Compendium* (1998: 17) reported that 30 percent of the FBOP prisoner population is chronically or critically ill. Sadly for those who in addition to suffering the pains of prison also struggle with physical and mental illness, money available for health care services is decreasing relative to the increasing prison population.

The Graying Prison Population

In addition to the rapid growth in the overall prison population, there is the alarming growth in the subpopulation of older prisoners. In prisons, age 50 and above is the benchmark for "older convicts" because the health of an average convict age 50 and above approximates the average health condition of those 10 years older in the free community (Falter, 1993: 27).[7] The prison population is "graying, and will continue to grow older as a result of current sentencing strategies such as elimination of good time, implementation of three strikes laws, and mandatory minimum sentencing" (Enter, 1995: 15).[8]

Associated health care costs escalate with age. It is estimated that by 2005, health care costs for elderly inmates will increase by 14-fold and that many prisons will become geriatric centers (also see Vito and Wilson, 1985; Wilson and Vito, 1988; Flynn, 1992; Allen and Simonsen, 1998). Aging is associated with sharp increases in morbidity and daily living limitations owing to chronic impairments and disease. These conditions directly relate to health care expenditures incurred by the FBOP, and, therefore, to the substantive quality of health care provided. Merianos et al. (1997) report:

> Prison organizations no doubt will be called on to expend more budgetary and programming resources on the elderly population subgroup. The cost of delivering health services to this group will grow in the years to come. If the general health conditions of these inmates worsen while they are in prison (i.e., increased morbidity), then this decline certainly will demand that prison organizations increase their expenditures to maintain the health of elderly offenders. (298–313)

A vital area of concern in caring for the elderly subpopulation is the lack of adequately trained prison staff. Aday (1994) reports:

> As one prison official confessed, "I know how to run prisons, not old-age homes." Training involving administrative personnel, line security staff, and health providers, should include an increased knowledge of growing old and how this knowledge specifically affects the elderly in a prison environment. Prison staff needs to be specifically trained to understand more fully the social and emotional needs of the elderly, dynamics of death and dying, procedures for identifying depression, and a system for referring older inmates to experts in the community. (47–54)

HIV/AIDS and Tuberculosis

Infectious diseases such as HIV/AIDS and tuberculosis (TB) pose enormous policy problems for the administration of correctional facilities. There is an overrepresentation of AIDS cases in prisons. For instance, the National Institute of Justice (NIJ), in conjunction with the Centers for Disease Control and Prevention (CDC), conducted a survey of the FBOP, the 50 state correctional systems, and 29 of the 50 largest city and county jail systems in the country.

> The survey, which was conducted between May and December 1994, found that 4,588 prisoners have died of AIDS since the beginning of the epidemic, and that during 1994, at least 5,297 adult prisoners with AIDS were incarcerated in prisons and jails. At year-end 1995, 2.3 percent of all state and federal prisoners were reported by prison authorities to be infected with the human immunodeficiency virus (HIV). This equates to 24,226 prisoners who are HIV positive. (R. Braithwaite et al., 1998: 108)[9]

In 1987, AIDS deaths accounted for 22.0 percent of total deaths in prison. In 1995, death due to AIDS accounted for 33.1 percent of total deaths in prison. It is projected that in the year 2000, 42.5 percent of deaths in prison will be attributable to AIDS (Camp and Camp, 1996). In 1991, the National Commission on Acquired Immune Deficiency Syndrome reported:

> By choosing mass imprisonment as the Federal and State governments' response to the use of drugs, we have created a de facto policy of incarcerat-

ing more individuals with HIV infection. Under the present policy, the percentage of drug offenders in the Federal Bureau of Prison system will rise by 1995 from 47 percent to 70 percent. Clearly, we are thus concentrating the HIV disease problem in our prisons and must take immediate action to deal with it. (32)

The health care delivery system of the FBOP is strained due to the expense of treating AIDS patients. "Treatments for HIV are becoming more costly, with the latest combination therapies costing between \$600–900 per month per prisoner" (McDonald, 1999: 427–478).[10] The opposing dynamics of an increasing proportion of the FBOP population who are infected with HIV/AIDS and the limited health care budget has resulted in reduced quality of care provided sick and dying convicts.

Tuberculosis poses another serious challenge to the health care delivery system of the FBOP. "Prisons and jails are high risk settings for the spread of TB infection. Living conditions are invariably crowded, and many facilities have extremely poor ventilation and air circulation" (R. Braithwaite et al., 1998: 108; see also Hammet, 1994; Greifinger, 1996; McDonald, 1999). As of 1997, the FBOP was operating at 119 percent of capacity (Gillard and Beck, 1998; Caplow and Simon, 1999). McDonald (1999) reports:

> TB infection, especially in combination with immunocompromised inmates, amounts to a kind of public health dynamite. Correctional facilities are nearly ideal places for transmitting the disease, and large numbers of prisoners return to the free community to live among others who are already at high risk of infection. (108)

"TB rates in prisons and jails typically are five times higher than in the general population" (Mueller, 1996: 100). Especially challenging to the health care delivery system of the FBOP is the emergence of drug-resistant TB. Treatment for strains of TB that are drug resistant can take up to two years and treatment efficacy is poor.

How is the FBOP going to meet the health care needs associated with the contagious diseases AIDS/HIV and tuberculosis? What effect does the spread of these diseases in prison have on society at large? Greifinger (1996) reports: "Penal populations are always tidal populations, with an outgoing as well as an incoming tide. It therefore means much more to the community as to what a man is when he comes out of prison, for he becomes a local factor in the social problem" (328).

CONCLUSION AND RECOMMENDATIONS

Many prisoners are condemned to death due to the lack of basic medical care in federal prisons. The FBOP attempts to balance limited funds available for health care services with increasing demands on its services. It is Congress that approves, or disapproves, FBOP funding requests. And, during the 1990s they passed the retributive sentencing laws that created an explosion in the federal prison population. The imbalance between finances available for health care services and the exploding prison population results in the rationing of health care available to the convict. Budget constraints are reducing health care services below the cruel and unusual punishment threshold established in the Eighth Amendment. The quality of health care provided in the FBOP does not rise to the level of acceptable community standards. The draconian sentencing policies of "throw away the key" have created human warehousing heretofore unseen.

As members of a civilized society, those imprisoned are entitled to humane treatment. By reducing the present rush to punishment, thousands of first-time, nonviolent offenders would be deflected from the prison system. This would stem the tide in the process of prison construction. Refocusing social conscience would greatly reduce budgetary demands on the FBOP.

Many who enter prisons come from a background of poverty. By providing prisoners' health management training, prison-related health care expenses would be reduced because the health status of the convict would improve over the course of incarceration. Upon release, the excon would be better equipped to maintain a healthy lifestyle and thus effect a reduction in social costs associated with subsidized health care. Additionally, improved health status might lead to a reduction in criminal activity and thus reduce recidivism.

It is imperative that an independent agency be established to campaign for the health care rights of convicts. If a prisoner does not have someone on the outside to fight for medical care on his/her behalf, that individual will be subject to rationed medical care. If an individual is not familiar with how to initiate a court proceeding to force the delivery of health care, that individual will be subject to discretionary care. An independent advocate would facilitate the right to timely and adequate medical care on the convict's behalf.

The compassionate release process must be streamlined. A maximum 60 days must be the limit for a compassionate release to run its course. It is unconscionable that men and women are dying in prison because the bureaucratic process drags on for many months. An independent advocate would represent the interests of the dying prisoner. A convict dying in the indignation of prison is not in a position to do battle with the bureaucracy of the FBOP.

An alternative would be the development of community-based facilities where terminally ill prisoners could be transferred, allowing them to be close to loved ones. Placing the incurably sick convict in this kind of setting near home, or under home confinement, would allow the prisoner to die with dignity.

In this environment, the custodial emphasis of prison would be replaced with the human requirements of the dying convict. Such facilities would drastically reduce the overall costs associated with dying in prison. For positive change to occur, first, the public must be informed of the reality of health care services within the FBOP, and second, an outcry by society is required, forcing politicians to address the misery of critical illness and death hidden behind the bars and razor wire of the FBOP.

NOTES

1. Admittedly, some convicts injure themselves on purpose because they believe that time spent in an FMC will be easier, or in order to get access to drugs that will help them to get high. One of the reasons why medical care is poor is because of the constant turnover of staff. The more qualified and mobile staff do not stay long in these facilities because they deplore the working conditions.

2. Prior to incarceration I earned a bachelor of science degree in sociology, University of Wisconsin-Madison. While incarcerated, I implemented my training as a sociologist to capture sociologically significant concepts occurring behind the razor wire. Since release (April 1997), I have earned a master's degree in sociology and am currently completing my Ph.D. within the Department of Sociology, Iowa State University. However, my area of concentration is criminology, an academic specialty often housed within a university's Department of Sociology.

3. While imprisoned I became what is known in prison argot as a "jail [prison] house attorney." I spent four years researching and learning federal criminal law.

4. The actual quality of health care provided prisoners in the FBOP does not rise to the stated standards as contained in the U.S. DOJ Health Care Manual (U.S. DOJ, 1997).

5. Delineation of health care requirements for prisoners of the FBOP is symbolic rhetoric put forth for public consumption. Please note directives of the FBOP, as compared to the firsthand accounts of those provided [deprived of] medical care by the FBOP.

6. Please see constitutional mandate contained in the Eighth, Fourteen, and Fifteenth Amendments of the U.S. Constitution. Also see congressional rulings [supra], as well as Supreme Court decisions that dictate health care delivery requirements within the FBOP.

7. Also see McDonald (1999).

8. Also see McDonald (1999).

9. Also see Hammet (1994); McDonald (1994, 1999).

10. Also see "Prisons Must Adhere" (1998).

13

Convict Criminology and the Mentally Ill Offender

Prisoners of Confinement

BRUCE A. ARRIGO

Mentally disordered individuals are a distinct and growing subgroup within the penal system (e.g., Steadman et al., 1989; Arrigo, 1996a; Lamb and Weinberger, 1998; Wettstein, 1998). Consequently, listening to their voices and the manner in which they seek to be heard (Henry and Milovanovic, 1996: 6) entails a careful assessment of the everyday reality of psychiatric citizens.

In this context, convict criminology is not simply about "doing time" in prison (Austin and Irwin, 2001). At its most basic level, this approach examines the manner in which the civil and criminal confinement systems, and all those responsible for the large-scale social engineering efforts of the past 200 years (e.g., Foucault, 1965; Rothman, 1971, 1980; Isaac and Armat, 1990), repeatedly failed to adopt genuinely humane responses to the problems posed by deviance, violence, and crime (Toch, 1998). In the wake of these miscalculations, the ones who have suffered the most are the very people for whom such grand reformist interventions were originally designed (McCleary, 1978/1992: ix). Mentally ill offenders are no exception to this travesty. They are civilly and criminally institutionalized and, as a result, typically experience profound alienation from and disillusionment with the systems of which they are a part, others similarly situated, and even themselves (Arrigo, 1993, 1996a).

Admittedly, reformist efforts historically have considered the public's interests as well (e.g., Rothman, 1980), particularly in the context of meaningful patient care and citizen safety. For example, during the early decades of the twentieth century, confinement of the psychiatrically disordered was linked to public hygiene, the psychopathic hospital, and curative treatment (Morrissey

267

and Goldman, 1986). The belief was that with enough "science," mentally ill offenders could be corrected and made functionally well. Ultimately, the hope was that they would return to society capable of maintaining productive, normal lives (Foucault, 1977). Unfortunately, efforts such as these were shortsighted at best.

Indeed, for many psychiatrically disordered citizens a process called *transcarceration* pervades their everyday interactions (Arrigo, 1997a). Transcarceration entails the ongoing routing of mentally ill offenders (MIOs) to and from the mental health and the criminal justice systems. This constant channeling of psychiatric subjects is also significant for convict criminology. When persons with psychiatric disabilities are perpetually and alternately housed in the civil and criminal systems of institutional control, they become prisoners of confinement; that is, the process of transcarceration substantially restricts the capacity of MIOs to vary their role performances or to renegotiate their identities. They live out their deviantly defined (i.e., "mad" and "bad") statuses and are largely powerless to alter them. Mentally ill offenders, then, are "silenced" through the activity of transcarceration, and they assume their oppressive position as a marginalized and captive group.

In my own penological scholarship, I have emphasized how the mental health and criminal justice communities work in concert to exclude the voices of (1994a) and ways of knowing for (1996b) persons confined, producing both social repression (1996c) and psychological punishment (1995a, 1996d). Moreover, in much of this research, I have relied heavily on the critical potential of postmodern criminological theory to considerably advance our understanding of how intrapsychic pain and interpersonal violence are enacted for MIOs through the "expert" forensic decision making of the medicolegal establishment (e.g., Arrigo and Tasca, 1999; Arrigo and Williams, 1999a, 1999b). Missing from these investigations, however, has been any significant contextualizing or ethnographic data that could confirm (or deny) the theoretical conclusions reached. This chapter addresses this gap in the literature.

In addition, although the studies cited above are conceptually grouped under the broad intellectual banner of critical criminology, they are not directly (or indirectly) positioned within the new school of convict criminology. This oversight needs to be rectified. Accordingly, this chapter demonstrates how critically inspired research on psychiatrically disordered offenders necessarily contributes to our knowledge of convict criminology.

In order to address these matters, the chapter is divided into four sections. First, selected elements of constitutive criminological thought are presented. This perspective represents an important strain of postmodern analysis conducive to the enterprise outlined above. Second, three distinct case studies of persons with identifiable mental illness subjected to civil and/or criminal confinement are described. These life stories dramatically reveal how transcarceration uniquely impacted their everyday experiences. Third, the selected principles of constitutive criminology are applied to the three representative case studies. This level of inquiry demonstrates where and how transcarceration functioned for these disordered citizens and the extent to which each person was a prisoner of confinement. Fourth, the chapter concludes by speculating on the future of convict criminology in relation to mentally ill offenders. The attending implications for subsequent scholarship in this area are also explored.

CONSTITUTIVE CRIMINOLOGICAL THEORY: AN OVERVIEW

Constitutive thought has firmly established itself as an important and leading postmodern orientation accounting for major developments within the sociology of law (A. Hunt, 1993) and criminological theory (Henry and Milovanovic, 1996). Selected application studies have addressed such diverse matters as sociolegal studies and their "critical" discontents (A. Hunt, 1987), psychoanalysis and the constitution of crime (Arrigo, 1998a, 1998b), the coproductive forces of law in American history (Salyer, 1991), media images in crime (Barak, 1993), and an integrated theory of social justice (Barak and Henry, 1999). Moreover, a recently released anthology by Henry and Milovanovic (1999) spells out a number of areas in crime and justice where the conceptual tools of constitutive theory are prominently and aptly displayed.

Several noteworthy schools of thought inform the constitutive perspective: existential phenomenology, labeling sociology, social constructionism, and poststructuralism. The intellectual history of constitutive theory also includes the post-Foucauldian investigations of Fitzpatrick (1984) and Coombe (1989), the structuration analysis of Giddens (1984, 1990), the social control taxonomy of Stanley Cohen (1985, 1988/1992), the sociology of knowledge formulations of Bourdieu (1977, 1987), the symbolic interactionism of Blumer (1969), and the political economy of Marx (1967). Clearly, the "constitution" of constitutive theory represents an eclectic orientation to understanding society and social phenomena, and this is certainly the case with constitutive studies in law and criminology (Arrigo, 1997b).

As with any substantive theory, there are a number of central principles comprising constitutive thought. For purposes of this study, four concepts integral to the composition of the theory will be enumerated. These concepts include (1) the decentered subject; (2) the recovering subject; (3) the social structure as deconstructive and reconstructive; and (4) the definition of crime. The selection process is not arbitrary. These four tenets were chosen because of their unique capacity to advance our awareness of mentally ill offenders, transcarceration, and convict criminology. In what follows, I briefly describe each of these constitutive principles.

Decentered Subject

Constitutive theory's reliance on the notion of a decentered or "divided" subject stems from the psychoanalytic semiotics of Jacques Lacan (e.g., 1977, 1981; for various applications in law and criminology see Milovanovic, 1997). Lacan (1977: 166) argued that identity (agency) and meaning (knowledge) are intimately connected to the language we use to convey our thoughts, impulses, feelings, attitudes, judgments, and so on. However, the language that we use typically speaks *through* us; that is, it represents a stand-in for the "real" subject, whose identity, regrettably, remains dormant, silenced, and/or oppressed (Lacan, 1977: 193–194, 310–316, 1988: 243; Henry and Milovanovic, 1996: 28–34). This posturing by discourse can be traced to the implicit values and hidden assumptions embedded in words and/or phrases that, unwittingly, are conveyed when we speak or otherwise communicate with others.

Elsewhere, I have shown how this process operates in civil (1993) and criminal (1996a) forensic settings. Words or expressions such as "dangerous," "incompetent to stand trial," "psychotic," "guilty but mentally ill," "diseased," "in need of treatment," "criminally insane," and the like are used by medicolegal decision brokers to render judgments about the confinement of disordered citizens. These terms, however, as part of a coordinated and specialized language system (i.e., psycholegal discourse) represent a "master (juridical) narrative . . . produc[ing] a circumscribed knowledge understood [to be] *psychiatric justice*" (1997a: 32). Indeed, the joint operation of the medical and legal establishment fills in these terms with selected meanings, consistent with their unstated values, effectively reducing the otherwise assorted interpretations of these terms to limited possibilities (1996c: 174–175).

For example, to define a person as "diseased" or "in need of treatment" is to imply that the individual is not well and is not able to care for her/himself. The hidden value unconsciously at work with these descriptors, then, is that the person is a passive, rather than an active, architect of his/her life and, therefore, is not in control of it. Corrective action is necessary so that the individual can normatively function and be made well (Arrigo and Williams, 1999b).

What is troubling about this conclusion is that alternative interpretations for persons with mental disabilities do not find their way into psycholegal discourse. Words or expressions such as "consumer," "mental health systems user," "psychiatric survivor," "disordered citizen," "differently abled," and their corresponding assumptions and values are denied affirmative recognition within mental health law circles. Indeed, as a practical matter, in order for persons with psychiatric disabilities to petition for release from civil and/or criminal custody, they must adopt the preexisting parameters of meaning that already define them. To resist these linguistically structured medicolegal categories of sense making is to risk sustained confinement in the prison or the hospital (Arrigo, 1994a: 25–31, 1996a: 151–173). In this context, disordered subjects contribute, knowingly or not, to the very victimization of self and denial of identity they seek to renounce.

According to Lacan (1977, 1981), this struggle in discourse is how the concealment of one's true or authentic self occurs. It is hegemony (Laclau and Mouffe, 1985) assuming a linguistic form (Henry and Milovanovic, 1996: 158, 160–162). The subject in speech is therefore *unstable* rather than stable, *decentered* rather than centered (MacCabe, 1979: 153). The mentally ill offender, then, is "the embodiment of multiple, overlapping, and contradictory expressions of desire, representing discordant voices [that are] temporarily unified by way of a dominant grammar and language system" (Arrigo, 1996c: 168).

Recovering Subject

Although language, as a stand-in, speaks *for* the subject (e.g., Pecheux, 1982; Silverman, 1983; Deleuze and Guattari, 1987), it does not follow that human agency is without implication in the activity of naming or defining reality. Indeed, the divided or decentered subject confronts the dialectics of (linguistic) struggle (Henry and Milovanovic, 1996: 170–177). For example, although structural forces (e.g., the criminal justice and mental health systems) delimit the humanity of MIOs, disordered citizens can and do contribute to that which defines them (e.g., participation in consumer self-help groups). As Bourdieu and Wacquant explain (1992: 167–168): "Social agents are knowing agents who, even when they are subjected to determinisms, contribute to producing the efficacy of that which determines them in so far as they structure what determines them." Thus, subjects help develop or produce the very social forms or structural conditions of which they are a part.

Recovering subjects, however, are not necessarily cognizant of the world that they coshape. Indeed, "the world produced by human agency is only episodically perceived as the outcome of its own authorship: much of the time we are forgetful producers of our world" (Henry and Milovanovic, 1996: 37). This forgetfulness returns us to the power of those social and structural forces that define our existences and mark our realities, in ways that are never neutral, saturated as they are in cloaked values and concealed assumptions that inconspicuously convey something more about our identities. The stock of our cultural and personal experiences, the expanse of our philosophical, political, and religious alliances, the magnitude of our institutional, organizational, and corporate allegiances all inform our uniquely lived realities (Bourdieu, 1984; Rosenau, 1992: 59). "The substance of being human must, therefore, entail what preceded us as biography, what looms ahead as prospect, caught in the contingent moment of the here and now, plowed by the discordant strands of unconscious processes" (Henry and Milovanovic, 1996: 36).

But in this scripted process of being decentered, the subject can be retrieved. Without ongoing, active engagement from individuals there would be no world, cultures, social conditions, and habitus. "Human agency is connected to the structures that it makes, as are the human agents to each other in making those structures" (Henry and Milovanovic, 1996: 39). Discourse is pivotal to how agents recover from their historically mediated, discursively constituted, and structurally situated existences. Recovering agency and being, then, involves reclaiming one's affirmative place in the dialectical play of speech. As Freire observed (1972: 76), "To exist, humanly, is to *name* the world, to change it. Once named the world . . . reappears to the namers as a problem and requires of them a new *naming*. Men [and women] are not built in silence, but in word, in work, in action-reflection."

The constitutive challenge for the recovering subject is to resist the organizing parameters of meaning that "speak" the person; that is, through discourse, human investment in the linguistic (and therefore social) reproduction of established structures must be displaced. To effect this end, human agency and, thus, one's potential liberation, must be in flux, mutable, in process (Kristeva, 1984). Transformation for the recovering subject necessarily includes the development of alternative vocabularies of meaning. These are "replacement discourses" (Henry and Milovanovic, 1996: 41, 214–229) that embody the disparate voices of and ways of knowing for those marginalized by the prevailing language system in use (e.g., medicolegal discourse). Through these alternative vocabularies, "the aim is to [replace] an inchoate life narrative [with] a congruent one, and [to] transform . . . [the] meanings that previously blocked the person's story with new ones" (Omer and Strenger, 1992: 253).

This approach acknowledges that people are "their own authors and can become [their own] poets" (Parry and Doan, 1994: 47, 27). Thus, reclaiming one's rightful place as the architect of one's life means that people must be given the requisite (reflective) space within which to speak "true words" (Freire, 1972: 56–67) about themselves, their interpersonal exchanges, and the social world humans develop.

Social Structure as Deconstructive/Reconstructive

Although the decentered subject can be retrieved, and although the recovering subject struggles in speech to fashion new or alternative vocabularies of meaning in which one's identity is more completely embodied, agency is inexorably connected to the material world in which it exists. But the constitutive position on structure or form does not subscribe to an objective, reductionistic, or historically fixed characterization for social order.

Indeed, "social structure is a cluster of ideas and images about order and its maintenance, a collection of humans oriented to uphold their version of these images, the reality of the outcomes that follow from actions they take to bring this about, and the potential to transform these images, actions and outcomes" (65). Thus, the construction of social reality is a *coproduction* in which "structure (the individual-social) and agency (active-passive) are mutually implicated in any production of knowledge" (Henry and Milovanovic, 1996: 65; see also Giddens, 1984).

Constitutive theory acknowledges that the principal means by which structural or organizational forces are defined as such is through language, and it is through the spoken or written word that the dialectical play of meanings (and their differential effects) embedded in these phenomena are given expressive form (e.g., Derrida, 1973, 1978). Thus, for example, execution of the mentally ill who invoke a right to refuse treatment (Arrigo and Tasca, 1999) is intimately linked to how the *prison system* and its *agents* interpret competency, treatment refusal, and mental illness (Arrigo and Williams, 1999b). As a constructed text or narrative, the structural response (i.e., execution or stay of execution) is laden with a multitude of meanings anchored in a coordinated language system (i.e., medicolegal discourse), producing circumscribed images about MIOs on death row (prisoners as diseased, deviant, and dangerous) taken to be de facto reality. These are summary representations (Knorr-Cetina, 1981: 36–7) in which spoken meanings become everyday constructions, given the behavior organized around them (e.g., forensic psychiatrists assessing competency and predicting dangerousness, approaching mental illness as a disease, and testifying in court as "experts" about both). As a result, these images and selected meanings establish themselves as concrete entities; that is, "real" categories of classification, in spite of the provisional, relational, positional, and thus, unstable nature of social forms and structures (Arrigo, 1995b: 452–454).

The preceding analysis, then, anchors our understanding of how social structure can be deconstructed and reconstructed. Indeed, the discursive co-production of reality leaves open the door to possible transformation. Constitutive theory allows us to critically comment on what is, and to reflectively suggest what could be. Organizational and social conditions, once constituted as summary representations, depend on the investment of humans to sustain these constructions in everyday discourse, with their implied values and hidden assumptions (Henry and Milovanovic, 1996: 68). But these constructions, particularly those that are marginalizing and alienating, can be exposed, reversed, destabilized, and dismantled. The activity of deconstruction (e.g., Derrida, 1973; Balkin, 1987) allows us to decode the meanings embedded in the words or phrases used to name the very oppressive forms or images we help to create.

In addition, a reidentification with nonterritorialized modes of communication (Deleuze and Guattari, 1987), more fully affirming of the speaking being, is possible provided we accept the "relative autonomy of structures and subject as well as their dependence in the co-production of social reality" (Henry and Milovanovic, 1996: 69). This is what Giddens (1984) means when describing the *duality* or mutuality of structure and agency. Both have meaning apart from and because of one another. Thus, in relation to the deconstructive/reconstructive possibilities for structure we conclude that

> the social properties of social systems are both medium and outcome of the practices they recursively organize. Structure is not "external" to individuals . . . , it is in a certain sense more "internal" than exterior to their activities. Structure is not to be equated with constraint but is always both constraining and enabling. (Giddens, 1984: 25)

The Definition of Crime as Power to Harm

An important facet of constitutive criminology is its explanation of crime. Both the passive (decentered) and active (recovering) subject dialectic, along with the deconstructive/reconstructive dynamics of social structure, substantially inform the constitutive understanding of crime. As a summary statement, crime is more than "symbolic violence" (Bourdieu, 1977: 192), or the will to harm others where overt and acknowledged domination psychically fosters power differentials in which autonomous subjects become objects of control, victimization, and oppression (Bourdieu and Wacquant, 1992: 167). Constitutively speaking, "crime is the expression of some agency's energy to make a difference on others and it is the exclusion of those others who in the instant are rendered powerless to maintain their humanity. . . . Crime then is the power to deny others their ability to make a difference" (Henry and Milovanovic, 1996: 116). This is expressed in one of two ways: harms of reduction or harms of repression (Henry and Milovanovic, 1996: 101; see Henry and Lanier, 1998: 622 for a more visually dynamic overview).

Harms of reduction refer to the denial of a person's overall identity or to the loss of a distinct quality constituting the individual. Thus, as a discursive construction, the offended party is somehow restricted from being who he/she is because of the actions of another. For example, when psychiatrically disordered citizens are thwarted in their request to be found not guilty by reason of insanity (NGRI), because of their difference (Arrigo, 1994a), or are found guilty, but mentally ill in spite of their difference (Arrigo, 1996b), then they experience a loss because of who they are.

Harms of repression refer to the denial of a person's potential to be other or more than who the individual is (Tifft, 1995: 9). Thus, as a discursive construction, the offended party is restricted in or prevented from "achieving a desired position or standing" (Henry and Milovanovic, 1996: 103). For example, when persons with mental disabilities are denied access to community-situated housing because their speech, thought, and behavior are appreciably different from others in the neighborhood, then they suffer a loss given their restricted access to a desired position (Arrigo, 1992).

Both harms of reduction and harms of repression are committed by "excessive investors" in power (Henry and Milovanovic, 1996: 220: 230; Henry and Lanier, 1998: 615). Excessive investors place considerable energy in the control of others, conveyed through language, where the "victim of crime is . . . rendered a non-person, a non-human, or a less complete being" (Henry and Milovanovic, 1996: 116). Harms of reduction and repression, then, are exemplars of power where difference is territorialized, criminalized, and vanquished.

THREE CASE STUDIES ON
CONFINEMENT: AN ETHNOGRAPHY

Between the years 1984 and 1991 I worked as a mental health outreach worker in Pittsburgh, Pennsylvania. Much of my time was spent in soup kitchens, sandwich lines, psychiatric facilities, abandoned buildings, deserted alleyways, welfare hotels, chemical dependency units, and prisons. The people with whom I worked were homeless, marginally housed, or soon to be discharged from psychiatric hospitals or released from jail or prison. Much of my time was spent in the communities in which they lived. My contact with them was mostly informal—unstaged, but streetwise. Many, though not all, of the people I met experienced bouts of depression, addiction, and unemployment, whereas others had been civilly and/or criminally confined. All of them lived on a social margin (Stonequist, 1934) and struggled to survive day to day (see Arrigo, 1997c, for some "criminal" subgroup applications exploring this phenomenon).

During the period of time that I worked as a mental health outreach worker, I attempted to establish rapport with these people and to assist them, both socially and psychologically, in coping with their life circumstances and changing them if they so desired. Most individuals spoke of wanting to alter their lives; few were successful (see Arrigo, 1994b for a model of successful community reintegration). This was particularly the case for persons who had been civilly and/or criminally confined.

In what follows, I briefly recount the stories of three persons whose lives were dramatically, though differentially, connected to the phenomenon of transcarceration. The ethnographic comments that follow are drawn from my previous field research (Arrigo, 1996a: 104–115) exploring the impact of mental health laws that produce "casualties of confinement" (Arrigo, 1996a: 104).[1] Missing from these findings, however, was any targeted assessment of social structure and human agency and their interactive capacity to coproduce the reality of transcarceration, rendering subjects prisoners of institutional control. Accordingly, I provide background on how three typical mental health citizens defined themselves, how they spoke about the civil and/or criminal justice systems of which they were a part, and what became of them in the wake of both.

On Being Mentally Ill: The Case of Edith

Edith lived in Pittsburgh's notorious Hill District. The "Hill" was well known for its urban poverty, drug culture, housing projects, and civic unrest. In many ways, the Hill District was an abandoned community, devastated by the transition from the city's manufacturing-based steel and iron industries to its service-based health and human service economies. When neighborhoods are ignored, the people in it are often forgotten. They succumb to the ravages of social disorganization. This was certainly the case for many people who lived in the Hill.

By her own admission, Edith was loud and obnoxious. She was a confirmed alcoholic who drank daily, clearly to the brink of excess, often to the verge of passing out. Edith lived alone except for an unnamed cat in a basement flat of a deserted apartment building. Her living quarters were festooned with debris, tattered clothing, jarred food (take-out meals from the nearby soup kitchen), and several stacks of assorted newspapers and magazines. I visited her weekly and we spoke mainly about drinking and death.

Edith was also prone to depression and had attempted to take her life several times. "When I'm shit-faced I don't feel so bad about things. . . . It's this drinking or I die." When she spoke, her speech was alternately slowed and pressured. She was prone to outbursts of anger, sometimes even rage, only to quiet herself suddenly in a fist full of tears and self-pity. "[Screaming] Look at me!! Look at *me!!* What do I have . . . nothing! [Crying] I ain't no good, damn it. I can't do nothin' 'bout my life, now. It's over for me."

On one occasion, Edith described how she had jumped from a seven-story building, shattering a number of bones in her left leg and leaving her an invalid. "I just did it, ya know? I had to. I couldn't take being this way [referring to depression] any more and I was tired of the booze." She spoke about her "emotional problems" but never articulated the source of her obvious pain.

> Maybe this is it for me. Maybe I'm suppose to be like this . . . stupid, depressed, and drunk all the time. [Laughing] I'm a real fuck-up and I have to deal with it, ya know? I have to accept my shit. [Angrily] It's *my* shit. . . . It's me and my life and that's all there is to it. Why can't I get over it? Why?

Edith had been involuntarily hospitalized in the past. She believed she needed to be permanently hospitalized. She spoke about being civilly committed and felt it was an answer to much of her mental anguish.

> I've got an illness, a disease. It's not my fault. I can't stop myself from thinking. I can't stop myself from thinking. [Holding her head with her hands firmly and crying] Look at me. I'm nothing. I'm already dead. The drinking, it's about being dead. I need to go to the hospital. I'm dead [crying]. I'm *all* dead! If they put me away at least I can die like the crazy fool that I am. At least I can die there with my illness.

On one particular occasion, in the midst of Edith's fierce depression, I drove her to a psychiatric facility for possible inpatient treatment. The attending physician diagnosed her as mentally ill and chemically addicted. The hospital stipulated that before any intensive psychiatric care could be extended to Edith, she would have to go through a 72-hour alcohol detoxification program and participate in a 28-day rehabilitation plan. The community mental health hospital was not in a position to ensure that Edith would be placed in an alcohol recovery unit, and encouraged her to pursue this course of action on her own. Indeed, hospital staff made clear that scarce financial resources and long waiting lists would delay prospects for immediate intervention and sustained services any time in the near future. However, following successful completion of an alcohol rehabilitation program, psychiatric treatment would be reconsidered.

Edith was faced with a profoundly frustrating dilemma: On the one hand, she was not "mentally ill" in the clinicolegal sense and, thus, could not receive psychiatric attention; on the other hand, she was an alcoholic but could not address her chemical abuse problem because of inadequate subsidies and limited placements. The hospital did not believe that drinking to death was, on its own, sufficient to diagnose Edith as a chronic depressive personality with extreme suicidal tendencies. As a result, she found herself stuck in a seemingly endless cycle of drinking to deaden the depression and feeling suicidal when sober because of the alcohol abuse. Trapped in and tormented by these restricted roles, neither the mental health nor the chemical dependency systems offered her much respite or relief. She died two years later, alone in her apartment. Although eventually Edith had been prescribed the alcohol inhibitor antabuse, she drank nonetheless, causing uncontrollable convulsions to her body that resulted in a fatal heart attack.

The Cycle of Psychiatric Treatment: The Story of James

James lived in Pittsburgh's downtown YMCA at a time when the facility housed a vulnerable tenant population (e.g., the mentally ill, the frail elderly, the chemically addicted) without offering the requisite support services many residents needed. The building was structured as an SRO (single-room occupancy): Living quarters included basic amenities (e.g., bed, walk-in closet, night stand, chair); semi-private bathroom facilities on each of the facility's floors were shared. Although the YMCA provided affordable housing, tenants remained mostly unknown to each other. Some preferred their anonymity; others, like Jim, suffered quietly because of it.

I first met James after some concern was expressed by building management that a tenant had been locked away in his flat for some time. After repeated attempts over a few days to gain access to his room, Jim unbolted his door and allowed me to enter. As I stepped into his living quarters, the stench of spoiled food and urine-soaked clothing filled the air. Papers, books, clothing, and other paraphernalia cluttered the space. A large color television filled much of the room and was playing loudly as an episode of a soap opera unfolded. James moved about slowly, awkwardly, listlessly. His speech was barely audible. His voice was expressionless. He was a mass of unmet needs: His hair was matted and unkempt, his shirt and pants were torn and frayed, his thoughts were incoherent and disorganized, his face was unwashed and unshaven, his body was limp and emaciated.

Following some preliminary discussions with James about his background, I realized that he was partially paralyzed. This explained the motor difficulties and the organic impairment. I also discovered that he was a veteran and a frequent inpatient at the Veteran's Administration local mental health hospital. A severe cardiac arrest, before his arrival at the YMCA, along with a history of depression and chronic organic brain syndrome (OBS), had all been diagnosed and treated there.

After a series of limited exchanges over several weeks, I asked James about his television and why the channel was always set to a daytime drama. On each previous visit, regardless of the time we met, James's TV was turned on and he intently watched one soap opera program after another. "I like the doctors." He said this a few times and smiled until his voice gave way to silence. I pressed him for more information and then he told me: "I'm a doctor."

It was hard to imagine how this man, seemingly lost, forgotten, and confused as he was, could ever have been a physician. The truth is, he was. Piled deep within a stack of papers scattered across his desk, Jim pulled out his college and medical school diplomas, his honorable discharge papers from military service, and several pay stubs documenting that he had worked at Pittsburgh's Allegheny County Morgue as a forensic pathologist. With this information in hand and with his permission, I was able to track down Jim's complete medical and psychological history.

Of particular significance was the number of involuntary commitments for which he had been treated. On four separate occasions within an eight-year period, Jim had been involuntarily hospitalized for depression. Three of these commitments lasted 28 days, and the remaining civil confinement lasted 90 days. In each instance, hospital's admitting staff determined that Jim was gravely disabled (i.e., deteriorating to the point of not eating, not sleeping, or generally not caring for himself). The hospital eventually discharged Jim following each episode of institutionalization.

According to mental health law, when a person is no longer a danger to him- or herself (i.e., caring for one's physical well being), the person must be released from confinement ("Guidelines," 1983: 674–677; Perlin, 1999: 127). In James's case, after some initial medical intervention and drug treatment, he agreed to frequent the veterans' hospital for subsequent medication monitoring and periodic therapy. In time, given the nature of his illness, hospital contact became more infrequent until it stopped altogether. Returning to his single room at the YMCA, Jim would retreat into the privacy of his living space. The prescription drugs would run out, the psychiatric symptoms would resurface, the decompensation would run its course again, and he would suffer alone in his anonymity.

This was the cycle of James's mental health treatment. The system of which he was part and the system of which he spoke did little to ensure that ongoing noncrisis care was made available to him. James said, "This is where I live. I'm a doctor and sometimes I go to the hospital but I don't stay. I can't stay. It's not possible for me to stay." James negotiated his limited identity as a sick patient receiving "revolving door" treatment (Arrigo, 1996a: 100–101). He was caught in a cycle of hospital care that restricted his ability to remain there as an inpatient and did not make it possible for him to thrive in the community as an outpatient. In the end, given the degree of sustained deterioration to his physical and mental condition, James was hospitalized on a psychogeriatric unit at the veterans' hospital where he passed away some five years later.

The Mentally Ill "Offender": The Case of Larry

Larry was a young man in his early 30s, small of stature, but sturdy of frame, who lived alone on the South Side of Pittsburgh. He frequented the city's soup kitchens and sandwich lines, and collected a modest subsidized income from the government. His head was completely shaved except for a thick batch of long brown hair that flowed from his crown to the small of his back, his ears were multiply pierced, and his body was appreciably tattooed. He wore a goatee and fashioned a patch over his left eye. A colorful bandanna was carefully placed around his head.

I first met Larry at a downtown sandwich line. He had difficulty standing still and paced incessantly. He spoke to himself, sometimes shouting obscenities, followed by muttering compliments. When I addressed him, he would modulate his personality without provocation or inducement: At times he was polite and overly gracious, and at other times he was enraged and extremely abrasive. When I asked Larry about this he would say, "It's like I'm always different, thank you. [Angrily] I'm a fuckin' asshole! Yep, I am. [Smiling] I am. Please don't get pissed-off at me. Sorry! [Screaming] Please don't get pissed off at me. Thank you!!"

I had enough training and field exposure to realize that Larry was a schizophrenic. He worked incredibly hard to contain his "demons" but was not always as successful as he wished he could be. His behavior and demeanor were problematic for another reason. Typically, people were offended by his more hostile comments and this led to intense verbal altercations, occasional scuffles, and some full-fledged brawls.

Larry had been criminally incarcerated and civilly committed. Usually, he was placed in the county jail following a fistfight where police were called in to resolve the dispute. Unfortunately for Larry, his more violent tendencies surfaced while in the local lockup, resulting in the filing of additional criminal charges. Jail personnel were aware of Larry's psychiatric condition (he had been incarcerated numerous times), and police personnel would later transfer him to a community mental health facility for immediate psychiatric care. His schizophrenia was treated through forced medication. Once the symptoms that had given rise to his violent outbursts dissipated, he was discharged and released so that he could return to his South Side apartment.

On several occasions, I asked Larry about what happened to him and how he felt about being confined. It was during these instances that I came to realize just how tormented he was and how angry his transcarcerative experiences made him. In one of his more lucid moments, he summarized his feelings as follows:

> They put me away, man. It's not right. That's all I mean to them. I'm someone to put away to rot. I'm not an animal, no sir. You can't put me away like that, can't treat me that way. Sure I get upset. Everybody gets upset. Then I'm supposed to take this medicine [showing me a pill container] and be good. I *am* good, right? They put me in the hospital with crazy people. I know I'm sick but I'm not crazy, right? I don't think I'm crazy. [Laughing] Crazy people can't think straight. Look at me. I got a place to live. I get my money and eat and take care of myself. And then they lock me up in the jail. [Angrily] I'm *not* a criminal? I get upset. I get upset, that's all. People get on my nerves sometimes, that's all. They don't understand me. I'm just a little sick but you can't tell me I'm crazy, and I'm not someone who, like, robs a bank or something. That's not me.

Larry continued on his course of clinical decompensation and criminal misconduct, with intermittent residence in psychiatric hospitals, jail, and his low-rent apartment. He negotiated his identity through the alternating role performances of the diseased-minded and danger-prone characterizations implied in the responses offered to him by the mental health and criminal justice systems. Ultimately, Larry found himself sentenced to a prison for a protracted period of time. The accumulation of criminal charges, coupled with failed inpatient psychiatric treatment, resulted in long-term confinement on a forensic unit of a correctional facility. With this placement secured, Larry became the embodiment of transcarceration: he assumed his socially structured and psychically inscribed role as both the "mad" and the "bad" offender.

CONSTITUTIVE THEORY,
THE MENTALLY ILL OFFENDER,
AND CONVICT CRIMINOLOGY:
AN APPLICATION

The three ethnographies differentially demonstrate the power of language, constitutively produced through agency and structure, to define the respective realities of Edith, James, and Larry. Each subject uniquely became a prisoner of confinement. In what follows, I provisionally demonstrate how the selected principles of constitutive theory apply to the three cases presented. In this process, I describe as well the relationship between mentally ill offenders and convict criminology.

Revisiting the Decentered Subject

The decentered subject experiences a lack in discourse; that is, one's essential being and one's interiorized meanings are silenced through language. Discourse "speaks the subject." The stories of Edith, James, and Larry reveal how words and expressions convey (unconscious) intents that alienate and oppress people. Edith's dilemma involved the definition of mental illness. James's predicament centered around the explanation for psychiatric treatment. Larry's problem entailed the meaning of violence.

Edith's forced choice (i.e., become "ill" in the clinicolegal sense or endure as a chronically depressed alcoholic) left her little room to re-articulate her identity. She was so thoroughly consumed by this choice that her persona was unmistakable: "I'm no good," "I'm nothing," "I'm dead." Indeed, so powerful was the established medicolegal meaning of mental illness that it stripped Edith of even this desired identity.

James's condition gave rise to a cycle of institutional treatment. His obvious and understandable identification with physicians resulted in repeated voluntary and involuntary hospitalizations that constituted and reaffirmed him as a "sick" patient. His listlessness, emaciation, and expressionlessness were all exemplars of his lack, conveyed quietly through seclusion and anonymity. James disappeared in thought and action. Words escaped him. He vanished in discourse. It spoke, as a stand-in, for him.

Larry's identity was linked to the fluctuating roles he assumed as a criminal and as a schizophrenic. These statuses collapsed into one when he was placed in a correctional forensic setting. Violence (both verbal and physical) engulfed Larry's reality. From the way he dressed and kept his hair, to the pierced ears and eye patch, to the body tattoos and ferocious outbursts, Larry assumed the character of a menacing, conflicted, and troubled figure. He became the quintessential mentally ill offender and this defined his everyday existence.

Revisiting the Recovering Subject

The recovering subject attempts to transcend, through language, the preconfigured parameters of meaning that symbolize the person's identity. Retrieving one's identity involves an active engagement with discourse. Subjects must resist alienating and marginalizing words, phrases, and language systems (i.e., medicolegal discourse), and replace them with vocabularies of sense making that restore their humanity and liberate them from oppression. Edith was unable to emancipate herself through speech, reflection, and action. James struggled, mostly unsuccessfully, to recover his identity. Larry actively resisted the assigned meanings embedded in the descriptor "mentally ill offender" and was punished for his opposition.

Edith wanted to be civilly confined. She made clear that she had an "illness, a disease," and that she wanted "to die" in a hospital because her life was "over." Edith felt as if she was already "dead," and that she had "nothing." Even when she questioned her existence, her words and thoughts returned her to the decentered state in which she suffered. "Maybe this is it for me. . . . Maybe I'm supposed to be like this [i.e., depressed, suicidal, and alcoholic]? Why can't I get over it? Why?" Edith could not retrieve her humanity even in words. As a result, she died. She was imprisoned by her thoughts, numbed as they were with alcohol, confined by the depression that spoke her identity.

James, too, sought and valued confinement. Where Edith longed for institutionalization as a means of quieting her suffering, James dreamed of involuntary hospitalization as a way of rediscovering his previous identity. James said very little; however, he made clear he was a physician. The power of the statement, "I'm a doctor," stood in stark, seemingly unimaginable contrast to the manner in which he lived. But it was in uttering this phrase that Jim, disheveled, incoherent, and emaciated as he was, struggled desperately to liberate himself from his deteriorating existence. His fixation with daytime dramas and actors who portrayed doctors was a constant reminder of who he had been and what he might be yet again. These words and actions, as the locus of potential transformation for James, were not enough. His identity as a gravely disabled, organically dysfunctional person consumed him as he cycled in and out of mental health hospitals.

Larry did not want to be civilly or criminally confined. He wanted to live without regulation from systems of institutional control. He wanted to be "good." He feared being "crazy." He did not believe he was a "criminal." Larry's resistance in words and actions was a continual struggle to keep his violence at bay. Often, he overcompensated by being polite, almost to the point of being disingenuous. This was a deliberate attempt at being a "good" citizen. After all, Larry, like most ordinary, "decent" people had "a place to live," and he had "money and [ate], and t[ook] care of [him]self." Larry's outrage at being "put away" and his resistance to the labels "crazy" and "criminal" were efforts to resituate himself as someone who was merely a victim of circumstances. "I get upset. I get upset, that's all. People get on my nerves sometimes, that's all. They [the mental health and criminal justice systems] don't understand me . . . . That's not me." The more that Larry defined his own reality and the more that Larry insisted on who he was, the harder it became for him to control his fierce temper. His steadfast refusal (verbally and physically) to accept his predefined status as a mentally ill offender was *the* source of his confinement. The language and logic of transcarceration rendered him a prisoner. He was captive to a process that restricted him from being anything more or anything other than the very contained "animal" he said he would not be and could not be.

Revisiting Social Structure as
Deconstructive/Reconstructive

Human agents are inexorably connected to the social and organizational structures that they define and of which they are a part.

In this context, the naming of social forms and organizational images are both independent of and linked to the subjects who constitute them. Sustaining the mental health and criminal justice systems and the manner in which they operate, then, depends as much on how they are defined as they do on the continued investment of humans to endorse these very identifications. This structure (individual-social) and agency (active-passive) duality makes possible the deconstruction and reconstruction of images and forms, especially those that are alienating, marginalizing, and oppressive. The structure of civil confinement for Edith was that she actively constituted the mental health system as a psychopathologized place in which to die. The structure of civil confinement for James was that he passively defined the hospital as a restorative place in which to live. The structure of civil and criminal confinement for Larry was that he actively constituted the mental health and criminal justice systems as punitive places in which to suffer.

The psychiatric hospital was where Edith wanted to die. She believed that she belonged there. "If they put me away at least I can die like the crazy fool that I am. At least I can die there with my illness." The system to which she professed such intense allegiance, however, refused her long-term admission. Much as Edith believed, the mental health facility existed to hospitalize and treat people with "an illness, a disease"; however, the system did not define Edith as someone who needed immediate psychiatric attention. Indeed, the hospital determined that, in her case, alcohol detoxification and rehabilitation were warranted. Edith was not interested in redefining her reality or the psychiatric system's role in her life. Instead, she vehemently maintained her investment in being mentally ill (i.e., depressed), and endorsed the psychiatric hospital as a place in which sick people could end their emotionally troubled lives.

The mental health hospital was where James wanted to live. He believed that his place was with other physicians. He vicariously experienced this sentiment while watching daytime soap opera dramas in his room. "I'm a doctor," he said. "I'm a doctor." Jim passively pronounced his identification with the hospital. He (James the doctor) disappeared in his silence. The psychiatric system defined its role as one in which to treat people like James; however, intervention could only be short-lived. After all, he recovered while hospitalized and became well enough to be discharged. Once in the community, James would return to the privacy of his flat. The medication would run out, the symptoms of decompensation would return, and the depression would intensify. In his quiet but powerful way, James decidedly maintained his investment in "revolving door" psychiatric treatment and passively endorsed the hospital as a place in which to retrieve his past. The system of which he was a part willingly, albeit incompletely and temporarily, availed him of institutional services.

Larry resisted civil and criminal confinement. "I'm not crazy . . . I'm not a criminal." The more intensely he renounced these descriptors (and systems), the more he became a part of them. Ultimately, he was fused to them. The mental health community defined its role as treating psychiatrically disordered people. The criminal justice community defined its role as handling overtly violent citizens. Larry was identified as both diseased and dangerous. His words, thoughts, and behaviors became synonymous with the meaning for the mentally ill offender. Although he actively resisted this characterization, his resistance was interpreted as an indication that he was, indeed, both diseased and dangerous. He was a schizophrenic and a menace. Larry actively maintained his opposition to civil and criminal confinement, alleging that they were places for "animals," places to "rot." For Larry, being "put away" was like a punishment; it was a place in which to suffer. The more that Larry spoke of transcarceration this way, the more it became the very structure of despair and imprisonment that he so forcefully rejected.

The Crimes of the Medical and Criminal Justice System

The constitutive power to harm denies people of their ability to make a difference. It denies them of their given humanity. This repudiation in discourse occurs through harms of reduction and repression. Harms of reduction restrict a person from being who he/she is through the actions of another. The person is treated as somehow less than his/her identity would otherwise allow. Harms of repression thwart a person in her/his efforts to be something more or something other than the individual already is. The subject is prevented from reaching a certain objective or particular standing in life. Edith was the victim of crime. The mental health system presented her with a forced choice that denied her difference. Thus, the harm perpetrated against her was one of reduction. James was the victim of crime. The mental health system refused to accept him indefinitely for psychiatric treatment until it was too late. Thus, the harm perpetrated against him was one of reduction. Larry was the victim of crime. The mental health and criminal justice systems denied him of the potential to live as he chose. Thus, the crime perpetrated against him was one of repression.

The psychiatric community refused to accept Edith for immediate inpatient treatment. It defined her as a dual-diagnosed (i.e., mentally ill and chemically addicted) client. But the implicit meaning of the dual diagnosis compelled Edith to confront an unreasonable dilemma: become psychiatrically disabled in the medicolegal sense *or* admit drug dependency and receive alcohol treatment. The problem was that Edith was both and she articulated her reality accordingly. The only system to which she could turn refused to embrace her spoken difference (i.e., simultaneously addicted and depressed). This denial of difference was the expression of state-sponsored power that reduced her humanity.

The psychiatric establishment subjected James to repeated institutional confinement, while typically ignoring prospects for chronic care. Although the system acknowledged that James was gravely disabled, it did not adequately support him once he returned to the community. The medicolegal community embraced his mental illness, but it did so only partially and impermanently. As long as James fit the gravely disabled description, he received psychiatric care. The problem was that James's illness extended beyond the limits of revolving-door institutional treatment. His dysfunctional and debilitating life as an SRO resident (e.g., without food, companionship, socialization), traceable to his forgotten past as a doctor, was similarly a part of his identity. The mental health system ignored (or dismissed) this dimension of his articulated reality and, at best, interpreted it as symptomatic of his cycle of decompensation. Thus, James was forced into the limiting role of an occasionally depressed patient. He was not perceived as more or less mentally ill than this, and his identification as a forensic pathologist was ostensibly disregarded. James was denied his existence and quietly suffered because of it. This denial of difference was the expression of state-endorsed crime that repudiated the fullness of his humanity.

Larry refused to accept that he was mentally ill or criminally dangerous. He struggled to be neither, managing to secure an apartment and living independently. For Larry, these were clear indicators of being a "good" person. Larry's efforts to maintain this standing and thrive in the face of it were restricted by both the mental health and criminal justice systems. Larry cycled in and between the psychiatric hospital and the county jail. His transcarceration, and the unstated values embedded in this ongoing process, significantly prevented him from rising above the restricted role performances he was compelled to live out. Eventually, not only was he hindered from returning to his autonomous existence on Pittsburgh's South Side, he was precluded from redefining himself as anything other than a mentally ill offender. Larry was denied the potential to be free and self-sufficient. He was denied the possibility to be other than "mad" and "bad." This articulated refusal was the power of state-regulated crime to quash, through words and actions, the dignity and humanity of vulnerable persons.

IMPLICATIONS, FUTURE RESEARCH, AND CONCLUSIONS

Transcarceration is a process by which persons with psychiatric disabilities are repeatedly and alternately contained in the mental health and/or criminal justice systems. Convict criminology is a new school of thought that attends to the felt experiences of prisoners in a more direct and intimate way, allowing us to more carefully and completely understand the presence of crime and the prospects for justice in the lives of those who are institutionalized. This chapter has explored how transcarceration differentially impacted the lives of three disordered citizens, uniquely rendering them captives of disciplinary control.

The method of analysis relied heavily on constitutive theory, informed by the ethnographic reporting of the researcher. What we discovered is how language, and the agency-structure duality implicated in the coproduction of reality, limited the role performances of the three individuals, leaving them little room to renegotiate their identities. Edith, James, and Larry were caught in a process that consumed and defined their existences. They distinctively invoked the discourse of "disease" and/or "dangerousness" (with their implicit values and hidden assumptions) to specify their experiences, and the psychiatric and/or penal institutions of which they were a part responded accordingly. Edith and James died because of it. Larry suffered in the face of it.

Future research in the area of constitutive theory, convict criminology, and the mentally ill would do well to examine how additional facets of agency and structure contribute (or not) to the activity of transcarceration. For example, this study did not consider the contextualizing variables of family history, political economy, religion, or the media. Indeed, it is easy to imagine how a history of mental illness in a subject's family might contribute to the articulation on his/her own reality, the structural and organizational forces the person coshapes, and the interpersonal exchanges the individual coconstitutes. The same may be said for other variables not directly or indirectly examined in this study.

Given this, the application in this chapter can be described as provisional at best. Accordingly, it follows that future scholarship in the area would do well to assess more systematically the utility of constitutive theory in relation to the psychiatrically disordered and convict criminology.

Finally, the conclusions reached from this chapter might lead one to assume that all mentally ill persons are prisoners of confinement. This is an oversimplification and overgeneralization not intended by this research. The expressed purpose of this study was to demonstrate how the process of transcarceration could and did work in the lives of some psychiatrically disordered subjects. What is disturbing about the conclusions reached is that, in the three cases examined, the effects of transcarceration were, without question, devastating. Future investigators need to examine how agency and structure coproduce victimization in words and behavior, and how, if at all, replacement discourses (e.g., MIOs as "psychiatric *survivors*," "mental health *consumers*," "differently *abled*") reduce prospects for harm in speech and action.

With these observations in mind, I acknowledge the shortcomings of my fieldwork and the limited implications that follow. Nevertheless, the study is suggestive on a number of fronts. First, language was significant to how Edith, James, and Larry defined their identities, and it was integral to how the civil and criminal systems of institutional control were interpreted and functioned in their lives. The selection of words, phrases, gestures, and silences (and the meanings embedded in them and the meanings subjects attached to them) illustrates the power of discourse to shape reality.

Second, the language explored in this study draws our attention to how people were harmed and how crimes were enacted. Edith, James, and Larry were victims of disciplinary forces because of their spoken differences. The systems to which they turned (or attempted to resist) coshaped their identities. Edith's insistence on being mentally ill (and chemically addicted) was repressed by the psychiatric system. James's desire to be permanently confined as a chronically ill, rather than occasionally depressed, patient was (largely) repressed by the mental health system. Larry's potential existence as a free and self-sufficient citizen was so reduced by the criminal and civil confinement systems that he became the "mad" and "bad" person he so vehemently renounced.

Third, the descriptor "mentally ill offender" signifies something more than psychiatrically disordered persons who are incarcerated. Based on the preliminary research findings of this study, the meaning of the MIO label is threefold: (1) it refers to psychiatrically disabled persons who are so offensive to society, because they are different from their non–mentally ill counterparts, that they are civilly confined; (2) it refers to psychiatrically disordered persons who are so offensive to society, because they are different from their non–mentally ill counterparts, that they are criminally confined; and (3) it refers to psychiatrically disabled (or disordered) persons who are so offensive to society, because they are different from their non–mentally ill counterparts, that they may be civilly and/or criminally confined. These conclusions suggest that being an "offender" has as much to do with one's articulated mental illness as it does with one's possible criminal conduct.

Fourth, transcarceration, constitutively interpreted, is the process that figuratively and literally condemns individuals to restrictive role performances (i.e., "bad," "mad," or both). Transcarceration renders subjects prisoners of confinement discourse. The result is that mentally ill citizens succumb to the marginalization, alienation, and victimization structurally embedded in the civil and criminal systems of institutional control, and linguistically reinforced by the very words and expressions subjects use to define and sustain them.

Although certainly limited in application, the three subjects ethnographically investigated in this article participated in transcarceration. Their felt pain was real; their articulated suffering was deep. As victims of the language and logic of a restrictive process, their lives were unmistakably and dramatically altered. Edith, James, and Larry became prisoners of confinement, and they could do little to change their marginalizing and alienating identities.

NOTE

1. The information collected during the 1984–1991 time period included initial client contact data, personal interviews, case reports, psychosocial histories, content and processes progress notes, and criminal confinement and psychiatric hospitalization records. Documentation for the last two required client/patient releases of information. Much of the field reporting described here was direct, personal, and recorded verbatim. During the eight-year period in which client information was documented, I interviewed more than 350 individuals. The case studies described in this study are representative of three types of mentally ill offenders: (1) persons who are defined as chemically addicted and experience difficulty with receiving ongoing mental health services (the case of Edith); (2) persons who are defined as mentally ill and cycle in and out of psychiatric treatment centers (the case of Jim); and (3) persons who are defined as mentally ill and criminally responsible, repeatedly and alternately institutionalized and incarcerated (the case of Larry).

14

Soar Like an Eagle, Dive Like a Loon

Human Diversity and Social Justice in the Native American Prison Experience

WILLIAM G. ARCHAMBEAULT

E agles and loons exemplify the great diversity that exists among birds of prey that attack from the sky. The eagle attacks its quarry in the air, on the ground, or near the surface of a body of water. The eagle's speed, cunning, and strength allow it to dominate the sky, to locate its prey while circling hundreds of feet above the earth or water, then swoop down upon it. However, if its quarry is in the water and can dive deep and quickly enough, it can escape the clutches of the eagle's talons. By contrast, the gangly loon flies much closer to the water and is much slower. Yet, the loon hunts its aquatic prey by diving deep into the water, staying submerged for many minutes. Both the eagle and the loon are highly respected in many American Indian cultures because each represents specific strengths that are the other's weaknesses. Nature's strength and resiliency derive from its diversity. Diversity has been the strength of America's First Peoples as well.

Human diversity, both in culture and genetic characteristics, allows the descendants of some of the indigenous peoples of *Turtle Island*[1] to survive to this day. These descendants are recognized by common ethnic labels,[2] including Native American, American Indian, First Peoples, indigenous or aboriginal peoples, and First Nations, as well as by many different tribal names.[3] Finally, many tribes are known by other sacred names, sometimes known only to tribal members.[4]

Earlier versions of this paper were presented at the annual Western Social Sciences Association Conference, San Diego, and at the Academy of Criminal Justice Sciences meeting, New Orleans, March 2000.

Contrary to popular stereotypes, there are no archetypal American Indians in physical appearance or culture. In reality, great cultural diversity and genetic heterogeneity have always existed between Indian nations.[5] Furthermore, significant diversity in culture, traditions, and language, as well as heterogeneity in physical appearance, often exists among members of the same band, tribe, or nation—diversity that is as great as differences between peoples of different tribes.

The simple fact that human diversity exists among native peoples continues to elude academics, legal scholars, and policymakers today much as it did in 1492 when Columbus[6] mistakenly labeled the America's native peoples "Indians."

American Indian studies scholars, such as Vine Deloria, point out that Eurocentric bias in contemporary science and traditional academic disciplines continues to prevent Native American histories, cultural traditions, societies, religions, and biology from being accurately studied, interpreted, or understood.[7] As a consequence, well-meaning, educated individuals in government and the courts continue to impose repressive and discriminating policies on native peoples today. Nowhere is this oppression more obvious than in the management of America's jails and prisons.

Each year tens of thousands of Native Americans are confined in jails and prisons throughout the United States. Although much is known about the prison experiences of other minorities, especially African and Latino Americans, comparatively little is known about Native American prisoners and their experiences. Historically, American Indian crime, justice, and correctional experiences were ignored until the end of the twentieth century. Contributing further to the lack of information about Native American criminogenic issues is that too often national studies obfuscated relevant issues, distorted population distributions, and ignored human diversity among native peoples.

This chapter addresses some of these issues. First it explores the issue of human diversity among Native Americans and discusses the effects of ethnic legal labels. Then, the focus shifts to Native American prison populations, related research and experiences, and First Amendment issues. Lastly, the chapter presents a classification schema for comprehending diversity among Native American prisoners.

It should be noted that the information presented in this chapter is derived from a variety of sources, including informal interviews with Native American medicine people[8] (some of whom worked with Native Americans in prison and some of whom had experienced incarceration themselves), former and current wardens and correctional workers, exconvicts, and a review of published literature. In addition, the author was allowed access to traditional ceremonies that are not commonly open and to medicine people who are not usually available to researchers because of his own mixed-blood ancestry (French Métis-Chippewa, Lakota, and Cherokee) and familiarity with some medicine traditions. Out of respect for these traditions and to protect the identities of individuals who shared information, no firsthand accounts are reported. Where information is used, the facts are generalized so that they cannot be traced to any source.

HUMAN DIVERSITY AMONG
AMERICA'S INDIGENOUS PEOPLES

The original peoples of the Americas have always been highly diverse in all aspects of their human existence: biological, cultural, societal, and religious. America's ancient indigenous peoples left two sources of proof that they actually even existed: human gene pools and culture. Some ancient groups have died out, leaving only traces and artifacts of once viable cultures and societies. Only fragments of ancestral gene pools and culture survive today for other groups.

Currently, culture and human gene pools remain least altered only among those native peoples who live in remote areas of the Americas and who had the least contact with white Euro-Americans. For example, the physical isolation of Inuit and Eskimo populations in the Arctic and Subarctic regions of North America, and the desert remoteness of Navajo, Zuni, and Hopi allowed these First Nation peoples to retain many of the characteristics of their ancestors, both in terms of culture and physical attributes.

By contrast, native peoples who had the most contact with Euro-Americans or who suffered most from the centuries of repression and forced assimilation tended to lose both genetic and cultural characteristics of their ancestors to varying degrees. The Cherokee, for example, are the largest officially recognized Indian tribe in the United States. Although some Cherokee who hold tribal membership retain both the physical appearance and culture of their ancestors, many more look and act more like their Euro-American or African ancestors.

Tens of thousands of people in the United States today can trace their lineage to Native American ancestors. Some native peoples exist today only because their ancestors married or mated with whites or were sold into slavery. Many trace their lineage to sixteenth-, seventeenth-, or eighteenth-century tribal customs that encouraged Indian women to mate with European white males during the fur trade era. During the nineteenth century, United States government policies of forced removal encouraged native women to marry white males in order to survive. Also, from the late nineteenth century through 1978 (when the practice became illegal), Indian babies were removed from their Indian families and adopted by (or sometimes sold to) white families.[9] Still others trace their lineage to other mixed-blood European and African ancestors.

From a native peoples perspective, American history is a continuous story of European, and later U.S. government, invasion of sovereign Indian lands since Columbus first conquered and enslaved the Tiano Nation (Deloria, 1969, 1994, 1995; Deloria and Lytle, 1983, 1984; Josephy, 1991; Means, 1995). The methods used to appropriate the land from American Indian control were varied, ranging from military conquest to political subterfuge, and from "ethnic cleansing" or physical extermination to cultural genocide[10] and boarding school "reeducation."[11]

Despite these efforts, some indigenous peoples and segments of their cultures did survive.[12] The collateral consequences of this history are many. One is the fact that many people of Native American ancestry do not retain many of the physical characteristics of their indigenous ancestors, while others do. Some people have maintained contact with tribal culture, traditions, and reservations, while others have not. Other native peoples who physically look like their Anglo or African American neighbors follow the spiritual and social traditions of specific tribes, while others who "look like Indians" do not. Some people with native ancestry have been able to retain much of the historical culture, while others have not. In short, there are people who "look like Indians" that reject native traditions and culture, and there are other people who "look Euro/African American" as well as those that "look Indian" that accept tribal customs and maintain tribal traditions.

Today, in order for a person to qualify as a tribal member, the person must be on a tribe's official rolls. In turn, eligibility for enrollment requires that the individual have a certain percentage or "quantum" of tribal ancestry. Issues of "blood quantum" and "tribal enrollment" did not become problematic until the late nineteenth century when the United States (and Canada) forced Native Americans onto reservations (or reserves, as they are called in Canada).[13]

Historically, although variance existed in customs of different tribes, most tribal cultures automatically recognized as full tribal members people who were the child of a tribal member, outsiders adopted into the tribe, outsiders who married tribal members, and captives and slaves who were adopted into the tribe.[14] Tribal enrollment and "blood quantum" issues today have their origins in the "land allotment" policies that went into effect after the reservation systems[15] were established. These aimed at stealing more tribal lands.[16] Tribal enrollment and "blood quantum" tests provide the rationale for ethnic labeling, discussed next.

ETHNIC LEGAL LABELS
AND THEIR EFFECTS

In the United States, the ethnic labels "Native American" and "American Indian" are legal terms that are political and controversial on many levels. Between tribes and government are those revolving around tribal sovereignty, land and compensation claims, federal and/or state recognition, and state and federal tax status, among many others. Political issues exist among tribes as well, such as contested ancestral land claims of the Hopi and Navajo.[17] Controversy exists too at the individual level, where "head rights" or per capita distribution of tribal funds are concerned. Finally, conflict exists between descendants of America's first indigenous peoples—those who are officially recognized as being tribal members, even Native Americans—and those who are not.

To appreciate the complexity of issues and controversy that blankets the experience of Native Americans in jails and prisons, it is necessary to understand three "Indian" legal statuses: U.S. government–certified Indians, state-only–certified Indians, and Indians without status. These classifications reflect more than mere semantics for the confined prisoner. In reality, these statuses directly impact the ability of a person in jail or prison to exercise his or her First Amendment rights concerning the practice of religion as well as to express cultural identity.

U.S. Government–Certified Indians

Some "Native Americans" are officially recognized by the United States Government (Bureau of Indian Affairs [BIA]) because they are enrolled in federally recognized tribes.[18] As of December 1998, the BIA, U.S. Department of the Interior, officially recognized approximately 330 different tribal nations in the lower 48 states and approximately 280 Eskimo-Aleut, Inuit, and other indigenous peoples in Alaska. According to the 1990 census,[19] which is frequently criticized for undercounting Native Americans, there were approximately 1.96 million Native Americans in the United States.[20] Of these, approximately 37.7 percent lived on reservations, trust lands, tribal jurisdiction, or designated statistical areas, including Alaskan native villages. Most of the remaining 62.3 percent lived in cities, with a few in rural areas that were not part of any designated Native American area.

The five largest "officially recognized" tribes in the United States, based on the 1990 census, were, in order from the largest to smallest: Cherokee (308,000), Navajo (219,000), Chippewa (104,000), Sioux (103,000), and Choctaw (82,000). These numbers[21] do not include indigenous peoples from Canada or those from Mexico, and Central and South America who come to the United States. Neither do these statistics include "native peoples without status," discussed later in this section.

Native American populations were greatest in the states of California, Arizona, New Mexico, and Oklahoma, which had populations exceeding 100,000. Next were the states of Washington, Oregon, Montana, North and South Dakota, Minnesota, Wisconsin, Michigan, New York, Colorado, North Carolina, Florida, and Texas, with populations in excess of 25,000. It is not surprising, then, that states with the largest Native American populations have the largest numbers of Native Americans in their prisons.

State-Only–Certified Indians

Most states recognize from 1 to 10 other Native American tribes or communities within their borders that are not recognized by the Federal Bureau of Indian Affairs. Some members of these "state-only" recognized tribes are included in the 1990 census numbers, whereas others are not. Some qualify as "Indian" for some things, whereas others cannot qualify for anything. For example, the United Houma Nation tribe in Louisiana and the Lumbee of North Carolina are recognized by state but not federal government. Their tribal members do not have Bureau of Indian Affairs registration cards and are *not* legally recognized as "Native Americans" by the federal government for treaty benefit purposes.[22]

Indians without Status

Still other individuals and aboriginal communities are not recognized either by the federal or state governments as "Indians." Three examples of these are the

Métis, the nonrecognized Native American communities and individuals of insufficient "blood quantum" who live either on or off reservations.

Métis are descendants of the aboriginal peoples of French-Indian or Scotch/Irish/Welsh-Indian ancestry. In Canada, Métis have a legal aboriginal or minority status equal to that of Indian nations, but in the United States, they have no federally recognized minority status, despite the fact that tens of thousands of mixed-blood peoples live in the United States, especially in states near the U.S.-Canadian Medicine Line[23] or border. Only the state of Montana recognizes Métis as an ethnic minority. The paradox is that Métis, or "mixed bloods," comprise significant portions, ranging from 40 to over 90 percent, of officially recognized tribal membership on both sides of the U.S.-Canadian border.[24]

"Nonrecognized Native American communities" refers to the hundreds of small communities of people living in rural areas or communities of people in large metropolitan areas without tribal affiliations. These are people without either federal or state recognition. Yet, many families have Native American ancestries that are as logically compelling as those living on reservations. These people "look like Indians." Often family ancestors refused to sell their land or to receive land allocations on ethical and religious grounds; consequently their names were never entered onto official rolls. Just as often, small bands or family clans of Indian peoples left tribal territory and moved elsewhere, avoiding armed conflict with land-hungry whites. Other ancestors escaped forced removal or reservations, married whites seeking better lives for themselves and their children, or were removed from their families and placed with whites to be raised without benefit of their tribal heritage. Legally, these people are neither "American Indians" nor "Native Americans."

There are many people of mixed ancestry who were born, reared, and educated as Native Americans, some of whom still live on reservations today, that do not meet "blood quantum" requirements[25] for tribal enrollment. The irony is that just because a person lives on a reservation, looks like a "Indian," and has been acculturated into tribal reservation society, he or she will not necessarily be recognized by the federal or state government or a tribe.

The reasons are many, but the net effect is similar. Throughout the United States there are thousands of people (individuals, bands, clans, and communities) whose claims to "Native American" legal status and culture are as valid and compelling as any, but who are not recognized by any government. Beyond the political issues of ethnic labeling, however, are the spiritual and personal identities of First Peoples and their descendants, and their personal affinity to sacred lands. These, in turn, are complicated because not everyone of indigenous ancestry experiences the connectivity to ancestral spirituality, traditions, and lands in the same way or at the same time.

The relevance of these issues to the study of Native Americans in prison is that prisoners without the legal label of "Native American" or "American Indian" may not be counted as Native American and may be denied the opportunity to follow tribal, cultural, or spiritual healing traditions.

CRIMINOLOGICAL RESEARCH
ON NATIVE AMERICANS

No one really knows how many Native Americans are confined in American jails and prisons. The reasons are many; four need to be mentioned here. Each set of factors, both separately and collectively, distort current research on Native Americans in prison. First, *the politics of state and local government directly influence how Native Americans are ethnically classified in prisons and jails.* States and local governments with high percentages of Native American voters respond to this political reality by not only counting Native American prisoners as minorities, but also by providing them with special cultural programs. By contrast, states such as Louisiana and Vermont, and local governments with small or insignificant Native American voting populations, not only do not count Native Americans separately as minorities but also do not provide different programs and services to native peoples.

Second, distortions occur in the official counts of Native Americans in prisons because of the *policies of intentional exclusion,* which are simply logical extensions of the first point. One way that some correctional facilities deny Native American prisoners the moral and spiritual support of their ancestral culture is by allowing *only* BIA-certified "Indians" to participate in Native American healing ceremonies. For example, in 1995, the Louisiana State Department of Corrections and Public Safety,[26] which did not even count Native Americans as minorities at the time, adopted guidelines that allowed prisoners to participate in traditional ceremonies only if participants met the following criteria: inmate must have a BIA number or be ethnically Native American.[27]

Third, some state prison systems follow a policy of *inmate self-labeling.* In many jurisdictions Native American cultural and spiritual traditions come under the heading of "religious" rights. In these states, prisoners have the right to identify themselves as to ethnicity and religious preference. The end result is that the convict is classified as Native American, if the prisoner claims to be Native American during the prison intake process,[28] and the inmate has a right to participate in native ceremonies based on that self-labeling. If the inmate claims to be Native American, he or she is classified as such without having to provide any proof. The one exception to this is participation in sweat lodge ceremonies, which is left up to the medicine person who runs the lodge.[29]

Fourth, *much government-funded crime-related research allows distortion to take place in the reporting of findings by lumping together Native Americans with other ethnic populations.*[30] Such confusion is discriminatory and hides the struggles of Native Americans to assert their own rights. It makes it impossible to accurately know how many Native Americans, either full- or mixed bloods, are confined in the jails and prisons in the United States.

Official Crime and Victimization Data (Adults only)

In February 1999, the federal Bureau of Justice Statistics (BJS) published a report entitled "American Indians and Crime" (Greenfeld and Smith, 1999).[31] Among the findings of this study for the years 1992–1996 are these: American

Indians experience twice the per capita rate of violence of the U.S. population as a whole and twice that of blacks. The murder rate for Indian people is similar to that for whites and Asians, but approximately one-quarter of that for blacks. Native American youth between 18 and 24 years of age experienced a higher rate of victimization caused by violence than any other comparison group. The rate of violent crime experienced by native women was 50 percent higher than that experienced by black males. Seventy percent of violent American Indian victimizations were committed by persons not of the same race. American Indian murder victims were less likely to have been murdered by a handgun than all other races. These data were fairly consistent with several other pieces of research.

Homicide rates for Native Americans are approximately twice that of the general population. Correspondingly, suicide rates are approximately 1.5 times greater as well (Wallace et al., 1996). Homicides, suicides, domestic assaults, and alcohol and substance abuse–related violence are all significantly higher on Native American reservations in the United States than corresponding rates found among the general population (Bachman, 1992). Disproportionately high numbers of Native Americans become involved with the criminal justice system as perpetrators (Bynum and Paternoster, 1996: 228–238; Grobsmith, 1994: 278–287) and as convicts in prisons.

As the proportion of females on Indian reservations entering the workforce has increased, so also has the homicide rate for Native American children (T. Young and French, 1997). The rate of reported child sexual abuse is significantly higher on Indian reservations than for general populations (National Indian Justice Center, 1995). A 1991 study found that medical resources were significantly less available for Native American populations than for the general population, whereas the suicide rate was 105 percent greater and homicide rates 172 percent greater in comparable areas (T. Young, 1991).

Native Americans are most often arrested, convicted, and sentenced for substance abuse–related crimes and violent crimes, particularly when the crime involves abuse toward family members. Greenfeld and Smith (1999) found that the annual violent crime rate among native peoples was 124/100,000 (12 and older) population—this is about 2.5 times the national rate. The aggravated assault rate (35/1,000) among native peoples was more than three times that of the national average (11/1,000) and twice that of blacks (16/1,000).

Devastating cycles of alcoholism and family violence and abuse are common among members of many Native American communities. However, the Greenfeld and Smith (1999) BJS study also reported that the rate of intimate and family violence was comparable to that of the general population, yet the percent was lower for intimate violence (general, 10.7 percent; American Indian [AI], 8.9 percent) and stranger violence (general, 50.8 percent; AI, 45.7 percent), but higher for family violence (general, 4.7 percent; AI, 6.7 percent) and acquaintance violence (general, 33.7 percent; AI, 38.7 percent).

Racial discrimination was a major factor in victimization involving violence. According to the Greenfeld and Smith (1999) BJS study, 60 percent of people assaulting native peoples were "white," 30 percent native, and the remainder "other non-Indian races." In 90 percent of the rape or sexual assault cases involving native women, the assailant was either "white" or "black." In more than 75 percent of robberies, aggravated, and simple assaults where the victim was an American Indian, the assailant was a non-Indian.

Discrimination, in terms of the handling of their cases, is also common. Native Americans were 10 times more likely to be arrested than whites and three times more likely than African Americans based on data from the Uniform Crime Reports (Harring, 1982). Native Americans also receive more severe sentences than do whites (Dommersheim and Wise, 1989; Feimer et al., 1990).[32] It is not surprising, then, that other research shows that incarcerated Native American women see prison as culture bound and racist, perceive that their lives, both in freedom and in prison, are continuous cycles of violence, and that their response to this violence is criminalizing (J. Ross, 1998b).

Official Data on Native
Peoples under Correctional Control

The Greenfeld and Smith (1999) BJS report estimates that 63,000 American Indians were under some form of correction control[33] in 1997, or about 4,193 per 100,000 population, compared to the U.S. average of 2,907 for all races and 9,863 for blacks. Gillard and Beck (1998: 1, 9), using similar 1997 data, found that there were nearly 1.25 million prisoners under the jurisdiction of federal or state adult correctional facilities in the United States, with fewer than 2 percent of this population classified as Native Americans. The Greenfeld and Smith (1999) BJS report found that about 2,000/100,000 American Indians were on probation and 300/100,000 were on parole; these rates were about average for the U.S. population as a whole. However, there were 1,083/100,000 American Indians being held in jails—the highest for any group.

The research on Native American crime and incarceration is still slim. Only a few studies have examined conditions for Native Americans in prison in any depth (French, 1982; Feimer et al, 1990; Grobsmith, 1994). Furthermore, only one recent publication (Lester, 1999) discusses why the causes of Native American criminal behavior may differ from those associated with crime patterns of other ethnic groups.

NATIVE AMERICAN
PRISON EXPERIENCES

When any person of indigenous ancestry enters a jail or prison in the United States, his or her experience is shaped by a complex set of interactive and interdependent personal, social, and contextual variables. Some of these are beyond the rational control of either the inmate or the prison, while others are within the rational control of one, the other, or both.[34]

Discrimination

Among some of the factors that are beyond rational control for any human being are gender, ethnicity and ethnic culture, patterns of socialization and nurturing, and early childhood learning. Also beyond the individual's control are community and criminal justice system biases toward these factors. Gender, ethnicity, and physical features of the individual play an important role in determining how different communities, law enforcement officials, judges, and corrections officials view the actions of an offender. In these sociopolitical settings, indigenous peoples who possess stereotypical "Indian" features tend to be treated differently throughout the justice system, than those who do not have such obvious "Indian" characteristics, especially in areas surrounding reservations (Harring, 1982; Dommersheim and Wise, 1989; Feimer et al., 1990). Not only are "American Indians" more than twice as likely to become victims of violent crimes than the national average, but they may experience 10 times greater victimization than average in the rural and small community areas immediately beyond reservation boundaries (Greenfield & Smith, 1999).

The stereotypical "Indian" features of the individual, whether male or female, shape how staff and other prisoners view and react to the confined person. This is particularly true in states with large Native American populations, such as Arizona, California, Oklahoma, Minnesota, New Mexico, and North and South Dakota, among others. People who "look like Indians" are treated like "Indians" according to the norms of the given community in which the jail or prison is located.

Discrimination, on the other hand, can work in reverse too. Persons of indigenous ancestry who do not look typically "Indian" may be prevented from exercising Native American rights or traditions while in prison because they *do not* look Indian enough. These individuals may even be ridiculed by other Native Americans who do possess stereotypical "Indian features"; this may be true of both guards and other prisoners alike.

Access to Native American Prison Programs

Not all jail and prison systems provide special programs for Native Americans and the types provided are substantially different for women than those available for men. In prison systems such as Minnesota's, which offer systemwide specialized programs for Native Americans, the experiences of the Indian female inmate are different from those of her male counterpart for two reasons. First, the tribal traditions that are taught or provided in prisons follow general guidelines of the Native American people who constitute the dominant indigenous peoples' tribal groups of the area. In Minnesota, Chippewa/Objibwa and Sioux traditions tend to be followed in prison cultural programs because these are the dominant Indian nations in the state. Second, tribal traditions, customs, and ceremonies are different for women and men. For example, both male and female prisons receive mentoring from elders, culture awareness programs that teach basic tribal customs by tribal members who are brought into the prison, sweat lodge ceremonies, and smudging. In addition, men perform frequent pipe ceremonies, but women rarely participate; instead they make and hang tobacco ties. Additionally, the subject matter in cultural awareness programs differs for men and women within the respective Chippewa and Sioux cultures.

Another set of factors that shapes the prison experience is that different individuals enter prison with different backgrounds and choose to react differently to the opportunities to learn more about native ways. Learning native or tribal customs is a highly individualized experience. Some individuals enter prison with a firm foundation of tribal cultural and religious beliefs, whereas others enter with little or no background.

While incarcerated, some native peoples come to understand, sometimes for the first time, their own cultural heritage. Still others enter prison with religious beliefs of a Christian denomination or other "mainstream" religions. Some individuals have integrated Native American and Christian traditions into their own value system, whereas others have not. Some indigenous peoples who hold fast their tribal traditions reject all non–Native American forms of religious practices.[35]

Special programs for Native American prison populations may vary dramatically in content and approach from one part of the country to another. However, some states, such as Louisiana and Vermont, neither provide any special programs nor count Native Americans as minorities.

First Amendment Rights of Native American Prisoners

Prison administrators have a wide range of tasks, objectives, and goals for which they are both civilly and criminally responsible. Prisons are primarily responsible for ensuring the life, health, and safety of the public, staff, and inmates; to maintain order within the prison; and to prevent prisoner escapes (Archambeault, 1982; Archambeault and Fenwick, 1988; Archambeault, 1983, 1985, 1988). The legitimate authority of prison officials to create policies and to implement operational procedures revolves around these primary responsibilities. The prison has the obligation of protecting inmates' rights, and one of the most important of these is the First Amendment right to practice religion.

The First Amendment provides that "Congress shall make no law respecting an establishment of religion, or prohibiting the free exercise thereof." Upon conviction and confinement in a jail or prison, no prisoner forfeits his or her constitutional rights, and he or she clearly retains the protections of the First Amendment. However, prisoners do not retain "unfettered rights," nor do they retain the "unrestricted use of rights." In the hierarchical logic of legal decision making, the duty of any prison to achieve its primary objectives (i.e., safety, protection of life and property) is a higher or greater right, than is the inmate's right to "unfettered" or "unrestricted use of constitutionally guaranteed rights." It is, therefore, necessary for prisons to place "reasonable" restrictions on the inmates' exercise of rights, including those to worship and practice religion according to individual conscience. When the issue of "reasonable restrictions" is examined in the courts, the task of the prison is to justify its actions (in restricting any inmate right) against the primary mission of the prison, which revolves around the issues of ensuring safety, protecting life and property, and preventing escape.

As this hierarchy of legal reasoning is applied to the right of Native American peoples to honor their own traditions and religious practices while being incarcerated, a variety of historical and contemporary factors often result in the application of inconsistent and discriminatory practices on the part of prison officials. Historically, until the 1960s only traditional religions (i.e., Christian, Jewish) were permitted in prisons and Christian biases against Native American spirituality as being "pagan, devil worship" prevailed. From the late 1960s forward, changes began occurring; Islamic, Black Muslim, Buddhism, and other religions and philosophies became permitted. In certain states (such as Minnesota, the Dakotas, California) with large Native American populations and in the Federal Bureau of Prisons, the introduction of traditional Native American forms of healing and spirituality began to be inconsistently provided from the 1970s onward.

In 1979, the United States Congress passed the American Indian Religious Freedom Act, which protects Native American ceremonies and culture under the First Amendment. In 1993, Congress enacted the Religious Freedom and Restoration Act (RFRA). This act essentially prohibited government, in any form, including prisons and jails, from "substantially" burdening a person's exercise of the First Amendment right of religion. This Act would have obligated every prison or jail in the United States to provide Native Americans with the means to worship and exercise their First Amendment rights according to tribal traditions and customs. However, in 1997 the U.S. Supreme Court struck RFRA down as being unconstitutional because the enactment legislation, as written by Congress, "exceeded the scope of its enforcement power under the Fourteenth Amendment."

Legitimate prison safety and health concerns in regard to Native American ceremonial practices are discussed in detail elsewhere (Archambeault, 2001). For the present, it suffices to note that sweat lodges pose a potential risk to prison safety and security because they involve the use of red-hot rocks, shovels and pitchforks, and activities carried on in the dark without staff supervision. Likewise, the possession of herbs, feathers, crystals, and other medicines can also pose possible health and safety risks. However, prison security and safety concerns can be addressed and balanced in ways that allow prisoners to follow their tribal and ancestral traditions. Prisons have an obligation to native peoples to work with communities both inside and out of prison to find ways of addressing these concerns.

Prisons also have the obligation of allowing native mentors and medicine people to enter prisons and to conduct cultural awareness training and instruction. Even without RFRA, prisons and jails have the moral obligation of providing American Indian cultural and spiritual programs. Prisons also have the obligation of training correctional staff and personnel to respect Native American customs and cultural traditions.

The experiences of American Indians in prisons are highly individualized, but, as noted below, imprisonment has a particularly traumatic impact on traditional and neotraditional individuals, native peoples who respect and follow tribal traditions and cultures. Yet, the destructive effects of prison life for many Native Americans is simply a continuation of the prisonization experience of the European and U.S. government systematic invasion of North America.

May or may not have "typical" Native American characteristics

Totally socialized into   Totally socialized into
values and beliefs of   values and beliefs of
tribal culture   dominant American culture

X——X
Traditionalist/Neotraditionalist   Culturally unaware

<————————————————————Adaptive————————————————————>
                  (Smoothly moves from one culture to another)

    [————Transitionist————]   [————Transitionist————]
              (In uneasy process of self-redefinition)

????????????????????????Marginal person????????????????????????
                  (Does not identify with any culture)

FIGURE 14.1 Continuum of idealized Native American prison roles

NATIVE AMERICAN PRISONER
ROLE SCHEMA

Informal field interviews with medicine people who work with convicts in prison suggest that there are at least five distinct dynamic and continuously changing roles found among Native American prisoners. Because no prior research exists on this matter, this writer designates these roles by the following terms:[36] traditionalist, neotraditionalist, adaptive, transitionist, marginalist, and culturally unaware. For purposes of illustration, these roles or role positions are organized along a continuum (Figure 14.1) based on the offender's personal commitment either to Native American/tribal cultural values or those of the dominant society. Over time, individuals may evolve or devolve into different roles. While a person occupies one of these positions, certain generalized patterns of behavior seem to be common.

Traditionalist and Neotraditionalist
Native American Prisoner Roles

At one extreme of the continuum are traditionalists and neotraditionalists. These types are similar in many ways, yet each has its unique differences. Both traditionalists and neotraditionalists are totally immersed into their native culture, language, and traditions.

Traditionalists Older traditionalists[37] and even some younger ones speak only the native language of the tribe or band. Most traditionalists will have physical characteristics of "full-bloods" from their particular tribe or village group. Their whole concept of self revolves around communal tribal and clan familial relationships. For some individuals, the word "I" cannot be separated from tribal culture or family group identity; in this, the traditionalist seems to share value systems that are typically found in Asian cultures, such as that of Japan or Korea.[38] Traditionalists who do not speak any language other than their own and who may be used to the freedom of the natural world find confinement in steel cages the most devastating.[39] Unless they are able to find someone who also speaks the same native tongue, they must endure the added imprisonment of silence, unable to communicate with other human beings.

Traditionalists today are not commonly found in most prisons in the lower 48 states. However, they can be found in substantial numbers in Alaskan prisons, and to a lesser degree in New Mexico, Arizona, Colorado, and those states beside the Canadian and Mexican borders. Their numbers will be greater among older prisoner populations. Historically, most Native American prisoners were traditionalists during most of the nineteenth century and the early part of the twentieth century.

Traditionalists who are scared and who cannot communicate with their correctional officers may become agitated and physically defensive. However, if they are able to talk with staff, if prison routines are explained to them, if their fears are addressed, and if they are allowed to find comfort in ways that are consistent with their tribal cultures, traditionalists will not become problems for correctional staff. Care should be taken, moreover, to protect traditionalists from other convicts in the general population who may prey on the traditionalists' lack of familiarity with prison ways of survival.

The Neotraditionalist   The neotraditionalist role is very close to that of the traditionalist. However, neotraditionalists also speak the language of the dominant society. Some are full-bloods with many stereotypic physical characteristics. However, others may be mixed bloods whose physical characteristics do not fit Native American Indian ideals. Regardless of physical features, however, their personal commitment of neotraditionalists to traditional tribal values is no less than that of traditionalists.

Many neotraditionalists are veterans of military service. Native men were drafted into World War I even though they were not citizens of either the United States or of the state in which the reservation was located,[40] and into World War II even though they were still not citizens of the state where they lived. Not "being a citizen" meant that, often, they could not vote, hold office, own property off the reservation, or enjoy the same level of due process protections as a white person.

Many others were drafted or volunteered for Korea and later Vietnam. After each of these wars,[41] returning veterans also brought back their dependence on cigarettes, alcohol, drugs, and training in the human violence of military conflict. All these had harmful effects on reservation life, and many veterans went to prison. However, along with the negatives came some very positive changes as well. Men and women learned how to better deal with white power structures. Many took advantage of educational opportunities, and a great many succeeded in the world of the dominant American culture. They also became the leaders who were able to revitalize their tribe's traditional religious and cultural life. Many became politically active for Native American causes.

During the 1970s, leaders of the American Indian Movement[42] who were confined in prison redefined the role of neotraditionalist, as later leaders also did in the 1980s and 1990s. In prison, these individuals know their rights and demand them in prison. Others become deeply committed to native healing and spirituality. Still others follow their own personal agendas and act in their own personal best interests. Many become convict leaders and spokesmen.

Some neotraditionalists have fathers and grandfathers who served time in prisons. Often alcohol or drugs were involved, and issues of honor are used as justification for the actions that put them in prison. Sometimes this group can be confrontational with institutional staff, especially where issues of culture and religious practice are concerned. Most of the time, however, if the staff and prison are making an honest effort to address the cultural and spiritual needs of the native population in prison, this group will have a generally calming and predictable influence on other native prisoners. Neotraditionalists may be seen as heroes or political prisoners by native peoples outside of the prison.

Some have made the transition from being a culturally unaware or marginalist to becoming a neotraditionalist. While in prison many came to know their own culture and its healing traditions for the first time.

Participation in Native American culture and spirituality are critically important in the maintenance of self–identity, balance, and self-control for both the traditionalist and neotraditionalist in prison. Neotraditionalists who are allowed to practice sacred ceremonies often become "ideal" inmates from the prison administration perspective. Consequently, traditional ceremonies and customs become critical to the institutional order. Without these aids, confinement may be not only more personally devastating than necessary, but also engender frustration within individuals that may lead to outbursts of violence. For these reasons, it is important for correctional staff to learn an appreciation for Native American spiritual values and ceremonies.

The Adaptive Native American Prisoner Role

The adaptive functions well in both the native and dominant society. Many are well educated or possess high levels of skills. They move smoothly back and forth from native or tribal culture and values to those of the dominant society. Many are college-educated business and professional people. Not many are found in state prisons, but slightly larger numbers may be found in federal facilities. They are often the most stable among the native population and most prone to defuse potentially volatile situations before they become confrontational incidents. They tend to be convicts who do their "own time." Some work with neotraditionalists on selected issues of concern.

Adaptives tend to follow multiple religious orientations. Outside of prison, this group may attend a mass or other worship service of a Christian tradition and then participate in sweat lodge ceremonies, pipe ceremonies, or other Native American traditional ceremonies. While in prison, adaptives may wish to continue doing the same. However, to the uninformed prison world, the spiritual needs and behavior of these natives may appear to be confused or contradictory. Correspondingly, to the traditionalist or neotraditionalist, the multiple spiritual approach of the adaptive may be seem like a threat or insult to traditional ways. As a consequence, the adaptive is often forced to choose either the native ways of the neotraditionalist or the ways of Western society. If the former is chosen, then the behavior of the adaptive may be very similar to that of the neotraditionalist. If the latter is chosen, the adaptive may lose him- or herself in the general inmate population. Only a few are able to maintain their balance between native and Western spiritual worlds while in prison.

The Transitionist Native American Prisoner Role

Transitionists are individuals progressing from one status to another. They may be evolving from marginal or culturally unaware roles into neotraditionalist or even adaptive roles. Progressing or changing takes place most often when the person becomes spiritually or politically awakened (or both) to indigenous or tribal beliefs, values, and culture. In contrast, the opposite may also occur in rare situations, such as if the person becomes disillusioned and withdraws from Native American values, traditions, or beliefs. Transitionists are often unpredictable and inconsistent during the period of self-redefinition. It may take a person many years to complete the change.

The Marginalist Native American Prisoner Role

The marginalist is the quintessential person who fits into neither the native nor the dominant society. Marginalists often have traumatic childhood backgrounds and memories that they associate with both the native culture and that of the dominant society. Females falling under this classification may have been sexually and psychologically abused. Similarly, male marginalists will have histories of physical and psychological abuse. Marginalists may constitute a large portion of indigenous prisoners in any prison.

Marginalists tend to be unpredictable, volatile, and unreliable whether in or out of prison. They may become confrontational with staff for any reason, often going out of their way to irritate guards and to create situations that push good correctional officers into overreacting. If guards overreact, then the marginalist tries to arouse other inmates to strike back at "another example of Indian abuse." At the same time, members of this group are likely to be using or selling drugs, "hooch," or other items of contraband. They tend to be followers and gang oriented. Or, they may be the "hangers-on" to a charismatic neotraditionalist.

The Culturally Unaware Prisoner Role

At the other extreme end of the continuum is the culturally unaware. The culturally unaware convict has little or no self-identity as a Native American or allegiance to tribal values or culture, and may actually reject indigenous values and culture. His or her knowledge of Native American values and culture is either nonexistent or suppressed for many different reasons. The culturally unaware does not care about indigenous issues or spirituality.

The culturally unaware person is often a living paradox. He or she may look like a Native American, may have lived on reservations, and may even hold tribal enrollment. However, for a host of different personal reasons, the individual feels absolutely no identification with any aspect of Native American culture. Or, the individual may be mixed blood with some but not many Native American physical traits, or may look like a person of Caucasian, African, Asian, or other non-Indian ancestry.

In some cases, the culturally unaware may be so totally immersed in Western or American cultural values and ideology that Native American values are rejected. In other cases, the person may have been intentionally removed from a Native American home or contact with tribal relatives as a child by a parent, guardian, court, or other entity and prevented from acquiring any indigenous self-identity or cultural knowledge.

Sometimes these individuals or their families experienced trauma as children over being labeled as an "Indian" and were forced to dissociate themselves from their heritage in order to survive. Individuals in this group disappear into the general inmate population within prison, often checking "white," "black," or "Latino" as their ethnicity upon entering prison. Because these individuals become indistinguishable from the general convict population, they are capable of the wide range of behaviors that are found in any prison.

If the individual has been reared according to a Western traditional religion, such as Christianity, the prisoner may find comfort in the practice of the same traditions while in prison, but will reject Native American traditions. On the other hand, the culturally unaware may be forced to confront many issues about him/herself while in prison, and may discover a hidden heritage that has otherwise remained dormant. Many people discover their native roots while in prison. When this happens, the person may begin to change. The culturally unaware may become a transitionist or marginalist.

CONCLUSION

In sum, there are four main points to consider in regard to the Native American prison experience. First, Native Americans are genetically and culturally diverse.[43] Some people who follow tribal traditions and culture have physical features that are associated with American Indians, and some do not. Some are card-carrying members of government-recognized tribes, and others are not. Second, the adjustment of any human being to prison is a highly individualized experience, and there is no typical Native American prison experience. Third, there remains a dearth of research that focuses on the prison experiences of American Indians. Fourth, existing correctional policy is often discriminatory in its dealing with Native American prisoners, especially those who choose to follow tribal traditions, because the issue of American Indian diversity is not considered. A complete rethinking of existing correctional management policies is required. The classification schema regarding prisoner roles offered in this chapter is meant as a means of better understanding the Native American experience of prison, with all the diversity that that implies.

The struggle to preserve and win back Native American identity, lands, cultural traditions, and spirituality continues. The battlefields of the twenty-first century are taking place in the courts of the United States, where the spiritual and cultural values of the survivors of America's indigenous peoples continue to collide with those of the dominant Western materialistic society.

The battles for Native American rights in prison continue as well. On the First Amendment freedom of religion issue, battles occur daily wherever native peoples are confined in prison. The United States legal system cannot comprehend that a person who is led to honor the Creator through the traditions of American Indian tribal culture should be entitled to the same rights to worship as a Christian, Jew, Muslim, Buddhist, or follower of other "mainstream" philosophies or religions.

Neither the U.S. courts nor most prison administrators understand that Native American identity cannot be determined by whether or not the person has a BIA tribal enrollment card. Rather, it is determined by what the Creator placed in the heart of that individual. To deny a Native American access to tobacco, sweet grass, the sacred pipe, smudging materials, feathers, or other items used in a traditional healing ceremony is parallel to denying a Catholic access to communion, a Jew access to a prayer cap or shawl, a Muslim access to the Koran, or a Buddhist the opportunity for introspection. To prevent a person whose traditions make use of a sweat lodge ceremony and whose institutional behavior does not pose a threat to institutional security is no different from denying a Baptist access to a Bible, a Catholic to confession, or forcing devout Jews and Muslims to eat pork.

For some American Indians, confinement in prisons is merely an extension of the imprisonment that their ancestors experienced being forced onto reservations and having to survive Indian boarding schools. Some Native Americans who are also military veterans view prison as less restrictive than boarding schools and less dangerous than war. Many consider themselves to be political prisoners.

In the future, criminology and criminal justice research can play an important role in protecting Native American rights. Future research must not only focus on Native American issues, but must also recognize the human diversity that exists among native peoples. Such focus and recognition are critical to understanding the Native American experience in prison, as well as many other American Indian issues.

NOTES

1. *Turtle Island* is the name used in most Native American cultures for the land mass that lies between the Atlantic and Pacific Oceans and between the Bering Strait and the Antarctic—a land mass known today as North, Central, and South America. Surviving native images of Turtle Island picture the mainland mass of North America as the back of the turtle, Central America as the tail, Florida as one back leg and Baja the other, Alaska and the Labrador Coast as the two front legs, and the Arctic Islands as the head.

2. The author apologizes to traditional Native American and American Indian people who may be offended by this grouping of categories. It is not meant to be disrespectful. However, the communication of salient issues requires that these terms be used interchangeably in this chapter.

3. Some of the recognized Indian tribes in the United States are Anishinabe (Chippewa, Objibwa), Apache, Arapaho, Aztec, Cherokee, Cheyenne, Choctaw, Colville, Creek, Eskimo, Flatheads, Hopi, Houma, Inuit, Iroquois, Navajo, Nez Perce, and Pueblo of the Southwest, Sac and Fox, Seminole, Sioux (Nakota, Lakota, Dakota), Winnebego, and Yakama.

4. For example, the medicine line dividing the United States from Canada divides the Chippewa/Objibwa Nation. In Canada, the tribe is called Objibwa, while in the United States, it is known as Chippewa. The People call themselves Anishenabe or descendants of "original man."

5. Each Indian nation is composed of different bands or tribal groupings. In turn, these are comprised of clans or family groupings. Gene pools and physical characteristics differ widely, not only between people of different nations, but between different bands of the same nation as well. Similarly, differences in language, culture, and traditions exist between bands of the same nation.

6. Columbus, and later Europeans, never realized that the Americas were inhabited by more than 500 independent nations, consisting of hundreds of bands and thousands of clan groups of indigenous peoples; or that 2,000 different language dialects were spoken; or that complex, sophisticated, and diversified cultures had evolved; or that American Indians had developed highly advanced medicines and treatments for illnesses that plague humankind even today (Deloria, 1994). Only fragments of this pool of knowledge survived the nineteenth- and early twentieth-century attempts at cultural genocide and boarding school "reeducation" (Crow Dog et al., 1995; Moses and Wilson, 1993; Deloria, 1994).

7. For a Native American critique of Eurocentric and Anglocentric science, academic disciplines, and knowledge, as well as Western religious bias, the reader is directed to Deloria (1994, 1995).

8. This writer continues to work with medicine people from the Chippewa/Objibwa Nation in both the United States and Canada. During the fall of 1998, the writer took a field sabbatical from his position at Louisiana State University to work with medicine people in both urban settings and on reservations, researching the use of traditional native healing programs both in and out of prisons. Much of the information came from medicine people working in the states of Minnesota, North and South Dakota, and the Canadian province of Manitoba. Through networking with medicine people in these states, information was also obtained from other medicine people working in the states of Utah, Arizona, and New Mexico.

9. In 1930 a U.S. Senate investigating committee confirmed that Navajo children were being systematically kidnapped and placed in church-run boarding schools (Neis, 1996: 331). Such practices had been widespread among many Indian nations since the 1800s.

10. Among some tribes, medicine knowledge and ceremonies were preserved for hundreds of generations within certain clan groups or secret medicine societies. In other instances, some parts of tribal culture and heritage were preserved by anthropological and archaeological efforts. In still other instances, many tribes who had lost nearly all their culture since first contact with Europeans have been able to reconstruct only parts of their heritage.

11. For a critical view of these policies see, for example, Means (1995).

12. By 1890, the Indian population in the United States had hit its lowest level. A 1900 census showed only about 237,196 Indians left (Neis, 1996: 300).

13. During the late 1800s, three rival solutions for resolving the "Indian problem" in the West were considered. The first was extermination or in current-day jargon, "ethnic cleansing." The killing of the buffalo, bounties paid for killing Indians, and

"open season" on "diggers" (word used for Indians in California) were all examples of attempts at physical extermination.

The second solution was to "Christianize" and "civilize" Indians by forcibly removing Indian children from their homes and placing them in government-approved boarding schools where they were taught to live as "whites" and severely punished for speaking their own language or observing any of their "Indian" customs. The boarding schools continued to operate in the United States until the middle of the twentieth century.

The third solution was to remove Indian children from their homes as infants and place them with white, Christian families. Tens of thousands of children were removed from Indian homes, often being placed by well-meaning fraternal organizations, such as the Improved Order of the Red Men Lodge. This policy continued until 1978, when it became illegal. See, for example, Deloria (1994, 1995) and Means (1995).

14. Consider these examples: The mother of the great Shawnee leader Tecumseh (Eckert, 1992) was a Cherokee who was taken captive by the Shawnee, made a slave, adopted into the tribe, and married to the chief. Another Shawnee leader, Yellowjacket, who was white, had been taken captive as a teenager and later adopted. Cynthia Parker was white, taken as captive of the Comanche, adopted by the tribe, married to a chief, and became the mother of Quanah Parker, the last free Comanche chief.

15. The term "concentration camp" was first used in describing the temporary stockades that were used to confine groups of Indians awaiting forced removal, and then later applied to "concentrating Indians on designated reservation lands."

16. For example, the 1887 Dawes Act, or General Allotment Act, dissolved tribal land holdings (land owned in common by the tribe) previously granted by treaties. Indian males were allotted 160 acres each. The remaining lands were declared to be surplus and sold to white speculators. During the 40-year period of allotment, more than 86 million acres or approximately 60 percent of Indian-held reservation lands were taken from Indian control. This pattern continued into the twentieth century. The latest attempt by the U.S. government to seize Indian lands was the 1953 Termination Act, which attempted to terminate American Indian reservations throughout the United States, making former reservation land government land so that it could be leased or sold to mining, forestry, or other private interests (Neis, 1996: 295–296, 355).

17. The U.S. government took lands belonging to the Navajo and compensated the nation by giving it land that had traditionally been Hopi. Many lives have been lost on both sides of this controversy.

18. Sometimes the term "card-carrying Indian" is used to describe a Native American who is officially enrolled in a BIA-recognized tribe.

19. The 2000 census is expected to reveal much higher numbers.

20. By comparison, the 1950 census showed only 377,273 Native Americans in the United States. Discussions with Native American leaders suggest that many feel that the undercounting in 1950 was due to a fear of racial prejudice.

21. Some aboriginal peoples, such as the Native Hawaiians and Native Pacific Islanders, tend to be excluded by both government definitions of Native Americans as well as in discussions of them, and unfortunately, this chapter will be no exception because of space considerations.

22. The diversity among non–federally recognized native peoples of today is illustrated by the contrasting examples of the Lumbee and the Houma. In the case of the Lumbee of North Carolina, the tribal peoples are generally satisfied with the "state-only" status because of the numerous grants and other means of financial support that are provided by the state. This tribe does not want federal recognition. In contrast, the Houma of Louisiana receive limited state support, and until 1964 were not even allowed to attend public schools.

23. Native Americans often call the U.S.-Canadian border a "medicine line" because it fits no logical geographic division. It

divides the historical tribal areas of many nations, especially the Anishenabe, who are called Chippewa on the U.S. side and Objibwa on the Canadian side. The medicine line makes visiting relatives and following tribal customs difficult for many Native Americans despite the Jay Treaty provisions. Feathers, tobacco, animal hides used in ceremonies, and so on, are seized at the borders. Some native peoples feel that they are subjected to closer scrutiny than non-Indians.

24. The designation of "mixed blood" traces back to Indian treaties of the eighteenth and nineteenth centuries in which "full-blood" and "mixed-blood" Indians were treated differently under treaty conditions. Today, the term "full-blood" is confusing. One meaning is that it simply designates that the person can trace tribal lineage back three generations. Another meaning is that when BIA ID cards are issued, they have "blood quantum" designations on them. Three generations of ancestors with more than 50 percent Indian blood can qualify as a "full-blood."

25. "Blood quantum" for enrollment purposes is complicated and varies from tribe to tribe. However, one experience is becoming increasingly more common. The offspring of a tribal member does not have sufficient ancestry to legally enroll in any tribe. For example, assume the standard for enrollment was one-quarter. Then, the child of an enrolled woman who was classified as one-quarter and whose father was not a tribal member would be one-eighth, which would not be sufficient for enrollment. Many children grow up on reservations only to find that when they reach 18, they are not tribal members and are not entitled to any tribal benefits or opportunities.

26. According to the 1990 census, Louisiana had fewer than 25,000 Native Americans living within its borders.

27. Such standards were upheld by the federal court for the Western District of Louisiana in 1997. (See *Michael Lloyd Combs et al. vs. Corrections Corp. of America et al.*, 977 F.Supp. 799; 1997 U.S. Dist. LEXIS 14709). As stated above this is the same Department of Corrections that does

not count Native Americans separately as a racial category.

28. It should be noted that many prison systems allow Native American medicine people to come into the prison to conduct ceremonies. In some ceremonies, such as a sweat lodge or purification ceremony, it is these medicine people who control which individuals participate. Most will not allow a non-Indian person to participate.

29. A few states, such as Minnesota, rely on Native American medicine people who are brought into the prison.

30. One of the worst distortions occurs when government research publications lump Native American populations in with "white" populations, such as reported in Table 11 of Gillard and Beck's *Prisoners of 1997* report (1998: 9). In other studies, the proportion of Native Americans in the general population is acknowledged, yet when it comes to tracking Native Americans in prison populations, they are either completely ignored or given only glancing mention.

Illustrative of the latter is Greenfeld and Snell (1999), *Special Report: Women Offenders*. In this report, 1998 population statistics of nearly 221 million people in the United States are estimated with 0.1 percent being male and another 0.1 percent being female Native Americans. Then, on all other statistical tables, Native Americans are lumped together with Aleuts, Asians, Eskimos, Pacific Islanders, and Native Hawaiians.

31. Report summaries were adjusted June 1999. The original and revised versions of the report are confusing. On some data tables, Native Americans included Aleuts, Eskimos, Native Hawaiians, and Pacific Islanders, while on other tables, Hawaiians and Pacific Islanders were counted as Asian.

32. These data are supported by the author's own field observations. While living on a reservation I noted that local law enforcement and judges often viewed the actions of Native American men and women differently than similar behavior exhibited by white people. Native people are perceived to be more of a threat than whites, are more likely to be arrested, be con-

victed, and be required to do more time than whites. These biases also carry over to prisons.

33. The term "under correctional control" refers to offenders who are in prison, in jail, on probation, on parole, or under some other form of official and legal control.

34. "Rational" means that it is logical or reasonable to expect that control can be exercised over these factors. "Beyond rational" means that it is not logical for control to be exercised.

35. For a discussion of correctional treatment implications, see, for example, Earle (1988) and D. Foster (1999).

36. These terms are the author's. Medicine people do not label people; they only described characteristics that were generalized into categories by the author.

37. Traditionalists often trace their tribal ancestry back many generations to times before the whites militarily defeated their people. They tell family stories about great grandfathers or grandfathers who lost the right to hunt for themselves, were confined to reservations where hunger and starvation were common, and where they lost the right even to visit friends and relatives on other reservations.

Well into the twentieth century, reservation Indians had to have written permission of the Indian agent to leave the reservation for any reason, and the consequence for being caught without a "pass" meant punishment that ranged from being shot to being imprisoned in the stockade to loss of food rations for one or more months for a man's family.

For some, the most painful experience was having their children forcibly taken from them and placed in boarding schools, only to return many years later having learned white man's ways and forgetting his tribal ways. For having learned white man's ways meant that the person—male or female—was often rejected by the native peoples, who followed traditional

tribal ways, as well as by white society. Some, however, were able to hold onto their cultural and religious traditions and language. These have been passed down to the present generations of traditionalists.

38. Referenced here are values of the Japanese and South Korean cultures that are discussed in Archambeault and Fenwick (1983, 1985, 1988).

39. For further background on nineteenth-century incarceration experiences of Native Americans, see, for example, La Fleshe (1963), Pratt (1964), Standing Bear (1975), Debo (1976), or Kalesnik (1993).

40. In 1924 American Indians were made citizens of the United States with the passage of the Indian Citizenship Act. However, it was not until 1948 that the courts declared in *Harrison v. Laveen* that Indians were citizens of the state in which they resided and that state laws denying Indians citizenship in these states were illegal (Neis, 1996: 328, 351).

41. Between 1941 and 1945 all Native American men were required to register for the draft even though they could not vote in several states. A total of 24,521 Indian men served in the U.S. armed services during World War II (Neis, 1996: 341).

42. To learn more about the personal experiences of neotraditionalists and prison, see Crow Dog, Brave Bird, and Erdoes (1990); Brave Bird and Erdoes (1993); Crow Dog and Erdoes (1995); Means (1995); and Peltier (1999).

43. An old medicine man once said to this writer: "If there is a decision to be made and there are five Indians making that decision, there will be from 6 to 16 different solutions proposed." His words were intended to convey a fundamental truth about Native Americans, namely, that in human diversity is the heart of native peoples. Each person is led to follow his or her own path in life as directed by the Creator.

15

Twenty Years Teaching College in Prison

WILLIAM S. TREGEA

People make mistakes, are convicted of crimes, and are sentenced to prison. While inside, and for a variety of reasons, they take college courses. Young adult prisoners know they need more formal education, that it will provide them with opportunities, and may help them lead a new life after release. On the other hand, older prisoners, like "nontraditional" students at universities, may want to take college courses, either as a means to better employment or simply to participate in "lifelong learning." In either case, every correctional institution has many men or women who desire the opportunity to further their education as a means to secure a new future that does not include returning to prison.

From the late 1960s to 1994, many convicts attended prison college.[1] In particular, the 1972 Pell Grants led to a hopeful era in which tens of thousands of U.S. prisoners earned postsecondary degrees or transferable credits. Then, because of punitive government policy, the college programs were stripped of federal and state support.

This chapter tells the story of prison college, as experienced by both convicts and teachers. I have spent the majority of my academic career as a prison college teacher. In short, in early 1981, lacking a Ph.D., I felt that the part-time

Special thanks to Stephen C. Richards and Jeffrey Ian Ross for their ideas, editing suggestions, and support, all of which improved this chapter. I would also like to thank the prisoner-students of the State Prison of Southern Michigan, Egler facility, for their insights.

adjunct teaching market was my only option, and the opportunity to teach in a prison sounded interesting.

Close to 20 years later, I was still at it. Because of this experience, I have learned that prisons are one of the best places to teach. Prison classrooms can be more poignant than college and university ones, and most prisoners are more dedicated to their studies than the typical college student because, as one prison college clerk at Jackson Penitentiary (MI) put it, "There are few alternatives on the inside to do anything positive." Receiving a Soros Foundation Grant (from the Open Society Institute) in 1997, I explored the situation of prison college in the current political climate (Tregea, 1998), and it is from both my experiences and that report that I draw on in this chapter.

MANY PRISONERS ARE READY FOR COLLEGE

Prison college offers an alternative community, which for some prisoners may be their only connection to the outside world (Newman, 1993; Duguid et al., 1998). Of course, there are different types of prisoners. Many grew up in poverty, with dysfunctional families, and/or in juvenile institutions. They may have served several prison terms. Still others may be mentally retarded or impaired, and are not capable of completing college courses (Clear and Cole, 1997: 110–34; Cole and Smith, 1998: 530). Rehabilitating criminals is not easy. They may be the victims of unfortunate circumstances, or they may have simply messed up their own lives (Moffitt, 1999: 42–50; Newbold, this volume).

Despite their problems and mistakes, hundreds of thousands of convicts are able to "glean" (Irwin, 1970: 104) from their prison environment positive experiences that can add to their chances of making it on the outside and that can improve their lives. Often prisoners enter a higher education program unfamiliar with being pushed to their intellectual capacity. No one has ever asked them to become academically accomplished. A large proportion of prisoners are African Americans or Hispanics, and their inner-city schools failed them (Sullivan, 1989: 29–57; Weissbourd, 1996: 169–186; Simon and Burns, 1997). Many of these prisoners never had a chance to succeed in secondary schools. The inner-city experience contributed to lives of crime (Hagan, 1994b; Tonry, 1994; J. G. Miller, 1996; J. W. Wilson, 1996).

Black, white, and Hispanic prisoners may have come from disadvantaged families, where their parents may often have failed them (Patterson and Forgatch, 1987; Sampson and Laub, 1993). Those who raised them may not have expected them to stay in high school or encouraged them to "make it" by completing high school and going to college (MacLeod, 1995: 83–110). Alternatively, maybe they never learned self-discipline at home or in school. Without self-control, many prisoners led lives as "leaves in the wind," overly influenced by peer pressure and street culture, without social support for conventional values (J. Braithwaite, 1989; Cullen, 1994).

Many readers of this chapter were expected to complete high school and go to college. They did not ask, "Why go?" but rather, "Which one to go to?" Thus, as children, many people have concrete goals for their future goals beyond high school. They were enfranchised in the social system, although their post–high school goals may have been vague. In contrast, the disenfranchised, who enter prison without a high school degree, may often complete their general equivalency degree (GED) in prison and discover themselves ready for college classes. In fact, over two-thirds of state prisoners have not finished high school and lack job skills (see Michigan Department of Corrections [MDOC], 1996: 1). It is an important experience for someone in their late 20s, 30s, or 40s, to finish a GED program and go to college in prison. Their sense of self-worth vastly increases (Wenda, 1997: 74–85).

Along with parental expectations about education, there is also the important issue of youth employment. Working a job, a teenager may be deterred from drifting into criminal activity, such as burglary, robbery, larceny, and drugs (Matza, 1964; Sullivan, 1989: 199–213). Many times I have taught business classes, teaching work-world concepts or skills, and the prisoner-students in their twenties would say, "I have never had a job."

Often their early years were characterized by family dependence on welfare checks, difficulties at school, trouble with police, and/or problems with juvenile justice authorities, resulting in years spent in and out of treatment and correctional facilities. Familiar with cops, courts, and corrections, these young adults are unfamiliar with the "real" world of work or with organizations not related to the welfare or criminal justice system. The state has been their guardian and parent, for better or worse. Coming from impoverished families, with histories of childhood neglect and abuse, they may have never learned to trust people (Currie, 1998: 120–128). For these prisoners, personal transformation, including a chance to become a productive member of society, requires carefully constructed prison programs, including postsecondary education (Duguid, 2000).

The discovery of self-efficacy through learning is a key area of opportunity. Prisons are responsible for "care and custody" but should also wean those who are ready away from the "state control culture," and help them develop self-leadership. Such a commitment also requires individuals developing a sense of being able to learn new concepts, information, and skills. All of these are part of a prison college programming.

Prison education demands performance from the uneducated prisoner. Prisoners need to be academically challenged. Unfortunately, most prisons offer only (remedial) adult basic education (ABE), GED tutoring, and low-tech vocational training. Prisoners need high-tech advanced skills training and accredited college programs to succeed in the present labor market. Postsecondary prison education, in particular, offers a certificate or degree earned through an outside accredited college, not a stigmatized "in house" prison vocational certificate.

PRISON COLLEGE IS
A PROGRAM THAT WORKS

Readers of *The Autobiography of Malcolm X* (Haley, 1964) may recall how Malcolm was a good student in Mason, Michigan, where he grew up. Nevertheless, he got sucked into the drug culture and became a "player" involved in crime. Later, in prison, he educated himself by excelling in classes, studying in the library, joining the debate team, and reading in his cell late into the night. My Michigan prisoner-students have written about the value of their prison postsecondary education. Comments included the following:

> Prisoner 1: I know firsthand that college has a positive effect. When I was first incarcerated 15 years ago, I was extremely antisocial and had a violent temper, which stemmed mostly from being illiterate. After I learned to read, however, I became energized to tackle other educational challenges and enrolled in a college program. I am not unique. I have seen prisoners engaged in behavioral trouble, but for those few who take advantage of the college program, this behavior stops! College enables prisoners to work toward self-improvement and positive growth that makes them realize that they have the power within their grasp to make a change.

> Prisoner 2: I have witnessed individual change within the prison setting from [men] just educating themselves.

> Prisoner 3: Coming to prison was an experience I needed. Just not for as long as I was sentenced to. College helped me grow in so many ways. Without it, I don't know where I would be.

In my prison classes many of the guys helped each other succeed. They may also have said to another prisoner who started to leave an exam early because he has not studied: "Loser!" Prison college offers the opportunity to prove oneself to be a winner.

Duguid and his colleagues have located specific mechanisms in prison college programs that are related to postrelease success, including "a record of improving academic performance, extra-curricular affairs, taking courses more consistently, and spending time in an education program" (Duguid et al., 1998; Duguid and Pawson, 1998; Duguid, 2000: 242). The components of a liberal arts education include a library, classes, writing, debates, and theater groups, all of which are important for forming an alternative community[2] (Newman, 1993; Murphy, 1998). The college program creates a different community where personal transformation may occur (Duguid and Pawson, 1998: 488). Prisoners grow as they reflect upon what they learn and consider instructor evaluations of their class work (Rosenberg and Kaplan, 1982: 174–177).

Prison college promotes self-leadership (Beckerman and Fontana, 1989: 174–179; Duguid et al., 1998: 95–97) and creates positive prisoner role models (J. Taylor and Tewksbury, 1998: 142–145). Accredited prison-based postsecondary education increases self-worth (Fraley, 1992: 178–181; Wenda, 1997: 24–28) and lowers recidivism (Jenkins et al., 1995: 20–24; Duguid et al., 1998: 88–105; J. Taylor and Tewksbury, 1998: 136–142). It also contributes to the likelihood that prisoners will seek further education after release (Duguid, 1992: 42, 2000: 242) and improves postrelease employability (Federal Bureau of Prisons, 1991: 1–13; J. Taylor, 1992: 133–134).

A TEACHER'S REFLECTIONS ON A PRISON CAREER

During the Pell Grant era (1972–1995), many Michigan prisons offered college programming. I worked as college teacher in several institutions, including the State Prison of Southern Michigan (SPSM), Cotton Facility, Michigan Reformatory (MR), the MR-dorm, Riverside, Ionia Temporary Facility (ITF), Carson City, and the Scott Facility (the women's prison). I also taught courses at the State Correctional Institution (SCI) at Soledad, California. I have worked with program administrators, on-site program supervisors, and taught over 35 preparations in business and management, composition, economics, philosophy, and sociology. Prisoners and teachers often talk about the many prisons they have been in. I will briefly describe my experiences below.

State Prison of Southern Michigan (SPSM)

In the spring of 1981, I began teaching at the SPSM, commonly referred to as Jackson Prison. This is the largest walled penitentiary in the world (1981 population approximately 7,000 men). On my first day, I met Paul Wreford, the director of the prison college program, in the main lobby.[3] We sat on blue plastic seats, while he introduced me to prison procedures: Law Enforcement Information Network (LEIN), clearance information (no outstanding warrants or felony record), where to get a photo ID, advice on do's and don'ts, and the advice that I should arrive early to allow time to get through all the security gates. Then, I walked through the high-security gates for the first time, wondering if I would ever get out; losing my sense of freedom, and thinking of all the awful things I had ever done, as the metal grills clanked behind me.

I had been in prison once before. As a high school student I visited a friend who landed up in this penitentiary for selling drugs. I can recall the same lobby with the blue plastic seats, institutional drabness, and shining floors. On that visit, I went through the first gate to the visiting room. But now, I was going through a series of gates to work all afternoon in a maximum-security area. I entered the penitentiary with trepidation. After my second week of teaching literature, the guys in class told me, "This place is going to blow." The next week Jackson Prison rioted, classes were canceled, and the spring semester was never completed.[4]

Returning in the fall to teach, I entered the first gate of the prison into the "bubble" (security space between the first two gates), signed in, went through a metal detector, was searched, picked up my ID, and went on my way to the college program. Located in the maximum-security area, known as central complex, it involved passing through two more gates. I was half-holding my breath the first few weeks of these walks. After the last heavy door shut behind me, I walked alone across the prisoner yard filled with thousands of convicts. This was a 200-foot tense stroll past basketball courts, lawn, and pavement, which brought me to the school building.

Entering the education building on the first floor, I found an auditorium, law library, three classrooms, and a small general library. This was where the bachelor-level courses were taught by Spring Arbor College. Eleven years later, after having completed my Ph.D., I would teach in this program. I then climbed the stairs to the second floor, where the Jackson Community College (JCC) "North Campus" was located, which included a program director's office, a general library, a reading and writing lab, the main college office, a book inventory room, and seven classrooms.

In 1981, this was a busy place, with several hundred students. The library was a particularly great place, with a full-time librarian, and lots of books, with quietly animated prisoner clerks and music playing in the background. The main office had several clerks, proud to work there. The writing lab had a full-time director. There was even an academic counselor. This was a good program, fully staffed, with a commitment to quality education. There were, however, no full-time prison college teachers. We were all hired on temporary contracts to teach specific classes.

Built in the 1920s, Jackson Penitentiary is an industrial prison covering an area of three-quarters of a square mile consisting of 12 housing blocks, surrounded by a tall wall guarded by numerous gun towers. This is an immense structure constructed with cell blocks four stories high, each level called a "gallery," some surrounding an open floor, others with a central tier. Each cell block held from 300 to 900 men. The building of this "big house" penitentiary reflected the business ideology of punishment under prohibition, a "Fordism" based on designing prisons like huge factories.

Walking through the Jackson Prison yard to the maximum-security classroom building gives one a sense of dull finality. This place is old, massive, and has changed little in 80 years. The convicts are doing hard time, many of them serving life sentences. This is a prison with a violent reputation; many of the prisoners are former residents of Michigan's industrial cities.

Maximum-security adult learners have a lot to say, and the classes are often interesting. Remaining nonjudgmental is an important part of any kind of teaching. However, in Jackson, I learned to say, when prisoners spoke of their crimes, "Spare me the details." An important finding of Wreford's (1990) study of the effect of prison college on recidivism was that the program worked well with "high-risk" prisoners. My classes were filled with men convicted of violent offenses, many of them my best students.

My Adjunct Positions Multiply
with Michigan's Prison Expansion

The prison classes offered an added dimension to my busy life. My first reactions of fear were replaced with a predictable routine: through the gate, teach the class, out the gate, go home. Meanwhile, as the Michigan prison system expanded, so did my employment opportunities. After two years at Jackson, I also began to teach simultaneously in another Michigan prison college program, the Montcalm Community College (MCC) College Opportunity Prisoner Education (COPE) program, which was located 80 miles north of Jackson, in the Ionia area.

The MCC programs were expanding to serve additional prison sites. This included the Michigan Reformatory (MR) and the MR-dorm for minimum-security prisoners. The program also offered classes at Riverside Prison, another old facility. In the mid-1980s, the Ionia Temporary Facility (ITF), and in the late 1980s, the upper mid–Michigan prison at Carson City, both newly constructed, were added to the MCC college program.

In this expanding prison system, the local stable of part-time prison college teachers would meet in the prison lobby, typically arriving several minutes early to prepare for class. We would say: "Hi, you teach for JCC?" "Me too." "Where are you driving from? Maybe we can share the drive?" A few weeks later we might say, "You drive this week, my car is in the garage, I will take next week." Saving money by ridesharing, sometimes we would have four or five instructors in a car.

After a few years of sharing drives we became friends. We had some great conversations on our 45-minute commutes from nearby cities (mostly Lansing). Over a dozen years, in the 1980s and 1990s, eight or nine of us taught in this expanding prison system, often at four places simultaneously—a community college, a business college, a liberal arts college, and perhaps at three or more prisons in both the JCC (Jackson) and the MCC (Ionia) programs. Seven courses per semester became a steady diet. This was our life. We shared our old cars, worries, and progress on finishing our Ph.D. degrees.

My gypsy scholar colleagues knew that prison teaching was important work. Many had taught in prison 10 years or more, and each of the old-timer prison instructors had his or her own character. One man completed a Ph.D. on Gramsci, another gave medieval skits in on-campus classes. One instructor was studying the Soviet Union. One woman taught writing classes and developed short story prison sketches. Another female instructor, who directed the writing lab, played city orchestra trombone and had been in a 1950s all-girl jazz band. I was doing a Ph.D. on social movements and occupations. There were also a few instructors with religious connections: a Methodist minister and an Islamic imam. We all had academic goals for the prisoners and could identify with the experiences of personal transformation. We had been there.

Part-time teaching in the prison college programs involved two types of instructors: old-timers with several years in prison teaching, and the new "once only" instructor. Some who try being prison instructors come, never to return. For example, a young lawyer came to teach paralegal studies, and then when his career improved, he was gone. Those who stayed became seasoned.

Meanwhile, the convicts were also busy, taking our classes and working in various prison industries. They had to push to do their homework after work. The men had few distractions. No families, parties, or sports got in the way of studying, but the prison routine prevented them from studying after hours, and access to the library was limited. The convicts were enthusiastic students, as the classes broke up the monotony of doing time. They never cut class and were devoted to their studies. Some of our students' biggest fears were that they might be transferred to another prison in the middle of a semester and lose their credit.

Michigan Reformatory (MR)

Built in 1860, the Michigan Reformatory (MR) is an ancient maximum-security prison. As opposed to penitentiaries, generally reserved for older convicts, this institution was designated to house younger inmates. At MR the prisoners ranged from 17 to 22 year olds with long sentences (mostly war-on-drugs mandatory minimums). These young prisoners were a definite contrast to the older, more experienced convicts at SPSM. Right off the inner-city streets, immature, and never having had a job, the guys coming into MR were tough and hard to handle. As I aged past 40, and then 50, I found it tiring to teach these young prisoners, but I was angry to see the program at MR end in the summer of 1997.

Trusty

Trusty, part of the massive Jackson Prison complex, also expanded in the early 1990s with modules and add-on buildings. College classes such as Human Relations in Business, Social Psychology, and Sales were popular because the guys were facing their "out date" within one year. Jolted out of their numb prison routines, they knew that before long they would have to support themselves in the real world. Self-concept, talk, and efficacy came alive as textbook concepts to prisoners, soon to be released, geared up for the street. The final graduation ceremony at Trusty took place in 1996. I was stunned when the program ended.

Cotton

In the 1980s, Cotton was built across the street from SPSM-Trusty, and housed 1,500 men. This is a medium-security prison for prisoners with less than fours years to their release. The institution is an example of the new "campus" design. Low-rise buildings are connected by open space and sidewalks, all of which is surrounded by a razor-wire fence. Teaching here I was impressed with the colorfully painted physical structures and smaller buildings. I might have gotten the mistaken impression that education would be supported in this new facility. Unfortunately, the prison college program ended in 1996.

Carson City Facility

Carson City, another new temporary prison, was part of the expansion of the prison system in rural towns and cities in the 1980s and 1990s. As Michigan's auto factories downsized and out-sourced, laying-off 500,000 workers, the new tough-on-crime and war-on-drugs policies had the latent function of tying small-town employment opportunities, and state politics, into a new rural prison building boom (P. Thomas, 1994; Walsh, 1994; Hernandez, 1996). We watched deer graze outside our prison classroom window as the prisoners studied economics.

Riverside

In 1983, at Riverside, a weathered brick prison built in the 1930s, two women prisoners appeared in my Business and Management class. Their long hair, lipstick, eye makeup, dresses, and movements attracted me. Still a novice prison teacher, I wondered which wing the women lived in. After two weeks the guys finally laughed at me and said, "You were really taken in by those two!" Who, of course, were men.

Ionia Temporary Facility (ITF)

Later that summer, I taught Entrepreneurship three miles up the road at the new Ionia Temporary Facility (ITF), another example of the new prisons constructed out of pole barn sheet metal and wire. Of course, none of these temporary prisons are going to be dismantled anytime soon. Temporary, in an era of prison expansion, is a euphemism for "cheap."

ADJUNCT TEACHING CONDITIONS
IN PRISON COLLEGE PROGRAMS

Physical mobility and changing assignments were characteristic of my adjunct teaching career. I was a "continuing contract," long-term, part-time adjunct at Lansing Community College, where I taught economics and sociology classes for 14 years; despite my long years there, that job could never, by contract, amount to more than three classes a semester, and it did not pay enough. So, I taught at many colleges.

The market for adjunct teaching positions is analogous to a number of horses (courses) on a set of merry-go-rounds (different college programs). Each community college, four-year college campus, and prison program director had various instructors "riding the horse" of numerous course preparations. You had to wait to "get on the horse." I might have to wait a year or two until another instructor left, and a position teaching that course on the merry-go-round opened up. Once you got off the horse, someone else got on. So, you needed to stay on as many horses in each program as you could. This often led to taking on a heavy teaching load just to cover your bases and make an adequate income.

For 20 years, I drove around Michigan, teaching at the various prisons and college campuses. Even after completing my sociology Ph.D. in 1993, it took five years more before I finally landed a tenure-track job. From 1995 to 2000, I taught at Egeler and Scott, the last prison college programs in Michigan. In 2000, my prison college teaching career ended when the Michigan Department of Corrections terminated funding for both of these programs.

WINNING BATTLES, BUT LOSING THE WAR: PRISON COLLEGE UNDERCUT BY "BIG POLITICS"

In 1994, the COPE program faltered with the ending of the Pell Grants but limped along, supported by the warden, while being funded by the Michigan Department of Corrections. I had taught at the Michigan Reformatory for 13 years, but, in the summer of 1997, I heard rumors this was the last semester for the COPE program.

One day our MR social science class was in the middle of studying some cultural history. We were discussing the contribution of northern African nations compared with European countries to world civilization. Then, in the middle of class, four inspectors and designers interrupted to measure the classroom walls and ceiling. They were assessing the classrooms for the next use. A month later prison college at the reformatory was gone.

I frequently think of my experience as doing "20 years in prison" (as a teacher). As the years, and the miles on the highway rolled on, life got into a rut. Battles had been won with particular program supervisors to get better classroom learning atmospheres, and materials such as videos screened and approved. Course preparations were honed to a fine edge. Learning accumulated on how to teach convicts, building in participation, oral presentations, and debates. Experience with troublemakers and their "ploys," and understanding different types of prisoners, helped the instructors become better and more effective. But the programs were ending. Experienced teachers now had to find other jobs.

The battles of how to run a quality prison college program had been fought valiantly, but the war of keeping such programs was lost. By the early 1990s, the public no longer seemed to support prison college, and the politicians rushed to cut funding. The "little politics" of daily program issues succumbed to the "big politics" of which politician was "tougher on crime" than the next politician (Stenson, 1991; Tonry, 1999).

CONVICT PERSPECTIVES ON ISSUES
IN PRISON HIGHER EDUCATION

We also need to examine what convicts, and exconvicts, have said about their prison college experiences. Interviews with former convicts who have achieved higher education degrees provide strong support for prison college. One of the convict criminology authors in this volume helped clarify many of the issues:

> Getting a real start in prison with college credit is important. If prisons could offer some college-credit courses, even an A.A. degree, this would make a big difference in recidivism.

Another convict criminologist in this book discusses how some convicts may decide to pursue higher education:

> I was helped by prison staff members and university professors. I think the point about "aging out of crime" is also related to how working-class whites and blacks may pursue a college education later in life. They may [have] never been supported by their parent[s] as young adults to go to college. Maybe while in the joint, they met a college graduate that gave them the idea to get an education when they got out. This may have been one of the college graduate prisoners who worked as volunteers one-on-one teaching GED in prison.
>
> Another related issue is college credit by correspondence. The University of Wisconsin-Extension (UW) has a fine program that serves prisoners, as well as military personnel. I completed 15 credits and a B.A. degree in federal prison through UW. Also, Ohio University has a college program by mail.

The prisoners in my classes shared their perspectives on problems and potentials in becoming accomplished college graduates. These included (1) experiences in being shifted around, or transferred, between prisons and different security levels (Rominger et al., 1993); (2) fear of violence in the yard and being drawn into prison deviance, or getting "tickets" (disciplinary reports), that would disrupt educational opportunity (they get sent to the hole) (G. Hunt et al., 1999); (3) concern about getting good quality classes; (4) complaints about toughened parole policy and getting "flops" (parole denial), so that it is difficult to plan prison vocational training, academic, career, and transition programs; and (5) worry about the transition to society, getting a job, and being discriminated against on the outside. They began to recognize their own maturing or "aging out" in new ways, through their exposure to higher education.

PRISONER GRADUATION CEREMONIES
REFLECT CRISES

In 1980, the "war on drugs" launched a punitive era eroding the political support for prison college. This led to a dramatic rise in prison construction, convict populations, and program cutbacks. By 1994, with the termination of federal Pell Grants, the higher education programs were in trouble. Two stories of prisoner graduation ceremonies reflect the crises for prisoners.

In 1986, I attended my first prison college graduation at Soledad Prison in California. Driving down from Berkeley for two years, I had taught business classes at the prison for Hartnell College. On the occasion of the graduation, about 150 prisoners and 50 teachers, administrators, and guests attended.

In most college graduation ceremonies the discussion is about the bright prospects ahead, the promise of the future. In contrast, this prison college graduation was a ceremony of dark warning. The talk was about how the pull of the street, the lack of employment, inadequate transition services, combined with the virulent addiction potential of drugs and alcohol and money from the drug trade could spell disaster for many graduating prisoner-students.

Meanwhile, the rising criticism of "those criminals getting a free college education" while in prison alarmed governors and members of Congress. In 1988, presidential hopeful Michael Dukakis was beaten up on the crime issue. Dozens of governors in the late 1980s and 1990s ran "tough-on-crime" campaigns (Davey, 1998). In the U.S. Senate, Jesse Helms (R–NC) led the way, and Congress, by 1994, ended support for federal Pell Grant eligibility for prisoners (Page, 1997). There had been 770 Pell Grant–funded prison postsecondary programs across the nation. Now, prison college was dead.

I attended my second graduation ceremony on 1996 at the Egeler facility (Jackson Prison). Michigan prison college programs were collapsing. Egeler was under a continuing federal consent decree to continue the college programs at the Jackson facility, but this court order was constantly being challenged by the Michigan Department of Corrections (MDOC). Two dozen graduating prisoner-students and an audience of 50 celebrated the achievement of the Bachelor of Arts degrees from Spring Arbor College. The valedictorian dutifully praised the accomplishments of the college and the students; referring, however, to recent corrections policies cutting the program, he said: "We're being cut back at Central and Trusty, the MDOC is eliminating prison college." He called for a movement of supporters, prisoners, staff, and interested people to struggle to reinstate prison college programs.[5]

These two crises, cutbacks in correctional programming, and the lure of the street, reveal how an expanding prison system that eliminates rehabilitative programs, and inner-city streets that continue to have high crime rates, begin to feed upon, and resemble, each other (Clear, 1996). As resilient adults (Higgins, 1994), many prisoners can escape the revolving door with some help, but there is a need to deliver quality prison programs that adequately prepare prisoners for legal employment.

QUALITY PRISON COLLEGE
INCLUDES MECHANISMS PROVEN
TO LOWER RECIDIVISM

When the prison college programs were being shut down, prison college teachers asked, "What can be done to save prison college?" Prisoners could finish their degrees through correspondence, but few had the money to do this. Could the Michigan Department of Corrections raise the pay scale for convicts employed in prison factories, so they could afford to pay for college credits? Would private foundations supply grants? The prisoners asked, "Aren't there studies that show prison college works?"

I knew there was research demonstrating a lowered recidivism rate for those who have taken prison college classes. But the last comprehensive literature review had been completed before the demise of these prison postsecondary programs (Gerber and Fritsch, 1995). So in 1997, I applied for an Open Society Institute (Soros Foundation) grant to study these matters and update the literature. In general, I found there is consensus about how to do quality prison college teaching. Many evaluations had established the evidence for the effectiveness of prison postsecondary. New studies proved that prison college programs lowered recidivism (Duguid et al., 1998; Duguid, 2000).

What makes for a quality prison college program that lowers recidivism? Quality can be attained in prison college programs by expanding the opportunities for prisoner involvement in roles such as clerks, tutors, and assistant teachers, and in activities such as debates and theater groups (Duguid et al., 1998; Duguid, 2000). Further, it is important to recognize that two sets of skills are needed for successful prisoner reintegration into society. First, education in liberal arts, including skills in writing, oral presentation, critical thinking, and problem solving, is needed for advanced students. Second, skills for traditional vocations, such as computer repair, software applications, auto mechanics, or those required for building, horticultural, custodial, and clerical positions, may be more appropriate for other prisoners (Tregea, 1998).

Another element of quality programs is experienced instructors. Good teachers are made, not born (Coffey, 1986; Duguid, 1992; Newman, 1993). Many of the best Pell Grant–era teachers, upon losing their prison positions, went on to other jobs. Some of this cohort of experienced teachers may be available to teach again.

TOWARD FUNDING QUALITY PRISON
POSTSECONDARY PROGRAMS

Federal and state government should support quality accredited prison postsecondary opportunities as a sane and humane prison policy, as well as a cost-effective way to reduce recidivism. But, where will the money come from? New federal money may become the replacement for the Pell Grants. Senator Specter, from Pennsylvania, was persuaded to sponsor an amendment to the "Youth Offender" section of the 1994 Crime Bill that provides for $1,500 a year in prison postsecondary tuition costs (and $300 in books) for prisoners 25 or under, with less than five years to first parole date, and convicted of a nonviolent crime. This legislation passed in 1997, with the first three years (1998–2001) of Specter Grant funding being $12 million a year to be divided among all states that applied. The next three-year funding cycle (2001–2004) is authorized at $14 million annual funding. Nearly all (44) states have applied, with each state receiving between $300,000 and $400,000 per year.

Specter Grants are still a vastly underfunded program, unable to serve enough prisoners or build quality prison postsecondary programs. There is not enough money to provide prisoners with a full staff at each prison program (director, counselor, writing lab, librarian). For example, just one prison college program, such as those at Jackson Prison, may cost $1 million annually. Three of the 44 states receiving Specter Grants (Texas, Florida, and Michigan) are not even using the funds for accredited postsecondary correctional education.[6]

Meanwhile, in Michigan the JCC prison library at Central Jackson Prison was closed in 1995 and sits boxed up in a storeroom. The college classrooms at the Michigan Reformatory, which were shutdown in 1997, have long since been converted to other purposes. Prison classrooms all across Michigan, and in the many other states that have no state-funded programs, sit empty.

Such states must plan reduced programs, moving to distance learning (for instance, canned college television programs watched in a prison cell, with monitored exams and no on-site teachers). Yet, the research evidence on the mechanisms that reduce recidivism has emphasized the importance, over time, of participation in program activities. The affiliation "I am a student" is greatly aided by the presence of an alternative community, which requires on-site teaching and program staff and extracurricular activities. Distance learning may be necessary under contemporary conditions, but measurable effects from on-site, instructor-based education are lost (Duguid, 2000).

The politics of our "imprisonment binge" (Austin and Irwin, 2001) has made it appear that there is enough money for prison expansion (bed space), but not enough for prison-based prevention programs. An additional investment of $3,000 for prison postsecondary education per eligible prisoner could materially reduce the recidivism rate (Belenko and Peugh, 1998: 53–60; J. Freeman, 1998). Where will the money for accredited advanced skills training and education come from?

One funding idea is to augment Specter funds with state tuition grants or loans. The Ohio legislature supported 2,700 inmates taking accredited advanced skills training with $1,500 state tuition grants. Another idea is for a state to launch a revolving loan fund so prisoners can borrow money to pay tuition credits. A combination of the state grants and loan approach is currently being advocated by a prisoner advocacy group in New York (CURE-NY, 2000). Still another suggestion is to have a modest prisoner copayment and to beef up prisoner benefit fund activities to help support prison postsecondary education.

With longer prison sentences, increased denial of parole, rising numbers of parole violations, and high recidivism, the money in corrections budgets continues to go for the steel, bricks, and mortar of prison expansion and operation. The problem is not merely budgetary but cultural and political (Stenson, 1991; Tonry, 1999). There must be a challenge to prison expansion. This includes working to reduce long sentences, depoliticizing parole decisions, advocating graduated parole violation sanctions instead of automatic return to prison for technical violations, and replacing tolerance of the "revolving door" with efforts to lower prison admittance. Without such a challenge, there will continue to be very little left over in state budgets for prison-based programming and community-based prevention (Citizens Alliance on Prisons and Public Safety [CAPPS], 1999).

CONCLUSION

As a country, we are experiencing an old familiar trend in prison policy: treatment gives way to control (Sykes, 1958).[7] For the past two decades, prison programs have been reduced as the prison population exploded. It is time to face the hard facts that prisons have become the new public housing for the poor, the mentally impaired, the alcoholic, the drug addicted, the homeless, and the unemployed. Sentenced to prison, warehoused in cages and dormitories, without prison programs, they will only become a bigger social problem when released.

The first order of business is to shorten prison sentences for many prisoners (Austin and Irwin, 2001: 245–247). The second priority is to provide prisoners with programs that improve their chances to adjust to life after prison (Austin and Irwin, 2001: 165–167). Colvin (1992: 214) argued that the funding for incentive-based programs like prison postsecondary education "will only come from legislators who see rehabilitation as the ultimate goal of corrections."

Currently, we may be seeing a pendulum swing, not back to the individual rehabilitative ideal, but rather toward a focus on community crime prevention. Can the role of the prison shift more toward crime prevention and prisoner reintegration? Or will prison policy continue on the path of "punishment as the solution," without thought to prisoner transition back to society?

I suggest we need to hold prison administrators accountable for what works to reduce recidivism. If government legislatures mandated "recidivism guidelines" as well as "sentencing guidelines," prisons would be forced to restore education programs. The primary evaluation criterion for prison administrators is the rate of institutional disorder—how many disturbances, riots, escapes, assaults happen per year. If transitioning programs (education, vocational, release) were as important as "no disturbances," then correctional programming in state prisons would become one of the key variables in assessing prison management.

In sum, we need to reduce the political rhetoric on crime, reverse the trend toward long sentences, be more sensible and less punitive toward drug use and treatment, stop building more prisons, and invest more tax dollars in improving the ones we already have.[8]

NOTES

1. Some prisoners, who completed a few college credits while in prison, return to the community to finish bachelor's degrees at universities (Lanier et al., 1994). A very small number, like many of the contributors to this book, complete graduate degrees. In fact, the exconvict authors in this book are all, more or less, products of college prison programs (Irwin, Jones, Lanier, Mobley, Murphy, Newbold, Richards, Terry, and Tromanhauser, in this volume).

2. The control world of secure custody is an oppositional culture of hacks and cons. The treatment world is a culture of professional and client. The prison alternative community that reduces recidivism requires a democratic culture. Personal development requires a degree of unstructuredness and choice (Rogers, 1977).

3. The prison college program day-to-day quality depends on the full-time on-site supervisor. In the JCC program at Jackson Prison, Director Wreford was there every day in Central Complex, and also supervised Trusty and Northside. In the MCC program, Director Herman spent most days at the Michigan Reformatory but also went across the valley to Riverside and Ionia Temporary Facility, and up the road 35 miles to Carson City. Different persons appeared in the MCC prison program as on-site supervisors, but they never seemed to last. Some rotated out of their prison locations back to a position at the community college campus. There was a lack of continuity of leadership.

4. See Useem and Kimball (1991: 114–160) for a description of the 1981 Jackson Prison riot. Administrators in the Michigan Department of Corrections (MDOC) have had several prisons, especially the Jackson complex, under federal court oversight since the 1981 Jackson Prison riot. Under the U.S. District Court oversight, the MDOC agreed through a consent decree to rebuild the aging and dangerous old "big house" blocks at Jackson into smaller podular-modular "unit management" design, at a cost of $116 million.

5. Recognizing that MDOC was not likely to fund prison college on its own without a signal from the state legislature, a group of prison instructors and former program administrators have been talking to state legislators. Would the new federal Specter Grant funds be used by the MDOC to fund Michigan prison college programs? The answer was no. The MDOC (along with the Florida and Texas departments of corrections) found a way to use Specter Grant money for "in-house" vocational (computer and auto mechanic equipment upgrades) and not for postsecondary programming.

6. Personal communication from Richard Smith, director of the U.S. Department of Education's Office of Correctional Education (June 2000).

7. Prison administrators make insufficient effort to balance treatment and control. Training prisoners in democratic culture helps reduce recidivism. Administrators should work harder to protect the "technical core" of alternative community, which facilitates transition-to-society success, and not repeatedly sacrifice this effect to the "technical core" of secure custody (Thompson, 1967). Put another way, the rulification and bureaucratization of prison management erodes the flexibility and initiative needed by staff to do correctional work (Stojkovic et al., 1999: 5). Moreover, there is evidence that remunerative controls (incentives like advanced skills training and education) work better than coercive controls (the control or bureaucratic model) in lowering disorder in high-security state prisons (Reisig, 1998).

8. Building a coalition to reinstate prison college is tied up with a critique of prison expansion. Prison expansion is creating a crisis in state priorities. Michigan, for example, has gone from seven prisons in 1980 to 48 prisons in 2000, despite a 31 percent decrease in new crimes since 1992. The money put into continuing prison expansion could be better spent through cost-effective mental health services, substance abuse treatment, education and vocational training, and community corrections (Citizens Alliance on Prisons and Public Safety [CAPPS], 2000).

16

Kids in Jail

"I Mean You Ain't Really Learning Nothin [Productive]"

PRESTON ELROD
AND MICHAEL T. BROOKS

The incarceration of youths in adult jails is nothing new. Since the colonial era, children have been placed in adult jails. What is new, however, is that the number of persons under 18 who are confined in these institutions has been growing in recent years. According to a recent report issued by the Bureau of Justice Assistance, the number of juveniles placed in adult jails has increased substantially since the early 1980s, from 1,736 in 1983 to 8,090 in 1998 (Austin et al., 2000). These juveniles are placed in adult jails because they have been transferred to adult courts for trial, have been difficult to control in juvenile institutions, or there are no or limited juvenile facilities within a particular jurisdiction.

Perhaps most disconcerting about the recent increase is that we have known for a long time that the jailing of children is bad social and correctional policy. Indeed, efforts to remove children from adult jails was a primary concern of the Child Savers, who played a major role in the development of the first legislatively established juvenile court at the turn of the last century (Platt, 1977). In 1869, the General Assembly of Illinois established a Board of State Commissioners of Public Charities to examine the treatment of persons in various state institutions. In that same year, agents of the Board inspected 78 jails in Illinois and found that 40 of those jails housed persons under 16 years of age.

An earlier version of this paper was presented at the American Society of Criminology meeting, San Francisco, 2000.

Furthermore, the inspections documented the appalling conditions facing children in these institutions. For example, the inspection of the Cook County Jail (Chicago) revealed that 14 children were among the 114 persons that were crowded into 32 poorly ventilated cells in the basement of the courthouse. Their report stated, "The jail is so dark, that it is necessary to keep the gas burning in the corridors both day and night. The cells are filthy and full of vermin." The Board noted that these facilities failed to separate young and old, and characterized the jails as "moral plague spots" and "dark, damp, and fetid places" that "confirm criminal tendencies instead of eliminating them" (Platt, 1977: 119).

During the 1970s, further attention was given to the negative consequences associated with placing children in adult jails. Testifying before a Senate subcommittee in 1973, Rosemary Sarri, a noted expert on juvenile justice, indicated that most jails "were more than 50 years old, dilapidated, and designed to service only the most dangerous offenders. Almost none had been constructed to permit humane segregation of juveniles from adults or unsentenced from sentenced offenders. Sanitary conditions, food, exercise facilities, fire control, and so forth, almost never met basic minimal public health requirements" (cited in Schwartz, 1989: 69).

In 1974, an important piece of federal legislation, the Juvenile Justice and Delinquency Prevention Act, became law. This Act contained a section mandating that juveniles be separated from adults in jails. However, it was clear to many that this legislation, although important for other reasons, failed to provide adequate protection for children, who continued to be placed in jails around the country. A report issued by the Children's Defense Fund (1976: 4) noted:

> The conditions of most of the jails in which we found children are abysmal, subjecting them to cruel and unusual punishment through physical neglect and abuse. Solitary confinement in dank basement or closet-like enclosures for the sole child in an adult jail removes him or her from other inmates, but also from the attention of caretakers and can have severe traumatic effects on an already troubled and frightened youngster.

Indeed, during the 1970s, research clearly documented that the rate of suicide among children held in adult jails was significantly greater than that for children placed in juvenile detention centers or in the general population, and this occurred even though they were frequently being separated from adult prisoners (Community Research Forum, 1980).

The historical evidence is incontrovertible. Jails are not designed and operated in ways that adequately meet the needs of children. Adult jails often lack the space, appropriately trained personnel, and the treatment resources to adequately meet the needs of youths. Indeed, a major problem faced by correctional staff in adult institutions is that the strategies they typically rely on to manage adult offenders are often ineffective when applied to children (Glick, 1998).

This becomes an additional problem for jail administrators, who often face severe overcrowding problems, a constantly changing population, and who struggle to separate offenders by age, gender, and processing stage (awaiting trial or serving a sentence). More important, however, the very nature of the jail, an institution that is ultimately intended for the short-term management of problem populations (Irwin, 1985a; Richards, this volume), makes it inherently unsuitable as a placement for youths. As a result, children who are in adult jails are much more likely to engage in various self-destructive or problem behaviors, ranging from suicide (Community Research Forum, 1980) to disciplinary infractions (Flanagan, 1983; Goetting and Howsen, 1986; McShane and Williams, 1989; Kerle, 1998).

As Irwin (1985a) discussed in his classic study *The Jail,* despite the history and popularity of the jail as a mechanism of social control, social scientists have almost completely ignored this institution. Irwin's work aside, we know relatively little about jails and even less about the people who inhabit them or work in them. We know even less about children who are locked up in jails and how they experience incarceration in adult facilities.[1] Moreover, much of what we do know is limited by the methodological approaches that are typically used to study correctional institutions.

This chapter is intended to explore how children understand their jail experience. It begins with a description of the methodology employed and the setting within which the research took place. Next, it focuses on a number of central themes that dominate the social world of the jail and reveals a reality that stands in opposition to official descriptions of the jail. We conclude with an examination of the academic and policy implications of this research.

THE RESEARCH METHODOLOGY

In 1996, we began our research. The project was initiated by jail administrators who sought to develop better mechanisms for meeting the needs of juvenile jail "inmates" and the correctional staff that works with them, and to reduce the number of discipline infractions committed by juvenile residents. We used the following methodological procedures to collect our data. First, semistructured interviews with the chief jail administrator, the administrator responsible for daily jail operations, and the director of inmate programs were conducted to identify issues that they felt should be addressed.

Next, a series of observations of the juvenile unit or "pod" were conducted, accompanied by semistructured interviews with line correctional staff and impromptu discussions with residents in the juvenile unit. These interviews, observations, and discussions were used to further identify issues that could be tapped through a series of resident surveys that were administered to all available juvenile prisoners, excluding those in court and a small number who declined to participate between 1996 and 1998. The total number of juveniles surveyed was 130. During and subsequent to the prisoner surveys, additional interviews with correctional staff and inmates were undertaken; the last of these, involving in-depth interviews with inmate volunteers, were completed in March 2000.[2]

THE RESEARCH SETTING

This study was conducted in one of two jail facilities in a large metropolitan area that houses, on any given day, over 400 residents. It is a modern "new generation" jail that houses up to 56 prisoners in each of the 11 pods that make up the facility. Physically, the juvenile pod is a separate living unit that houses prisoners under 18 years old, some as young as 14. Like other living areas in the facility, the juvenile unit is clean and bright and residents are assigned individual cells arranged in two tiers around a common area that can be observed by the correctional officer on duty.

The common area contains card tables (that double as lunch tables during meals), chairs, and several sofas that are placed in front of two television sets that are located on each side of the unit. Toilet and shower facilities are located in an area on one side of the pod, and there is an enclosed recreational area where prisoners can play basketball during their free time. In addition, the pod has two "wet cells" containing toilet facilities where prisoners can be placed for extended periods of time for violations of jail rules. The physical design of the new generation facility is intended to allow staff to constantly observe small groups of residents in a self-contained unit, thereby enhancing the ability of staff to control residents and ensure staff and resident safety (Zupan, 1991).

As in other jails, daily operation follows a strict regimen. The prisoners' day begins with wake-up at 4:30 A.M. and ends at 9:00 P.M., when they are required to return to their rooms. During this timeframe, prisoners participate in physical training, are served three meals in the pod, and receive three to six hours of academic instruction. Room inspections are conducted, and pod cleanups are completed by selected groups of inmates at least three times each day. In addition, juveniles are required to participate in programs focusing on domestic violence, drug education, teen health, and life skills development; they may also participate in voluntary religious programs that are offered on certain days.[3]

Operationally, the facility and the juvenile pod are officially governed by the principles of direct supervision, a major component of the "new generation" management style. These principles are as follows:

1. Staff, rather than inmates, will control the facility and inmates' behavior.
2. Inmates will be directly and continuously supervised and custodial staff, rather than inmates, will direct and control the behavior of all inmates.
3. Rewards and punishments will be structured to ensure compliant inmate behavior.
4. Open communication will be maintained between the custodial staff and inmates, and between staff members.
5. Inmates will be advised of the expectations and rules of the facility.
6. Inmates will be treated in a manner consistent with "constitutional standards and other applicable codes and court decisions," and will be treated equitably and fairly regardless of their personal characteristics or the rea-

sons for which they are in jail (Nelson and O'Toole, 1983; Gettinger, 1984, cited in Zupan, 1991: 105).

Practically, applying the principles of direct supervision in the pod is the responsibility of one correctional officer, who supervises the juvenile unit during a six-hour shift. Importantly, in a new generation jail, officers are in direct physical contact with inmates and, ideally, they rely on "sophisticated management and leadership skills to maintain order" within the pod (Zupan, 1991: 106).

In many respects, this is like other jails. There is an obvious concern with custody and security, and the daily lives of prisoners are marked by routine. It houses a diverse and continually changing population of persons. Some prisoners may only spend the night whereas others will spend many months. Some are in jail awaiting trial and others spend their time serving sentences for various crimes ranging from minor theft offenses to homicide, although most have been charged with a nonviolent offense.

The prisoner population ranges in age from 14 to 76, although the average age is just under 30 years old. They are mostly males; 10 percent are females, and disproportionate numbers of these persons are minorities (about 80 percent). They tend to be poor, they have little formal education, and they report few ties with conventional social networks outside of jail (Elrod et al., 1999). In short, the prisoners in this study are similar to those in jails around the country in terms of their demographic (Maguire and Pastore, 1999) and social (Irwin, 1985) characteristics.

In others respects, however, the facility examined in this study differs from many other jails. Physically and operationally it differs in a number of ways from old-style linear jails and appears to reflect the latest in correctional thinking. The majority of prisoners in this facility feel reasonably safe from violence (M. Brooks, 1999). There are a number of programs that are offered to prisoners that, if nothing else, keep them busy and make the routinization of jail life more tolerable. Some correctional staff have implemented a variety of informal programs during their shifts that focus on physical fitness and social skills.

Moreover, correctional administrators line staff, at least when it comes to adolescent residents, express rather progressive sentiments about the youths under their supervision. As the facility administrator noted during our first meeting to discuss the project, "We need to look at the jail as a positive opportunity to help inmates make changes, to turn things around. We also need to get staff more involved, to act as problem solvers, not just as guards."

AN EXAMINATION OF THE SOCIAL WORLD OF ADOLESCENT PRISONERS

Jails, like other institutions, do not represent monolithic social worlds. Like other total institutions, the world of the jail is understood and perceived differently by the individuals that live and work there (Goffman, 1961). Sometimes these differences in understanding are rather dramatic. This is most clearly reflected in the discrepancy between the official descriptions of the jail presented by correctional staff and those expressed by juvenile prisoners. In other instances, differences in perceptions of the jail are quite subtle, which is apparent when we compare the responses of staff and prisoners.

Our task in this section is to examine the more apparent discrepancies between the official descriptions of the jail and those presented by adolescent prisoners. Official descriptions of the jail represent characterizations that are given to outsiders about the purpose and operation of the jail. These depictions of the jail are typically found in documents prepared for public consumption, in presentations provided jail visitors and tour groups, and in interactions with members of the press and other outsiders, including researchers, who are interested in learning more about the jail (see Goffman, 1959, introduction). Furthermore, official descriptions of the jail can be bolstered by positive expressions of concern for adolescent prisoners, by the physical appearance of the facility, by the cursory remarks of prisoners themselves, and by research methodologies that employ surveys of prisoners and correctional staff that tend to produce a surface understanding of institutions and how people adapt to life within highly structured and bureaucratic settings.

Altogether, utterances made, nonverbal signs, and the physical trappings of the institution help convey a certain picture of the jail that is intended for public consumption. This official characterization of the jail, however, is a sanitized and simplified version of the realities experienced by those who live and work there. The official portrayal of the institution, then, does not tell the whole story.

Instead, it presents a reality that is constructed by jail administrators and some correctional staff that masks the complex understanding of jails held by those who are incarcerated within their walls as well as other correctional workers. For example, the above descriptions of the jail population and the research setting, as well as our surveys of jail residents, indicate that most juveniles feel safe in the jail, and it conveys a particular impression of the jail that fits well with official accounts of the institution. Yet, our observations and interviews of jail prisoners indicate that these official descriptions reflect a very narrow understanding of the realities of incarceration as experienced by the inmate.

Indeed, there are a number of interrelated themes that better typify the operation of jails and influence inmates. These have surfaced in the course of our research and deserve further attention. In the following sections, we explore these themes and analyze what they tell us about the realities of jail from the perspective of adolescent prisoners.

THE CONTROL OF PRISONERS

One inescapable reality of the jail, with which both prisoners and staff must contend, is the concern with control. As Goffman (1961: 4) noted, jails are one form of total institution, an institution that is "symbolized by the barrier to social intercourse with the outside and to departure that is often built into the physical plant, such as locked doors, high walls, barbed wire." As one juvenile prisoner, Rasheed, remarked, "You don't touch the ground, you're on cement, everywhere you go you got bricks around . . . you feel like you are in a box."[4] Moreover, the control exerted by the jail goes beyond limiting one's freedom of movement; it also invades more intimate aspects of one's daily life. As Bobby revealed, "If you got to go to the bathroom, most of the time they'll [correctional officers] make you hold it, you know 'till you come out [of your cell]. You just got to sit and hold it for about an hour sometimes, or two hours."

Within the jail, control is exerted and reinforced through at least three mechanisms: (1) hardware, (2) symbolic representations of control that are reflected in formal jail rules and operations, and (3) informal mechanisms of control employed by correctional workers. The most obvious manifestation of the concern with control is the physical hardware that is used to limit the movements of prisoners and their contact with those on the outside. The heavy metal doors, the perimeter fences topped with razor wire, the glass that prevents the prisoner from touching their loved ones during visits, the existence of segregation or "wet cells" in the unit that are used to discipline those who violate jail rules, and the use of frequent lockdowns (sometimes for simply being too loud) are clear reminders of the power of correctional staff over residents.

In addition to the more obvious manifestations of control found in the jail, there are also a variety of symbolic representations of control that convey to the prisoners that their lives are carefully regulated by others. Many prisoners are aware that the lights, doors to units and cells, toilets, intercom, surveillance cameras, and other electrical and mechanical components of the jail can be controlled by the Central Control Room, a darkened video arcade–like room containing touch-sensitive video screens that cannot be seen by prisoners. As one resident remarked, "It ain't your world anymore, they're in control of your program . . . you're a robot."

Some of the symbols of control are quite explicit, such as the list of 155 rules that are given to prisoners that cover everything from the 25-cent charge for calls to the commissary (a store in the jail that sells at a profit a variety of items to inmates such as snacks, clothing, and personal hygiene products) to prohibitions against fighting and disorderly conduct. However, other symbols of control are more subtle and are found in the daily regimen to which prisoners are expected to acquiesce—the lack of privacy, the types of programming seen on the two televisions in the unit, the selection of "safe" eating utensils at meals, and the content of meals served. In addition, correctional staff employ a number of informal mechanisms in their efforts to control residents, such as showing favoritism to some residents and using some prisoners to dominate others, even though this is in violation of the principles of direct supervision.

In their daily interactions with prisoners, correctional staff use three primary strategies to achieve control: punishment, or its implied threat, manipulation, and negotiation. Prisoners are well aware that they can be placed in "wet cells" within the unit or removed to a specialized segregation unit if they violate the rules. They are also aware that correctional staff can use force in order to direct prisoners' behavior. From the perspective of the prisoner, correctional staff employ a number of punishments, or the threat of punishment, in order to exert control. A common punishment used in the jail is a lockdown, but others are used as well, as noted in the following statement by Rasheed:

> Lockdowns bother you worse than anything, like you do something wrong they make you go to your room and take your mat [mattress] and if that don't bother you they send you to the hole, they'll take your mat all day and you get your mat back at night, and if they find that don't bother you, they just try to take your phone privileges and stuff like that, stuff and anything like that, that will hurt you, they'll try and take it and use it for control. Like now they've got like a point system, you got to get a certain amount of points . . . they're trying to use that to control people's attitudes, and like self-control and stuff like that.

Although correctional staff can and occasionally do use force to exert control over inmates, a more common strategy is to manipulate compliance with jail rules through the threat of punishment.[5] These threats are not seen as part of the official "sophisticated management and leadership skills" that are integral to direct supervision. Instead, they are part of the informal system of control that governs jail life. The existence of this informal system of control is one of many examples of the failure of jail management to effectively translate the theory of direct supervision jail management into practice. Recognizing that a primary function of correctional staff is to maintain control of the unit, but lacking an understanding of alternative means of gaining inmate compliance with pod rules, correctional officers will resort to threats that range from lockdowns of the entire pod and turning off the telephones (which effectively severs the inmates' one tie to the outside world) to the placement of prisoners in their rooms, in "wet cells" for extended periods of time, or in a segregation unit for problem prisoners.

CHICKENSHIT RULES

The mechanisms used to control prisoners do have purpose; to some degree prisoners and correctional staff depend on the rules for stability and safety. Yet many of the regulations can be seen as "chickenshit rules" that are more designed to add to the deprivations of jail life than to keep the prisoner safe (Austin and Irwin, 2001). For example, jail rules prohibit prisoners from getting under their bed covers during the day when they are in their rooms. In addition, inmates are required to wear jail-issued clothing that resembles hospital scrubs without pockets and are prohibited from putting their hands and arms inside their shirts or pants. Although the temperature of the jail is supposedly kept at 70 degrees, it feels considerably cooler. As Jermaine noted, "I mean they keep the air condition on 24-7 . . . . Man, I mean, it's cold." Indeed, jail residents frequently complain about the temperature in the unit and rules that prohibit them from getting under their bed covers during the day. Moreover, when they are out of their rooms, they often keep their arms inside their clothes in order to keep warm, although this is a violation of still another jail rule. In recounting an interaction with one of the correctional staff over this issue, Bobby shared the following:

> I had my hands in my pants . . . and then that was when the lady was like, "Why you got your hands in your pants?" I was like, "My hands are cold." She was like, "Well, that's your problem." And I was like, "They should've made pockets on the suits or something to keep our hands warm." And then she was like, "Well I'm going to tell you like this, I'm going to give you a zero and see who going to be laughing now."

From the perspective of the prisoner, many jail rules are unnecessary and petty. More important, however, they are perceived as additional punishments that compound the discomforts of jail and add to the resentment prisoners feel toward the institution and correctional staff.

PRISONER RESISTANCE

Although the symbols of control are omnipresent in the jail, submission is not given over freely. Juvenile prisoners attempt to resist in a variety of ways. Sometimes, this resistance takes the form of direct challenges to correctional staff and blatant violations of jail rules. More often, however, resistance is expressed in subtle challenges to the constraints of the jail. As Jermaine stated:

> There's a lot of it [resistance] . . . like lockdown, when they be calling us to go down for lockdown, people go to the bathroom, sit in the bathroom for 30 to 45 minutes, talking, playing cards, so there's a way around that . . . I mean, eventually, you going to go to your room, but you've beaten half the time you supposed to be in your room.

There is a precarious stability that typically dominates the world of the jail, and both prisoners and correctional staff are aware of the negotiated nature of control. As Rasheed noted:

> If somebody don't want to do something, no matter what they do, they're going to do it. You can't control nobody who don't want to be controlled . . . The way I feel is like this, if I want to do something, I'm going to do it, no matter what it is, there's no way they're going to stop me . . . that's how most inmates feel. That's why there is a lot of trouble going on in the pod with the officers and inmates arguing with each other . . . They abuse their powers trying to use them like say they got the power to lock you down. Say they tell you do something but you don't do it the way they want, they lock you down.

Or as Jermaine said:

> Really, if we wanted to, we could take over this jail. They ain't got no
> guns, only thing they got is mace and that ain't going to burn but so long.
> It ain't nothing but one supervisor per pod and all them inmates . . . I
> mean when the inmates get tired enough, they going to really take over
> this jail . . . It's only going to hold for so long before somebody starts flip-
> pin [becoming extremely angry or upset].

Although "flippin" may appear to be an understandable response for some,
prisoners believe that there are other consequences associated with creating
problems in the jail. When Jermaine was asked why more inmates don't openly
rebel, he stated the following: "Freedom . . . a lot of inmates . . . they don't
want to really do nothing wrong cause they're afraid what might happen in
court . . . When they go to court, the judge might give 'em more time or might
not release them, so most of 'em try to do right."

INCONSISTENCY IN
PRISONER MANAGEMENT

The daily regimen of the jail is marked by routine, but correctional officers'
efforts to control prisoners are marked by inconsistency. This has two causes.
First, each correctional officer has considerable discretion in how he/she man-
ages the unit during his/her shift. According to one member of the correctional
staff, "The duty officer can run the pod any way they want to . . . they can go
by the book or break the rules." Second, correctional workers often lack a coherent understanding of the theory of direct supervision and how to apply the
principles of direct supervision within the unit. Devoid of the knowledge and
skills necessary to respond in more effective ways to inmates, correctional staff
resort to a variety of informal mechanisms of maintaining control.

The ability of correctional staff to use a variety of formal and informal control mechanisms produces considerable variation in pod management from shift
to shift. Not surprisingly, prisoners regularly complain about differential treatment. However, there is also frequent within-shift variation in the management
of the pod. Although inmates feel that some differences in the management
styles of correctional staff are normal, they have more trouble understanding
why some officers show favoritism to some prisoners and are hostile to others.
When asked if he felt the correctional officers treat everyone the same, Rasheed
replied:

> Nah . . . some officers come in and show favoritism . . . They pick certain
> people to clean every day . . . they say no talking in the pod. One officer
> [will] like me but not like the person I'm talking to and lock that person
> down, but not say anything to me . . . It causes a lot of problems in the
> pod between the officers and inmates and makes inmates do stuff to get

back at the officers. Causes a lot of feuds . . . between inmates . . . you get mad . . . causes anger, jealousy, and all that.

Or as Jermaine noted:

[Correctional officers] show favoritism to certain inmates. I mean certain staff show certain inmates different things, like locking somebody down because they got up out of bed too late and then tell another inmate, well, you can stay under your covers . . . but if another person stay under their covers they come strip their room . . . They [officers] let other inmates run the pod for them. Make their day go by easier.

The perception that correctional workers treat some inmates differently than others is a common complaint among adolescent inmates, who are astute observers of situations both in and outside the jail where adults do not "walk the talk." Within the jail, inconsistency in the management of inmates and the lack of fairness become additional evidence of the focus on punishment that pervades daily life in the jail, and confirms in inmates' minds that they are also victims of a system that is itself unfair and corrupt. It also leads to considerable conflict within the prisoner population and between line staff and inmates. As we note in the next section, the differential treatment of inmates is one fuel for the conflict that is another common feature of the jail environment.

CONFLICT WITHIN THE JAIL

Jails are characterized by conflict. Sometimes the antagonisms that pervade the jail are overt. Physical altercations and heated arguments are common features of the correctional environment. More frequently, however, the discord that marks jail life is covert. One way that this conflict is experienced is in a constant tension and uneasiness that permeates the social organization of the jail.[6] The most obvious expression of tension is one that exists between correctional staff and prisoners. Yet, there are also tensions among prisoners and within the ranks of the correctional staff.[7]

Many factors contribute to the discord found in jails. The formal and informal mechanisms used to control inmates, inconsistencies in the treatment of prisoners; feelings of inequity, unfairness, deprivation, and corruption within the jail; a lack of sensitivity on the part of correctional staff; and a generalized feeling of victimization contribute to an institutional environment that is a breeding ground for conflict. Consider the following statements about conflict within the jail from Rasheed's perspective:

Officers cause most of the problems between inmates by showing favoritism . . . They punish everybody to get to the main one . . . Some officers are nasty, they think they are bad because they got power . . . Say they come in the morning and they got an attitude, things might not be going their way before they left home, they come in planning to take it out on us.

Insensitivity, particularly what is perceived as uncaring attitudes on the part of correctional workers, and corruption within the jail are acutely felt by many adolescent inmates. The lack of sensitivity to their needs and the corruption among guards who violate their own rules are clearly reflected in the following comments by Jermaine when he was asked if correctional staff are sensitive to the inmates' living conditions:

> No . . . I asked for a . . . different pair of pants this morning, well last night, on another shift. I ain't got 'em yet. So I know they don't care . . . Like when they [other inmates] be holding the phone [preventing others from making a call] . . . they'll [the officers] be like . . . well go up and take the phone then, if you really want it. Then most people be scared of half the people that be on the phone . . . So staff, man really don't care. Like . . . in the hole, if you talk junk to a staff, they'll pop . . . they'll let the people in the hole that's bad, that they know is going to be up there a long time, give 'em a snack or something . . . [Officers will say] I'm going to get you something off of somebody else's tray . . . pop their lock and let them in somebody room. [So they will encourage one inmate to victimize another inmate?] Uh, huh. That's why I know they don't care . . . Ain't never seen no staff member sit down and talk to you [about your problems], but there is some that are fair, they'll look out for everybody . . . But there are some that are dang dirty.

Life in jail produces a heightened sense of deprivation where even the smallest things take on value that far surpasses the value of those entities on the outside. For example, for the prisoner a piece of cake or candy, a phone call, or a period of privacy can take on a value that far exceeds its worth outside of the jail.[8] Moreover, obtaining valued items becomes the primary goal of gambling, which is common among prisoners and leads to considerable conflict. As Jermaine stated:

> Most of it [conflict] comes with the gambling, playing cards for snacks off trays or playing cards for half your main [entree]. Like, half main is half your tray. Be a lot of conflicts over that. People be cheating, just to win half somebody's main, get somebody's snack . . . The phone and TV. Certain people want to watch something, other people want to watch something. They'll fall out over it . . . People owing other people snacks . . . like, say for instance if he owe me a snack, but he owe somebody else a snack, if he owe me first and ole boy get his snack before I do, we going to have a conflict over that, because I gotta get paid first.

It is not unusual for inmates to acknowledge their victimization of others and to feel that some punishment is a justified response to their offense. However, the prisoners face a clear paradox in jail. On the one hand, they feel that some penalty for their criminal actions is appropriate. On the other hand, they view much of the punishment that is inflicted upon them in jail as unnecessary, unjust, and often counterproductive.

Indeed, the inmate, and this may be particularly true of the adolescent inmate, not only has a keen sense of what constitutes fair and just reactions to illegal behavior, but what jail should ideally be like. The jail, however, never lives up to these expectations.[9] Instead, the jail becomes another example of injustice and confirms the inmates' belief that the criminal justice system is a "game" that is rigged against them. The result is resentment, anger, and the feeling of being victimized. These feelings are reflected in the following conversation with Jermaine when he was asked about prices in the jail commissary:

> Cookies that you can buy at the store . . . for 25 or 50 cents . . . you're paying $2.00 for a pack . . . That's what I want to know, what they doing with the money they get, cause they sure not spending it on us. I mean not if we got the same uniform somebody done wore from whenever they opened this jail . . . I feel that they getting over on us for being locked up, I mean I know we got no freedom, no privileges really, but damn, you ain't got to play us like that . . . Say you order six pack of Jolly Ranchers [from the commissary] and they run out of Jolly Ranchers and only bring you four packs, they still keep their money . . . [So they charge you for whatever you order, not what they have in stock?] Yep. They don't put the money back in your account or nothing, they keep it. The next time you order, they don't send it to you, or none of that, so you get beat across the head. Like I say, charge it to the game.

Much of the discord found in the jail is the product of the jail itself and how inmates respond to the deprivations associated with incarceration (Sykes, 1958), but other sources of conflict originate outside the jail (Irwin and Cressey, 1962). Two external and often interrelated sources of conflict are race/ethnicity and gang/clique affiliation. Although some inmates coexist with persons from other racial or ethnic groups without difficulty, others experience more problems with the racial and ethnic diversity of the jail. This is particularly evident for blacks and "rednecks." Moreover, there are usually small groups of Hispanics and Asians, many of whom speak little or no English, and these individuals often keep to themselves.

Although there is some fragmentation among prisoners along racial and ethnic lines, there are also antagonisms evident within racial groups, and these often result from gang or clique rivalries. A number of the residents of the pod were acquainted with other prisoners before their incarceration. They went to the same school, lived in the same neighborhood, belonged to the same gang, or otherwise associated with one another in some way.

When persons arrive in the unit they tend to gravitate toward those they already know. As Bobby stated, "I have a group of friends that I hang out with . . . Everybody sits with their little section." Observations of the pod reveal that particular areas serve as gathering places for the same groups of inmates each day. These acquaintances give the individual someone to talk to, help them pass the time, provide them with information on how to cope with jail, serve as a conduit for information to others on the outside, and act as allies who can help the individual defend himself against attack by hostile groups or individuals.

In fact, a prisoner who is not a member of a group that can offer protection in the event of violence is at a distinct disadvantage in the jail. The inmate's associations are important because the jail is not only a confusing place where friends are relied on for advice on how to best cope with the jail environment, but it can be a dangerous place where having the right connections can mean the difference between life and death. As Bobby noted:

> I'm really not worrying about nobody running up on me cause the people I hang around, I know if something go down they got my back. They going to be there for me . . . no matter what . . . The people I hang with got a reputation not to be messed with, I mean they don't mess with us. I mean we don't mess with nobody either, but it's just to the point where they know that if you mess with him . . . they going to get on you, so they don't do it.

Those without friends in jail can also be disadvantaged in other ways. For example, if a prisoner does not have someone to send him money to be placed in his spending account, he will not be able to purchase a variety of valued items, particularly food items, from the commissary. Access to food is important to prisoners because they are only served three meals per day and the quality and quantity of the food they receive leaves much to be desired. Friends in jail can be helpful in these circumstances, as Bobby indicated when asked if everyone has access to the commissary:

> If they parents don't send them money they short . . . I look out for some of the people [the guys he hangs out with]. I look out for 'em . . . give 'em a soup, or some cookies, or something because I know how it feels. They be hungry . . . and I don't like it, so I try to look out as much as I can.

DISORIENTED AND DISCONNECTED

As Irwin (1985a: 53) noted, "The process of being arrested and held in jail often produces a profound state of internal disorganization and demoralization." Indeed, the transition from being an autonomous individual with freedom to make decisions to being a prisoner who is in a totally subservient status is disconcerting. Talking about his arrest and incarceration, Rasheed stated, "[I] felt like I wasn't getting out, like I was just gone, in a daze, dream, I was just, put me in a car, wasn't coming home anymore. Like everything went down a drain, like you won't see anybody for a long time."

When arrested and placed in the jail, the individual is forced to confront a number of frightening possibilities that may include severe restrictions on his freedom of movement; facing the shame and embarrassment that is often associated with legal troubles; separation from family, friends, and other familiar things; being victimized by other inmates, correctional staff, or both; and having little knowledge about what will happen in the future. From the prisoner's point of view, the jail is often seen as a surreal world characterized by a physical plant constructed of concrete and steel, daily operating procedures, and correctional staff who work in opposition to the needs of inmates and challenges their conceptions of what is just, fair, and reasonable.

It is a world of contrast where the apparent brightness and cleanliness of the new generation facility obscures a reality experienced by many prisoners who never feel clean. As Michael noted, "I don't feel clean in this place. I've got bumps on my arms. There's something about this place that makes you feel unclean; my face is greasy." Or as Jermaine noted about the food:

> That shit be nasty, you don't know who be cooking your food man or who be playing over it. I mean there been time that inmates done got hair in they food. I seen spit in they food. All kinda shit . . . I mean, you don't know who be playing around with food . . . That's why I trade . . . I eat my breakfast . . . so I trade from lunch to dinner, I don't eat that. I done trade all that for commissary or I go get me some noodles . . . I know like . . . when he's [another inmate] trying to eat his food, when he flipped his meat over, he had hair all in it.

One of the most difficult things that many inmates wrestle with is a profound sense of disconnectedness from all things familiar and a pervasive sense of uncertainty about the future. Many jail inmates have limited prosocial community support networks that they can rely on in times of trouble (Elrod et al., 1999). Furthermore, the jail does nothing to help prisoners develop these networks. Jermaine commented, "You feel lonely . . . I wanted to call my mom or someone in my family to see how they were doing . . . I disconnected myself from them, and when I got locked up . . . I really need them, I wanted to talk with them all the time." Instead of helping inmates develop connections to others, the jail acts as a barrier to the development of positive social relations. Importantly, the physical characteristics of the jail, the formal and informal mechanisms of control employed, and the social relations that develop between many inmates and between inmates and staff hinder the development of positive connections to others both within and outside the institution.

Moreover, this sense of disconnectedness occurs despite the fact that prisoners have regular access to phones and are allowed weekly visits from family and friends. But as is always the case in jail, there is a cost to be paid.[10] Violations of jail rules often result in prisoners losing telephone or visiting privileges. Also, all calls from prisoners are collect calls that cost the receiving party 25 cents per minute. This is seen by inmates as an exorbitant amount of money for families, especially when they have limited financial resources to pay their bills, which may include lawyer fees, fines, and court costs. As a result, prisoners feel trapped. On one hand, they want, often desperately, to communicate with those outside the jail. On the other, they realize that there can be considerable financial costs associated with their communications that will have to be borne by family and friends.

Incarcerated adolescents appreciate receiving visits from family and friends. To some extent, the opportunity to maintain links with the familiar eases some of the pain of incarceration. In talking about weekly visits by his family, Bobby noted, "It helps a little bit to know that they're still there and they care for me and whatever, but it still don't beat being out there with them."

Prisoners are often discomforted, however, over the conditions that surround visitation, particularly the fact that even during visits the jail continues to reinforce disconnectedness, as typified in this comment by Rasheed, "When you get visitation like you behind a glass, you got to talk through a phone to talk to your people, that make you feel like you're really separated from everybody else."

There is both a positive and negative side to contact with those on the outside. Adolescent inmates often look forward to seeing family and friends in person, but they can also experience considerable uneasiness as a result of their status as prisoners and because of the shame, disappointment, and difficulty they have caused others. Moreover, some prisoners are well aware that visitation can also be used as a mechanism of control. For example, prisoners may be allowed to have family visits through security glass (no physical contact), or contact visits (no glass barrier, limited physical contact allowed). In contrast, the staff used denial of all visits or contact visits as a means of punishing prisoners. When Bobby was asked if he feels contact visits would be a good idea, he responded as follows:

> Yeah, it's a good thing, but it can also hurt you cause some of the people in here, they [some of the correctional officers and teachers] don't like you. Just because you in here, they try to treat you any kinda way and they'll just throw anything on the sheet [allege that the inmate has committed some discipline infraction that would deny him a contact visit].

Part of the disconnectedness experienced by jail inmates is a product of uncertainty about the future. For the prisoner, the ability to learn about his legal troubles, family, and friends is limited to what he can discover through the telephone, visits, jail personnel, and acquaintances in jail. This places the prisoner in a disadvantaged position when it comes to ascertaining timely and accurate information about a host of things related to his legal and social condition.

Indeed, it is common to hear inmates complain about not understanding the status of their legal case, having little concrete information about how long they may have to stay in jail, being uncertain as to how their incarceration is affecting relationships with family and friends, and being concerned about how their legal troubles and incarceration will influence their future. Concerns about the future are exacerbated because adolescent inmates are considered adults and face the prospect of incarceration in adult prisons. This feeling of uncertainty that many prisoners experience is clearly reflected in the following comments by Jermaine:

> I know what I was here for, but I still ain't talked to my lawyer yet. I mean I don't know the results of what they [the judge in criminal court] are going to do . . . I don't know if I am going to be here longer, or if they

are going to release me or not. I go to court Friday, but I don't know what's going to happen. My mother says they are going to give me time served, and then again you can never believe that because it's all on the judge. Sometimes I feel mad, sometimes you're afraid. I'm just angry.

The uncertainty that many inmates feel about the future and the anger that results is reinforced by many jail personnel, who are perceived by prisoners as uncaring and mean spirited. In talking about how some correctional workers treat inmates, Bobby stated the following:

Some of the officers . . . when they come in they'll just be like such and such go to your room and don't come out . . . cause they nasty. And then everything they say to you, they got to cuss you out and make the other people in the pod laugh . . . Every time you say something . . . [the officers will be] cursing and stuff . . . trying to make you feel bad.

From the prisoners' perspective, the actions of many jail staff are evidence that their primary concern is with the control and punishment of inmates, not helping the prisoners with the problems they face. When asked if there was anyone at the jail to help him understand the status of his case, Jermaine said:

There's supposed to be . . . When you first come, they send you to a case manager. He talk your head up like he's really going to be there for you, he's going to help you do all this, and all this when you get out. He going to help you do right in here. He'll find out more information, what's going to happen and all this. But I've been here two weeks and I'm still stuck in the same spot. I talked with my probation officer, he said he was going to come get me . . . That was last week . . . I haven't talked with him since then.

Or as Bobby noted:

Most of the [correctional] officers don't care. You know, most of 'em . . . want to see you do bad . . . They want you to get in trouble, you know what I'm saying, so they can blank [react in a punitive way] while you in here. Like say, if we out in the pod playing cards or whatever, if one person talk or laugh loud or something, they'll lock the whole pod down for about two hours and they be throwing you in a "wet" cell. And a wet cell they ain't even sanitary cause they make you sleep on steel . . . and then the steel be rusted where you can get lead poisoning or whatever cause it be rusty and everything. And then, there be piss and stuff everywhere . . . Stank in there, then it be cold and you don't get no covers or nothin so you liable to get sick, so it's hard.

REHABILITATION AND DEBILITATION

Officially, the new generation jail described in this study was concerned about the safety and well being of inmates, with doing more than simply warehousing adolescent offenders. For example, the jail operated a number of mandatory programs that were intended to help adolescent inmates develop a range of academic and social skills that can assist them in making a successful transition to the community. These programs included a GED program, a full-day high school program, and classes that discussed domestic violence, substance abuse, teen health, and life skills. Moreover, it is clear that a number of correctional administrators and line staff were genuinely concerned about the adolescent charges in their care.

Nevertheless, official descriptions of jail operations are often at odds with daily operations of the institution. In reality, many correctional personnel did not share the same concern for adolescent inmates expressed by their more progressive counterparts. The result was a program replete with contradiction, where a number of supposedly rehabilitative programs operated in ways or in a larger context that obscured or negated their intended purpose. Indeed, as we have documented throughout this study, the jail existed to punish and control. Although some prisoners did gain something positive from their experience in jail, these benefits were largely in spite of the social organizational context of the institution. In talking about how he saw the jail, Jermaine stated the following:

> Jail ain't nothing but a big time gambling place. I mean, if I was running the jail, I would occupy a lot of people's time, cause the grown-ups, they ain't gotta go to school, they can sit in the pod all day and watch TV, talk on the phone . . . all they want. Juveniles, they make us go to school, shit I be making the grown-ups go to school, they'll be having to work, somethin to occupy their time . . . Jail ain't nothin but, I mean, a waste of time . . . To me, that's all it is. Cause you, I mean, you really ain't learning nothing . . . they say jail supposed to help you learn from your mistakes, but once you get in here you ain't around nothin but a bunch of criminals . . . people in here for stealing cars and all that and they telling other people how to steal cars . . . break in houses and all this. That's all you doing, learning more criminal ways, so when you get out you can be a better criminal. How not to get caught, that's how I see it. I mean it's like they say, when you come to jail, it ain't helping you better yourself, it's just teaching you more conniving ways, of scheming on people, of how to get around stuff.

These young prisoners learned that many if not most of the people who work in the criminal justice system are callous and uncaring; that jail, like so much of life, is a game to be played, but also one that is rigged so that they have little chance of winning. They discovered that criminal justice is really about "you ain't really learning nothin productive, just how to do time." If they derived anything positive out of the jail experience, it was probably in spite of themselves and the correctional staff, who were supposed to be concerned with their treatment and rehabilitation.

Unfortunately, during their time as child prisoners they may have begun to acquire the attitudes, jargon, and postures that will help prepare them for future trips to adult correctional institutions. In short, the lessons that young people might learn in jail confirm their worst fears about adult authority and correctional institutions, and help prepare them for lives as prisoners as opposed to productive adults.

CONCLUSION

Jails have long been used as a mechanism for controlling and punishing problem youths (Kerle, 1998). Moreover, it is recognized that the placement of youths in adult jails is both counterintuitive and harmful. Historically, the placement of children in jails has resulted in extreme cases of child neglect and abuse at the hands of guards and other inmates. Indeed, the conditions faced by children in jails during the later 1800s was a primary concern of the Child Savers, who were instrumental in the development of the first juvenile court around the turn of the last century. More recently, concerns about the plight of children in jails, particularly the fact that children placed in jails are at higher risk of engaging in self-destructive behaviors such as suicide, has prompted federal efforts to support the removal of children from adult jails and to separate children from adults when detention in adult jails occurs. Unfortunately, neither of these efforts has been successful.

Of course, corrections, including jails, has changed considerably over time. The dark, dank, linear dungeons of the past have, in many places, given way to bright, clean, new generation facilities. Moreover, the management of inmate populations, which in the past was often based on terror, has in many instances given way to newer correctional philosophies that, officially, preach the gospel of humane management in institutions where the "symbolic" vestiges of control (e.g., bars, grates, metal furnishings) are replaced by self-contained housing modules characterized by open spaces and a variety of colors and textures that are intended to lessen the "incarcerative feel" of the jail (see, Zupan, 1991). Arguably, if one accepts the official view, new generation facilities may be capable of meeting the needs of the adolescent inmate. This research seriously questions this assumption.

As Fishman (1922: 793), the lone prison inspector for the federal government in the 1920s, noted, when one is placed in jail for 30 days, one is subjected to more than confinement in an institution. According to Fishman:

> If the facts were known, in most instances the sentence would actually read: "I not only sentence you to confinement for 30 days in a bare, narrow cell in a gloomy building, during which time you will be deprived of your family, friends, occupation, earning power, and all other human liberties and privileges, but in addition, I sentence you to a putrid mire, demoralizing to body, mind, and soul, where every rule of civilization is violated, where you are given every opportunity to deteriorate, but none to improve, and where the tendency to wrong-doing cannot be corrected but only aggravated.

Although conditions in the new generation facility that is the site of this research are undoubtedly better in may ways than the jails visited by Fishman, in other ways jails have not changed at all. As Fishman (1922) and Irwin (1985a) made clear, jails have been and are about more than incarceration. The jail continues to be "the special social device for controlling offensive rabble" (Irwin, 1985a: 3). It is often about disintegration of ties to significant others and to society in general, confusion, guilt, shame, personal degradation, and the maintenance and reproduction of a disadvantaged rabble class (Irwin, 1985a). It is about punishment, pain, control, conflict, boredom, loneliness, bad food, hunger, inconsistency, and contradiction. It is also about the countless other indignities and feelings experienced by those who live and work in jails and their efforts to cope with these realities.

Our research in a large urban new generation facility over the past four years has revealed that official descriptions of the jail presented by correctional administrators and many line staff are incongruent with the jail experiences of adolescent prisoners. Despite the apparent cleanliness of the facility, brightness of the self-contained "pods" in which prisoners live, development of a number of programs for adolescent residents, use of direct supervision to manage inmate behavior, and the progressive attitudes of some correctional administrators and line staff, there is an opposing reality that dominates the daily lives of adolescent inmates. From the prisoners' perspective, jail is often experienced as a confusing, uncaring place, characterized by control, punishment, pain, conflict, disconnectedness, debilitation, contradiction, and injustice.

This research suggests a number of policy responses ranging from the importance of expanding the ways that we study jails and other correctional institutions to changes in the training, supervision, and operation of the particular jail that served as the site of this study. There are, of course, a number of methods that can, and should, be used to study jails and other correctional settings. During the time that we have been involved in this project we have completed a series of surveys of inmates and correctional staff and have learned many important things about the jail environment.

Indeed, we would argue that surveys of prisoners and correctional personnel are important tools that can aid our efforts to understand and improve jail conditions for inmates and correctional staff. However, we would also argue that there are many things that we need to understand about correctional environments that can be best learned through lengthy observations and intensive interviews of inmates and correctional staff. As this research makes clear, prisoners have powerful stories to tell, and their insights help us understand a world that would be difficult to otherwise comprehend. As one inmate (James) remarked to one of the researchers during an overnight observation, "The only way to learn about it is to be locked up and not be able to leave." Consequently, researchers who are interested in understanding correctional environments should make use of methodologies that allow the voice of the prisoner to become more explicit.

Allowing us to better understand the jail is an acceptable reason to conduct research on jails, and this knowledge can also be used to inform correctional policy. Based on our research, it could be argued that the breakdown between the more humane vision of the jail espoused by some correctional administrators and line staff and the actual operation of the jail could be remedied by improved screening and training of correctional staff. Particularly evident is the need for staff who can relate appropriately to adolescent prisoners and who are educated in child and adolescent development. Also obvious is the need for jail personnel to engage in serious program design efforts intended to create effective ways to apply the principles of child and adolescent development within a correctional setting.

There is also a need for an examination of present training that focuses on the theory and application of direct supervision. In addition, better quality assurance mechanisms that assess the degree to which correctional staff are implementing direct supervision are needed. As this research indicates, the principles of direct supervision are not being implemented with integrity, and this creates a variety of problems for prisoners. Importantly, these are not "quick fixes." They will require considerable investment of time and energy, a fact that may preclude their implementation, although they have some potential for improving conditions within the jail for both prisoners and correctional personnel.

There is one other policy implication that can be derived from this study. There is the possibility that today's modern jails, despite their spit and polish and commitment to new correctional philosophies, are inappropriate placements for adolescents. In this case, a more prudent policy would be to remove youths from adult jails.

NOTES

1. For a good overview of issues related to the placement of juveniles in adult facilities see James Austin, Kelley D. Johnson, and Maria Gregoriou (2000).

2. The adolescent prisoners' voices that appear in this chapter were chosen because of their ability to articulate the themes that were identified through inmate surveys and jail observations.

3. All juvenile residents of the jail are required to participate in academic classes, unless they have completed high school or have a GED diploma.

4. We did not use the real names of prisoners interviewed for this study. Any name used in this study that resembles that of a resident of the jail during the time we conducted this research is purely coincidental.

5. The use of manipulation is common in correctional environments; however, discussions of manipulation typically focus

on its use by inmates rather than correctional staff (see B. Allen and Bosta, 1981; Zupan, 1991).

6. By "social organization" we mean the complex set of social relationships that exist among all of those individuals (correctional staff, prisoners, and others) who make up the jail.

7. It is important to note that correctional staff as well as prisoners are influenced in a variety of negative ways by their experiences in jail. As a result, high turnover among correctional staff is a frequent complaint of administrators.

8. Because connection to the outside world is so valued by prisoners, considerable conflict revolves around the use of telephones. A common way of antagonizing another inmate is to tie up the phone just to prevent someone else from using it.

9. Although many prisoners have had negative experiences with the criminal justice system and other formal social institutions, they maintain idealized perceptions of how these institutions should operate.

10. Prisoners are charged for a variety of services and supplies that they receive in jail. Inmates' accounts are charged for personal hygiene products beyond the most basic necessities, sick calls, medications, and items from the commissary such as thermal tops and bottoms to keep warm, tennis shoes, and food items.

CONCLUSION

An Invitation to the Criminology/Criminal Justice Community

STEPHEN C. RICHARDS
AND JEFFREY IAN ROSS

C onvict criminology is the result of a long journey that has had as its primary mission the introduction of an emerging type of criminological writing, research, and analysis. The question that we must answer is, Where do we go from here? In order to accomplish this goal, we need to step back and reflect upon what we have achieved. Thus, this chapter thanks the authors in the book, pays our respects to other convict writers, reviews the themes in the project, and then suggests a series of recommendations for reforming not only the study of criminology, criminal justice, and corrections, but policy and practice in these fields.

AUTHORS IN THIS BOOK

As the coeditors of this book, we wanted the chapters to begin a new academic discourse. Our effort was to create realistic criminology that impacts the reader in ways typical academic research and writing fails to do. We encouraged the authors to write in the first person, provide biographical details, and go beyond the existing research in the field. Almost all the contributors in this volume have firsthand experience with the criminal justice system and prisons in particular. We want to thank these authors for their demonstrated courage and dedication to this project.

The exconvict authors (Irwin, Jones, Lanier, Mobley, Murphy, Newbold, Richards, Terry, Tromanhauser) have shared their stories about arrest, court, jail, prison, release, and other post-prison experiences. These individuals discussed their convictions (e.g., drug possession, drug conspiracy, armed robbery, burglary), addictions, deviant lifestyles, and time in prison. They have taken serious risks in publicly discussing their lives. A number of them told us that this was the most difficult writing they ever attempted. In some cases, these admissions were painful and even frightening. Many still struggle with the guilt of surviving prison, while their convict friends are still incarcerated, and the pain they may have caused others, including their own families and loved ones. Some may suffer from post-traumatic stress disorder related to remembering their former criminal activities and time incarcerated. All of them have expressed their appreciation for the many mentors and supporters that have helped them with the difficult transition from the life of a convict in the penitentiary, to a being a professor in the university.

Many of these exconvicts, after serving years in penitentiaries and/or correctional institutions, have discussed with us how they are enjoying their new lives and the opportunities the academic setting provides for teaching, research, writing, and making new friends. A few of the authors joked about how prison may actually be good training for being a professor, which may be a surprise to some people. In some cases, living in a high-security prison cell block may not be that different from working in some academic departments. Generally, the trick is to mind your own business, be polite, do your job, stay out of trouble with administrators, and be real careful of the "lifers" who having nothing left to lose. Of course, at the university the food is better, the pay is higher, you can come and go as you please, and you do not get shot for failure to obey. Besides, most students love convict tattoos and prison stories.

Most of the non-exconvict authors (Archambeault, Arrigo, Austin, Brooks, Elrod, Fisher-Giorlando, Owen, Ross, Tregea) have also provided autobiographical elements in their chapters. They too broke from the standard scholarly format and attempted the difficult task of merging first- with third-person writing. A number of these chapters are stories; some are ethnographic, each of them deliberately modified from how they might have appeared in another book or academic journal. All of these contributors, because they never served prison time, struggled with their own good fortune and our requirement that their chapters include convict voices.

PAYING OUR RESPECTS TO THE CONVICT AUTHORS STILL IN PRISON

A number of the authors in this book continue friendships and working relationships with writers in penitentiaries, some of whom are well published in criminology (e.g., Victor Hassine, Wilbert Rideau, Jon Marc Taylor). We all owe a debt of gratitude to the many men and women who live inside prison and continue to write and publish their ideas, thoughts, and observations. Correspondence, phone calls, and prison visits with many prisoners help us to stay current with the conditions inside correctional facilities.

Contributors to this project pay their respects to the prisoners that have and are attempting to write serious commentaries on prison life (e.g., Abbott, 1981; Rideau and Wikberg, 1992; Abu-Jamal, 1996, 2000; J. Taylor, 1995; Hassine, 1996; Peltier, 1999). We recognize that much of their research and writing, while critically informed, is based on their experiences inside prisons, and may only be partially grounded in the academic literature. After all, many of these authors lack or have difficulties obtaining the typical amenities that most scholars take for granted (e.g., a computer for writing, university library, and colleagues educated in criminology who might provide feedback on their work). They struggle to write by hand, or with broken and/or worn out typewriters and copy machines, and lack of office supplies (typewriter ribbons, paper, envelopes, stamps, etc.). In addition, their phone calls are monitored and recorded, and all their mail, sent or received, is opened, searched, and read by prison authorities. In many cases they suffer the retribution of prison authorities, including denial of parole, loss of good time credit, physical threats from staff or inmates, frequent cell searches, confiscation of papers, trips to the hole, and disciplinary transfers to other prisons.

The convict criminologists that are included in this book, both the excons and noncons, have it easier. They have benefited from superior resources in order to open the window on a subterranean world of confinement that few people know.

REFORMING CRIMINOLOGY
AND CRIMINAL JUSTICE

If our project is to have long-lasting meaning, it will lead to progressive public policy reforms. The notion of reform is nothing new in the academic disciplines of criminology and criminal justice. One might even argue that the entire field was originally conceived in an effort to replace the historical use of brutal corporal punishment with civilized solutions. We have come a long way since the use of death, torture, and mutilation were common penalties for minor offenses.

Still, we are shocked by the number of criminologists who although they claim to be experts have little or no firsthand experience with how human beings experience the criminal justice system. Whether it is because they have never worked in a prison, or in a police department, been charged or convicted of a crime, or victimized by crime, the numbers are staggering. They simply do not comprehend the profound impact that imprisonment has on many individuals. The result is criminology and criminal justice writing that is dominated by academic technicians that manipulate data sets and publish statistical trivia from the safety of their offices.

Unfortunately, much of this number crunching, which masquerades as objective science, only obscures the truth and supports the functions of managerial elites. The analytical interpretation of aggregate data does not replace the need to go to the streets, visit penal institutions, and observe and interview the victims of the criminal "justice juggernaut" (Gordon, 1990).

By the same token, we have difficulty understanding why many classroom instructors avoid firsthand experience with the criminal justice system (Fisher-Giorlando, Tregea, this volume). At the very least, we need to know more about our subject than what we read in books or view in videos. One modest beginning is to have students do ride-a-longs in police squad cars, tour a correctional facility, or invite exconvicts to be guest speakers in class. The fact is, adequate instruction in criminology, criminal justice, and corrections requires field experiences to supplement what is learned in university classrooms.

Throughout this book, either directly or indirectly, we have argued for the primacy of ethnographic methods, or those that involve speaking, observing, or interacting with prisoners. This approach requires researchers to take some chances, get a little "dirty" as they sample reality, and even, although this may be considered an "academic felony" or "scholar's sin," get emotionally involved with their subject. Objectivity is an illusion that illustrates the class privilege and social distance of the armchair technician from the sordid lives of criminals and convicts. In contrast, the prison ethnographer, by entering prisons and spending time with convicts, and learning to understand their concerns as legitimate, surrenders any pretense to being value free. He or she becomes partisan (Gouldner, 1968), as it should be. Once you have ventured forth to spend enough time behind prison walls, observed the way human beings live caged like animals, and listened carefully to what they have to say, you will know why you have to take a side.

AN INVITATION TO JOIN US:
CHANGING CORRECTIONS

Unfortunately, the primary focus of correctional work has been on controlling prisoners rather than providing them with services, programs, and opportunities for reintegration into mainstream society. The real problem is finding ways to control the abuse of legal authority that allows the state to imprison millions of poor, minority, and young Americans by criminalizing common nonviolent activity and behavior (J. Ross, 1995/2000; Richards and Avey, 2000; Irwin et al., 2000; J. Ross and Richards, 2002).

The convict perspective suggests several policy recommendations for civilizing corrections, reducing the number of men and women in prison, and lowering the rate of recidivism. First, we advocate dramatic reductions in the national prison population through diversion to probation or other community programs.

Today, many persons are being sentenced to prison for nonviolent crime. These people should be evaluated as candidates for early release, with the remainder of their sentence to be served under community supervision. The only good reason for locking up a person in a cage is that he or she presents a danger to the community. A prisoner should have an opportunity to reduce his or her sentence by earning "good time credit" for good behavior and program participation. Unfortunately, many state correctional systems, following the federal model (Richards, this volume), have moved toward determinate sentencing, so-called truth in sentencing with limited provisions for "good time" reductions in sentences, and no parole. We need to return good behavior incentives to correctional practice.

One criticism of our suggestion to reduce the prison population through diversion to community programs, already discussed by Irwin, Austin, and Tromanhauser earlier in this volume, is the question of how we might predict who will or will not offend or reoffend. Despite numerous attempts by social science, we still have no reliable instruments to predict the potential risk of either first-time or subsequent criminal behavior by either free or incarcerated individuals. The problems are many, including "false positives," which predict a person to be a risk who is not. Conversely, "false negatives" are persons predicted not to be dangerous who turn out to be so. The fact that our science is so primitive, and as yet unsuccessful, at devising classification schemes and prediction scales is not adequate rationale for failing to support reductions in prison admissions and population.

Second, along with the reduction in prison population, we support the closing of large-scale penitentiaries and reformatories, where prisoners are warehoused in massive cell blocks. Over many decades, the design and operation of these "big house" prisons has resulted in murder, assault, and sexual predation that continues unabated. A smaller prison population housed in smaller institutions would be accomplished by constructing or redesigning prison housing units with single cells or rooms. It is well known that single-occupancy cells and rooms is one requirement for lowering the rate of institutional violence. Smaller prisons, for example, with a maximum of 500 prisoners, with single cells or rooms, should become the correctional standard when we begin to seriously consider the legal requirement for safe and secure institutions.

Third, we need to listen carefully to the prisoner demands for better food and clothing. This is the most common complaint of men and women locked up in U.S. jails and prisons. Well-fed and -clothed prisoners are easier to manage, less alienated, and more amenable to correctional treatments. Every parent and correctional administrator knows hungry people are irritable.

Fourth, we have strong evidence that prison programs are underfunded, as administrators and legislators continue to emphasize custody at the expense of treatment. We advocate prisoners be provided with opportunities for paid institutional employment, vocational training, higher education, and family skills programs. It is true that most institutions have "token" programs that serve a small number of prisoners. For example, a prison may have paid jobs for 20 percent of its prisoners, low-tech training, a GED program, and occasional classes in life skills or group therapy sessions. The problem is that these services are dramatically limited in scope and availability.

We need to ask convicts what services and programs they want and need to improve their ability to live law-abiding lives rather than assume and then implement what we believe is good for them. One recommendation is that prisoners be provided with paid employment, either inside or outside of the prison, where they will earn enough to pay for their own college credit tuition (see Tregea, this volume). At the very least, all prisons should have a program that supports prisoners to complete college credit course by correspondence.

In addition, we suggest voting rights for all prisoners and felons, voluntary drug education therapy, an end to the use of prison snitches, and the termination of the drug war. We are one the few advanced industrial countries that continues to deny prisoners and felons voting rights. Understanding that voting rights are decided by state legislation, we suggest that if convicts could vote, many of the recommendations we advocate would become policy because the politicians would be forced to campaign for convict votes. State and federal government will only begin to address the deplorable conditions in our prisons when prisoners and felons become voters. We do not see prisoners as any less interested than free persons in exercising the right to vote. To the contrary, if voting booths were installed in jails and prisons, we think the voter turnout would be higher than in most outside communities.

Voluntary drug education therapy should be available to all Americans in the community or prison. Many taxpayers would be surprised to know that persons sentenced to prison for alcohol- or drug-related offenses are provided with few opportunities for treatment and therapy. Like the programs discussed above, these services are limited to token programs for a few inmates.

Fifth, we advocate that prisoners released from prison should have enough "gate money" to pay for three months worth of rent and food (Tromanhauser, this volume). The excons could earn some of this money working in prison industries, with the balance provided by the institution. All prisoners exiting correctional institutions should have clothing suitable for applying for employment, eye glasses (if needed), identification (social security card, state ID, or drivers' license), and a copy of their institutional medical records. They should be given credit for time served on parole supervision. Finally, we need to address the use of drug and alcohol testing as the primary cause of parole violations (J. Ross and Richards, 2002: Chapter 12).

Our most controversial policy recommendations include eliminating the snitch system in prison and ending the drug war. The snitch system is used by "guards" in old-style institutions to supplement their surveillance of convicts. It is used to control prisoners by turning them against each other, and is therefore responsible for ongoing institutional violence. If our recommendations for a smaller population, housed in single cells or rooms, with better food and clothing, voting rights, and well-funded institutional programming were implemented, the snitch system would be unnecessary. In a small prison, with these progressive reforms, prison staff would no longer be forced to behave as guards, instead having the opportunity to actively "do corrections" as correctional workers. The staff would be their own eyes and ears, because they would be actively involved in the care and treatment of prisoners.

Along with these recommendations we recognize that the proliferation of prisons and prisoners does not help the victims of crime, and thus we advocate continued use of victim-offender reconciliation programs, particularly those that include elements of restorative justice. Although these have limitations for all parties, those willing to participate may find benefit in these endeavors.

Finally, we support the termination of the drug war. Military metaphors continue to confuse our thinking and complicate our approach to crime and drug addiction. For example, the theory of judicial deterrence, discussed as a rationale for sentencing in nearly every criminal justice textbook, is derived from the "Cold War" idea of nuclear deterrence. This idea evolved into mutually assured destruction (MAD), which was the American rationale for building thousands of nuclear bombs to deter a possible Soviet nuclear attack. The use of deterrence and war has now bled over from the military strategic thinking to colonize criminal justice. The result is another cold war, this one against our own people. We advocate an end to the drug war, amnesty for drug offenders, and a reexamination of how our criminal justice priorities are set. These recommendations will be further developed and debated by colleagues concerned with the humanitarian reform of criminal justice.

Indeed, more research must be conducted and essays written from a convict criminology perspective. We already have plans for a number of prison studies to be conducted by authors in this volume. Additionally, perhaps those who are still in the closet, excons with Ph.D.'s who do not want to reveal their status, or exconvict graduate students, or members of the criminology/criminal justice community, may feel empowered by this book. We invite you to join us.

References

Abbott, Jack Henry. 1981. *In the Belly of the Beast: Letters from Prison.* New York: Random House.

Abbott, Jack Henry, and Naomi Zack. 1987. *My Return.* Buffalo, NY: Prometheus Books.

Abramsky, Sasha. 1999. "Crime: When They Get Out." *Atlantic Monthly* 283 (6): 30–36.

———. 2002. *Hard Time Blues: How Politics Built a Prison Nation.* New York: St. Martin's Press.

Abu-Jamal, Mumia. 1995. *Live from Death Row.* New York: Avon Books.

———. 2000. *All Things Censored.* New York: Seven Stories Press.

"Access Prisons." 1998. *The Quill* 86 (4): 4.

Acoca, Leslie. 1998. "Defusing the Time Bomb: Understanding and Meeting the Growing Health Care Needs of Incarcerated Women in America." *Crime and Delinquency* 44 (1): 49–70.

Aday, Ronald H. 1994. "Golden Years behind Bars: Special Programs and Facilities for Elderly Inmates." *Federal Probation* 58:47–54.

Adler, Patricia, and Peter Adler. 1989. "The Gloried Self: The Aggrandizement and the Constriction of the Self." *Social Psychology Quarterly* 52: 299–310.

Allen, Bud, and Diana Bosta. 1981. *Games Criminals Play.* Susanville, CA: Rae John Publishers.

Allen, F. 1981. *The Decline of the Rehabilitation Ideal.* New Haven: Yale University Press.

Allen, Harry E., and Clifford E. Simonsen. 1998. *Corrections in America: An Introduction.* 8th ed. Upper Saddle River, NJ: Prentice-Hall.

American Correctional Association. 1990. *The Female Offender: What does the Future Hold?* Washington, DC: St. Mary's Press.

American Friends Service Committee. 1971. *Struggle for Justice.* New York: Hill and Wang.

America's Prisons: Opposing Viewpoints. 1997. San Diego: Greenhaven Press.

Anderson, David. 1995. *Crime and the Politics of Hysteria: How the Willie Horton*

Story Changed American Justice. New York: New York Times Books.

Anderson, Elijah. 1999. *Code of the Street: Decency, Violence, and the Moral Life of the Inner City*. New York: Norton.

Annin, Peter. 1998. "Inside the New Alcatraz: The ADX 'Supermax' Prison Redefines Hard Time." *Newsweek*, July 13, p. 35.

Anno, Jaye B. 1977. *Analysis of Inmate/Patient Profile Data*. Washington, DC: Blackstone.

———. 1979. *Analysis of Inmate/Patient Profile Data, Year Two*. Silver Springs, MD: Anno.

———. 1991. *Prison Health Care: Guidelines for the Management of an Adequate Delivery System*. Silver Springs, MD: Anno.

Archambeault, William G. 2001. "Prison Management and Traditional Native Healing: A Comparative Analysis of Conflicting Cultures and Values." In Larry Gould and Jeffery Ross (eds.), *A Comparative Analysis of Native Americans and the Criminal Justice System: Theoretical and Policy Directions*. Lincoln: University of Nebraska Press.

Archambeault, William G., and Betty J. Archambeault. 1982. *Correctional Supervisory Management: Principles of Organization, Policy and Law*. Englewood Cliffs, NJ: Prentice-Hall.

Archambeault, William G., and Charles R. Fenwick. 1983. "Comparative Analysis of Japanese and American Police Organizational Management Practices." *Police Studies* 6 (1): 3–12.

———. 1985. "Differential Effects of Organizational Management Styles in Cultural Context: A Comparative Analysis of South Korean, Japanese, and American Law Enforcement." *Police Studies* 1 (March): 13.

———. 1988. "A Comparative Analysis of Culture, Safety, and Organizational Management Factors in Japanese and United States Prisons." *Prison Journal* 68:3–23.

Arrigo, Bruce A. 1992. "The Right to Community-Based Treatment for the Institutionalized Mentally Disabled: The Logic of Identity and the Politics of Justice." *New England Journal on Criminal and Civil Confinement* 18 (1): 1–31.

———. 1993. *Madness, Language, and the Law*. New York: Harrow and Heston.

———. 1994a. "Legal Discourse and the Disordered Criminal Defendant." *Legal Studies Forum* 18 (1): 93–112.

———. 1994b. "Rooms for the Misbegotten: On Social Design and Social Deviance." *Journal of Sociology and Social Welfare* 21 (4): 95–113.

———. 1995a. "Subjectivity in Law, Medicine, and Science: A Semiotic Perspective on Punishment." In C. Sistare (ed.), *Punishment: Social Control and Coercion*. New York: P. Lang, pp. 69–92.

———. 1995b. "The Peripheral Core of Law and Criminology: On Postmodern Social Theory and Conceptual Integration." *Justice Quarterly* 12 (3): 447–472.

———. 1996a. *The Contours of Psychiatric Justice: A Postmodern Critique of Mental Illness, Criminal Insanity, and the Law*. New York: Garland.

———. 1996b. "The Behavior of Law and Psychiatry: Re-thinking Knowledge Construction and the Guilty-but-Mentally Ill Verdict." *Criminal Justice and Behavior* 23 (4): 572–592.

———. 1996c. "Desire in the Psychiatric Courtroom: On Lacan and the Dialectics of Linguistic Oppression." *Current Perspectives in Social Theory* 16:159–187.

———. 1996d. "Toward a Theory of Punishment in the Psychiatric Courtroom: On Language, Law, and Lacan." *Journal of Crime and Justice* 19 (1): 15–32.

———. 1997a. "Transcarceration: Notes on a Psychoanalytically Informed Theory of Social Practice in the Criminal Justice and Mental Health Systems." *Crime, Law, and Social Change* 27 (1): 31–48.

———. 1997b. "The Constitution of Constitutive Theory in Law and Criminology: Revisiting the Past and

Forging the Future." *Theoretical Criminology* 1 (3): 392–396.

———. 1997c. "Recommunalizing Drug Offenders: The 'Drug Peace' Agenda." *Journal of Offender Rehabilitation* 23 (3/4): 53–73.

———. 1998a. "Marxist Criminology and Lacanian Psychoanalysis: Outline for a General Constitutive Theory of Crime." In Jeffrey Ian Ross (ed.), *Cutting the Edge: Current Perspectives in Radical and Critical Criminology.* New York: Praeger, pp. 40–62.

———. 1998b. *Social Justice: The Maturation of Critical Theory in Law, Crime, and Deviance.* Belmont, CA: Wadsworth.

Arrigo, Bruce A., and J. J. Tasca. 1999. "The Right to Refuse Treatment, Competency to Be Executed and Therapeutic Jurisprudence: Toward a Systematic Analysis." *Law and Psychology Review* 23:1–47.

Arrigo, Bruce A., and C. R. Williams. 1999a. "Chaos Theory and the Social Control Thesis: A Post-Foucauldian Analysis of Mental Illness and Involuntary Civil Commitment." *Social Justice* 26 (1): 177–207.

———. 1999b. "Law, Ideology and Critical Inquiry: The Case of Treatment Refusal for Incompetent Prisoners Awaiting Execution." *New England Journal on Criminal and Civil Confinement* 25 (2): 367–412.

Ashcroft, Bill, Gareth Griffiths, and Helen Tiffin. 1989. *The Empire Writes Back.* London: Routledge.

Auerhahn, Kathleen. 1999. "Selective Incapacitation and the Problem of Prediction." *Criminology* 37 (4): 703–734.

Austin, James. 1996. "Are Prisons Really a Bargain." *Spectrum* 69 (2): 6–14.

Austin, James, Marino A. Bruce, Leo Carroll, Patricia L. McCall, and Stephen C. Richards. 2001. "The Use of Incarceration in the United States." American Society of Criminology National Policy Committee. *Critical Criminology* 10 (1): 17–41.

Austin, James, and John Irwin. 2001. *It's about Time.* Belmont, CA: Wadsworth.

Austin, James, Kelley D. Johnson, and Maria Gregoriou. 2000. *Juveniles in Adult Prisons and Jail: A National Assessment.* Washington, DC: U.S. Department of Justice, Bureau of Justice Assistance.

Ayers, Edward. 1984. *Vengeance and Justice Crime and Punishment in the Nineteenth-Century American South.* New York: Oxford University Press.

Bachman, R. 1992. *Death and Violence on the Reservation: Homicide, Family Violence, and Suicide in American Indian Populations.* Westport, CT: Greenwood.

Bakker, Leon, and David Riley. 1999. *Recidivism: How to Measure a Fall from Grace.* Unpublished draft.

Balkin, J. M. 1987. "Deconstructive Practice and Legal Theory." *Yale Law Journal* 96 (4): 743–786.

Barak, Gregg. 1991. *Crimes by the Capitalist State.* Albany: SUNY Press.

———. 1993. "Media, Crime, and Justice: A Case for Constitutive Criminology." *Humanity and Society* 17 (3): 272–296.

———. 1995. "Media, Crime and Justice: A Case for Constitutive Criminology." In Jeff Ferrell and Clinton R. Sanders (eds.), *Cultural Criminology.* Boston: Northeastern University Press, pp. 142–168.

Barak, Gregg, and Stuart Henry. 1999. "An Integrated-Constitutive Theory of Crime, Law, and Social Justice." In Bruce A. Arrigo (ed.), *Social Justice/Criminal Justice: The Maturation of Critical Theory in Law, Crime, and Deviance.* Belmont, CA: West/Wadsworth, pp. 152–175.

Barksdale v. King, 699 F.2d. 744, 1983.

Barnes, Harry E. 1972. *The Story of Punishment.* Montcliff, NJ: Patterson Smith.

Barry, Ellen. 1985. "Children of Prisoners: Punishing the Innocent." *Youth Law News* 12:12–18.

Bartollas, Clemens, and John P. Conrad. 1992. *Introduction to Corrections.* New York: Harper-Collins.

Bauhofer, Valerie S. 1985. "Policy Formulation, Policy Modification and Perception of the Application: A Correctional Case Study." Ph.D. diss., Cornell University, Ithaca, NY.

Beccaria, Cesare. 1764/1963. *On Crimes and Punishments*. New York: Macmillan.

Beck, Allen J. 2000. "Prison and Jail Inmates at Midyear 1999." *Bureau of Justice Statistics Bulletin*. Washington, DC: U.S. Department of Justice.

Becker, Harold S. 1963. *Studies in the Sociology of Deviance*. New York: Free Press.

Beckerman, A., and L. Fontana. 1989. "Professional Education in a Maximum Security Prison: A Comparative Study." *Journal of Correctional Education* 40 (4): 174–180.

Beckett, Katherine, and Theodore Sasson. 2000. *The Politics of Injustice: Crime and Punishment in America*. Thousand Oaks, CA: Pine Forge Press.

Belenko, Steven, and Jordon Peugh. 1998. "Fighting Crime by Treating Substance Abuse." *Issues in Science and Technology* 15 (1): 53–60.

Belknap, Joanne. 1996. *The Invisible Woman: Gender, Crime, and Justice*. Belmont, CA: Wadsworth.

Bell v. Wolfish, 441 U.S. 520, 99 S. Ct. 1861, L. Ed. 2d 447, 1979.

Bentham, Jeremy. 1789/1961. *An Introduction to the Principles of Morals and Legislation*. Garden City, NY: Doubleday.

Berger, Peter L., and Thomas Luckmann. 1966. *The Social Construction of Reality*. New York: Anchor.

Bergner, Daniel. 1998. *The God of the Rodeo: The Quest for Redemption in Louisiana's Angola Prison*. New York: Ballantine.

Berkman, Alan. 1995. "Prison Health: The Breaking Point." *American Journal of Public Health* 85:1616–1618.

Bloom, Barbara, and Meda Chesney-Lind. 2000. "Women in Prison: Vengeful Equity." In Roslyn Muraskin (ed.), *It's a Crime: Women and Criminal Justice*. 2d ed. Upper Saddle River, NJ: Prentice-Hall, pp. 183–204.

Bloom, Barbara, Meda Chesney-Lind, and Barbara Owen. 1994. *Women in California Prisons: Hidden Victims of the War on Drugs*. San Francisco: Center on Juvenile and Criminal Justice.

Blumberg, Mark. 1991. "AIDS: The Impact on Corrections." In Kenneth C. Haas and Geoffrey P. Alpert (eds.), *The Dilemmas of Corrections*. Prospect Heights, IL: Waveland, pp. 517–538.

Blumer, H. 1969. *Symbolic Interactionism: Perspective and Method*. Englewood Cliffs, NJ: Prentice-Hall.

Blumstein, Alfred, Jacqueline Cohen, and Daniel Nagin. 1978. *Deterrence and Incapacitation: Estimating the Effects of Criminal Sanctions on Crime Rates*. Washington, DC: National Academy of Sciences.

Blumstein, Alfred, Jacqueline Cohen, Jeffrey Roth, and Christy A. Visher, eds. 1986. *Career Criminals and "Career Criminals."* 2 vols. Washington, DC: National Academy Press.

Board of Control. 1859. "Report of the Board of Control of the Louisiana Penitentiary to the General Assembly." Baton Rouge, LA: n.p.

Bottoms, A. E., and Ronald Preston. 1980. *The Coming Penal Crisis: A Criminological and Theological Exploration*. Edinburgh, UK: Scottish Academic Press.

Bourdieu, P. 1977. *Outline of a Theory of Practice*. Cambridge, UK: Cambridge University Press.

———. 1987. "The Force of Law: Toward a Sociology of the Juridical Field." *The Hastings Law Journal* 38:814–853.

———. 1994. *Distinction: A Social Critique of the Judgment of Taste*. Cambridge: Harvard University Press.

Bourdieu, P., and L. J. D. Wacquant. 1992. *An Invitation to Reflexive Sociology*. Chicago: University of Chicago Press.

Bowker, Lee. 1977. *Prisoner Subcultures*. Lexington, MA: Lexington Books.

Braithwaite, John. 1989. *Crime, Shame and Reintegration*. Cambridge, UK: Cambridge University Press.

Braithwaite, Ronald L., Braithwaite, Kisha, and Ronald Poulson. 1998.

"HIV and TB in Prison." *Corrections Today* (April): 108.

Brave Bird, Mary, and Richard Erdoes. 1993. *Ohitka Woman*. New York: Harper Perennial.

Braybrook, Bev, and Rose O'Neill. 1988. *A Census of Prison Inmates*. Wellington: New Zealand Department of Justice.

Brenner, Eric. 1998. "Fathers in Prison: A Review of the Data." National Center on Fathers and Families [online brief]. Available at http://fatherfamilylink .gse.upenn.edu/org/ncoff/briefs/ briefs.htm (accessed July 10, 2000).

Brooks, Justin, and Kimberly Bahna. 1994. "'It's a Family Affair'— The Incarceration of the American Family: Confronting Legal and Social Issues." *University of San Francisco Law Review* 28: 271–308.

Brooks, Michael T. 1999. *A Multidimensional Analysis of Jail Inmates' Adjustment: The Factors That Influence Adolescent Inmates' Behavior, Emotional Reactions, and Perceptions of Safety*. Master's thesis, University of North Carolina at Charlotte.

Browne, Angela, Brenda Miller, and Eugene Maquin. 1999. "Prevalence and Severity of Lifetime Physical and Sexual Victimization among Incarcerated Women." *International Journal of Law and Psychiatry* 22 (2–3): 301–322.

Brownstein, Henry. 1995. "The Media and the Construction of Random Drug Violence." In Jeff Ferrell and Clinton R. Sanders (eds.), *Cultural Criminology*. Boston: Northeastern University Press, pp. 45–65.

Bruno, Robert. 1999. *Steelworker Alley*. Ithaca, NY: Cornell University Press.

Burstein, Jules. 1977. *Conjugal Visits in Prisons: Psychological and Social Consequences*. Lexington, MA: Lexington Books.

Burton, Velmer, Francis T. Cullen, and Lawrence Travis. 1987. "The Collateral Consequences of a Felony Conviction: A National Study of State Statutes." *Federal Probation* 51 (4): 52–60.

Burton-Rose, Daniel, with Dan Pens and Paul Wright, eds. 1998. *The Celling of America: An Inside Look at the U.S. Prison Industry*. Monroe, ME: Common Courage Press.

Bush-Baskette, Stephanie. 1998. "The War on Drugs as a War on Black Women." In Susan Miller (ed.), *Crime Control and Women*. Thousand Oaks, CA: Sage, pp. 113–129.

Butler, Anne, and C. Murray Henderson. 1990. *Angola: Louisiana State Penitentiary, A Half-Century of Rage and Reform*. Lafayette: Center for Louisiana Studies, University of Southwestern Louisiana.

———. 1992. *Dying to Tell: Angola— Crime Consequence, Conclusion at Louisiana State Penitentiary*. Lafayette: Center for Louisiana Studies, University of Southwestern Louisiana.

Bynum, Timothy S., and Raymond Paternoster. 1996. "Discrimination Revisited." In Robert A. Silverman and Marianne O. Nielsen (eds.), *Native Americans, Crime and Justice*. Boulder, CO: Westview, pp. 228–238.

Caban v. Mohammed, 441 U.S. 380, 1979.

Camp, George, and Camille Camp. 1996. *The Corrections Yearbook*. South Salem, NY: Criminal Justice Institute.

Caplow, Theodore, and Jonathan Simon. 1999. "Understanding Prison Policy and Population Trends." In Michael Tonry and Joan Petersilia (eds.), *Prisons, Crime and Justice: A Review of Research*. Vol. 26. Chicago: University of Chicago Press, pp. 63–119.

Cardona, Mercedes M. 2000. "Benetton Ad Shift Expected in the Wake of Toscani Exit." *Advertising Age* 71 (20): 4.

Carleton, Mark T. 1971. *Politics and Punishment: The History of the Louisiana State Penal System*. Baton Rouge: Louisiana State University Press.

Carlson, Norman A., Karen M. Hess, and Christine M. H. Orthmann. 1999. *Corrections in the Twenty-First Century*. Belmont, CA: Wadsworth.

Census and Statistics Office of the Dominion of New Zealand. 1925. *The New Zealand Official Yearbook*.

Wellington: New Zealand Government Printer.

Chaiken, Jan M., and Marcia R. Chaiken. 1982. *Varieties of Criminal Behavior.* Santa Monica, CA: Rand.

Cheatwood, Darryl. 1998. "Prison Movies: Films about Adult, Male, Civilian Prisons: 1929–1995." In Frankie Bayley and Donna Hale (eds.), *Popular Culture, Crime and Justice.* Belmont, CA: Wadsworth, pp. 209–231.

Chermack, Steven. 1998. "Police, Courts, Corrections in the Media." In Frankie Bailey and Donna Hale (eds.), *Popular Culture, Crime and Justice.* Belmont, CA: Wadsworth, pp. 87–99.

Chesney-Lind, Meda. 1991. "Patriarchy, Prisons, and Jails: A Critical Look at Trends in Women's Incarceration." *The Prison Journal* 63:47–65.

———. 1997. *The Female Offender: Girls, Women and Crime.* Thousand Oaks, CA: Sage.

Chessman, Caryl. 1954. *Cell 2455 Death Row.* New York: Prentice-Hall.

———. 1955. *Trial by Ordeal.* New York: Prentice-Hall.

———. 1957. *The Face of Justice.* New York: Prentice-Hall.

Chevigny, Bell Gale. 2000. *Doing Time: 25 Years of Prison Writing.* New York: Arcade.

Children's Defense Fund. 1976. "Children in Adult Jails." Washington, DC: Washington Research Project.

Christie, Nils. 1993. *Crime Control as Industry.* London: Routledge.

Churchill, Ward, and Jim J. Vanderwall, eds. 1992. *Cages of Steel: The Politics of Imprisonment.* Washington, DC: Maisonneuve Press.

Citizens Alliance on Prisons and Public Safety [CAPPS]. 1999. "Factors Affecting Prison Expansion: A Briefing for Legislators." Lansing, MI: Citizens Alliance on Prisons and Public Safety.

Citizens United for the Rehabilitation of Errants. Available at http://www.curenational.org (accessed April 2000).

"Civic Genics on the Front Lines of America's Battle with the Destructive Cycle of Addiction-Criminality-Imprisonment." Available at http://www.prnewswire.com (accessed July 26, 2000).

Clark, John. 1998. *Report to the Attorney General: Inspection and Review of the Northeast Ohio Correctional Center.* Washington, DC: Office of the Corrections Trustee.

Clark, John, James Austin, and Henry D. Alan. 1999. "Three Strikes and You're Out: A Review of State Legislation." In Chris Eskridge (ed.), *Criminal Justice: Concepts and Issues.* Los Angeles: Roxbury, pp. 279–287.

Clark, Stephen H. 1974. "Getting 'Em Out of Circulation: Does Incarceration of Juvenile Offenders Reduce Crime?" *Journal of Criminal Law and Criminology* 65 (4): 528–535.

Clear, Todd R. 1994. *Harm in American Penology.* Albany: SUNY Press.

———. 1996. "Backfire: When Incarceration Increases Crime." *Journal of the Oklahoma Criminal Justice Research Consortium* 3:7–17.

Clear, Todd R., and George Cole. 1997. *American Corrections.* 4th ed. Belmont, CA: Wadsworth.

Cleaver, Eldridge. 1968. *Soul on Ice.* New York: Dell.

Clemmer, Donald. 1940/1958. *The Prison Community.* New York: Holt, Rinehart, and Winston.

Clines, Francis X. 1995. "Ron Wikberg." In Burk Foster, Wilbert Rideau, and Douglas Dennis (eds.), *Wall Is Strong: Corrections in Louisiana.* Lafayette: Center for Louisiana Studies, University of Southwestern Louisiana, pp. xv–xvi.

Cobean, S., and P. Power. 1978. "The Role of the Family in the Rehabilitation of the Offender." *International Journal of Offender Therapy and Comparative Criminology* 22:29–38.

Coffey, Osa D. 1986. "T.I.E.: Integrating Training, Industry, and Education." *Journal of Correctional Education* 37 (3): 104–108.

Cohen, Albert. 1955. *Delinquent Boys: The Culture of the Gang.* New York: Free Press.

Cohen, Jacqueline. 1978. *Incapacitating Criminals: Recent Research Findings of Justice.* Washington, DC: USGPO.

———. 1986. "Research on Criminal Career: Individual Frequency Rates and Offense Seriousness." In Alfred Blumstein, Jacqueline Cohen, Jeffrey Roth, and Christy A. Visher (eds.), *Career Criminals and "Career Criminals."* Vol. 1. Washington, DC: National Academy Press.

Cohen, Mark A. 1988. "Pain, Suffering, and Jury Awards: A Study of the Cost of Crime to Victims." *Law and Society Review* 22 (3): 537–555.

———. 2000. Measuring the Costs and Benefits of Crime and Justice. *Criminal Justice* 4:263–315.

Cohen, Stanley. 1985. *Visions of Social Control.* Oxford, UK: Polity Press.

———. 1988/1992. *Against Criminology.* New Brunswick, NJ: Transaction.

Cole, George, and Christopher Smith. 1998. *The American System of Criminal Justice.* Belmont, CA: Wadsworth.

Colvin, Mark. 1982. "The New Mexico Prison Riot." *Social Problems* 29 (5): 449–463.

———. 1992. *The Penitentiary in Crisis: From Accommodation to Riot in New Mexico.* Albany: SUNY Press.

Community Research Forum. 1980. "An Assessment of the National Incidence of Juvenile Suicide in Adult Jails, Lockups, and Juvenile Detention Centers." Champaign: University of Illinois.

Conover, Ted. 2000. *Newjack: Guarding Sing Sing.* New York: Random House.

Conrad, John. 1981. "Where There's Hope There's Life." In David Fogel and Joe Hudson (eds.), *Justice as Fairness.* Cincinnati, OH: Anderson, pp. 3–21.

Consultants' Report Submitted to Committee on the Judiciary, U.S. House of Representatives, 1984. *The United States Penitentiary, Marion, Illinois.* Washington, DC: USGPO.

Coombe, R. J. 1989. "Room for Maneuver: Toward a Theory of Practice in Critical Legal Studies." *Law and Social Inquiry* 14:69–121.

Cordilia, Ann. 1983. *The Making of an Inmate: Prison as a Way of Life.* Cambridge, MA: Schenkman.

Cordozo-Freeman, Inez, with Eugene Delorme. 1984. *The Joint: Language and Culture in a Maximum Security Prison.* Springfield, IL: Thomas Publishers.

Cornish, Derek B., and Ronald V. Clark. 1999. "Crime as Rational Choice." In Francis T. Cullen and Robert Agnew (eds.), *Criminological Theory: Past to Present.* Los Angeles: Roxbury, pp. 254–257.

Corrections Compendium. 1996. Vol. 21, no. 10, p. 3.

———. 1998. Vol. 23, no. 11, p. 13, and no. 23, p. 17.

"Corrections and the Media." 1989. *Corrections Today,* 51.

A Course in Miracles. 1992. Glen Ellen, CA: Foundation for Inner Peace.

Crawford, Cheryl A., and Marilyn C. Moses. 1995. "NIJ Reports Help Practitioners through Health Care Maze." *Corrections Today* 57:120–121.

Cressey, Donald R. 1955. "Changing Criminals: The Application of the Theory of Differential Association." *American Journal of Sociology* 61:116–120.

———. 1961. *The Prison: Studies in Institutional Organization and Change.* New York: Holt, Rinehart and Winston.

———. 1963. *Other People's Money.* New York: Free Press.

Criminal Justice Newsletter. 1989. November 15.

Criminal Justice Policy Group. 1998. *The Use of Imprisonment in New Zealand.* Wellington: New Zealand Ministry of Justice.

Cromwell, Paul, ed. 1996. *In Their Own Words: Criminals on Crime.* Los Angeles: Roxbury.

Crossen, Cynthia. 1994. *Tainted Truth: The Manipulation of Fact in America.* New York: Simon and Schuster.

Crow Dog, Leonard, Mary Brave Bird, and Richard Erdoes. 1990. *Lakota Woman.* New York: Harper Perennial.

Crow Dog, Leonard, and Richard Erdoes. 1995. *Crow Dog: Four Generations of Sioux Medicine Men.* New York: Harper-Collins.

Crowther, Bruce. 1989. *Captured on Film: The Prison Movie.* London: B. T. Batsform.

Cullen, Francis T. 1994. "Social Support and Crime." In Francis Cullen and Robert Agnew (eds.), *Criminological Theory.* Los Angeles: Roxbury, pp. 236–245.

———. 1995. "Assessing the Penal Harm Movement." *Journal of Research in Crime and Delinquency* 32:330–358.

Cummins, Eric. 1994. *The Rise and Fall of California's Radical Prison Reform Movement.* Stanford, CA: Stanford University Press.

Currie, Elliott. 1993. *Reckoning: Drugs, the Cities, and the American Future.* New York: Hill and Wang.

———. 1998. *Crime and Punishment in America.* New York: Henry Holt.

Dale, Mitchell. 1976. "Barriers to the Rehabilitation of Ex-Offenders." *Crime and Delinquency* 22:322–337.

Daly, Kathleen. 1994. *Gender, Crime and Punishment.* New Haven: Yale University Press.

Daly, Kathleen, and Meda Chesney-Lind. 1988. "Feminism and Criminology." *Justice Quarterly* 5 (4): 497–535.

Davey, Joseph Dillon. 1998. *The Politics of Prison Expansion: Winning Elections by Waging War on Crime.* Westport, CT: Praeger.

Davidson, R. Theodore. 1974. *Chicano Prisoners: The Key to San Quentin.* Prospect Heights, IL: Waveland.

Davis, Fred. 1992. *Fashion, Culture, and Identity.* Chicago: University of Chicago Press.

Dearing, Susan. 2000. "The Invitation: An Answer to Women's Experience

with Social Services, Jails, and Community Punishments." Paper presented to the Academy of Criminal Justice Sciences, New Orleans.

Debo, Angi. 1976. *Geronimo: The Man, His Time, His Place.* Norman: University of Oklahoma Press.

Deleuze, F., and G. Guattari. 1987. *A Thousand Plateaus.* Minneapolis: University of Minnesota Press.

Della Famina, Jerry. 2000. "Manager's Journal: Benetton Ad Models Are Dressed to Kill Sales." *Wall Street Journal,* March 20, p. A34.

Deloria, Vine, Jr. 1969. *Custer Died for Your Sins: An Indian Manifesto.* New York: Avon.

———. 1994. *God Is Red: A Native View of Religion.* Golden, CO: Fulcrum.

———. 1995. *Red Earth, White Lies: Native Americans and the Myth of Scientific Fact.* New York: Scribner's.

Deloria, Vine, Jr., and Clifford Lytle. 1983. *American Indians, American Justice.* Austin: University of Texas Press.

———. 1984. *The Nation Within: The Past and Future of American Indian Sovereignty.* New York: Pantheon.

Derrida, J. 1973. *Of Grammatology.* Baltimore: Johns Hopkins University Press.

———. 1978. *Writing and Difference.* Evanston, IL: Northwestern University Press.

De Shaney v. Winnebago County Social Services, 489 U.S. 189, 109 S.Ct. 998, 103 L.Ed. 2d. 249, 1989.

Dickey, Walter. 1989. "From the Bottom Up: Probation and Parole in Milwaukee." Madison: University of Wisconsin Law School, Continuing Education and Outreach.

DiIulio, John J., Jr. 1987. *Governing Prisons: A Comparative Study of Correctional Management.* New York: Free Press.

———. 1989. *Prisons That Work: An Overview of Management in the Federal Bureau of Prisons.* Washington, DC: National Institute of Corrections.

———. 1990. "Prisons That Work— Management is the Key." *Federal Prisons Journal* 1 (4).

————. 1991. *No Escape: The Future of American Corrections.* New York: Basic Books.

DiMaggio, Paul. 1982. "Culture Capital and School Success: The Impact of Status Culture Participation on the Grades of U.S. High School Students." *American Sociological Review* 47:189–201.

Dinkmeyer, Don C., and Gary D. McKay. 1982. *The Parents Handbook: Systematic Training for Effective Parenting.* New York: Random House.

Dommersheim, F., and S. Wise. 1989. "Going to the Penitentiary: A Study of Disparate Sentences in South Dakota." *Criminal Justice and Behavior* 16 (2): 155–165.

Douglas, Cynthia. 1996. *Adult Corrections Systems.* Baton Rouge: Louisiana House Legislative Services.

Douglas, Jack D. 1992. "Betraying Scientific Truth." *Society* (November/ December).

Douglas, Theola, and Lynette Mundey. 1995. "Making Managed Care Principles Work in the Correctional Setting." *Corrections Today* 57:98–100.

Dowd, Nancy E. 1996. "Rethinking Fatherhood." *Florida Law Review* 48: 523–537.

Du Cane, Edmund. 1885. *The Punishment and Prevention of Crime.* London: Macmillan.

Duguid, Stephen. 1992. "Becoming Interested in Other Things: The Impact of Education in Prison." *Journal of Correctional Education* 47 (2): 74–85.

————. 2000. "Subjects and Objects in Modern Corrections." *Journal of Correctional Education* 51 (2): 241–255.

Duguid, Stephen, and Ray Pawson. 1998. "Education, Change, and Transformation: The Prison Experience." *Evaluation Review* 22 (4): 470–495.

Duguid, Stephen, Colleen Hawkey, and Wane Knights. 1998. "Measuring the Impact of Post-Secondary Education in Prison: A Report from British Columbia." *Journal of Offender Rehabilitation* 27 (1/2): 87–106.

Duncan, Martha Grace. 1988. "'Cradled on the Sea: Positive Images of Prison and Theories of Punishment." *California Law Review* 76 (6): 1202–1247.

————. 1996. *Romantic Outlaws, Beloved Prisons.* New York: New York University Press.

Durkheim, Emile. 1964. *The Division of Labor in Society.* New York: Free Press.

Dyer, J. 1999. *The Perpetual Incarceration Machine: How America Profits from Crime.* Boulder, CO: Westview.

Earle, Kathleen. 1999. "Harvest Festival." *Families in Society* 80 (3): 213–215.

Earley, Pete. 1993. *Hot House: Life inside Leavenworth Prison.* New York: Bantam.

Education as Crime Prevention. 1997. [Soros Report, online] Available at www.soros .org/crime (accessed January 1998).

Ebaugh, Helen Rose Fuchs. 1988. *Becoming an Ex: The Process of Role Exit.* Chicago: University of Chicago Press.

Eckert, Allan W. 1992. *A Sorrow in Our Hearts: The Life of Tecumseh.* New York: Bantam.

Elrod, Preston, Michael Brooks, and Beth Bjerregaard. 1999. "Correctional Environment Improvement Study: Community Support Networks for Jail Inmates." Paper presented at the Academy of Criminal Justice Sciences, Orlando, FL.

English, Kim, and Mary Mande. 1991. "Community Corrections in Colorado: Why Do Some Clients Succeed and Others Fail?" Denver: Department of Public Safety, Colorado Division of Criminal Justice.

Enter, Jack 1995. "Aging Populations in a Correctional Facility." *Corrections Manager's Report* (June/July): 11, 15.

Estelle v. Gamble, 429 U.S. 97, 97 S. Ct. 285, 50 L. Ed. 2d. 251, 1976.

Faith, Karlene. 1993. *Unruly Women: The Politics of Confinement and Resistance.* Vancouver, BC: Press Gang Publishers.

————. 1997. "Media, Myths and Masculinization: Images of Women in Prison." In Ellen Adelberg and Claudia Currie (eds.), *Too Few to Count:*

Canadian Women in Conflict with the Law. Vancouver, BC: Press Gang Publishers, pp. 181–219.

Falter, Robert G. 1993. "Selected Predictors of Service Needs of Inmates over Age 50." Ph.D. diss., Walden University, Naples, FL.

Farkas, Mary A. 1992. "The Impact of the Correctional Field Setting in the Research Experience." *Journal of Crime and Justice* 15:177–184.

Farrington, David P., Lloyd Ohlin, and James Q. Wilson. 1986. *Understanding and Controlling Crime: Towards a New Research Strategy.* New York: Springer-Verlag.

Federal Bureau of Prisons. 1991. *Post Release Employment Project.* Office of Research and Evaluation. Washington, DC. BOP Home Page. Available at www. bop.gov/ (accessed June 2000).

Federal Bureau of Prisons Fact Card. 1995. Washington, DC: U.S. Department of Justice, Federal Bureau of Prisons.

Feigns, John. 1990. U.S. District Court, Eastern District of Michigan, Southern Division. Findings of Fact. Civil Action No. 80-73581-DT (*Radix v. Johnson*).

Feimer, S., F. Pommersheim, and S. Wise. 1990. "Marking Time: Does Race Make a Difference? A Study of Disparate Sentencing in South Dakota." *Journal of Crime and Justice* 13 (1): 86–102.

Fergusson, David M. 1998. "The Christchurch Health and Development Study: An Overview and Some Key Findings." *Social Policy Journal of New Zealand* 10:154–176.

Fergusson, David M., and John L. Horwood. 1997. "Physical Punishment/Maltreatment during Childhood and Adjustment in Young Adulthood." *Child Abuse and Neglect* 21 (7): 617–630.

Ferrell, Jeff. 1993. "The World Politics of Wall Painting. *Social Justice* 20:188–202.

———. 1994. "Confronting the Agenda of Authority: Critical Criminology, Anarchism, and Urban Graffiti." In

Greg Barak (ed.), *Varieties of Criminology Readings from a Dynamic Discipline.* Westport, CT: Praeger, pp. 161–178.

———. 1995. "Style Matters: Criminal Identity and Social Control." In Jeff Ferrell and Clinton R. Sanders (eds.), *Cultural Criminology.* Boston: Northeastern University Press, pp. 169–189.

———. 1996. *Crimes of Style.* Boston: Northeastern University Press.

———. 1998. "Stumbling toward a Critical Criminology." In Jeffrey Ian Ross (ed.), *Cutting the Edge: Current Perspectives in Radical/Critical Criminology and Criminal Justice.* Westport, CT: Praeger, pp. 63–76.

Ferrell, Jeff, and Mark S. Hamm, eds. 1998. *Ethnography at the Edge: Crime, Deviance, and Field Research.* Boston: Northeastern University Press.

Ferrell, Jeff, and Clinton R. Sanders. 1995a. *Cultural Criminology.* Boston: Northeastern University Press.

———. 1995b. "Culture, Crime, and Criminology." In Jeff Ferrell and Clinton R. Sanders (eds.), *Cultural Criminology.* Boston: Northeastern University Press, pp. 3–21.

———. 1995c. "Toward a Cultural Criminology." In Jeff Ferrell and Clinton R. Sanders (eds.), *Cultural Criminology.* Boston: Northeastern University Press, pp. 297–326.

Field, Adrian, and Sally Casswell. 1999. *Drugs in New Zealand: National Survey, 1998.* Auckland, N.Z.: Alcohol and Public Health Research Unit.

Fierce, Milfred C. 1994. *Slavery Revisited: Blacks and the Southern Convict Lease System 1865–1933.* New York: Brooklyn College, City University of New York.

Fisher-Giorlando, Marianne. 1987. "Prison Culture: Using Music as Data." Ph.D. diss., Ohio State University.

———. 1992. Review of *Life Sentences: Rage and Survival behind Bars,* ed. Wilbert C. Rideau and Ron Wikberg. *The Criminologist* 18:24–25.

———. 1995. "Women in the Walls: The Imprisonment of Women at the Baton

Rouge Penitentiary 1835–1862." In Burk Foster, Wilbert Rideau, and Douglas Dennis (eds.), *The Wall Is Strong: Corrections in Louisiana*. Lafayette: Center for Louisiana Studies, University of Southwestern Louisiana, pp. 16–25.

Fisher-Giorlando, Marianne, and Shanhe Jiang. 2000. "Race and Disciplinary Reports: An Empirical Study of Correctional Officers." *Sociological Spectrum* 20 (2): 169–194.

Fishman, Joseph F. 1922. "The American Jail: Pages from the Diary of a Prison Inspector." *Atlantic Monthly* 130:792–805.

Fitzpatrick, P. 1984. "Law and Societies." *Osgoode Hall Law Journal* 22:115–138.

Flanagan, Timothy J. 1983. "Correlates of Institutional Misconduct among State Prisoners." *Criminology* 21:29–39.

———. 1995. *Long-Term Imprisonment*. Thousand Oaks, CA: Sage.

Fleischer, Steven. 1998. "Termination of Parental Rights: An Additional Sentence for Incarcerated Parents." *Seton Hall Law Review* 29:312–341.

Fleisher, Mark S. 1989. *Warehousing Violence*. Newbury Park, CA: Sage.

———. 1995. *Beggars and Thieves: Lives of Urban Street Criminals*. Madison: University of Wisconsin Press.

Fleisher, Mark S., and Richard H. Rison. 1997. "Health Care in the Federal Bureau of Prisons." In James W. Marquart and Jonathan R. Sorensen (eds.), *Correctional Contexts: Contemporary and Classical Readings*. Los Angeles: Roxbury, pp. 327–334.

Flynn, Edith E. 1992. "The Graying of America's Prison Population." *Prison Journal* 72 (1/2): 77–98.

Fogel, David. 1975. *We Are the Living Proof*. Cincinnati, OH: Anderson.

Fonow, Mary Margaret, and Judith A. Cook, eds. 1990. *Beyond Methodology: Feminist Scholarship in Lived Research*. Bloomington: Indiana University Press.

Foster, Burk. 1995. "Plantation Days at Angola: Major James and the Origins

of Modern Corrections in Louisiana." In Burk Foster, Wilbert Rideau, and Douglas Dennis (eds.), *The Wall Is Strong: Corrections in Louisiana*. Lafayette: Center for Louisiana Studies, University of Southwestern Louisiana, pp. 1–3.

Foster, Burk, Wilbert Rideau, and Douglas Dennis, eds. 1995. *The Wall Is Strong: Corrections in Louisiana*. Lafayette: Center for Louisiana Studies, University of Southwestern Louisiana.

Foster, Daniel. 1988. "Consideration of Treatment Issues with Native American Indians Detained in the Federal Bureau of Prisons." *Psychiatric Annals* 18 (12): 698–701.

Foucault, M. 1965. *Madness and Civilization: A History of Insanity in the Age of Reason*. New York: Vintage.

———. 1970. *The Order of Things*. New York: Vintage.

———. 1977. *Discipline and Punish: The Birth of a Prison*. New York: Pantheon.

Fox, James G. 1983. "The New Right and Social Justice: Implications for the Prisoners Movement." *Social Justice* 20:63–75.

Fox, Vernon. 1956. *Violence behind Bars: An Explosive Report on Prison Violence in the United States*. Westport, CT: Greenwood.

Fraley, Stephen E. 1992. "From Self-Blame to Self-Acceptance: Freeing Myself in a Prison Undergraduate Program." *Journal of Correctional Education* 43 (4): 178–181.

Franklin, H. Bruce. 1982. *Prison Literature in America: The Victim as Criminal and Artist*. Westport, CT: Lawrence Hill and Company.

———, ed. 1998. *Prison Writing in Twentieth-Century America*. New York: Penguin.

"Freedom of Information." 1998. *The Quill* 1 (86): 29.

Freeman v. Lockhart, 503 F.2d. 1016, 1974.

Freeman, John (D-Madison Heights, Chair, Michigan House Corrections Committee). 1998. Hearings, Lansing and Detroit (February).

Freeman, Robert M. 1998. "Public Perception and Corrections: Correctional Officers as Smug Hacks." In Frankie Bailey and Donna Hale (eds.), *Popular Culture, Crime and Justice.* Belmont, CA: Wadsworth, pp. 196–208.

———. 2000. *Popular Culture and Corrections.* Lanham, MD: American Correctional Association.

Freire, P. 1972. *Pedagogy of the Oppressed.* New York: Herder and Herder.

French, Lawrence, ed. 1982. *Indians and Criminal Justice.* New York: Allanheld, Osmun and Co.

French v. Owens, 538 F. Supp. 910, 1982.

Friedrichs, David O. 1996. *Trusted Criminals.* Belmont, CA: Wadsworth.

Gabor, Thomas. 1995. *Everybody Does It! Crime by the Public.* Toronto: University of Toronto Press.

Garabedian, Peter. 1963. "Social Roles and Processes of Socialization in the Prison Community." *Social Problems* 11:139–152.

Gaucher, Bob. 1998. "Punitive Justice and the Victim's Movement." *Journal of Prisoners on Prisons* 9 (2): 2–16.

———. 1999. "Inside Looking Out: Writers in Prison." *Journal of Prisoners on Prisons* 10 (1/2): 14–31.

Gellert, Lawrence. 1936. *Negro Songs of Protest.* New York: American Music League.

———. 1939. *Me and My Captain: Chain Gang Negro Songs of Protest.* New York: Hours Press.

Gendreau, Paul, and Robert R. Ross. 1986. "Correctional Treatment: Some Recommendations for Effective Intervention." In Kenneth C. Haas and Geoffrey P. Alpert (eds.), *The Dilemmas of Punishment: Readings in Contemporary Corrections.* Prospect Heights, IL: Waveland, pp. 315–236.

Genet, Jean. 1949a. *Haute Surveillance* (Death Watch). Paris: Libraire Gallimard.

———. 1949b. *Journal du Voleur* (A Thief's Journal). Paris: Libraire Gallimard.

Genisio, Margaret H. 1996. "Breaking Barriers with Books: A Father's Book-Sharing Program from Prison." *Journal of Adolescent and Adult Literacy* 40 (2): 92–100.

Genty, Philip M. 1991/1992. "Procedural Due Process Rights of Incarcerated Parents in Termination of Parental Rights Proceedings: A Fifty State Analysis." *Journal of Family Law* 30: 757–846.

Gerber, Jurg, and Eric J. Fritsch. 1995. "Adult Academic and Vocational Correctional Educational Programs: A Review of Recent Research." *Journal of Offender Rehabilitation* 22 (1/2): 119–142.

Gettinger, Stephen H. 1984. *New Generation Jails: An Innovative Approach to an Age-Old Problem.* Washington, DC: National Institute of Corrections.

Giallombardo, Rose. 1966. *Society of Women: A Study of a Women's Prison.* New York: Wiley.

Giddens, A. 1984. *The Constitution of Society: Outline of the Theory of Structuration.* Oxford, UK: Polity Press.

———. 1990. *The Consequences of Modernity.* Stanford, CA: Stanford University Press.

Gillard, Darrell K., and Allen J. Beck. 1998. *Prisoners in 1997.* Washington, DC: U.S. Department of Justice, Bureau of Justice Statistics.

Glazer, Barney, and Anselm Strauss. 1967. *The Discovery of Grounded Theory.* Chicago: Aldine.

Glick, Barry. 1998. "Kids in Adult Correctional Systems: An Understanding of Adolescent Development Can Aid Staff in Managing Youthful Offender Populations." *Corrections Today* 60: 96–99.

Goetting, Ann, and Roy M. Howsen. 1986. "Correlates of Prisoner Misconduct." *Journal of Quantitative Criminology* 2:49–67.

Goffman, Erving. 1959. *The Presentation of Self in Everyday Life.* Garden City, NY: Doubleday.

———. 1961. *Asylums: Essays on the Social Situation of Mental Patients and Other Inmates.* Garden City, NY: Doubleday.

————. 1963. *Stigma: Notes on the Management of Spoiled Identity*. Englewood Cliffs, NJ: Prentice-Hall.

Goldsmith, Seth B. 1975. *Prison Health: Travesty of Justice*. New York: Prodist Publications.

Goodstein, Lynne, and Kevin Wright. 1989. "Inmate Adjustment to Prison." In L. Goodstein and Doris Mackenzie (eds.), *The American Prison: Issues in Research and Policy*. New York: Plenum, pp. 229–251.

Gordon, Dianna R. 1990. *The Justice Juggernaut: Fighting Street Crime, Controlling Citizens*. New Brunswick, NJ: Rutgers University Press.

————. 1994. *The Return of the Dangerous Classes: Drug Prohibition and Policy Politics*. New York: Norton.

Gottfredson, Michael, and Travis Hirschi. 1986. "The True Value of Lambda Would Appear to Be Zero: An Essay on Career Criminals, Criminal Careers, Selective Incapacitation, Cohort Studies, and Related Topics," *Criminology* 24(2):213–233.

Gould, Stephen Jay. 1981. *The Mismeasure of Man*. New York: Norton.

Gouldner, Alvin. 1968. "The Sociologist as Partisan: Sociology and the Welfare State." *American Sociologist* 3:103–116.

Greenberg, David F. 1975. "The Incapacitation Effects of Imprisonment: Some Estimates." *Law and Society* 9 (4): 541–586.

————. 1991. "Modeling Criminal Careers." *Criminology* 29 (1): 17–44.

Greenberg, Maury. 1988. "Prison Medicine." *American Family Physician* 38: 167–170.

Greenfeld, Lawrence, and Steven Smith. 1999. *American Indians and Crime*. Bureau of Justice Statistics. Washington, DC: U.S. Department of Justice, Office of Justice Programs.

Greenfeld, Lawrence, and Tracy Snell. 1999. *Women Offenders. Bulletin:* Bureau of Justice Statistics. Washington, DC: U.S. Department of Justice, Office of Justice Programs.

Greenfield, L. A., and S. K. Smith. 1999. *American Indians and Crime*. Washington, DC: Bureau of Justice Statistics, U.S. Department of Justice. NCJ 173386, pp. v–vii.

Greenwood, Peter W., and Allan Abrahamse. 1982. *Selective Incapacitation*. Santa Monica, CA: Rand.

Greenwood, Peter W., and Susan Turner. 1987. *Selected Incapacitation Revisited: Why the High-Rate Offenders Are Hard to Predict*. Santa Monica, CA: Rand.

Gregg v. Georgia, 428 U.S. 153, 182–183, 96 S.Ct. 2909, 49 L.Ed. 2d. 859, 1976.

Greifinger, Robert B. 1996. "TB Testing of Inmates." *Public Health Reports* 111 (July/August): 328.

Grobsmith, E. S. 1994. *Indians in Prison: Incarcerated Native Americans in Nebraska*. Lincoln: University of Nebraska Press.

————1996. "The Future for Native American Prisoners." In Robert A. Silverman and Marianne O. Nielsen and (eds.), *Native Americans, Crime and Justice*. Boulder, CO: Westview, pp. 278–287.

Grogger, J. 1989. *Employment and Crime*. Sacramento, CA: Bureau of Criminal Statistics and Special Services.

"Guidelines for Legislation on the Psychiatric Hospitalization of Adults." 1983. *American Journal of Psychiatry* 140: 672–679.

Hagan, John. 1994a. "Social Capital and Crime." In Francis Cullen and Robert Agnew (eds.), *Criminological Theory*. Los Angeles: Roxbury, pp. 332–339.

————. 1994b. *Crime and Disrepute*. Thousand Oaks, CA: Pine Forge Press.

Hairston, Creasie F. 1989. "Men in Prison: Family Characteristics and Parenting Views." *Journal of Offender Counseling, Services and Rehabilitation* 14:23–30.

————. 1995. "Fathers in Prison." In Katherine Gabel and Denise Johnston (eds.), *Children of Incarcerated Fathers*. New York: Lexington Books, pp. 31–40.

————. 1996a. "How Correctional Policies Impact Father-Child Relationships." *Family and Corrections Network Report* 8:3–4.

———. 1996b. "Fathers in Prison and Their Children: Visiting Policy Guidelines." *Social Policy and Research Notes* [online brief]. Available at http://www.fcnetwork.org/reading/hairston2.html (accessed July 2000).

———. 1998. "The Forgotten Parent: Understanding the Forces that Influence Incarcerated Fathers' Relationships with Their Children." *Child Welfare* 77 (5): 617–639.

Hairston, Creasie F., and Patricia Lockett. 1985. "Parents in Prison: A Child Abuse and Neglect Prevention Strategy." *Child Abuse and Neglect* 9: 471–477.

———. 1987. "Parents in Prison: New Directions for Social Services." *Social Work* 32 (2): 162–164.

Haley, Alex. 1964. *Autobiography of Malcolm X*. New York: Grove.

Hallinan, Joseph T. 2001. *Going up the River: Travels in a Prison Nation*. New York: Random House.

Hamilton, Arthur, and William Banks. 1993. *Fathers behind Bars*. Waco, TX: W. R. S. Publishing.

Hamm, Mark S. 1991. "The Abandoned Ones: A History of the Oakdale and Atlanta Prison Riots." In Gregg Barak (ed.), *Crimes by the Capitalist State*. Albany: SUNY Press, pp. 145–180.

———. 1995. *The Abandoned Ones*. Boston: Northeastern University Press.

———. 1997. *Apocalypse in Oklahoma: Waco and Ruby Ridge Revenged*. Boston: Northeastern University Press.

Hamm, Mark S., Terese Coupez, Frances E. Hoze, and Corey Weinstein. 1994. "The Myth of Humane Imprisonment: A Critical Analysis of Severe Discipline in U.S. Maximum Security Prisons, 1945–1990." In Michael Braswell, Reid Montgomery Jr., and Lucien X. Lobardo (eds.), *Prison Violence in America*. 2d ed. Cincinnati, OH: Anderson, pp. 167–200.

Hamm, Mark S., and Jeff Ferrell. 1994. "Rap, Cops, and Crime: Clarifying the Cop Killer Controversy." *ACJS Today* 13: 1, 3, 29.

Hammet, Douglas. 1994. "Update: HIV/AIDS in Correctional Facilities." *NIJ Issues and Practices,* January (NCJ 143399).

Hammett, Theodore, and Lynne Harrold. 1994. "Tuberculosis in Correctional Facilities." *Issues and Practices in Criminal Justice* (January). Washington, DC: National Institute of Justice.

Hampton v. Holmesburg Prison Officials, 546 F.2d, 1977, 1976.

Harland, Ann. 1995. *Victimisation in New Zealand—As Measured by the 1992 International Crime Survey.* Wellington: New Zealand Ministry of Justice.

Harring, Stephen. 1982. "Native American Crime in the United States." In Lawrence French (ed.), *Indians and Criminal Justice*. New York: Allanheld, Osmun and Co., pp. 83–108.

Harrison, Kim. 1997. "Parental Training for Incarcerated Fathers: Effects on Attitudes, Self-Esteem, and Children's Self-Perceptions." *Journal of Social Psychology* 137 (5): 588–593.

Hassine, Victor. 1996. *Life without Parole: Living in Prison Today*. Los Angeles: Roxbury.

Hay, Douglas. 1975. *Albion's Fatal Tree: Crime and Society in Eighteenth-Century England*. New York: Pantheon.

Hayano, Dan M. 1979. "Auto-Ethnography: Paradigms, Problems, and Prospects." *Human Organization: Journal of the Society for Applied Anthropology* 38 (1): 99–104.

Heffernan, Esther. 1972. *Making It in Prison: The Square, the Cool, and the Life*. New York: Wiley.

Henry, Stuart, and Mark Lanier. 1998. "The Prison of Crime: Arguments for an Integrated Definition of Crime." *Justice Quarterly* 15 (4): 609–629.

Henry, Stuart, and Dragan Milovanovic. 1996. *Constitutive Criminology: Beyond Postmodernism*. London: Sage.

———. 1999. *Constitutive Theory at Work: Applications in Crime and Justice*. Albany: SUNY Press.

Hernandez, Raymond. 1996. "Give Them the Maximum: Small Towns Clamor for the Boon a Big Prison Could Bring." *New York Times,* February 26, p. B1.

Hershberger, Gregory L. 1979. "The Development of the Federal Prison System." *Federal Probation* 43 (December): 13–23.

Higgins, Gina O'Connell. 1994. *Resilient Adults: Overcoming a Cruel Past.* San Francisco: Jossey-Bass.

Hincle, Pia. 1996. "Prisons to Journalists: Drop Dead: At a Time of Unprecedented Growth and Controversy State Prison Systems Are Clamping Down on Media Access." *Extra! Newsletter of Fair,* July 1, 9, 4: 13.

Hirschi, Travis. 1969. *Causes of Delinquency.* Berkeley: University of California Press.

Hoffer, Eric. 1951/1980. *The True Believer: Thoughts on the Nature of Mass Movements.* Alexandria, VA: Time-Life Books.

Holt, Norman, and Donald Miller. 1972. "Explorations in Inmate-Family Relationships." Sacramento: California Department of Corrections, Report 46.

Homer, E. 1979. "Inmate-Family Ties: Desirable but Difficult." *Federal Probation,* March: 47–52.

Horwitz, Allen V., and Teresa L. Scheid. 1999. *A Handbook for the Study of Mental Health: Social Contexts, Theories, and Systems.* Cambridge, UK: Cambridge University Press.

Howard, John. 1777/1929. *The State of the Prisons in England and Wales.* London: John Dent.

Howell, Robert, I. Reed, J. Paye, and Allan Rose. 1971. "Differences among Behavioral Variables, Personal Characteristics, and Personality Scores of Tattooed and Nontattooed Prison Inmates." *Journal of Research in Crime and Delinquency* 8 (1): 32–37.

Hughes, Robert. 1988. *The Fatal Shore: The Epic of Australia's Founding.* New York: Random House.

Human Rights Watch. 1996. *All Too Familiar: Sexual Abuse of Women in U.S. State Prisons.* New York: Author.

Hunt, A. 1987. "The Critique of Law: What is 'Critical' about Critical Theory?" *Journal of Law and Society* 14: 5–19.

———. 1993. *Exploration in Law and Society: A Constitutive Theory of Law.* New York: Routledge.

Hunt, Geoffrey, Stephanie Riegel, Thomas Morales, and Dan Waldorf. 1999. "Changes in Prison Culture: Prison Gangs and The Case of the 'Pepsi Generation.'" In Paul Cromwell (ed.), *In Their Own Words: Criminals on Crime.* Los Angeles: Roxbury, pp. 175–184.

Immarigeon, Russ, and Meda Chesney-Lind. 1992. *Women's Prisons: Overcrowded and Overused.* San Francisco: National Council on Crime and Delinquency.

Inciardi, James. 1999. *Criminal Justice.* Fort Worth, TX: Harcourt Brace.

Irwin, John. 1970. *The Felon.* Englewood Cliffs, NJ: Prentice-Hall.

———. 1980. *Prisons in Turmoil.* Boston: Little, Brown.

———. 1985a. *The Jail.* Berkeley: University of California Press.

———. 1985b. "The Return of the Bogeyman." Keynote Address at American Society of Criminology, San Diego.

Irwin, John, and Donald Cressey. 1962. "Thieves, Convicts and Inmate Culture." *Social Problems* 10: 142–155.

Irwin, John, Vincent Schiraldi, and Jason Ziedenberg. 2000. "America's One Million Nonviolent Prisoners." *Social Justice* 27 (2): 135–147.

Isaac, R. J., and V. C. Armat. 1990. *Madness in the Streets: How Law and Psychiatry Abandoned the Mentally Ill.* New York: Free Press.

Jackson, Bruce. 1972. *Wake Up Dead Man: Afro-American Worksongs from Texas Prisons.* Cambridge: Harvard University Press.

Jackson, George. 1970. *Soledad Brother: The Prison Letters of George Jackson.* New York: Coward, McCann.

———. 1972. *Blood in My Eye.* New York: Random House.

Jacobs, James B. 1977a. "Macrosociology and Imprisonment." *Corrections and Punishment* 87:89–107.

———. 1977b. *Stateville.* Chicago: University of Chicago Press.

———. 1980. "The Prisoners' Rights Movement and Its Impacts, 1960–1980." *Crime and Justice* 2:429–470.

———. 1983. "The Mass Media and Prison News." In James B. Jacobs (ed.), *New Perspectives on Prisons and Imprisonment.* Ithaca, NY: Cornell University Press, pp. 106–115.

Jacobs, James B., and Helen A. Brooks. 1983. "The Mass Media and Prison News." In James B. Jacobs (ed.), *New Perspectives on Prisons and Imprisonment.* Ithaca, NY: Cornell University Press, pp. 106–115.

Jacobs, Susan. 1995. "AIDS in Correctional Facilities: Current Status of Legal Issues Critical to Policy Development." *Journal of Criminal Justice* 23 (3): 209–221.

Janus, Michael, Jerome Mabli, and J. D. Williams. 1986. "Security and Custody: Monitoring the Federal Bureau of Prisons' Classification System." *Federal Probation* 50: 35–41.

Jenkins, H. David, S. J. Steurer, and J. Pendry. 1995. "A Post Release Follow-Up of Correctional Education Program Completers Released in 1990–1991." *Journal of Correctional Education* 46 (1): 20–24.

Johns, Christina Jacqueline, and Jose Maria Borrero. 1991. "The War on Drugs: Nothing Succeeds Like Failure." In Gregg Barak (ed.), *Crimes by the Capitalist State: An Introduction to State Criminality.* Albany: SUNY Press, pp. 67–100.

Johnson, Jean M., and Christa N. Flowers. 1998. "You Can Never Go Home Again: The Florida Legislature Adds Incarceration to the List of Statutory Grounds for Termination of Parental Rights." *Florida State University Law Review* 25:335–350.

Johnson, Robert. 1996. *Hard Time: Understanding and Reforming the Prison.* Belmont, CA: Wadsworth.

Johnson, Robert, and Hans Toch, eds. 1999. *Crime and Punishment: Inside Views.* Los Angeles: Roxbury.

Jones, David A. 1976. *The Health Risk of an Imprisonment.* Lexington, MA: Lexington Books.

Jones, Edward, Amerigo Farina, Albert Hastorf, Hazel Marcus, Dale Miller, and Robert Scott. 1984. *Social Stigma: The Psychology of Marked Relationships.* New York: W. H. Freeman.

Jones, Richard S. 1995. "Uncovering the Hidden Social World: Insider Research in Prison." *Journal of Contemporary Criminal Justice* 11:106–118.

Jones, Richard S., and Thomas Schmid. 1989. "Inmates' Conception of Prison Sexual Assault." *Prison Journal* 69: 53–61.

———. 1993. "Ambivalent Actions: Prison Adaptation Strategies of First-Time, Short-Term Inmates." *Journal of Contemporary Ethnography* 21 (4): 439–463.

———. 2000. *Doing Time: Prison Experience and Identity among First Time Inmates.* Stamford, CT: JAI Press.

Josephy, Alvin M., Jr. 1991. *The Indian Heritage of America.* Boston: Houghton Mifflin.

Kalesnik, Frank. 1993. "Caged Tigers: Native American Prisoners in Florida, 1875–1888." *Dissertation Abstracts International* 53-10A: 3652.

Kamin, Leon J. 1986. "Is Crime in the Genes? The Answer May Depend on Who Chooses What Evidence." *Scientific American* (February): 22–27.

Kappeler, Victor E., Mark Blumberg, and Gary W. Potter. 1996. *The Mythology of Crime and Criminal Justice.* Prospect Heights, IL: Waveland.

Kappeler, Victor E., Richard D. Sluder, and Geoffrey P. Alpert. 1994. *Forces of Deviance: Understanding the Dark Side of Policing.* Prospect Heights, IL: Waveland.

Karmen, Andrew. 2001. *Crime Victims: An Introduction to Victimology.* Belmont, CA: Wadsworth.

Katz, Jack. 1988. *Seductions of Crime: Moral and Sensual Attractions in Doing Evil.* New York: Basic Books.

Kerle, Kenneth E. 1998. *American Jails: Looking to the Future.* Boston: Butterworth-Heinemann.

Kessler, Ronald, et al. 1994. "National Comorbidity Survey." National Institute of Mental Health. "The Prevalence of Mental Illness." In Allan V. Horwitz and Teresa L. Scheid (eds.), *A Handbook for the Study of Mental Health: Social Context, Theories, and Systems.* Cambridge, UK: Cambridge University Press.

Keve, Paul W. 1991. *Prisons and the American Conscience: A History of Federal Corrections.* Carbondale: Southern Illinois University Press.

Keyes, Ken, Jr. 1975. *Handbook to Higher Consciousness.* Berkeley, CA: Living Love Center.

Killinger, George, and Paul Cromwell. 1973. *Penology.* St. Paul, MN: West.

Kindel, Tip. 1998. "Media Access: Where Should You Draw the Line." *Corrections Today* 59:22–24.

King, Harry, with William J. Chambliss. 1984. *Harry King.* New York: Macmillan.

King, Lambert, and Bindu Desai. 1979. *Management of Common Medical Problems in Correctional Institutions: Epilepsy and Tuberculosis.* Chicago: National Correctional Council on Health Care.

Klein, Dorie. 1973. "The Etiology of Female Crime: A Review of the Literature." *Issues in Criminology* 8 (2): 3–30.

Klein, Naomi. 2000. *No Logo: Taking Aim at the Brand Bullies.* Toronto: Vintage Canada.

Knorr-Cetina, K. 1981. "Introduction: The Micro-Sociological Challenge of Macro-Sociology: Towards a Reconstruction of Social Theory and Methodology." In K. Knorr-Cetina and A. V. Cicourel (eds.), *Advances in Social Theory and Methodology: Toward an Integration of Micro- and Micro-Sociologies.* London: Routledge and Kegan Paul.

Koban, Linda A. 1983. "Parents in Prison: A Comparative Analysis of the Effects of Incarceration on the Families of Men and Women." *Research in Law, Deviance and Social Control* 5:171–183.

Koestler, Arthur. 1941. *Darkness at Noon.* New York: Bantam.

Kolfas, John, and Hans Toch. 1982. "The Guard Subculture Myth." *Journal of Research in Crime and Delinquency* 192: 238–254.

Konrad, George. 1982. *The Loser.* New York: Harcourt Brace Jovanovich.

Krane, Karina M., Molly S. Parece, and John R. Miles. 1998. "Intervening among the Invisible Population: The CDC Examines Correctional Health Care." *Corrections Today* 60 (2): 124.

Kratcoski, Peter C., and George A. Pownall. 1989. "Federal Bureau of Prisons: Programming for Older Offenders." *Federal Probation* 53 (March): 28–35.

Kristeva, J. 1984. *Revolution in Poetic Language.* New York: Columbia University Press.

Lacan, J. 1977. *Écrits: A Selection.* Translated by S. Sheridan. New York: Norton.

———. 1981. *The Four Fundamental Principles of Psycho-analysis.* New York: Norton.

———. 1988. *The Seminars of Jacques Lacan, Book II: The Ego in Freud's Theory and the Technique of Psychoanalysis 1954–1955.* Cambridge, UK: Cambridge University Press.

Laclau, E., and C. Mouffe. 1985. *Hegemony and Socialist Strategy.* New York: Verso.

La Flesche, Francis. 1963. *The Middle Five: Indian Schoolboys of the Omaha Tribe.* Madison: University of Wisconsin Press.

Lamb, R. H., and L. E. Weinberger. 1998. "Persons with Severe Mental Illness in Jails and Prisons: A Review." *Psychiatric Services* 49:483–492.

Landreth, Garry L., and Alan F. Lobaugh. 1998. "Filial Therapy with Incarcerated Fathers: Effects on Parental Acceptance of Child, Parental Stress, and Child Adjustment." *Journal of Counseling and Development* 76 (2): 157–165.

Lanier, Charles S. 1987. "Fathers in Prison: A Psychosocial Exploration." Master's thesis, State University of New York.

———. 1989. "Fathers in Prison: A Psychosocial Exploration." *Voices and Visions: The Family and Corrections.* Proceedings from the First National Conference on the Family and Corrections, Family and Corrections Network, Sacramento, CA.

———. 1990/1991. "Dimensions of Father-Child Interaction in a New York State Prison Population." *Journal of Offender Rehabilitation* 16/17:27–42.

———. 1993. "Affective States of Fathers in Prison." *Justice Quarterly* 10 (1): 51–68.

———. 1995. "Incarcerated Fathers: A Research Agenda." *Forum on Corrections Research* 7 (2): 34–36.

———. 1996. "Children of Prisoners: Fathers' Issues." In Marilyn D. McShane and Frank P. Williams (eds.), *Encyclopedia of American Prisons.* New York: Garland, pp. 79–83.

Lanier, Charles S., and Glenn Fisher. 1989. "The Eastern Fathers' Group: An Educational and Mutual Support Program for Incarcerated Fathers." In Stephen Duguid (ed.), *Yearbook of Correctional Education: 1989.* Stephen Institute for the Humanities, Simon Fraser University, Burnaby, BC, Canada, pp. 155–173.

———. 1990. "A Prisoners' Parenting Center (PPC): A Promising Resource Strategy for Incarcerated Fathers." *Journal of Correctional Education* 41 (4): 158–165.

Lanier, Charles S., Susan Philliber, and William W. Philliber. 1994. "Prisoners with a Profession: Earning Graduate Degrees behind Bars." *Journal of Criminal Justice Education* 5 (1): 15–29.

Lansing, Douglas, Joseph B. Bogan, and Loren Karacki. 1977. "Unit Management: Implementing a Different Correctional Approach." *Federal Probation* 41:43–49.

Lash, Barb. 1998. *Census of Prison Inmates.* Wellington: New Zealand Ministry of Justice.

Leder, Drew, ed. 1999. *The Soul Knows No Bars: Inmates Reflect on Life, Death and Hope.* Oxford, UK: Rowman and Littlefield.

Lemert, Edwin M. 1967. *Human Deviance: Social Problems and Social Control.* Englewood Cliffs, NJ: Prentice-Hall.

Lenihan, K. 1975. "The Financial Condition of Released Prisoners." *Crime and Delinquency* (July): 226–281.

Lester, David. 1999. *Crime and the Native American.* Springfield, IL: Charles C. Thomas.

Levasseur, Ray Luc. 1998a. "From USP Marion to ADX Florence (and Back Again): The Fire Inside." In Daniel Burton-Rose, with Dan Pens and Paul Wright (eds.), *The Celling of America: An Inside Look at the U.S. Prison Industry.* Monroe, ME: Common Courage Press, pp. 200–205.

———. 1998b. "Trouble Coming Everyday: ADX, One Year Later." In Daniel Burton-Rose, with Dan Pens and Paul Wright (eds.), *The Celling of America: An Inside Look at the U.S. Prison Industry.* Monroe, ME: Common Courage Press, pp. 206–211.

Levine, Stephan. 1979. *A Gradual Awakening.* Garden City, NJ: Anchor.

Levinson, Robert B. 1994. "The Development of Classification and Programming." In John W. Roberts (ed.), *Escaping Prison Myths: Selected Topics in the History of Federal Corrections.* Washington, DC: American University Press, pp. 95–109.

Levinson, Robert B., and J. D. Williams. 1979. "Inmate Classification: Security/Custody Considerations." *Federal Probation* 43:37–43.

Lichter, Robert S., Stanley Rothman, and Linda S. Lichter. 1986. *The Media Elite.* Bethesda, MD: Adler and Adler.

Lindesmith, Alfred R., and Anselm Strauss. 1972. "Language and the Structure of

Thought." In Howard M. Shapiro and Robert Gliner (eds.), *Human Perspectives: Introductory Readings for Sociology*. New York: Free Press, pp. 75–83.

Lockwood, Daniel. 1980. *Prison Sexual Violence*. New York: Elsevier.

Loconte, Joe. 1997. "Jailhouse Rock of Ages." *Policy Review* 84:12–14.

Lomax, John A., and Alan Lomax. 1936. *Negro Folk Songs as Sung by Leadbelly*. New York: Macmillan.

———. 1966. *Folk Song U.S.A.* New York: New American Library.

Lombardo, Lucien. 1989. *Guards in Prison: Correctional Officers at Work*. Cincinnati, OH: Anderson.

Lopiano-Misdom, Janine, and Joanne De Luca. 1997. *Street Trends: Today's Alternative Youth Cultures Are Creating Tomorrow's Mainstream Markets*. New York: HarperCollins Business.

Lord, Elaine. 1995. "A Prison Superintendent's Perspective on Women in Prison." *Prison Journal* 75 (2): 257–269.

Lozoff, Bo. 1985. *We're All Doing Time*. Durham, NC: Human Kindness Foundation.

Lynch, Michael J. 1996. "Assessing the State of Radical Criminology." In Peter Cordella and Larry Siegel (eds.), *Readings in Contemporary Criminological Theory*. Boston: Northeastern University Press, pp. 294–304.

Lynch, Michael J., and W. Byron Groves. 1986/1989. *A Primer in Radical Criminology*. Albany: Harrow and Heston.

Lynd, Staughton. 1983. *The Fight against Shutdowns: Youngstown's Steel Mill Closings*. San Pedro, CA: Singlejack.

M.L.B. v. S.L.J., 519 U.S. 102, 1996.

MacCabe, C. 1979. *James Joyce and the Revolution of the World*. London: Macmillan.

MacCormick, Austin H. 1954. "Behind the Prison Riots." *Annals of the American Academy of Political and Social Science* 293:17–27.

MacLeod, Jay. 1995. *Ain't No Makin' It: Aspirations and Attainment in a Low-Income Neighborhood*. Boulder, CO: Westview.

Maguire, Kathleen, and Ann L. Pastore, eds. 1995. *Sourcebook of Criminal Justice Statistics 1994*. U.S. Department of Justice, Bureau of Justice Statistics. Washington, DC: USGPO.

———. 1998. *Sourcebook of Criminal Justice Statistics 1997*. U.S. Department of Justice, Bureau of Justice Statistics. Washington, DC: USGPO.

———. 1999. *Sourcebook of Criminal Justice Statistics 1998*. U.S. Department of Justice, Bureau of Justice Statistics. Washington, DC: USGPO.

———. 2000. *Sourcebook of Criminal Justice Statistics 1999* [online]. Table 6.26. Available at http://www.albany.edu/sourcebook (accessed March 15, 2001).

Mancini, Matthew J., and Alan Lomax. 1996. *One Dies, Get Another: Convict Leasing in the South, 1866–1928*. Columbia: University of South Carolina Press.

Mandell, Betty Reid. 1975. *Welfare in America: Controlling the "Dangerous Classes."* Englewood Cliffs, NJ: Prentice-Hall.

Manning, Peter K. 1997. *Police Work: The Social Organization of Policing*. Prospect Heights, IL: Waveland.

Marquart, James W., Dorothy E. Merianos, Steven J. Cuvelier, and Leo Carrol. 1996. "Thinking about the Relationship between Health Dynamics in the Free Community and Prison." *Crime and Delinquency* 42 (July): 331–360.

Marquez, Gabriel Garcia. 1970. *One Hundred Years of Solitude*. New York: Harper and Row.

Marsh, Robert L. 1983. "Services for Families: A Model Project to Provide Services for Families of Prisoners." *International Journal of Offender Therapy and Comparative Criminology* 27 (2): 156–162.

Martin, Dannie M., with Peter Y. Sussman. 1995. *Committing Journalism: The Prison Writings of Red Hog*. New York: Norton.

Martinson, Robert. 1974. "What Works? Questions and Answers about Prison Reform." *The Public Interest* 35:22–54.

———. 1979. "Symposium on Sentencing, Part II." *Hofstra Law Review* 7 (2): 243–258.

Martinson, Robert, and Judith Wilks. 1977. "Save Parole Supervision." *Federal Probation* 41:63–76.

Maruna, Shadd. 2002. *Making Good: How Ex-Convicts Reform and Rebuild Their Lives*. Washington, DC: American Psychological Association.

Marx, Karl. 1967. *Capital*. New York: International Publishing House.

Massey, Dennis. 1989. *Doing Time in American Prisons: A Study of Modern Novels*. New York: Greenwood.

Matza, David. 1964. *Delinquency and Drift*. New York: Wiley.

Mauer, Marc, Cathy Potler, and Richard Wolf. 1999. *Gender and Justice: Women Drugs and Sentencing Policy*. Washington, DC: The Sentencing Project.

Maurer, David W. 1981. *Language of the Underworld*. Lexington, KY: University of Kentucky Press.

May, John P., ed. 2000. *Building Violence: How America's Rush to Incarcerate Creates More Violence*. Thousand Oaks, CA: Sage.

Mays, G. Larry, and L. Thomas Winfree. 1998. *Contemporary Corrections*. Belmont, CA: Wadsworth.

McAuley, L. 1994. "Exploding Myths about Correctional Industries." *Corrections Today* 56:8.

McCleary, Richard. 1978/1992. *Dangerous Men: The Sociology of Parole*. New York: Harrow and Heston.

McDonald, Douglas. 1994. "Managing Prison Health Care and Costs." *NIJ Issues and Practices*, March (NCJ 152768).

———. 1999. "Medical Care in Prisons." In Michael Tonry and Joan Petersilia (eds.), *Prisons*. Chicago: University of Chicago Press, pp. 427–478.

McKelvey, Blake. 1977. *American Prisons: A History of Good Intentions*. Montclair, NJ: Patterson Smith.

McLaren, John. 1997. "Prisoners' Rights: The Pendulum Swings." In Joycelyn M. Pollock (ed.), *Prisons: Today and Tomorrow*. Gaithersburg, MD: Aspen, pp. 369–371.

McLaren, Kaye. 1992. *Reducing Reoffending: What Works Now*. Wellington: New Zealand Department of Justice.

McLellan, Velma, Greg Newbold, and Kay Saville-Smith. 1996. *Escape Pressures: Inside Views for the Reasons for Prison Escapes*. Wellington: New Zealand Ministry of Justice.

McShane, Marilyn D., and Frank P. Williams, III. 1989. "The Prison Adjustment of Juvenile Offenders." *Crime and Delinquency* 35 (2): 254–269.

Means, Russell. 1995. *Where White Men Fear to Tread*. New York: St. Martin's.

Meatto, Keith. 2000. "Jailhouse Rock." *Mother Jones,* May/June, p. 81.

Menninger, Karl. 1968. *The Crime of Punishment*. New York: Penguin.

Merianos, Dorothy E., James W. Marquart, Kelly Damphouse, and Jaimie L. Hebert. 1997. "From the Outside in: Using Public Health Data to Make Inferences about Older Inmates." *Crime and Delinquency* 43:298–313.

Michael Lloyd Combs et al. vs. Corrections Corp. of America et al. 1997. United States District Court for the Western District of Louisiana, Alexandria Division. 977 F. Supp. 799.

Michels, Roberto. 1911/1962. *Political Parties: A Sociological Study of Oligarchical Tendencies in Modern Democracy*. New York: Macmillan.

Michigan Department of Corrections. 1996. "Prisoners in Michigan." Public Information and Communication Pamphlet F: 1–3.

Miller, Eleanor M. 1986. *Street Women*. Philadelphia: Temple University Press.

Miller, J. Mitchell, and Richard Tewksbury. 2000. *Extreme Methods: Innovative Approaches to Social Science Research*. Needham, MA: Allyn and Bacon.

Miller, Jerome G. 1996. *Search and Destroy: African-American Males in the Criminal*

Justice System. New York: Cambridge University Press.

Miller, Jody. 1995. "Struggles over the Symbolic: Gang Style and the Meanings of Social Control." In Jeff Ferrell and Clinton R. Sanders (eds.), *Cultural Criminology.* Boston: Northeastern University Press, pp. 213–234.

Miller, Ted. R., Mark A. Cohen, and Brian Wiersema. 1996. *Victim Costs and Consequences.* Research Report. Washington, DC: U.S. Department of Justice, National Institute of Justice.

Mills, C. Wright. 1959. *The Sociological Imagination.* New York: Oxford University Press.

Milovanovic, Dragan, ed. 1996. "Postmodern Criminology: Mapping the Terrain." *Justice Quarterly* 13:567–610.

———. 1997. *Postmodern Criminology.* New York: Garland.

Missen, Eric A. 1971. *The History of New Zealand Penal Policy.* Criminology Seminar in Changes to Attitudes to Punishment, September 3–4, Department of University Extension, Victoria University, Wellington, N.Z.

Mitford, Jessica. 1973. *Kind and Usual Punishment.* New York: Knopf.

Mobley, Alan, and Gilbert Geis. 2000. "The Corrections Corporation of America AKA the Prison Realty Trust." In Michael Gilbert and David Shichor (eds.), *Privatization in Criminal Justice: Past, Present and Future.* Cincinnati, OH: Anderson, pp. 202–226.

Moffitt, Terrie E. 1999. "Pathways in the Life Course to Crime." In Francis Cullen and Robert Agnew (eds.), *Criminological Theory.* Los Angeles: Roxbury, pp. 41–58.

Morey, Anne. 1995. "The Judge Called Me an Accessory: Women's Prison Films, 1950–1962." *Journal of Popular Film and Television* 23 (2): 80–87.

Morris, James McGrath. 1998. *Jailhouse Journalism: The Fourth Estate behind Bars.* New York: McFarland.

Morris, Norval, and Gordon Hawkins. 1970. *The Honest Politician's Guide to*

Crime Control. Chicago: University of Chicago Press.

Morrissey, J., and H. H. Goldman. 1986. "Care and Treatment of the Mentally Ill in the United States: Historical Developments and Reforms." *Annals of the American Academy of Political and Social Science* 484:12–27.

Moses, Lawrence, and Raymond Wilson, eds. 1993. *Indian Lives: Essays on Nineteenth- and Twentieth-Century Native American Leaders.* Albuquerque: University of New Mexico Press.

Mueller, Julie. 1996. "Locking Up Tuberculosis." *Corrections Today,* October, p. 100.

Munro-Bjorklund, Vicky. 1991. "Popular Cultural Images of Criminals and Convicts since Attica." *Social Justice* 18 (3): 48–70.

Murphy, P. J. 1998. "Some Post-Mortem Reflections on the Cancellation of University Programs in Canada's Prisons." *Journal of Prisoners on Prisons* 9 (1): 37–52.

Murton, Tom, and Joe Hyams. 1969. *Accomplices to the Crime: The Arkansas Prison Scandal.* New York: Grove.

Nacci, Peter, and Thomas Kane. 1983. "The Incidence of Sex and Sexual Aggression in Federal Prisons." *Federal Probation* 47:31–36.

National Center on Addiction and Substance Abuse [CASA]. 1998. *Behind Bars: Substance Abuse and America's Prison Population.* New York: Columbia University.

National Commission on Acquired Immune Deficiency Syndrome. 1991. *HIV Disease in Correctional Institutions.* Washington, DC: National Commission on Acquired Immune Deficiency Syndrome.

National Indian Justice Center. 1995. *Child Sexual Abuse.* Washington, DC: U.S. Department of Justice, Office of Justice Programs, Office for Victims of Crime, National Institute of Justice, National Criminal Justice Reference No. 167686.

Neilson, J. 1990. *Feminist Research Methods: Exemplary Readings in the Social Sciences.* Boulder, CO: Westview.

Neis, Judith. 1996. *Native American History: A Chronology of a Culture's Vast Achievements and Their Links to World Events.* New York: Ballantine Books.

Nelson, W. Raymond, and Michael O'Toole. 1983. *New Generation Jails.* Boulder, CO: Library Information Specialists.

Neuman v. Alabama, 349 F. Supp. 285 (M.D. Ala. 1972); aff'd 503 F. 2d 1320 (5th Circuit, 1974).

Newbold, Greg. 1982/1985. *The Big Huey.* Auckland, N.Z.: Collins.

———. 1989. *Punishment and Politics: The Maximum Security Prison in New Zealand.* Auckland, N.Z.: Oxford University Press.

———. 1992. "What Works in Prison Management: Effects of Administrative Change in New Zealand." *Federal Probation* 56 (4): 53–57.

———. 2000. *Crime in New Zealand.* Palmerston North, N.Z.: Dunmore.

Newbold, Greg, and Chris Eskridge. 1996. "History and Development of Modern Correctional Practices in New Zealand." In Charles Fields and Richter Moore (eds.), *Comparative Criminal Justice.* Prospect Heights, IL: Waveland, pp. 453–476.

Newbold, Greg, and Robert Ivory. 1993. "Policing Serious Fraud in New Zealand." *Crime, Law and Social Change* 20:233–248.

Newland, Francesca. 1999. "HHCL Extends Pot Noodle Prison Theme with Puppets." *Campaign,* May 28, p. 7.

Newman, Annabel. 1993. "Prison Literacy: Implications for Program and Assessment Policy." Technical Report TR-93-1. Philadelphia: National Center on Adult Literacy.

Omer, H., and C. Strenger. 1992. "The Pluralist Revolution: From One True Meaning to an Infinity of Constructed Ones." *Psychotherapy* 29 (2): 253–261.

"On Prisoners and Parenting: Preserving the Tie That Binds." 1978. *Yale Law Journal* 87:1408–1429.

Oshinsky, David M. 1996. *"Worse Than Slavery": Parchman Farm and the Ordeal of Jim Crow Justice.* New York: Free Press.

Oster, Harry. 1969. *Living Country Blues.* Detroit: Folklore Associates.

Owen, Barbara. 1985. "Socialization Experiences of Women Correctional Workers." *Resources for Feminist Research* 13 (4): 53–56.

———. 1986. "Race and Gender among Prison Workers." *Crime and Delinquency* 31 (1): 147–159.

———. 1988. *The Reproduction of Social Control: A Study of Prison Workers in San Quentin.* New York: Praeger.

———. 1998. *"In the Mix": Struggle and Survival in a Women's Prison.* Albany: SUNY Press.

Owen, Barbara, and Barbara Bloom. 1995a. "Profiling Women Prisoners: Findings from National Survey and a California Sample." *Prison Journal* 75 (1): 165–185.

———. 1995b. *Profiling the Needs of California's Female Prisoners: A Needs Assessment.* Washington, DC: National Institute of Corrections.

———. 1999. "Final Report: Modeling Gender-Specific Services in Juvenile Justice." Sacramento, CA: Office of Criminal Justice Planning.

Owen, Barbara, Barbara Bloom, Elizabeth Deschenes, and Jill Rosenbaum. 1998. *Modeling Gender-Specific Services in Juvenile Justice: Policy and Program Recommendations.* State of California Office of Criminal Justice Planning, Grant 96-JF-FX-0006.

Pace, Arthur. 1993. "Religious Volunteers Form Partnership with the Military's Chaplaincy Program." *Corrections Today* 55:114, 116.

Page, Clarence. 1997. "Helm's Heavy Hand Chops Prison Frills." *Detroit News,* November 2, p. 9B.

Palmer, John W. 1994. *Constitutional Rights of Prisoners.* Cincinnati, OH: Anderson.

Palmer, Ted. 1986. "The 'Effectiveness' Issue Today." In Kenneth C. Haas and Geoffrey P. Alpert (eds.), *The Dilem-*

mas of Punishment: Readings in Contemporary Corrections. Prospect Heights, IL: Waveland, pp. 299–314.

Parenti, Christian. 1999. Lockdown America: Police and Prisons in the Age of Crisis. New York: Verso.

Parenti, Michael. 1995. Democracy for the Few. New York: St. Martin's.

Pareto, Vilfredo. 1916/1935. The Mind and Society. Translated by A. Bongiorno and A. Livingston. New York: Harcourt, Brace, Jovanovich.

Parish, James Robert. 1991. Prison Pictures from Hollywood. Jefferson, NC: McFarland.

Parker, Edward A., and Charles S. Lanier. 1997. "An Exploration of Self-Concepts among Incarcerated Fathers." In James W. Marquart and Jonathan R. Sorensen (eds.), Correctional Contexts: Classical and Contemporary Readings. Los Angeles: Roxbury, pp. 335–340.

Parry, A., and R. Doan. 1994. Story Re-Visions: Narrative Therapy in the Postmodern World. New York: Guilford.

Patterson, Gerald, and Marion Forgatch. 1987. Parents and Adolescents: Living Together. Eugene, OR: Castalia.

Patton, William W. 1999. "Mommy's Gone, Daddy's in Prison, Now What About Me? Family Reunification for Children of Single Custodial Fathers in Prison—Will the Sins of Incarcerated Fathers Be Inherited by Their Children?" North Dakota Law Review 75:179–204.

Paulus, Paul. 1988. Prison Crowding: A Psychological Perspective. New York: Springer-Verlag.

Peak, Ken. 1985. "Correctional Research in Theory and Practice: Political and Operational Hindrances." Criminal Justice Review 10:21–31.

Pecheux, M. 1982. Language, Semantics, and Ideology. New York: St. Martin's.

Pell v. Procunier, 4147 U.S. 817, 1974.

Peltier, Leonard. 1999. Prison Writings: My Life Is My Sundance. New York: St. Martin's.

Pens, Dan. 1998. "Federal Prisons Erupt." In Daniel Burton-Rose, with Dan Pens

and Paul Wright (eds.), The Celling of America: An Inside Look at the U.S. Prison Industry. Monroe, ME: Common Courage Press, pp. 244–249.

Pepinsky, Harold E. 1991. The Geometry of Violence and Democracy. Bloomington: Indiana University Press.

Pepinsky, Harold E., and Paul Jesilow. 1985. Myths That Cause Crime. Cabin John, MD: Seven Locks Press.

Pepinsky, Harold E., and Richard Quinney. 1991. Criminology as Peacemaking. Bloomington: Indiana University Press.

Perlin, M. 1999. Mental Disability Law. Durham, NC: Carolina Academic Press.

Petersilia, Joan, and Peter W. Greenwood. 1978. "Mandatory Prison Sentences: Their Projected Effects on Crime and Prison Populations." Journal of Criminal Law and Criminology 69:604–615.

Petersilia, Joan, Peter W. Greenwood, and M. Lavin. 1978. Criminal Careers of Habitual Felons. Washington, DC: National Institute of Law Enforcement and Criminal Justice.

Petersilia, Joan, and Paul Honig. 1980. The Prison Experience of Career Criminals. Santa Monica, CA: Rand.

Peterson, M. A., H. B. Braiker, and S. M. Polich. 1981. Who Commits Crimes: A Survey of Prison Inmates. Rand Corporation, Department of Justice Grant No. 77-NI-99-0053. Washington, DC: National Institute of Justice.

Peterson, Rebecca D., and Dennis J. Palumbo. 1997. "The Social Construction of Intermediate Punishment." Prison Journal 77 (1): 77–91.

Platt, Anthony M. 1977. The Child Savers: The Invention of Delinquency. 2d ed. Chicago: University of Chicago Press.

Pollock-Bryne, J. M. 1990. Women, Prison, and Crime. Pacific Grove, CA: Brooks/Cole.

"Pot Noodle Hard Cell in Latest TV Work." 1998. Marketing, January 22, p. 3.

Powers, E., and Helen Witmer. 1970. "The Cambridge-Somerville Study." In Norman Johnston, Leonard Savitz, and Marvin E. Wolfgang (eds.), *The Sociology of Punishment and Correction.* New York: Wiley, pp. 587–600.

Pownell, George. 1969. *Employment Problems of Released Offenders.* Washington, DC: U.S. Department of Labor Report.

Pratt, Robert. 1964. *Battlefield and Classroom: Four Decades with the American Indian.* New Haven: Yale University Press.

President's Commission on Law Enforcement and the Administration of Justice. 1967. [Task Force Reports on Police, Courts, and Corrections.] Washington, DC: USGPO.

Prison Discipline Study. 1996. "Exposing the Myth of Humane Imprisonment in the United States." In Elihu Rosenblatt (ed.), *Criminal Injustice: Confronting the Prison Crisis.* Boston: South End Press, pp. 92–99.

"Prison Envelope Art: Imagery in Motion." 1992. *Artpaper* 12:16–17.

"Prisons Must Adhere to Evolving Standard of HIV Care." 1998. *AIDS Policy and Law* 13 (3): 6–7.

"A Proposal: A Partnership in Education with the Prisoner Tuition Reimbursement Program." 2000. Address: CURE-NY, Box 102, Katonah, NY 10536.

Quinney, Richard. 1995. "Socialist Humanism and the Problem of Crime: Thinking about Erich Fromm in the Development of Critical/Peacemaking Criminology." *Crime, Law and Social Change* 23:147–156.

———. 1998. "Criminology as Moral Philosophy: Criminologist as Witness." *Contemporary Justice Review* 1: 347–364.

Rafter, Nicole H. 1985. *Partial Justice: Women in State Prisons, 1800–1935.* Boston: New England University Press.

———. 1990. *Partial Justice: Women, Prisons, and Social Control.* New Brunswick, NJ: Transaction Books.

———. 1992. "Criminal Anthropology in the United States." *Criminology* 30 (4): 525–545.

———. 2000. *Shots in the Mirror: Crime Films and Society.* New York: Oxford University Press.

Ransom, Rainey E. 1993. "Doing Time Together: An Exploratory Study of Incarcerated Fathers and Their Kids." Ph.D. diss., American University.

Reiman, Jeffrey. 1995. *The Rich Get Richer and the Poor Get Prison.* Needham Heights, MA: Allyn and Bacon.

Reisig, Michael D. 1998. "Rates of Disorder in Higher-Custody State Prisons: A Comparative Analysis of Managerial Practices." *Crime and Delinquency* 44 (2): 229–244.

Renzetti, Claire. M. 1997. "Confessions of a Reformed Positivist." In Martin D. Schwartz (ed.), *Researching Sexual Violence against Women: Methodological and Personal Perspectives.* Thousand Oaks, CA: Sage, pp. 131–143.

Richards, Stephen C. 1990. "The Sociological Penetration of the American Gulag." *Wisconsin Sociologist* 27 (4): 18–28.

———. 1995a. *The Structure of Prison Release.* New York: McGraw-Hill.

———. 1995b. *The Sociological Significance of Tattoos.* New York: McGraw-Hill.

———. 1998. "Critical and Radical Perspectives on Community Punishment: Lesson from the Darkness." In Jeffrey Ian Ross (ed.), *Cutting the Edge: Current Perspectives in Radical/Critical Criminology and Criminal Justice.* Westport, CT: Praeger, pp. 122–144.

———. 2003. *USP Marion: The First Super Max Penitentiary.* Carbondale: Southern Illinois University Press (forthcoming).

Richards, Stephen C., and Michael J. Avey. 2000. "Controlling State Crime in the United States of America: What Can We Do about the Thug State?" In Jeffrey Ian Ross (ed.), *Varieties of State Crime and Its Control.* Monsey, NY: Criminal Justice Press, pp. 31–57.

Richards, Stephen C., and Richard S. Jones. 1997. "Perpetual Incarceration Machine: Structural Impediments to Postprison Success." *Journal of Contemporary Criminal Justice* 13 (1): 4–22.

Richards, Stephen C., and Jeffrey Ian Ross. 2001. "The New School of Convict Criminology." *Social Justice* 28 (1): 177–190.

Richards, Stephen C., Charles M. Terry, and Daniel S. Murphy. 2002. "Lady Hacks and Gentlemen Convicts." In Leanne Fiftal Alarid and Paul Cromwell (eds.), *Contemporary Correctional Perspectives: Academic, Practitioner, and Prisoner.* Los Angeles: Roxbury, pp. 207–216.

Rideau, Wilbert. 1994. "Why Prisons Don't Work." *New York Times,* March 21, p. 80.

———. 1995. "The Clubs." In Wilbert Rideau and Ron Wikberg (eds.), *Life Sentences: Rage and Survival behind Bars.* New York: Times Books, pp. 107–110.

Rideau, Wilbert, and Ron Wikberg, eds. 1992. *Life Sentences: Rage and Survival behind Bars.* New York: Times Books.

Roberts, John W., ed. 1994. *Escaping Prison Myths: Selected Topics in the History of Federal Corrections.* Washington, DC: American University Press.

Robins, L. N., and D. A. Regier, eds. 1991. *Psychiatric Disorder in America: The Epidemiological Catchment Area Study.* New York: Free Press.

Robinson, Matthew B., and Barbara H. Zaitzow. 1999. "Criminologists: Are We What We Study? A National Self-Report Study of Crime Experts." *The Criminologist* 24 (2): 1–4, 17.

Rogers, Joseph W. 1977. *Why Are You Not a Criminal?* Englewood Cliffs, NJ: Prentice-Hall.

Romero, Phillip J. 1994. *How Incarcerating More Felons Will Benefit California's Economy.* Sacramento, CA: California Governor's Office of Planning and Research.

Rominger, Duane A., L. G. Christenson, and J. W. Mercer. 1993. "The Condition of Correctional Education in Minnesota: Toward a Vision for Learning." *State Council on Vocational Technical Education Report.* Minneapolis.

Rosenau, P. M. 1992. *Postmodernism and the Social Sciences: Insights, Inroads, and Intrusions.* Princeton, NJ: Princeton University Press.

Rosenbaum, Marsha. 1981. *Women on Heroin.* New Brunswick, NJ: Rutgers University Press.

Rosenberg, Morris, and Howard B. Kaplan, eds. 1982. *Social Psychology of the Self-Concept.* Arlington Heights, IL: Harlan Davidson.

Rosenblatt, Elihu, ed. 1996. *Criminal Injustice: Confronting the Prison Crisis.* Boston: South End Press.

Ross, Jeffrey Ian. 2000a. "Grants-R-US: Inside a Federal Grant-Making Agency." *American Behavioral Scientist* 43 (10): 1704–1723.

———. 2000b. *Varieties of State Crime and Its Control.* Monsey, NY: Criminal Justice Press.

———. 2000c. *Making News of Police Violence: A Comparative Study of Toronto and New York City.* Greenwood, CT: Praeger.

———, ed. 1998a. "Situating the Academic Study of Controlling State Crime." *Crime, Law, and Social Change,* 29:331–340.

———. 1998b. *Cutting the Edge: Current Perspectives in Radical/Critical Criminology and Criminal Justice.* Westport, CT: Praeger.

———. 1998c. "The Role of the Media in the Creation of Public Police Violence." In Frankie Bayley and Donna Hale (eds.), *Popular Culture, Crime and Justice.* Belmont, CA: Wadsworth, pp. 100–110.

———. 1999. "The Frequency and Nature of Prison Reporting in the Baltimore Sun." Unpublished paper, available from author.

———. 1995/2000. *Controlling State Crime.* New Brunswick, NJ: Transaction Press.

Ross, Jeffrey Ian, and Stephen C. Richards. 2002. *Behind Bars: Surviving Prison.* Indianapolis: Alpha.

Ross, L. 1998. *Inventing the Savage: The Social Construction of Native American Criminality.* Austin: University of Texas Press.

Rothman, David J. 1971. *The Discovery of the Asylum: Social Order in the New Republic.* Boston: Little, Brown.

———. 1980. *Conscience and Convenience: The Asylum and Its Alternative in Progressive America.* Boston: Little, Brown.

Rubenstein, Ruth P. 1995. *Dress Codes: Meanings and Messages in American Culture.* Boulder, CO: Westview.

Samenow, Stanton, and Samuel Yochelson. 1977. *The Criminal Personality.* New York: Jason Aronson.

Sampson, Robert J., and John H. Laub. 1993. *Crime in the Making: Pathways and Turning Points through Life.* Cambridge: Harvard University Press.

Sanders, Clinton R. 1988. "Marks of Mischief." *Journal of Contemporary Ethnography* 16 (4): 395–432.

———. 1989. *Customizing the Body: The Art and Culture of Tattooing.* Philadelphia: Temple University Press.

Santosky v. Kramer, 455 U.S. 745, 1982.

Saum, C., H. Surratt, J. Inciardi, and R. Bennett. 1995. "Sex in Prison: Exploring the Myths and Realities." *Prison Journal* 75:413–431.

Saxbe v. Washington Post, 417 U.S. 843, 1974.

Sayler, L. 1991. "The Constitutive Nature of Law in American History." *Legal Studies Forum* 15 (1): 61–64.

Schafer, N. 1978. "Prison Visiting: A Background for Change." *Federal Probation* 42:47–50.

Schicher, D. 1992. "Myths and Realities in Prison Setting." *Crime and Delinquency* 38:70–88.

Schiller, Herbert I. 1989. *Culture Inc.: The Corporate Takeover of Public Expression.* New York: Oxford University Press.

Schlosser, Eric. 1998. "The Prison-Industrial Complex." *Atlantic Monthly,* December, pp. 51–77.

Schmalleger, Frank. 1991. *Criminal Justice Today: An Introductory Text for the Twenty-First Century.* Englewood Cliffs, NJ: Prentice-Hall.

Schrag, Clarence 1960. "The Sociology of Prison Riots." *Proceedings of the American Correctional Association* 90: 136–145.

Schultz, Robert. 1991. "Life in SHU: An Ethnographic Study of Pelican Bay State Prison." M.S. thesis, Humboldt State University, Arcata, CA.

Schur, Edwin M. 1968. *Law and Society: A Sociological View.* New York: Random House.

Schwartz, Ira M. 1989. *(In)Justice for Juveniles.* Lexington, MA: Lexington Books.

Sellin, J. Thorsten. 1971. "The Sociology of Crime and Delinquency." In Marvin Wolfgang (ed.), *Crime and Delinquency: A Sociological Approach.* New York: Wiley.

———. 1976. *Slavery and the Penal System.* New York: Elsevier.

Senate Journal. 1832. Governor A. B. Roman's Address to the Third Session of the Tenth Legislature of the State of Louisiana. New Orleans: n.p., January 3, 1832.

———. 1833. Governor A. B. Roman's Address to the First Session of the Eleventh Legislature. New Orleans: n.p., January 7, 1833.

Shadoian, Jack. 1979. *Dreams and Dead Ends: The American Gangster/Crime Film.* Cambridge, MA: MIT Press.

Shelden, Randall G. 2001. *Controlling the Dangerous Classes: A Critical Introduction to the History of Criminal Justice.* Boston: Allyn and Bacon.

Sherman, Lawrence, and Richard Berk. 1984. *The Minneapolis Domestic Violence Experiment.* Washington, DC: The Police Foundation.

Shibutani, Tomatsu. 1955. "Reference Groups as Perspectives." *The American Journal of Sociology* 60:562–569.

Shinnar, Shlomo, and Reuel Shinnar. 1975. "The Effects of the Criminal Justice System on the Control of Crime: A Quantitative Approach." *Law and Society Review* 9:581–611.

Shover, Neal. 1996. *Great Pretenders: Pursuits and Careers of Persistent Thieves.* Boulder, CO: Westview.

Shover, Neal, and David Honaker. 1999. "The Socially Bounded Decision Making of Persistent Property Offenders." In Paul Cromwell (ed.), *In Their Own Words: Criminals on Crime.* Los Angeles: Roxbury, pp. 10–22.

Silberman, Matthew. 1995. *A World of Violence: Corrections in America.* Belmont, CA: Wadsworth.

Silverman, K. 1983. *The Subject of Semiotics.* New York: Oxford University Press.

Simon, David, and Edward Burns. 1997. *The Corner: A Year in the Life of an Inner-City Neighborhood.* Broadway, NY: Broadway Books.

Smith, R. 1984. "Reported Ex-Offender Employment in American Adult Corrections." *Journal of Offender Counseling, Services and Rehabilitation* 8:5–13.

Smith v. Sullivan, 553 F.2d. 373, 1977.

Spier, P. 1998. *Conviction and Sentencing of Offenders in New Zealand: 1988 to 1997.* Wellington, N.Z.: Ministry of Justice.

Stack, Jonathan, Liz Garbus, and Wilbert Rideau (Directors). 1998. *The Farm: Angola USA.* Arts and Entertainment Home Video.

Standing Bear, Luther. 1975. *My People Sioux.* Lincoln: University of Nebraska Press.

Stanley v. Illinois, 405 U.S. 645, 1982.

Statistics New Zealand. 1997. *Census 96: National Summary.* Wellington: Statistics New Zealand.

Steadman, H. J., D. W. McCarty, and J. P. Morrissey. 1989. *The Mentally Ill in Jail: Planning for Essential Services.* New York: Guilford.

Steffensmeier, Darrell, and Emilie Allan. 1998. "The Nature of Female Offending: Patterns and Explanations." In Ruth Zupan (ed.), *Female Offenders: Critical Perspectives and Interventions.* Gaithersburg, MD: Aspen, pp. 5–30.

Stenson, Kevin. 1991. "Making Sense of Crime Control." In Kevin Stenson and David Cowell (eds.), *The Politics of Crime Control.* London: Sage, pp. 1–32.

Stojkovic, Stan, John Klofas, and David Kalinich, eds. 1999. *The Administration of Criminal Justice Organizations: Readings.* Prospect Heights, IL: Waveland.

Stolberg, Sheryl. 1995. "Schools Out for Convicts: Taxpayers Have Stopped Paying for Inmates' College Degrees in a Backlash against Prison Reform." *Los Angeles Times,* September 14, p. A1.

Stonequist, E. V. 1934. *The Marginal Man.* New York: Scribner's.

Stuever, Hank. 2000. "Radical Chic: Bennetton Takes on the Death Penalty." *Washington Post,* January 25, p. C1.

Sullivan, Mercer L. 1989. *Getting Paid: Youth Crime and Work in the Inner City.* Ithaca, NY: Cornell University Press.

Surrette, Ray. 1998. "Some Unpopular Thoughts about Popular Culture." In Frankie Bailey and Donna Hale (eds.), *Popular Culture, Crime and Justice.* Belmont, CA: Wadsworth, pp. xiv–xxiv.

Sutherland, Edwin H. 1924. *Criminology.* Philadelphia: Lippincott.

———. 1937. *The Professional Thief.* Chicago: University of Chicago Press.

Sutherland, Edwin H., and Donald R. Cressey. 1960. *Principles of Criminology.* Chicago: Lippincott.

———. 1978. *Criminology.* 10th ed. Philadelphia: Lippincott.

Sutherland, Edwin H., Donald R. Cressey, and David F. Luckenbill. 1992. *Principles of Criminology.* Dix Hills, NY: General Hall.

Sykes, Gresham M. 1956. "Men, Merchants, and Toughs: A Study of Reactions to Imprisonment." *Social Problems* 4:130–138.

———. 1958. *The Society of Captives.* Princeton, NJ: Princeton University Press.

Sykes, Gresham M., and Sheldon L. Messinger. 1960. "Inmate Social System." In Richard A. Cloward, Donald R. Cressey, G. H. Grosser, Richard H.

McCleery, Lloyd E. Ohlin, Gresham. M. Sykes, and Sheldon L. Messinger, eds. *Theoretical Studies in Social Organization of the Prison*. New York: Social Science Research Council, pp. 5–19.

Sylvestor, Sawyer, John Reed, and David Nelson. 1977. *Prison Homicide*. New York: Spectrum.

Talbott, Frederick. 1988. "Reporting from behind the Walls." *The Quill* 76:16–20.

———. 1989. "Covering Prisons." *Editor and Publisher,* April 22, pp. 74–78.

Taylor, Ian, Paul Walton, and Jock Young. 1973. *The New Criminology*. London: Routledge and Kegan Paul.

———. 1975. *Critical Criminology*. Boston: Routledge and Kegan Paul.

Taylor, Jon Marc. 1992. "Post-Secondary Correctional Education: Evaluation of Effectiveness and Efficiency." *Journal of Correctional Education* 43 (3): 132–141.

———. 1995. "The Resurrection of the Dangerous Classes." *Journal of Prisoners on Prisons* 6 (2): 7–16.

Taylor, Jon Marc, and Richard Tewksbury. 1998. "Post-Secondary Correctional Education: The Imprisoned University." In Ted Alleman and Rosemary Gido (eds.), *Turnstile Justice: Issues in American Corrections*. Upper Saddle River, NJ: Prentice-Hall, pp. 126–158.

Teeters, Negley K. 1955. *The Cradle of the Penitentiary*. Philadelphia: Pennsylvania Prison Society.

Terry, Charles M. 1997. "The Function of Humor for Prison Inmates." *Journal of Contemporary Criminal Justice* 13 (1): 23–40.

Thomas, Jo. 2000. "Drug Agency Looks Again at an Informer's Career: Man Who Lied on the Stand Is Suspended." *New York Times,* June 28, p. A14.

Thomas, Paulette. 1994. "Rural Regions Look to Prisons for Prosperity." *Wall Street Journal,* July 11, p. B1.

Thompson, James. 1967. *Organizations in Action*. New York: McGraw-Hill.

Thompson, Joel A., and Larry G. Mays. 1991. *American Jails: Public Policy Issues*. Chicago: Nelson-Hall.

Tifft, L. L. 1995. "Social Harm Definitions of Crime." *Critical Criminologist* 7:9–13.

Toch, Hans. 1982. "The Disturbed Disruptive Inmate." *Journal of Psychiatry and Law* (fall): 327–349.

———. 1998. *Corrections: A Humanistic Perspective*. New York: Harrow and Heston.

Tonry, Michael. 1993. "The Failure of the U.S. Sentencing Commission's Guidelines." *Crime and Delinquency* 39 (2): 131–149.

———. 1994. *Malign Neglect: Race, Crime and Punishment in America*. New York: Oxford University Press.

———. 1999. "Why Are U.S. Incarceration Rates So High?" *Crime and Delinquency* 45 (4): 419–437.

Travisino, A. P. 1980. "Brubaker: The Crusader Strikes Out." *On the Line* 3 (6): 1.

Trebay, Guy. 2000. "In Jailhouse Chic, an Anti-Style Turns into a Style Itself." *New York Times,* June 13, p. A23.

Tregea, William S. 1998. "Prison Post-Secondary, Recidivism, and the Current Political Climate." Center on Crime, Communities, and Culture (Soros Foundation).

Tremblay, Pierre, and Carlo Morselli. 2000. "Patterns in Criminal Achievement: Wilson and Abrahamse Revisited." *Criminology* 38 (2): 633–675.

Tripney, Billy. 2000. "Stories from Ma Cell." *Relational Justice Bulletin* 7:5.

Tropin, L. A. 1977. "Testimony before the U.S. House Judiciary Subcommittee on Crime." September 27. Washington, DC.

Tunnell, Kenneth S. 1992. "99 Years Is Almost for Life: Punishment for Violent Crime in Bluegrass Music." *Journal of Popular Culture* 26:165–181.

———. 1995. "A Cultural Approach to Crime and Punishment, Bluegrass Style." In Jeff Ferrell and Clinton R.

Sanders (eds.), *Cultural Criminology.* Boston: Northeastern University Press, pp. 80–105.

———. 2000. *Living off Crime.* Chicago: Burnham.

U.S. Department of Justice. 1997. P.S. 6000.05 Health Services Manual, p. 1.

U.S. Department of Justice. Bureau of Justice Statistics. 1994. *Women in Prison.* Washington, DC: USGPO.

———. 1995. *Prisoners in 1994.* Washington, DC: USGPO.

———. 1998. NCJ 170014 (August). Washington, DC: USGPO.

———. 1998. *Prisoners in 1997.* Washington, DC: U.S. Department of Justice.

———. 1999. *Prisoners in 1998.* Washington, DC: USGPO.

———.1999. *Special Report: Women Offenders.* Washington, DC: USGPO.

———. 2000. *Incarcerated Parents and Their Children.* NCJ 182335. Washington, DC: USGPO.

Useem, Bert, and Peter Kimball. 1991. *States of Siege: U.S. Prison Riots 1971–1986.* New York: Oxford University Press.

U.S. General Accounting Office. 1994. "Bureau of Prisons Health Care: Inmate's Access to Health Care Is Limited by Lack of Clinical Staff." *Report to the Chairman, Subcommittee on Intellectual Property and Judicial Administration, Committee on the Judiciary, House of Representatives.*

Van Dine, Steve, Simon Dinitz, and John Conrad. 1977. "Incapacitation of the Dangerous Offender—A Statistical Experiment." *Journal of Research in Crime and Delinquency* 14 (1): 22–34.

Vaughn, Michael S., and Linda G. Smith. 1999. "Practicing Penal Harm Medicine in the United States: Prisoners' Voices from Jail." *Justice Quarterly* 16: 175–232.

Visher, Christy A. 1986. "Rand Inmate Survey—A Reanalysis." In Alfred Blumstein, Jacqueline Cohen, Jeffrey Roth, and Christy A. Visher (eds.), *Criminal Careers and "Career Crimi-*

nals." Vol. 2. Washington, DC: National Academy Press, pp. 161–211.

———. 1987. "Incapacitation and Crime Control: Does a 'Lock 'em Up' Strategy Reduce Crime?" *Justice Quarterly* 4 (4): 513–543.

Vito, Gennaro, and Deborah Wilson. 1985. "Forgotten People: Elderly Inmates." *Federal Probation* 49:18–24.

Vold, George B., and Thomas Bernard. 1996. *Theoretical Criminology.* New York: Oxford University Press.

"Volunteers: Corrections' Unsung Heroes." 1993. Special issue of *Corrections Today* 55 (5).

Walens, Susann. 1997. *War Stories: An Oral History of Life behind Bars.* Westport, CT: Praeger.

Walker, Nigel. 1983. "Side-effects of Incarceration." *British Journal of Criminology* 23:61–71.

Wallace, L., A. Calhoun, K. Powell, J. O'Neil, and S. James. 1996. *Homicide and Suicide among Native Americans 1979–1992.* Washington, DC: U.S. Department of Health and Human Services, National Center for Injury Prevention and Control, CDC, Division of Violence Prevention. NIJ 167056.

Walsh, Edward. 1994. "Strapped Small Towns Try to Lock Up Prisons." *New York Times,* December 24, p. B1.

Ward, David A. 1994. "Alcatraz and Marion: Confinement in Super Maximum Custody." In John W. Roberts (ed.), *Escaping Prison Myths: Selected Topics in the History of Federal Corrections.* Washington, DC: American University Press, pp. 81–93.

Ward, David A., and Gene Kassebaum. 1965. *Women's Prison: Sex and Social Structure.* Chicago: Aldine.

Warren, Carol A. 1980. "Destigmatization of Identity: From Deviance to Charismatic." *Qualitative Sociology* 3:59–72.

Watts, Alan. 1957. *The Way of Zen.* New York: Pantheon Books.

"WCC Awarded Two Contracts in Texas; Annualized Contract Revenues Exceed $12.3 Million." Available at http://

www.prnewswire.com (accessed July 21, 2000).

Webb, Patricia. 1982. *A History of Custodial and Related Penalties in New Zealand.* Wellington: New Zealand Government Printer.

Weis, Joseph G. 1986. "Issues in the Measurement of Criminal Careers." In Alfred Blumstein, Jacqueline Cohen, Jeffrey Roth, and Christy A. Visher (eds.), *Criminal Careers and "Career Criminals."* Vol. 2. Washington, DC: National Academy Press, pp. 1–51.

Weissbourd, Richard. 1996. *The Vulnerable Child: What Really Hurts America's Children and What We Can Do about It.* Reading, MA: Addison-Wesley.

Welch, Michael. 1994. "Jail Overcrowding: Social Sanitation and the Warehousing of the Urban Underclass." In Albert Roberts (ed.), *Critical Issues in Crime and Justice.* Thousand Oaks, CA: Sage, pp. 251–276.

———. 1996. *Corrections: A Critical Approach.* New York: McGraw-Hill.

———. 1999. *Punishment in America: Social Control and the Ironies of Imprisonment.* Thousand Oaks, CA: Sage.

Wellisch, Jean M., Douglas Anglin, and Michael Prendergast. 1994. "Treatment Strategies for Drug-Abusing Women Offenders." In James Inciardi (ed.), *Drug Treatment and the Criminal Justice System.* Thousand Oaks, CA: Sage, pp. 5–25.

Wenda, Walter. 1997. "The Relationship between Life-Skills Literacy and Vocational Education and Self-Perception of Eleven Domains and Global Self-Worth of Adult Incarcerated Males." *Journal of Correctional Education* 47 (2): 74–85.

Wettstein, R., ed. 1998. *Treatment of Offenders with Mental Disorders.* New York: Guilford.

Wheeler, Stanton. 1961. "Socialization in Correctional Communities." *American Sociological Review* 26:697–712.

Wicker, Tom. 1975. *A Time to Die.* New York: Quadrangle.

Wideman, John Edgar. 1984. *Brothers and Keepers.* New York: Holt.

Wilczak, Ginger L., and Carol A. Markstrom. 1999. "The Effects of Parent Education on Parental Locus of Control and Satisfaction of Incarcerated Fathers." *International Journal of Offender Therapy and Comparative Criminology* 43 (1): 90–102.

Wilson, Deborah, and Gennaro Vito. 1988. "Long-Term Inmates: Special Need and Management Considerations." *Federal Probation* 52:21–26.

Wilson, James Q. 1986. "'What Works?' Revisited: New Findings on Criminal Rehabilitation." In K. C. Haas and G. P. Alpert, *The Dilemmas of Punishment: Readings in Contemporary Corrections.* Prospect Heights, IL: Waveland, pp. 327–341.

Wilson, James Q., and Allen F. Abrahamse. 1992. "Does Crime Pay?" *Justice Quarterly* 9 (3): 357–377.

Wilson, James Q., and Richard J. Hernstein. 1985. *Crime and Human Nature.* New York: Simon and Schuster.

Wilson, Julius William. 1996. *When Work Disappears: The World of the New Urban Poor.* New York: Vintage.

Winfree, L. Thomas. 1996. "Attica." In Marilyn D. McShane and Frank P. Williams (eds.), *Encyclopedia of American Prisons.* New York and London: Garland, pp. 43–45.

Winfree, L. Thomas, and Howard Abadinsky. 1996. *Understanding Crime: Theory and Practice.* Chicago: Nelson Hall.

Wojda, Grace, Raymond G. Wojda, Norman Erik Smith, and Richard K. Jones. 1991. *Behind Bars.* Laurel, MD: American Correctional Association.

Wojda, Raymond G., and Judy Rowse. 1996. *Women behind Bars.* Lanham, MD: American Correctional Association.

Wolf v. McDonnell, 418 U.S. 539, 555–56, 94 S. Ct. 2963, 41 L. Ed. 2d 935, 1974.

Wolfgang, Larry D. 1999. *Fathers in Prison.* Paxinos, PA: Stone Creek Publishing.

Wolfgang, Marvin E., Robert Figlio, and Thorsten Sellin. 1972. *Delinquency in a Birth Cohort*. Chicago: University of Chicago Press.

Women Prisoners of the District of Columbia Department of Corrections v. District of Columbia, 877 F. Supp. 634 D.D.C., 1994.

Wooden, Wayne S., and Jay Parker. 1983. *Men behind Bars: Sexual Exploitation in Prison*. New York: Da Capo Press.

Wormith, S. 1984. "The Controversy over the Effects of Long-Term Incarceration." *Canadian Journal of Criminology* 26:423–435.

Wreford, Paul. 1990. "Prison College Programs and Recidivism." Ph.D. diss., Wayne State University.

Young, Jock, and Roger Matthews. 1992. *Rethinking Criminology: The Realist Debate*. London: Sage.

Young, Thomas. 1991. "Medical Resources, Suicides and Homicides among Native Americans." *Corrective and Social Psychiatry and Journal of Behavior Technology Methods and Therapy* 37 (3): 3.

Young, Thomas, and Lawrence French. 1997. "Homicide Rates among Native American Children: The Status Integration Hypothesis." *Adolescence* 32 (spring): 57–59.

Zamble, Edward, and Frank Porporino. 1988. *Coping, Behavior and Adaptation in Prison Inmates*. New York: Springer-Verlag.

Zaner, Laura Ochipiniti. 1989. "The Screen Test: Has Hollywood Hurt Corrections' Image?" *Corrections Today* 51:64–66, 94–95, 98.

Zealand, Elise. 1998. "Protecting the Ties that Bind from behind Bars: A Call for Equal Opportunities for Incarcerated Fathers and Their Children to Maintain the Parent-Child Relationship." *Columbia Journal of Law and Social Problems* 31:247–281.

Zedlewski, Edwin W. 1987. *Making Confinement Decisions*. Washington, DC: Department of Justice, National Institute of Justice.

Zimmerman, Don, and D. Lawrence Wieder. 1977. "The Diary: Diary-Interview Method." *Urban Life* 5: 479–498.

Zimring, Franklin E., and Gordon Hawkins. 1988. "The New Mathematics of Imprisonment." *Crime and Delinquency* 34:425–36.

———. 1995. *Incapacitation: Penal Confinement and the Restraint of Crime*. New York: Oxford University Press.

Zupan, Linda L. 1991. *Jails: Reform and the New Generation Philosophy*. Cincinnati, OH: Anderson.

Index